GW00771927

GAME PROGRAMMING GEMS 8

Edited by Adam Lake

Course Technology PTR
A part of Cengage Learning

COURSE TECHNOLOGY
CENGAGE Learning™

Australia, Brazil, Japan, Korea, Mexico, Singapore, Spain, United Kingdom, United States

COURSE TECHNOLOGY
CENGAGE Learning

Game Programming Gems 8
Edited by Adam Lake

Publisher and General Manager,
Course Technology PTR:
Stacy L. Hiquet

Associate Director of Marketing:
Sarah Panella

Manager of Editorial Services:
Heather Talbot

Marketing Manager:
Jordan Castellani

Senior Acquisitions Editor:
Emi Smith

Project and Copy Editor:
Cathleen D. Small

Interior Layout:
Shawn Morningstar

Cover Designer:
Mike Tanamachi

CD-ROM Producer:
Brandon Penticuff

Indexer:
Katherine Stimson

Proofreader:
Heather Urschel

For product information and technology assistance, contact us at
Cengage Learning Customer & Sales Support, 1-800-354-9706

For permission to use material from this text or product, submit all requests online at **cengage.com/permissions**
Further permissions questions can be emailed to
permissionrequest@cengage.com

All trademarks are the property of their respective owners.
Cover image used courtesy of Valve Corporation.
All other images © Cengage Learning unless otherwise noted.

Library of Congress Control Number: 2010920327

ISBN-13: 978-1-58450-702-4

ISBN-10: 1-58450-702-0

Course Technology, a part of Cengage Learning
20 Channel Center Street
Boston, MA 02210
USA

Cengage Learning is a leading provider of customized learning solutions with office locations around the globe, including Singapore, the United Kingdom, Australia, Mexico, Brazil, and Japan. Locate your local office at:
international.cengage.com/region

Cengage Learning products are represented in Canada by Nelson Education, Ltd.

For your lifelong learning solutions, visit **courseptr.com**

Visit our corporate website at **cengage.com**

Printed in the United States of America
1 2 3 4 5 6 7 12 11 10

Contents

Preface

Welcome to the eighth edition of the *Game Programming Gems* series, started by Mark DeLoura in 2000. The first edition was inspired by Andrew Glassner's popular *Graphics Gems* series. Since then, other *Gems* series have started, including *AI Gems* and a new series focused on the capabilities of programmable graphics, the *ShaderX* series. These tomes serve as an opportunity to share our experience and best practices with the rest of the industry.

Many readers think of the *Game Programming Gems* series as a collection of articles with sections that target specialists. For me, I've read through them as a way to get exposure to the diverse subsystems used to create games and stay abreast of the latest techniques. For example, I may not be a specialist in networking, but reading this section will often enlighten and stimulate connections that I may not have made between areas in which I have expertise and ones in which I do not.

One statement I've heard recently regarding our industry is the idea that we now have all the horsepower we need to create games, so innovations by hardware companies are not needed. I believe this argument is flawed in many ways. First, there are continued advancements in graphical realism in academia, in R&D labs, and in the film industry that have yet to be incorporated into our real-time pipelines. As developers adopt these new features, computational requirements of software will continue to increase. Second, and the more important issue, is that this concept of play isn't entirely correct—the very notion of what gaming serves from an anthropological perspective. Play is fundamental, not just to the human condition, but to the sentient condition. We invent interactive experiences on any platform, be it a deck of cards, a set of cardboard cutouts, or a next-gen PC platform with multi-terabyte data and multi-threaded, multi-gigahertz, multi-processor environments. It's as natural as the pursuit of food. This play inspires real-world applications and pushes the next generation of platform requirements. It enables affordability of ever-increased computational horsepower in our computing platforms.

The extension of gaming into other arenas, mobile and netbook platforms, serves only to prove the point. While the same ideas and themes may be used in these environments, the experience available to the player is different if the designer is to leverage the full capabilities and differentiating features of the platform.

There is an often-chanted "ever increasing cost of game development" quote for console and PC platforms. In the same breath, it's alluded that this spiral of cost cannot continue. I believe these issues are of short-term concern. If there is a community willing to play, our economies will figure out a way to satisfy those needs. This will open up new opportunities for venture capital and middleware to reduce those platform complexities and cross-industry development costs, fueling the next generation of interactive experiences. I do believe the process has changed and will continue to evolve, but game development will continue to thrive. Will there be 15 first-person military simulations on a single platform? Perhaps not, but will there continue to be compelling multiplayer and single-player experiences? I believe so. The ingenuity of the game developer, when brought to the task of leveraging new incarnations of silicon, will continue to create enriching interactive experiences for ever-increasing audiences.

Finally, I'd like to take a moment to address another issue often mentioned in the press. In November 2009, the *Wall Street Journal* ran an article by Jonathan V. Last from the *Weekly Standard* discussing the social implications of gaming. The majority of his article, "Videogames—Not Only for the Lonely," was making this observation in the context of a holiday gathering of family members of many generations sharing experiences with their Nintendo Wii. Near the end of the article, he refers to the fact that "the shift to videogames might be lamenting if it meant that people who would otherwise be playing mini-golf or Monopoly were sealing themselves off and playing *Halo 3* death matches across the Internet." Much to the contrary, I have personally spent many quality multiplayer hours interacting socially with longtime friends when playing multiplayer games. A few days ago, I was having a conversation with an acquaintance who was thrilled that she could maintain her relationship with her brother on the East Coast by playing *World of Warcraft* with him. Ultimately, whether we are discussing our individual game experiences with others or interacting directly while playing, games do what they have always done across generations and platforms—they bring us together with shared experiences, whether it be cardboard cutouts, a deck of cards, or multiplayer capture the flag. Despite the overall informed message of the article, the writer encouraged a myth I see repeated in the mainstream press by those out of touch with the multiplayer, socially interactive game experiences that are common today, including *Halo 3*.

Overview of Content

The graphics section in this edition covers several topics of recent interest, leveraging new features of graphics APIs such as Compute Shader, tessellation using DirectX 11, and two gems on the implementation details of Screen Space Ambient Occlusion (SSAO). In the physics and animation section, we have selected a number of gems that advance beyond the basics of the topics such as IK solvers or fluid simulation in general. Instead, these gems go deeper with improvements to existing published techniques based on real-world experience with the current state of the art—for example, a simple, fast, and accurate IK solver, leveraging swarm systems for animation, and modeling air and fluid resistance.

Artificial intelligence, AI, is one of the hottest areas in game development these days. Game players want worlds that don't just look real, but that also feel and act real. The acting part is the responsibility of the AI programmer. Gems in the AI section are diverse, covering areas such as decision making, detailed character simulation, and player modeling to solve the problem of gold farm detection. The innovations discussed are sure to influence future gems.

In the general programming section, we have a number of tools to help with the development, performance, and testing of our game engines. We include gems that deal with multi-threading using Intel's Thread Building Blocks, an open-source multi-threading library, memory allocation and profiling, as well as a useful code coverage system used by the developers at Crytek. The gems in the networking and multiplayer section cover architecture, security, scalability, and the leveraging of social networking applications to create multiplayer experiences.

The audio section had fewer submissions than in past years. Why is this? Is the area of audio lacking in innovation? Has it matured to the point where developers are buying off-the-shelf components? Regardless, we've assembled a collection of gems for audio that we think will be of interest. In one of the articles in the audio section, we discuss a relatively new idea—the notion of real-time calculation of the audio signal based on the actual physics instead of using the traditional technique of playing a pre-recorded processed sound. As games become more interactive and physics driven, there will be a corresponding demand for more realistic sound environments generated by such techniques enabled with the increasing computational horsepower Moore's Law continues to deliver to game developers.

I'm excited to introduce a new section in this edition of *Game Programming Gems 8* that I'm calling "General Purpose Computing on GPUs." This is a new area for the *Gems* series, and we wanted to have a real-world case study of a game developer using the GPU for non-graphics tasks. We've collected three gems for this section. The first is about OpenCL, a new open standard for programming heterogeneous platforms of today, and we also have two gems that leverage PhysX for collision detection and fluid simulation. The PhysX components were used in *Batman: Arkham Asylum* by Rocksteady Studios Ltd. As the computing capabilities of the platform evolve, I expect game developers will face the decision of what to compute, where to compute, and how to manage the data being operated upon. These articles serve as case studies in what others have done in their games. I expect this to be an exciting area of future development.

While we all have our areas of specialty, I think it's fair to say game developers are a hungry bunch, with a common desire to learn, develop, and challenge ourselves and our abilities. These gems are meant to inspire, enlighten, and evolve the industry. As always, we look forward to the contributions and feedback developers have when putting these gems into practice.

Adam Lake
Adam_t_lake@yahoo.com

About the Cover Image

© Valve Corporation

The cover of *Game Programming Gems 8* features the Engineer from Valve's *Team Fortress 2*. With their follow-up to the original class-based multiplayer shooter *Team Fortress*, Valve chose to depart from the typical photorealistic military themes of the genre. Instead, they employed an "illustrative" non-photorealistic rendering style, reminiscent of American commercial illustrators of the 1920s. This was motivated by the need for players to be able to quickly visually identify each other's team, class, and weapon choices in the game. The novel art style and rendering techniques of *Team Fortress 2* allowed Valve's designers to visually separate the character classes from each other and from the game's environments through the use of strong silhouettes and strategic distribution of color value.

CD-ROM Downloads

If you purchased an ebook version of this book, and the book had a companion CD-ROM, we will mail you a copy of the disc. Please send ptrsupplements@cengage.com the title of the book, the ISBN, your name, address, and phone number. Thank you.

Acknowledgments

I'd like to take a moment to acknowledge the section editors that I worked with to create this tome. They are the best and brightest in the industry. The quality of submissions and content in this book is a testament to this fact. They worked incredibly hard to bring this book together, and I thank them for their time and expertise. Also, I appreciate the time and patience that Emi Smith and Cathleen Small at Cengage Learning have put into this first-time book editor. They were essential in taking care of all the details necessary for publication. Finally, I'd like to acknowledge the artists at Valve who provided the cover image for this edition of *Game Programming Gems*.

I have been blessed to have had exposure to numerous inspirational individuals—friends who refused to accept norms, parents who satiated my educational desires, teachers willing to spend a few extra minutes on a random tangent, instructors to teach not just what we know about the world, but also to make me aware of the things we do not. Most importantly, I want to acknowledge my wife, Stacey Lake, who remained supportive while I toiled away in the evenings and weekends for the better part of a year on this book.

I dedicate these efforts to my mother, Amanda Lake. I thank her for teaching me that education is an enjoyable lifelong endeavor.

Contributors

Full bios for those contributors who submitted one can be found at www.courseptr.com/ downloads. Contributors to this book include:

Dr. Doug Binks, D.Phil.
Udeepta Bordoloi
Igor Borovikov
Cyril Brom
Eric Brown
Phil Carlisle
Michael Dailly
Peter Dalton
Kevin Dill
Jean-Francois Dube
Dominic Filion
Marco Fratarcangeli
Nico Galoppo
Benedict R. Gaster
Gero Gerber
Robert Jay Gould
Neil Gower
Joshua Grass, Ph.D.
Hunter Hale
Mark Harris
Thomas Hartley
Kevin He
Claus Höfele
Allen Hux
Peter Iliev
Matthew Jack
Aleksey Kadukin
Nikhil S. Ketkar
Hyunwoo Ki
Adam Lake
Michael Lewin
Chris Lomont, Ph.D.

Ricky Lung
Khaled Mamou
Dave Mark
Quasim Mehdi
Krzysztof Mieloszyk
Jason Mitchell
Ben Nicholson
Ian Ni-Lewis
Mat Noguchi
Borut Pfeifer
Brian Pickrell
Tomas Poch
Steve Rabin
Mike Ramsey
B. Charles Rasco, Ph.D.
João Lucas G. Raza
Aurelio Reis
Zhimin Ren
Marc Romankewicz
Dario Sancho
Rahul Sathe
Simon Schirm
Brian Schmidt
Ondřej Šerý
Philip Taylor
Richard Tonge
Steven Tovey
Gabriel Ware
Ben Wyatt
G. Michael Youngblood
Jason Zink
Robert Zubek

GRAPHICS

Introduction

Jason Mitchell, Valve

jason@pixelmaven.com

In this edition of the *Game Programming Gems* series, we explore a wide range of important real-time graphics topics, from lynchpin systems such as font rendering to cutting-edge hardware architectures, such as Larrabee, PlayStation 3, and the DirectX 11 compute shader. Developers in the trenches at top industry studios such as Blizzard, id, Bizarre Creations, Nexon, and Intel's Advanced Visual Computing group share their insights on optimally exploiting graphics hardware to create high-quality visuals for games.

To kick off this section, Aurelio Reis of id Software compares several methods for accelerating font rendering by exploiting GPU instancing, settling on a constant-buffer-based method that achieves the best performance.

We then move on to two chapters discussing the popular image-space techniques of Screen Space Ambient Occlusion (SSAO) and deferred shading. Dominic Filion of Blizzard Entertainment discusses the SSAO algorithms used in *StarCraft II*, including novel controls that allowed Blizzard's artists to tune the look of the effect to suit their vision. Hyunwoo Ki of Nexon then describes a multi-resolution acceleration method for deferred shading that computes low-frequency lighting information at a lower spatial frequency and uses a novel method for handling high-frequency edge cases.

For the remainder of the section, we concentrate on techniques that take advantage of the very latest graphics hardware, from DirectX 11's tessellator and compute shader to Larrabee and the PlayStation 3. Rahul Sathe of Intel presents a method for culling of Bezier patches in the context of the new DirectX 11 pipeline. Jason Zink then describes the new DirectX 11 compute shader architecture, using Screen Space Ambient Occlusion as a case study to illustrate the novel aspects of this new hardware architecture. In a pair of articles from Intel, Nico Galoppo and Allen Hux describe a method for integrating anti-aliasing into the irregular shadow mapping algorithm as well as a software task system that allows highly programmable systems such as Larrabee to achieve maximum throughput on this type of technique. We conclude the section with Steven Tovey's look at the SPU units on the PlayStation 3 and techniques for achieving maximum performance in the vehicle damage and light pre-pass rendering systems in the racing game *Blur* from Bizarre Creations.

1.1

Fast Font Rendering with Instancing

Aurelio Reis, id Software
AurelioReis@gmail.com

Font rendering is an essential component of almost all interactive applications, and while techniques exist to allow for fully scalable vector-based font rendering using modern GPUs, the so-called "bitmap font" is still the most versatile, efficient, and easy-to-implement solution. When implemented on typical graphics APIs, however, this technique uses run-time updated vertex buffers to store per-glyph geometry, resulting in inefficient rendering performance by potentially stalling the graphics pipeline. By leveraging efficient particle system rendering techniques that were developed previously, it is possible to render thousands of glyphs in a single batch without ever touching the vertex buffer.

In this article, I propose a simple and efficient method to render fonts utilizing modern graphics hardware when compared to other similar methods. This technique is also useful in that it can be generalized for use in rendering other 2D elements, such as sprites and graphical user interface (GUI) elements.

Text-Rendering Basics

The most common font format is the vector-based TrueType format. This format represents font glyphs (in other words, alphabetic characters and other symbols) as vector data, specifically, quadratic Bezier curves and line segments. As a result, TrueType fonts are compact, easy to author, and scale well with different display resolutions. The downside of a vector font, however, is that it is not straightforward to directly render this type of data on graphics hardware. There are, however, a few different ways to map the vector representation to a form that graphics hardware can render.

One way is to generate geometry directly from the vector curves, as shown in Figure 1.1.1. However, while modern GPUs are quite efficient at rendering large numbers of triangles, the number of polygons generated from converting a large number of complex vector curves to a triangle mesh could number in the tens of thousands. This increase in triangle throughput can greatly decrease application performance.

Some optimizations to this way of rendering fonts have been introduced, such as the technique described by Loop and Blinn in which the polygonal mesh consists merely of the curve control points while the curve pixels are generated using a simple and efficient pixel shader [Loop05]. While this is a great improvement over the naive triangulation approach, the number of polygons generated in this approach is still prohibitively high on older graphics hardware (and that of the current console generation—the target of this article).

Times New Roman

Figure 1.1.1   Vector curves converted into polygonal geometry.

Because of these limitations, the most common approach relies on rasterizing vector graphics into a bitmap and displaying each glyph as a rectangle composed of two triangles (from here on referred to as a *quad*), as shown in Figure 1.1.2. A font texture page is generated with an additional UV offset table that maps glyphs to a location in that texture very similar to how a texture atlas is used [NVIDIA04]. The most obvious drawback is the resolution dependence caused by the font page being rasterized at a predefined resolution, which leads to distortion when rendering a font at a non-native resolution. Additional techniques exist to supplement this approach with higher quality results while mitigating the resolution dependence that leads to blurry and aliased textures, such as the approach described by [Green07]. Overall, the benefits of the raster approach outweigh the drawbacks, because rendering bitmap fonts is incredibly easy and efficient.

Figure 1.1.2   A font page and a glyph rendered on a quad.

To draw glyphs for a bitmap font, the program must bind the texture page matching the intended glyph set and draw a quad for each glyph, taking into account spacing for kerning or other character-related offsets. While this technique yields very good performance, it can still be inefficient, as the buffers containing the geometry for each batch of glyphs must be continually updated. Constantly touching these buffers is a sure way to cause GPU stalls, resulting in decreased performance. For text- or GUI-heavy games, this can lead to an unacceptable overall performance hit.

Improving Performance

One way to draw the glyphs for the GUI is to create a GUI model that maintains buffers on the graphics card for drawing a predefined maximum number of indexed triangles as quads. Whenever a new glyph is to be drawn, its quad is inserted into a list, and the vertex buffer for the model is eventually updated with the needed geometry at a convenient point in the graphics pipeline. When the time comes to render the GUI model, assuming the same texture page is used, only a single draw call is required. As previously mentioned, this buffer must be updated each frame and for each draw batch that must be drawn. Ideally, as few draw batches as possible are needed, as the font texture page should contain all the individual glyphs that would need to be rendered, but on occasion (such as for high-resolution fonts or Asian fonts with many glyphs), it's not possible to fit them all on one page. In the situation where a font glyph must be rendered from a different page, the batch is broken and must be presented immediately so that a new one can be started with the new texture. This holds true for any unique rendering states that a glyph may hold, such as blending modes or custom shaders.

Lock-Discard

The slowest part of the process is when the per-glyph geometry must be uploaded to the graphics card. Placing the buffer memory as close to AGP memory as possible (using API hints) helps, but locking and unlocking vertex buffers can still be quite expensive. To alleviate the expense, it is possible to use a buffer that is marked to "discard" its existing buffer if the GPU is currently busy with it. By telling the API to discard the existing buffer, a new one is created, which can be written to immediately. Eventually, the old buffer is purged by the API under the covers. This use of lock-discard prevents the CPU from waiting on the GPU to finish consuming the buffer (for example, in the case where it was being rendered at the same time). You can specify this with the `D3DLOCK_DISCARD` flag in Direct3D or by passing a NULL pointer to `glBufferDataARB` and then calling `glMapBufferARB()`. Be aware that although this is quite an improvement, it is still not an ideal solution, as the entire buffer must be discarded. Essentially, this makes initiating a small update to the buffer impossible.

Vertex Compression

Another step in improving performance is reducing the amount of memory that needs to be sent to the video card. The vertex structure for sending a quad looks something like this and takes 28 bytes per vertex (and 112 bytes for each quad):

```
struct GPU_QUAD_VERTEX_POS_TC_COLOR
{
        D3DXVECTOR4 Position;
        D3DXVECTOR2 Texcoord;
        D3DCOLOR Color;
};
```

Since the bandwidth across the AGP bus to the video card is not infinite, it is important to be aware of how much memory is being pushed through it. One way to reduce the memory costs is to use an additional vertex stream to update only that information that has changed on a per-frame basis. Unfortunately, the three essential quad attributes (position, texture dimensions, and color) could be in a state of constant flux, so there is little frame-to-frame coherency we can exploit.

There is one very easy way to reduce at least some of the data that must be sent to the video card, however. Traditionally, each vertex represents a corner of a quad. This is not ideal, because this data is relatively static. That is, the size and position of a quad changes, but not the fact that it is a quad. Hicks describes a shader technique that allows for aligning a billboarded quad toward the screen by storing a rightFactor and upFactor for each corner of the billboard and projecting those vertices along the camera axes [Hicks03]. This technique is attractive, as it puts the computation of offsetting the vertices on the GPU and potentially limits the need for vertex buffer locks to update the quad positions.

By using a separate vertex stream that contains unique data, it is possible to represent the width and height of the quad corners as a 4D unsigned byte vector. (Technically, you could go as small as a Bool if that was supported on modern hardware.) In the vertex declaration, it is possible to map the position information to specific vertex semantics, which can then be accessed directly in the vertex shader. The vertex structure would look something like this:

```
struct GPU_QUAD_VERTEX
{
        BYTE OffsetXY[ 4 ];
};
```

Although this may seem like an improvement, it really isn't, since the same amount of memory must be used to represent the quad attributes (more so since we're supplying a 4-byte offset now). There is an easy way to supply this additional information without requiring the redundancy of all those additional vertices.

Instancing Quad Geometry

If you're lucky enough to support a Shader Model 3 profile, you have hardware support for some form of geometry instancing. OpenGL 2.0 has support for instancing using pseudo-instancing [GLSL04] and the EXT_draw_instanced [EXT06] extension, which uses the glDrawArraysInstancedEXT and glDrawElementsInstancedEXT routines to render up to 1,024 instanced primitives that are referenced via an instance identifier in shader code.

As of DirectX 9, Direct3D also supports instancing, which can be utilized by creating a vertex buffer containing the instance geometry and an additional vertex buffer with the per-instance data. By using instancing, we're able to completely eliminate our redundant quad vertices (and index buffer) at the cost of an additional but smaller buffer that holds only the per-instance data. This buffer is directly hooked up to the vertex shader via input semantics and can be easily accessed with almost no additional work to the previous method. While this solution sounds ideal, we have found that instancing actually comes with quite a bit of per-batch overhead and also requires quite a bit of instanced data to become a win. As a result, it should be noted that performance does not scale quite so well and in some situations can be as poor as that of the original buffer approach (or worse on certain hardware)! This is likely attributed to the fact that the graphics hardware must still point to this data in some way or another, and while space is saved, additional logic is required to compute the proper vertex strides.

Constant Array Instancing

Another way to achieve similar results with better performance is to perform shader instancing using constant arrays. By creating a constant array for each of the separate quad attributes (in other words, position/size, texture coordinate position/size, color), it is possible to represent all the necessary information without the need for a heavyweight vertex structure. See Figure 1.1.3.

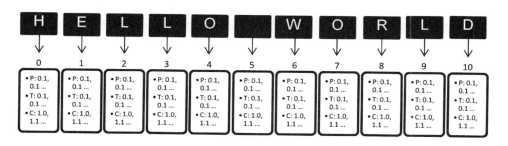

Figure 1.1.3 A number of glyphs referencing their data from a constant array.

Similar to indexed vertex blending (a.k.a. matrix palette skinning), an index is assigned for each group of four vertices required to render a quad, as shown in Figure 1.1.4. To get the value for the current vertex, all that is needed is to index into the constant array using this value. Because the number of constants available is usually below 256 on pre–Shader Model 4 hardware, this index can be packed directly as an additional element in the vertex offset vector (thus requiring no additional storage space). It's also possible to use geometry instancing to just pass in the quad ID/index in order to bypass the need for a large buffer of four vertices per quad. However, as mentioned previously, we have found that instancing can be unreliable in practice.

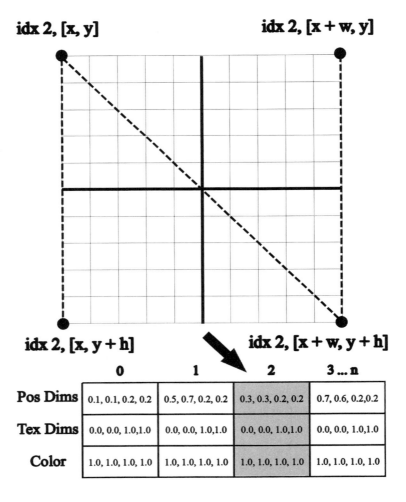

idx 2, [x, y]   **idx 2, [x + w, y]**

idx 2, [x, y + h]   **idx 2, [x + w, y + h]**

	0	1	2	3 ... n
Pos Dims	0.1, 0.1, 0.2, 0.2	0.5, 0.7, 0.2, 0.2	0.3, 0.3, 0.2, 0.2	0.7, 0.6, 0.2,0.2
Tex Dims	0.0, 0.0, 1.0,1.0	0.0, 0.0, 1.0,1.0	0.0, 0.0, 1.0,1.0	0.0, 0.0, 1.0,1.0
Color	1.0, 1.0, 1.0, 1.0	1.0, 1.0, 1.0, 1.0	1.0, 1.0, 1.0, 1.0	1.0, 1.0, 1.0, 1.0

Figure 1.1.4   A quad referencing an element within the attribute constant array.

This technique yields fantastic performance but has the downside of only allowing a certain number of constants, depending on your shader profile. The vertex structure is incredibly compact, weighing in at a mere 4 bytes (16 bytes per quad) with an additional channel still available for use:

```
struct GPU_QUAD_VERTEX
{
        BYTE OffsetXY_IndexZ[ 4 ];
};
```

Given the three quad attributes presented above and with a limit of 256 constants, up to 85 quads can be rendered per batch. Despite this limitation, performance can still be quite a bit better than the other approaches, especially as the number of state changes increases (driving up the number of batches and driving down the number of quads per batch).

Additional Considerations

I will now describe some small but important facets of font rendering, notably an efficient use of clip-space position and a cheap but effective sorting method. Also, in the sample code for this chapter on the book's CD, I have provided source code for a texture atlasing solution that readers may find useful in their font rendering systems.

Sorting

Fonts are typically drawn in a back-to-front fashion, relying on the painter's algorithm to achieve correct occlusion. Although this is suitable for most applications, certain situations may require that quads be layered in a different sort order than that in which they were drawn. This is easily implemented by using the remaining available value in the vertex structure offset/index vector as a z value for the quad, allowing for up to 256 layers.

Clip-Space Positions

To save a few instructions and the constant space for the world-view-projection matrix (the clip matrix), it's possible to specify the position directly in clip-space to forego having to transform the vertices from perspective to orthographic space, as illustrated in Figure 1.1.5. Clip-space positions range from −1 to 1 in the X and Y directions. To remap an absolute screen-space coordinate to clip space, we can just use the equation [cx = −1 + x * (2 / screen_width)], [cy = 1 − y * (2 / screen_height)], where x and y are the screen-space coordinates up to a max of screen_width and screen_height, respectively.

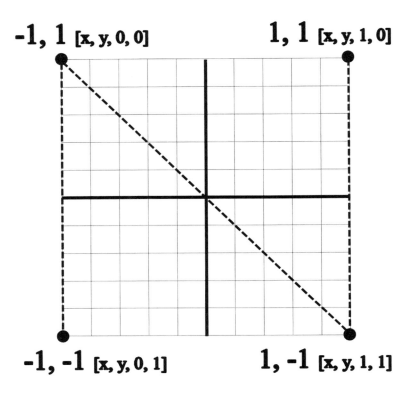

Figure 1.1.5   A quad/billboard being expanded.

Texture Atlasing

On the book's CD, I have provided code for a simple virtual texture system that uses atlases to reduce batches. This system attempts to load an atlased version of a texture if possible and otherwise loads a texture directly from disk. There are some switches (documented in the code) that demonstrate how to turn this system on and off to demonstrate how important it can be toward reducing the number of batches and maintaining a high level of performance.

Future Work

The techniques demonstrated in this chapter were tailored to work on current console technology, which is limited to Shader Model 3. In the future, I would like to extend these techniques to take advantage of new hardware features, such as Geometry Shaders and StreamOut, to further increase performance, image fidelity, and ease of use.

Demo

On the accompanying disc, you'll find a Direct3D sample application that demonstrates each of the discussed techniques in a text- and GUI-rich presentation. Two scenes are presented: One displays a cityscape for a typical 2D tile-based game, and the other displays a Strange Attractor simulation. In addition, there is an option to go overboard with the text rendering. Feel free to play around with the code until you get a feel for the strengths and weaknesses of the different approaches.

The main shader file (Font.fx) contains the shaders of interest as well as some additional functionality (such as font anti-aliasing/filtering). Please note that certain aspects (such as quad expansion) were made for optimum efficiency and not necessarily readability. In general, most of the code was meant to be very accessible, and it will be helpful to periodically cross-reference the files GuiModel.cpp and Font.fx.

Conclusion

In this gem, I demonstrated a way to render font and GUI elements easily and efficiently by taking advantage of readily available hardware features, such as instancing, multiple stream support, and constant array indexing. As a takeaway item, you should be able to easily incorporate such a system into your technology base or improve an existing system with only minor changes.

References

[EXT06] "EXT_draw_instanced." 2006. Open GL. n.d. <http://www.opengl.org/registry/specs/EXT/draw_instanced.txt>.

[GLSL04] "GLSL Pseudo-Instancing." 17 Nov. 2004. NVIDIA. n.d. <http://http.download.nvidia.com/developer/SDK/Individual_Samples/DEMOS/OpenGL/src/glsl_pseudo_instancing/docs/glsl_pseudo_instancing.pdf>.

[Green07] Green, Chris. "Improved Alpha-Tested Magnification for Vector Textures and Special Effects." Course on Advanced Real-Time Rendering in 3D Graphics and Games. SIGGRAPH 2007. San Diego Convention Center, San Diego, CA. 8 August 2007.

[Hicks03] Hicks, O'Dell. "Screen-aligned Particles with Minimal VertexBuffer Locking." *ShaderX2: Shader Programming Tips and Tricks with DirectX 9.0*. Ed. Wolfgang F. Engel. Plano, TX: Wordware Publishing, Inc., 2004. 107–112.

[Loop05] Loop, Charles and Jim Blinn. "Resolution Independent Curve Rendering Using Programmable Graphics Hardware." 2005. Microsoft. n.d. <http://research.microsoft.com/en-us/um/people/cloop/loopblinn05.pdf>.

[NVIDIA04] "Improve Batching Using Texture Atlases." 2004. NVIDIA. n.d. <http://http.download.nvidia.com/developer/NVTextureSuite/Atlas_Tools/Texture_Atlas_Whitepaper.pdf>.

Principles and Practice of Screen Space Ambient Occlusion

Dominic Filion, Blizzard Entertainment
dfilion@blizzard.com

Simulation of direct lighting in modern video games is a well-understood concept, as virtually all of real-time graphics has standardized on the Lambertian and Blinn models for simulating direct lighting. However, indirect lighting (also referred to as *global illumination*) is still an active area of research with a variety of approaches being explored. Moreover, although some simulation of indirect lighting is possible in real time, full simulation of all its effects in real time is very challenging, even on the latest hardware.

Global illumination is based on simulating the effects of light bouncing around a scene multiple times as light is reflected on light surfaces. Computational methods such as radiosity attempt to directly model this physical process by modeling the interactions of lights and surfaces in an environment, including the bouncing of light off of surfaces. Although highly realistic, sophisticated global illumination methods are typically too computationally intensive to perform in real time, especially for games, and thus to achieve the complex shadowing and bounced lighting effects in games, one has to look for simplifications to achieve a comparable result.

One possible simplification is to focus on the visual effects of global illumination instead of the physical process and furthermore to aim at a particular subset of effects that global illumination achieves. Ambient occlusion is one such subset. Ambient occlusion simplifies the problem space by assuming all indirect light is equally distributed throughout the scene. With this assumption, the amount of indirect light hitting a point on a surface will be directly proportional to how much that point is exposed to the scene around it. A point on a plane surface can receive light from a full 180-degree hemisphere around that point and above the plane. In another example, a point in a room's corner, as shown in Figure 1.2.1, could receive a smaller amount of light than a point in the middle of the floor, since a greater amount of its "upper hemisphere" is occluded by the nearby walls. The resulting effect is a crude approximation of global illumination that enhances depth in the scene by shrouding corners, nooks, and crannies in a scene. Artistically, the effect can be controlled by varying the size of the hemisphere within which other objects are considered to occlude neighboring points; large hemisphere ranges will extend the shadow shroud outward from corners and recesses.

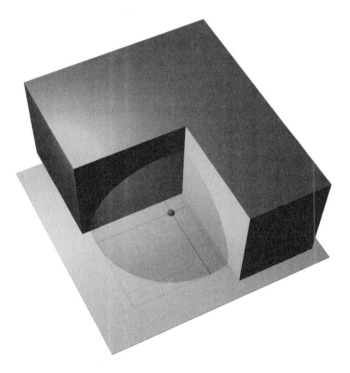

Figure 1.2.1   Ambient occlusion relies on finding how much of the hemisphere around the sampling point is blocked by the environment.

Although the global illumination problem has been vastly simplified through this approach, it can still be prohibitively expensive to compute in real time. Every point on every scene surface needs to cast many rays around it to test whether an occluding object might be blocking the light, and an ambient occlusion term is computed based on how many rays were occluded from the total amount of rays emitted from that point. Performing arbitrary ray intersections with the full scene is also difficult to implement on graphics hardware. We need further simplification.

Screen Space Ambient Occlusion

What is needed is a way to structure the scene so that we can quickly and easily determine whether a given surface point is occluded by nearby geometry. It turns out that the standard depth buffer, which graphics engines already use to perform hidden surface removal, can be used to approximate local occlusion [Shanmugam07, Mittring07]. By definition, the depth buffer contains the depth of every visible point in the scene. From these depths, we can reconstruct the 3D positions of the visible surface points. Points that can potentially occlude other points are located close to each other in both screen space and world space, making the search for potential occluders straightforward. We need to align a hemisphere around each point's upper hemisphere as defined by its normal. We will thus need a normal buffer that will encode the normal of every corresponding point in the depth buffer in screen space.

Rather than doing a full ray intersection, we can simply inspect the depths of neighboring points to establish the likelihood that each is occluding the current point. Any neighbor whose 2D position does not fall within the 2D coverage of the hemisphere could not possibly be an occluder. If it does lie within the hemisphere, then the closer the neighbor point's depth is to the target point, the higher the odds it is an occluder. If the neighbor's depth is behind the point being tested for occlusion, then no occlusion is assumed to occur. All of these calculations can be performed using the screen space buffer of normals and depths, hence the name Screen Space Ambient Occlusion (SSAO).

At first glance, this may seem like a gross oversimplification. After all, the depth buffer doesn't contain the whole scene, just the visible parts of it, and as such is only a partial reconstruction of the scene. For example, a point in the background could be occluded by an object that is hidden behind another object in the foreground, which a depth buffer would completely miss. Thus, there would be pixels in the image that

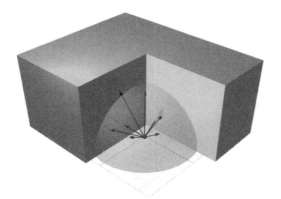
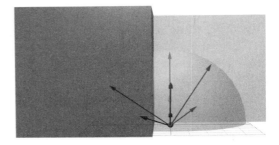

Figure 1.2.2 SSAO samples neighbor points to discover the likelihood of occlusion. Lighter arrows are behind the center point and are considered occluded samples.

should have some amount of occlusion but don't due to the incomplete representation we have of the scene's geometry.

It turns out that these kinds of artifacts are not especially objectionable in practice. The eye focuses first on cues from objects within the scene, and missing cues from objects hidden behind one another are not as disturbing. Furthermore, ambient occlusion is a low-frequency phenomenon; what matters more is the general effect rather than specific detailed cues, and taking shortcuts to achieve a similar yet incorrect effect is a fine tradeoff in this case. Discovering where the artifacts lie should be more a process of rationalizing the errors than of simply catching them with the untrained eye.

From this brief overview, we can outline the steps we will take to implement Screen Space Ambient Occlusion.

- We will first need to have a depth buffer and a normal buffer at our disposal from which we can extract information.
- From these screen space maps, we can derive our algorithm. Each pixel in screen space will generate a corresponding ambient occlusion value for that pixel and store that information in a separate render target. For each pixel in our depth buffer, we extract that point's position and sample n neighboring pixels within the hemisphere aligned around the point's normal.
- The ratio of occluding versus non-occluding points will be our ambient occlusion term result.
- The ambient occlusion render target can then be blended with the color output from the scene generated afterward.

I will now describe our Screen Space Ambient Occlusion algorithm in greater detail.

Generating the Source Data

The first step in setting up the SSAO algorithm is to prepare the necessary incoming data. Depending on how the final compositing is to be done, this can be accomplished in one of two ways.

The first method requires that the scene be rendered twice. The first pass will render the depth and normal data only. The SSAO algorithm can then generate the ambient occlusion output in an intermediate step, and the scene can be rendered again in full color. With this approach, the ambient occlusion map (in screen space) can be sampled by direct lights from the scene to have their contribution modulated by the ambient occlusion term as well, which can help make the contributions from direct and indirect lighting more coherent with each other. This approach is the most flexible but is somewhat less efficient because the geometry has to be passed to the hardware twice, doubling the API batch count and, of course, the geometry processing load.

A different approach is to render the scene only once, using multiple render targets bound as output to generate the depth and normal information as the scene is first rendered without an ambient lighting term. SSAO data is then generated as a post-step, and the ambient lighting term can simply be added. This is a faster approach, but in practice artists lose the flexibility to decide which individual lights in the scene may or may not be affected by the ambient occlusion term, should they want to do so. Using a fully deferred renderer and pushing the entire scene lighting stage to a post-processing step can get around this limitation to allow the entire lighting setup to be configurable to use ambient occlusion per light.

Whether to use the single-pass or dual-pass method will depend on the constraints that are most important to a given graphics engine. In all cases, a suitable format must be chosen to store the depth and normal information. When supported, a 16-bit floating-point format will be the easiest to work with, storing the normal components in the red, green, and blue components and storing depth as the alpha component.

Screen Space Ambient Occlusion is very bandwidth intensive, and minimizing sampling bandwidth is necessary to achieve optimal performance. Moreover, if using the single-pass multi-render target approach, all bound render targets typically need to be of the same bit depth on the graphics hardware. If the main color output is 32-bit RGBA, then outputting to a 16-bit floating-point buffer at the same time won't be possible. To minimize bandwidth and storage, the depth and normal can be encoded in as little as a single 32-bit RGBA color, storing the x and y components of the normal in the 8-bit red and green channels while storing a 16-bit depth value in the blue and alpha channels. The HLSL shader code for encoding and decoding the normal and depth values is shown in Listing 1.2.1.

LISTING 1.2.1   HLSL code to decode the normal on subsequent passes as well as HLSL code used to encode and decode the 16-bit depth value

```
// Normal encoding simply outputs x and y components in R and G in
// the range 0..1
float3 DecodeNormal( float2 cInput ) {
    float3 vNormal.xy = 2.0f * cInput.rg - 1.0f;
    vNormal.z = sqrt(max(0, 1 - dot(vNormal.xy, vNormal.xy)));
    return vNormal;
}


// Encode depth to B and A
float2 DepthEncode( float fDepth ) {
    float2 vResult;
    // Input depth must be mapped to 0..1 range
    fDepth = fDepth / p_fScalingFactor;

    // R = Basis = 8 bits = 256 possible values
    // G = fractional part with each 1/256th slice
    vResult.ba = frac( float2( fDepth, fDepth * 256.0f ) );
    return vResult;
}

float3 DecodeDepth( float4 cInput ) {
    return dot ( cInput.ba, float2( 1.0f, 1.0f / 256.0f ) *
                p_fScalingFactor;
}
```

Sampling Process

With the input data in hand, we can begin the ambient occlusion generation process itself. At any visible point on a surface on the screen, we need to explore neighboring points to determine whether they could occlude our current point. Multiple samples are thus taken from neighboring points in the scene using a filtering process described by the HLSL shader code in Listing 1.2.2.

LISTING 1.2.2   Screen Space Ambient Occlusion filter described in HLSL code

```
// i_VPOS is screen pixel coordinate as given by HLSL VPOS interpolant.
// p_vSSAOSamplePoints is a distribution of sample offsets for each sample.
float4 PostProcessSSAO( float3 i_VPOS )
{
    float2 vScreenUV;          // ▪ This will become useful later.
    float3 vViewPos = 2DToViewPos( i_VPOS, vScreenUV );

    half fAccumBlock = 0.0f;
    for ( int i = 0; i < iSampleCount; i++ )
    {
        float3 vSamplePointDelta = p_vSSAOSamplePoints[i];
        float fBlock = TestOcclusion(
                        vViewPos,
                            vSamplePointDelta,
                        p_fOcclusionRadius,
                        p_fFullOcclusionThreshold,
                        p_fNoOcclusionThreshold,
                        p_fOcclusionPower ) )
        fAccumBlock += fBlock;
    }
    fAccumBlock /= iSampleCount;

    return 1.0f - fAccumBlock;
}
```

We start with the current point, p, whose occlusion we are computing. We have the point's 2D coordinate in screen space. Sampling the depth buffer at the corresponding UV coordinates, we can retrieve that point's depth. From these three pieces of information, the 3D position of the point within can be reconstructed using the shader code shown in Listing 1.2.3.

LISTING 1.2.3   HLSL shader code used to map a pixel from screen space to view space

```
// vRecipDepthBufferSize = 1.0 / depth buffer width and height in pixels.
// p_vCameraFrustrumSize = Full width and height of camera frustum at the
// camera's near plane in world space.
float2 p_vRecipDepthBufferSize;
float2 p_vCameraFrustrumSize;
```

```
float3 2DPosToViewPos( float3 i_VPOS, out float2 vScreenUV )
{
    float2 vViewSpaceUV = i_VPOS * p_vRecipDepthBufferSize;
    vScreenUV    = vViewSpaceUV;

    // From 0..1 to to 0..2
    vViewSpaceUV = vViewSpaceUV * float2( 2.0f, -2.0f );
    // From 0..2 to -1..1
    vViewSpaceUV = vViewSpaceUV + float2( -1.0f, 1.0f );
    vViewSpaceUV = vViewSpaceUV * p_vCameraFrustrumSize * 0.5f;

    return float3( vViewSpaceUV.x, vViewSpaceUV.y, 1.0f ) *
                  tex2D( p_sDepthBuffer, vScreenUV ).r;
}
```

We will need to sample the surrounding area of the point p along multiple offsets from its position, giving us n neighbor positions qi. Sampling the normal buffer will give us the normal around which we can align our set of offset vectors, ensuring that all sample offsets fall within point p's upper hemisphere. Transforming each offset vector by a matrix can be expensive, and one alternative is to perform a dot product between the offset vector and the normal vector at that point and to flip the offset vector if the dot product is negative, as shown in Figure 1.2.3. This is a cheaper way to solve for the offset vectors without doing a full matrix transform, but it has the drawback of using fewer samples when samples are rejected due to falling behind the plane of the surface of the point p.

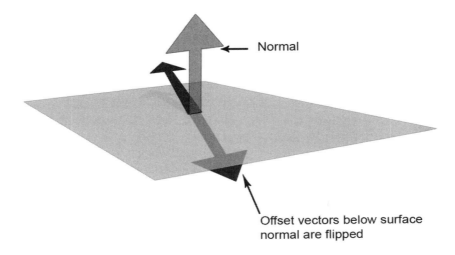

Figure 1.2.3   Samples behind the hemisphere are flipped
over to stay within the hemisphere.

Each neighbor's 3D position can then be transformed back to screen space in 2D, and the depth of the neighbor point can be sampled from the depth buffer. From this neighboring depth value, we can establish whether an object likely occupies that space at the neighbor point. Listing 1.2.4 shows shader code to test for this occlusion.

LISTING 1.2.4   HLSL code used to test occlusion by a neighboring pixel

```
float TestOcclusion( float3 vViewPos,
                     float3 vSamplePointDelta,
                float fOcclusionRadius,
                     float fFullOcclusionThreshold,
                     float fNoOcclusionThreshold,
    float fOcclusionPower )
{
    float3 vSamplePoint = vViewPos + fOcclusionRadius * vSamplePointDelta;
    float2 vSamplePointUV;
    vSamplePointUV = vSamplePoint.xy / vSamplePoint.z;
    vSamplePointUV = vSamplePointUV / p_vCameraSize / 0.5f;
    vSamplePointUV = vSamplePointUV + float2( 1.0f, -1.0f );
    vSamplePointUV = vSamplePointUV * float2( 0.5f, -0.5f );

    float fSampleDepth = tex2D( p_sDepthBuffer, vSamplePointUV ).r;
    float fDistance = vSamplePoint.z - fSampleDepth;
    return OcclusionFunction( fDistance, fFullOcclusionThreshold,
                              fNoOcclusionThreshold, fOcclusionPower );
}
```

We now have the 3D positions of both our point p and the neighboring points qi. We also have the depth di of the frontmost object along the ray that connects the eye to each neighboring point. How do we determine ambient occlusion?

The depth di gives us some hints as to whether a solid object occupies the space at each of the sampled neighboring points. Clearly, if the depth di is behind the sampled point's depth, it cannot occupy the space at the sampled point. The depth buffer does not give us the thickness of the object along the ray from the viewer; thus, if the depth of the object is anywhere in front of p, it may occupy the space, though without thickness information, we can't know for sure. We can devise some reasonable heuristics with the information we do have and use a probabilistic method.

The further in front of the sample point the depth is, the less likely it is to occupy that space. Also, the greater the distance between the point p and the neighbor point, the lesser the occlusion, as the object covers a smaller part of the hemisphere. Thus, we can derive some occlusion heuristics based on:

- The difference between the sampled depth d_i and the depth of the point q_i
- The distance between p and q_i

For the first relationship, we can formulate an occlusion function to map the depth deltas to occlusion values.

If the aim is to be physically correct, then the occlusion function should be quadratic. In our case we are more concerned about being able to let our artists adjust the occlusion function, and thus the occlusion function can be arbitrary. Really, the occlusion function can be any function that adheres to the following criteria:

- Negative depth deltas should give zero occlusion. (The occluding surface is behind the sample point.)
- Smaller depth deltas should give higher occlusion values.
- The occlusion value needs to fall to zero again beyond a certain depth delta value, as the object is too far away to occlude.

For our implementation, we simply chose a linearly stepped function that is entirely controlled by the artist. A graph of our occlusion function is shown in Figure 1.2.4. There is a full-occlusion threshold where every positive depth delta smaller than this value gets complete occlusion of one, and a no-occlusion threshold beyond which no occlusion occurs. Depth deltas between these two extremes fall off linearly from one to zero, and the value is exponentially raised to a specified occlusion power value. If a more complex occlusion function is required, it can be pre-computed in a small 1D texture to be looked up on demand.

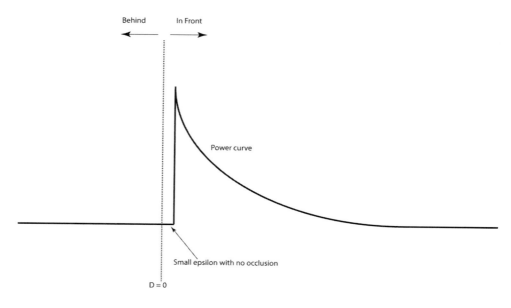

Figure 1.2.4   SSAO blocker function.

LISTING 1.2.5   HLSL code used to implement occlusion function

```
float OcclusionFunction( float fDistance,
                         float fNoOcclusionThreshold,
float fFullOcclusionThreshold,
float fOcclusionPower )
{
    const c_occlusionEpsilon = 0.01f;

    if ( fDistance > c_ occlusionEpsilon )
    {
        // Past this distance there is no occlusion.
        float fNoOcclusionRange = fNoOcclusionThreshold -
                          fFullOcclusionThreshold;
        if ( fDistance < fFullOcclusionThreshold )
            return 1.0f;
        else return max( 1.0f - pow( ( ( fDistance -
            fFullOcclusionThreshold ) / fNoOcclusionRange,
            fOcclusionPower ) ), 0.0f );
    } else return 0.0f;
}
```

Once we have gathered an occlusion value for each sample point, we can take the average of these, weighted by the distance of each sample point to p, and the average will be our ambient occlusion value for that pixel.

Sampling Randomization

Sampling neighboring pixels at regular vector offsets will produce glaring artifacts to the eye, as shown in Figure 1.2.5.

To smooth out the results of the SSAO lookups, the offset vectors can be randomized. A good approach is to generate a 2D texture of random normal vectors and perform a lookup on this texture in screen space, thus fetching a unique random vector per pixel on the screen, as illustrated in Figure 1.2.6 [Mittring07]. We have n neighbors we must sample, and thus we will need to generate a set of n unique vectors per pixel on the screen. These will be generated by passing a set of offset vectors in the pixel shader constant registers and reflecting these vectors through the sampled random vector, resulting in a semi-random set of vectors at each pixel, as illustrated by Listing 1.2.6. The set of vectors passed in as registers is not normalized—having varying lengths helps to smooth out the noise pattern and produces a more even distribution of the samples inside the occlusion hemisphere. The offset vectors must not be too short to avoid clustering samples too close to the source point p. In general, varying the offset vectors from half to full length of the occlusion hemisphere radius produces good results. The size of the occlusion hemisphere becomes a parameter controllable by the artist that determines the size of the sampling area.

Figure 1.2.5   SSAO without random sampling.

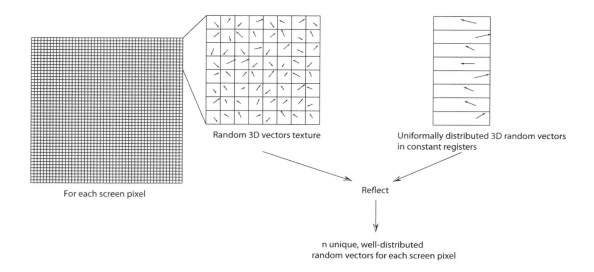

For each screen pixel

Random 3D vectors texture

Uniformally distributed 3D random vectors in constant registers

Reflect

n unique, well-distributed random vectors for each screen pixel

Figure 1.2.6   Randomized sampling process.

LISTING 1.2.6 HLSL code used to generate a set of semi-random 3D vectors at each pixel

```
float3 reflect( float3 vSample, float3 vNormal )
{
    return normalize( vSample - 2.0f * dot( vSample, vNormal ) * vNormal );
}

float3x3 MakeRotation( float fAngle, float3 vAxis )
{
    float fS;
    float fC;
    sincos( fAngle, fS, fC );
    float fXX       = vAxis.x * vAxis.x;
    float fYY       = vAxis.y * vAxis.y;
    float fZZ       = vAxis.z * vAxis.z;
    float fXY       = vAxis.x * vAxis.y;
    float fYZ       = vAxis.y * vAxis.z;
    float fZX       = vAxis.z * vAxis.x;
    float fXS       = vAxis.x * fS;
    float fYS       = vAxis.y * fS;
    float fZS       = vAxis.z * fS;
    float fOneC     = 1.0f - fC;

    float3x3 result = float3x3(
        fOneC * fXX +  fC, fOneC * fXY + fZS, fOneC * fZX - fYS,
        fOneC * fXY - fZS, fOneC * fYY +  fC, fOneC * fYZ + fXS,
        fOneC * fZX + fYS, fOneC * fYZ - fXS, fOneC * fZZ +  fC
    );
    return result;
}

float4 PostProcessSSAO( float3 i_VPOS )
{

    ...

    const float c_scalingConstant = 256.0f;
    float3 vRandomNormal = ( normalize( tex2D( p_sSSAONoise, vScreenUV *
                            p_vSrcImageSize / c_scalingConstant ).xyz * 2.0f
                            - 1.0f ) );
    float3x3 rotMatrix = MakeRotation( 1.0f, vNormal );

    half fAccumBlock = 0.0f;
    for ( int i = 0; i < iSampleCount; i++ ) {
        float3 vSamplePointDelta = reflect( p_vSSAOSamplePoints[i],
                                            vRandomNormal );
        float fBlock = TestOcclusion(
                        vViewPos,
    vSamplePointDelta,
                            p_fOcclusionRadius,
                            p_fFullOcclusionThreshold,
                            p_fNoOcclusionThreshold,
                            p_fOcclusionPower ) ) {
```

```
        fAccumBlock += fBlock;
    }

    ...

}
```

Ambient Occlusion Post-Processing

As shown in Figure 1.2.7, the previous step helps to break up the noise pattern, producing a finer-grained pattern that is less objectionable. With wider sampling areas, however, a further blurring of the ambient occlusion result becomes necessary. The ambient occlusion results are low frequency, and losing some of the high-frequency detail due to blurring is generally preferable to the noisy result obtained by the previous steps.

Figure 1.2.7 SSAO term after random sampling applied. Applying blur passes will further reduce the noise to achieve the final look.

To smooth out the noise, a separable Gaussian blur can be applied to the ambient occlusion buffer. However, the ambient occlusion must not bleed through edges to objects that are physically separate within the scene. A form of bilateral filtering is used. This filter samples the nearby pixels as a regular Gaussian blur shader would, yet the normal and depth for each of the Gaussian samples are sampled as well. (Encoding the normal and depth in the same render targets presents significant advantages here.) If the depth from the Gaussian sample differs from the center tap by more than a certain threshold, or the dot product of the Gaussian sample and the center tap normal is less than a certain threshold value, then the Gaussian weight is reduced to zero. The sum of the Gaussian samples is then renormalized to account for the missing samples.

LISTING 1.2.7 HLSL code used to blur the ambient occlusion image

```
// i_UV : UV of center tap
// p_fBlurWeights Array of gaussian weights
// i_GaussianBlurSample: Array of interpolants, with each interpolants
// packing 2 gaussian sample positions.
float4 PostProcessGaussianBlur( VertexTransport vertOut )
{
    float2 vCenterTap    = i_UV.xy;
    float4 cValue        = tex2D( p_sSrcMap, vCenterTap.xy );
    float4 cResult       = cValue * p_fBlurWeights[0];
    float fTotalWeight   = p_fBlurWeights[0];

    // Sample normal & depth for center tap
    float4 vNormalDepth = tex2D( p_sNormalDepthMap, vCenterTap.xy ).a;
    for ( int i = 0; i < b_iSampleInterpolantCount; i++ )
    {
        half4 cValue = tex2D( p_sSrcMap,
                            i_GaussianBlurSample[i].xy );
        half fWeight = p_fBlurWeights[i * 2 + 1];

        float4 vSampleNormalDepth = tex2D( p_sNormalDepthMap,
                            i_GaussianBlurSample[i].xy );
        if ( dot( vSampleNormalDepth.rgb, vNormalDepth.rgb) < 0.9f ||
            abs( vSampleNormalDepth.a — vNormalDepth.a ) > 0.01f )
            fWeight = 0.0f;

        cResult += cValue * fWeight;
        fTotalWeight += fWeight;

        cValue = tex2D( p_sSeparateBlurMap,
                            INTERPOLANT_GaussianBlurSample[i].zw );
        fWeight = p_fBlurWeights[i * 2 + 2];
        vSampleNormalDepth = tex2D( p_sSrcMap,
                            INTERPOLANT_GaussianBlurSample[i].zw );
        if ( dot( vSampleNormalDepth.rgb, vNormalDepth .rgb < 0.9f ) ||
                abs( vSampleNormalDepth.a — vNormalDepth.a ) > 0.01f )
            fWeight = 0.0f;
        cResult += cValue * fWeight;
        fTotalWeight += fWeight;
    }

    // Rescale result according to number of discarded samples.
    cResult *= 1.0f / fTotalWeight;

    return cResult;
}
```

Several blur passes can thus be applied to the ambient occlusion output to completely eliminate the noisy pattern, trading off some higher-frequency detail in exchange.

Figure 1.2.8   Result of Gaussian blur.

Handling Edge Cases

The offset vectors are in view space, not screen space, and thus the length of the offset vectors will vary depending on how far away they are from the viewer. This can result in using an insufficient number of samples at close-up pixels, resulting in a noisier result for these pixels. Of course, samples can also go outside the 2D bounds of the screen. Naturally, depth information outside of the screen is not available. In our implementation, we ensure that samples outside the screen return a large depth value, ensuring they would never occlude any neighboring pixels. This can be achieved through the "border color" texture wrapping state, setting the border color to a suitably high depth value.

To prevent unacceptable breakdown of the SSAO quality in extreme close-ups, the number of samples can be increased dynamically in the shader based on the distance of the point p to the viewer. This can improve the quality of the visual results but can result in erratic performance. Alternatively, the 2D offset vector lengths can be artificially capped to some threshold value regardless of distance from viewer. In effect, if the camera is very close to an object and the SSAO samples end up being too wide, the SSAO area consistency constraint is violated so that the noise pattern doesn't become too noticeable.

Optimizing Performance

Screen Space Ambient Occlusion can have a significant payoff in terms of mood and visual quality of the image, but it can be quite an expensive effect. The main bottleneck of the algorithm is the sampling itself. The semi-random nature of the sampling, which is necessary to minimize banding, wreaks havoc with the GPU's texture cache system and can become a problem if not managed. The performance of the texture cache will also be very dependent on the sampling area size, with wider areas straining the cache more and yielding poorer performance. Our artists quickly got in the habit of using SSAO to achieve a faked global illumination look that suited their purposes. This required more samples and wider sampling areas, so extensive optimization became necessary for us.

One method to bring SSAO to an acceptable performance level relies on the fact that ambient occlusion is a low-frequency phenomenon. Thus, there is generally no need for the depth buffer sampled by the SSAO algorithm to be at full-screen resolution. The initial depth buffer can be generated at screen resolution, since the depth information is generally reused for other effects, and it potentially has to fit the size of other render targets, but it can thereafter be downsampled to a smaller depth buffer that is a quarter size of the original on each side. The downsampling itself does have some cost, but the payback in improved throughput is very significant. Downsampling the depth buffer also makes it possible to convert it from a wide 16-bit floating-point format to a more bandwidth-friendly 32-bit packed format.

Fake Global Illumination and Artistic Styling

If the ambient occlusion hemisphere is large enough, the SSAO algorithm eventually starts to mimic behavior seen from general global illumination; a character relatively far away from a wall could cause the wall to catch some of the subtle shadowing cues a global illumination algorithm would detect. If the sampling area of the SSAO is wide enough, the look of the scene changes from darkness in nooks and crannies to a softer, ambient feel.

This can pull the art direction in two somewhat conflicting directions: on the one hand, the need for tighter, high-contrast occluded zones in deeper recesses, and on the other hand, the desire for the larger, softer, ambient look of the wide-area sampling.

One approach is to split the SSAO samples between two different sets of SSAO parameters: Some samples are concentrated in a small area with a rapidly increasing occlusion function (generally a quarter of all samples), while the remaining samples

Figure 1.2.9   SSAO with different sampling-area radii.

use a wide sampling area with a gentler function slope. The two sets are then averaged independently, and the final result uses the value from the set that produces the most (darkest) occlusion. This is the approach that was used in *StarCraft II*.

The edge-enhancing component of the ambient occlusion does not require as many samples as the global illumination one, thus a quarter of the samples can be assigned to crease enhancement while the remainder are assigned for the larger area threshold.

Though SSAO provides for important lighting cues to enhance the depth of the scene, there was still a demand from our artist for more accurate control that was only feasible through the use of some painted-in ambient occlusion. The creases from SSAO in particular cannot reach the accuracy that using a simple texture can without using an enormous amount of samples. Thus the usage of SSAO does not preclude the need for some static ambient occlusion maps to be blended in with the final ambient occlusion result, which we have done here.

Figure 1.2.10   Combined small- and large-area SSAO result.

For our project, complaints about image noise, balanced with concerns about performance, were the main issues to deal with for the technique to gain acceptance among our artists. Increasing SSAO samples helps improve the noise, yet it takes an ever-increasing number of samples to get ever smaller gains in image quality. Past 16 samples, we've found it's more effective to use additional blur passes to smooth away the noise pattern, at the expense of some loss of definition around depth discontinuities in the image.

Transparency

It should be noted the depth buffer can only contain one depth value per pixel, and thus transparencies cannot be fully supported. This is generally a problem with all algorithms that rely on screen space depth information. There is no easy solution to this, and the SSAO process itself is intensive enough that dealing with edge cases can push the algorithm outside of the real-time realm. In practice, for the vast majority of scenes, correct ambient occlusion for transparencies is a luxury that can be skimped on. Very transparent objects will typically be barely visible either way. For transparent objects that are nearly opaque, the choice can be given to the artist to allow some transparencies to write to the depth buffer input to the SSAO algorithm (not the z-buffer used for hidden surface removal), overriding opaque objects behind them.

Final Results

Color Plate 1 shows some results portraying what the algorithm contributes in its final form. The top-left pane shows lighting without the ambient occlusion, while the top-right pane shows lighting with the SSAO component mixed in. The final colored result is shown in the bottom pane. Here the SSAO samples are very wide, bathing the background area with an effect that would otherwise only be obtained with a full global illumination algorithm. The SSAO term adds depth to the scene and helps anchor the characters within the environment.

Color Plate 2 shows the contrast between the large-area, low-contrast SSAO sampling component on the bar surface and background and the tighter, higher-contrast SSAO samples apparent within the helmet, nooks, and crannies found on the character's spacesuit.

Conclusion

This gem has described the Screen Space Ambient Occlusion technique used at Blizzard and presented various problems and solutions that arise. Screen Space Ambient Occlusion offers a different perspective in achieving results that closely resemble what the eye expects from ambient occlusion. The technique is reasonably simple to implement and amenable to artistic tweaks in real time to make it ideal to fit an artistic vision.

References

[Bavoil] Bavoil, Louis and Miguel Sainz. "Image-Space Horizon-Based Ambient Occlusion." *ShaderX7: Advanced Rendering Techniques.* Ed. Wolfgang F. Engel. Boston: Charles River Media, 2009. Section 6.2.

[Bavoil09] Bavoil, Louis and Miguel Sainz. "Multi-Layer Dual-Resolution Screen-Space Ambient Occlusion." 2009. NVIDIA. n.d. <http://developer.download.nvidia.com/presentations/2009/SIGGRAPH/Bavoil_MultiLayerDualResolutionSSAO.pdf>.

[Bavoil08] Bavoil, Louis and Miguel Sainz. "Screen Space Ambient Occlusion." Sept. 2008. NVIDIA. n.d. <http://developer.download.nvidia.com/SDK/10.5/direct3d/Source/ScreenSpaceAO/doc/ScreenSpaceAO.pdf>.

[Fox08] Fox, Megan. "Ambient Occlusive Crease Shading." *Game Developer.* March 2008.

[Kajalin] Kajalin, Vladimir. "Screen Space Ambient Occlusion." *ShaderX7: Advanced Rendering Techniques.* Ed. Wolfgang F. Engel. Boston: Charles River Media, 2009. Section 6.1.

[Lajzer] Lajzer, Brett and Dan Nottingham. "Combining Screen-Space Ambient Occlusion and Cartoon Rendering on Graphics Hardware." n.d. Brett Lajzer. n.d.<http://brettlajzer.com/pub/graphics/final/nprssao_final_presentation.pdf>.

[Luft06] Luft, Thomas, Carsten Colditz, and Oliver Deussen. "Image Enhancement by Unsharp Masking the Depth Buffer." Course on Non-Photorealistic Rendering. SIGGRAPH 2006. Boston Convention and Exhibition Center, Boston, MA. 3 August 2006.

[Mittring07] Mittring, Martin. "Finding Next Gen—CryEngine 2.0." Course on Advanced Real-Time Rendering in 3D Graphics and Games. SIGGRAPH 2007. San Diego Convention Center, San Diego, CA. 8 August 2007.

[Pesce] Pesce, Angelo. "Variance Methods for Screen-Space Ambient Occlusion." *ShaderX7: Advanced Rendering Techniques*. Ed. Wolfgang F. Engel. Boston: Charles River Media, 2009. Section 6.7.

[Ritschel09] Ritschel, Tobias, Thorsten Grosch, and Hans-Peter Seidel. "Approximating Dynamic Global Illumination in Image Space." 2009. Max Planck Institut Informatik. n.d. <http://www.mpi-inf.mpg.de/~ritschel/Papers/SSDO.pdf>.

[Sains08] Sains, Miguel. "Real-Time Depth Buffer Based Ambient Occlusion." Game Developers Conference. Moscone Center, San Francisco, CA. 18–22 February 2008.

[Shamugan07] Shanmugam, Perumaal and Okan Arikan. "Hardware Accelerated Ambient Occlusion Techniques on GPUs." 2007. Google Sites. n.d.<http://perumaal.googlepages.com/ao.pdf>.

[Sloan07] Sloan, Peter-Pike, Naga K. Govindaraju, Derek Nowrouzezahrai, and John Snyder. "Image-Based Proxy Accumulation for Real-Time Soft Global Illumination." Pacific Graphics Conference. The Royal Lahaina Resort, Maui, Hawaii. 29 October 2007.

[Tomasi98] Tomasi, Carlo and Roberto Manduchi. "Bilateral Filtering for Gray and Color Images." IEEE International Conference on Computer Vision. Homi Bhabha Auditorium, Bombay, India. 7 January 1998.

1.3

Multi-Resolution Deferred Shading

Hyunwoo Ki, INNOACE Co., Ltd
psykinu@gmail.com

Recently, deferred shading has become a popular rendering technique for real-time games. Deferred shading enables game engines to handle many local lights without repeated geometry processing because it replaces geometry processing with pixel processing [Saito90, Shishkovtsov05, Valient07, Koonce07, Engel09, Kircher09]. In other words, shading costs are independent of geometric complexity, which is important as the CPU cost of scene-graph traversal and the GPU cost of geometry processing grows with scene complexity. Despite this decoupling of shading cost from geometric complexity, we still seek to optimize the pixel processing necessary to handle many local lights, soft shadows, and other per-pixel effects. In this gem, we present a technique that we call multi-resolution deferred shading, which provides adaptive sub-sampling using a hierarchical approach to shading by exploiting spatial coherence of the scene. Multi-resolution deferred shading efficiently reduces pixel shading costs as compared to traditional deferred shading without noticeable aliasing. As shown in Figure 1.3.1, our technique allows us to achieve a significant improvement in performance with negligible visual degradation relative to a more expensive full-resolution deferred shading approach.

Figure 1.3.1   Deferred shading (left: 20 fps), multi-resolution deferred shading (center: 38 fps), and their difference image (right). There are 40 spot lights, including fuzzy shadows (1024×1024 pixels with 24 shadow samples per pixel).

Deferred Shading

Unlike traditional forward rendering approaches, deferred shading costs are independent of scene complexity. This is because deferred shading techniques store geometry information in textures, often called *G-buffers*, replacing geometry processing with pixel processing [Saito90, Shishkovtsov05, Valient07, Koonce07].

Deferred shading techniques start by rendering the scene into a G-buffer, which is typically implemented using multiple render targets to store geometry information, such as positions, normals, and other quantities instead of final shading results. Next, deferred shading systems render a screen-aligned quad to invoke a pixel shader at all pixels in the output image. The pixel shader retrieves the geometry information from the G-buffer and performs shading operations as a post process. Naturally, one must carefully choose the data formats and precise quantities to store in a G-buffer in order to make the best possible use of both memory and memory bandwidth. For example, the game *Killzone 2* utilizes four buffers containing lighting accumulation and intensity, normal XY in 16-bit floating-point format, motion vector XY, specular and diffuse albedo, and sun occlusion [Valient07]. The Z component of the normal is computed from normal XY, and position is computed from depth and pixel coordinates. These types of encodings are a tradeoff between decode/encode cost and the memory and memory bandwidth consumed by the G-buffer. As shown in Color Plate 3, we simply use two four-channel buffers of 16-bit floating-point precision per channel without any advanced encoding schemes for ease of description and implementation. The first of our buffers contains view-space position in the RGB channels and a material ID in the alpha channel. The other buffer contains view-space normal in the RGB channels and depth in the alpha channel.

We could also use material buffers that store diffuse reflectance, specular reflectance, shininess, and so on. However, material buffers are not necessary if we separate lighting and material phases from the shading phase using light pre-pass rendering [Engel09]. Unlike traditional deferred shading, light pre-pass rendering first computes lighting results instead of full shading. This method can then incorporate material properties in an additional material phase with forward rendering. Although this technique requires a second geometry rendering pass, such separation of lighting and material phases gives added flexibility during material shading and is compatible with hardware multi-sample anti-aliasing. A related technique, inferred lighting, stores lighting results in a single low-resolution buffer instead of the full-resolution buffer [Kircher09]. To avoid discontinuity problems, this technique filters edges using depth and object ID comparison in the material phase. As we will describe in the next section, our technique is similar to inferred lighting, but our method finds discontinuous areas based on spatial proximity and then solves the discontinuity problems using a multi-resolution approach during the lighting (or shading) phase.

Multi-Resolution Deferred Shading

Although deferred shading improves lighting efficiency, computing illumination for every pixel is still expensive, despite the fact that it is often fairly low frequency. We have developed a multi-resolution deferred shading approach to exploit the low-frequency nature of illumination. We perform lighting in a lower-resolution buffer for spatially coherent areas and then interpolate results into a higher-resolution buffer. This key concept is based upon our prior work [Ki07a]. Here, we generalize this work and improve upon it to reduce aliasing.

The algorithm has three steps, as shown in Color Plate 4: geometry pass, multi-resolution rendering pass, and composite pass. The geometry pass populates the G-buffers. Our technique is compatible with any sort of G-buffer organization, but for ease of explanation, we will stick with the 8-channel G-buffer layout described previously.

The next step is multi-resolution rendering, which consists of resolution selection (non-edge detection), shading (lighting), and interpolation (up-sampling). We allocate buffers to store rendering results at various resolutions. We call these buffers *R-buffers*, where the "R" stands for "Result" or "Resolution." In this chapter, we will use three R-buffers: full resolution, quarter resolution, and 1/16th resolution (for example, 1280×1024, 640×512, and 320×256). If the full-resolution image is especially high, we could choose to decrease the resolutions of the R-buffers even more drastically than just one-quarter resolution in each step.

Multi-resolution rendering uses rendering iterations from lower-resolution to higher-resolution R-buffers. We prevent repeated pixel processing by exploiting early-Z culling to skip pixels processed in earlier iterations using lower-resolution R-buffers [Mitchell04]. To start shading our R-buffers, we set the lowest-resolution R-buffer as the current render target and clear its depth buffer with one depth (farthest). Next, we determine pixels being rendered in this resolution by rendering a screen-aligned quad with $\mathbf{Z_i} = \mathbf{1.0 - i * 0.1}$, where $\mathbf{i}$ is the current iteration, writing only depth. During this pass, the pixel shader reads geometry information from mip-mapped versions of our G-buffers and estimates spatial proximity for non-edge detection. To estimate spatial proximity, we first compare the current pixel's material ID with the material IDs of neighboring pixels. Then, we compare the difference of normal and depth values using tunable thresholds. If spatial proximity is low for the current pixel, we should use a higher-resolution R-buffer for better quality, and thus we discard the current pixel in the shader to skip writing Z. After this pass, pixels whose spatial proximity is high (in other words, non-edge) in the current resolution contain meaningful Z values because they were not discarded. The pixels whose spatial proximity is low (in other words, edges) still have farthest Z values left over from the initial clear.

We then perform shading (or lighting) by rendering a screen-aligned quad with $\mathbf{Z_i} = \mathbf{1.0 - i * 0.1}$ again, but the Z function is changed to Equal. This means that only spatially coherent pixels in this resolution will pass the Z-test, as illustrated in Color Plate 4. In the pixel shader, we read geometric data from G-buffers and compute illumination as in light pre-pass rendering. On a textured surface, such as wall and floor, although spatial proximity between neighboring pixels is high, these pixel colors are often different. Such cases can cause serious aliasing in the resulting images. To solve this problem, we store only lighting results instead of full shading results into R-buffers, and we handle material properties with stored illumination in R-buffers in the composite pass.

After shading, we copy the current shading/lighting results and depth to the next higher-resolution R-buffer, allowing the hardware's bilinear units to do a simple interpolation as we up-sample. We have found that bilinear filtering is adequate, though we could use bi-cubic filtering or other higher-order filtering for better quality.

We repeat the process described above at the next higher resolution, estimating spatial proximity and writing Z and computing illumination until we reach the full-resolution R-buffer. A full-screen quad is drawn three times per iteration. If a given pixel was shaded on a prior iteration in a lower-resolution R-buffer, that pixel is not shaded again at the higher resolution due to early-Z culling. In this way, we are able to perform our screen-space shading operations at the appropriate resolution for different regions of the screen. In Figure 1.3.2, we visualize the distribution of pixels shaded at each level of our hierarchy.

Because this approach exploits image scaling from low resolution to high resolution with interpolation, discontinuity artifacts can appear at boundaries of lighting or shadows. We address this issue during the multi-resolution rendering phase. We write 1.0 to the alpha channel of R-buffer pixels that are lit; otherwise, we write zero. If pixels are lit by the same lights (or the same number of lights), their neighbors' alpha values will be equal. Therefore, we interpolate these pixels to a higher-resolution buffer. Otherwise, we consider these pixels within the boundary, and thus we discard them in the interpolation pass (see Figure 1.3.3). We can handle shadow boundaries similarly.

Figure 1.3.2 Visualization of hierarchical pixel processing.
Non-black pixels were shaded in the first pass at 1/16th resolution as in the image on the left.
The middle image shows the pixels shaded in the second iteration at one-quarter
resolution, and only the pixels in the image on the right were shaded at full image resolution.

If shadow color is neither zero nor one (in other words, penumbra), we also set a
pixel alpha to zero and thus discard it in the interpolation work.

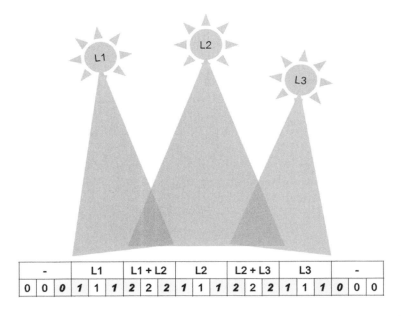

Figure 1.3.3 A boundary-check algorithm. If a pixel is lit by a light, we add one
alpha for this pixel in the lighting phase. In the interpolation pass, we consider pixels
that are in boundaries whose neighbor pixels' alpha values are different to others,
and thus we use a higher-resolution buffer without interpolation.

In the composite pass, we render a screen-aligned quad, reading shading results from the full-resolution R-buffer and material properties such as albedo to compute the final shading result. We could draw scene geometry instead of drawing a screen quad for MSAA, similar to light pre-pass rendering.

In contrast to traditional deferred shading and light pre-pass rendering, multi-resolution deferred shading reduces rendering costs for low-frequency pixels. Our multi-resolution deferred shading is also more efficient than inferred lighting due to the hierarchical approach. Multi-resolution deferred shading can also be used for other rendering techniques, such as the GPU-based light clustering technique for diffuse interreflection and subsurface light diffusion called Light Pyramids [Ki08]. The Light Pyramids technique stores first-bounced lights in shadow maps and groups them by considering their angular and spatial similarity. Although such light clustering dramatically reduces the number of lights, it still requires hundreds of lights for each pixel. Figure 1.3.4 shows an example of a combination of Light Pyramids and multi-resolution deferred shading. Thanks to our pixel clustering, we achieved a performance improvement of approximately 1.5 to 2.0 times without noticeable quality loss. As pixel processing increases in complexity—for example, using higher resolution or using more lights—the relative performance improvement also increases.

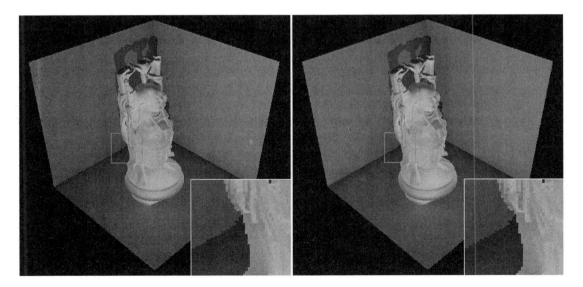

Figure 1.3.4 Indirect illumination using Light Pyramids [Ki08] based on traditional deferred shading (left) and multi-resolution deferred shading (right: 1.7 times faster).

Conclusion and Future Work

We have presented a multi-resolution deferred shading technique that performs lighting and shading computations at appropriate screen-space frequency in order to improve the efficiency of deferred shading without aliasing. In the future, we would also like to develop even more efficient resolution-selection algorithms, and we also seek to handle a wider variety of surface reflection models. We also hope to integrate transparent rendering of inferred lighting into our method. We believe that our method could be applied for not only lighting but also other rendering operations with high per-pixel overhead, such as per-pixel displacement mapping [Ki07b].

References

[Engel09] Engel, Wolfgang. "Designing a Renderer for Multiple Lights: The Light Pre-Pass Renderer." *ShaderX7: Advanced Rendering Techniques.* Ed. Wolfgang F. Engel. Boston: Charles River Media, 2009. 655-666.

[Ki08] Ki, Hyunwoo. "A GPU-Based Light Hierarchy for Real-Time Approximate Illumination." *The Visual Computer* 24.7–9 (July 2008): 649–658.

[Ki07a] Ki, Hyunwoo. "Hierarchical Rendering Techniques for Real-Time Approximate Illumination on Programmable Graphics Hardware." Master's Thesis. Soongsil University, 2007.

[Ki07b] Ki, Hyunwoo and Kyoungsu Oh. "Accurate Per-Pixel Displacement Mapping using a Pyramid Structure." 2007. Hyunwoo Ki. n.d. <http://ki-h.com/article/ipdm.html>.

 [Kircher09] Kircher, Scott and Alan Lawrance. "Inferred Lighting: Fast Dynamic Lighting and Shadows for Opaque and Translucent Objects." Course on 3D and the Cinematic in Games. SIGGRAPH 2009. Ernest N. Morial Convention Center, New Orleans, LA. 6 August 2009.

[Koonce07] Koonce, Rusty. "Deferred Shading in Tabula Rasa." *GPU Gems 3.* Ed. Hurbert Nguyen. Kendallville, KY: Addison-Wesley, 2007. 429–458.

[Mitchell04] Mitchell, Jason and Pedro Sander. "Applications of Explicit Early-Z Culling." Course on Real-Time Shading. SIGGRAPH 2004. Los Angeles Convention Center, Los Angeles, CA. 8 August 2004.

[Saito90] Saito, Takafumi and Tokiichiro Takahashi. "Comprehensible Rendering of 3-D Shapes." *ACM SIGGRAPH Computer Graphics* 24.4 (August 1990): 197–206.

[Shishkovtsov05] Shishkovtsov, Oles. "Deferred Shading in S.T.A.L.K.E.R." *GPU Gems 2: Programming Techniques for High-Performance Graphics and General Purpose Computation.* Ed. Matt Pharr. Kendallville, Ky: Addison-Wesley, 2005. 143–166.

[Valient07] Valient, Michal. "Deferred Rendering in *Killzone 2*." Develop Conference 2007. Brighton Hilton Metropole, Brighton, England, UK. 25 July 2007.

1.4

View Frustum Culling of Catmull-Clark Patches in DirectX 11

Rahul P. Sathe,
Advanced Visual Computing, Intel Corp

rahul.p.sathe@intel.com

DirectX 11 has introduced hardware tessellation in order to enable high geometric detail without increasing memory usage or memory bandwidth demands. Higher-order surface patches with displacements are of prime interest to game developers, and we would like to render them as efficiently as possible. For example, we would like to cull subdivision surface patches (instead of the resulting triangles) that will not affect the final image. Culling a given patch avoids higher-order surface evaluation of domain points in that patch as well as processing of the triangles generated for the patch. The nature of higher-order surface patches coupled with displacements and animation make the process of culling them non-trivial, since the exact geometric bounds are not known until well after the opportunity to cull a given patch. In this chapter, we will present an algorithm that evaluates conservative bounding boxes for displaced approximate Catmull-Clark subdivision surface patches at run time, allowing us to perform view frustum culling on the patches. With this method, we achieve performance improvement with minimal overhead.

Background

Before describing our culling strategy, we must review the fundamentals of Catmull-Clark subdivision surfaces, displacement mapping, and the methods that are currently in use to approximate Catmull-Clark subdivision surfaces on DirectX 11.

Displaced Subdivision Surfaces and Catmull-Clark Surfaces

Catmull-Clark subdivision surfaces have become an increasingly popular modeling primitive and have been extensively used in offline rendering [DeRose98]. In general, subdivision surfaces can be described as recursive refinement of a polygonal mesh. Starting with a coarse polygonal mesh *M0*, one can introduce new vertices along the edges and faces and update the connectivity to get a mesh *M1*, and repeat this process to get meshes *M2*, *M3*, and so on. In the limit, this process approaches a smooth surface *S*. This smooth surface *S* is called the *subdivision limit surface*, and the original mesh *M0* is often referred to as the *control mesh*.

The control mesh consists of vertices connected to each other to form edges and faces. The number of other vertices that a given vertex is connected to directly by shared edges is called the *valence* of a vertex. In the realm of Catmull-Clark subdivision surfaces, a vertex is called a *regular* or *ordinary* vertex if it has a valence of four. If the valences of all of the vertices of a given quad are four, then that quad is called an *ordinary quad* or an *ordinary patch*. The faces that have at least one vertex that is not valence four are called *extraordinary faces* (or *patches*).

Approximate Catmull-Clark Subdivision Surfaces

Recently, Loop and Schaefer introduced a hardware-friendly method of rendering Approximate Catmull Clark (ACC) subdivision surfaces, which maps very naturally to the DirectX 11 pipeline [Loop08]. At its core, the ACC scheme maps each quadrilateral from the original control mesh to a bi-cubic Bezier patch. Loop and Schaefer show that, for ordinary patches, the bi-cubic Bezier corresponds exactly to the Catmull-Clark limit surface. Extraordinary patches do not correspond exactly to the limit surface, but Loop and Schaefer decouple the patch description for position attributes and normal attributes in order to reduce the visual impact of the resulting discontinuities. To do this, for extraordinary patches, ACC generates separate normal and bi-tangent patches in order to impose G^N continuity at patch boundaries. The word "approximate" in ACC has its roots in the fact that these extraordinary patches are G^N continuous, and this G^N continuity only guarantees the same direction of partial derivatives but not the magnitudes across the patch boundaries. The ACC scheme describes the normals and bi-tangents using additional Bezier patches, which results in a continuous normal field even across edges of extraordinary patches.

Displacement

Although it is very empowering to be able to generate smooth surfaces from polygonal meshes procedurally, such smooth surfaces are rarely encountered in real life and lack realism without additional high-frequency geometric detail. This is where displacement maps come into the picture. Displacement maps are simply textures that can be used to store geometric perturbations from a smooth surface. Although normal maps and displacement maps have the similar effect of adding high-frequency detail, the difference is notable around the silhouettes of objects. A normal mapped object's silhouette lacks geometric detail because only per-pixel normals are perturbed and not the underlying geometry, as illustrated in Figure 1.4.1. To add this high-frequency detail, displacement maps can be applied to subdivision surfaces.

Figure 1.4.1 Normal mapping versus displacement mapping.

DirectX 11 Pipeline

DirectX 11 has introduced three new stages to the graphics pipeline to enable dynamic on chip tessellation, as shown in Figure 1.4.4. The two new programmable pipeline stages are the *hull shader* and the *domain shader*. Between these two programmable stages lies a new fixed function stage, the *tessellator*. Fortunately for us, ACC and Direct3D 11 were designed with each other in mind, and there is a natural mapping of the ACC algorithm onto the Direct3D 11 pipeline.

Hull Shader

As illustrated in Figure 1.4.1, the new hull shader stage follows the traditional vertex shader. In a typical implementation of ACC on Direct3D 11, the vertex shader is responsible for performing animation of the control mesh vertices. In the hull shader, each quadrilateral's four vertices and its one-ring neighborhood are gathered from the output of the vertex shader. These vertices are used to define the control points of a bi-cubic Bezier patch. This basis conversion process that generates the Bezier patch control points is SIMD friendly, and every output control point can be calculated independently of others. In order to exploit this opportunity for parallelism, this control point phase of the hull shader is invoked once per control point. In the case of ACC, the basis conversion process depends on the topology of the incoming patch, but the output control points are always a 4×4 Bezier control mesh. Please refer to the sample code on the CD.

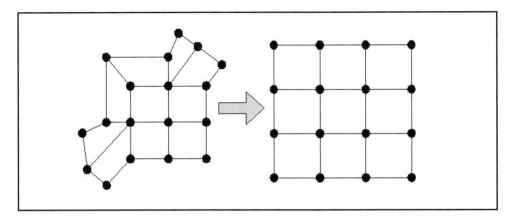

Figure 1.4.2   Basis conversion for an irregular patch.

In addition to the computation of the Bezier control points, the hull shader can optionally calculate edge tessellation factors in order to manage level of detail. One can assign arbitrary tessellation factors to the edges of a patch (within some constraints, defined by the DirectX 11 tessellator specifications). Because the hull shader is programmable, one can choose any metric to calculate edge tessellation factors. Typical metrics may include screen space projection, proximity to silhouette, luminosity reaching the patch, and so on. The calculation of each edge tessellation factor is typically independent of the others, and hence the edge tessellation factors can also be computed in parallel in a separate phase of the hull shader called the *fork phase*. The final stage of hull shader is called the *join phase* (or *patch constant phase*) and is a phase in which the shader can efficiently compute data that is constant for the entire patch. This stage is of most interest to us in this chapter.

Tessellator

The tessellator accepts edge LODs of a patch and other tessellator-specific states that control how it generates domain locations and connectivity. Some of these states include patch topology (quad, tri, or isoline), inside reduction function (how to calculate inner tessellation factor(s) using outer tessellation factors), one-axis versus two-axis reduction (whether to reduce only one inner tessellation factor or two—once per each domain axis), and scale (how much to scale inner LOD). The tessellator feeds domain values to the domain shader and connectivity information to the rest of the pipeline via the geometry shader.

Domain Shader

In the case of quadrilateral patch rendering, the *domain shader* is invoked at domain values (u,v) determined by the tessellator. (In the case of triangular patches, the barycentric coordinates (u,v,w); $w = 1 - u - v$ are used.) Naturally, the domain shader has access to output control points from the hull shader. Typically, the domain shader evaluates a higher-order surface at these domain locations using the control points provided by the hull shader as the basis. After evaluating the surface, the domain shader can perform arbitrary operations on the surface position, such as displacing the geometry using a displacement map.

In ACC, we evaluate position using bi-cubic polynomials for a given *(u,v)*. Our domain shader interpolates texture coordinates *(s,t)* from the four vertices using bilinear interpolation to generate the texture coordinates for the given *(u,v)*. We also optionally sample a displacement map at these interpolated texture coordinates. As mentioned earlier, normal calculation is different for ordinary and extraordinary patches. For ordinary patches, we just calculate *d/du* and *d/dv* of the position and take the cross-product. For extraordinary patches, we evaluate tangent and bi-tangent patches separately and take their cross-product.

Culling

The mapping of ACC to the DirectX 11 pipeline that we have described allows us to render smooth surfaces with adaptive tessellation and displacement mapping, resulting in a compelling visual quality improvement while maintaining a modest memory footprint. At the end of the day, however, we are still rendering triangles, and the remaining stages of the graphics pipeline are largely unchanged, including the hardware stages that perform triangle setup and culling. This means that we perform vertex shading, domain shading, tessellation, and hull shading of all patches submitted to the graphics pipeline, including those patches that are completely outside of the view frustum. Clearly, this provides an opportunity for optimization. The main contribution of this chapter is a method for frustum culling patches early in the pipeline in order to avoid unnecessary computations. Of course, we must account for mesh animation and displacement, both of which deform a given patch in a way that complicates culling. An elegant generalized solution to surface patch culling has been proposed by Hasselgren *et al.* that generates culling shaders, looking at domain shaders using Taylor Arithmetic [Hasselgren09]. This article proposes a simplified version of ideas discussed in their work to cull the approximate Catmull-Clark patches against view frustum.

Pre-Processing Step

We perform a pre-processing step on a given control mesh and displacement map in order to find the maximum displacement for each patch. Please note, although the positions are evaluated as bi-cubic polynomials using the new basis, the texture coordinates for those points are the result of bilinear interpolation of texture coordinates of the corners. This is due to the fact that the local (per-patch) uv-parameterization used to describe the Catmull-Clark surface and the global uv-parameterization done while creating the displacement map are linearly dependent on each other. Figure 1.4.3 shows one such patch. This linear dependence means that straight lines *u=0*, *v=0*, *u=1*, and *v=1* in the patch parameterization are also straight lines in the global parameterization. Due to this linear relationship, we know the exact area in the displacement map from which the displacements will be sampled in the domain shader for that patch. The maximum displacement in the given patch can be found by calculating the maximum displacement in the region confined by patch boundaries in the displacement map. Even if the displacement map stores vector-valued displacements, the mapping is still linear, so we can still find the magnitude of the maximum displacement for a given patch. Based on this, we can create a buffer for the entire mesh that stores this maximum displacement per patch.

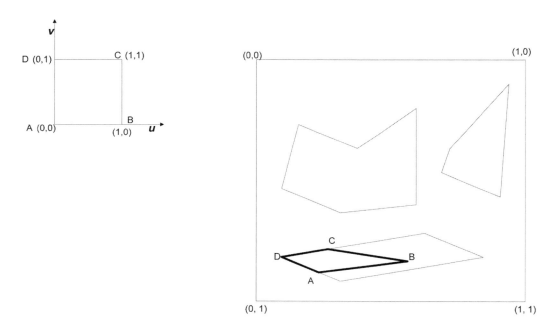

Figure 1.4.3   Mapping between global (*s-t*) and local (*u-v*) parameterization is linear. The figure on the left shows (*u,v*) parameterization that is used for patch evaluation. The figure on the right shows the global parameterization (*s,t*) that was used while unwrapping original mesh. Bold lines correspond to *u=0, v=0, u=1*, and *v=1* lines in the figure on the left.

Run-Time Step

At run time, the patch vertices of the control mesh go through the vertex shader, which animates the control mesh. The hull shader then operates on each quad patch, performing the basis transformation to Bezier control points. One convenient property of Bezier patches is that they always stay within the convex hull of the control mesh defining the patch. Using the maximum displacement computed previously, we can move the convex hull planes of a given patch outward by the maximum displacement, resulting in conservative bounds suitable for culling a given patch. Although moving the convex hull planes out by the max displacement may give tighter bounds compared to an axis-aligned bounding box (AABB) for the control mesh, calculating the corner points can be tricky because it requires calculation of plane intersections. It is simpler and more efficient to compute an AABB of the control mesh and offset the AABB planes by the maximum displacement.

In Figure 1.4.5, we show a 2D representation of this process for illustration. Dotted black lines represent the basis-converted Bezier control mesh. The actual Bezier curve is shown in bold black, displacements along the curve normal (scalar valued displacements) are shown in solid gray, and the maximum displacement for this curve segment is denoted as d. An AABB for the Bezier curve is shown in dashed lines (the inner bounding box), and the conservative AABB that takes displacements into account is shown in dashed and dotted lines (the outer bounding box).

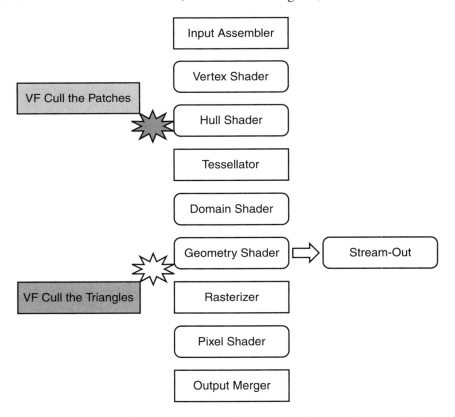

Figure 1.4.4   The DirectX11 pipeline. Normally, triangles get culled after primitive assembly, just before rasterization. The proposed scheme culls the patches in the hull shader, and all the associated triangles from that patch get culled as a result, freeing up compute resources.

As you can see, the corners of inner and outer enclosures are more than d distance apart, so we are being more conservative than we need to be for the ease and speed of computation.

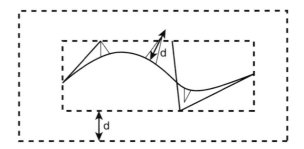

Figure 1.4.5   Conservative AABB for a displaced Bezier curve. The Bezier curve is shown in bold black, the control mesh in dotted lines, and displacements in solid gray lines. AABB for the Bezier curve without displacements is shown in dashed lines (inner bounding box), and conservative AABB for the displaced Bezier curve is shown in dashed and dotted lines (outer bounding box).

At this point, we have a conservative patch AABB that takes displacements into account. If the AABB for a patch is outside the view frustum, we know that the entire patch is outside the view frustum and can be safely culled. If we make the view frustum's plane equations available as shader constants, then our shader can test the AABB using in-out tests for view frustum. Alternatively, one can transform the AABB into normalized device coordinates (NDC), and the in-out tests can be done in NDC space. In-out tests in NDC space are easier than world space tests because they involve comparing only with +1 or −1. If the AABB is outside the view frustum, we set the edge LODs for that patch to be negative, which indicates to the graphics hardware that the patch should be culled. We perform the culling test during the join phase (a.k.a. patch constant phase) of the hull shader because this operation only needs to be performed once per patch.

Performance

For each culled patch, we eliminate unnecessary tessellator and domain shader work for that patch. All patches, whether or not they're culled, take on the additional computational burden of computing the conservative AABB and testing against the view frustum. When most of the character is visible on the screen (for example, Figure 1.4.9 (a)), culling overhead is at its worst. Figure 1.4.6 shows that, even in this case, culling overhead is minimal and is seen only at very low levels of tessellation. At LOD=3, the gains due to culling a very small number of patches (around the character's feet) start offsetting the cycles spent on culling tests.

When about half of the patches in our test model are outside of the view frustum (see Figure 1.4.9 (b)), the overhead of the AABB computations is offset by the gains from culling the offscreen patches. The gains from culling patches are more noticeable at higher levels of tessellation. This is shown graphically in Figures 1.4.7 and 1.4.8. Figure 1.4.7 shows how fps changes with the edge tessellation factor (edge LOD) when about half of the patches are culled. As you can see, at moderate levels of tessellation, we strike the balance between benefits of the proposed algorithm at increased level of detail. Figure 1.4.8 shows the same data as percentage speed-up.

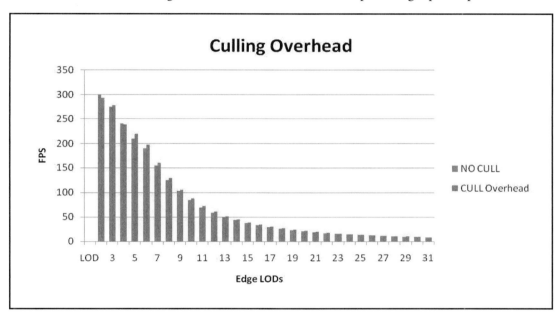

Figure 1.4.6 Culling overhead is the worst when nothing gets culled. Culling overhead is minimal except at very low levels of tessellation. "NO CULL" indicates the fps measured when no culling code was running. "CULL Overhead" shows the fps measured when culling code was running in the patch constant phase of shaders.

We performed all our tests on the ATI Radeon 5870 card, with 1 GB GDDR. The benefits of this algorithm increase with domain shader complexity and tessellation level, whereas the per-patch overhead of the culling tests remains constant. It is easy to imagine an application strategy that first tests an object's bounding box against the frustum to determine whether patch culling should be performed at all for a given object, thus avoiding the culling overhead for objects that are known to be mostly onscreen.

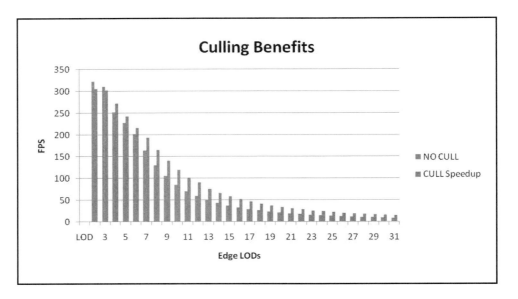

Figure 1.4.7   Culling benefits go up with the level of tessellation, except at the super-high levels of tessellation where culling patches doesn't help. At moderate levels of tessellation, we get benefits of the proposed algorithm and still see high geometric details.

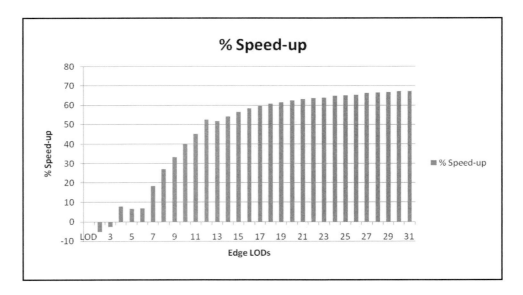

Figure 1.4.8   Culling benefits shown as percentage increase in fps against edge LODs (edge tessellation factor).

Conclusion

We have presented a method for culling Catmull-Clark patches against the view frustum using the DirectX 11 pipeline. Applications will benefit the most from this algorithm at moderate to high levels of tessellation. In the future, we would like to extend this technique to account for occluded and back-facing patches with displacements.

Figure 1.4.9   Screenshots showing our algorithm in action. We saw about 8.9 fps for the view on the left and 15.1 fps for the view on the right on the ATI Radeon 5870. Increase in the frame rate was due to view frustum culling patches.

References

[DeRose98] DeRose, Tony, Michael Kass, and Tien Truong. "Subdivision Surfaces in Character Animation." *Proceedings of the 25th Annual Conference on Computer Graphics and Interactive Techniques.* 1998. ACM SIGGRAPH. n.d. <http://doi.acm.org/10.1145/280814.280826>.

[Hasselgren09] Hasselgren, Jon, Jacob Munkberg, and Tomas Akenine-Möller. "Automatic Pre-Tessellation Culling." *ACM Transactions on Graphics* 28.2 (April 2009): n.p. *ACM Portal.*

[Loop08] Loop, Charles and Scott Schaefer. "Approximating Catmull-Clark Subdivision Surfaces with Bicubic Patches." *ACM Transactions on Graphics* 27.1 (March 2008): n.p. *ACM Portal.*

[Microsoft09] Microsoft Corporation. DirectX SDK. August 2009.

[Reif95] Reif, Ulrich. "A Unified Approach to Subdivision Algorithms Near Extraordinary Vertices." *Computer Aided Geometric Design* 12.2 (March 1995): 153–174. *ACM Portal.*

[Stam98] Stam, Jos. "Exact Evaluation of Catmull-Clark Subdivision Surfaces at Arbitrary Parameter Values." *Proceedings of the 25th Annual Conference on Computer Graphics and Interactive Techniques* (1998): 395–404. *ACM Portal.*

[Zorin2000] Zorin, Dennis and Peter Schroder. "Subdivision for Modeling and Animation." SIGGRAPH. 2000. 85–94.

1.5

Ambient Occlusion Using DirectX Compute Shader

Jason Zink

jzink_1@yahoo.com

Microsoft has recently released DirectX 11, which brings with it significant changes in several of its APIs. Among these new and updated APIs is the latest version of Direct3D. Direct3D 11 provides the ability to perform multi-threaded rendering calls, a shader interface system for providing an abstraction layer to shader code, and the addition of several new programmable shader stages. One of these new shader stages is the compute shader, which provides a significantly more flexible processing paradigm than was available in previous iterations of the Direct3D API. Specifically, the compute shader allows for a controllable threading model, sharing memory between processing threads, synchronization of primitive functions, and several new resource types to allow read/write access to resources.

This gem will provide an introduction to the compute shader and its new features. In addition, we will take an in-depth look at a Screen Space Ambient Occlusion (SSAO) algorithm implemented on the compute shader to show how to take advantage of this new processing paradigm. We will examine the SSAO algorithm in detail and provide a sample implementation to demonstrate how the compute shader can work together with the traditional rendering pipeline. Finally, we will wrap up with a discussion of our results and future work.

The Compute Shader

Before we begin to apply the compute shader's capabilities to a particular problem domain, let's take a closer look at the compute shader itself and the general concepts needed to program it.

Overview

The compute shader is a new programmable shader stage that is actually not simply inserted into the traditional rendering pipeline like some of the other new DirectX 11 pipeline stages discussed in Sathe's Gem 1.4. Rather, the compute shader is conceptually a standalone processing element that has access to the majority of the functionality available in the common shader core, but with some important additional functionality. The two most important new mechanics are fine-grained control over how each thread is used in a given shader invocation and new synchronization primitives that allow threads to synchronize. The threads also have read/write access to a common memory pool, which provides the opportunity for threads to share intermediate calculations with one another. These new capabilities are the basic building blocks for advanced algorithms that have yet to be developed, while at the same time allowing for traditional algorithms to be implemented in different ways in order to achieve performance improvements.

Compute Shader Threading Model

To use the compute shader, we need to understand its threading model. The main concept is that of a *Thread Group*. A Thread Group defines the number of threads that will be executing in parallel that will have the ability to communicate with one another. The threads within the Thread Group are conceptually organized in a 3D grid layout, as shown in Figure 1.5.1, with the sizes along each axis of the grid determined by the developer. The choice of the layout provides a simple addressing scheme used in the compute shader code to have each thread perform an operation on a particular portion of the input resources. When a particular thread is running, it executes the compute shader code and has access to several system value input attributes that uniquely identify the given thread.

To actually execute the compute shader, we tell the API to execute a given number of Thread Groups via the Dispatch method, as illustrated in Figure 1.5.2.

With these two layout definitions in mind, we can look at how they affect the addressing scheme of the compute shader. The following list of system values is available to the compute shader:

- **SV_GroupID.** This system value identifies the Thread Group that a thread belongs to with a 3-tuple of zero-based indices.
- **SV_GroupThreadID.** This system value identifies the thread index within the current Thread Group with a 3-tuple of zero-based indices.

- **SV_DispatchThreadID.** This system value identifies the current thread identifier over a complete Dispatch call with a 3-tuple of zero-based indices.
- **SV_GroupIndex.** This system value is a single integer value representing a flat index of the current thread within the group.

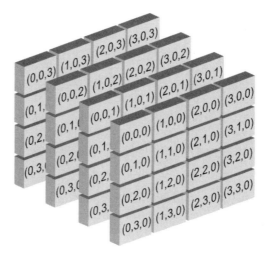

Figure 1.5.1   Thread Groups visualized as a 3D volume.

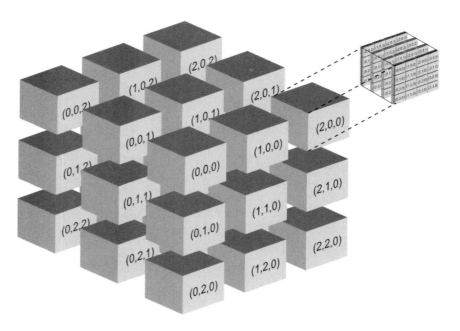

Figure 1.5.2   Visualization of the Dispatch method.

The individual threads running the compute shader have access to these system values and can use the values to determine, for example, which portions of input to use or which output resources to compute. For example, if we wanted a compute shader to perform an operation on each pixel of an input texture, we would define the thread group to be of size (x, y, 1) and call the Dispatch method with a size of (m, n, 1) where x^*m is the width of the image and y^*n is the height of the image. In this case, the shader code would use the SV_DispatchThreadID system value to determine the location in the input image from which to load data and where the result should be stored in the output image.

Figure 1.5.3 illustrates one way in which a 2D workload might be partitioned using this method. In this example, we have an image with a size of 32×32 pixels. If we wanted to process the image with a total of 4×4 (m = 4, n = 4) Thread Groups as shown, then we would need to define the Thread Groups to each have 8×8 (x = 8 and y = 8) threads. This gives us the total number of threads needed to process all 32×32 (x^*m and y^*n) pixels of the input image.

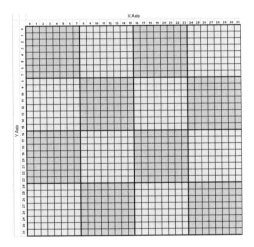

Figure 1.5.3 Visualization of Thread Group distribution for a 2D workload, where the number of Thread Groups (m = 4, n = 4) and the number of threads (x = 8, y = 8) are shown.

Compute Shader Thread Interactions

In addition to providing an easy-to-use thread addressing scheme, the compute shader also allows each Thread Group to declare a block of Group Shared Memory (GSM). This memory is basically defined as an array of variables that are accessible to all of the threads in the Thread Group. The array itself can be composed of any native data types as well as structures, allowing for flexible grouping of data. In practice, the Group

Shared Memory is expected to be on-chip register-based memory that should be significantly faster to access than general texture memory, which can have unpredictable performance depending on access patterns.

Similar to CPU-based multi-threaded programming, when you have multiple threads reading and writing to the same area of memory there is the potential that the same memory can be accessed simultaneously by more than one thread. To provide some form of control over the sequences of access, the compute shader introduces several atomic functions for thread synchronization. For example, there is an atomic function for adding called `InterlockedAdd`. This can be used to have all threads perform a test sequence and then use the `InterlockedAdd` function to increment a variable in the Group Shared Memory to tabulate an overall number of test sequences that produce a particular result.

Another atomic function is the `InterlockedCompareExchange` function, which compares a shared variable with one argument and sets the variable to a second argument if the variable has the same value as the first argument. This provides the basic building blocks of creating a mutex system in the compute shader, where a shared variable serves as the mutex. Each thread can call this function on the mutex variable and only take action if it is able to update the variable to its own identifier. Since the compute shader is intended to provide massively parallel execution, a mutex is not really a preferred choice, but in some situations it may be a desirable avenue to follow, such as when a single resource must be shared across many threads. The Direct3D 11 documentation can be referenced for a complete list of these atomic functions and how they can be used.

Also similar to CPU-based multi-threaded programming is the fact that it is more efficient to design your algorithms to operate in parallel while minimizing the number of times that they must synchronize data with one another. The fastest synchronization operation is the one that you don't have to perform!

Compute Shader Resources

New resource types introduced in Direct3D 11 include Structured Buffers, Byte Address Buffers, and Append/Consume Buffers. Structured Buffers provide what they sound like—1D buffers of structures available in your shader code. The Byte Address Buffers are similar, except that they are a general block of 32-bit memory elements.

The Append/Consume Buffers allow for stack/queue-like access to a resource, allowing the shader to consume the elements of a buffer one at a time and append results to an output buffer one at a time. This should also provide some simplified processing paradigms in which the absolute position of an element is less important than the relative order in which it was added to the buffer.

To further facilitate the compute shader's parallel-processing capabilities, Direct3D 11 provides a new resource view called an Unordered Access View (UAV). This type of view allows the compute shader (as well as the pixel shader) to have read and write access to a resource, where any thread can access any portion of the resource.

This is a big departure from the traditional shader resource access paradigm; typically, a shader can only read from or write to a given resource during a shader invocation, but not both. The UAV can be used to provide random access to both the new and existing resource types, which provides significant freedom in designing the input and output structure of compute shader–based algorithms.

With a general understanding of the new capabilities of the compute shader, we can now take a look at a concrete example in order to better understand the details. We will discuss the general concepts of the SSAO algorithm and then describe how we can use the compute shader's features to build an efficient implementation of the technique.

Screen Space Ambient Occlusion

Screen Space Ambient Occlusion is a relatively recently developed technique for approximating global illumination in the ambient lighting term based solely on the information present in a given frame's depth buffer [Mittring07]. As described in detail in Gem 1.2 by Filion, an approximate amount of ambient light that reaches a given pixel can be computed by sampling the area around the pixel in screen space. This technique provides a convincing approximation to global illumination and performs at a usable speed for high-end applications.

The quality of the algorithm depends on the number of samples and subsequent calculations that are performed for each pixel. In the past few years, a variety of techniques have been proposed to modify the general SSAO algorithm with varying levels of quality versus performance tradeoffs, such as HBAO [Bavoil09a] and SSDO [Ritschel09]. While these new variants of the original algorithm provide improvements in image quality or performance, the basic underlying concepts are shared across all implementations, and hence the compute shader should be applicable in general.

We will now review some of these recent SSAO techniques and discuss several areas of the underlying algorithm that can benefit from the compute shader's new capabilities. Then we will look at an implementation that takes advantage of some of these possible improvements.

SSAO Algorithm

Ambient occlusion techniques have been around for some time and have found uses primarily in offline rendering applications [Landis02]. The concept behind these techniques is to utilize the geometric shape of a model to calculate which portions of the model would be more likely to be occluded than others. If a given point on a model is located on a flat surface, it will be less occluded than another point that is located at a fold in the surface. This relationship is based on the following integral for the reflected radiance:

$$L(\vec{n}) = \int (L_{in}(\vec{\omega}) \cdot \vec{n}) d\omega$$

In this integral, L_{in} is the incident radiation from direction ω, and the surface normal vector is n. This integral indicates that the amount of light reflected at a given surface point is a function of the incident radiance and the angle at which it reaches that point. If there is nearby geometry blocking some portion of the surface surrounding the surface point, then we can generally conclude that less radiant energy will reach the surface. With this in mind, the ambient lighting term can be modulated by an occlusion factor to approximately represent this geometric relationship.

One way to perform this geometric calculation is to project a series of rays from each surface point being tested. The amount of occlusion is then calculated depending on the number of rays that intersect another part of the model within a given radius from the surface point. This effectively determines how much "background" light can reach that point by performing the inverse operation of the radiance integral described previously. Instead of integrating the incident radiance coming into that point over the surface of a hemisphere, we shoot rays out from the surface point over the hemisphere to test for occlusion within the immediate area. The overall occlusion factor is then calculated by accumulating the ray test results and finding the ratio of occluded rays versus non-occluded rays. Once it is calculated, this occlusion factor is then stored either per vertex or per pixel in a texture map and is used to modulate the ambient lighting term of that object when rendered. This produces a rough approximation of global illumination. Figure 1.5.4 demonstrates this ray casting technique.

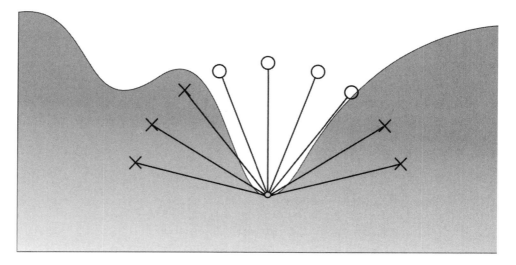

Figure 1.5.4   Side profile of a ray casting technique for approximating occlusion.

This technique works quite well for static scenes or individual static geometric models, but the pre-computation requirements are not practical for dynamic geometry, such as skinned meshes. Several alternative techniques have been suggested to allow for dynamic ambient occlusion calculations, such as [Bunnell05], which generalizes the geometric object into disks to reduce the computational complexity of the occlusion calculations. This allows real-time operation of the algorithm, but it still requires some pre-processing of the models being rendered to determine where to place the disks in the approximated models. In addition, the cost of performing the occlusion calculation scales with increased scene complexity.

The Screen Space Ambient Occlusion algorithm provides an interesting alternative technique for determining an approximate occlusion value. Instead of computing an occlusion value based on the geometric representation of a scene by performing ray casting, the occlusion calculation is delayed until after the scene has been rasterized. Once the scene has been rasterized, an approximated amount of occlusion is determined by inspecting the contents of the scene's depth buffer only—the geometric queries are carried out on the depth buffer instead of on the geometric models. This effectively moves the operation from an object space operation to a screen space operation—which is one of the major benefits of this algorithm. Since it operates at the screen space level, the algorithm's performance is less sensitive to the amount of geometry being rendered and is more sensitive to the resolution of the buffers being used.

The scene's depth buffer can be obtained by utilizing the actual Z-buffer used during rendering, by performing a separate rendering pass that writes the linear depth to a render target, or by using the depth information from a deferred rendering G-buffer. Regardless of how the buffer is generated, the algorithm performs a processing pass that uses the depth buffer as an input and generates an output texture that holds the occlusion values for the entire visible scene. Each pixel of the output is calculated using the depth information within a given radius of its local area, which can be considered an approximation to ambient occlusion. I will refer to this output in the remainder of this document as the *occlusion buffer*. When the final scene rendering is performed, the occlusion buffer is sampled based on screen space location and used to modulate the ambient term of each object in the final scene.

SSAO Algorithm Details

Screen Space Ambient Occlusion has provided a significant improvement over previous ambient occlusion algorithms. Due to the fact that the algorithm runs after a scene is rendered, it focuses the processing time on only the portion of the scene that is visible for the current frame, saving a significant amount of computation and allowing the algorithm to be run in real-time applications without pre-computation. However, the use of the depth buffer also introduces a few obstacles to overcome.

There is the potential that some occluders will not be visible in the depth buffer if there is another object in front of it. Since the depth buffer only records one depth sample per pixel, there is no additional information about the occluders behind the foreground object. This is typically handled by defaulting to zero occlusion if the depth sample read from the depth buffer is too far away from the current pixel being processed. If a more accurate solution is needed, depth peeling can be used to perform multiple occlusion queries, as described in [Bavoil09b].

Additionally, if an object is offscreen but is still occluding an object that is visible onscreen, then the occlusion is not taken into account. This leads to some incorrect occlusion calculations around the outer edge of the image, but solutions have also been proposed to minimize or eliminate these issues. One possibility is to render the depth buffer with a larger field of view than the final rendering to allow objects to be visible to the algorithm around the perimeter of the view port [Bavoil09a].

Another issue with the algorithm is that a relatively large number of samples needs to be taken in order to generate a complete representation of the geometry around each pixel. If performance were not a concern, we could sample the entire area around the pixel P in a regular sampling pattern, but in real-time applications this quickly becomes impractical. Instead of a regular sampling pattern, a common solution is to use a sparse sampling kernel to choose sampling points around the current pixel. This roughly approximates the surrounding area, but the decreased sampling rate may miss some detail.

To compensate for the decreased sampling, it is common to use a stochastic sampling technique instead. By varying the sampling kernel shape and/or orientation for each pixel and then sharing the results between neighboring pixels, an approximation to the more expensive regular sampling pattern can be achieved. Since a typical 3D scene is composed of groups of connected triangles, the majority of the contents of the depth buffer will contain roughly similar depth values in neighborhoods of pixels except at geometric silhouette edges. The variation of the sampling kernel between pixels in combination with this spatial coherence of the depth buffer allows us to share a combined larger number of sample results per pixel while reducing the overall number of calculations that need to be performed.

This helps to effectively widen the sampling kernel, but it also introduces some additional high-frequency noise into the occlusion buffer. To compensate for this effect, it is common to perform a filtering pass over the entire occlusion buffer that blurs the occlusion values without bleeding across object boundaries. This type of a filter is referred to as a *bilateral filter*, which takes into account both the spatial distance between pixels and the intensity values stored in neighboring pixels when calculating the weights to apply to a sample [Tomasi98]. This allows the filter to remove high-frequency noise and at the same time preserve the edges that are present in the occlusion buffer. In addition, the randomization process can be repeated over a small range to facilitate easier filtering later on. Figures 1.5.5 and 1.5.6 show ambient occlusion results before and after bilateral filtering.

Figure 1.5.5 A sample scene rendered without bilateral filtering.

Figure 1.5.6 A sample scene after bilateral filtering.

As mentioned before, the algorithm is performed after rasterization, meaning that its performance is directly related to the screen resolution being used. In fact, this dependency on screen resolution has been exploited to speed up the algorithm as described in Gem 1.3. The depth buffer and/or the occlusion buffer can be generated at a decreased resolution. If the screen resolution is decreased by a factor of 2 in the x and y directions, there is an overall factor of 4 reduction in the number of occlusion pixels that need to be calculated. Then the occlusion buffer can either be upsampled with a bilateral filter or just directly used at the lower resolution.

This strategy can still lead to fairly pleasing results, since the contents of the occlusion buffer are relatively low frequency.

SSAO Meets the Compute Shader

When looking at the block diagram of the SSAO algorithm in Figure 1.5.7, we can begin to compare these high-level operations with the new capabilities of the compute shader to see how we can build a more efficient implementation. We will now go over the steps of the algorithm and discuss potential strategies for mapping to the compute shader.

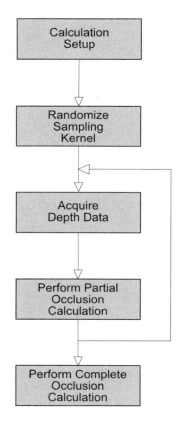

Figure 1.5.7   Block diagram of the SSAO algorithm.

Calculation Setup

The first step shown in the block diagram is to initialize the computations for the current pixel. This entails sampling the depth buffer to obtain the pixel's depth. One of the benefits of having a Group Shared Memory that can be shared by all threads in a Thread Group is the possibility to share texture samples among the entire Thread Group.

Because the shared memory is supposed to be significantly faster than a direct texture sample, if each thread requests a depth sample to initialize its own calculations, then it can also write that depth value to the shared memory for use later on by other threads. The net effect of every thread in a Thread Group doing this is to have a copy of the complete local depth data in the Group Shared Memory. Later, as each thread begins calculating the relative occlusion against the local area, it can read the needed depth values from the Group Shared Memory instead of directly loading from texture memory. Figure 1.5.8 shows this process.

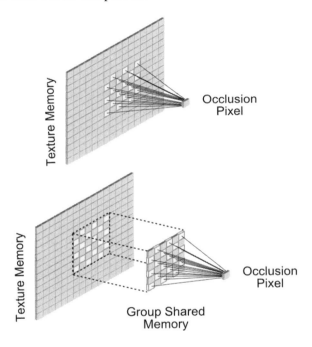

Figure 1.5.8 Comparison of directly sampling versus using the Group Shared Memory for cached sampling.

There are a few additional notes to consider on this topic, however. There is some overhead associated with reading the depth values and then storing them to the Group Shared Memory. In addition, the texture cache can often provide very fast results from memory sample requests if the result was in the cache. Thus, depending on the hardware being run and the patterns and frequency of memory access, it may or may not provide a speed increase to use the Group Shared Memory in practice.

Randomize Sampling Kernel

The next step in the SSAO block diagram is to somehow randomize the sampling kernel that will be used to later look up the surrounding area. This is typically done by acquiring a random vector and then performing a "reflect" operation on each of the sampling kernel vectors around the random vector. Probably the most common way to acquire this vector is to build a small texture with randomized normal vectors inside. The shader can load a single normalized reflection vector based on the screen space position of the pixel being processed [Kajalin09]. This makes removing the "salt-and-pepper" noise easier in the filtering stage of the algorithm.

In the past, SSAO was performed in the pixel shader, which means that the pixel shader required a screen space position as a fragment attribute to be passed by the vertex or geometry shader. The compute shader can help to simplify this operation somewhat. By utilizing the Dispatch ID system value, we can automatically receive the integer ID of each pixel being processed in our compute shader code. To create our repeating pattern of reflection vectors in screen space, we can simply perform a bitwise AND operation on the least significant bits of the dispatch ID—in other words, if we wanted to repeat every 4×4 block of pixels, we would mask off all but the two least significant bits of the ID.

In fact, we can even store the randomized vectors as an array of constants in our shader. This eliminates the need for a texture sample and the repeating texture of normalized reflection vectors altogether. Of course this is predicated on the fact that we don't use too many vectors, but we could always use the standard approach if that is needed.

Acquire Depth Data

Once the sampling kernel has been randomized, we can acquire each individual depth sample. In a traditional SSAO algorithm, this is done with a sampler that uses the x and y coordinates of the current sampling kernel vector to offset from the current pixel location. Since the sampling kernel has been pseudo-randomized, there is a potential for reduced texture cache efficiency if the sampling kernel width is large enough.

If we utilize the Group Shared Memory as described previously, then the depth values that we need to acquire could already be available in the GSM. However, there are several points to consider before embarking on this strategy as well. Since the Thread Group will only be operating on one block of the depth data at a time—for example, a 16×16 block—then we need to consider what happens at the edges of that block. The pixels along the outer edges of the block will need access to the depth samples within our sampling radius, and they would not already be pre-loaded. This provides a choice—we could either pre-load a larger portion of the depth buffer to include the surrounding area or we could dynamically check to see whether the data has been loaded to the GSM yet, and, if not, then directly get it from the depth buffer.

Both options could have performance penalties. Pre-loading large bands of depth data around each block may end up increasing the number of depth samples to the point that it would be just as efficient to perform the sampling in the traditional manner. If we dynamically decide whether or not to fetch data from the depth buffer, then we could perform a large number of dynamic branches in the shader, which could also be detrimental to performance. These factors need to be weighed against the increased access speed provided by using the GSM instead of direct sampling. With the texture cache providing similar fast access for at least a portion of the texture samples, it is altogether possible that the standard approach would be faster. Of course, any discussion of texture cache performance depends on the hardware that the algorithm is running on, so this should be tested against your target platform to see which would be a better choice.

The other point to consider with using the GSM is that there is no native support for bilinear filtering of the GSM data. If you wanted to filter the depth values for each depth sample based on the floating-point values of the kernel offset vector, then you would need to implement this functionality in the shader code itself. However, since the depth buffer contains relatively low-frequency data, this is not likely to affect image quality in this case.

Perform Partial Occlusion Calculation (per Sample)

Once we have obtained a depth sample to compare to our current pixel depth, we can move to the partial occlusion calculations. In this step, we determine whether our sample depth causes any occlusion at the current pixel. There are many different varieties of calculations available to perform here, from a binary test of the sample point being above or below the kernel offset vector [Kajalin09] all the way up to a piecewise defined function read from a texture [Filion08].

Regardless of how the calculation is performed, there is an interesting possibility that the compute shader introduces if the calculation is only a function of the depth delta—sharing occlusion calculations between pixels. If we call our current pixel point P and our current sample point S, then the occlusion caused at point P by point S is inherently related to the inverse occlusion at point S by point P. Since the compute shader can perform scatter operations, a single thread can calculate the occlusion for one pair of locations and then write the result to point P and the inverse of the calculation to point S.

This would save the number of required calculations by nearly a factor of 2, but it would also introduce the need for some type of communication mechanism to get the values to both occlusion buffer values. Since there is the possibility that multiple pixels would be trying to write a result to the same pixel, we could attempt to use the atomic operations for updating the values, but this could lead to a large number of synchronization events between threads. At the same time, these occlusion values can be accumulated in the GSM for fast access by each thread. Again, the cost of the synchronization events will likely vary across hardware, so further testing would be needed to see how much of a benefit could come from this implementation.

Perform Complete Occlusion Calculation

The final step in this process is to calculate the final occlusion value that will end up in the occlusion buffer for use in the final rendering. This is normally done by performing a simple average of all of the partial occlusion calculations. In this way, we can scale the number of samples used to calculate the occlusion according to the performance level of the target hardware.

As described earlier, there is typically some form of a bilateral filter applied to the occlusion buffer after all pixels have a final occlusion value calculated. In general, filtering is one area that could potentially see huge benefits from compute shader implementations. Since filtering generally has an exact predetermined access pattern for the input image, the Group Shared Memory can directly be used to pre-load the exact texture data needed. This is especially beneficial when implementing 2D separable filters due to the ability to perform the filtering pass in one direction, store the result into the GSM, then perform the second filtering pass in the other direction over the values in the GSM without ever writing the results back to the output buffer in between steps. Even though the bilateral filter is non-separable, it has been shown that a decent approximation of it can be achieved with a separable implementation [Pham05].

Compute Shader Implementation Details

After reviewing some of the new features available in the compute shader and how they can be used with the SSAO algorithm, we can now look at a sample implementation. Since the compute shader techniques are relatively new, the focus of this implementation will be to demonstrate some of its new features and draw some conclusions about appropriate-use cases for them. These features are described briefly here, with additional detail provided in the following sections.

This implementation will utilize two different-size thread groups, 16×16 and 32×32, to generate the occlusion buffer. Using two different sizes will allow us to see whether the Thread Group size has any effect on the performance of the algorithm. We will also demonstrate the use of the GSM as a cache for the depth values and compare how well this tactic performs relative to directly loading samples from the depth buffer. In addition to using the GSM, we also utilize the Gather sampling function for filling the GSM with depth values to see whether there is any impact on overall performance. The randomization system will utilize one of the new thread addressing system values to select a reflection vector, eliminating the need for a randomization texture. After the occlusion buffer has been generated, we will utilize a separable version of the bilateral filter to demonstrate the ability of the compute shader to efficiently perform filtering operations.

Implementation Overview

The process is started by rendering a linear depth buffer at full-screen resolution with the traditional rendering pipeline. Stored along with the depth value is the view space normal vector, which will be used during the occlusion calculations. This depth/normal buffer serves as the primary input to the compute shader to calculate a raw, unfiltered occlusion buffer. Finally, we use the depth/normal buffer and the raw occlusion buffer to perform separable bilateral filtering to produce a final occlusion buffer suitable for rendering the scene with the standard rendering pipeline.

Depth/Normal Buffer Generation

The depth/normal buffer will consist of a four-component floating-point texture, and each of the occlusion buffers will consist of a single floating-point component. The depth/normal vectors are generated by rendering the linear view space depth and view space normal vectors into the depth/normal buffer. The depth value is calculated by simply scaling the view space depth by the distance to the far clipping plane. This ensures an output in the range of [0,1]. The normal vector is calculated by transforming the normal vector into view space and then scaling and biasing the vector components. Listing 1.5.1 shows the code for doing so.

LISTING 1.5.1   Generation of the view space depth and normal vector buffer

```
output.position =
    mul( float4( v.position, 1.0f ), WorldViewProjMatrix );

float3 ViewSpaceNormals =
    mul( float4( v.normal, 0.0f ), WorldViewMatrix ).xyz;

output.depth.xyz = ViewSpaceNormals * 0.5f + 0.5f;
output.depth.w = output.position.w / 50.0f;
```

Depending on the depth precision required for your scene, you can choose an appropriate image format—either 16 or 32 bits. This sample implementation utilizes 16-bit formats.

Raw Occlusion Buffer Generation

Next, we generate the raw occlusion buffer in the compute shader. This represents the heart of the SSAO algorithm. As mentioned earlier, we will utilize two different Thread Group sizes. The occlusion calculations will be performed in Thread Groups of size 16×16×1 and 32×32×1. Since we can adjust the number of Thread Groups executed in the application's Dispatch call, either Thread Group size can be used to generate the raw occlusion buffer. However, if there is any performance difference between the two Thread Group sizes, this will provide some insight into the proper usage of the compute shader.

Regardless of the size of the Thread Groups, each one will generate one portion of the raw occlusion buffer equivalent to its size. Each thread will calculate a single pixel of the raw occlusion buffer that corresponds to the thread's Dispatch thread ID system value. This Dispatch thread ID is also used to determine the appropriate location in the depth/normal buffer to load. The depth value and normal vector are loaded from the texture and converted back into their original formats for use later.

Depth Value Cache with the GSM

We will also set up the compute shader to cache local depth values in the GSM. Once the depth values of the surrounding area are loaded into the GSM, all subsequent depth sampling can be performed on the GSM instead of loading directly from texture memory.

Before we discuss how to set up and use the GSM, we need to consider the desired layout for the data. Since we are utilizing two different Thread Group sizes, we will specify a different layout for each. Each of the Thread Groups requires the corresponding depth region that it represents to be present in the GSM. In addition, the area surrounding the Thread Group's boundary is also needed to allow the occlusion calculations for the border pixels to be carried out correctly. This requires each thread to sample not only its own depth/normal vector, but also some additional depth values to properly load the GSM for use later. If we stipulate that each thread will load four depth values into the GSM, then our 16×16 thread group will provide a 32×32 overall region in the GSM (the original 16×16 block with an 8-pixel boundary). The 32×32 Thread Group size will provide a 64×64 region (the original 32×32 block with a 16-pixel boundary).

Fortunately, the Gather instruction can be utilized to increase the number of depth values that are sampled for each thread. The Gather instruction returns the four point-sampled single component texture samples that would normally have been used for bilinear interpolation—which is perfect for pre-loading the GSM since we are using only single component depth values. This effectively increases the number of depth samples per texture instruction by a factor of 4. If we use each thread to perform a single Gather instruction, then we can easily fill the required areas of 32×32 and 64×64. The required samples are obtained by having each thread perform the Gather instruction and store the results in the GSM for all other threads within the group to utilize. This is demonstrated in Listing 1.5.2.

LISTING 1.5.2   Declaring and populating the Group Shared Memory with depth data

```
#define USE_GSM

#ifdef USE_GSM
    // Declare enough shared memory for the padded thread group size
    groupshared float LoadedDepths[padded_x][padded_y];
#endif

    int3 OffsetLocation =
        int3( GroupID.x*size_x - kernel_x, GroupID.y*size_y - kernel_y, 0 );
    int3 ThreadLocation = GroupThreadID * 2;

    float2 fGatherSample;
    fGatherSample.x = ((float)GroupID.x * (float)size_x -
        (float)kernel_x + (float)GroupThreadID.x * 2.0f ) / xres;
    fGatherSample.y = ((float)GroupID.y * (float)size_y -
        (float)kernel_y + (float)GroupThreadID.y * 2.0f ) / yres;

    float4 fDepths = DepthMap.GatherAlpha( DepthSampler, fGatherSample +
        float2( 0.5f / (float)xres, 0.5f / (float)yres ) ) * zf;

    LoadedDepths[ThreadLocation.x][ThreadLocation.y] = fDepths.w;
    LoadedDepths[ThreadLocation.x+1][ThreadLocation.y] = fDepths.z;
    LoadedDepths[ThreadLocation.x+1][ThreadLocation.y+1] = fDepths.y;
    LoadedDepths[ThreadLocation.x][ThreadLocation.y+1] = fDepths.x;

    GroupMemoryBarrierWithGroupSync();
```

The number of depth values loaded into the GSM can be increased as needed by having each thread perform additional Gather instructions. The Group Shared Memory is defined as a 2D array corresponding to the size of the area that will be loaded and cached. After all of the depth values have been loaded, we introduce a synchronization among threads in the Thread Group with the `GroupMemoryBarrierWithGroupSync()` intrinsic function. This function ensures that all threads have finished writing to the GSM up to this point in the compute shader before continuing execution.

A compile-time switch is provided in the sample code to allow switching between filling the GSM to use the cached depth values or to directly access the depth texture. Since the GSM has the potential to improve the sampling performance depending on the access pattern, this will allow an easy switch between techniques for a clear efficiency comparison.

Next, we initialize the randomization of the sampling kernel with the lowest four bits of the Dispatch thread ID x and y coordinates, as shown in Listing 1.5.3. The lowest four bits in each direction are used to select a reflection vector from a 2D array of rotation vectors, which are predefined and stored in a constant array. This eliminates the need for a separate texture and range expansion calculations, but it requires a relatively large array to be loaded when the compute shader is loaded. After it is selected, the reflection vector is then used to modify the orientation of the sampling kernel by reflecting each of the kernel vectors about the reflection vector. This provides a different sampling kernel for each consecutive pixel in the occlusion buffer.

LISTING 1.5.3   Definition of the sampling kernel and selection of the randomization vector

```
const float3 kernel[8] =
{
    normalize( float3(  1, 1, 1 ) ),
    normalize( float3( -1,-1,-1 ) ),
    normalize( float3( -1,-1, 1 ) ),
    normalize( float3( -1, 1,-1 ) ),
    normalize( float3( -1, 1 ,1 ) ),
    normalize( float3(  1,-1,-1 ) ),
    normalize( float3(  1,-1, 1 ) ),
    normalize( float3(  1, 1,-1 ) )
};

const float3 rotation[16][16] =
{
    { {...},{...},{...},{...}, ... }
};

int rotx = DispatchThreadID.x & 0xF;
int roty = DispatchThreadID.y & 0xF;
float3 reflection = rotation[rotx][roty];
```

With a random reflection vector selected, we can begin the iteration process by sampling a depth value at the location determined by the randomized sampling kernel offsets. The sample location is found by determining the current pixel's view space 3D position and then adding the reoriented sampling kernel vectors as offsets from the pixel's location. This new view space position is then converted back to screen space, producing an (x, y) coordinate pair that can then be used to select the depth sample from either the GSM or the depth/normal texture. This is shown in Listing 1.5.4.

LISTING 1.5.4   Sampling location flipping and re-projection from view space to screen space

```
    float3 vRotatedOffset =
        reflect( kernel[y], rotation[rotx][roty] );

    float fSign = dot( fPixelNormal, vRotatedOffset );
    if ( fSign < 0.0f )
        vFlippedOffset = -vFlippedOffset;

    float3 Sample3D = PixelPosVS + vFlippedOffset * scale;
    int3 newoffset = ViewPosToScreenPos( Sample3D );

#ifndef USE_GSM
    float fSample = DepthMap.Load( iNewOffset ).w * zf;
#else
    float fSample = LoadDepth( iNewOffset - OffsetLocation );
#endif
```

The pixel's view space normal vector is used to determine whether the kernel off-set vector points away from the current pixel. If so, then the direction of the offset vector is negated to provide an additional sample that is more relevant for determining occlusion. This provides additional samples in the visible hemisphere of the pixel, which increases the usable sample density for the pixel. The final screen space sample location is then used to look up the depth sample either directly from the texture or from the GSM by calling the LoadDepth() function.

After the depth has been loaded, the occlusion at the current pixel from this sample is calculated. The calculation that is used is similar to the one presented in [Filion08] and [Lake10], using a linear occlusion falloff function raised to a power. This produces a smooth gradual falloff from full occlusion to zero occlusion and provides easy-to-use parameters for adjusting the occlusion values.

The partial occlusion calculation is repeated for a given number of samples, implemented as a multiple of the number of elements in the sampling kernel. In this implementation, the number of samples can be chosen in multiples of eight. All of these individual occlusion values are averaged and then stored in the raw occlusion buffer for further processing.

Separable Bilateral Filter

The final step in our occlusion value generation is to perform the bilateral blur. As described earlier, we are able to use a separable version of the filter, even though it is not perfectly accurate to do so. The bilateral filter passes are implemented in the compute shader, with each of the separable passes being performed in an individual dispatch call. Since we are only processing one direction at a time, we will first use one Thread Group for each row of the image and then process the resulting image with one Thread Group for each column of the image. In this arrangement, we can load the entire contents of a Thread Group's row or column into the GSM, and then each thread can directly read its neighbor values from it. This should minimize the cost of sampling a texture for filtering and allow larger filter sizes to be used. This implementation uses 7×7 bilateral filters, but this can easily be increased or decreased as needed. Listing 1.5.5 shows how the separable filter pass loads its data into the GSM.

LISTING 1.5.5   Loading and storing the depth and occlusion values into the GSM for the horizontal portion of a separable bilateral filter

```
// Declare enough shared memory for the padded group size
groupshared float2 horizontalpoints[totalsize_x];
...

int textureindex = DispatchThreadID.x + DispatchThreadID.y * totalsize_x;

// Each thread will load its own depth/occlusion values
float fCenterDepth = DepthMap.Load(DispatchThreadID).w;
float fCenterOcclusion = AmbientOcclusionTarget[textureindex].x;

// Then store them in the GSM for everyone to use
horizontalpoints[GroupIndex].x = fCenterDepth;
horizontalpoints[GroupIndex].y = fCenterOcclusion;

// Synchronize all threads
GroupMemoryBarrierWithGroupSync();
```

One thread is declared for each pixel of the row/column, and each thread loads a single value out of the raw occlusion buffer and stores that value in the GSM. Once the value has been stored, a synchronization point is used to ensure that all of the memory accesses have completed and that the values that have been stored can be safely read by other threads.

The bilateral filter weights consist of two components: a spatially based weighting and a range-based weighting. The spatial weights utilize a fixed Gaussian kernel with a size of 7 taps in each direction. A separate Gaussian weighting value is calculated based on the difference between the center pixel and each of the samples to determine the weighting to apply to that sample. Modifying the sigma values used in the range-based Gaussian allows for easy adjustment of the range-filtering properties of the bilateral filter. Listing 1.5.6 shows how this calculation is performed.

LISTING 1.5.6   Horizontal portion of a separable bilateral filter in the compute shader

```
const float avKernel7 =
{ 0.004431f, 0.05402f, 0.2420f, 0.3990f, 0.2420f, 0.05402f, 0.004431f };

const float rsigma = 0.0051f;
float fBilateral = 0.0f;
float fWeight = 0.0f;

for ( int x = -3; x <= 3; x++ )
{
    int location = GroupIndex + x;
    float fSampleDepth = horizontalpoints[location].x;
    float fSampleOcclusion = horizontalpoints[location].y;

    float fDelta = fCenterDepth - fSampleDepth;
    float fRange =
        exp( ( -1.0f * fDelta * fDelta ) / ( 2.0f * rsigma * rsigma ) );

    fBilateral += fSampleOcclusion * fRange * avKernel[x+3];
    fWeight += fRange * avKernel[x+3];
}

AmbientOcclusionTarget[textureindex] = fBilateral / fWeight;
```

Finally, once both passes of the bilateral filter are performed, the values written to the final output buffer can be used to supply the ambient lighting term of an output image. The value stored in the occlusion buffer represents visibility, and thus can be directly used as the ambient lighting term without modification. The sample implementation provides its output using only the occlusion value—no other lighting is applied to the scene.

Results

Figure 1.5.9 shows the end result of our compute shader–based implementation of the algorithm. All images and performance numbers were generated on an AMD 57xx series GPU. The following image was generated using 32 depth samples for each occlusion pixel and with the 7×7 separable bilateral filter applied twice.

To gain some insight into how well the new implementation techniques perform, we can review the overall frame time for each of our optional configurations. Table 1.5.1 provides the performance metrics for the two Thread Group sizes for varying numbers of samples used in the occlusion calculation. These frames-per-second figures were generated with the direct sampling technique on a 640×480 render target with no bilateral filtering applied.

The two Thread Group sizes produce nearly identical performance numbers. This indicates that the Thread Group size does not have a significant impact on this type of iterative algorithm. When considering the actual frame time for each test (the inverse of the fps), we see a linear increase in frame time for each of the additional sets of samples.

Figure 1.5.9   Final results of the compute shader SSAO implementation.

TABLE 1.5.1

NO GSM	8	16	24	32	40	48	56	64
16×16	947	608	437	349	288	241	212	188
32×32	961	610	445	350	288	245	214	187

In comparison, Table 1.5.2 provides the same metrics generated with the GSM caching technique.

TABLE 1.5.2

W/ GSM	8	16	24	32	40	48	56	64
16×16	811	699	531	426	357	306	269	240
32×32	764	625	485	391	330	286	252	225

Table 1.5.2 shows a different performance characteristic. When compared to the direct loading technique, we see the GSM technique performs slower at the 8-sample level. However, for all sample levels above this, the GSM technique significantly outperforms the direct sampling method. For all of these higher sampling levels, we see a similar linear increase in frame time but a smaller slope than the direct sampling method. Figure 1.5.10 shows the frame times for the four different cases.

The slower performance with the GSM at lower sampling rates can be attributed to the overhead of loading and storing all of the additional depth data. However, there is a clear performance gain for each additional sample used in the occlusion calculation.

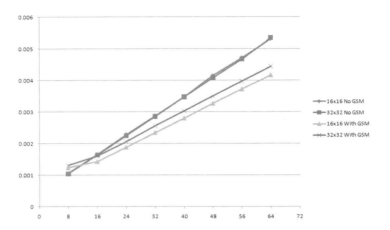

Figure 1.5.10   Comparison of frame times with and without the GSM as a cache.

With this performance advantage also comes some limitations. In both Thread Group sizes, we defined a fixed border size. In some cases, when a pixel is close to the viewer, the offset vector can produce a screen space offset much larger than this border size. This can be overcome either by scaling the size of the sampling kernel according to the distance from the camera or by dynamically determining whether the sample location is available in the GSM and directly loading the sample if needed.

Conclusion and Future Work

In this chapter, we have applied the compute shader to the Screen Space Ambient Occlusion algorithm and discussed the implications of various implementation choices. This implementation provides a basic framework upon which further proposed extensions can be implemented relatively easily. Additional research can be directed at sharing partial occlusion values between neighboring pixels for each occlusion calculation, which is now possible due to the scatter capabilities of the compute shader. In addition, further exploration on the use of the GSM as a caching mechanism for regional depth averages could be investigated. Finally, there have been several recent findings using multi-resolution rendering solutions for SSAO, which should also benefit from the compute shader implementations.

References

[Bavoil09a] Bavoil, Louis and Miguel Sainz. "Image-Space Horizon-Based Ambient Occlusion." *ShaderX7: Advanced Rendering Techniques*. Ed. Wolfgang F. Engel. Boston: Charles River Media, 2009. Section 6.2.

[Bavoil09b] Bavoil, Louis and Miguel Sainz. "Multi-Layer Dual-Resolution Screen-Space Ambient Occlusion." 2009. SlideShare. n.d. <http://www.slideshare.net/NVIDIA/multilayer-dualresolution-screenspace-ambient-occlusion>.

[Bunnell05] Bunnell, Michael. "Dynamic Ambient Occlusion and Indirect Lighting." 2005. Gamedev.net. n.d. <http://downloads.gamedev.net/pdf/Pharr_ch14.pdf>.

[Filion08] Filion, Dominic and Rob McNaughton. "Effects and Techniques." Course on Advances in Real-Time Rendering in 3D Graphics and Games Course. SIGGRAPH 2008. Los Angeles Convention Center, Los Angeles, CA. 11 August 2008.

[Kajalin09] Kajalin, Vladimir. "Screen Space Ambient Occlusion." *ShaderX7: Advanced Rendering Techniques*. Ed. Wolfgang F. Engel. Boston: Charles River Media, 2009. Section 6.1.

[Lake10] Lake, Adam, ed. *Game Programming Gems 8*. Boston: Charles River Media, 2010.

[Landis02] Landis, Hayden. "Production-Ready Global Illumination." Course notes on RenderMan in Production. SIGGRAPH 2002. Henry B. Gonzalez Convention Center, San Antonio, TX. 21 July 2002. Chapter 5.

[Mittring07] Mittring, Martin. "Finding Next Gen – CryEngine 2.0." Course notes on Advanced Real-Time Rendering in 3D Graphics and Games. SIGGRAPH 2007. San Diego Convention Center, San Diego, CA. 8 August 2007. 97–121.

[Pham05] Pham, T.Q. and L.J. van Vliet. "Separable Bilateral Filtering for Fast Video Processing." IEEE International Conference on Multimedia and Expo. Amsterdam, The Netherlands. July 2005.

[Ritschel09] Ritschel, Tobias, Thorsten Grosch, and Hans-Peter Seidel. "Approximating Dynamic Global Illumination in Image Space." *Proceedings of the 2009 Symposium on Interactive 3D Graphics and Games* (2009): 75–82.

[Tomasi98] Tomasi, Carlo and Roberto Manduchi. "Bilateral Filtering for Gray and Color Images." *Proceedings of the Sixth International Conference on Computer Vision.* (1998): 839–846.

1.6

Eye-View Pixel Anti-Aliasing for Irregular Shadow Mapping

Nico Galoppo,
Intel Advanced Visual Computing (AVC)
nico.galoppo@intel.com

The irregular shadows algorithm (also known as *Irregular Z-Buffer shadows*) combines the image quality and sampling characteristics of ray-traced shadows with the performance advantages of depth buffer–based hardware pipelines [Johnson04]. Irregular shadows are free from aliasing from the perspective of the light source because the occlusion of each eye-view sample is evaluated at sub-pixel precision in the light view. However, irregular shadow mapping suffers from *pixel aliasing* in the final shadowed image due to the fact that shadow edges and high-frequency shadows are not correctly captured by the resolution of the eye-view image. Brute-force super-sampling of eye-view pixels decreases shadow aliasing overall but incurs impractical memory and computational requirements.

In this gem, we present an efficient algorithm to compute anti-aliased occlusion values. Rather than brute-force super-sampling all pixels, we propose adaptively adding shadow evaluation samples for a small fraction of potentially aliased pixels. We construct a conservative estimate of eye-view pixels that are not fully lit and not fully occluded. Multiple shadow samples are then inserted into the irregular Z-buffer based on the footprint of the light-view projection of potentially aliased pixels. Finally, the individual shadow sample occlusion values are combined into fractional and properly anti-aliased occlusion values. Our algorithm requires minimal additional storage and shadow evaluation cost but results in significantly better image quality of shadow edges and improved temporal behavior of high-frequency shadow content.

Previously, architectural constraints of traditional GPUs have inhibited per-frame construction and traversal of irregular data structures in terms of both performance and programmer flexibility. Our implementation of anti-aliased irregular shadow mapping exploits many strengths of the Larrabee architecture, one of which is the ability to write to run-time computed addresses in global memory space. Additionally, we were able to do so using the conventional C programming model and incorporate the adaptive nature of our technique with little effort. In comparison, traditional GPU architectures do not offer programming semantics for such global scatter operations, or they do so at extremely low performance due to their highly specialized but constrained (localized) memory hierarchy (for example, the CUDA programming model), in the worst case falling back to main memory writes [Sintorn08, Baumann05].

Background and Problem: Shadow Edge Aliasing

In this section, we'll describe the characteristics of various popular shadow generation algorithms and how they cope with different forms of aliasing, and we'll describe the problem of screen-space shadow edge aliasing, which affects many current algorithms.

Pixel-Perfect Shadows with the Irregular Z-Buffer

Conventional shadow mapping renders the scene from the eye and the light, and in the final compositing pass, the two views are compared to identify points that are in shadow [Williams78]. Light-view aliasing results from misalignment of these two views, as shown in Figure 1.6.1(a). There are several variants of shadow mapping that reduce but do not eliminate sampling and self-shadowing artifacts [Fernando01, Stamminger02, Sen03, Lloyd08, Lefohn07], because none of them resolves the fundamental mismatch in sampling patterns between the eye and light views, which is the root cause of most shadow mapping artifacts.

Irregular shadow mapping addresses the root cause of visual artifacts in conventional shadow mapping by basing the light-view sampling pattern on the positions of pixels in the eye-view raster and their corresponding depth values, therefore perfectly aligning the compared occluder surface point with the projection of the shadow sample, as illustrated in Figure 1.6.1(b) [Johnson04, Johnson05]. The density of shadow samples varies significantly across the image plane (as seen in Figure 1.6.2), which illustrates the need for an irregular data structure during the light pass.

Irregular shadow mapping utilizes the irregular Z-buffer in this context. This data structure explicitly stores all of the sample locations in a two-dimensional spatial data structure rather than implicitly representing them with a regular pattern. The data structure can be any spatial data structure that supports efficient range queries, such as a k-d tree or a grid. Just as in conventional shadow mapping, irregular shadow mapping projects triangles onto the light-view image plane one at a time and then determines which samples lie inside a triangle. Unlike conventional shadow mapping, this determination is made by querying the irregular Z-buffer. Finally, for each sample inside a triangle, irregular shadow mapping performs the standard depth comparison and updates the sample's occlusion value.

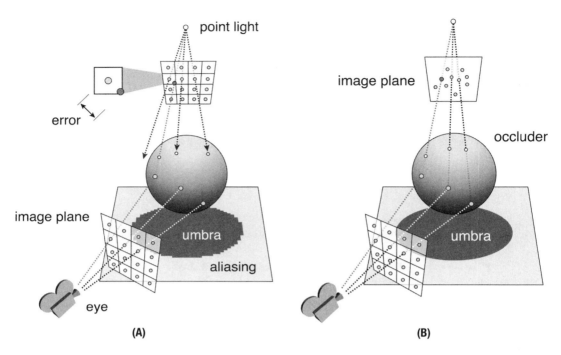

Figure 1.6.1   Conventional versus irregular shadow mapping. In conventional shadow mapping (left), both the eye-view and light-view images are rendered with the classic Z-buffer, leading to a mismatch between the desired and actual sample locations in the shadow map. Irregular shadow mapping (right) avoids this mismatch by rendering the light-view image with the irregular Z-buffer.

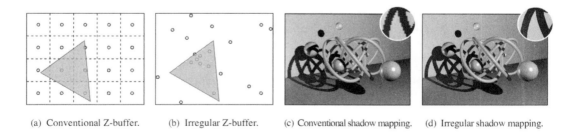

(a) Conventional Z-buffer.   (b) Irregular Z-buffer.   (c) Conventional shadow mapping.   (d) Irregular shadow mapping.

Figure 1.6.2   The classic Z-buffer (a) samples a scene at regularly spaced points on the light image plane. The irregular Z-buffer (b) samples a scene at arbitrary points on the light image plane. Irregular shadow mapping (d) eliminates aliasing artifacts typically associated with conventional shadow mapping (c).

Note that when a conventional rasterizer is used during light-view projection of occluder triangles, it is necessary to scan-convert expanded triangles to ensure fragments will be generated for any cell touched by the unexpanded triangle (also known as *conservative rasterization* [Akenine-Möller05]), since irregular Z-buffer samples may lie anywhere within the cell bounds, as illustrated in Figure 1.6.3. For reference, [Hasselgren05] describes a shader implementation with example code. On the other hand, the advantage of a software rasterizer (for example, on Larrabee) is that a special rasterization path can be implemented to apply custom rasterization rules that enable conservative rasterization directly without triangle expansion.

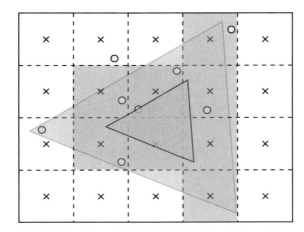

Figure 1.6.3   Conservative rasterization versus conventional rasterization. Scan-converted triangles have to be expanded during light-view projection to ensure fragments will be generated for any cell touched by the unexpanded triangle (shaded cells), since irregular Z-buffer samples (circles) may lie anywhere within the pixel bounds.

Eye-View Aliasing

While irregular shadow mapping is free of light-view aliasing, it still suffers from eye-view aliasing of pixels, as illustrated in Figure 1.6.4. Such aliasing is a common problem in computer graphics. For example, it is also encountered in ray casting with a single eye ray per pixel. The problem is that thin geometry (high-frequency screen content) cannot be captured by a single ray, because the rays of two neighboring pixels may miss some geometry even though the geometry projects to part of those pixels. Similarly, in the case of shadows in a rasterizer, it is possible that a surface point projected to the center of an eye-view pixel is lit, but the entire area of the pixel is not lit. This phenomenon, known as *eye-view shadow aliasing*, is caused by the fact that a single bit occlusion value is not sufficient to represent the occlusion value of aliased pixels. Anti-aliased occlusion values are fractional values that represent the fraction of the total pixel area that is lit. Recently, a few novel shadow mapping techniques [Brabec01, Lauritzen06, Salvi08] have addressed this problem and provide good solutions for eye-view aliasing but still expose light-view aliasing.

Figure 1.6.4   The thin geometry in the tower causes eye-view aliasing of the projected shadow. Note that some of the tower's connected features are disconnected in the shadow.

The most obvious approach to produce anti-aliased shadows with irregular shadow mapping is super-sampling of the entire screen by generating and evaluating multiple shadow samples for each eye-view pixel. The anti-aliased occlusion value for a pixel is then simply the average of the individual sample occlusion values. While this brute-force approach certainly works, as illustrated in Figure 1.6.5, the computational and storage costs quickly become impractical. Data structure construction, traversal times, and storage requirements of the irregular Z-buffer are proportional to the number of shadow samples, making real-time performance impossible on current hardware for even as little as four shadow samples per pixel.

The recent method by [Robison09] provides a solution to compute anti-aliased shadows from the (aliased) output of irregular shadow mapping, but in essence it is also a brute-force approach in screen space that does not exploit the irregular Z-buffer acceleration structure and is therefore at a computational disadvantage compared to our approach.

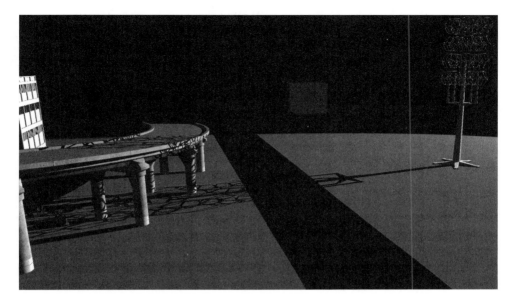

Figure 1.6.5 A four-times super-sampled irregular shadow
mapping result image of the tower scene.

Solution: Adaptive Multi-Sampling of Irregular Shadows

We observed in Figure 1.6.5 that accumulating shadow evaluation results of multiple
samples per eye-view pixels provides a nice anti-aliased shadow and that potentially
shadow-aliased pixels are those pixels that lie on a projected shadow edge. Therefore, we
propose an efficient algorithm for anti-aliased irregular shadow mapping by *adaptive*
multi-sampling of *only* those pixels that potentially lie on a shadow edge. Since only a
marginal fraction of all screen pixels are shadow-edge pixels, this approach results in substantial gains in computational and storage costs compared to the brute-force approach.

Essentially, our method is an extension of the original irregular shadow mapping
algorithm, where the irregular Z-buffer acceleration structure remains a light space–
oriented acceleration structure for the projected eye-view shadow samples. However,
during irregular Z-buffer construction, potential shadow edge pixels are detected
using a conservative shadow edge stencil buffer. Such pixels generate multiple shadow
samples distributed over the pixel's extent and are inserted in the irregular Z-buffer
(shadow sample splatting). Non-shadow-edge pixels are treated just as in the original
irregular shadow mapping algorithm—a single shadow sample is sufficient to detect
the occlusion value of the entire pixel. In the final shadow evaluation step, shadow
occlusion values are averaged over each eye-view pixel's sample, resulting in a properly
anti-aliased fractional occlusion value. This value approximates the fraction of the pixel's
area that is occluded, and it goes toward the true value in the limit as the number of
samples per pixel increases.

Algorithm: Anti-Aliased Irregular Shadow Mapping

We will now give an overview of the complete algorithm to provide structure to the remainder of the algorithm description in this section. Then we describe how to determine which pixels are potentially aliased by constructing a conservative shadow edge stencil buffer and how to splat multiple samples into the irregular Z-buffer efficiently. Finally, we put it all together and present the complete algorithm in practice.

We can formulate our approach in the following top-level description of our algorithm:

1. Render the scene conservatively from the light's point of view to a variance shadow map.
2. Render the scene from the eye point to a conventional Z-buffer—depth values only (gives points P_0).
3. Construct a conservative shadow edge stencil buffer using a variance shadow map and light-space projection of P_0.
4. Using the stencil in Step 3, generate N extra eye-view samples P_i *for potential shadow edge pixels only*.
5. Transform eye-view samples P_i to light space P'_i (shadow sample splatting).
6. Insert all samples P'_i in the irregular Z-buffer.
7. Render the scene from the light's point of view while testing against samples in the irregular Z-buffer, tagging occluded samples.
8. Render the scene from the eye point, using the result from Step 7 and the conservative shadow edge stencil buffer. Multi-sampled eye-view pixels accumulate shadow sample values into a fractional (anti-aliased) shadow value.

Conservative Shadow Edge Stencil Buffer

To adaptively add shadow samples at shadow-edge pixels, we construct a special stencil buffer that answers the following question: Is there any chance that this eye-space pixel is partially occluded by geometry in this light-space texel? We call this stencil buffer the *conservative shadow edge stencil buffer*. Giving an exact answer to the aforementioned question is impossible because it is essentially solving the shadowing problem. However, we can use a probabilistic technique to answer the question *conservatively* with sufficient confidence. A conservative answer is sufficient for our purpose, since multi-sampling of non-shadow-edge pixels does not alter the correctness of the result —it only adds some extra cost. Obviously, we strive to make the stencil buffer only as conservative as necessary.

We employ a technique called *Variance Shadow Mapping* [Lauritzen06]. Variance shadow maps encode a distribution of depths at each light-space texel by determining the mean and variance of depth (the first two moments of the depth distribution). These moments are constructed through mip-mapping of the variance shadow map.

When querying the variance shadow map, we use these moments to compute an upper bound on the fraction of the distribution that is more distant than the surface being shaded, and therefore this bound can be used to cull eye-view pixels that have very little probability to be in shadow.

In particular, the cumulative distribution function $F(t) = P(x \geq t)$ can be used as a measure of the fraction of the eye-view fragment that is lit, where t is the distance of the eye-view sample to the light, x is the occluder depth distribution, and P stands for the probability function. While we cannot compute this function $F(t)$ exactly, Chebyshev's inequality gives an upper bound:

$$P_{lit}(t) \equiv P(x \geq t) \leq p_{max}(t) \equiv \frac{\sigma^2}{\sigma^2 + (t - \mu)^2} \qquad \text{for } t < \mu$$

$$\leq p_{max}(t) \equiv 1 \qquad \text{for } t \geq \mu$$

The upper bound $P_{max}(t)$ and the true probability $P_{lit}(t)$ are depicted in Figure 1.6.6. Thus, we can determine that it is almost certain that a projected eye-view sample with light depth t is in shadow (for example, with 99-percent certainty) by comparing P_{max} to 1% ($P_{max} <$ implies $P_{lit}(t) < 0.01$).

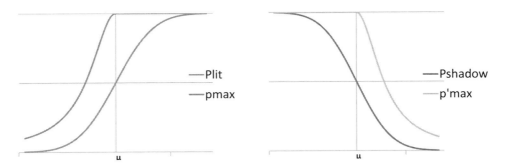

Figure 1.6.6 $P_{in\ shadow}(t)$ and $P_{lit}(t)$, in addition to their conservative upper bounds $P_{max}(t)$ and $p'_{max}(t)$.

Conversely, we can use the same distribution to construct a bound to cull eye-view pixels that have very high probability of being lit:

$$P_{in\ shadow}(t) \equiv P(x \leq t) \leq p'_{max}(t) \equiv \frac{\sigma^2}{\sigma^2 + (t - \mu)^2} \qquad \text{for } t > \mu$$

$$\leq p'_{max}(t) \equiv 1 \qquad \text{for } t \leq \mu$$

In summary, the conservative shadow edge stencil buffer can be constructed in the following steps:

1. Render the scene from the light's point of view, writing out depth x and depth squared x^2 to a variance shadow map texture (VSM).
2. Mip-map the resulting texture, effectively computing $E(x)$ and $E(x^2)$, the mean and variance of the depth distribution.
3. Render the scene from the eye point, computing for each sample:
   a. The light depth t by projection of the sample to light space.
   b. $E(x)$ and $E(x^2)$ by texture-sampling the mip-mapped VSM with the appropriate filter width, determined by the extent of the light projection of the pixel area.
   c. $\mu = E(x)$, $\sigma^2 = E(x^2) - E(x)$ and $P_{max}(t)$, $p'_{max}(t)$
4. Compare $P_{max}(t)$ and $p'_{max}(t)$ to a chosen threshold (for example, 1 percent). Set the stencil buffer bit if *either* one is smaller than the threshold.

These steps can be implemented in HLSL shader pseudocode, as shown in Listing 1.6.1.

LISTING 1.6.1   Conservative shadow edge stencil buffer construction HLSL shader

```
float2 ComputeMoments(float Depth)
{
    // Compute first few moments of depth
    float2 Moments;
    Moments.x = Depth;
    Moments.y = Depth * Depth;
    return Moments;
}

float ChebyshevUpperBound(
  float2 moments, float mean, float minVariance)
{
    // Compute variance
    float variance = max(
             minVariance,
             moments.y - (moments.x * moments.x));
    float d       = mean - moments.x;
    float pMax    = variance / (variance + (d * d));

    // One-tailed Chebyshev's Inequality
    return (mean <= moments.x ? 1.0f : pMax);
}

bool IsPotentialShadowEdge(float2 texCoord,
                           float2 texCoordDX,
                           float2 texCoordDY,
                           float  depth)
{
    float4 occluderData;
```

```
// Variance Shadow Map mip-mapped LOD tex lookup
occluderData = texShadowMap.SampleGrad(
  sampShadowMap,
  texCoord, texCoordDX, texCoordDY);

float2 posMoments = occluderData.xy;

// Minimum variance to take account for variance
// across entire pixel
float gMinVariance = 0.000001f;

float pMaxLit = ChebyshevUpperBound(
    posMoments, depth, gMinVariance);
float pMaxShadow = ChebyshevLowerBound(
    posMoments, depth, gMinVariance);

if (PMaxLit < .01 || PMaxShadow < .01) {
  return true;
}

return false;
}
```

Note that while conventional rasterization of the scene from the light's point of view in Step 1 earlier is sufficient for generating a conventional variance shadow map, it is not sufficient for generating our conservative stencil buffer. Conventional rasterization does not guarantee that a primitive's depth contributes to the minimum depth of each light-view texel that it touches. Hence, the conservativeness of the stencil buffer would not be preserved as illustrated in Figure 1.6.7, which depicts potential shadow-edge pixels in overlay but misses quite a few due to the low resolution of the variance shadow map.

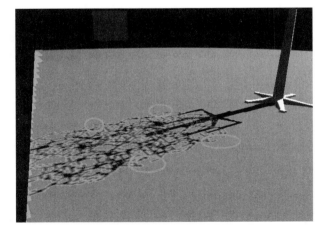

Figure 1.6.7 Conservative shadow edge stencil map with regular rasterization. Many potential shadow-edge pixels (overlay) are missed due to low resolution of the variance shadow map.

To preserve conservativeness, it is required to perform conservative rasterization in the light-view render of Step 1, just as we do during the light-view render of irregular shadow mapping illustrated in Figure 1.6.3. Figure 1.6.8 depicts correctly detected potential shadow-edge pixels in overlay, regardless of the variance shadow map resolution.

Figure 1.6.8   Conservative shadow edge stencil map with conservative rasterization. All potential shadow-edge pixels are detected (overlay), regardless of the variance shadow map resolution.

Shadow Sample Splatting

In the irregular Z-buffer construction phase, when the time comes to generate additional samples for potentially aliased pixels, as defined by the conservative shadow edge stencil buffer, we insert the eye-view samples in each light-view grid cell that is touched by the pixel samples. We call this process *shadow sample splatting,* because we conceptually *splat* the projection of the pixel footprint into the light space grid data structure. This process is as follows:

1. In addition to light view coordinates of the eye-view pixel center, also generate multiple samples per eye-view pixel. We have achieved very good results with rotated grid 4× multi-sampling, but higher sample rates and even jittered sampling strategies can be used to increase the quality of the anti-aliasing.
2. Project all samples into light space as in the original irregular shadow algorithm.
3. Insert all samples into the irregular Z-buffer as in the conventional irregular shadowing algorithm. Potentially multiple light grid cells are touched by the set of samples of a pixel.

Results and Discussion

We will now show the results of our algorithm for two different scenes. The first scene consists of a tower construction with fine geometry casting high-frequency shadows onto the rest of the scene. The second scene is the view of a fan at the end of a tunnel, viewed from the inside. The fan geometry casts high-frequency shadows on the inside walls of the tunnel. The tunnel walls are almost parallel to the eye and light directions, a setup that is particularly hard for many shadow mapping algorithms. Irregular shadow mapping shows its strength in the tunnel scene because no shadow map resolution management is required to avoid light-view aliasing. However, severe eye-view aliasing artifacts are present for the single-sample irregular shadow algorithm (see Figures 1.6.10(a) and 1.6.11(a)). Figure 1.6.9 illustrates the result of computing the conservative shadow edge stencil buffer on both scenes: Potential shadow edge pixels are rendered with an overlay. Figure 1.6.10 compares single-sample irregular shadows with 4× rotated grid multi-sampling on potential shadow edge pixels only. Note the significant improvement in the tower shadow, where many disconnected features in the shadow are now correctly connected in the improved algorithm. Figure 1.6.11 illustrates the same comparison for the tunnel scene. There is a great improvement in shadow quality toward the far end of the tunnel, where high-frequency shadows cause significant aliasing when using only a single eye-view shadow sample.

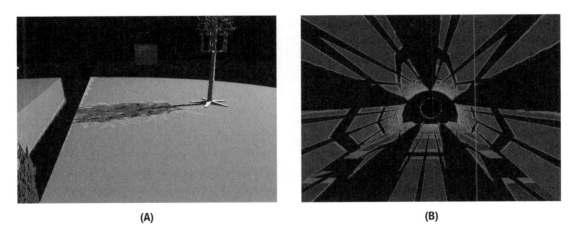

(A)   (B)

Figure 1.6.9   Result of the conservative shadow edge stencil buffer on the tower (a) and tunnel (b) scenes. Potential shadow edge pixels are rendered with an overlay.

(A)   (B)

Figure 1.6.10   Tower scene: (a) Single-sample irregular shadows and
(b) 4× rotated grid multi-sampling on potential shadow edge pixels only.
Note the significant improvement in the tower shadow, where many disconnected
features in the shadow are now correctly connected in the improved algorithm.

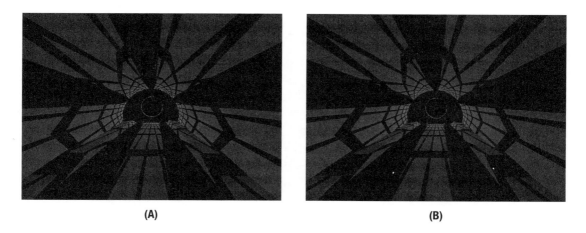

(A)   (B)

Figure 1.6.11   Tunnel scene: (a) Single-sample irregular shadows and
(b) 4× rotated grid multi-sampling on potential shadow edge pixels only.
There is a great improvement in shadow quality toward the end of the tunnel,
where high-frequency shadows caused significant anti-aliasing when using
only a single eye-view shadow sample.

Implementation Details

On Larrabee, we have implemented Steps 2 and 3 of our algorithm in an efficient post-process over all eye-view pixels in parallel. However, Step 3 is identical to the conventional irregular shadowing algorithm; therefore, it could be implemented as in [Arvo07] as well.

Conceptually, we use a grid-of-lists representation for the irregular Z-buffer. This representation is well-suited to parallel and streaming computer architectures and produces high-quality shadows in real time in game scenes [Johnson05]. The following chapter of this book [Hux10], in particular Figure 1.7.1, explains our grid-of-lists representation and its construction in more detail.

Finally, our solution was implemented in a deferred renderer, but it could also be implemented in a forward renderer with a few modifications.

Compute Requirements

Since only a marginal fraction of all screen pixels are shadow-edge pixels, this approach results in substantial gains in computational and storage costs compared to the brute-force approach. Compared to the single-sample irregular shadow maps, the additional computational cost is relatively small. For example, let's assume the number of potential shadow-edge pixels is ~10 percent of all eye-view pixels, and that we generate N additional samples per potential shadow-edge pixel. Since data structure construction and traversal times are proportional to the number of shadow map samples, this means an additional cost of $10N$ percent for anti-aliasing.

Additionally, there is an extra cost associated with creating the conservative shadow edge stencil buffer. In our implementation inside a deferred rendering, much of the required information was already computed—therefore, that extra cost is small. However, our algorithm does require an extra light-space pass, per light, to capture the depth distribution into the variance shadow map.

Storage Requirements

The storage cost is the same as the standard irregular Z-buffer, proportional to the number of samples. Again, for 10-percent extra samples, $10N$-percent extra storage is required, depending on the implementation. Storage of the stencil buffer requires only 1 bit per eye-view pixel and can easily be packed into one of the existing eye-view buffers of the irregular shadowing algorithm.

Future Work

Going forward, we would like to investigate the benefits of merging our algorithm that adaptively samples potential shadow edge pixels multiple times with conventional multi-sampling techniques that adaptively sample the geometry silhouette pixels multiple times—for best performance, preferably through the use of common data structures and shared rendering passes. Additionally, it should be fairly straightforward to extend our approach to *soft* irregular shadow mapping, where the concept of anti-aliasing is implicit, as both the soft and hard irregular shadow mapping algorithms share the same algorithmic framework [Johnson09]. For soft shadows, one may envision extending the conservative stencil to shadow penumbra detection.

Conclusion

The main advantage of irregular shadow maps with respect to conventional shadow maps is that they bear no light-view aliasing. However, irregular shadow maps are affected by eye-view aliasing of the shadow result. Recent pre-filterable shadow mapping algorithms and brute-force eye-view techniques have provided solutions for anti-aliased shadows, but none of them exploits the irregular Z-buffer acceleration structure directly. The method in this chapter is an extension of irregular shadow mapping, exploits the same irregular data structure, and is therefore the first algorithm to produce anti-aliased shadows by means of adaptive multi-sampling of irregular shadow maps, while keeping all its other positive characteristics, such as pixel-perfect ray-traced quality shadows and the complete lack of light-view aliasing.

Acknowledgements

We'd like to thank the people at the 3D Graphics and Advanced Rendering teams at the Intel Visual Computing group for their continued input while developing the methods described here. Many thanks go out in particular to Jeffery A. Williams for providing the art assets in the tower and tunnel scenes and to David Bookout for persistent support and feedback.

References

[Akenine-Möller05] Akenine-Möller, Tomas and Timo Aila. "Conservative and Tiled Rasterization Using a Modified Triangle Setup." *Journal of Graphics, GPU, and Game Tools* 10.3 (2005): 1–8.

[Arvo07] Arvo, Jukka. "Alias-Free Shadow Maps using Graphics Hardware." *Journal of Graphics, GPU, and Game Tools* 12.1 (2007): 47–59.

[Baumann05] Baumann, Dave. "ATI Xenos: Xbox 360 Graphics Demystified." 13 June 2005. Beyond 3D. n.d. http://www.beyond3d.com/content/articles/4/>.

[Brabec01] Brabec, Stefan and Hans-Peter Seidel. "Hardware-Accelerated Rendering of Antialiased Shadows with Shadow Maps." *Proceedings of the International Conference on Computer Graphics* (July 2001): 209. *ACM Portal.*

[Fernando01] Fernando, Randima, Sebastian Fernandez, Kavita Bala, and Donald P. Greenberg. "Adaptive Shadow Maps." *Proceedings of the 28th Annual Conference on Computer Graphics and interactive Techniques* (2001): 387–390. *ACM Portal.*

[Hasselgren05] Hasselgren, Jon, Tomas Akenine-Möller, and Lennart Ohlsson. "Conservative Rasterization." *GPU Gems 2.* 2005. NVIDIA. n.d. <http://http.developer.nvidia.com/ GPUGems2/gpugems2_chapter42.html>.

[Hux10] Hux, Allen. "Overlapped Execution on Programmable Graphics Hardware." *Game Programming Gems 8*. Ed. Adam Lake. Boston: Charles River Media, 2010.

[Johnson04] Johnson, Gregory S., William R. Mark, and Christopher A. Burns. "The Irregular Z-Buffer and its Application to Shadow Mapping." April 2004. The University of Texas at Austin. n.d. <http://www.cs.utexas.edu/ftp/pub/techreports/tr04-09.pdf>.

[Johnson05] Johnson, Gregory S., Juhyun Lee, Christopher A. Burns, and William R. Mark. "The Irregular Z-Buffer: Hardware Acceleration for Irregular Data Structures." *ACM Transactions on Graphics* 24.4 (October 2005): 1462–1482. *ACM Portal*.

[Johnson09] Johnson, Gregory S., Allen Hux, Christopher A. Burns, Warren A. Hunt, William R. Mark, and Stephen Junkins. "Soft Irregular Shadow Mapping: Fast, High-Quality, and Robust Soft Shadows." *Proceedings of the 2009 Symposium on Interactive 3D Graphics and Games*. (2009): 57–66. *ACM Portal*.

[Lauritzen06] Lauritzen, Andrew and William Donnelly. "Variance Shadow Maps." *Proceedings of the 2006 Symposium on Interactive 3D Graphics and Games*. (2006): 161–165. *ACM Portal*.

[Lefohn07] Lefohn, Aaron E., Shubhabrata Sengupta, and John D. Owens. "Resolution-Matched Shadow Maps." *ACM Transactions on Graphics* 26.4 (Oct. 2007): 20. *ACM Portal*.

[Lloyd08] Lloyd, D. Brandon, Naga K. Govindaraju, Cory Quammen, Steven E. Molnar, and Dinesh Manocha. "Logarithmic Perspective Shadow Maps." *ACM Transactions on Graphics* 27.4 (Oct. 2008): 1–32. *ACM Portal*.

[Robison09] Robison, Austin, and Peter Shirley. "Image Space Gathering." *Proceedings of the Conference on High Performance Graphics 2009* (2009): 91–98. *ACM Portal*.

[Salvi08] Salvi, Marco. "Rendering Filtered Shadows with Exponential Shadow Maps." *ShaderX6: Advanced Rendering Techniques*. Ed. Wolfgang Engel. Boston: Charles River Media, 2008. 257–274.

[Sen03] Sen, Pradeep, Mike Cammarano, and Pat Hanrahan. "Shadow Silhouette Maps." *ACM Transactions on Graphics* 22.3 (July 2003): 521–526. *ACM Portal*.

[Sintorn08] Sintorn, Erik, Elmar Eisemann, and Ulf Assarsson. "Sample Based Visibility for Soft Shadows using Alias-free Shadow Maps." *Computer Graphics Forum: Proceedings of the Eurographics Symposium on Rendering 2008* 27.4 (June 2008): 1285–1292.

[Stamminger02] Stamminger, Marc and George Drettakis. "Perspective Shadow Maps." *Proceedings of the 29th Annual Conference on Computer Graphics and Interactive Techniques* (2002): 557–562. *ACM Portal*.

[Williams78] Williams, Lance. "Casting Curved Shadows on Curved Surfaces." *ACM SIGGRAPH Computer Graphics* 12.3 (Aug. 1978): 270–274. *ACM Portal*.

1.7

Overlapped Execution on Programmable Graphics Hardware

Allen Hux,
Intel Advanced Visual Computing (AVC)

allen.hux@intel.com

Some graphics algorithms require data structure construction and traversal steps that do not map well to constrained graphics pipelines. Additionally, because of the dependencies between rendering and non-rendering passes, much (or all) of the compute power of the device may go idle between steps of a given algorithm. In this gem, we examine techniques for executing non-rendering algorithms concurrently with traditional rendering on programmable graphics hardware, such as Larrabee. Such programmable graphics devices enable fine-grained signaling and event graphs, allowing algorithmic stages to "overlap." As a working model, we present an implementation of Irregular Z-Buffer (IZB) shadows—an algorithm requiring both standard rendering passes (for example, depth-only pre-pass) and parallelized data structure construction. Identification of rendering and non-rendering work that is not dependent reveals opportunities to remove the stalls that currently occur when switching between the two types of workloads. The APIs discussed in this article are examples and not necessarily representative of APIs provided with a particular product.

Introduction to Irregular Z-Buffer Shadows

The simplest shadow mapping algorithm requires two passes. First, render the scene from the light view to get a light-view depth buffer (at one resolution). Second, render the scene from the eye view (at the same or different resolution). For each point, test the visibility of that point by projecting it into the light view and comparing its depth to the one found in the first pass. If the eye-view depth is greater, then something must be between the light and the point being tested, and therefore it must be in shadow. This algorithm fits entirely within conventional rendering pipelines [Williams78].

The problem with this approach is aliasing: The resolution of the light-view plane will never precisely match the sampling frequency when projecting from the eye view, resulting in visual artifacts. As described in the previous gem, an irregular Z-buffer stores precise eye-view positions in the light-view grid, enabling accurate shadow determination from the eye view [Johnson04, Johnson09, Galoppo10]. Shadow mapping with an irregular Z-buffer is a multi-step process involving three rendering passes interleaved with two non-rendering steps.

1. Render the scene from the eye view, depth only.
2. Transform the eye-view points to light view.

    a. For each point, atomic increment the corresponding pixel in the light-view plane. (A bigger plane improves parallelism at the cost of memory.)

    b. Parallel prefix sum the indices, resulting in a mapping from each eye-view receiver to a light-view pixel.

    c. Scatter the light-view values into a light-view-friendly 1D structure. Indices into the 1D structure are stored in the light-view plane.

3. Render the scene from the light view. Instead of executing a traditional pixel shader, test the triangle bounds against the points in the data structure (referring to the indices from Step 2c). Points that are inside and behind the triangle are in shadow. Set a bit in the data structure marking this point as in shadow (occluded).
4. Create a standard shadow map by traversing the data structure and scattering out the occlusion value to a traditional 2D image. We call this the "deswizzle" step.
5. Render the scene from the eye view again, using the shadow map.

For our purposes, this serves as an example of an algorithm that has some rasterization steps intermingled with some algorithmic work one might normally implement in C++. The second step in particular can result in quite a bit of idle hardware, because it requires a dependency chain of parallel and serial workloads.

Assuming we have a graphics system capable of performing the compute steps of IZB (shown in Figure 1.7.1) and executing a pixel shader capable of traversing the IZB data structure, we get the simple dependency graph of tasks shown in Figure 1.7.2. Each stage in the graph cannot start until the last thread completes the last task of the prior stage.

Because there is almost always a "long pole" that determines the duration of a stage in the algorithm, nearly every thread in the system experiences some amount of idle time. This is suggested by the activity bars in Figure 1.7.2. (Imagine these correspond to the execution time on a system with four threads.) In the remainder of the gem, we will describe how we can reclaim some of those lost cycles on a programmable architecture, such as Larrabee.

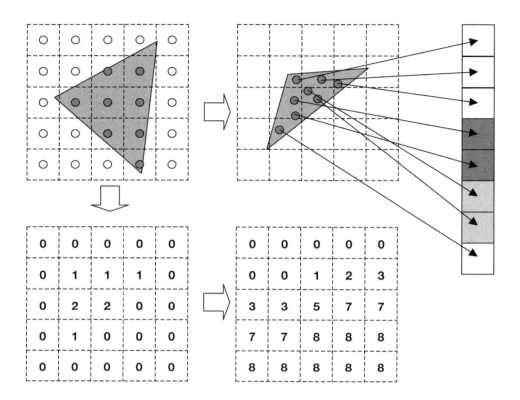

Figure 1.7.1   Building the IZB data structure, effectively a grid of lists.
Regular points from the eye view (top left) are transformed into the light view
(top middle). A count of the number of pixels is kept in the light grid (bottom left).
A prefix sum of the counters in the light grid results in offsets (bottom right)
into the 1D data structure (top right). Point data is scattered to the 1D data
structure, including position and occlusion state (initially 0). The number
of points in a light-view pixel can be determined by subtracting the
current pixel value from the value to the right. The offset table combined
with the 1D data structure forms the grid-of-lists IZB data structure.

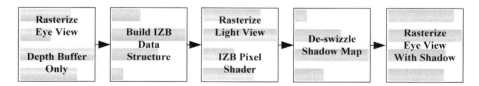

Figure 1.7.2   IZB dependency graph. (Tasks are completed
in the order they are submitted.)

Overview of Programmable Graphics Hardware

As graphics devices become more general, they can be viewed as many-core compute devices with threads that can communicate amongst themselves (for example, via global variables and atomic instructions). Consider a representative programmable graphics architecture, Larrabee. Larrabee consists of many in-order cores on a single chip, each executing four threads in round-robin fashion, with an extended instruction set supporting 16-element vectors [Seiler08]. The cores are connected by a very high-bandwidth ring that maintains cache coherency. Several hardware texture samplers are distributed around the ring, as well as connections to GDDR. Traditional graphics APIs (DirectX, OpenGL) could be implemented on Larrabee as a typical process running within a relatively conventional operating system [Abrash09a].

A Larrabee architecture device could be an add-in adapter discrete from the traditional host CPU, it could be on-chip or on-die with the host CPU, or it could be the only processor in the system. For the purposes of this gem, we ignore the transport mechanism that enables our programs to run on the device, but it is important to realize that the techniques and code that follow are designed to execute directly on an architecture such as Larrabee.

Implementing an efficient rasterizer within a many-threaded, 16-wide SIMD platform is beyond the scope of this chapter, but we can summarize it here. Maximizing parallelism is the main design goal. (Keeping the cores busy will be a recurring theme.) The approach described by Abrash [Abrash09b] is to use a binning architecture where the bin dimensions are chosen such that the data accessed by each core (the depth buffer format and the pixel format) does not exceed the cache size of the core (256 KB L2, 32 KB L1 in the current Larrabee architecture). Done properly, operations such as depth tests would require no off-core bandwidth (neither ring nor GDDR accesses)—unless, of course, something wants to access that depth buffer later, which merely requires a one-time write at the end. Remember that textures are accessed via hardware texture samplers, which have their own caches. Despite the attention to bandwidth, the primary motivation for binning is to produce a lot of independent work that can be executed in parallel.

A programmable graphics device, such as a software rasterizer, would build a dependency graph of rendering tasks to complete (which we will call a *render graph*). We can expect rendering tasks to be roughly divided between front end (for example, vertex processing/binning) and back end (rasterization/pixel shading). A dependency graph enables independent tasks to run concurrently; for example, if a core completes pixel shading within a bin, it can work on a different bin or begin vertex shading for the next frame. Dependencies can be defined in terms of resources—for example, a render task may signal that it has completed writing to a render target resource (write dependency) or wait to start until a shadow map resource (texture) is ready for use (read dependency). The task affected (front end or back end) is a function of whether the resource is bound to the vertex shader or pixel shader.

Commands can be inserted within the graph to be executed when a resource is ready—for example, `CopySubResource` of a render target. We can also create nodes in the graph that are signaled by outside events, such as direct memory access (DMA) transfer completions. We will discuss dependency graphs in more detail in the subsequent sections.

Overview of Task-Based Parallelism

Non-rendering algorithms hoping to effectively use many-core architectures require an efficient tasking system, such as Cilk [Blumofe95]. Such a task system leverages a thread pool (where the number of software threads is less than or equal to the number of hardware threads) to avoid operating system overhead from switching between threads. A good tasking system also provides the following features:

- The ability to create individual tasks or sets of tasks (*task sets*). A task set calls the same task function a user-defined number of times (in parallel).
- Tasks and task sets may depend upon each other. Specifically, a task or task set will not start until the tasks or task sets it depends on have completed.
- Tasks and task sets may also depend upon user-defined events. Events can be signaled by simply calling a NotifyEvent API.
- An efficient work-stealing scheduler to automatically spawn and load-balance among independent tasks.

Following is an example of what such a task API might look like. Tasks call a user function with user data. Task sets call a user function with user data and a number indicating which instance this is (0..numTasks-1).

```
// create an individual work item
typedef void (* const TaskFunction)
    (void* in_pTaskFunctionArg);
SyncObject CreateTask(
    TaskFunction in_pTaskFunc, void* in_pData,
    SyncObject* in_pDependencies,
    int in_numDependencies);

// create work items that do a subset of work
typedef void (* const TaskSetFunction)
    (void* in_pTaskSetFunctionArg,
    int in_taskIndex, int in_taskSetSize);
SyncObject CreateTaskSet(
    int in_numTasksInSet,
    TaskSetFunction in_pTaskFunc, void* in_pData,
    SyncObject* in_pDependencies,
    int in_numDependencies);

SyncObject CreateEvent(bool initialState);
```

Since the task system itself is software, common-sense performance heuristics apply: The amount of work done in the task should be sufficient to compensate for the overhead of the tasking system, which includes the function call into the task as well as some amount of communication to synchronize with internal task queues. For example, to perform an operation across a 1024×1024 image, don't create one million tasks. Instead, create a multiple of the number of hardware threads in the system. For a system with 100 hardware threads, 400 or 500 equally sized tasks would give the task system some opportunity to greedily load balance, while each task of approximately 2,000 pixels would give good opportunities for prefetching and loop unrolling. (A Larrabee optimized routine would operate on 16 pixels at a time, hence a loop of only about 100 iterations.) Our experiments on desktop x86 machines show that tasks of a few thousand clocks each achieve 90 percent or better overall efficiency.

Efficient graphics processing requires thread affinity knowledge. That is, the rasterizer assigns threads to cores with the expectation that those threads will share render target data in their cache. Non-rendering tasks typically function more opportunistically, executing whenever a thread becomes idle. Hence, we design our tasks to be independent of the threads they may execute on. Since the hardware is programmable, finer control is possible but adds complexity.

Even with equal-sized tasks, in a machine with that many threads, contention for resources (caches and GDDR bandwidth) will cause tasks to have variable durations. For very irregular workloads, such as irregular Z-buffer, optimal performance may require thousands of tasks—it all depends on the algorithm.

Combining Render Graphs and Task Graphs

The ability to create non-rendering task sets that depend on, or are dependencies of, rendering tasks is the key to achieving maximum hardware utilization for these mixed-usage algorithms. To do this, we need a way to interact with the rendering dependency graph from user code. Following is a method to inject a non-rendering task into the render graph, referring to the current render context (analogous to a DirectX or OpenGL context), a function to call when the dependencies are met, user data to pass to the function, and a list of all the resource dependencies.

```
void CreateRenderTask(in_pRenderContext,
    in_pUserFunc, in_pUserData,
    in_pReadDependencies, in_numReadDependencies,
    in_pWriteDependencies, in_numWriteDependencies,
    out_pRenderTask);
```

We then need a way to notify the render system that the render task and its read and write dependencies, as declared above, are complete and available.

```
void NotifyRenderTaskComplete(in_pRenderTask);
```

Now we have a way for tasks created using our task system to define dependencies with rendering tasks and for rendering tasks to very finely interact with our task system. For example, if a render pass has pixel shaders bound to a resource declared as a write dependency of a user task, the front end of the render pass can start (transform/ bin), but the back end cannot (rasterize/pixel shade).

We need a little helper glue to efficiently communicate between "render" work and the tasks created for our "client" work. Following, we show how an event that waits on a task set can call `NotifyRenderTaskComplete()` to enable dependent render work. We also show how render work can cause a callback declared in `CreateRenderTask()` to signal an event, thereby starting dependent client work.

On the left side of Figure 1.7.3, we show how a render pass can be made to wait on client work. First, create a task set that does some client work, such as builds a data structure. Next, create a render task with the data structure (resource) written to by the task set as a write dependency, no read dependencies, and no callback. Then, create a render pass with the data structure resource as a read dependency. Finally, create a task that depends on the task set that will call `NotifyRenderTaskComplete()`. The render pass cannot start until the task set is complete.

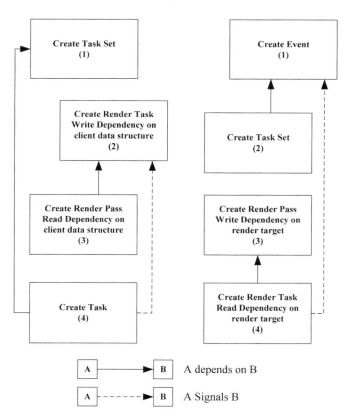

Figure 1.7.3   Detail of connecting client task sets to render passes via render tasks.

On the right side of Figure 1.7.3, we show how client work can be made dependent on a render pass. First, create an event that we will signal and a task set that depends on the event. (It would do work on the render target.) Next, create the render pass, which in this case writes to a render target (write dependency). Finally, create a render task with the render target as a read dependency and a callback that will set the event. The task set cannot start until the render pass is complete.

Combined Dependency Graph

To reduce the idle time, we need to build a complete dependency graph including both rendering and non-rendering tasks. Below, we work with the following constraints:

- Tasks or task sets must have their dependencies described at creation time.
- Tasks or tasks sets can depend on tasks, task sets, or events.

These constraints force us to work from the end of the algorithm backwards. Since a task will start immediately if it has no dependencies, we create events in a not-signaled state to act as gates for the task sets.

1. Create a build data structure event (not signaled).
2. Create a build data structure task set that depends on event (1).
3. Create a deswizzle event (not signaled).
4. Create a deswizzle task set that depends on event (3).
5. Create a light-view render pass where:
   a. Rasterization depends on resource from task set (2).
   b. Render target resource complete signals event (3).

6. Create a final eye-view render pass where rasterization depends on the shadow map resource from task set (4).
7. Create a depth-only eye-view render pass that signals event (1) when its render target resource is complete.

As soon as we complete the seventh step, creating the depth-only eye-view render with no dependencies, the whole algorithm will fall into place. As shown in Figure 1.7.4, when the depth-only pass (7) completes, it signals the build event (1), which enables the build task set (2) to start. Completion of the build task set (2) enables the light-view rasterization (5) to start. (Transform and binning should already be complete.) When the light-view render (5) completes, it signals the deswizzle event (3), which enables the deswizzle task set (4) to start. When the deswizzle task set (4) completes, it enables the final eye-view rasterization (6) to start. (Transform and binning should already be complete.)

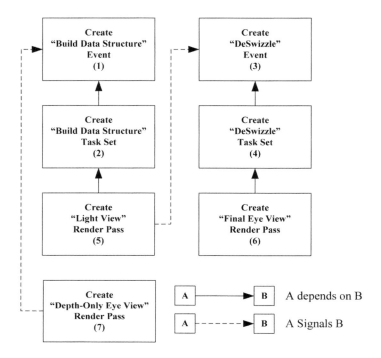

Figure 1.7.4   Order of creation of events, task sets, and
render graph nodes for overlapped execution of IZB.

Idle-Free Irregular Z-Buffer Shadows

Figure 1.7.5 shows the naïve linear dependency graph of the IZB algorithm discussed earlier, showing the render stages expanded into front end (transform + binning) and back end (rasterization + pixel shading) for a total of eight stages, or task sets.

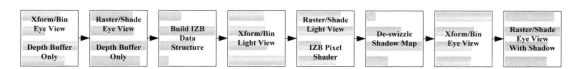

Figure 1.7.5   IZB dependency graph with render stages expanded into front and back end.

Figure 1.7.6 shows how threads that would otherwise have become idle can instead work on non-dependent front-end rendering tasks if we start all three render passes immediately. This overlapped execution is especially helpful for improving the performance of our irregular shadow-mapping tasks, allowing us (in this example) to fully hide the cost of the front-end rendering tasks. Another way to interpret this is that the compute part of irregular shadow mapping is essentially free when overlapped with rendering.

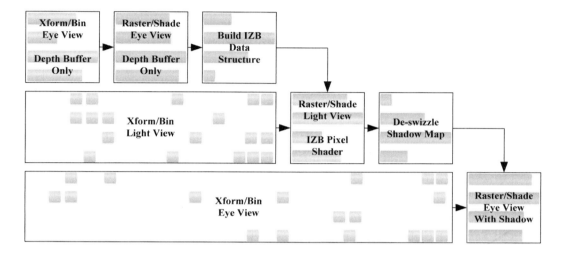

Figure 1.7.6   IZB with dependency graph integrated with flexible rendering pipeline. Xform/bin tasks can complete as threads become available from non-rendering tasks, filling in gaps in execution.

This demonstrates another advantage of programmable hardware: Maximum performance is achieved by enabling flexible hardware to execute whatever tasks are available, rather than by partitioning the hardware into dedicated islands of computation. Compare this to the early days of graphics devices with dedicated pixel shader and vertex shader hardware: When there was more vertex work than pixel work, the idle pixel shading hardware could not be reconfigured to help out. In modern architectures, graphics processors dynamically load balance across all execution units. On a programmable architecture such as Larrabee, this load balancing can be controlled by the programmer, enabling the overlap of rendering and non-rendering tasks.

Conclusion

Maximizing performance on modern, many-core platforms requires identifying independent work to be executed in parallel. Non-graphics workloads leverage a system of dependent tasks and task sets to manage parallel computation. On programmable graphics devices such as Larrabee, a similar system of task dependencies can be used to identify independent and dependent graphics work—for example, binning versus pixel shading. By connecting these graphs, we can further exploit available execution units by exposing more opportunities for independent tasks to run concurrently.

References

[Abrash09a] Abrash, Michael. "A First Look at the Larrabee New Instructions (LRBni)." Dr. Dobb's. 1 April 2009. <http://www.ddj.com/hpc-high-performance-computing/216402188>.

[Abrash09b] Abrash, Michael. "Rasterization on Larrabee: A First Look at the Larrabee New Instructions (LRBni) in Action." Intel. March 2009. <http://software.intel.com/file/15542>.

[Blumofe95] Blumofe, Robert D., Christopher F. Joerg, Bradley C. Kuszmaul, Charles E. Leiserson, Keith H. Randall, and Yuli Zhou. "Cilk: An Efficient Multithreaded Runtime System." *Proceedings of the Fifth ACM SIGPLAN Symposium on Principles and Practice of Parallel Programming* (July 1995): 207–216.

[Galoppo10] Galoppo, Nico. "Eye-view Pixel Anti-Aliasing for Irregular Shadow Mapping." *Game Programming Gems 8*. Ed. Adam Lake. Boston: Charles River Media, 2010.

[Johnson04] Johnson, Gregory S., William R. Mark, and Christopher A. Burns. "The Irregular Z-Buffer and its Application to Shadow Mapping." April 2004. The University of Texas at Austin. n.d. <http://www.cs.utexas.edu/ftp/pub/techreports/tr04-09.pdf>.

[Johnson09] Johnson, Gregory S., Allen Hux, Christopher A. Burns, Warren A. Hunt, William R. Mark, and Stephen Junkins. "Soft Irregular Shadow Mapping: Fast, High-Quality, and Robust Soft Shadows." *Proceedings of the 2009 Symposium on Interactive 3D Graphics and Games*. (2009): 57–66. *ACM Portal*.

[Seiler08] Seiler, Larry, et al. "Larrabee: A Many Core x86 Architecture for Visual Computing." *ACM Transactions on Graphics* 27.3 (Aug. 2008): n.p. *ACM Portal*.

[Williams78] Williams, Lance. "Casting Curved Shadows on Curved Surfaces." *ACM SIGGRAPH Computer Graphics* 12.3 (Aug. 1978): 270–274. *ACM Portal*.

1.8

Techniques for Effective Vertex and Fragment Shading on the SPUs

Steven Tovey, Bizarre Creations Ltd.
steven.tovey@bizarrecreations.com

When the Cell Broadband Engine was designed, Sony and the other corporations in the STI coalition always had one eye on the Cell's ability to support a GPU in its processing activities [Shippy09]. The Cell has been with us for three years now, and like any new piece of hardware, it has taken time for developers to understand the best ways of pushing the hardware to its limits. The likes of Mike Acton and the Insomniac Games Technology Team have been instrumental in pushing general development and coding strategies for the Cell forward, but there has been little discussion about ways that the SPUs can support a GPU in its processing activities *specifically*. This chapter aims to introduce fundamental techniques that can be employed when developing code for the CBE that will allow it to aid the GPU in performing rendering tasks.

The CBE as Part of a Real-World System

Understanding Cell's place in a real-world system is useful to our discussion, and, as such, we will use Sony's PlayStation 3 as our case study. PlayStation 3 contains the Cell Broadband Engine, which was developed jointly by Sony Computer Entertainment, Toshiba Inc., and IBM Corp. [Shippy09, Möller08, IBM08]. The Cell forms part of the overall architecture of the console along with the Reality Synthesizer, RSX, and two types of memory. Figure 1.8.1 shows a high-level view of the architecture.

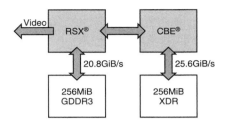

Figure 1.8.1   The PlayStation 3 architecture
(illustration modeled after [Möller08, Perthuis06]).

The Cell contains two distinctly different types of processor: the PowerPC Processing Element (PPE) and the Synergistic Processing Element (SPE). The PPE is essentially the brains of the chip [Shippy09] and is capable of running an operating system in addition to coordinating the processing activities of its counterpart processing elements, the SPEs. Inside PlayStation 3, there are eight SPEs. However, to increase chip yield, one is locked out, and Sony reserves another for their operating system, leaving a total of six SPEs available for application programmers. All processing elements in the Cell are connected by a token-ring bus, as shown in Figure 1.8.2.

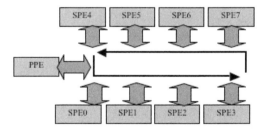

Figure 1.8.2   The Cell Broadband Engine (modeled after [IBM08]).

Because the SPEs are the main focus of this chapter, they are discussed in much greater detail in the forthcoming sections.

The SPEs

Each Synergistic Processing Element is composed of two major components: the Synergistic Processing Unit (SPU) and the Memory Flow Controller (MFC).

The SPU

Detailed knowledge of the SPU instruction set and internal execution model are critical to achieving peak performance on the PlayStation 3. In the following sections, we will highlight some important facets of this unique processor.

The Synergistic Execution Unit and SPU ISA

The Synergistic Execution Unit (SXU), part of the SPU, is responsible for the execution of instructions. Inside the SXU are two pipelines: the odd pipeline and the even pipeline. Instructions are issued to exactly one of these pipelines, depending on the group the issued instruction falls into (see Table 1.8.1). The SXU supports the dual issue of instructions (one from each pipeline) if and only if a very strict set of requirements is met. We will discuss these requirements in detail later.

TABLE 1.8.1 A List of Instruction Groups Together with Their Associated Execution Pipes and Latencies

Instruction Group	Pipeline	Latency (Cycles)	Issue (Cycles)
Single precision floating-point operations	EVEN	6	1
Double precision floating-point operations	EVEN	7	6
Integer multiplies, integer/float conversions, and interpolation	EVEN	7	1
Immediate loads, logical operations, integer addition/subtraction, carry/borrow generate	EVEN	2	1
Element-wise rotates and shifts, special byte operations	EVEN	4	1
Loads and stores, branch hints, channel operations	ODD	6	1
Shuffle bytes, qword rotates and shifts, estimates, gather, selection mask formation and branches	ODD	4	1

The SPU has a particularly large register file to facilitate the execution of pipelined, unrolled code without the need for excessive register spilling. Unlike its counterpart, the PPE, the register file of the SPU is unified. That is, floating-point, integer, and vector operations act on the same registers without having to move through memory. As the SPU is a vector processing unit at its heart, its Instruction Set Architecture (ISA) is designed specifically for vector processing [IBM08a]. All 128 of the SPU's registers are 16 bytes in size, allowing for up to four 32-bit floating-point values or eight 16-bit integers to be processed with each instruction.

While a full analysis of the SPU's ISA is beyond the scope of this gem, there are a number of instructions worth discussing in greater detail that are particularly important for efficient programming of the SPU. The first of these instructions is `selb`, or "select bits." The `selb` instruction performs branchless selection on a bitwise basis and takes the form `selb rt, ra, rb, rm`. For each bit of a quadword, this instruction uses the mask register (`rm`) to determine which bits of the source registers (`ra` and `rb`) should be placed in the corresponding bits of the target register (`rt`). Comparison instructions all return a quadword selection mask that can be used with `selb`[1].

[1] The `fsmbi` instruction is also very useful for efficiently constructing a selection mask for use with `selb`.

The shuffle bytes instruction, shufb, is the key instruction in data manipulation on the SPU. The shufb instruction takes four operands, all of which are registers. The first operand, rt, is the target register. The next two operands, ra and rb, are the two quadwords that will be manipulated by the quadword pattern from the fourth operand, rp. The manipulations controlled by this fourth operand, known as the *shuffle pattern*, are particularly interesting.

A shuffle pattern is a quadword value that works on a byte level. Each of the 16 bytes in the quadword controls the contents of the corresponding byte in the target register. For example, the 0th byte of the pattern quadword controls the value that will ultimately be placed into the 0th byte of the target register, the 1th byte controls the value of the 1th byte placed into the target register, and so on, for all 16 bytes of the quad word. Listing 1.8.1 provides an example shuffle pattern.

LISTING 1.8.1   An example shuffle pattern

```
const vector unsigned char _example1 =
{ 0x00, 0x11, 0x02, 0x13,
  0x04, 0x15, 0x06, 0x17,
  0x08, 0x19, 0x0a, 0x1b,
  0x0c, 0x1d, 0x0e, 0x1f };
```

The above pattern performs a perfect shuffle, but on a byte level. (The term "perfect shuffle" typically refers to the interleaving of bits from two words.) The lower 4 bits of each byte can essentially be thought of as an index into the bytes of the first or second operand quadword. Similarly, the upper 4 bits can be thought of as an index into the registers referred to in the instruction's operands. Since there are only two, we need only concern ourselves with the LSB of this 4-bit group—in other words, $0x0x$ (where x denotes some other value of the lower 4 bits of the byte) would index into the contents of the ra register, and $0x1x$ would access the second. It is worth noting that there are special case values that can be used to load constants with shufb; an interested reader can refer to [IBM08a] for details. A further example in Listing 1.8.2 will aid us in our understanding.

LISTING 1.8.2   An example of using shufb

```
const vector unsigned char _example2 =
{ 0x00, 0x01, 0x02, 0x03,
  0x14, 0x15, 0x16, 0x17,
  0x08, 0x09, 0x0a, 0x0b,
  0x1c, 0x1d, 0x1e, 0x1f };

qword pattern = (const qword)_example2;
qword ra = si_ilhu(0x3f80); // ra contains: 1.0f, 1.0f, 1.0f, 1.0f
qword rb = si_ilhu(0x4000); // rb contains: 2.0f, 2.0f, 2.0f, 2.0f

// result contains: 1.0f, 2.0f, 1.0f, 2.0f
qword result = si_shufb(ra, rb, pattern);
```

In many programs, simply inlining of shuffle patterns for data manipulation requirements will suffice, but since the terminal operand to shufb is simply a register, there is nothing to stop you from computing the patterns dynamically in your program or from forming them with the constant formation instructions (as should be preferred when lower latency can be achieved than the 6-cycle load from the local store). As it turns out, dynamic shuffle pattern computation is actually critical to performing unaligned loads from the local store in a vaguely efficient manner, as we shall see later. In-depth details of the SPU ISA can be found in [IBM08a].

Local Store and Memory Flow Controller

As previously mentioned, each of the SPUs in the Cell is individually endowed with its own memory, known as its *local store*. The local store is (at least on current implementations of the CBE) 256 KB in size and can essentially be thought of as an L1 cache for the Synergistic Execution Unit. Data can be copied into and out of the local store by way of the DMA engine in the MFC, which resides on each SPE and acts asynchronously of the SXU. Loads and stores to and from the local store are always 16-byte aligned and sized. Hence, processing data smaller than 16 bytes requires use of a less-than-efficient load-modify-store pattern. Accesses to the local store are arbitrated by the SPU Store and Load unit (SLS) based on a priority; the DMA engine always has priority over the SXU for local store accesses.

Each DMA is part of a programmer-specified tag group. This provides a mechanism for a programmer to poll the state of the MFC to find out if a specific DMA has completed. A tag group is able to contain multiple DMAs. The tag group is denoted by a 5-bit value internally, and, as such, the MFC supports 32 distinct tag groups [Bader07]. The DMA queue (DMAQ) is 16 entries deep in current implementations of the CBE.

Data Management

In many ways, the choice of data structure is more important than the efficiency of the operations that must be performed on it. In the following sections, we will describe a variety of data management strategies and their tradeoffs in the context of the SPU.

Multi-Buffering

All graphics programmers will be familiar with the concept of a double buffer. The multi-buffer is simply a term that generalizes the concept to an arbitrary number of buffers. In many cases two buffers will be sufficient, but sometimes a third buffer will be required to effectively hide the latency of transfers to and from the effective address space. Figure 1.8.3 shows the concept of multi-buffering.

Bader suggests that each buffer should use a separate tag group in order to prevent unnecessary stalling of the SPU waiting for data that will be processed sometime in the future. Barriers and fences should be used to order DMAs within a tag group and the DMA queue, respectively [Bader07]. Multi-buffering can yield significant performance increases, but it does have a downside. Because the buffers are resident in the local store, it does mean that SPE programs must be careful not to exceed the 256-KB limit.

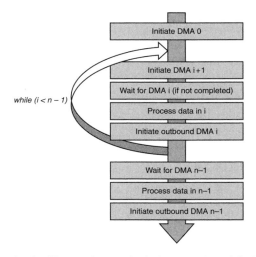

Figure 1.8.3   Multi-buffering data to hide latency (modeled after [Bader07]).

Using a reasonable size for each of the buffers in your multi-buffer (about 16 KB) in order to allow the SPU to process several vertices or pixels before requiring more data from the main address space is a fine strategy. However, the pointer wrangling can become a little complicated if one's goal is to support a list of arbitrarily sized (and hence aligned) vertex formats. Conversely, alignments do tend to be a little more favorable and can be easily controlled by carefully selecting a reasonably sized unit of work when processing pixels.

Structure-of-Arrays versus Array-of-Structures

The design of data is paramount when hoping to write performant software for the SPU. Since the SPU is a SIMD vector processor, concepts familiar to those who have programmed with other vector ISAs, such as SSE on Intel chips, Altivec on PowerPC chips, or even the VU on the PlayStation 2, are immediately transferable to the SPU. One such concept is parallel array data layout, better known as Structure-of-Arrays (SOA). By laying data out in a format that is the transpose of its natural layout (Array-of-Structures), as can be seen in Figure 1.8.4, a programmer is often able to produce much more efficient code (most notably in those cases where vectorized data is interacting with scalar data).

The benefits of using an SOA layout are substantial in a lot of common cases. Listing 1.8.3 illustrates this by way of computing the squared length of a vector.

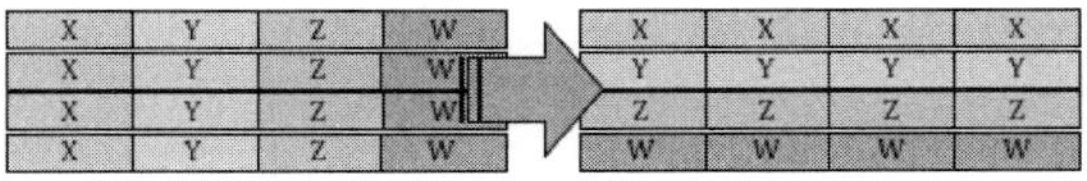

Figure 1.8.4 An Array-of-Structures layout on the left is transposed into a Structure-of-Arrays layout (illustration modeled after [Tovey10]).

LISTING 1.8.3 Two versions of a function to calculate the squared length of a vector. The first assumes Array-of-Structures data layout, and the second Structure-of-Arrays layout.

```
// Version 1: AOS mode — 1 vector, ~18 cycles.
    qword dot_xx                = si_fm(v, v);
    qword dot_xx_r4             = si_rotqbyi(dot_xx, 4);
          dot_xx               = si_fa(dot_xx, dot_xx_r4);
    qword dot_xx_r8            = si_rotqbyi(dot_xx, 8);
          dot_xx               = si_fa(dot_xx, dot_xx_r8);
    return si_to_float(dot_xx);

    // Version 2: SOA mode — 4 vectors, ~8 cycles.
    qword dot_x                = si_fm(x, x);
    qword dot_y                = si_fma(y, y, dot_x);
    qword dot_z                = si_fma(z, z, dot_y);
    return dot_z;
```

Branch-Free DMAs

The cost of badly predicted branches on the SPU is quite significant. Given that the SPU does not contain any dedicated branch prediction hardware[2], the burden of responsibility falls squarely on the shoulders of the programmer (or in the majority of cases, the compiler). There are built-in language extensions available in most SPU compilers that allow the programmer to supply branch hints, but such things assume that you have sufficient time in order to make the prediction (that is, more than 11 cycles) and that the branch is intrinsically predictable, which may not be the case. It is therefore recommended that programmers avoid branches entirely [Acton08]. Others have discussed this topic at length [Acton08, Kapoulkine09], so I will refrain from doing so here; however, I do wish to touch upon one common case where branch avoidance is not entirely obvious but is entirely trivial.

IBM's SDK provides several MFC functions to initiate DMA without resorting to the manual writing of registers[3]. An unfortunate side effect of such functions is that they seem to actively encourage code such as that presented in Listing 1.8.4.

---

[2] The SXU adopts the default prediction strategy that all branches are *not* taken.

[3] SPU-initiated DMAs are performed by the writing of special-purpose registers in the MFC using the wrch instruction. There are six such registers that must be written in order to initiate a DMA. These may be written arbitrarily as long as the command register is written terminally [IBM08].

LISTING 1.8.4   All-too-often encountered code to avoid issuing unwanted DMAs

```
if(si_to_uint(counter) > 0))
    mfc_put(si_to_uint(lsa),
                si_to_uint(ea),
                si_to_uint(size),
                si_to_uint(tag));
```

However, a little knowledge of the MFC can help avoid the branch in this case. The MFC contains the DMA queue (DMAQ). This queue contains SPU-initiated commands to the MFC's DMA engine. Similar to a CPU or GPU, the MFC supports the concept of a NOP. A NOP is an operation that can be inserted into the DMAQ but doesn't result in any data being transferred. A NOP for the MFC is denoted by any DMA command being written that has zero size. The resulting code looks something like Listing 1.8.5.

LISTING 1.8.5   Branch-free issue of DMA

```
qword cmp_mask     = si_cgti(counter, 0x0);
qword cmp          = si_andi(cmp_mask, 0x1); // bottom bit only.
qword dma_size     = si_mpy(size, cmp);      // size < 2^16
                   mfc_put(si_to_uint(lsa),
                               si_to_uint(ea),
                               si_to_uint(dma_size),
                               si_to_uint(tag));
```

Unfortunately, the hardware is not smart enough to discard zero-sized DMA commands immediately upon the command register being written, and these commands are inserted into the 16-entry DMAQ for processing. The entry into the queue is immediately discarded when the DMA engine attempts to process this element of the queue. However, this causes a subtle downside to the employment of this technique for branch avoidance. SPE programs that issue a lot of DMAs can quickly back up the DMAQ, and issuing a zero-sized DMA can stall the SPU while it flushes the entire DMAQ. Luckily, this state of affairs can be almost entirely mitigated by a well-designed SPE program, which issues fewer, but larger DMAs.

Vertex/Geometry Shading

The SPUs can also lend a hand in various vertex processing tasks and, because of their general nature, can help overcome some of the shortcomings of the GPU programming model. In *Blur*, we were able to use the SPU to deal with awkward vertex sizes and to optimize the vehicle damage system.

Handling Strange Alignments When Multi-Buffering

Vertex data comes in all shapes and sizes, and, as a result, multi-buffering this type of data presents some challenges. When vertex buffers are created, contiguous vertices are packed tightly together in the buffer to both save memory and improve the performance of the pre-transform cache on the GPU. This presents an SPU programmer with a challenge when attempting to process buffers whose per-vertex alignment may not be a multiple of 16 bytes. This is a problem for two reasons. First, the DMA engine in the MFC transfers 1, 2, 4, 8, or multiples of 16 bytes, meaning that we must be careful not to overwrite parts of the buffer that we do not mean to modify. Second, loads and stores performed by the SXU itself are always 16-byte aligned [IBM08].

There are a lot of cases where a single vertex will straddle the boundary of two multi-buffers, due to vertex structures that have alignments that are sub-optimal from an SPU processing point of view. The best way of coding around this problem is to simply copy the end of a multi-buffer to its nearest 16-byte boundary into the start of the second multi-buffer and offset the pointer to the element you are currently processing. This means that when the second multi-buffer is transferred back to the main address space, it will not corrupt the vertices you had previously processed and transferred out of the first multi-buffer, as shown in Figure 1.8.5. Listing 1.8.6 contains code demonstrating how to handle unaligned loads from the local store.

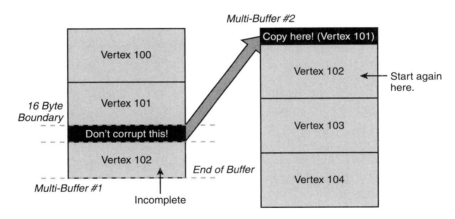

Figure 1.8.5 Avoid buffer corruption by copying a small chunk from the end of one multi-buffer into the start of another.

Case Study: Car Damage in Blur

The car damage system in *Blur* works by manipulating a lattice of nodes that roughly represent the volume of the car. The GPU implementation makes use of a volume texture containing vectors representing the offset of these nodes' positions from their original positions. This is then sampled based on the position of a vertex being processed relative to a volume that loosely represents the car in order to calculate position and normal offsets (see Figure 1.8.6). The texture is updated each time impacts are applied to the lattice, or when the car is repaired.

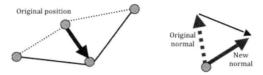

Figure 1.8.6   Position and normal offsets are applied to each
vertex based on deltas stored in a volume texture.

The GPU performs the deformation every frame because the damage is stateless
and a function of the volume texture and the undamaged vertex data. Given the
amount of work involved and the additional performance hit from sampling textures
in the vertex unit, the performance of rendering cars in *Blur* was heavily vertex limited. This was something we wanted to tackle, and the SPUs were useful in doing so.
Porting the entire vertex shader to the SPU was not practical given the timeframe and
memory budgets, so instead we focused on moving just the damage calculations to the
SPUs. This meant that the car damage vertex processing would only occur when damage needed to be inflicted on the car (instead of every frame with the equivalent GPU
implementation), and it would greatly reduce the complexity of the vertex shader running on the GPU.

The damage offsets are a function of the vertex's position and the state of the
node lattice. Given the need for original position, we must transfer the vertex data for
the cars to the local store via DMA and read the position data corresponding to each
vertex. This is done using a multi-buffering strategy. Because different components of
the car utilize different materials (and hence have different vertex formats), we were
also forced to a variety of vertex alignments as described earlier. With the vertex data
of the car in the SPU local store, we are able to calculate a position and normal offset
for each vertex and write these out to a separate vertex buffer. Each of these values is
stored as a `float4`, which means the additional vertex stream has a stride of 32 bytes
per vertex. An astute GPU programmer will notice the potential to pack this data into
fewer bits to improve cache utilization. This is undesirable, however. The data in its
32-bytes-per-vertex form is ideal for the DMA engine because the MFC natively
works in 16-byte chunks, meaning from the point of view of other processing elements (in our case, the GPU), a given vertex is either deformed or it is not. This is one
of the tradeoffs made to mitigate the use of a double buffer. Color Plate 5 has a screenshot of this technique.

To GPU Types and Back Again

For the most part, GPUs do their best to support common type formats found in
CPUs. The IEEE754 floating-point format is (for better or worse) the de facto floating-
point standard on pretty much all modern hardware that supports floating point[4].

---

[4] Ironically, the SPUs do not offer full IEEE754 support, but it's very close.

However, in addition to the IEEE754 standard 32-bit floats and 64-bit doubles, most shading languages offer a 16-bit counterpart known as *half*. The format of the half is not defined by any standard, and, as such, chip designers are free to implement their own floating-point formats for this data type on their GPUs. Fortunately, almost all GPU vendors have adopted the half format formalized by Industrial Light & Magic for their OpenEXR HDR file format [ILM09]. This format uses a single bit to denote the sign of the number, 5 bits for the exponent, and the remaining 10 bits for its mantissa or significand.

Since the half type is regrettably absent from the C98 and C++ standards, it falls to the programmer to write routines to convert to other data types. Acton has made available an entirely branch-free version of these conversion functions at [Acton06]. For the general case, you would be hard-pressed to better Acton's code (assuming you don't have the memory for a lookup table as in [ILM09]). However, in many constrained cases, we have knowledge about our data that allows us to omit support for floating-point special cases that require heavyweight conversion logic (NaNs and de-normalized numbers). Listing 1.8.6 contains code to convert between an unaligned `half4` and `float4` but omits support for NaNs. This is an optimization that was employed in *Blur*'s damage system. The inverse of this function is left as an exercise for the reader.

LISTING 1.8.6 Code to convert an unaligned `half4` to a `qword`

```
static inline const qword ld_float16_4(void* __restrict__ addr)
{
    const vector unsigned char _loader =
    { 0x80, 0x80, 0x00, 0x01,
      0x80, 0x80, 0x02, 0x03,
      0x80, 0x80, 0x04, 0x05,
      0x80, 0x80, 0x06, 0x07 };
    const vector unsigned char _shft =
    { 0x00, 0x01, 0x02, 0x03,
      0x04, 0x05, 0x06, 0x07,
      0x08, 0x09, 0x0a, 0x0b,
      0x0c, 0x0d, 0x0e, 0x0f };

    qword target        = si_from_ptr(addr);
    qword val_lo         = si_lqd(target, 0x00);
    qword val_hi         = si_lqd(target, 0x10);
    qword sign_bit_mask  = si_ilhu(0x0);
          sign_bit_mask  = si_iohl(sign_bit_mask, 0x8000);
    qword mant_bit_mask  = si_ilhu(0x0);
          mant_bit_mask  = si_iohl(mant_bit_mask, 0x7fff);
    qword expo_bias      = si_ilhu(0x3800);
    qword loader         = (const qword)_loader;
    qword shft           = (const qword)_shft;
    qword offset         = si_andi(target, 0x0f);
    qword lo_byte_pat    = si_ilh(0x0303);
    qword offset_pat     = si_shufb(offset, offset, lo_byte_pat);
```

```
    qword mod_shuf              = si_a(shft, offset_pat);
    qword val                   = si_shufb(val_lo, val_hi, mod_shuf);
    qword result                = si_shufb(val, val, loader); // aligned
    qword sign_bit              = si_and(result, sign_bit_mask);
          sign_bit              = si_shli(sign_bit, 0x10);
    qword significand           = si_and(result, mant_bit_mask);
          significand           = si_shli(significand, 0xd);
    qword is_zero_mask          = si_cgti(significand, 0x0);
          expo_bias             = si_and(is_zero_mask, expo_bias);
    qword exponent_bias         = si_a(significand, expo_bias);
    qword final_result          = si_or(exponent_bias, sign_bit);
    return final_result;
}
```

Benefits versus Drawbacks

Processing vertex data on the SPUs has a number of advantages; one of the most significant is that the rigidity of the GPU's processing model is largely circumvented as you are performing processing on a general-purpose CPU. Access to mesh topology is supported, but one must be careful that these accesses do not introduce unwanted stalls as the data is fetched from the main address space. In addition, since we are using a CPU capable of general-purpose program execution, we are able to employ higher-level optimization tactics, such as early outs or faster code paths, which would be tricky or impossible under the rigid processing model adopted by GPUs. The ability to split workloads between the SPUs and the GPU is also useful in striking the ideal balance for a given application.

As with most things in graphics programming, there are some tradeoffs to be made. Vertex processing on the SPU can in many cases require that vertex buffers are double buffered, meaning a significantly increased memory footprint. The situation is only aggravated if there is a requirement to support multiple instances of the same model. In this case, each instance of the base model may also require a double buffer. This can be mitigated to some extent by carefully designing the vertex format to support atomic writes of individual elements by the DMA engine, but the practicality of this is highly application-specific and certainly doesn't work in the case of instances. Clever use of a ring buffer can also solve this problem to some extent, but it introduces additional problems with SPU/GPU inter-processor communication.

Fragment Shading

Fragment shading in the traditional sense is heavily tied to the output of the GPU's rasterizer. Arbitrarily "hooking into" the graphics pipeline to have the SPUs perform general-purpose fragment shading with current generations of graphics hardware is effectively impossible. However, performing the heavy lifting for certain types of fragment shading that do not necessarily require the use of the rasterizer, or even helping out the GPU with some pre-processing as in [Swoboda09], is certainly feasible and in our experience has yielded significant performance benefits in real-world applications [Tovey10]. This section discusses some of the techniques that will help you get the most out of the SPUs when shading fragments.

Batch! Batch! Batch!

It might be tempting with initial implementations of pixel processing code on the SPU to adopt the approach of video hardware, such as the RSX. RSX processes pixels in groups of four, known as *quads* [Möller08]. For sufficiently interleavable program code—in other words, program code that contains little dependency between operations that follow one another—this may be a good approach. However, in our experience, larger batches can produce better results with respect to pixel throughput because there is a greater volume of interleavable operations. Too few pixels result in large stalls between dependant operations, time that could be better spent performing pixel shading, while larger batches cause high register pressure and ultimately spilling. Moreover, in many applications that have a fixed setup cost for each processing batch, you are doing more work for little to no extra setup overhead.

So, what is the upper bound on the number of pixels to process in a single batch of work? Can we simply process the entire buffer at once? The answer to this is not obvious and depends on a number of factors, including the complexity of your fragment program and the number of intermediate values that you have occupying registers at any one time. Typically, the two are inextricably linked.

As mentioned earlier, the SXU contains 128 registers, each 16 bytes in size. It is the task of the compiler to multiplex all live variables in your program onto a limited register file[5]. When there are more live variables than there are registers—in other words, when register pressure is high—the contents of some or all of the registers (depending on the size of the register file) have to be written back to main memory and restored later. This is known as *spilling* registers. The more pixels one attempts to process in a batch, the higher the register pressure for that function will be, and the likelihood that the compiler will have to spill registers back to the stack becomes greater. Spilling registers can become very expensive if done to excess. The optimum batch size is hence the largest number of pixels that one can reasonably process without spilling any registers back to the local store and without adding expense to the setup code for the batch of pixels.

Pipeline Balance Is Key!

An efficient, well-written program will be limited by the number of instructions issued to the processor. Those processors with dual-issue capabilities, such as the SPU, have the potential to dramatically decrease the number of cycles that a program consumes.

---

[5] The process of mapping multiple live variables onto a limited register file is known as *register coloring*. Register coloring is a topic in its own right, and we will not cover it in detail here.

Pipeline balance between the odd and even execution pipelines is critical to achieving good performance with SPU programs. We will now discuss the requirements for instruction dual-issue and touch briefly on techniques to maximize instruction issue (through dual-issue) for those programmers writing in assembly.

The SPU can dual-issue instructions under a very specific set of circumstances. Instructions are fetched in pairs from two very small instruction buffers [Bader07], and the following must all be true if dual-issue is to occur:

- The instructions in the fetch group must be capable of dispatch to separate execution pipelines.
- The alignment of the instructions must be such that the even pipeline instruction occupies an even-aligned address in the fetch group, and the odd pipeline in the odd-aligned address.
- Finally, there must be no dependencies either between the two instructions in the fetch group or between any one of the instructions in the fetch group and another instruction currently being executed in either of the pipelines.

Programmers writing code with intrinsics rarely need to worry about instruction alignment. The addition of nops and lnops in intrinsic form does not typically help the compiler to better align your code for dual-issue, and, in many cases, the compiler will do a reasonable job of instruction balancing. However, if you're programming in assembly language, the use of nop (and its odd-pipeline equivalent, lnop) will be useful in ensuring that code is correctly aligned for dual-issue. Of course, care must be taken not to overdo it and actually make the resulting code slower. A good rule of thumb is never to insert more than two nops/lnops.

Case Study: Light Pre-Pass Rendering in Blur

Light pre-pass rendering is a variant of deferred shading first introduced by Wolfgang Engel on his blog [Engel08] and later in [Engel09, Engel09a] at the same time it was derived independently by Balestra et al. for use in *Uncharted: Drake's Fortune* [Balestra08]. The techniques behind light pre-pass rendering are well understood and are discussed elsewhere [Engel08, Balestra08, Engel09, Engel09a, Tovey10], so a brief summary will suffice here.

As with all deferred rendering, the shading of pixels is decoupled from scene complexity by rendering out "fat" frame buffers for use in an image space pass [Deering88, Saito90]. Light pre-pass rendering differs slightly from traditional deferred shading in that only the data required for lighting calculations is written to the frame buffer during an initial rendering pass of the scene. This has several advantages, including a warm Z-buffer and a reduced impact on bandwidth requirements, at the expense of rendering the scene geometry twice.

Because one of the main requirements for the new engine written for *Blur* was that it should be equipped to handle a large number of dynamic lights, the light pre-pass renderer was a very attractive option. After implementing a light pre-pass renderer for *Blur* (which ran on the RSX), it became apparent that we could get significant performance gains from offloading the screen-space lighting pass to the SPUs[6].

The lighting calculations in *Blur* are performed on the SPU in parallel with other non-dependent parts of the frame. This means that as long as we have enough rendering work for the RSX, the lighting has no impact on the latency of a frame. Processing of the lighting buffer is done in tiles, the selection of which is managed through the use of the SPE's atomic unit. When the tiles are processed, the RSX is free to access the lighting buffer during the rendering of the main pass. The results of our technique are shown in Color Plate 6 and discussed in greater detail in [Swoboda09, Tovey10].

Benefits versus Drawbacks

The SPUs are powerful enough to perform fragment processing. This has been demonstrated by developers with deferred shading, post-processing, and so on [Swoboda09, van der Leeuw09, Tovey10]. While general-purpose fragment shading is not possible, it is possible to perform a plethora of image-space techniques on the SPUs, including motion blur, depth of field, shadowing, and lighting. Parallelization with other non-related rendering work on the GPU can provide an extra gain if one's goal is to minimize frame latency. Such gains can even be made without the expense of an increased memory footprint.

Rasterization on the SPUs has been achieved by a number of studios with good results, but the use cases for this technique are somewhat restricted, usually being reserved for occlusion culling and the like rather than general-purpose rendering. Rasterization aside, the most serious drawback to performing fragment shading on the SPUs is the lack of dedicated texture-mapping hardware. Small textures may be feasible, as they will fit in the limited local store, but for larger textures or multiple textures, software caching is currently considered to be the best approach [Swoboda09].

Further Work

Due to the highly flexible nature of the SPUs in augmenting the processing power of the GPU, it is hard to suggest avenues of further work with any certainty. However, there are a few significant challenges that warrant additional research efforts in order to further improve the feasibility of some graphics techniques on the SPUs.

Texture mapping is one such avenue of research. Currently, the best that has been done is the use of a good software cache [Swoboda09] to try and minimize the latency of texture accesses from the SPUs. Taking inspiration from other convergent architectures, namely Intel Larrabee [Seiler08], we believe that the employment of user-level threads on the SPUs as a mechanism for hiding latency could certainly go some way

---

[6] Coincidentally, it was around this time that Matt Swoboda presented his work in a similar area, in which he moved a fully deferred renderer to the SPUs in [Swoboda09]; Matt's work and willingness to communicate with us was useful in laying the ground work for our implementation in *Blur*.

to helping the prohibitively slow texture access speeds currently endured by graphics programmers seeking to help the GPU along with the SPUs. Running two to four copies of the same SPU program (albeit with offline modifications to the program's byte code) could allow a programmer to trade space in the local store for processing speed. The idea is simple: Each time a DMA is initiated, the programmer performs a lightweight context-switch to another version of the program residing in the local store, which can be done cheaply if the second copy does not make use of the same registers. The hope is that by the time we return the original copy, the data we requested has arrived in the local store, allowing us to process it without delay. Such a scheme would impose some limitations but could be feasible for small-stream kernels, such as shaders.

Conclusion

The SPUs are fast enough to perform high-end vertex and fragment processing. While they are almost certainly not going to beat the GPU in a like-for-like race (in other words, the implementation of a full graphics pipeline), they can be used in synergy with the GPU to supplement processing activities traditionally associated with rendering. The option to split work between the two processing elements makes them great tools for optimizing the rendering of specific objects in a scene. The deferred lighting and car damage systems in *Blur* demonstrate the potential of the SPUs to work harmoniously with the GPU to produce impressive results.

Looking to the future, the ever-growing popularity and prevalence of deferred rendering techniques in current generations of hardware further empower the SPUs to deliver impressive improvements to the latency of a frame and allow game developers to get closer to synthesizing reality than ever before.

Acknowledgements

I would like to thank the supremely talented individuals of the Bizarre Creations Core Technologies Team for being such a great bunch to work with, with special thanks reserved for Steve McAuley for being my partner in crime with our SPU lighting implementation. Thanks also go to Andrew Newton and Neil Purvey at Juice Games for our numerous discussions about SPU coding, to Matt Swoboda of SCEE R&D for our useful discussions about SPU-based image processing, and to Wade Brainerd of Activision Central Technology for his helpful comments, corrections, and suggestions. Last but not least, thanks also to Jason Mitchell of Valve for being an understanding and knowledgeable section editor!

References

[Acton06] Acton, Mike. "Branch-Free Implementation of Half Precision Floating Point." *CellPerformance*. 17 July 2006. Mike Acton. 2 July 2009. <http://cellperformance.beyond3d.com/articles/2006/07/update-19-july-06-added.html>.

[Acton08] Acton, Mike and Eric Christensen. "Insomniac SPU Best Practices." *Insomniac Games.* 2008. Insomniac Games. 2 July 2009. <http://www.insomniacgames.com/tech/articles/0208/files/insomniac_spu_programming_gdc08.ppt>.

[Bader07] Bader, David A. "Cell Programming Tips & Techniques." *One-Day IBM Cell Programming Workshop at Georgia Tech.* 6 Feb. 2007. Georgia Tech College of Computing. 2 July 2009. <http://www.cc.gatech.edu/~bader/CellProgramming.html>.

[Balestra08] Balestra, Christophe and Pal-Kristian Engstad. "The Technology of *Uncharted: Drake's Fortune.*" Game Developers Conference. 2008. Naughty Dog Inc. n.d. <http://www.naughtydog.com/docs/Naughty-Dog-GDC08-UNCHARTED-Tech.pdf>.

[Deering88] Deering, Michael, et al. "The Triangle Processor and Normal Vector Shader: A VLSI System for High Performance Graphics.*" Proceedings of the 15th Annual Conference on Computer Graphics and Interactive Techniques* (1988): 21–30. *ACM Portal.*

[Engel08] Engel, Wolfgang. "Light Pre-Pass Renderer." *Diary of a Graphics Programmer.* 16 March 2008. Blogspot.com. 4 July 2009. <http://diaryofagraphicsprogrammer.blogspot.com/2008/03/light-pre-pass-renderer.html>.

[Engel09] Engel, Wolfgang. "Designing a Renderer for Multiple Lights: The Light Pre-Pass Renderer." *ShaderX7: Advanced Rendering Techniques.* Ed. Wolfgang Engel. Boston: Charles River Media, 2009. 655–666.

[Engel09a] Engel, Wolfgang. "The Light Pre-Pass Renderer Mach III." To appear in proceedings of ACM SIGGRAPH09, 2009.

[IBM08] "Cell Broadband Engine Programming Handbook." *IBM.* 19 April 2006. IBM. n.d. https://www-01.ibm.com/chips/techlib/techlib.nsf/techdocs/7A77CCDF14FE70D5852575CA0074E8ED>.

[IBM08a] "Synergistic Processing Unit Instruction Set Architecture." *IBM.* 27 Jan. 2007. IBM. n.d. <https://www-01.ibm.com/chips/techlib/techlib.nsf/techdocs/76CA6C7304210F3987257060006F2C44/$file/SPU_ISA_v1.2_27Jan2007_pub.pdf.>

[IBM09] "The Cell Project at IBM Research." *IBM.* n.d. IBM. 4 July 2009. <http://researchweb.watson.ibm.com/cell/home.html>.

[ILM09] "OpenEXR." *OpenEXR.* n.d. Lucas Digital Limited. 4 July 2009. <http://www.openexr.com>.

[Kapoulkine09] Kapoulkine, Arseny. "View frustum culling optimization—never let me branch." *What Your Mother Never Told You About Graphics Development.* 1 March 2009. Blogspot.com. 21 July 2009. <http://zeuxcg.blogspot.com/2009/03/view-frustum-culling-optimization-never.html>.

[Möller08] Akenine-Möller, Thomas, Eric Haines, and Naty Hoffman. *Real-Time Rendering, 3rd Edition.* Wellesley, MA: A.K. Peters, Ltd, 2008.

[Perthuis06] Perthuis, Cedric. "Introduction to the Graphics Pipeline of the PS3." Eurographics 2006. Austrian Academy of Sciences, Vienna, Austria. 6 Sept. 2006.

[Saito90] Saito, Takafumi and Tokiichiro Takahashi. "Comprehensible Rendering of 3-D Shapes." *ACM SIGGRAPH Computer Graphics* 24.4 (1990): 197-206. *ACM Portal.*

[Seiler08] Seiler, Larry, et al. "Larrabee: A Many Core x86 Architecture for Visual Computing." *ACM Transactions on Graphics* 27.3 (Aug. 2008): n.p. *ACM Portal.*

[Shippy09] Shippy, David and Mickie Phipps. *The Race for a New Games Machine: Creating the Chips Inside The New Xbox360 & The Playstation 3.* New York: Citadel Press, 2009.

[Swoboda09] Swoboda, Matt. "Deferred Lighting and Post Processing on PLAYSTATION®3." Game Developers Conference. 2009. Sony Computer Entertainment Eurpoe, Ltd. n.d. <http://www.technology.scee.net/files/presentations/gdc2009/ DeferredLightingandPostProcessingonPS3.ppt>.

[Tovey10] Tovey, Steven and Steven McAuley. "Parallelized Light Pre-Pass Rendering with the Cell Broadband Engine™." *GPU Pro: Advanced Rendering Techniques.* Natick, MA: A K Peters Ltd., 2010.

[van der Leeuw09] van der Leeuw, Michiel. "The PLAYSTATION3's SPUs in the Real World—KILLZONE2 Case Study." Game Developers Conference 2009. Moscone Center, San Francisco, CA. 25 March 2009.

PHYSICS AND ANIMATION

Introduction

Jeff Lander, Darwin 3D, LLC

jeffl@darwin3d.com

Game creation as a business and an art has become much more mature, in years of experience, in complexity, and in controversy of the material covered. For the most part, long gone are the days when text adventures, simple frame flipping, and sprite-based animation ruled the top-ten lists of gamers' hearts. Our games need to be much more real and complex to compete with the ever-increasing expectations of our audience.

Nowhere is this more evident than in the character performances and physical simulations of real (or imaginary) worlds. Players exposed to the amazing worlds that television and filmmakers can create with visual effects rightly believe that their games should reflect these advances and expectations as well. We need to bring our characters to life. We need to create worlds where the rules and systems that govern the reality have a basis in physical realism and have a consistency that is at once familiar and exciting for our players. We are past the point where players can be amazed by a simple animation clip of a character running or watching a ball bounce on the ground. They have seen that all before. They now expect a game's characters to react to the worlds around them in an intelligent way, as well as interact with the world in a way that models the physical interactions in our real-life experiences.

The gems in this section represent the intersection of the physical interactions and animated performances that we need in order to bring more of the illusion of life to our characters and worlds. In "A Versatile and Interactive Anatomical Human Face Model," Marco Fratarcangeli discusses how to bring more realistic movement to facial animation to directly attack the problems with facial performance. This gem models the underlying facial animation systems with physical simulation. In this same way, physical simulation is used in the gems "Application of Quasi-Fluid Dynamics for Arbitrary Closed Meshes" and "What a Drag: Modeling Realistic Three-Dimensional Air and Fluid Resistance" to improve the realism in our interactive worlds. "Particle Swarm Optimization for Game Programming" discusses applying easy-to-use particle simulation techniques to a variety of optimization problems. Much of this is pretty advanced stuff. We will not be discussing how to play back an animation on a hierarchical character or how to simulate and detect a collision between two objects. You are expected to be masters of that kind of low-level system by now.

We are attacking larger problems now. For example, it is no longer sufficient for our characters to follow a simple piecewise linear path when moving across a space. That simply looks too mechanical and robotic. In "Curved Paths for Seamless Character Animation," Michael Lewin discusses how it is necessary to smooth the results from our AI pathfinding systems to create a movement path that follows a much more realistic curve, while still avoiding all the obstacles that may be in the way. Adding to our character performance improvements, in Philip Taylor's "Non-Iterative, Closed-Form, Inverse Kinematic Chain Solver," the existing iterative IK techniques are improved with an easy-to-understand, closed-form solution. It is also not enough to take for granted little code snippets for numerical integration we have seen posted on the net. It is important now for us to have a deeper understanding of what is going on when we use something such as Euler integration for a physical simulation and why it is important that we understand the error inherent in these algorithms. "Improved Numerical Integration with Analytical Techniques" looks directly at these issues and proposes methods to increase the accuracy in our simulations.

As we continue to create amazing new projects and push the envelope for what is possible to do in a game, I believe some of the most important steps forward will come at this intersection of animation and physics. As our animated characters become more physically aware and grounded in our game environments, and our simulated worlds become inhabited by these responsive and emotional characters, our games will make huge leaps forward in connecting to our audience. I hope these gems provoke some new ideas and encourage you all to inject just a little more life into your virtual creations.

2.1

A Versatile and Interactive Anatomical Human Face Model

Marco Fratarcangeli

frat@dis.uniroma1.it

In a compelling virtual world, virtual humans play an important role in improving the illusion of life and interacting with the user in a natural way. In particular, face motion is crucial to represent a talking person and convey emotive states. In a modern video game, approximately 5 to 10 percent of the frame cycle is devoted to the animation and rendering of virtual characters, including face, body, hair, cloth, and interaction with the surrounding virtual environment and with the final user. Facial blend shapes are commonly adopted in the industry to efficiently animate virtual faces. Each blend shape represents a key pose of the face while performing an action (for example, a smiling face or raised eyebrows). By interpolating the blend shapes with each other, as depicted in Figure 2.1.1, the artist can achieve a great number of facial expressions in real time at a negligible computational cost.

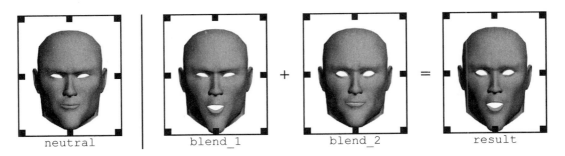

Figure 2.1.1 Blend shapes interpolation.

However, creation of the facial blend shapes is a difficult and time-consuming task, and, more likely than not, it is still heavily dependant on the manual work of talented artists.

In this gem, I share principles and ideas for a tool that assists the artist in authoring humanoid facial blend shapes. It is based on a physical simulation of the human head, which is able to mimic the dynamic behavior of the skull, passive tissues, muscles, and skin. The idea is to let the artist design blend shapes by simply adjusting the contraction of the virtual muscles and rotating the bony jaw. The anatomical simulation is fast enough to feed back the results in real time, allowing the artist to tune the anatomical parameters interactively.

Overview

Our objective is to build a virtual model of the human head that simulates its anatomy and can be adapted to simulate the dynamics of different facial meshes. The artist models a static face mesh, and then the anatomical simulation is used to generate its blend shapes. The goal of the simulation is to create shapes that generate realistic motion. The exact accuracy of the individual muscles in a real anatomical model is not the goal.

The anatomical elements are simple yet expressive and able to capture the dynamics of a real head. The anatomical simulation must also be fast enough to be interactive (in other words, run at least at 30 fps) to allow the artist to quickly sketch, prototype, tune, and, where needed, discard facial poses.

The basic anatomical element is the skull. The anatomical model is not bound to the polygonal resolution or to the shape of the skull mesh; we require only that the skull mesh has a movable jaw. On top of the skull, the artist may design several layers of muscles and passive tissue (such as the fat under the cheeks), the so-called *muscle map*. The skull and the muscle map form the musculoskeletal structure that can be saved and reused for different faces. The musculoskeletal structure is morphed to fit the shape of the target face. Then, the face is bound to the muscles and to the skull, and thus it is animated through a simple and efficient numerical integration scheme.

Numerical Simulation

The anatomical model is composed of different parts, most of which are deformable bodies, such as muscles, fat, and the skin. The dynamics algorithm must be stable enough to allow interaction among these parts, it must be computationally cheap to carry out the computation at an interactive rate, and it must be controllable to allow precise tuning of the muscles' contractions. To meet these requirements, we will use Position Based Dynamics (PBD), a method introduced in [Müller06] and recently embedded in the PhysX and Bullet engines. A less formal (although limited) description was introduced in [Jakobsen03] and employed in the popular game *Hitman: Codename 47*.

For an easy-to-understand and complete formulation of PBD, as well as other useful knowledge about physics-based animation, you can review the publicly available SIGGRAPH course [Müller08]. In this gem, I describe PBD from an implementation point of view and focus on the aspects needed for the anatomical simulation.

In most of the numerical methods used in games, the position of particles is computed starting from the forces that are applied to the physical system. For each integration step at a given time, we obtain velocities by integrating forces, and eventually we obtain the particle's position by integrating velocities. This means that, in general, we can only influence a particle's position through forces.

PBD works in a different way. It is based on a simple yet effective concept: The current position of particles can be directly set according to a customizable set of geometrical constraints $C(\vec{p}) = 0$, where $\vec{p}$ is the set of particles involved in the simulation. Because the constraints could cause the resulting position to change slightly, the velocity must be recalculated using the new position and the position at the previous time step. As the position is computed, the velocity is adjusted according to the current position and the position at the previous time step. The integration steps are:

(1) **for each** particle i **do** $\vec{v}_i(t + \Delta t) = \vec{v}_i(t) + \vec{a}_i(t)\Delta t$

(2) for each particle i do $\vec{p}_i(t + \Delta t) = \vec{p}_i(t) + \vec{v}_i(t + \Delta t)\Delta t$

(3) **loop** nbIterations **times**

(4)   **solve** $C(\vec{p}(t + \Delta t)) = 0$

(5) **for each** particle i

(6) $\vec{v}_i(t + \Delta t) = \big(\vec{p}_i(t + \Delta t) - \vec{p}_i(t)\big)/\Delta t$

For example, let us consider the simple case of two particles traveling in the space, which must stick to a fixed distance d from each other. In this case, there is only one constraint C, which is:

$$C(\vec{p}) = \left\| \vec{p}_1 - \vec{p}_2 \right\| - d = 0 \qquad\qquad (1)$$

Assuming a particle mass $m = 1Kg$, Step (3) in the Algorithm 1 is solved by:

$$\Delta p_1 = -\frac{1}{2}\left(\left\| \vec{p}_1 - \vec{p}_2 \right\| - d\right)\frac{\vec{p}_1 - \vec{p}_2}{\left\| \vec{p}_1 - \vec{p}_2 \right\|}$$

$$\Delta p_2 = +\frac{1}{2}\left(\left\| \vec{p}_1 - \vec{p}_2 \right\| - d\right)\frac{\vec{p}_1 - \vec{p}_2}{\left\| \vec{p}_1 - \vec{p}_2 \right\|}$$

In this example, if a force is applied to $\vec{p}_1$, it will gain acceleration in the direction of the force, and it will move. Then, both $\vec{p}_1$ and $\vec{p}_2$ will be displaced in Step (3) in order to maintain the given distance d.

Given $C(\vec{p})$, finding the change in position Δp_i for each particle is not difficult; however, it requires some notions of vectorial calculus, which are outside the scope of this gem. The process is explained in [Müller06, Müller08] and partly extended in [Müller08b].

Steps (3) and (4) solve the set of constraints in an iterative way. That is, each constraint is solved separately, one after the other. When the last constraint is solved, the iteration starts again from the first one, and the loop is repeated `nbIterations` times, eventually converging to a solution. Then, the velocity is accommodated in order to compensate the change in position Δp_i. In general, using a high value for `nbIterations` improves the precision of the solution and the stiffness of the system, but it slows the computation. Furthermore, an exact solution is not always guaranteed because the solution of a constraint may violate another constraint.

This issue is partly solved by simply multiplying the change in position Δp_i by a scalar constant $k \in [0,..,1]$, the so-called constraint stiffness. For example, choosing $k <$ for a distance constraint leads to a dynamics behavior similar to the one of a soft spring. Using soft constraints leads to soft dynamics and improves drastically the probability of finding an acceptable (and approximated) solution for the constraint set. For example, think about two rigid spheres that must be accommodated inside a cube with a diagonal length smaller than the sum of the diameters of the two spheres: The spheres simply will not fit. However, if the spheres were soft enough, they would change shape and eventually find a steady configuration to fit in the cube. This is exactly how soft constraints work: If they are soft enough, they will adapt and converge toward a steady state.

In my experiments, I used a time step of 16.6 ms and found that one iteration is enough in most of the cases to solve the set of constraints. Rarely did I use more iterations, and never beyond four.

Similar to the distance constraint, other constraints can be formulated considering further geometric entities, such as areas, angles, or volumes. The set of constraints defined over the particles defines the dynamics of a deformable body represented by the triangulated mesh. I provide the source code for the distance, bending, triangular area, and volume constraints on the companion CD-ROM. You are encouraged to experiment with PBD and build deformable bodies following the examples in the source code.

PBD has several advantages:

- The overshooting problem typical of force-driven techniques, such as mass-spring networks, is avoided.
- You can control exactly the position of a subset of particles by applying proper constraints; thus, the remaining particles will displace accordingly.
- PBD scales up very well with spatial dimensions because the constraint stiffness parameter is an adimensional number, without unit of measure.

Building the Anatomical Model

We begin the process of building our virtual head by building up the low-level pieces that make up the foundation of the physical motion. To do this, we take an anatomical approach.

The Skull

The skull is the basis upon which the entire computational model of the face is built. It is represented by a triangulated mesh chosen by the artist. Figure 2.1.2 illustrates an example of the mesh used in our prototype. The skull mesh is divided in two parts: the fixed upper skull and the movable mandible. The latter will move by applying the rigid transformation depicted in Figure 2.1.2.

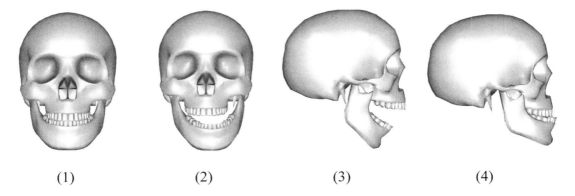

(1)   (2)   (3)   (4)

Figure 2.1.2   (1) Example skull mesh, (2) jaw lateral slide, (3) jaw opening, (4) jaw protruding.

Interactive Sketching of the Muscles

In our model, muscles are represented by rectangular parallelepipeds, which are deformed to match the shape of the facial muscles. To define the shape of the muscles, we draw a closed contour directly on the skull surface and the already-made muscles. Figure 2.1.3 shows an example of the definition of the initial shape of a muscle in rest state. The closed contour is defined upon underlying anatomical structures—in this case, the skull. Then, a hexahedral mesh M is morphed to fit the contour. M is passively deformed as the skull moves.

The closed contour is drawn through a simple ray-casting algorithm. The position of the pointing device (I used a mouse) is projected into the 3D scene, and a ray is cast from the near plane of the frustum to the far plane, as shown in Figure 2.1.4.

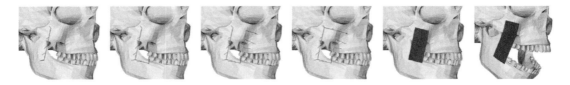

Figure 2.1.3   Defining the shape of a muscle on the skull.

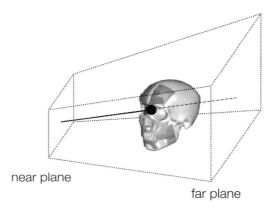

Figure 2.1.4   Casting a ray to determine the intersection point.

The intersection points form the basis of the muscle geometry, the so-called *action lines*.

An action line is a piecewise linear curve lying on at least one mesh. The purpose of the action lines is twofold: (1) They define the bottom contour of the muscle geometry during the simulation, and (2) they provide a mechanism to control the active contraction of the muscle itself. A surface point is a point sp in S, where S is the surface represented by the mesh. A surface point sp is uniquely described by the homogeneous barycentric coordinates (t_1, t_2, t_3) with respect to the vertices $A_1A_2A_3$ of the triangular facet to which it belongs, as shown in Figure 2.1.5.

The relevant attributes of a surface point are position and normal; both of them are obtained through the linear combination of the barycentric coordinates with the corresponding attributes of the triangle vertices. When the latter displace due to a deformation of the triangle, the new position and normal of sp are updated and use the new attributes of the vertices (Figure 2.1.5 (b)). Each linear segment of the action line is defined by two surface points; thus, an action line is completely described by the ordered list of its surface points. Note that each single surface point may belong to a different surface S. So, for example, an action line may start on a surface, continue on another surface, and finish on a third surface. When the underlying surfaces deform, the surface points displace, and the action line deforms accordingly.

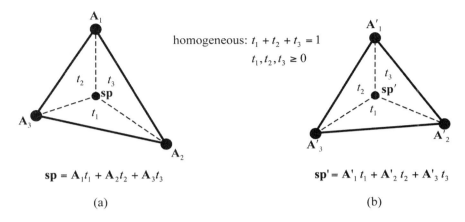

Figure 2.1.5 (a) A surface point *sp* in $A_1A_2A_3$ is defined by the homogeneous barycentric coordinates (t_1, t_2, t_3) with respect to the triangle vertices. (b) When the triangle deforms, the triple (t_1, t_2, t_3) does not change, and *sp* is updated to *sp'*.

Soft Model for a Facial Muscle

Starting from a triangulated, rectangular parallelepiped (or hexahedron), each vertex is considered as a particle with mass $m = 1$; particles are connected with each other to form a network of distance constraints, as shown in Figure 2.1.6.

These constraints replicate some aspects of the dynamic behavior of a real face muscle, in particular resistance to in-plane compression, shearing, and tension stresses. Note that distance constraints are placed over the surface of the hexahedron, not internally. For completing the muscle model, we add bending constraints among the triangular faces of the mesh to conserve superficial tension. We also add a further volume constraint over all the particles, which makes the muscle thicker due to compression and thinner due to elongation.

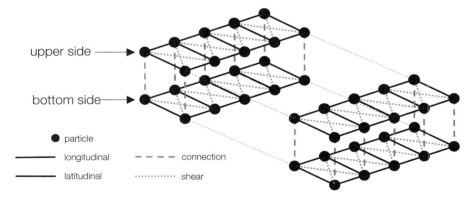

Figure 2.1.6 Distance constraints used in the muscle model.

The Muscle Map

Using the interactive editor to sketch the shape of the soft tissues over the skull, we define the structure made up of intertwined muscles, cartilage, and facial tissue, mostly fat. The muscles are organized in layers. Each layer influences the deformation of the layers on top of it, but not those underlying it. See Figure 2.1.7.

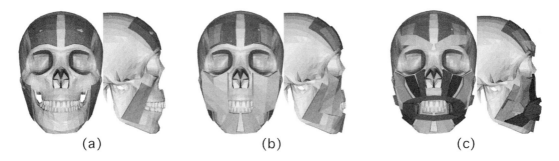

(a)   (b)   (c)

Figure 2.1.7   Different layers forming the muscle map used in the experiments.

The muscle map comprises 25 linear muscles and one circular muscle. This map does not represent the real muscular structure of the human head; this is due to the simulated muscle model, which has simplified dynamics compared to the real musculoskeletal system. However, even though there may be not a one-to-one mapping with the muscle map in a real head, this virtual muscle map has been devised to mimic all the main expressive functionalities of the real one.

For instance, on the forehead area of a real head, there is a single large, flat sheet muscle, the *frontalis belly*, which causes almost all the motion of the eyebrows. In the virtual model, this has been represented by two separate groups of muscles, each one on a separate side of the forehead. Each group is formed by a flat linear muscle (the *frontalis*) and on top of it two additional muscles (named, for convenience, *frontalis inner* and *frontalis outer*). On top of them, there is the corrugator, which ends on the nasal region of the skull. Combining these muscles, the dynamics of the real *frontalis belly* are reproduced with a satisfying degree of visual realism, even though the single linear muscle models have simple dynamics compared to the corresponding real ones.

Each simulated muscle is linked to the underlying structures through position constraints following the position of surface points. Thus, when an anatomical structure deforms, the entire set of surface points lying on it moves as well, which in turn influences the motion of the above linked structures. For instance, when the jaw, which is part of the deepest layer, rotates, all the deformable tissues that totally or partially lie on it will be deformed as well, and so on, in a sort of chain reaction that eventually arrives at the skin.

Active contraction of a muscle is achieved by simply moving the surface points along the action lines. Given that the bottom surface of the muscles is anchored to the surface points through position constraints, when the latter move, the muscle contracts or elongates, depending on the direction of motion of the surface points.

 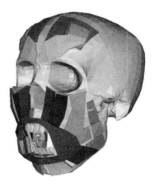

Figure 2.1.8   The example muscle map is deformed by rotating the jaw and contracting the *frontalis belly*. Note how all the above muscles are properly deformed.

Morphing the Muscle Map into the Target Face Mesh

Once the skull and the muscle map are ready, they can be morphed to fit inside the target facial mesh, which represents the external skin. The morphing is done through an interpolation function, which relies on the so-called Radial Basis Functions [Fang96]. We define two sets of 3D points, P and Q. P is a set of points defined over the surface of the skull and the muscles, and Q is a set of points defined over the skin mesh. Each point of P corresponds to one, and only one, point of Q. The position of the points in P and Q are illustrated in Figure 2.1.9 (a) and must be manually picked by the artist. These positions have been proven to be effective for describing the shape of the skull and of the human face in the context of image-based coding [Pandzic and Forchheimer02]. Given P and Q, we find the interpolation function $G(p)$, which transforms a point p_i in P and a point q_i in Q. Once $G(p)$ is defined, we apply it to all the vertices of the skull and muscle meshes, fitting them in the target mesh.

Finding the interpolation function $G(p)$ requires solving a system of linear independent equations. For each couple $\langle p_i, q_i \rangle$, where p_i is in P and q_i is the corresponding point in Q, we set an equation like:

$$q_j = \sum_{i=1}^{n} h_i \cdot \left(d_i^2 \left(p_j \right) + r_i^2 \right)^{\frac{1}{2}}$$

Where n is the number of points in each set, d_i is the distance of p_i from p_j, r_i is a positive number that controls the "stiffness" of the morphing, and h_i is the unknown.

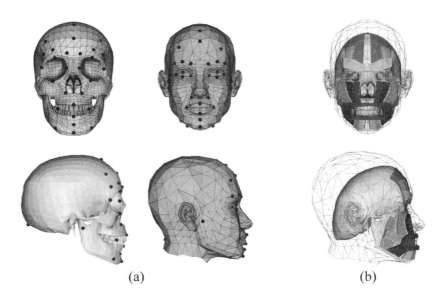

(a)   (b)

Figure 2.1.9   (a) The set of points P and Q picked on the skull and on the face
mesh, respectively. (b) The outcome of the morphing technique.

Solving the system leads to the values of h_i, i = 1, .., n, and thus $G(p)$:

$$G(p) = \sum_{i=1}^{n} h_i \cdot \left(d_i^2(p) + r_i^2\right)^{\frac{1}{2}}$$

This particular form of Radial Basis Functions is demonstrated to always have a
solution, it is computationally cheap, and it is particularly effective when the number
of points in P and Q is scarce. Figure 2.1.9 (b) shows an example of fitting the skull
into a target skin mesh.

Skin

Skin is modeled as a deformable body; its properties are defined by geometrical constraints in a similar way to the muscles. The skin is built starting from the target face
mesh provided in input. Each vertex in the mesh is handled as a particle with a mass,
which is set to 1.0. After the skull and the muscle map are fitted onto the skin mesh,
further constraints are defined to bind the skin to the underlying musculoskeletal
structure. For each particle p in the skin mesh, a ray is cast along the normal that is
toward the outer direction. In fact, after the fitting, portions of some muscles may
stay outside the skin. By projecting in the outer direction, the skin vertices are first
bound to these muscles. If no intersection is found, then another ray is cast in the

opposite direction of the normal, toward the inner part of the head. The ray is tested against the muscles from the most superficial to the deepest one. If the ray does not intersect any muscle, then the skull is tested. The normal of the skin particle is created by averaging the normals of the star of faces to which the particle belongs.

If an intersection is found, then it is defined as a surface point sp on the intersected triangular face in the position where the ray intersects the face. A particle q is added to the system, and it is bound through a position constraint to sp. A stretching constraint is placed among the particles p and q. When the skull and the muscles move, the position of the surface points will change accordingly. The set of added particle q is updated as well because it is bound to the surface points through the corresponding position constraint and will displace the skin particles, whose final motion will depend also on the other involved constraints.

Conclusion

Although not very accurate from the point of view of biomechanics, the presented anatomical model is able to simulate convincing facial poses, including macro-wrinkles, which can be used as blend shapes, as shown in Color Plate 7. The model is stable, robust, and controllable, which is critical in interactive tools for producing video game content. The anatomical model is adaptive enough to animate directly the face mesh provided by the artist, thus it does not lead to the artifacts associated with motion retargeting. It does not require expensive hardware, and it may run on a consumer-class PC while still providing interactive feedback to the artist.

References

[Fang96] Fang, Shiaofen, Raghu Raghavan, and Joan T. Richtsmeier. "Volume Morphing Methods for Landmark Based 3D Image Deformation." *International Symposium on Medical Imaging*. 2710 (1996): 404–415.

[Fratarcangeli08]. Fratarcangeli, Marco. "A Computational Musco-Skeletal Model for Animating Virtual Faces." Ph.D. thesis, Universitá degli Studi di Roma "La Sapienza." 2008.

[Pandzic and Forchheimer02] Pandzic, Igor S. and Robert Forchheimer. *MPEG-4 Facial Animation—The Standard, Implementation and Applications*, 1st ed. John Wiley & Sons, 2002.

[Jakobsen03] Jakobsen, T. "Advanced Character Physics." 2003. Gamasutra. n.d. <http://www.gamasutra.com/view/feature/2904/advanced_character_physics.php, 2003>.

[Müller06] Müller, M., B. Heidelberger, M. Hennix, and J. Ratcliff. "Position Based Dynamics." *J. Vis. Commun.* 18.2 (2007): 109–118.

[Müller08] Müller M., D. James, J. Stam, and N. Thuerey. "Real Time Physics." 2008. Matthias Muller. n.d. <http://www.matthiasmueller.info/realtimephysics/index.html>.

[Müller08b] Müller, M. "Hierarchical Position Based Dynamics." *Proceedings of Virtual Reality Interactions and Physical Simulations*. Grenoble, 2008.

2.2

Curved Paths for Seamless Character Animation

Michael Lewin
mikelewin@cantab.net

The latest generation of consoles brings with it the promise of almost lifelike graphics and animation. Yet for all the beautiful artwork, we are still seeing artifacts, such as character *sliding*, that break the illusion of the virtual world. Sliding occurs when we apply any extra rotation or translation to an animation that does not correspond to the way the character's limbs are moving. This causes movement in which the feet are not planted firmly on the ground, such as running on the spot, shifting left or right while walking, rotating unnaturally while walking or standing, or sliding upwards or downwards while walking on stairs.

A tension exists between our desire for realistic human animation and our need to maintain precise control of the character's position, orientation, and velocity. In many projects, there is not sufficient synergy between the AI and animation layers to satisfy both requirements simultaneously. This gem presents a general way to adapt pathfinding techniques to better interact with animation selection. We developed a technique at Sony Computer Entertainment that uses cubic Bezier curves to allow the AI system to be more closely coupled with dynamics and animation, considering the constraints of the character's movement.

Related Work

[Johnson06] describes a method for fitting Bezier curves inside the cells of a navigation mesh to create a smooth path. This gem describes in a more general way that Bezier curves can be fitted to any piecewise linear path.

Finding a Path

All characters need to move around their environment, which usually involves fast-paced dynamic changes and contains unpredicted obstacles. This problem is just as relevant to robot motion planning in the real world as it is to character movement in simulations such as games, and there is a wealth of literature on the subject applied to both domains.

The vast majority of pathfinding solutions create a piecewise linear path first and then fit a curved path to it. There are a few examples where this intermediate step is not needed, such as using potential fields [Ratering95], but they do not give the same level of control as other methods. I will not consider them further in this article.

There are many different choices of representation when constructing a piecewise linear path. The A* algorithm is usually applied because it is simple, fast, and guaranteed to be optimal. Where techniques for generating pathfinding solutions differ lies in how to represent the physical space. It can be represented as a set of connected cells or points. I briefly explain some of the main techniques; a thorough review can be found in [Tozour03] or [Latombe91], and an edifying demo can be downloaded at [Tozour05]. Figure 2.2.1 shows an example that compares the results of using the various methods.

The simplest method is to divide up the space into a grid of regular rectangular cells with a resolution that is small compared to the size of obstacles. A slightly more sophisticated version of this is to use a quad tree instead of identical rectangles, so that areas of different resolution are defined as needed.

Navigation meshes, as described in [Snook00, Tozour02], are an increasingly popular alternative to the grid solutions described previously. They partition the space using a variety of irregular polygons so that each cell is either entirely filled by an obstacle or entirely empty. The partitioning may be performed by hand when the environment is authored, or it can be generated automatically and then hand-edited later. [Axelrod08, Marden08] describe algorithms for dynamically recalculating the mesh to account for moving obstacles.

Voronoi diagrams are on first appearance similar to navigation meshes, but they yield quite different paths. Obstacles are represented as a finite set of points, and the space is partitioned such that each point is inside a region, where that region is defined as the set of points closer to that obstacle point than any other. The edges of the resulting diagram can define paths around the space provided that all edges that pass through an obstacle are removed first.

Visibility graphs are different from the previously described methods because they generate a set of waypoints rather than partitioning the space into cells. The graph is defined by points in the environment, in which pairs of points are connected by an edge if they can be joined by a straight line without intersecting any obstacles. The points are selected to be close to the corners of obstacles (this is known as a corner graph), so that the character can pass close to obstacles without colliding with them. A good demonstration of the technique can be seen at [Paluszewski]. These methods are shown in Figure 2.2.1.

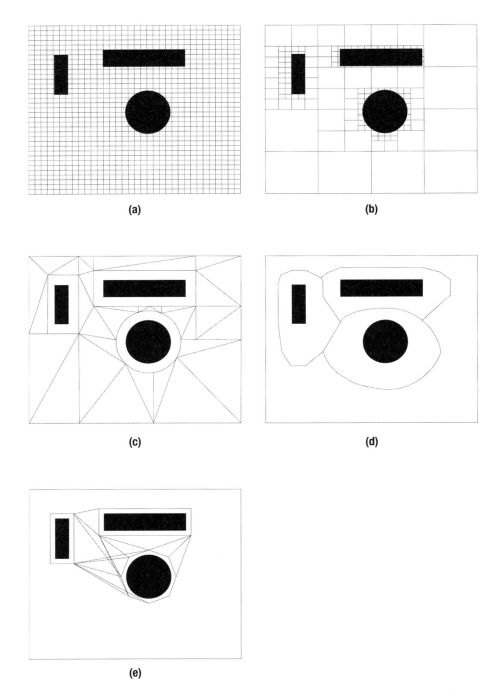

Figure 2.2.1 The various methods of creating a piecewise linear path: (a) regular grid, (b) quad tree, (c) navigation mesh, (d) Voronoi diagram, and (e) visibility graph.

Smoothing the Path

The AI programmer's challenge is to create a piecewise linear path through the environment so that the character appears as lifelike and natural as possible, which means it cannot include jagged edges. Piecewise polynomial parametric curves, more commonly known as splines, are well suited to this task, and in particular cubic Bezier curves. This is a parametric curve of the form:

$$\mathbf{B}(t) = (1\text{-}t)^3\, \mathbf{P_0} + 3(1\text{-}t)^2\, t\, \mathbf{P_1} + 3(1\text{-}t)t^2\, \mathbf{P_2} + t^3 \mathbf{P_3} \text{ for } t \in [0,1] \quad (1)$$

As Figure 2.2.2 illustrates, the control points P_0 and P_3 define the start and end points, respectively, while the control points P_1 and P_2 define the curvature at the end points. The vectors P_1-P_0 and P_3-P_2 are referred to as the start and end velocity, respectively, because they define the tangent and curvature at the two end points. In practical terms, this means we can adjust their direction to control the character's initial and final direction of motion, and we can adjust their magnitude to control the curvature of the curve. Another useful property is that the curve will always lie within the boundary of the quadrilateral convex hull defined by the four control points.

Having constructed a piecewise linear path, we can fit cubic Bezier curves to it for a smooth path. By choosing the control points so that for each consecutive pair of curves the output direction of the first matches the input direction of the second, we achieve continuity and smoothness at the endpoints. Our objective is to adhere to the linear path only as much as necessary. If the character's momentum is high and a large sweeping curve looks most natural, and provided there are no obstacles in the way of that path, we want to select such a path rather than sticking rigidly to the linear path. However, if the path is very close to obstacles and there is little room to maneuver, we want a path that is as curved as possible but still avoids those obstacles.

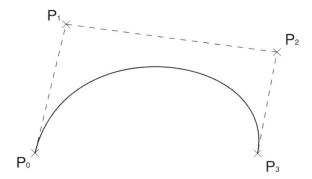

Figure 2.2.2   Bezier curves are well suited to path fitting. The four control points define the curve's position, shape, and curvature. The curve will always be contained inside the convex hull defined by the control points.

The solution to this problem comes from an unlikely source: The open source graph plotting software Graphviz [Graphviz] makes use of the same technique for drawing edges between its nodes [Dobkin97]. The inspiration comes from a 1990 article in the first *Graphics Gems* book that was presented as a way to render fonts using vector graphics [Schneider90, Schneider90_2]. The basic principle is described by the following pseudocode:

```
Fitcurve(startPos, endPos, startVel, endVel)

create a Bezier curve from startPos to endPos,
using startVel and endVel to define the control points

while the curve intersects an obstacle:
    reduce startVel and endVel
    recalculate the Bezier curve
    if startVel and endVel reach a user-defined minimum:
        break

if the curve still intersects an obstacle:
    divide the path in two by choosing a point newPos along path
    set newVel using the vector between two neighbors of newPos
    Fitcurve(startPos, newPos, startVel, newVel)
    Fitcurve(newPos, endPos, newVel, endVel)
```

The whole process of calculating the piecewise linear path and fitting the curved path to it is fast enough to run in a single frame. The path can therefore be recalculated whenever a new obstacle renders the current path unfeasible. Note that the above recursive algorithm is guaranteed to terminate with a valid path because, in the limiting case, we are left with the same piecewise linear path that we began with.

Figure 2.2.3 shows an example. A piecewise linear path is created that avoids an obstacle. Then a single cubic Bezier curve is fitted to it, which takes into account the character's starting momentum. But this curve intersects with another obstacle, so a new path is created, using two cubic Bezier curves, that passes through another point on the piecewise linear path.

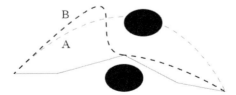

Figure 2.2.3   Fitting a curve that accounts for character momentum. A single cubic Bezier curve *A* (light dashed line) is fitted to the piecewise linear curve (light filled line). But this passes through another obstacle, so a new path *B* (heavy dashed line) is constructed from two cubic Bezier curves that passes through an intermediate point on the piecewise linear path.

In order for a character to walk along the Bezier path, we need to choose the maximum and minimum velocities for the curve. Consider the distance d from the start point to the end point of a single Bezier curve. If the sum of the magnitudes of the start and end velocities exceeds d, the resulting curve can contain a loop. Usually we do not want this, so we can impose $d/2$ as a maximum. A value of zero works perfectly well for a minimum, but we can also use this as an opportunity to impose constraints based on the character's initial momentum, so that sharp turns are not allowed if the character is moving fast. Unfortunately, the character's physical velocity is not identical to the concept of velocity in the Bezier curve. This is because the latter is related to the curve's internal parametrization and therefore varies with curvature and curve length. Nonetheless, good results can be achieved by imposing a minimum kv/d, where v is the character's speed and k is a constant calculated empirically.

Animation Selection

Thus we have created a smooth path to the end point that avoids any obstacles in the environment. All that remains is to select the appropriate animation for the character that will take it along this path. There is a wealth of literature on this complicated topic, using techniques such as motion graphs and inverse kinematics, which are beyond the scope of this article. Instead, I will present a simple solution using animation blending that gives a satisfactory degree of accuracy.

To test the system, I created a character with a family of hand-designed animations for each different gait (for example, walking, running, sprinting). Within each family, all the animations had the same duration and path length but different amounts of rotation (for example, 0, 22.5, 45, 90 degrees). In this way, we can generate motion with any amount of rotation by blending two of the animations together. Linear blending of two or more animations simply means averaging the position and rotation of the skeleton joints. This is done separately for each frame of the animation. The resulting output is therefore a mixture of the inputs. This will only look natural when the animations are quite similar to begin with, as is the case here. Figure 2.2.4 shows an example.

We can chain the animations together because each one begins and ends at the same point in the character's stride. We can transition seamlessly between different gaits using transition animations, authored in the same way as a family of animations with different degrees of rotation.

As one animation ends, a new one must be selected. It is possible at this moment that the character's position and orientation do not perfectly match the curved path. We could choose an animation that will return the character to the path, but if his orientation is wrong, this will result in a zigzagging motion as the character veers too far one way with one step and then too far the other way with the next. It is better to ensure the character's final orientation matches the tangent to the path, even if this means there is some error in his position.

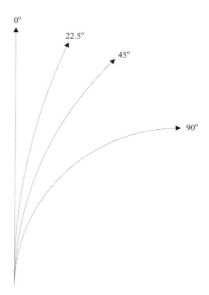

Figure 2.2.4   A family of animations that can be blended together. Each has the same path length but a different amount of rotation (0, 22.5, 45, and 90 degrees).

The method described gave sufficiently accurate results with a wide range of walking and running gaits; Figure 2.2.5 shows an example. This technique is limited, however, as Figure 2.2.6 shows. The animations we can create by blending in this way always describe a circular arc. All we can do is set the curvature of this arc. Some portions of a Bezier curve, however, cannot be described by a circular arc, and this is what causes the character to deviate from the path. For this reason, more sophisticated animation selection techniques would work better.

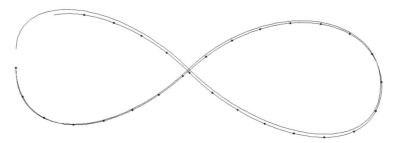

Figure 2.2.5   There is not much error between the dotted line, made of circular arcs, and the full line, made of four cubic Bezier curves. Each dot represents the start of a new arc.

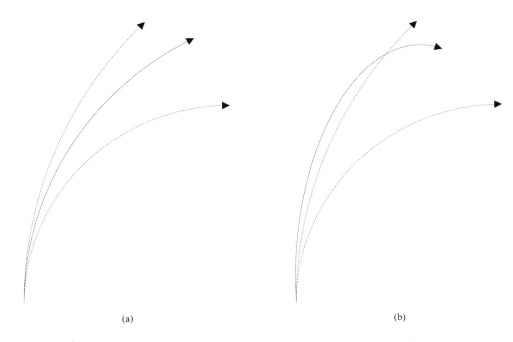

(a)   (b)

Figure 2.2.6   (a) A possible blended output: a circular arc with a rotation of 67.5 degrees. (b) An impossible output: No single circular arc can fit it.

Conclusion

In conclusion, this gem has presented a simple and effective way to generate a curved path from any piecewise linear path that facilitates animation selection and promotes interaction between the AI and animation layers of a character. Future work should look at applying this to common physical constraints, such as enforcing a run-up before jumping or picking up an object. An important future extension to this work is to address how best to manage features of a three-dimensional terrain, such as stairs, gaps, and ledges.

References

[Axelrod08] Axelrod, Ramon. "Navigation Graph Generation in Highly Dynamic Worlds." *AI Game Programming Wisdom 4*. Boston: Charles River Media, 2008.

[Dobkin97] Dobkin, David P., et al. "Implementing a General-Purpose Edge Router." *Proceedings of Graph Drawing* 1997: 262–271.

[Graphviz] Graphviz "Spline-o-matic." n.d. Graphviz. n.d. <http://www.graphviz.org/Misc/spline-o-matic/>.

[Johnson06] Johnson, Geraint. "Smoothing a Navigation Mesh Path." *AI Game Programming Wisdom 3*. Boston: Charles River Media, 2006.

[Latombe91] Latombe, Jean-Claude. *Robot Motion Planning*. Kluwer Academic Publishers, 1991.

[Marden08] Marden, Paul. "Dynamically Updating a Navigation Mesh via Efficient Polygon Subdivision." *AI Game Programming Wisdom 4*. Boston: Charles River Media, 2008.

[Paluszewski] Paluszewski, Martin. "Robot Motion Planning (applet)." n.d. University of Copenhagen. n.d. <http://people.binf.ku.dk/palu/robotmotion/index.html>.

[Ratering95] Ratering, Steven and Maria Gini. "Robot Navigation in a Known Environment with Unknown Moving Obstacles." *Autonomous Robots*. 1.1 (June 1995): n.p.

[Schneider90] Schneider, Philip J. "An Algorithm for Automatically Fitting Digitized Curves." *Graphics Gems*. Academic Press Professional, Inc., 1990.

[Schneider90_2] Schneider, Philip J. "A Bezier Curve-Based Root-Finder." *Graphics Gems*. Academic Press Professional, Inc., 1990.

[Snook00] Snook, Greg. "Simplified 3D Movement and Pathfinding Using Navigation Meshes." *Game Programming Gems*. Boston: Charles River Media, 2000.

[Tozour02] Tozour, Paul. "Building a Near-Optimal Navigation Mesh." *AI Game Programming Wisdom*. Boston: Charles River Media, 2002.

[Tozour03] Tozour, Paul. "Search Space Representations." *AI Game Programming Wisdom 2*. Boston: Charles River Media, 2003.

[Tozour05] Tozour, Paul. "Pathfinding Algorithms & Search Space Representations Demo." 16 July 2005. <http://www.ai-blog.net/archives/000091.html>.

2.3

Non-Iterative, Closed-Form, Inverse Kinematic Chain Solver (NCF IK)

Philip Taylor

ptaylor@trapdoorinc.com

Inverse kinematics (IK) has many uses in games. A primary use is to control the limbs of characters—to fit the pose of the character to the terrain it is standing on or to pin a foot while walking to reduce foot sliding, as described in [Forsyth04]. For many characters, a simple two-bone solver is all that is required because, as in the case of human characters, there are only two major bones in a chain that need to be modified.

The problem of solving a two-bone chain is often reduced to a two-dimensional problem by constraining the solution to lie on a plane, usually defined by the root of the chain, the IK goal, and an up-vector position value. These two-bone solutions are considered "closed form" because the solution can be found using trigonometry [Lander98]. When it comes to chains with more than two bones, there are several well-known algorithms used to solve this problem. Coordinate Cyclic Descent (CCD), Jacobian Transpose, or Pseudo-Inverse are commonly used.

These algorithms suffer from performance issues because multiple iterations are required to converge on a solution. Without sufficient iterations, the chain may not reach the goal within acceptable limits, and the chain may exhibit irregular movements between frames, causing visual artifacts. Additionally, they lack precise control over the resulting shape of the chain.

In this gem, I present a new method for solving inverse kinematics on chains comprising any number of bones by solving each bone separately in two dimensions. This solution is non-iterative in that only a single evaluation per bone is required, while guaranteeing a correct solution if the goal is within reach of the chain. The algorithm does not require extra parameters, such as up-vector position values or preferred angles. Instead, the algorithm attempts to preserve the initial shape of the chain while reaching for the goal, maintaining the integrity of any pose or animation data that was present on the chain prior to the IK solver's evaluation.

Context

Consider the context of the character within a game. We are usually not building a set of rotations to define the chain pose; rather, we are modifying a set of orientations to more closely fit a world space constraint.

During the evaluation of a game scene, the animation system is sampled to provide a local space transform per bone, and these local space pose transforms get concatenated together to build a global space pose. The pose at this point in the engine's evaluation is artist defined and part of what describes the style and personality of the character.

Maintaining the integrity of the character's pose, or motion, while introducing new constraints, such as foot planting or lever pulling, is desirable as significant investment has been made in defining these motions. Any modifications made to the pose should be minimized to avoid breaking the original intent of the motion.

In this gem, the pose defined by the animation system is referred to as the *forward kinematic pose*, or *FK pose*. Forward kinematic refers to the way that the pose was built, by accumulating local space transforms down through the hierarchy to generate global space transforms.

Bone Definition

For the purpose of this gem, a bone is defined as containing a position and an orientation. The position is represented as a vector triple, and the orientation is represented as a quaternion. As illustrated in Figure 2.3.1, we refer to the vector that runs along its length as the *bone length vector*, and the length of a bone is defined as the length of this vector. By convention, bones are aligned with their local X-axis. A chain is defined as a linear hierarchy of bones, usually lined end to end.

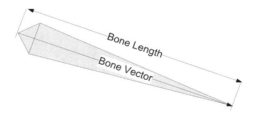

Figure 2.3.1   Bone definition.

IK Goal Position

Without considering hands, feet, or any other child bones of the chain, a solution is defined as solving the chain such that the tip of the last bone touches, or comes as close to touching as possible, some predetermined IK goal position. The exact location of this IK goal position is defined by the engine and is not within the scope of this gem.

The animation engine might be locking the foot to a plant position over the course of a character's step, or the hand of a character could be constrained to the steering wheel of a vehicle. In both cases, we have a bone chain with animation applied and a desired goal position, which is defined by the character's environment.

One-Bone IK

The simplest chain would only comprise one bone, and the closest valid solution would be to align the bone with the goal. While this example may appear trivial, the rest of this gem builds upon this concept.

The vector between the bone and the goal is called the *bone-to-goal vector*, and we refer to the desired angle between the bone length vector and the bone-to-goal vector as the *IK angle*.

When solving a chain comprising one bone, the best that can be achieved is to adjust the bone's pose such that the bone length vector is aimed at the IK goal, as shown in Figure 2.3.2. This is done by incrementing the rotation using the angle between the bone length vector and the bone-to-goal vector. The axis of rotation is perpendicular to both the bone length vector and the bone-to-goal vector. This rotation is the shortest arc of rotation that will transform the bone vector onto the bone-to-goal vector. Computing this quaternion directly is described in the article by [Melax06].

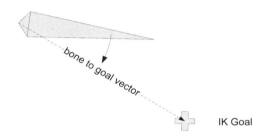

Figure 2.3.2   Aiming a bone at an IK goal position.

Two-Bone IK

When an additional bone is added into the system, the mathematics becomes more complex.

Aligning the Chain to the IK Goal

Maintaining the shape of the limb while solving IK requires that each bone retain the respective transforms with bones prior to it and after it in the chain. For example, if the bones in the chain all lie on one plane prior to solving, then after solving the bones should all still lie on a single plane.

The first step to solving a chain is to offset the orientation of each bone by the shortest arc between the root of the chain and the chain tip, and the root of the chain and the IK goal position, as shown in Figure 2.3.3. This step ensures that all further deformation will occur on the same plane with respect to the overall chain shape, as the original chain pose describes. This step also has the effect of biasing most of the deformation to the first joint in the chain. For most characters' limbs this is desirable, but joint limits can be imposed to restrict this deformation. See the "Future Work" section.

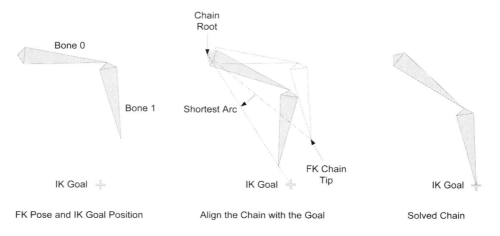

Figure 2.3.3   Aligning the chain to the IK goal.

We first apply the overall alignment to each bone and then solve using the appropriate method for that bone.

Calculating Bone 0 in a Two-Bone Chain

The vector from a bone to the tip of the chain prior to solving is called the *bone-to-chain-tip vector*, and the angle between the bone length vector and the bone-to-chain tip is the *FK angle*, as shown in Figure 2.3.4. To calculate the IK angle for Bone 0, we use the law of cosines equation providing the parameters *a*, *b*, and *c*.

$$a = \text{Bone 0 length}$$
$$b = \text{Bone 1 length}$$
$$c = \text{Bone to IK goal distance}$$

$$IKBoneAngle = \cos^{-1} \frac{a^2 + b^2 - c^2}{2ab} \qquad (1)$$

Once we have calculated the IK angle, we subtract this from the current angle between the bone length vector and the bone-to-goal vector to get a delta angle, which we will use to modify the bone's pose. The axis around which we rotate the bone is the cross product of the bone-to-goal vector and the bone-to-chain-tip vector. We then modify the bone's orientation by incrementing the rotation using the axis and the delta angle.

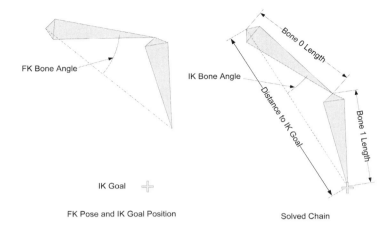

Figure 2.3.4   Solving the first bone in a two-bone chain.

Solving the Last Bone

Before any child bone can be solved, its new global position must be calculated by transforming the bone's length vector using the new orientation of its parent and adding it to the parent's position. Bone 1, or the last bone in any chain, is solved using the one-bone solution described previously in the section "One-Bone IK."

Three-Bone IK Solver

I have shown that a two-bone problem can be decomposed into two types of bones that are each solved using an appropriate method. The first thing to consider about a three-bone chain is that it encapsulates the two-bone chain described previously with one extra bone at the start of the chain, as shown in Figure 2.3.5. Therefore, once a solution can be found for Bone 0, then bones one and two can be derived using the previously described methods.

Maximum Bone Angles

Consider that the initial pose of the chain defines an ideal pose for the limb, and any modification of the limb pose must be minimized. By analyzing the FK pose of the chain, for example, in Figure 2.3.6, we can determine a value that describes how bent Bone 0 is with respect to the rest of the chain.

   We can use the law of cosines to calculate a value that defines the angle of Bone 0 if the remaining chain were to be laid out in a straight line. The remaining chain length, the distance to the FK chain tip, and the bone length are used to calculate the max bone angle. This angle is referred to as the *max FK bone angle*. Comparing this max FK bone angle to the actual FK bone angle gives us a value that defines our FK bone angle relative to the distance to the FK chain tip.

   bone angle fraction = FK bone angle / maximum FK bone angle   (2)

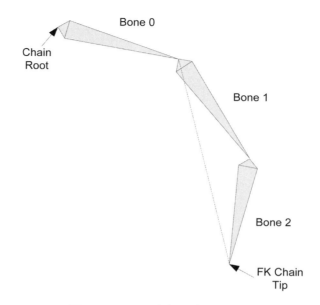

Figure 2.3.5   Three-bone chain.

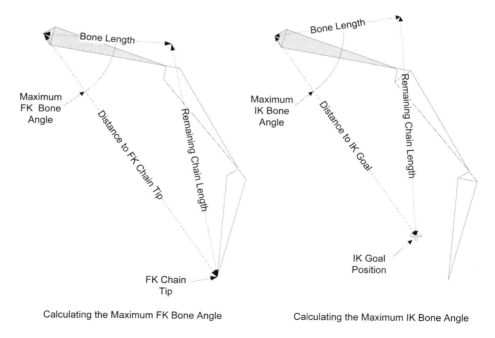

Calculating the Maximum FK Bone Angle   Calculating the Maximum IK Bone Angle

Figure 2.3.6   Calculating the bone angle and the maximum FK and IK bone angles.

The bone angle fraction is defined relative to the initial shape of the chain and is a correlation between the bone's orientation and the rest of the chain pose. Conversely, the remaining bone length can also be used to calculate the maximum possible angle that the bone can assume in IK. This maximum IK bone angle is multiplied by the bone angle fraction value to determine the new IK bone angle.

Four-Bone IK Solver

Figure 2.3.7 illustrates that with chains comprising three or more bones, the bones before the last two bones are all solved using the method described previously. Considering only the bone length, the remaining bone lengths, the distance to the FK chain tip, and the distance to the IK goal, a bone angle can be calculated. Once the IK bone angle has been calculated for Bone 0, then we simply continue down the chain, and Bone 0 can be solved in exactly the same way. Bone 2 can then be solved using trigonometry, and Bone 3 is simply aligned with the target.

N-Bone IK Solver

An N-bone chain consists of three categories of problems. Bones 0 to $N-3$ are all solved using the method described previously of calculating maximum IK and FK bone angles to derive an IK bone angle. Bone $N-2$ can be solved using trigonometry, and Bone $N-1$ is simply aligned with the goal.

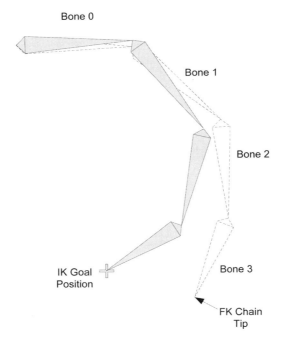

Figure 2.3.7 Applying the method to a four-bone chain.

```
Function SolveIKChain( chain )
begin
    calculate chain target alignment

    for each bone in chain
    begin
        apply chain target alignment to bone

        if bone is last bone
            aim bone at target
        else if bone is second last
            use trigonometry to calculate bone angle
        else
        begin
            determine FK bone angle
            determine maximum FK bone angle
            determine maximum IK bone angle

            IK bone angle = ( FK bone angle / maximum FK bone angle ) *
                            maximum IK bone angle
        end
    end
end
```

Handling Extreme Deformation

In some cases, the remaining chain length is greater than the bone length plus the distance to the chain tip or IK goal. In these cases, the technique described previously of using trigonometry to calculate the maximum FK and IK angles cannot generate a maximum angle greater than π. Furthermore, during animation there may be visual artifacts if the max IK bone angles hit this limit.

As shown in Figure 2.3.8, if the distance between the bone and the chain tip is greater than the remaining chain length, then trigonometry is used as described previously. Once the distance to the IK goal is less than the remaining chain length, the maximum IK and FK bone angle values can be calculated.

The following pseudocode describes how to calculate the maximum FK bone angle for a long chain.

```
if( distToFkChainTip > remainingChainLength )
{
    use trigonometry to calculate maximum bone angle
}
else
{
    maxFkBoneAngle = acos( ( boneLength/2 ) / remainingChainLength )
    maxFkBoneAngle += ( remainingChainLength - distToFkChainTip ) /
boneLength;
    }
```

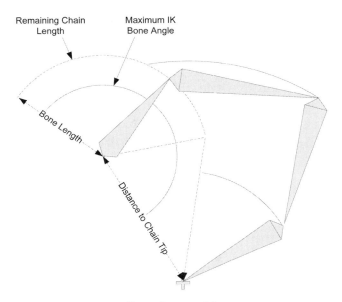

Figure 2.3.8   Handling chains with extreme curvature.

Effectively, the remaining chain length is applied in an arc around the one position, allowing us to define maximum angles greater than π. This technique gives a much greater range of angles for the maximum FK/IK bone angle values, while maintaining the important limits when the chain is extended.

Additional Details

We have only discussed the basic case in this gem. Here are some additional details that may be helpful for specific cases.

IK/FK Blending

In many cases, you will want to turn off IK because it may not be applicable. Simply disabling IK evaluation will cause a visual pop in the pose of your character. A better approach is to interpolate your IK pose back to your original FK pose before disabling IK. To do this, you need to keep an IK pose buffer separate from your FK pose buffer.

Animated Joint Offsets

So far in this gem, we have only considered chains with static local offsets along the local X-axis. This solver can readily be extended to support animated joint offsets.

The local position offset of a joint can be used as the bone length vector of the parent bone, as shown in Figure 2.3.9. The FK bone angle and max FK/IK bone angles are all calculated using this vector and its length, as described in this gem. This ensures that the bones pivot in the same position relative to their parent bone and that local position offsets are still applied in parent space. Because we are required to know the total length of the chain before solving, the entire chain's length needs to be measured prior to solving for IK.

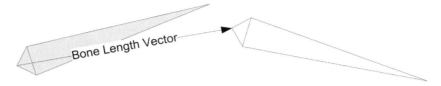

Figure 2.3.9   Animated joint offsets.

Extension Limit

One concern with applying inverse kinematics to a chain in a game is that often the IK solvers will generate artifacts in the motion of the limb when the limb reaches the limit of its extension. The term *hyperextension* refers to the visual pop that happens when a chain reaches the limits of its reach. Fixing this issue is a minor addition to the IK solver algorithm. In the code samples provided with the book, extension dampening has been implemented to show how this can be achieved.

Future Work

Our algorithm will not address all cases that you will come across. In the future, we plan to extend the system in several ways.

Sliding Joints

This IK solver will not currently calculate new local joint position offsets but only calculates orientation changes for each bone in the hierarchy. For example, it will not extend a hydraulic joint to reach the goal. Sliding joints could be implemented using a similar technique as that used to calculate angles. By defining the FK bone's local position relative to a slide vector, a new local offset position could be defined by comparing the distance to the FK chain tip and the actual distance to the IK goal.

Joint Limits

Aside from limiting the overall extension of the chain, it may be required that certain bones do not rotate beyond a certain limit or that they are not free to rotate on any plane. Because this chain is evaluated from top to bottom, it is possible to start imposing limits on angles. A simple way to do this is to limit the angle generated for each bone. In this way, we can limit the angle of a bone with respect to its parent.

DOF Constraints

Creature limbs are usually made up of a ball joint followed by a collection of hinge joints. In this gem, however, no twisting is ever applied to the chain, meaning that the solver only modifies the pose of the root bone on two axes, and every other joint rotates on only one axis. The axis used to modify the bone's orientation is assumed to be perpendicular to the bone vector and the bone-to-goal vector. Chains with limited degrees of freedom are not supported in the algorithm presented in this gem. If an axis of motion were defined for a particular bone, then solving would still be feasible by calculating the maximum bone angles projected onto the plane defined by this axis.

General-Purpose Programming on Graphics Processors

The algorithm presented in this gem does not employ any recursion, or major branching, and has a fixed cost per evaluation. These features make it an ideal candidate for implementations using some of the newer SIMT architectures, such as CUDA or OpenCL. Perhaps, as in the case of shaders, specific versions of the solver would be generated for categories of chains and the loops unrolled. A two-, three-, and four-bone version could be generated and the loops unrolled at compile time. Depending on the bone count, a chain would be solved in a batch with all other limbs of the same structure. This would avoid costly synchronization points, which would slow all chain evaluations to the cost of the longest chain.

Conclusion

In this gem, I have presented a new method for solving inverse kinematics on chains of bones that is simple, fast, and accurate. This is achieved by calculating bone angles directly using values derived from the initial pose of the chain and the position of the IK goal. This method minimizes the modification of the original chain's pose, while ensuring the goal is always reached if within range. There are many possibilities for further development to expand this concept beyond a simple chain solver.

References

[Forsyth04] Forsyth, Tom. "How to Walk." 2004. Game Tech. n.d. <http://www.game-tech.com/Talks/HowToWalk.ppt>.

[Lander98] Lander, Jeff. "Oh My God, I Inverted Kine!" *Game Developer*. (September 1998): 9–14.

[Melax06] Melax, Stan. "The Shortest Arc Quaternion." *Game Programming Gems*. Boston: Charles River Media, 2006. 214–218.

2.4

Particle Swarm Optimization for Game Programming

Dario L. Sancho-Pradel
dariosancho@gmail.com

This gem presents the foundations of Particle Swarm Optimization (PSO), a simple yet powerful meta-heuristic optimization technique that can be applied to complex non-linear problems, even in the absence of a precise analytical formulation of the system. As a result, PSO is used in a variety of engineering applications, such as artificial neural network training, mechanical design, and telecommunications. I have also applied this technique to robotic systems. PSO is related to other population-based search strategies, such as Genetic Algorithms (GA), and can solve similar problems. However, PSO works natively with real numbers and tends to be more efficient than GA, often reaching a near-optimal solution in fewer function evaluations [Hassan05]. Next-generation consoles are pushing the boundaries of realism and complexity in game development. Often, games contain large sets of parameters that drive or influence the behavior of various systems, such as physics, animation, or AI. More often than not, the final values of many of these parameters are the result of a manual selection process based on experience and trial and error. Under certain basic conditions, PSO can be a valuable tool for better tuning these parameters in an automated fashion.

A Few Words on Optimization

Optimization problems are typically modeled as finding the maximum or minimum value of a set of m-dimensional real functions, whose variables are normally subject to constraints. Maximizing a function f is equivalent to minimizing the function $-f$ and vice versa. Using vector notation, the optimization problem is reduced to finding the roots (solutions) of the vector function:

$$\mathbf{F(x)} = \mathbf{0} \qquad (1)$$

where, for the general case of p non-linear equations in m variables:

$$\mathbf{F}(\mathbf{x}) = [f_1(\mathbf{x}),...,f_p(\mathbf{x})]^T, \mathbf{x} = [x_1,...,x_m]^T \text{ and } \mathbf{0} = [0,...,0]^T$$

In some cases, Equation (1) may be solved analytically, which means that the optimum point (or set of points) can be calculated exactly. In most real applications, however, this is not possible, and numerical methods are applied to find an approximate solution.

Numerical Methods

Numerical methods are algorithms that return a numerical value that in most cases represents an approximation to the exact solution of a problem. Classical optimization techniques have been successful at solving many optimization problems common in industry and science. However, there are optimization scenarios that classical approaches cannot solve in a reasonable amount of time. Combinatorial optimization problems—in other words, problems with a discrete set of solutions from which we want to find the optimal one—and NP-hard problems in general are good examples. For those cases, approximate solutions can be obtained relatively quickly using meta-heuristic approaches (that is, high-level strategies used for guiding different heuristics in search problems).

No Free Lunch (NFL) Theorem for Optimization

Optimizing can be regarded as a search problem where the selected optimization method represents the particular style or mechanism of executing the search. The NFL theorem [Wolpert97] states that for finite spaces and algorithms that do not resample points, the performance of all search (optimization) algorithms averaged over all possible objective functions is the same. In practice, however, we do observe that some algorithms perform, on average, significantly better than others over certain objective functions. This is because the objective functions considered in most real optimization scenarios have a structure that is far from random. As a result, algorithms that exploit such a structure will perform, on average, better than "uninformed" search strategies (for example, a linear sequential search). The PSO search strategy is based on an exchange of information between members of a swarm of candidate solutions and operates under the assumption that "good solutions" are close together in the search space. If this is not the case, PSO will not perform better than a random search.

The PSO Paradigm and Its Canonical Formulation

PSO is a stochastic, population-based computer algorithm modeled on swarm intelligence. The PSO paradigm was originally developed by Dr. Eberhart and Dr. Kennedy [Kennedy95], an electrical engineer and a social psychologist, respectively, who had the idea of applying social behavior to continuous non-linear optimization problems.

They reasoned that social behavior is so ubiquitous in the animal kingdom because it optimizes results. Social behavior is the result of an exchange of information within the members of the society. The original PSO algorithm evolved from a bird flocking simulator into an optimization tool motivated by the hypothesis that social sharing of information among members of the society offers an evolutionary advantage. In order to implement and exploit that flow of information, each member was provided with a small amount of memory and a mechanism to exchange some knowledge with its social network (in other words, its neighbors). Although different improvements and variations have been proposed since the initial PSO algorithm was presented, most of them resemble closely the original formulation. A significant exception is the Quantum PSO (QPSO) algorithm [Sun04], which for reasons of space will not be covered here.

Canonical Equations of Motion

The way PSO works is by "flying" a swarm of collision-free particles over the search space (also called the *problem space*). Each particle represents a candidate solution of the optimization problem, and each element (dimension) of the particle represents a parameter to be optimized. The movement of each particle in the swarm is dictated by the equations of motion that the particular flavor of the PSO algorithm defines. In its canonical form, these equations can be expressed as:

$$\mathbf{V}(t + \Delta t) = \mathbf{V}_{Inertia}(t) + \mathbf{V}_{Cognitive}(t) + \mathbf{V}_{Social}(t)$$

$$\mathbf{x}(t + \Delta t) = \mathbf{x}(t) + \Delta t \cdot \mathbf{V}(t + \Delta t) \qquad (2)$$

where $\mathbf{x}(t)$ and $\mathbf{V}(t)$ represent respectively the particle's position and velocity at time t. By choosing $\Delta t = 1$, t becomes the iteration step. Note that $\mathbf{x}(t)$ and $\mathbf{V}(t)$ are m-dimensional vectors. At $t = 0$, the position of each particle is selected from a uniform random distribution, i.e. $x^j(0) = U(x^j \min, x^j \max)$, $j = 1,2,...m$, where $x^j \min$, $x^j \max$ are the search space boundaries for the j-th dimension. $\mathbf{V}(0)$ can either be randomly initialized or set equal to the zero vector.

Velocity Update

As Equation (2) shows, the search process is driven by the velocity update, based on:

- **Cognitive information.** Experience gained during the particle's search, expressed as the best location ever visited by the particle $\mathbf{x}_{Cognitive\_Best}$.
- **Socially exchanged information.** The best location found so far by any member of the particle's social network ($\mathbf{x}_{Social\_Best}$). The calculation of $\mathbf{x}_{Social\_Best}$ depends on the chosen network's topology. Figure 2.4.1 shows some common topologies. In a fully connected network (for example, Star), $\mathbf{x}_{Social\_Best}$ represents the best location found by any particle in the swarm, hence called *global best* ($\mathbf{g}_{Best}$). If the swarm is not fully connected $\mathbf{x}_{Social\_Best}$ becomes the best position found by any particle in its local neighborhood, hence called *local best* ($\mathbf{l}_{Best}$). Using $\mathbf{l}_{Best}$ tends

to provide more accurate results, whereas algorithms running g_{Best} execute faster [Engelbrecht02]. The neighborhood is typically defined based on the particles' indices, although spatial information could also be used. Allowing neighborhood overlapping helps the information exchange across the swarm.

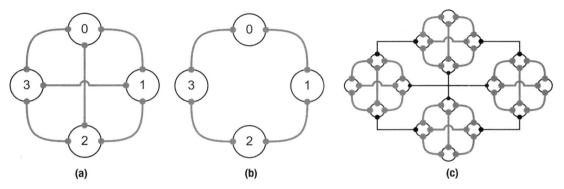

Figure 2.4.1   Three classical social network structures: (a) Star topology (fully connected), (b) Ring topology, (c) Cluster topology.

- **Inertia.** Provides certain continuity to the motion of the particle. Adding inertia to the velocity update helps to decrease the change in momentum between two consecutive iterations and provides a means of controlling the balance between the particle's *exploration* and *exploitation*. An exploratory strategy tends to direct the particle toward unexplored areas of the problem space. Exploitation refers to the movement of a particle around previously explored areas, resulting in a finer-grain search on these areas. Clearly, low inertia will favor exploitation, whereas higher values will result in a more exploratory behavior.

In general, the PSO strategy is to use the cognitive and social best positions as attractors in the search space of the particle. It achieves that by defining the particle's velocity vectors as:

$$\mathbf{V}_{Inertia}(t) = \omega \cdot \mathbf{V}(t)$$
$$\mathbf{V}_{Cognitive}(t) = c_{Cognitive} \cdot \mathbf{r}_1 \otimes (\mathbf{x}_{Cognitive\_Best} - \mathbf{x}(t))$$
$$\mathbf{V}_{Social}(t) = c_{Social} \cdot \mathbf{r}_2 \otimes (\mathbf{x}_{Social\_Best} - \mathbf{x}(t))$$

where $\omega \in (0,1)$. $\mathbf{r}_1$ and $\mathbf{r}_2$ are random m-dimensional vectors taken from a uniform random distribution, in other words, $\mathbf{r}_i = \{\mathbf{r}_{i^j} \in U(0,1)\}$, $j = 1,2,...,m$, $i = 1,2$. The values of the two acceleration coefficients are normally chosen to be the same (typically $c_{Cognitive} = c_{Social} \in (0,2.05]$). It is important to notice that here the operator $\otimes$ denotes a per-component multiplication of two vectors, and therefore its result is another vector.

Finally, the equations of motion for the basic canonical PSO system can be expressed as:

$$\mathbf{V}(t+1) = \omega \cdot \mathbf{V}(t) + c_{Cognitive} \cdot \mathbf{r}_1 \otimes (\mathbf{x}_{Cognitive\_Best} - \mathbf{x}(t)) + c_{Social} \cdot \mathbf{r}_2 \otimes (\mathbf{x}_{Social\_Best} - \mathbf{x}(t))$$
$$\mathbf{x}(t+1) = \mathbf{x}(t) + \mathbf{V}(t+1) \tag{3}$$

Algorithm 1 details the basic canonical PSO formulation implementing the $\mathbf{g}_{Best}$ strategy, and Figure 2.4.2 illustrates graphically the position and velocity update of one particle based on the equations of motion presented in Equation (3).

```
Algorithm 1: Canonical PSO (<<eq32.pdf>> version)
 1: // Create a swarm of N randomly distributed particles
 2: FOR EACH particle(P) i=1,…,N do
 3:         FOR EACH dimension j=1,..,M do
 4:             P[i].X[j] = Xmin[j]+rand(0,1)*(Xmax[j]- Xmin[j]);
 5:             P[i].V[j] = rand(0,1)*Vmax[j]*sign(rand(0,1)-0.5);// or =0;
 6:         END
 7: END
 8: g_Best = P[0];
 9: numIterations = 1;
10: // Iterative optimisation process
11: REPEAT
12:    FOR EACH particle(P) i=1,…,N do
13:         IF Eval(P[i].X) BETTER_THAN Eval(g_Best.X)
14:             g_Best = P[i];
15:         END
16:         IF Eval(P[i].X) BETTER_THAN Eval(P[i].x_best)
17:             P[i].x_best = P[i].X;
18:         END
19:    END
20:    // Apply_Equations_of_Motion
21:    FOR EACH particle i=1,…,N do
22:         FOR EACH dimension j=1,..,M do
23:             V_Inertia = w*P[i].V[j];
24:             V_social = c1*rand(0,1)*(g_Best.X[j] - P[i].X[j]);
25:             V_cognitive = c2*rand(0,1)*(P[i].x_best[j] - P[i].X[j]);
26:
27:             P[i].V[j] = V_Inertia + V_social + V_cognitive;
28:                 Clamp(P[i].V[j]); // optional
29:             P[i].X[j] = P[i].X[j] + P[i].V[j];
30:                 Clamp(P[i].X[j]); // or any other strategy
31:         END
32:    END
33:    numIterations++;
34: UNTIL (m_numIterations > MAX_NUM_ITER || GOOD_ENOUGH(Eval(g_Best)))
```

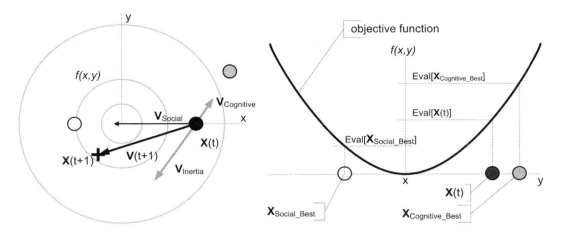

Figure 2.4.2 Illustration of the velocity and position updates of a particle during the optimization of a simple 2D parabolic function $f(x,y)$. (Left) Geometrical illustration showing contour lines of $f(x,y)$. (Right) Sketch of $f(x,y)$ illustrating the particle's relevant information and labels.

The position update may take the particle outside of the predefined boundary. In fact, it has been proven that in high-dimensional swarms, most of the particles will leave the search space after the first iteration [Helwig08]. Some strategies to constrain the particles to the search space include:

- Moving the particle to its closest boundary and setting its velocity to zero.
- Assuming a cyclic problem space. For instance, for $\varepsilon < \left| x^j{}_{max} - x^j{}_{min} \right|$, if $x^j(t) = x^j{}_{max} + \varepsilon$, then it is recalculated as $x^j(t) = x^j{}_{min} + \varepsilon$.
- Allowing the particle to leave the boundary, omitting its evaluation if the objective function is not defined at the new coordinates.
- Reinitializing all components whose values are outside of the search space.

Evaluating the Particles: The Objective Function

The objective function, also referred to as the *fitness function* or *cost function*, does not need to be the actual mathematical representation of the system to be optimized, but a measure of the quality of any solution found. Therefore, each call to Eval(P[i].X) in Algorithm 1 requires the simulation of the system using the parameters encoded in P[i]. During the simulation, various indicators related to the performance of the solution are recorded and combined in a function to provide a numerical measure of performance. This function is the objective function.

Imagine that we want to optimize the parameters that define the way an NPC performs a certain task, such as handling a car. Most likely, we do not have a dynamic model of the car and its controllers, so we cannot directly optimize the non-linear system of equations that defines the problem at hand. Nevertheless, by defining an objective function that penalizes, for instance, the time the NPC spends outside the training path and the time required to drive a predetermined distance, we are effectively giving the particles valid feedback to evaluate their quality, and therefore a means of improving in later iterations.

Add-Ons to the Classical Formulation

Beyond the basic formulation, we can add a few improvements to deal with specific cases that may come up in a particular use case.

Velocity Clamping

The formulation described so far may generate particles with increasingly large oscillations around a potential optimum due to an "explosion" in the velocity values. This issue was addressed in [Kennedy01] by the introduction of a positive velocity clamping parameter $\mathbf{V}_{max}$, which modifies the velocity update as follows:

$$V^j(t+1) = \begin{cases} V^j_{Calculated}(t+1) & \text{if } \left| V^j_{Calculated}(t+1) \right| < V_{max} \\ sign(V^j_{Calculated}(t+1)) \cdot V^j_{max} & otherwise \end{cases} \quad j = 1,2,...,m$$

where $V^j_{Calculated}(t+1)$ is the j-th component of the velocity vector calculated using Equation (3). The selection of $\mathbf{V}_{max}$ is problem dependent. Typically, each of its components is initialized within the size of the search space boundaries, in other words, $V^j_{max} = \kappa \cdot \left| x^j_{max} - x^j_{min} \right|$, $\kappa \in (0,1)$. Initially, we want κ to be close to 1 in order to favor exploration. During the optimization process, $\mathbf{V}_{max}$ can be periodically adjusted by:

- Setting $\mathbf{V}_{max}$ to the dynamic range of the particle.
- Using linearly or exponentially decaying $\mathbf{V}_{max}$ in order to progressively move toward exploitation (fine-grained searches) of the area around the best particle(s).
- Increasing or decreasing $\mathbf{V}_{max}$ after α iterations without improvement in the best found solution.

Variable Inertia Weight $\omega(t)$

The inertia coefficient has a clear influence in the particle's search strategy. Large values of ω favor exploring new areas, while small values favor the exploitation of known areas. Initially, we would like the algorithm to favor exploration, and as we approach the vicinity of the optimum, we could decrease the value of ω in order to perform finer-grain searches. There are many ways to define a decreasing $\omega(t)$. A common one is a linear interpolation between the desired values of $\omega_{Initial}$ and ω_{Final}:

$$\omega(t) = \omega_{Initial} - d\omega$$

$$d\omega = \frac{(\omega_{Initial} - \omega_{Final})}{T}$$

where t is the current iteration and T represents the number of iterations required to reach ω_{Final}, keeping $\omega(t) = \omega_{Final}$ for $t > T$. Another strategy is to select $T =$ MAX_NUM_ITER / N, resetting $\omega(t)$ and applying again the interpolation every N iterations.

Constriction Coefficient

Based on the dynamic analysis of a simplified and deterministic PSO model, Kennedy and Clerc [Clerc02] reformulated the velocity update in terms of the constriction coefficient χ. They also analyzed the convergence properties of the algorithm, obtaining a set of theoretical optimal values for the PSO parameters to control both convergence and the velocity explosion. A simple constriction model for velocity update can be expressed as:

$$\mathbf{V}(t+1) = \chi \cdot [\mathbf{V}(t) + \phi_1 \cdot (\mathbf{x}_{Cognitive\_Best} - \mathbf{x}(t)) + \phi_2 \cdot (\mathbf{x}_{Social\_Best} - \mathbf{x}(t))]$$
$$\mathbf{x}(t+1) = \mathbf{x}(t) + \mathbf{V}(t+1)$$

where χ is a diagonal matrix, whose elements are calculated as:

$$\chi_{jj} = \frac{2 \cdot \kappa}{\left| 2 - \phi_{jj} - \sqrt{\phi_{jj} \cdot (\phi_{jj} - 4)} \right|}$$

and:

$$\phi = \phi_1 + \phi_2, \quad \phi > 4, \quad \chi_{jj} \in (0,1), \quad \kappa \in (0,1)$$

Low values of κ encourage exploitation, whereas high values result in a more exploratory system. Typical values are $\chi_{jj} = 0.7298$ and $\phi_1 = \phi_2 = 2.05$. Notice that this model can be easily converted into the original inertia-based formulation.

Extended Full Model for Velocity Update

The velocity update could include both the global best and the local best particle:

$$\mathbf{V}(t+1) = \omega \cdot \mathbf{V}(t) + \mathbf{\Theta}_1 \otimes (\mathbf{x}_{Cognitive\_Best} - \mathbf{x}(t)) + \mathbf{\Theta}_2 \otimes (\mathbf{g}_{Best} - \mathbf{x}(t)) + \mathbf{\Theta}_3 \otimes (\mathbf{l}_{Best} - \mathbf{x}(t))$$

where typically $\mathbf{\Theta}_i \in U(0,1)$.

Adding Constraints

In an optimization scenario, the constraints define feasible subspaces within the search space of the unconstrained problem. In the original PSO algorithm, each dimension is bounded individually. (See Line 4 of Algorithm 1.) This translates into an axes-aligned hyper-rectangular search space. Therefore, constraints such as $g(\mathbf{x}) \leq \mathbf{b}$ cannot be generally defined. As a result, neither a simple circular search space ($x^2 + y^2 \leq radius^2$), nor a combination of constraints (for example, a rectangular search space with a rectangular hole inside), is supported. Different approaches have been proposed to extend the constraint-handling capabilities of evolutionary algorithms. (For a review, see [Michalewicz96] and [Mezura09].) A simple approach presented in [Hu02] uses the canonical PSO algorithm and introduces two modifications:

- All particles are initialized inside the feasible region.
- After evaluating the population, only particles within the feasible region can update the values of $\mathbf{x}_{Cognitive\_Best}$ and $\mathbf{x}_{Social\_Best}$.

Integer Optimization

Although PSO deals natively with optimization problems of continuous variables, it can also be modified to cope with discrete and mixed-parameter problems. The simplest way to do that is to use the same equations of motion, but round the results of the integer components (at least for the position update) to the nearest integer. In some cases this can result in invalid particles (for example, duplicated elements in a particle are generally not allowed in permutation problems), and particles need to be "fixed" after every position update. The fixing mechanism is problem dependent, but it may consist of making all the elements of a particle different, while keeping their values within a certain range.

Maintaining Diversity

A common problem in numerical optimization is premature convergence—in other words, getting trapped around a local optimum. In stochastic methods, the diversity of the population has a major effect on the convergence of the problem; hence, diversity loss is commonly regarded as a threat to the optimization process. Some ways of favoring diversity are:

- Alternating periodically PSO with other search methods.
- Every α iterations, reinitializing (randomizing) the location of a random number of particles in the swarm.
- Every β stalls, reinitializing the system.
- Including mutation and crossover operators and applying them to the position of a small subset of particles in the swarm.

- Running multiple independent swarms, allowing an occasional exchange of information (for example, $\mathbf{g}_{Best}$) and/or particles between swarms. Furthermore, each swarm could use different search strategies (for example, some could use $\mathbf{l}_{Best}$, some others could use $\mathbf{g}_{Best}$, some could use parameters that favor exploration, some others could use more exploitative ones, and so on).

It is important to notice that the selected networking strategy also has an impact on the diversity of the population. Distributed topologies, such as Ring or Cluster, generate a number of local attractors and tend to maintain higher levels of diversity, leading to good solutions more often than other centralized approaches.

A Note on Randomness

PSO is a stochastic optimization technique that initializes its particles by placing them randomly in the search space. In order to do so, pseudo-random values are drawn from a uniform distribution. The reason is that in the absence of any prior knowledge about the location of the optimum, it is best to distribute the particles randomly, covering as much of the problem space as possible. However, as Figure 2.4.3 (a) shows, the result may be less uniform than desired. The spatial uniformity of the randomized particles can be improved by using Halton point sets, which are uniformly distributed and stochastic-looking sampling patterns, generated by a deterministic formula at low computational cost [Wong97].

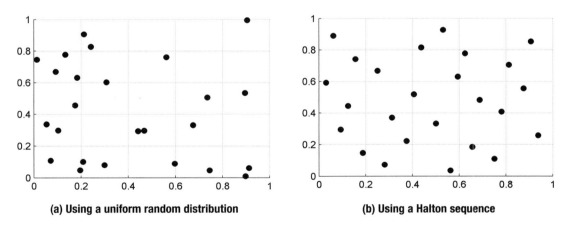

(a) Using a uniform random distribution   (b) Using a Halton sequence

Figure 2.4.3   One instance of two sets of 25 particles initialized in a two-dimensional space using (a) a uniform random distribution and (b) a Halton sequence.

Case Study 1: Typical Benchmarking Functions

There are sets of functions that are commonly used for benchmarking optimization algorithms. These functions tend to have areas with a very low gradient (for example, Rosenbrock's saddle) and/or numerous local optima (for example, Rastrigin's function). Figure 2.4.4 illustrates the 2D versions of three of them. The accompanying CD includes the multidimensional version of a larger set of benchmarking functions together with a PSO algorithm implementation. You are encouraged to experiment with the different PSO parameters, observing the variation in convergence speed and accuracy. More information about different benchmarking functions can be found in [Onwubolu04].

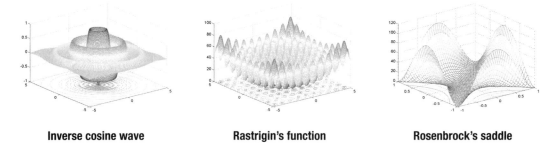

Inverse cosine wave   Rastrigin's function   Rosenbrock's saddle

Figure 2.4.4   2D versions of some common benchmarking functions.

Case Study 2:
Optimization of Physical Parameters for In-Game Vehicle Simulation

To obtain realistic vehicle responses in a game, simplified physical models of their key components are generated. These models contain a number of physical parameters that define the way the vehicle reacts in many situations. Those parameters are often obtained based on experience and a trial-and-error process of selection. Such a manual process tends to be inevitably slow, and as a result, little of the search space is often covered. It is clear that there is room for improvement, and PSO is a good candidate for automating the search process. The only prerequisite is to be able to estimate numerically the quality of each candidate solution. The following example illustrates the general principle. We want to optimize the performance of a car, whose simplified model is shown in Figure 2.4.5. The model includes friction between the tires and the ground, the suspension, and the car's mass distribution. Based on the model's parameters, the particle's components can be defined as:

```
P.X[0] = Forward Friction Coeff.; P.X[1] = Side Friction Coeff.;
P.X[2] = Spring Constant (Rear);  P.X[3] = Damper Constant (Rear);
P.X[4] = Spring Constant (Front); P.X[5] = Damper Constant (Front);
P.X[6] = Mass 1; P.X[7] = Mass 1 location (along Z); P.X[8] = Mass 2;
```

As an example of dimensionality reduction, the value and location of the mass *M3* and the location of the mass *M2* have been fixed. They can be included at any moment in the optimization by extending the dimensionality of the particle.

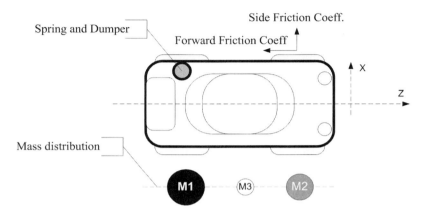

Figure 2.4.5   A simplified physics model of a car.

Most importantly, we need to define an objective function capable of quantifying the response of the vehicle while following a path along a network of roads. The objective function to be minimized could include the following variables: distance to goal on a crash, total distance driven without being on the marked spline, accumulated distance from the car's center of mass to the marked spline (shown as *d* in Figure 2.4.6 (b)), accumulated heading deviation with respect to the selected path, oscillations around the Z-axis, and tilt around the Z-axis on curves (c.f. Figure 2.4.6 (a)). The function can also include big penalties for crashing and in cases where only two wheels are in contact with the road. The final objective function could be a quadratic combination of each of these variables $\mathbf{r}_i$.

$$ObjFunc(\boldsymbol{r}) = \boldsymbol{k} \cdot \boldsymbol{r}_n = \sum_i k_i \cdot \left(\frac{r_i}{\eta_i}\right)^2$$

The normalization constant η_i ensures that all the variables have the same weight (typically between 0 and 1), regardless of their particular ranges. The relative importance of $\mathbf{r}_i$, with respect to the rest of the variables, is represented by the coefficient $\mathbf{k}_i$, which can also be used for scaling the objective function. Squaring $\mathbf{r}_i$ is useful in cases where only the magnitude of $\mathbf{r}_i$ is relevant, ensuring that the objective function does not decrease based on the sign of the variables.

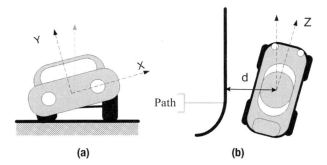

Figure 2.4.6   Illustration of some of the parameters included in the objective function.
(a) Tilt around the Z-axis during a curve. (b) Distance to the path's splines and heading error.

As Algorithm 1 showed, each iteration requires the evaluation of the whole population (in other words, N particles). Therefore, it would be convenient to evaluate N vehicles simultaneously following identical paths.

Case Study 3: Physics-Based Animation of Mechanical Systems

Physics-based animation can improve the gaming experience by adding physical realism and believability to the game. Cloth and hair procedural animation, ragdolls, and general collisions between rigid bodies are some examples featured in many titles. Extending this concept to complex mechanical systems, such as robotic NPCs and vehicles, can result in more realistic behaviors that are in accordance with our experience of how mechanical systems move.

Figure 2.4.7 shows a hexapod NPC robot exhibiting a tripod gait, which is a gait pattern often used by insects and other animals due to its performance and stability. Gait patterns can be defined by a series of parameters (for example, maximum joint angles, feet trajectory, stance phase offset, stance duty factor, step duration) whose values will depend on the physical characteristics of the robot, the environment, the pattern configuration, the task (for example, turn, go forward, climb, and so on), and the task qualifiers (for example, fast, safe, and so on). PSO can be used for finding good values for these parameters. Each gait could be optimized individually by using specialized objective functions and running single-gait simulations. Next, gait transitions could be worked out. Once the optimization is finished, the result would be a hexapod robotic NPC with newly acquired locomotion skills.

The design of the robot can be taken one step further. The configuration of the legs could be optimized by adding the length of their segments and the number of joints into the optimization's parameters list. Ultimately, PSO could be used as a tool for evolving different types of robots by including the number of legs and their position in body coordinates as optimization parameters.

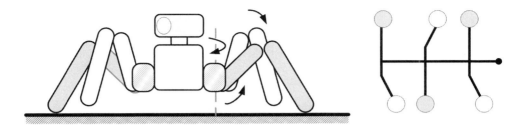

Figure 2.4.7   Snapshot of a hexapod NPC robot using a tripod gait.
The legs shown in white are lifted, while the darkened ones are in stance.

Once the robot design is finished and the gait parameters optimized, the gait controller of the robot would send the appropriate sequence of actions to the different joints, and the physics engine would do the rest. Incidentally, the controller of each joint (typically some flavor of proportional-integral-derivative controller, or PID) could also be optimized using PSO.

Let's see one final example. We want to find the parameters that generate the fastest walking gait for the particular robotic NPC illustrated in Figure 2.4.8. Figure 2.4.8 (b) shows the feet trajectory selected for this gait. This half-ellipse trajectory is defined by two parameters, namely the step height (h) and the step size (s). Another important parameter is the duration of the step (Ts). To improve stability, the torso of the robot is initially tilted sideways to shift its center of mass toward the supporting leg (refer to Figure 2.4.8 (a)). This can be parameterized by a maximum tilt angle (α) and the percentage of step time that the body is tilted toward the leg in stance (Tt) before shifting the weight to the other side. Assuming a 50-percent duty cycle for each leg, the structure of the particles could be P.X[ ]= {h, s, Ts, α, Tt}.

The objective function could be designed as in Case Study 2, taking into account the walking time, the distance to the goal before falling, the accumulative heading error, the accumulative position error with respect to the given path, and the stability of the gait measure in terms of oscillations around various axes. It is worth noticing that the gait parameters obtained are subject to external factors, such as the friction between the robot's feet and the ground. In principle, it could be possible to find a continuous mapping between the walking parameters and different types of terrains by feeding the friction data and the PSO solutions to a neural network or a fuzzy inference system. In that way, the robotic NPC could try to adapt its gait to optimize the walking performance when the type of terrain changes.

Gaits are not the only movements that could be optimized. Learning other actions, such as crouching (refer to Figure 2.4.8 (c)) or climbing stairs would follow the same principles.

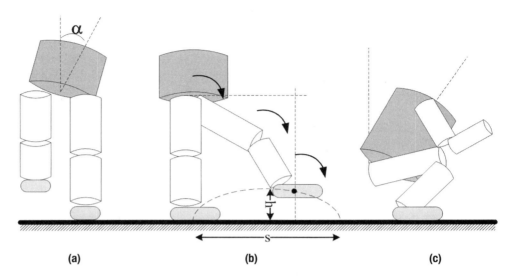

Figure 2.4.8 Illustration of some basic parameters in a humanoid-like robot.
(a) Weight-shifting angle for improving stability, (b) half-ellipse gate parameters,
(c) the different joint angles in a crouching action.

Conclusion

The aim of meta-heuristic optimization algorithms is to provide approximated solutions to complex non-linear optimization problems that more traditional approaches have difficulties addressing. These algorithms are not guaranteed to converge at a good solution, but they are designed to find good approximations to the global optimum with high probability. Population-based algorithms are sensitive to the diversity of their individuals and to their configuration parameters. PSO relies on a small set of intuitive parameters, such as the number of particles, the maximum number of iterations, and the topology of the social network. Often, the mapping between an optimization problem and the function that quantifies the quality of a solution is not unique. In these cases, the quality of the selected objective function has a significant impact on the convergence of the algorithm. This gem has shown a number of variations proposed around the canonical PSO algorithm. The simplicity of the PSO paradigm makes its extension a relatively simple task.

Games are becoming extremely complex and highly parameterized software products. In many cases, the response of different systems is driven, or at least influenced, by sets of parameters stored in configuration files. PSO could be a useful tool for optimizing some of these parameters in an automated fashion. AI, physics, and animation are examples of systems that could benefit from this optimization technique.

References

[Clerc02] Clerc, M. and J. Kennedy. "The Particle Swarm-Explosion, Stability and Convergence in a Multidimensional Complex Space." *IEEE Transactions on Evolutionary Computation* 6 (2002): 58–73.

[Engelbrecht02] Engelbrecht, A.P. *Computational Intelligence: An Introduction*. Wiley, 2002.

[Hassan05] Hassan, R., B. Cohanim, and O. de Weck. "A Comparison of Particle Swarm Optimization and the Genetic Algorithm." *Proceedings of 46th AIAA/ASME/ASCE/AHS/ASC Structures, Structural Dynamics and Materials Conference*. 2005.

[Helwig08] Helwig, S. and R. Wanka. "Theoretical Analysis of Initial Particle Swarm Behavior." *Proceedings of the 10th International Conference on Parallel Problem Solving from Nature* (Sept 2008): 889–898.

[Hu02] Hu, X. and R. Eberhart. "Solving Constrained Nonlinear Optimization Problems with Particle Swarm Optimization." *6th World Multiconference on Systemics, Cybernetics and Informatics* (SCI 2002): 203–206.

[Kennedy95] Kennedy, J. and R. Eberhart. "Particle Swarm Optimization." *Proceeding of IEEE International Conference on Neural Networks* 4 (Dec. 1995): 1942–1948.

[Kennedy01] Kennedy, J., R.C. Eberhart, and Y. Shi. *Swarm Intelligence*. Morgan Kaufmann Publishers, 2001.

[Mezura09] Mezura-Montes, E. *Constraint-Handling in Evolutionary Optimization*. Springer, 2009.

[Michalewicz96] Michalewicz, Z. and M. Schoenauer. "Evolutionary Algorithms for Constrained Parameter Optimization Problems." *Evolutionary Computation* 4 (1996): 1–32.

[Onwubolu04] Onwubolu, G. and B. Babu. *New Optimization Techniques in Engineering*. Springer, 2004.

[Sun04] Sun, J., B. Feng, and Wenbo Xu. "Particle Swarm Optimization with Particles Having Quantum Behavior." *Proc. Cong. Evolutionary Computation* 1 (June 2004): 325–331.

[Wolpert97] Wolpert, D.H. and W.G. Macready. "No Free Lunch Theorems for Search." *IEEE Transactions on Evolutionary Computation* 1.1 (April 1997): 67–82.

[Wong97] Wong, Tien-Tsin, Wai-Shing Luk, and Pheng-Ann Heng. "Sampling with Hammersley and Halton Points." *Journal of Graphics Tools* 2.2 (1997): 9–24.

Improved Numerical Integration with Analytical Techniques

Eric Brown
analytic.spinors@gmail.com

There is a fairly standard recipe for integrating the equation of motion in the context of a game physics engine. Usually the integration technique is based on the Symplectic Euler stepping equations. These equations are fed an acceleration, which is accumulated over the current time step. Such integration methods are useful when the exact nature of the forces acting on an object is unknown. In a video game, the forces that are acting on an object at any given moment are not known beforehand. Therefore, such a numerical technique is very appropriate.

However, though we may not know beforehand the exact nature of the forces that act on an object, we usually know the exact nature of forces that are currently acting on an object. If this were not so, we would not be able to provide the stepping equations with the current acceleration of the body. If it were possible to leverage our knowledge of these current forces, then we might expect to decrease the error of the integration dramatically.

This gem proposes such a method. This method allows for the separation of numerical integration from analytic integration. The numerical integration steps the state of the body forward in time, based on the previous state. The analytic integration takes into account the effect of acceleration acting over the course of the current time step. This gem describes in detail the differences and implications of the integration techniques to aid the physics developer in understanding design choices for position, velocity, and acceleration updates in physics simulation.

As we build up to the introduction of this method, we will first discuss a heuristic model for classifying errors of integration techniques.

Classifying Errors

Often, the method for classifying errors in integration techniques is to label them as first order, second order, and so on. Methods that are first order have an upper bound error on the order of the time step taken to the first power. Methods that are second order have an upper bound error on the order of the time step to the second power. Taking a small number to a large power makes the small number smaller. Thus, higher-order methods yield more accuracy.

Error can also be classified in terms of how well an integrator conserves energy. Integrators might add or remove energy from the system. Some integrators can conserve energy on average. For instance, the semi-implicit, or Symplectic Euler, method is a first-order method, but it conserves energy on average. If an integrator adds energy to the system, the system can become unstable and diverge, especially at higher time steps. The accuracy of a method can affect its stability, but it does not determine it, as shown by the Symplectic Euler method. More often than not, it is the stability of a method that we desire, more than the accuracy.

In this gem we will be taking a different approach to classifying error. This approach is based on the fact that the stepping equations usually assume that the acceleration is constant over the course of a time step. The kinematics of constant acceleration are a problem that can be solved easily and exactly. Comparing the kinematic equations of constant acceleration with the results of a numerical method provides qualitative insight into sources of error in the method.

When derivatives are discretized, it is done by means of a finite difference. Such a finite difference of positions implies that the velocity is constant over the course of the time step. In order to introduce a non-constant velocity, you must explicitly introduce an equation involving acceleration. Similarly, the only way to deal with non-constant acceleration is to explicitly introduce an equation involving the derivative of acceleration. Since many numerical methods do not involve any such equation, we are safe in making the comparison with the kinematic equations for constant acceleration, at least over the course of a single time step.

Kinematics of Constant Acceleration

We know the exact form of the trajectory of particles that are subject to a constant acceleration.

$$v_{n+1} = v_n + a_n \Delta t$$

$$x_{n+1} = x_n + v_n \Delta t + \frac{1}{2} a_n \Delta t^2$$

We can compare this set of equations to the results of common numerical methods in order to gain a qualitative idea about the error in the method. Consider the standard Euler method:

$$v_{n+1} = v_n + a_n \Delta t$$
$$x_{n+1} = x_n + v_n \Delta t$$

This set of equations can be transformed into a set that more closely resembles the kinematic equations by inserting the velocity equation into the position equation:

$$v_{n+1} = v_n + a_n \Delta t$$
$$x_{n+1} = x_n + v_{n-1} \Delta t + a_{n-1} \Delta t^2$$

The appearance of $\mathbf{v}_{n-1}$ in the position equation is due to the fact that we must insert $\mathbf{v}_n$ and must therefore re-index the velocity equation. The differences in form of this equation to the kinematic equations can be considered as qualitatively representative of the error of the method.

We may perform this same procedure with the Symplectic Euler method:

$$v_{n+1} = v_n + a_n \Delta t$$
$$x_{n+1} = x_n + v_{n+1} \Delta t$$

Insert the velocity equation into the position equation to transform to the kinematic form:

$$v_{n+1} = v_n + a_n \Delta t$$
$$x_{n+1} = x_n + v_n \Delta t + a_n \Delta t^2$$

This equation is a much closer match in form to the kinematic equations. We can use this resemblance to justify the fact that the Symplectic Euler method must in some way be better than the standard Euler method.

The Kinematic Integrator

If we are trying to find an integration method that when converted to a kinematic form is identical to the kinematic equations, why not just use the kinematic equations as the integration method?

$$v_{n+1} = v_n + a_n \Delta t$$
$$x_{n+1} = x_n + v_n \Delta t + \frac{1}{2} a_n \Delta t^2$$

If we do this, then we are guaranteed to get trajectories that are exact, within the assumption that acceleration is constant over the course of the time step. However, the accelerations we are usually interested in modeling are not constant over the course of the time step. We must use a value for the acceleration that encapsulates the fact that the acceleration is changing.

We could use the acceleration averaged over the time step, $\overline{a}_n$, as the constant acceleration value. By inserting the average acceleration into the kinematic equations, we achieve a method that we will refer to as the *average acceleration method*. In order to calculate this average exactly, we must analytically integrate the acceleration over the time step, which in many instances can be done easily. The average acceleration method therefore represents a blend between numerical and analytic integration. We are numerically integrating the current position and velocity from the previous position and velocity, but we are analytically integrating accelerations that are acting during the current time step.

Of course, calculating the average acceleration exactly requires that we know how to integrate the particular force in question. Luckily, most forces that are applied in game physics are analytic models that are easily integrated. Calculating the average acceleration from an analytic model of a force is usually just as easy as calculating the acceleration at an instant of time.

If the average acceleration is calculated analytically, then the velocity portion of the kinematic equations produces exact results. However, the position portion would require a double integral in order to achieve an exact result. If the forces that we are dealing with follow simple analytic models, then calculating a double integral is usually just as easy as calculating a single integral.

We will generalize the idea of the average acceleration method in order to introduce the *kinematic integrator*. The kinematic integrator is a set of stepping equations that allow for exact analytic calculation of both the velocity integral and the position integral.

$$v_{n+1} = v_n + dv$$
$$x_{n+1} = x_n + v_n \Delta t + dx$$

The *exact method* uses the following definitions for *dv* and *dx*:

$$dv = \int_0^{\Delta t} a_n \, dt$$

$$dx = \int_0^{\Delta t} \left(\int a_n \, dt \right) dt$$

If we are using the *average acceleration method*, then we define *dv* and *dx* as:

$$dv = \int_0^{\Delta t} a_n \, dt$$

$$dx = \frac{1}{2}(dv)\Delta t$$

In the case of constant acceleration, it is very easy to perform both the single and the double integral. The integral contributions of a constant acceleration are given as:

$$dv = a_n \Delta t$$

$$dx = \frac{1}{2} a_n \Delta t^2$$

If there are multiple forces acting on a body, we can express the integral contributions as a sum of contributions that are due to each force.

$$dv = dv_1 + dv_2 + ...$$

$$dx = dx_1 + dx_2 + ...$$

Thus for the kinematic integrator we accumulate dv's and dx's rather than accelerations. All forces acting on a body provide contributions to dv and dx. The amount that is contributed is dependent on the nature of the force and can usually be calculated exactly. If all forces acting on a body are integrable, then every contribution is exact.

The kinematic integrator can be used to perform the Symplectic Euler method with the following integral contributions:

$$dv = a_n \Delta t$$

$$dx = a_n \Delta t^2$$

This method is useful if the acceleration is not integrable (or if we are too lazy to calculate the integrals). These contributions are not going to be exact, but they will at least conserve energy, which will maintain stability.

The kinematic integrator does not represent a specific integration method, but rather the ability to isolate the portions of the stepping equations that actually require integration. Since the method used to evaluate the integral contributions is not explicitly specified, we have a degree of freedom in choosing which method might be best for a particular force. For instance, if there is a contribution from a constant gravitational force, then we can easily use the exact method. We will see that for some forces we will want to use the average acceleration method. Or we could use the Symplectic Euler method if the force in question is too complicated to integrate or if we are performing a first pass on the implementation of a particular force.

Integral Contributions Due to a Spring Force

Probably one of the most common forces, next to a constant uniform force, is a spring force. The spring force is proportional to the displacement of the spring from equilibrium. This results in the following equation of motion:

$$a = -\frac{k}{m}(x - l) = -\omega^2 (x - l)$$

The solution of this equation of motion is analytically solvable and is given by:

$$x - l = A\cos(\omega t) + B\sin(\omega t)$$
$$v = -\omega A\sin(\omega t) + \omega B\cos(\omega t)$$

Using this exact trajectory, we can determine the integral contributions:

$$dx = x_n(c-1) + v_n\left(\frac{s}{\omega} - \Delta t\right) + (l - lc)$$
$$dv = x_n(-\omega s) + v_n(c-1) + (\omega l s)$$

where c and s represent the cosine and sine, respectively, of $\omega(t)$. We could represent this calculation as a matrix operation.

$$\begin{pmatrix} dv \\ dx \end{pmatrix} = \begin{pmatrix} -\omega s & c-1 & \omega l s \\ c-1 & \dfrac{s}{\omega} - \Delta t & l - lc \end{pmatrix} \begin{pmatrix} x_n \\ v_n \\ 1 \end{pmatrix}$$

The components of this matrix depend on the size of the time step Δt, the mass of the body m, the strength of the spring k, and the equilibrium position of the spring l. The components of the matrix can be cached and reused until any of these parameters change. In many instances, these parameters do not change for the lifetime of the spring. Thus, the calculation of the integral contributions of a spring is relatively trivial—in other words, six multiplies and four adds.

We can consider that the spring that we have been discussing is anchored to an infinitely rigid object at the origin, since we have only taken into account the action of the spring on a single body, and the spring coordinates are the same as the body coordinates. It is only slightly more complicated to calculate the integral contributions due to a spring that connects two movable bodies.

Multiple Forces

Before discussing the integral contributions of other possible forces, we need to discuss what happens when multiple forces act on a body.

If all of the forces acting on a body depend only on time, then the result of accumulating exact integral contributions will be exact. But consider the case where at least one of the forces depends on the position of the body, such as the spring force.

The integral contribution of the spring takes into account the position of the body at intermediate values as the spring acts over the course of the time interval. However, the calculation is not aware of intermediate changes in position that are due to other forces. The result is a very slight numerical error in the resulting trajectory of the particle.

As an example, consider two springs that are acting on the same body. For simplicity, both springs are attached to an infinitely rigid body at the origin, and the rest length of both springs is zero. The springs have spring constants k_1 and k_2. The acceleration becomes:

$$a = -(\omega_1)^2 x - (\omega_2)^2 x$$

If we are to handle these forces separately, then we would exactly calculate the integral contributions of two springs, with frequencies ω_1 and ω_2, and accumulate the results.

The springs can also be combined into a single force.

$$a = -\left[\sqrt{(\omega_1)^2 + (\omega_2)^2}\right]^2 x$$

In this case, only a single integral contribution would be calculated. It might be surprising to discover that these two methods produce different results. The second method is exact, while the first contains a slight amount of numerical error. This seems to imply that:

$$\int(a_1 + a_2)dt \neq \int a_1 dt + \int a_2 dt$$

which is usually not true. However, in the current circumstance, if the acceleration is a function of the position, which in turn is a function of the acceleration, then the integrals have feedback. The effect of this feedback is that we cannot separate the sum into independent integrals, since the independent integrals will not receive feedback from each other.

If the acceleration only depends on time, there is no feedback, and the integrals can safely be separated. Because of this, you may want to separate out forces that depend only on time and accumulate their integral contributions as a group. The integral contributions of these forces can be safely added together without introducing numerical error. Unfortunately, most of the forces that are applicable to game physics depend on the position of the body.

Though the error due to multiple forces is incredibly small, it represents a tiny violation of energy conservation. If this violation persists for long enough, then the trajectory can eventually diverge. The error due to multiple forces is initially much less than the error in the Symplectic Euler method, but it can eventually grow until it is out of control.

Since we can integrate exactly the system with two springs, we can use this example to gauge the error present in the different methods for calculating the integral contributions. Results of this error calculation are contained in the figures. The first figure contains the results of integrating one spring; the second figure represents errors due to integrating two springs. The integration takes place over one half of the period of the two-spring system.

The Symplectic Euler method as well as the pulse method (which will be introduced later) both conserve energy on average. Neither the average acceleration method nor the exact method conserve energy over long intervals of time. It takes quite a while, but the exact method will eventually diverge. The average acceleration method will eventually dampen out. For this reason, the average acceleration method is preferred if the integration is going to take place over a long interval.

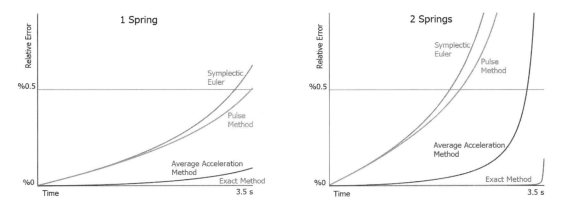

Figure 2.5.1 The relative errors in the case of one spring and two springs.

Integral Contributions of a Pulse

One solution to the problem due to multiple forces is to approximate the action of the force as a pulse. A pulse is a force that acts very briefly over the course of the time step. A perfect pulse acts instantaneously. Pulses acting at the beginning of the time step do not depend on intermediate values of position or velocity; therefore, pulses are immune to the multiple-force problems.

Consider a rectangular pulse. The area under the curve of a rectangular pulse is $dv = adt$, where dt is the width of the pulse, and a is the magnitude of the pulse. It is possible to shrink the width of the pulse while maintaining the same area. To do this, we must, of course, increase the magnitude of the pulse. If we allow the pulse width to go to zero, the height diverges to infinity. However, the product of the width and the height is still equal to dv. In the case where $dv = 1$, there is a special name for this infinite pulse. It is called a *delta function*, and is denoted as $\delta(t)$. The delta function is zero at all values of t, except at $t = 0$. At $t = 0$, the delta function is equal to infinity. Integrating the delta function is very easy to do.

$$\int_a^b \delta(t)dt = 1$$

for all values of a and b where $a < 0 < b$. If the interval between a and b does not contain zero, then the result of the integral is zero.

To represent the force as a pulse, we define the acceleration as:

$$a = dv\delta(t)$$

Here, dv is the area under the curve of this instantaneous pulse, as previously described. Integrating this acceleration is easy to do:

$$\int a\,dt = dv$$

Integrating the position contribution is now just integrating a constant.

$$dx = dv\int_0^{\Delta t} dt = dv\Delta t$$

We can choose dv as the amount of acceleration we want to pack into the pulse. If we want to pack all of the acceleration due to an arbitrary force into the pulse, then we use the average value of the acceleration $\overline{a}_n$. This produces stepping equations of the form:

$$v_{n+1} = v_n + \overline{a}_n\Delta t$$

$$x_{n+1} = x_n + v_n\Delta t + \overline{a}_n\Delta t^2$$

In a more familiar form, the stepping equations for the pulse would appear as:

$$v_{n+1} = v_n + \overline{a}_n\Delta t$$

$$x_{n+1} = x_n + v_{n+1}\Delta t$$

If you make the assumption that the acceleration is constant over the time interval, then you can replace $\overline{a}_n$ with a_n. Doing this, you will arrive back at the stepping equations for the standard Symplectic Euler method. This gives meaningful insight into the Symplectic Euler method. It is a method that assumes that the acceleration is constant over the course of the time step and delivers all of the acceleration in an instantaneous pulse at the beginning of the time step. Since pulses can be accumulated without introducing error, the Symplectic Euler method can be considered to be an exact solution to forces of an approximated form. Since the method is exact, it intrinsically conserves energy. The error in the method is entirely due to the differences between the actual form of the force and the approximate form of the pulse.

Integral Contributions of Collision Forces

One very common thing that needs to be done in a game physics engine is to resolve collisions. To calculate our collision, we will assume that the forces due to the collision act within some subinterval that fits entirely within our given time interval. The nature of the force does not matter as much as the fact that it operates on a very small timescale and achieves the desired result.

For simplicity, we will assume that the object has normal incidence with a plane boundary. We will also assume that the collision with the boundary is going to take place within the time interval.

To handle the collision correctly, we should sweep the trajectory of the body between x_n and x_{n+1} and find the exact position and the exact time where the collision begins to take place. If we want to find the projected position at the next time step x_{n+1}, we should wait to apply the collision force until all other forces have been applied, so that the projected next position is as accurate as possible.

For the purpose of simplification, we will consider that the trajectory is a straight line that connects the position x_n with x_{n+1}. The position of the body at some intermediate value of the time step is given by:

$$x_f = x_n(1-f) + x_{n+1}(f)$$

where f is the fraction of the time step that represents the moment of impact. The intermediate velocity is simplified as well, to be:

$$v_f = v_n(1-f) + v_{n+1}(f)$$

With this physically inaccurate yet simplified trajectory, we can perform a sweep of the body against the collision boundary. The result of this sweep will determine the time fraction f. This will tell us the position and velocity (almost) of the body at the moment of impact. To determine the force that is applied in order to resolve the collision, we need to apply a pulse force that reflects the component of velocity v_f about the contact plane. This reflection incorporates the interaction of the body with the contact surface; thus, the result should incorporate surface friction. For now, we will assume that there is no friction.

To apply the pulse force, we will begin by applying a constant force over a small subinterval of the time step. The subinterval begins at time $f\Delta t$ and ends at $(f + df)\Delta t$. The velocity of the body at the end of the subinterval is given by:

$$v_{f+df} = v_f + a_v df$$

According to our initial simplification, the velocity is aligned with the normal of the contact plane. Thus, all of the velocity is reflected. We choose a_v to enact this reflection.

$$a_v = \frac{-2v_f}{df}$$

The integral contributions of this force in the limit that $df \rightarrow 0$ are given by:

$$dv_v - 2v_f$$

$$dx_v = 0$$

Since this force pulse does not contribute anything to the position integral, the application of this force does not change the value of x_{n+1} from what it would have been. Thus, the value of x_{n+1} will still violate the collision constraint.

We need to apply a second force pulse, which moves the position of the body out of the collision surface. Assuming that the body has normal incidence to the plane, then the amount the body needs to be pushed is given by $\Delta x = x_f - x_{n+1}$. Again, we are going to apply a constant force on a subinterval. The acceleration of this force a_x is determined by considering the kinematic equations for constant acceleration.

$$a_x = \frac{2(\Delta x - v_f df)}{df^2}$$

The integral contributions for this acceleration as $df \to 0$ are:

$$dv_x = -2\left(\frac{x_{n+1} - x_n}{\Delta t} - vf\right)$$

$$dx_x = -\Delta x$$

Adding these two sets of contributions together gives the final result for the collision force. This set of contributions can be expressed in terms of the position at the beginning and end of the interval, as well as the parameter f, which represents the moment when the collision first begins to happen.

$$dv = -2\left(\frac{x_{n+1} - x_n}{\Delta t}\right)$$

$$dx = -(x_{n+1} - x_n)(1 - f)$$

Integral Contributions of Viscous Forces

A viscous force is a force that is related to, and usually opposing, the velocity of an object.

$$F = -kv$$

The equation can be solved for the velocity in terms of the constant k and the mass m. This is done by expressing the acceleration as the derivative of velocity.

$$\frac{\partial v}{\partial t} = -\frac{k}{m}v$$

This equation can be integrated to get:

$$v = v_n e^{-\frac{k}{m}t}$$

$$x = x_n - v_n \frac{m}{k} e^{-\frac{k}{m}t}$$

The integral contributions of this force can be determined exactly and are given by:

$$dv = v_n \left(e^{-\frac{k}{m}\Delta t} - 1 \right)$$

$$dx = -v_n \left(\frac{m}{k} e^{-\frac{k}{m}\Delta t} + \Delta t \right)$$

It may very well be sufficient to approximate the exponent function with the first-order Taylor series expansion. Since the force dissipates energy, exactness for the sake of accuracy is not required.

$$dv = -\frac{k}{m} v_n \Delta t$$

$$dx = -\frac{m}{k} v_n$$

Viscosity can be applied in an anisotropic fashion, meaning that the viscosity constant k can actually be a vector $\vec{k}$. The viscosity force then contains the dot product of $\vec{k}$ with v_n.

A simple method of introducing surface contact friction is to generate an anisotropic viscous force in the event that a collision is determined. The viscosity in the direction of the collision surface normal can be tuned separately from the components in the surface plane in order to decouple the restitution of reflected velocity with sliding friction. Of course, this general viscosity force does not accurately model dry friction, where there is a transition from static to kinetic friction. But it is a good place to start.

Integral Contributions of Constraint Forces

Many physics engines offer a variety of constraints on objects. We will not calculate the integral contributions of every possible constraint, but rather suggest a general mechanism of determining resolution forces to enforce that constraints are satisfied. In many physics engines, collisions are handled as constraints. The pattern for evaluating the resolution forces for a collision can apply to all constraints. This general pattern is as follows.

1. Approximate the trajectory and find the value of f, which represents the moment when the constraint violation began.
2. Forces are applied as pulses. Using the Jacobian of the constraint equations to determine the direction of the force, the magnitude is calculated in order to bring the velocity v_{n+1} into compliance with the constraint.
3. If needed, another force pulse is applied in the same direction in order to bring the position v_{n+1} into compliance.
4. The contributions for both pulses are added together.

Summary

When using the kinematic integrator, the state of a body is defined by the position x_n and velocity v_n at the beginning of the current time step t_n.

The state of a body is stepped forward in time using the kinematic integration equations:

$$v_{n+1} = v_n + dv$$

$$x_{n+1} = x_n + v_n \Delta t + dx$$

The quantities dv and dx represent the portions of the stepping equations that can be analytically integrated per force and accumulated.

The integral contributions can be calculated using the exact method as:

$$dv = \int_0^{\Delta t} a_n \, dt$$

$$dx = \int_0^{\Delta t} \left(\int a_n \, dt \right) dt$$

where the inner integral of dx is indefinite, and the outer integral is a definite integral.

The integral contributions for the average acceleration method are:

$$dv = \int_0^{\Delta t} a_n \, dt$$

$$dx = \frac{1}{2} dv \Delta t$$

The integral contributions for a pulse are:

$$dv = \int_0^{\Delta t} a_n \, dt$$

$$dx = dv \Delta t$$

If desired the integral contributions of the Symplectic Euler method are defined as:

$$dv = a_n \Delta t$$

$$dx = a_n \Delta t^2$$

These different methods can be mixed, depending on the desired results. When there is more than one force applied that depends on position, then the average acceleration method can be much more accurate than the exact method.

The acceleration contributions for the spring with a spring constant k and a natural length l are:

$$\omega = \sqrt{\frac{k}{m}}$$

$$c = \cos(\omega \Delta t)$$

$$s = \sin(\omega \Delta t)$$

$$dv = x_n(-\omega s) + v_n(c - 1) + (\omega l s)$$

$$dx = x_n(c - 1) + v_n\left(\frac{s}{\omega} - \Delta t\right) + (l - lc)$$

The contribution of a viscous force, with a viscosity constant v, is:

$$dv = -\frac{k}{m}v_n \Delta t$$

$$dx = -\frac{m}{k}v_n$$

For a collision response force, the integral contributions are defined as:

$$dv = -2\frac{x_{n+1} - x_n}{\Delta t}$$

$$dx = -(x_{n+1} - x_n)(1 - f)$$

where f is the fraction of the time step when the collision begins.

For a general constraint, the generic framework is as follows:

1. Approximate the trajectory and find the value of f, which represents the moment when the constraint violation began.

2. Forces are applied as pulses. Using the Jacobian of the constraint equations to determine the direction of the force, the magnitude is calculated in order to bring the velocity v_{n+1} into compliance with the constraint.

3. If needed, another force pulse is applied in the same direction in order to bring the position x_{n+1} into compliance.

4. The contributions for both pulses are added together.

Conclusion

Using a well-chosen mix of numerical integration and analytic integration, it is possible to achieve exact trajectories for some force models. If there are multiple forces applied, error may accumulate, since the analytic integration of individual forces cannot take other forces into account. Using the average acceleration method for calculating the integral contributions can result in relative errors that are millions of times smaller than the errors from the Symplectic Euler method alone.

We have seen that the Symplectic Euler method can be thought of as an exact method, which approximates the force as pulses. The errors in this method are due to this misrepresentation of the force.

This gem has demonstrated the fact that the kinematics of simple physical models, which are prevalent in game-related physics, can be leveraged to dramatically reduce and sometimes eliminate the error of integration methods.

Going forward, work on this topic might include determining the integral contributions due to the different flavors of translational and rotational constraints. Also, determining whether there is a way to pre-accumulate elements of the acceleration integrands prior to integration would provide a very natural solution to the problems that arise because of multiple forces that depend on position.

2.6

What a Drag: Modeling Realistic Three-Dimensional Air and Fluid Resistance

B. Charles Rasco, Ph.D., President, Smarter Than You Software

charlie@smarterthanyou.com

Basic physics simulations have been around in games for quite a while. But beyond simple gravity, simple 2D collisions, and not-so-simple 3D collisions, there is a lack of further refinement of object motion. Drag physics is one area that has not been adequately addressed. Most games simulate drag physics with a simple linear model, if they simulate it at all. This gem demonstrates and contrasts two different mathematical models that simulate drag: a linear drag model and a quadratic drag model. The quadratic drag model is more realistic, but both models have applicability to different situations in physical simulations for many different types of games. The gem also defines and explains relevant parameters of drag physics, such as the terminal velocity and the characteristic decay time.

The linear three-dimensional drag problem and both the one-dimensional linear and parts of the quadratic drag problems are discussed in [Davis86]. This gem adds a stable implementation of quadratic drag in three dimensions. The integrals used in this article may be found in any calculus book or on the web [Salas82, MathWorld].

Games could use improved drag physics for many things: artillery shells, bullets from smaller guns, golf ball trajectories, car racing games (air resistance is the main force that limits how fast a car can go), boats in water, and space games that involve landing on alien planets. Even casual games could use improved drag physics. The quadratic drag model in this gem was developed to make the iPhone and iPod Touch app *Golf Globe* by ProGyr. In this game, the user tries to get a golf ball onto a tee inside a snow globe. Originally the game was designed with linear water resistance, but it did not feel quite right. This was the motivation to improve the water resistance to the more realistic, and more complicated, quadratic model. I have a real golf ball in a snow globe and have never been able to get it onto the tee. To be honest, I have never gotten the ball on the tee in the *Golf Globe* game on the 3D eagle level, but in the game the easy levels are much simpler because the easier levels are two-dimensional.

Physics

This section provides the general mathematics and physics background for both the linear and the quadratic drag models.

Three-Dimensional Physics

The forces for the linear model are:

$$\boldsymbol{F} = m\boldsymbol{a} = -mg\hat{\boldsymbol{k}} - \alpha\boldsymbol{v}$$

And the forces for the quadratic model are given by:

$$\boldsymbol{F} = m\boldsymbol{a} = -mg\hat{\boldsymbol{k}} - \beta v^2 \hat{\boldsymbol{n}}$$

where $v^2 = v_x^{\,2} + v_y^{\,2} + v_z^{\,2}$ is the velocity squared, and $\hat{\boldsymbol{n}} = \boldsymbol{v}/|\boldsymbol{v}| = \left(n_x, n_y, n_z \right)$ is the unit vector that points in the direction of the velocity.

The first term of both equations is the force due to gravity, and in my representation down is the negative z direction. The direction of gravity depends on your coordinate system. The second term of both equations is the drag term. I chose the alpha and beta as different labels for the drag coefficient in order to keep it clear which version of air resistance I am referencing. For both models, if this value is big, there is a lot of fluid resistance, and if it is small, there is little fluid resistance. This parameter should always have positive value and does not actually need to remain constant. It can change if an object changes shape or angle from the direction of the fluid motion. A sail in the wind does not have a constant value, but changes depending on how taut the sail is and how perpendicular it is relative to the wind, among other factors. The velocity in these equations is the velocity of the object in the fluid, so if there is wind, then it would be the velocity of the object minus the velocity of the wind.

The linear equation is solvable in a complete analytical closed-form solution. Since the quadratic mixes all of the components of the velocity vector together, it is not solvable in a closed form, but we can solve it numerically. In addition, the quadratic drag model has the advantage of being a better approximation of realistic air and fluid resistance. Interestingly, both are exactly solvable when considered as one-dimensional problems. This will be discussed in more detail later in this gem.

Conversion from Three-Dimensional Physics to One-Dimensional Physics

To convert the drag problem from three dimensions into one dimension, we need to break the object's motion into two components: motion along the velocity (one dimension) and motion perpendicular to the current velocity (two dimensions). The drag force only acts along the current direction of velocity; thus, we can treat it as a one-dimensional problem.

The unit vector in the direction of the velocity is given by $\hat{n} = v/|v| = (n_x, n_y, n_z)$, or if the velocity is zero it is valid to set $\hat{n} = 0$. Setting the normal to zero works because if the object is not moving, there will be no fluid resistance. The components of the forces along the direction of motion and perpendicular to the direction of motion are shown in Figure 2.6.1. We can update the velocity along the current direction of motion as well as perpendicular to it once it is decomposed this way.

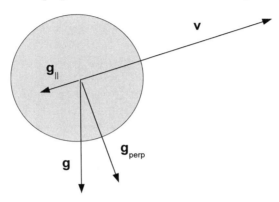

Figure 2.6.1 Breaking three-dimensional space into components along the direction of motion and perpendicular to the current direction of motion.

One-Dimensional Solutions

For a one-dimensional solution, we start from the one-dimensional version of Newton's Second Law, $F = MA$, and from the definition of acceleration, $a = dv/dt$. If the force is a function of the velocity alone, then these two equations can be combined to get time as a function of velocity, as shown here:

$$t = \int_0^t dt = \int_{v_0}^{v_f} \frac{m\,dv}{F(v)}$$

The force equations that are relevant to the present matter are $\mathbf{F} = mg\cos(\theta) - \alpha\mathbf{v}$, the linear fluid resistance equation, and $\mathbf{F} = mg\cos(\theta) \pm \beta v^2$, the quadratic fluid resistance equation. The cosine in these equations is the cosine of the angle between the current velocity and the vertical. For the linear equation, the negative sign in front of the velocity term means the force always opposes the direction of motion. If the velocity is positive, then the force is in the negative direction. If the velocity is negative, then the force is in the positive direction, which is taken care of automatically by the linear equation. In the quadratic equation, the different sign must be applied based on which way the object is traveling, since squaring the velocity loses the directional information.

For the linear equation, we have:

$$t = \int_0^t dt = \int_{v_0}^{v_f} \frac{m dv}{mg\cos(\theta) - \alpha v} = \frac{1}{g\cos(\theta)} \int_{v_0}^{v_f} \frac{dv}{1 - v/v_{t1}}$$

where $v_{t1} = mg\cos(\theta)/\alpha$ is the terminal velocity. There is one other variable that describes the motion, and that is the characteristic time, $\tau_1 = m/\alpha$. The characteristic time is a measure of how quickly (or slowly) the object speeds up or slows down to the terminal velocity, and it shows up in the equations after we integrate. The formula for the quadratic drag model's terminal velocity and characteristic time is different than the linear drag model's characteristic time and terminal velocity. The linear drag models are labeled with subscript 1s. Another way to calculate the terminal velocity is to set the force equation to zero and solve for the velocity. This integral is evaluated with a change of variables $x = 1 - v/v_{t1}$, so that $dx = -dv/v_{t1}$.

$$t = -\tau_1 \int_{1-v_0/v_{t1}}^{1-v_f/v_{t1}} dx/x = -\tau_1 \log\left(\frac{1 - v_f/v_{t1}}{1 - v_0/v_{t1}}\right)$$

Lastly, we solve this somewhat intimidating equation for v_f, which turns out nicely as:

$$v_{f1} = (v_0 - v_{t1})\exp(-t/\tau_1) + v_{t1} \quad (1)$$

If you feel like practicing taking limits, see what happens when the air resistance coefficient goes to zero. The traditional $v_f = v_0 + g\cos(\theta)t$ pops up. The first few terms in this expansion are useful if you want to approximate the exact solution in order to avoid the expensive exponential function calls.

For the quadratic case, we solve the equations in the same way. We start with the general equation:

$$t = \int_{v_0}^{v_f} \frac{m dv}{mg\cos(\theta) \pm \beta v^2} = \frac{m}{\beta} \int_{v_0}^{v_f} \frac{dv}{mg\cos(\theta)/\beta \pm v^2} = \frac{m}{\beta} \int_{v_0}^{v_f} \frac{dv}{v_{t2}^2 \pm v^2}$$

From this equation we define the terminal velocity, $v_{t2} = \sqrt{mg\cos(\theta)/\beta}$, and the characteristic time is (not obvious from the equation) $\tau_2 = \sqrt{m/\beta g \cos(\theta)}$, which shows up after we integrate. Integrating this equation is straightforward. Although related, the plus version and the minus version are different integrals, and we need to evaluate both.

First, let us do the integral when the terminal velocity term (labeled with subscript 2s for the quadratic model) and the velocity square terms have the same sign. This is the case where the force of gravity and the fluid resistance are in the same direction, which happens when the particle is traveling up and both forces are pointing down.

To keep track of the overall sign relative to the velocity direction, we introduce the variable, *sign*, which is either 1 or −1, on the outside of the integral. This is important to get the correct overall sign compared to the direction of the velocity unit vector, $\hat{n}$. We continue to solve for the time as a function of initial and final velocity to obtain:

$$t = sign\frac{m}{\beta}\int_{v_0}^{v_f}\frac{dv}{v^2 + v^2_{t2}} = sign\frac{m}{\beta}\frac{1}{v_{t2}}\left(\tan^{-1}\left(\frac{v_f}{v_{t2}}\right) - \tan^{-1}\left(\frac{v_0}{v_{t2}}\right)\right) = sign\,\tau_2\left(\tan^{-1}\left(\frac{v_f}{v_{t2}}\right) - \tan^{-1}\left(\frac{v_0}{v_{t2}}\right)\right)$$

Now we solve this equation for the final velocity and obtain:

$$v_f = v_t\tan\left(\tan^{-1}\left(\frac{v_0}{v_{t2}}\right) + sign\frac{t}{\tau_2}\right) \quad (2)$$

Secondly, we solve for the case where the terminal velocity and velocity squared terms have opposite signs:

$$t = sign\frac{m}{\beta}\int_{v_0}^{v_f}\frac{dv}{v^2 - v^2_{t2}} = sign\,\tau_2\left(\frac{1}{2}\ln\left(\left|\frac{v_f - v_{t2}}{v_f + v_{t2}}\right|\right) - \frac{1}{2}\ln\left(\left|\frac{v_0 - v_{t2}}{v_0 + v_{t2}}\right|\right)\right)$$

There is a relevant connection between the inverse hyperbolic tangent and the natural log of the form:

$$\tanh^{-1}(z) = \frac{1}{2}\ln(\frac{1+z}{1-z}) \text{ for } -1 < z < 1$$

The absolute value bars from the integral are important in order to get the equation to involve the inverse hyperbolic tangent correctly. We must answer whether the initial and final velocities are bigger than the terminal velocity. In addition, given that the initial velocity is less than the terminal velocity, is the final velocity necessarily less than the terminal velocity? It turns out that it is (see the solution below), and it is acceptable to convert both natural logarithms to inverse hyperbolic tangents. A similar question can be asked if the initial velocity is greater then the terminal velocity.

So there are four different cases with which we need to deal: $v_0 < v_{t2}$, $v_0 > v_{t2}$, $v_0 = v_{t2}$, and $v_{t2} = 0$.

For the first case $v_0 < v_{t2}$:

$$t = sign\,\tau_2\left(\frac{1}{2}\ln(\frac{v_{t2} - v_f}{v_{t2} + v_f}) - \frac{1}{2}\ln(\frac{v_{t2} - v_0}{v_{t2} + v_0})\right) = -sign\,\tau_2\left(\tan^{-1}(\frac{v_f}{v_{t2}}) - \tan^{-1}(\frac{v_0}{v_{t2}})\right)$$

and solving for the final velocity:

$$v_f = v_{t2}\tanh\left(\tanh^{-1}(\frac{v_0}{v_{t2}}) - sign\frac{t}{\tau_2})\right) \quad (3a)$$

For the second case $v_0 > v_{t2}$:

$$t = sign\, \tau_2 \left(\frac{1}{2} \ln(\frac{v_f - v_{t2}}{v_{t2} + v_f}) - \frac{1}{2} \ln(\frac{v_0 - v_{t2}}{v_{t2} + v_0}) \right) = -sign\, \tau_2 \left(\tan^{-1}(\frac{v_{t2}}{v_f}) - \tan^{-1}(\frac{v_{t2}}{v_0}) \right)$$

and solving for the final velocity:

$$v_f = v_{t2} \tanh\left(\tanh^{-1}(\frac{v_{t2}}{v_0}) - sign\frac{t}{\tau_2}) \right) \quad (3b)$$

For the third case, $v_0 = v_{t2}$, where the object begins traveling at the terminal velocity in the same direction as the force of gravity, we get:

$$v_f = v_0 \quad (3c)$$

There are several ways to arrive at this result. We can take a limit of both of the first two cases, Equations (3a) and (3b), or if we look at the force in the quadratic force equation, it is zero, hence the object must travel at a constant velocity.

And lastly is the case when the terminal velocity is identically zero, $v_{t2} = 0$. It is easiest to start from the original equation and solve like the previous cases.

$$t = -\frac{m}{\beta} \int_{v_0}^{v_f} \frac{dv}{v^2} = \frac{m}{\beta}\left(\frac{1}{v_f} - \frac{1}{v_0} \right)$$

As previously, we solve this for the final velocity:

$$v_f = \frac{v_0}{1 + \beta t v_0 / m} \quad (3d)$$

All right, this is all the information we need to solve for the linear and quadratic three-dimensional cases, and we now transition to solving the three-dimensional linear case.

Solution of the Three-Dimensional Linear Case

We could solve the linear three-dimensional case in a similar manner as we solve the quadratic version. However, we choose to treat it as three separate one-dimensional problems because the results can be used by the AI in your game. The previous equations are modified to suit each of the Cartesian directions x, y, and z. Again, gravity is in the negative z direction. The solutions of the three different velocity equations are:

$$v_{xf} = v_{x0} \exp(-t/\tau_1)$$
$$v_{yf} = v_{y0} \exp(-t/\tau_1)$$

and

$$v_{zf} = (v_{z0} - v_{tl}) \exp(-t/\tau_1) + v_{tl}$$

with $v_{tl} = -mg/\alpha$ and $\tau_1 = m/\alpha$. The terminal velocities in the horizontal direction are zero.

If we integrate these equations with respect to time, then we get the position as a function of time.

$$x = v_{x0}\tau_1(1 - \exp(-t/\tau_1)) + x_0$$
$$y = v_{y0}\tau_1(1 - \exp(-t/\tau_1)) + y_0$$

and

$$z = (v_{z0} - v_{tl})\tau_1(1 - \exp(-t/\tau_1)) + v_{tl}t + z_0$$

The complete distance equations are useful for AI targeting, AI pathfinding, and calculating targeting info for players, without actually propagating the solutions forward in time step by step. In general, the distance equations are well approximated for most video games with $x = x_0 + vt$, since the time for most games is very small and is much faster than updating with the complete position equations.

Solution of the Three-Dimensional Quadratic Case

The three-dimensional quadratic equations are $F = ma = -mg\hat{k} - \beta v^2 \hat{n}$, $v^2 = v_x^2 + v_y^2 + v_z^2$, $\hat{n} = v/|v| = (n_x, n_y, n_z)$. It is impossible to solve these as three independent equations since they are all coupled by the quadratic term of the fluid resistance. One way to solve this is to break the motion into two directions, along the current velocity and perpendicular to the current velocity, and then update the velocity based on the force calculated.

Along the direction of motion, the force is $F_{parallel} = -mgn_z - \beta v^2$, where n_z is the z component of $\hat{n}$ and is equal to negative of the cosine of the angle between the direction of motion $\hat{n}$ and the gravity vector. Notice that the drag term is always negative since it is in the opposite direction as the current velocity.

Perpendicular to the direction of motion, the forces are $F_{perp} = F - F_{parallel}\hat{n} = -mg\{n_x n_z, n_y n_z, 1 - n_z^2\}$. If the velocity is either straight up or straight down, $n_z = \pm 1$ and $n_x = n_y$, there is no component of force perpendicular to the current velocity. And if the velocity is completely horizontal, the perpendicular force is completely in the negative z direction. If you have a different coordinate system, this equation will look slightly different.

For the motion along the velocity normal, there are three different cases to consider: $n_z > 0$, $n_z < 0$, and $n_z = 0$. If $n_z > 0$, the object is moving upwards, the opposite direction from gravity, and the fluid resistance is in the same direction as gravity. If $n_z < 0$, then the object is moving in the same direction as gravity, and the fluid resistance force is in the opposite direction as gravity. Lastly, if $n_z = 0$, then the object is moving horizontally, and gravity has no effect on horizontal motion.

For $n_z > 0$, the relevant solution is Equation (2) with $v_{t2} = \sqrt{mgn_z/\beta}$, $\tau_2 = \sqrt{m/\beta gn_z}$, and $sign = -1$. The velocity is:

$$v_f = v_t \tan\left(\tan^{-1}\left(\frac{v_0}{v_{t2}}\right) - \frac{t}{\tau_2} \right)$$

For $n_z < 0$, the relevant solution is Equation (3a), (3b), (3c), or (3d) depending on the current velocity relevant to the current terminal velocity with $v_{t2} = \sqrt{mgn_z/\beta}$, $\tau_2 = \sqrt{m/\beta gn_z}$, and $sign = -1$. The velocity update is:

$$v_f = v_{t2} \tanh\left(\tanh^{-1}\left(\frac{v_0}{v_{t2}}\right) + \frac{t}{\tau_2} \right) \text{ for } v_0 < v_{t2}$$

$$v_f = v_{t2} \tanh\left(\tanh^{-1}\left(\frac{v_{t2}}{v_0}\right) + \frac{t}{\tau_2} \right) \text{ for } v_0 > v_{t2}$$

$$v_f = v_0 \text{ for } v_0 = v_{t2}$$

or

$$v_f = \frac{v_0}{1 + \beta t v_0 / m} \text{ for } v_{t2} = 0$$

Notice that the characteristic time for the last instance is undefined, but it is never used in the solution, so there should not be a problem.

For the force perpendicular to the initial velocity, the updated velocity is the same as Equation (3) with $v_0 = 0$ and its own distinct terminal velocity, $v_{t3} = \sqrt{-mg\sqrt{n_x^2 + n_y^2}/\beta}$, and characteristic time, $\tau_3 = \sqrt{-m/\beta g\sqrt{n_x^2 + n_y^2}}$. This leads to:

$$v_{fperp} = v_{t3} \tanh\left(\frac{t}{\tau_3}\right)\{n_x n_z, n_y n_z, 1 - n_z^2\}$$

For most cases this can be approximated (since the characteristic time is usually large and the update time is usually small for games) as:

$$v_{fperp} \approx \frac{v_{t3}t}{\tau_3}\{n_x n_z, n_y n_z, 1 - n_z^2\} = -gt\{n_x n_z, n_y n_z, 1 - n_z^2\} \tag{4}$$

This last equation should look familiar. So usually there is no need to calculate the separate terminal velocity or the characteristic time for the perpendicular motion if the mentioned approximations are valid.

There is one issue that occurs when a slow-moving object changes from traveling upward to going downward, as shown in Figure 2.6.2. If this case is not handled, then the object appears to go back in the direction it came from, when in fact it would stop traveling in the horizontal direction and travel down along the direction of gravity.

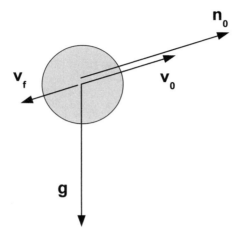

Figure 2.6.2   A bad thing that can happen for slow-moving particles and/or large update times.

There are several ways to handle this. The most straightforward approach is to propagate the object for the time it takes to get to the top with Equation (2) and then for the rest of the time propagate with Equation (3a). From Equation (2), we can calculate the time it takes to stop moving in the positive velocity direction. The result is:

$$t_{top} = \tau_2 \tan^{-1}\left(\frac{v_0}{v_{t2}}\right) \quad (5)$$

If the time to the top is less than the total time to propagate, then subtract the time to the top from the total time to propagate. Then use the downward velocity update for the time remaining *and* use zero as the initial velocity. There might be a slight discontinuity in the object's smooth motion on the screen, but usually there is not. If there is too much, then update the position in a more rigorous manner.

The last thing to consider is how to update the position. All of these equations are integrable, which is more accurate, but they provide little extra accuracy noticeable in a gaming environment and are computationally expensive to evaluate. For most game purposes, it is accurate enough to use Euler integration to calculate the position $x_f = x_0 + vt$, where the time, t, in the equation is the time since the last update and is not the global time. For the *Golf Globe* game on an iPod Touch, the game runs smoothly with no visible numerical issues at 60 frames per second by updating the position using Euler integration.

Pseudocode

This is the pseudocode for a function that calculates the final velocity, `velocityFinal`, given the initial velocity, `velocityInitial`, of an object by the time, `deltaTime`. This does not update the position of the object, which should be updated separately but with the same `deltaTime`.

```
void updateVelocityWithFluidResistance(
      const float deltaTime,
      const ThreeVector& velocityInitial,
      ThreeVector& velocityFinal )
{
      Calculate Velocity Normal or zero it.
      Calculate terminal velocity and characteristic time along velocity
normal.

      For objects going up use Equation (2), but first check
to make sure the velocity does not reach the top
Equation (5).

      For objects going down use either Equation (3a), (3b),
(3c), or (3d) as is appropriate to the initial velocity
at the beginning of the frame.

      Update the velocity perpendicular to the initial velocity with
Equation (4).
}
```

Comparison of Linear versus Quadratic Solutions

There are benefits to using either the linear version or the quadratic version. The computational advantages lie with the linear solution. The quadratic computational cost is hardly prohibitive, especially if there are not too many objects updated with the quadratic model. And the quadratic model looks and feels much nicer, especially in a game where the user is getting feedback from movement due to handheld motion, such as from the iPod Touch or another handheld device.

There are several advantages to the linear solution: There are exact velocity and position equations for all time, which is useful for AI and targeting; it is faster computationally; and the exponent in the solution is easily expanded, making it only minutely more computationally intense than updates with gravity only.

One disadvantage to the linear solution is that it is not as realistic, especially when compared directly to the quadratic case.

There are some advantages to using the quadratic solution: It is more realistic and it is not hugely more computationally intense (as long as there are not too many objects). There are several disadvantages to the quadratic solution: It is computationally more intense, especially if there are many objects; there is no analytic solution for all time, thus it is not as easy to use for AI and player targeting; and its approximations are more difficult and are more numerically touchy to the input drag parameters.

There is a possible way to balance the two approaches if there are too many objects to update with the quadratic drag model. Use the linear model for the vast majority of these objects and then use the quadratic for the more important, or highly visible, objects.

For both the linear and the quadratic solutions, it is a good approximation to use Euler integration to update the object position. It will save big on computational cost if there are many objects, especially for the quadratic case.

Conclusion

The concept of drag is simple: Slow things down in the opposite direction they are moving. However, it is difficult to implement in a numerically accurate and stable manner. The simple and mathematically accurate linear drag model as presented here would be an improvement to many current games. The mathematically and physically accurate quadratic model is an additional improvement. There are many areas of simulation in games that would visibly benefit from using the mathematically and physically accurate quadratic drag model instead of the linear drag model: boats, sailboats (both with respect to the water and the wind in the sails), parachutes, car racing, snow-globe games, golf ball trajectories, craft flying through atmospheres, and artillery shells.

Along the lines of this gem, there are several areas that would be interesting to research further. Physically based drag coefficients depend on all sorts of factors, including temperature, density, type of fluid, and the shape of the object. For spacecraft entering an atmosphere, several of these things are relevant and can make for some interesting gameplay while flying into land or chasing AIs or other players in a multiplayer game.

References

[Davis86] Davis, A. Douglas. *Classical Mechanics*. Academic Press, Inc., 1986.

[MathWorld] "Wolfram MathWorld." n.d. <http://mathworld.wolfram.com/>.

[Salas82] Salas, S. L. and Einar Hille. *Calculus: One and Several Variables with Analytic Geometry: Part 1*. John Wiley and Sons, 1982.

Application of Quasi-Fluid Dynamics for Arbitrary Closed Meshes

Krzysztof Mieloszyk,
Gdansk University of Technology
krzysztof.mieloszyk@gmail.com

Physics in real-time simulations as well as in computer games has been gaining importance. The game producers have observed that the advanced realism of the graphics is not enough to keep players content and that the virtual world created in a game should follow the rules of physics in order to behave more realistically. Until now, such realism has been mainly reflected by illustrating the interactions between the material objects. However, the phenomenon of reciprocity between such media as liquid or gas and more complex objects is also of high importance. With increasing processor power, the growing number of physics simulation methods that were initially developed purely for scientific reasons are being utilized in the entertainment market. However, simulation methods commonly used in games tend to be relatively simple in the computational sense or very focused on a specific case. An attempt to adapt them to other game variants is often impossible or requires an application of complicated parameters with values that are difficult to acquire. Hence, some more universal methods that allow for more easily modeled game physics are valuable and attractive tools for hobbyists and creators of later game extensions.

Requirements for the Mesh Representing the Object

Commonly, the medium is a physical factor that in various ways affects the complete surface of the object. Hence, for the purpose of fluid dynamics simulation, every shape needs to be represented as a closed body with all its faces pointing outward and fully covering its outside surface. The inside should be looked upon as full; it must not have any empty spaces or "bubbles." Every edge should directly contact exactly two surfaces, while the entire object mesh must fulfill the following condition:

$$V + F - E = 2 \qquad (1)$$

where V = vertices, F = faces, and E = edges.

Because the preliminary interaction value is calculated on points, it is convenient to organize the mesh in a list of points in the form of coordinates and a list of triangles represented as three sequential indices of its vertices. Additionally, every triangle should have a normal vector of its surface, as well as the surface value. In some cases, depending on the computational method used, the position of the triangle center can also be useful. In this article, we will sometimes refer to vertices as *points* and triangle meshes as *faces*.

Physical Rudiments

Using some physical basics of fluid mechanics (referring among others to Pascal's Law), pressure is defined as a quotient of force F, which exercises perpendicularly to the surface sector limiting the object given, and the surface S of this sector [Bilkowski83].

$$P = \frac{F}{S} \quad [Pa] = [N/m^2] \quad (2)$$

The total pressure affecting the body surface in a given medium point can be represented by a sum of two components: static and dynamic pressure.

$$P_{total} = P_{stat} + P_{dyn} \quad [Pa] \quad (3)$$

In order to define the static pressure that is needed to create buoyancy in a selected medium, we need the medium density ρ *[kg/m3]*, gravitational field intensity g *[m/s2]*, and the distance to the medium surface h. (In the case of air, the altitude is needed.)

$$P_{total} = \rho\, g\, h \quad [Pa] \quad (4)$$

Dynamic pressure originates from the kinetic energy pressure of the medium, which results from its movement and can be determined by knowing the medium density ρ as well as the fluid velocity V *[m/s]* at a selected position (applicable for subsonic speed).

$$P_{dyn} = \frac{\rho |V|^2}{2} \quad [Pa] \quad (5)$$

Equation (5) can be extended with a nondimensional pressure coefficient cp, whose value can be calculated as a cosine of the angle between the normal vector of the surface sector and the vector of the actual velocity in a selected point (see Figure 2.7.1). This can also be represented as a scalar product of the normal surface and the normalized velocity vector.

$$c_p = \cos(\alpha) \;=\; \mathbf{N} \circ \mathbf{V}_N = \frac{\mathbf{N} \circ \mathbf{V}}{|\mathbf{V}|} \quad (6)$$

As an effect, we obtain a general equation for dynamic pressure exerted on a segment of the surface shown in Equation (7). The method presented in this gem solves the computation of dynamic pressure based on velocity and assumes that we use a rigid body. The use of physical models based on joints or springs is also possible.

$$P_{dyn} = \frac{\rho\, c_p |\mathbf{V}|^2}{2} \quad [\text{Pa}] \quad (7)$$

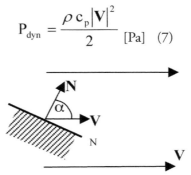

Figure 2.7.1   Normal vector of the surface and normal vector of velocity and the angle between them.

Pre-Computation Based on a Triangle Mesh

The whole issue of calculating the pressure distribution on a mesh comes down to computing the values on the mesh vertices (or center of triangles) taking into consideration the immersion, velocity, surface area, and normal of each of the triangles that form the object. This allows us to calculate the force of the pressure that influences the physical model. Additional problems arise in the case of the object being placed in two different media simultaneously. Here the division plane separates the object faces into those faces that are totally immersed in only one medium and faces that are located in both of them. The factors requiring serious consideration are characterized in the following section.

Calculating the Distance to Medium Boundary

For calculations of the static pressure affecting the object, it is necessary to define the distance h between the selected point and the medium boundary (for example, a water surface). For this, the scalar product can be applied, giving us the following Equation (8), schematically illustrated in Figure 2.7.2.

$$h_i = (\mathbf{P}_i - \mathbf{P}_{surface}) \circ \mathbf{N}_{surface} \quad [\text{m}] \quad (8)$$

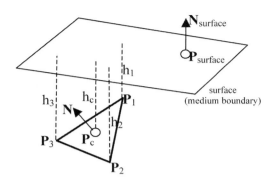

Figure 2.7.2 Defining the distance of the point from the surface.

Assuming that the normal vector of the surface is pointing upward, the negative value of the obtained distance means that the point is located under the "water" surface, and the positive is above its surface. In cases when the boundary is located at the virtual world "sea level," we know in which of the two media the point is located. To reduce the possibility of a calculation error, point *Psurface* (through which the surface dividing the media is crossing) should correspond to the projection of the object's center onto this surface, in accordance with its normal vector.

Calculating the Point Velocity

Because the objects simulated in the virtual world are frequently moving, one of the most important factors needing to be improved in their dynamics is the influence of the surrounding medium. Therefore, it is required to include the velocities of each of the object mesh points (Equation (9)) as a sum of the mass center's linear velocity *Vobj* and the object's angle velocity (Figure 2.7.3). The velocity *Vp* obtained this way represents the global velocity for selected point *P*. To calculate the dynamic pressure, the local velocity vector, which is equal to the negative global point velocity, is required [Padfield96].

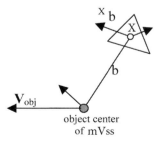

Figure 2.7.3 Velocity of the arbitrary point belonging to the moving object.

We represent this mathematically as follows:

$$\mathbf{V}_p = \mathbf{V}_{obj} + \omega \times \mathbf{r} \quad [m/s] \quad (9)$$

$$\mathbf{V}_{p\,local} = -\mathbf{V}_p$$

Morphing Shape Objects

The simulated object is not always a rigid body, because some objects move by changing their body shape. A fish or a bird can be used as an example here because various body fragments of those animals move with different velocities in relation to other parts. For such objects, when calculating the point velocity, it is necessary to take the so-called morphing effect into consideration. The simplest method here is to find the change between the old and new local positions of the mesh points (see Figure 2.7.4), followed by the velocity computation, keeping the time difference Dt between the morphing animation frames in mind. As a result and an extension to Equation (9), we obtain Equation (10), which is presented below.

$$\mathbf{V}_{p\,local} = -\left(\mathbf{V}_{obj} + \omega \times \mathbf{r} + \frac{\mathbf{P}_{i\,new} - \mathbf{P}_{i\,old}}{\Delta t}\right) \quad (10)$$

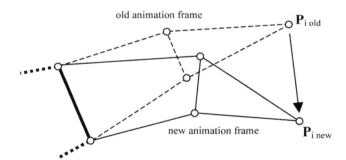

Figure 2.7.4   Moving vertex position in morphing mesh.

Triangle Clipping

Because there is a situation in which the object triangle can be located in both media simultaneously, it is necessary to determine the borderline and find those parts that are completely submerged in only one of the media. To achieve this, the triangle should be divided into three triangles calculated by cutting points of the edges that cross the medium border. By applying Equation (11), we obtain PAB, PAC, and dividing the triangle ABC, we create a triangle A PAB PAC, located in one medium, and two arbitrary triangles located in the other medium (for example, B C PAB and C PAC PAB), as presented in Figure 2.7.5.

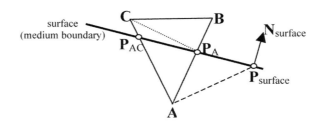

Figure 2.7.5 Assigning the cutting points on the surface by edge AB.

It is important to keep in mind that the newly created triangles must have the same normal vectors as the primary triangle. Even though each of the new triangles has the same normal, it is still necessary to recalculate the current surface area of each of those triangles. It might be very useful to apply the cross-product property, described in Equation (12), for the exemplary triangle ABC. This surface area can then be used to calculate the pressure force.

$$\mathbf{P}_{AB} = \mathbf{A} + \mathbf{AB}\frac{(\mathbf{P}_{surface} - \mathbf{A}) \circ \mathbf{N}_{surface}}{\mathbf{AB} \circ \mathbf{N}_{surface}} \quad (11)$$

$$S = \frac{|\mathbf{AB} \times \mathbf{AC}|}{2} \qquad \mathbf{N}_{\triangle ABC} = \frac{\mathbf{AB} \times \mathbf{AC}}{|\mathbf{AB} \times \mathbf{AC}|} \quad (12)$$

Calculation of the Pressure on the Triangle Surface

To calculate the pressure force exerted on the arbitrary triangle of the body, the pressure at each of the triangle vertices should be taken into consideration. Hence, we need to calculate the distance of each vertex from the medium surface for static pressure (Equation (6)) and the vertex local velocity, taking the angle between the velocity and the triangle surface normal into account, for dynamic pressure (Equation (7)). In the next step, the average complete pressure of the triangle vertices is calculated. However, it is useful to know that some simplifications are possible for cases when any mesh vertex has the velocity calculated from $\omega \times r$ that is considerably smaller than the object linear velocity *Vobj* or when ω is close to zero. As a result of this, the pressure gradient distribution is almost linear, and the calculation of the complete pressure exerted on the triangle surface is reduced to obtaining the pressure in the triangle center (based on *h* and *Vp*). Thus, the pressure force is a product of a triangle normal, its surface area, and pressure (Equation (2)). For models based on a rigid body, calculation of the complete force and the torque comes down to summing the pressure forces from each surface fragment, as well summing all torques as pressure force vector cross-products and the forces at the center of the triangles.

Simple Correction of Dynamic Pressure

The method for computing the static pressure presented in this gem is based solely on simple physical rules. However, the effect of dynamic pressure is one of the most complicated problems of the mechanics, for which no simple modeling method exists. The computational method used here is highly simplified and based on a heuristic parameter cp. This is sufficient for the purpose of physical simulation, which visually resembles the correct one; however, obtained values strongly diverge from the real values, resulting in too low of lift and too high of drag values. Hence, when calculating a force vector obtained from dynamic pressure, it is beneficial to introduce a correction in accordance with the velocity vector at a selected point. As in Equation (13), the factors used here are determined empirically and should be interpreted as recommended, not required. The corrected dynamic pressure force vector of the selected triangle has to be summed with the static pressure force vector occurring on its surface. The results obtained in that way approximate the results of the real object (for example, an airplane) for which the dynamic pressure is most important.

$$\mathbf{F}_{i \text{ corrected}} = 2.2\mathbf{F}_i - 1.6\mathbf{V}_{iN}\left(\mathbf{V}_{iN} \circ \mathbf{F}_i\right) \quad (13)$$

Conclusion

The simplified method of computing the flow around an arbitrary closed body presented here allows us to easily obtain approximate values of forces surrounding a medium. This is possible thanks to simulating some fundamental physical phenomena, such as static and dynamic pressure. Figure 2.7.6 shows screenshots from an application that interactively simulates real time using the algorithm presented here. This clearly shows a potential possibility for use in simulating the behavior of objects with fairly complicated shapes. The control here is carried out by changing the interaction between the medium and the object obtained, by morphing the shape of the object's surface, or by moving or rotating the object elements. This allows us to create controlled planes, ships, airships, submarines, hydrofoils, seaplanes, swimming surfers, or drifting objects, as well as objects that undergo morphing, such as birds or fish. All of this is simulated based on the object mesh only.

The simplifications used in the algorithm bring some inaccuracies. The main problem here is the lack of consideration for the reciprocal interferential influences for each face on the final pressure values. This is a consequence of analyzing each face separately, as if it were moving in the flow consistent with its own velocity. In reality, the velocity of the flow at a given fragment of the body surface depends on the velocity over the adjacent surface fragments [Wendt96, Ferziger96]. Dependence of the value on the pressure coefficient parameter cp (as angle cosine) is a generalization. In fact, this issue would require some more specialized characteristics. Another drawback of the material presented here is that the medium viscosity has not been taken into consideration, which also adds to inaccuracies in the results. These computation versus performance tradeoffs need to be evaluated when comparing real-time methods and those that may be used in fluid dynamics engineering and design.

Implementations of the equations in this article motivated by specific examples are available on the CD-ROM.

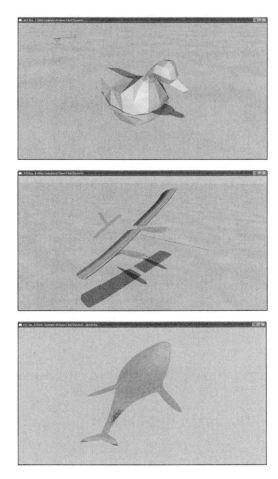

Figure 2.7.6   Examples of applications: drifting object (top),
static object (middle), morphing object (bottom).
(Grayscale marks the pressure distribution in the middle and bottom images.)

References

[Bilkowski83] Bilkowski, J. and J. Trylski. *Physics*. Warsaw: PWN, 1983.

[Ferziger96] Ferziger, Joel H. and Milovan Peri . *Computational Methods for Fluid Dynamics*. Berlin: Springer-Verlag, 1996.

[Padfield96] Padfield, Gareth D. *Helicopter Flight Dynamic*. Oxford: Blackwell Science Limited, 1996.

[Wendt96] Wendt, John F. *Computational Fluid Dynamics*. Berlin: Springer-Verlag 1996.

2.8

Approximate Convex Decomposition for Real-Time Collision Detection

Khaled Mamou

Khaled_mamou@yahoo.fr

Collision detection is essential for realistic physical interactions in video games and physically based modeling. To ensure real-time interactivity with the player, video game developers usually approximate the 3D models, such as game characters and static objects, with a set of simple convex shapes, such as ellipsoids, capsules, or convex hulls. While adequate for some simple interactions, these basic shapes provide poor approximations for concave surfaces and generate false collision detections (see Figure 2.8.1).

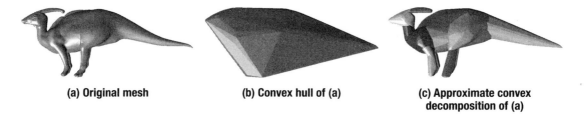

(a) Original mesh   (b) Convex hull of (a)   (c) Approximate convex decomposition of (a)

Figure 2.8.1 Convex hull versus approximate convex decomposition.

In this gem, we present a simple and efficient approach to decomposing a 3D mesh into a set of nearly convex surfaces. This decomposition is used to compute a faithful approximation of the original 3D mesh, particularly adapted to collision detection. First, we introduce the approximate convex decomposition problem. Next, our proposed segmentation technique and performance characteristics will be evaluated. Finally, we conclude with some areas of future work.

Approximate Convex Decomposition

Let S be a triangular mesh of connectivity κ and geometry γ. Intuitively, S is a piecewise linear surface composed of a set of triangles stitched along their edges. The connectivity κ is represented as a simplical complex describing the topology of the mesh. κ is composed of a set of vertices $\chi = \{v_1, v_2, \cdots, v_v\} \in IN$ (IN denotes the set of positive integers and V the number of vertices of κ), together with a set of non-empty subsets of χ, called *simplices* and verifying the following conditions:

- Each vertex $v \in \chi$ is a simplex of κ, and
- Each subset of a simplex of κ is also a simplex of κ.

A d-simplex is defined as a simplex composed of $d+1$ elements of χ. The 0-simplices correspond to the set of vertices of κ, the 1-simplices to the set of its edges, and the 2-simplices to the set of its triangles, denoted as $\theta = \{t_1, t_2, \cdots, t_T\}$. ($T$ represents the number of triangles.)

The geometry γ specifies the shape of the surface by associating 3D positions and usually surface normals to the vertices of κ. A surface S is convex if it is a subset of the boundary of its convex hull (in other words, the minimal convex volume containing S). Computing an exact convex decomposition of an arbitrary surface S consists of partitioning it into a minimal set of convex sub-surfaces. Chazelle, et al. prove that computing such decomposition is an NP-hard problem and evaluate different heuristics to resolve it [Chazelle95]. Lien, et al. claim that the exact convex decomposition algorithms are impractical since they produce a high number of clusters, as shown in Figure 2.8.2 [Lien04]. To provide a tractable solution, they propose to relax the exact convexity constraint and consider instead the problem of computing an approximate convex decomposition (ACD) of S. Here, for a fixed parameter $\varepsilon > 0$, the goal is to determine a partition $\Pi = \{\pi_1, \pi_2, \cdots, \pi_K\}$ of θ with a minimal number of clusters K and verify that each cluster has concavity lower than ε.

(a) Exact convex decomposition
[Chazelle95] generates 7,611 clusters

(b) Approximate convex decomposition
generates 11 clusters

Figure 2.8.2 Exact convex decomposition versus approximate convex decomposition.

The ACD problem has been addressed in a number of recent publications [Lien04, Lien08, Kraevoy07, Attene08]. Attene, et al. apply a hierarchical segmentation approach to a tetrahedral mesh generated from S [Attene08]. The tetrahedralization process exploited by Attene, et al. is, in practice, hard to compute and introduces extra computational complexity. Other methods avoid this limitation by considering the original 3D mesh directly [Lien04, Lien08, Kraevoy07]. Kraevoy, et al. introduce an incremental Lloyd-type segmentation technique exploiting a concavity-based seed placement strategy [Kraevoy07]. Here, the concavity measure is defined as the area weighted average of the distances from the clusters to their corresponding convex hulls. Lien, et al. claim that such concavity measure does not efficiently capture the important features of the surface [Lien04, Lien08]. They propose instead to compute the maximal distance between the mesh vertices and the clusters' convex hulls. Their divide-and-conquer approach iteratively divides the mesh until the concavity of each sub-part is lower than the threshold ε, as shown in Figure 2.8.3. Here, at each step i, the vertex v_i^* with the highest concavity is selected, and the cluster to which it belongs is divided into two sub-clusters by considering a bisection plane incident to v_i^*.

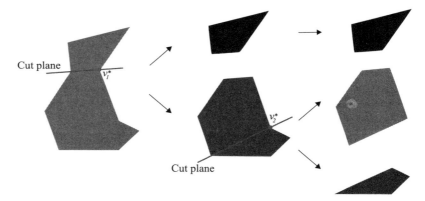

Figure 2.8.3 The divide-and-conquer ACD approach
introduced in [Lien04] and [Lien08].

The main limitation of this approach is related to the choice of the "best" cut plane, which requires a sophisticated analysis of the model's features. A public implementation of [Lien04] is provided in [Ratcliff06]. Here, the sophisticated feature analysis procedure is replaced by a simple cut plane selection strategy that splits each cluster according to its longest direction. This suboptimal choice generates over-segmentations, which are optimized by applying a post-processing procedure aiming at aggregating the maximal number of clusters while ensuring the maximal concavity constraint. As illustrated in Figure 2.8.7, the ACDs produced by Ratcliff are, in practice, suboptimal, since the aggregation procedure is applied to clusters generated only by plane-based bisections.

To overcome the aforementioned limitations, we introduce, in the next section, a simple and efficient hierarchical ACD approach for 3D meshes.

Hierarchical Approximate Convex Decomposition

Our proposed hierarchical approximate convex decomposition (HACD) proceeds as follows. First, the dual graph of the mesh is computed. (See the upcoming "Dual Graph" section.) Then, its vertices are iteratively clustered by successively applying topological decimation operations, while minimizing a cost function related to the concavity and the aspect ratio of the produced segmentation clusters. Finally, by approximating each cluster with the boundary of its convex hull [Preparata77], a faithful approximation of the original mesh is computed. This surface approximation is piecewise convex and has a low number of triangles (when compared to T), which makes it particularly well adapted for collision detection.

Let's first recall the definition of the dual graph associated with a 3D mesh.

Dual Graph

The dual graph S^* associated with the mesh S is defined as follows. Each vertex of S^* corresponds to a triangle of S. Two vertices of S^* are neighbors (in other words, connected by an edge of the dual graph) if and only if their corresponding triangles in S share an edge. Figure 2.8.4 illustrates an example of a dual graph for a simple 3D mesh.

Decimation Operator

Once the dual graph is computed, the algorithm starts the decimation stage, which consists of successively applying half-edge collapse operations to S^*. Each half-edge collapse operation applied to an edge (v, w), denoted *hecol* (v, w), merges the two vertices v and w, as illustrated in Figure 2.8.5. The vertex w is deleted, and all its incident edges are connected to v.

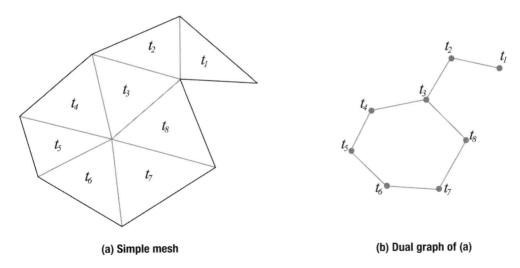

(a) Simple mesh   (b) Dual graph of (a)

Figure 2.8.4   Example of a dual graph.

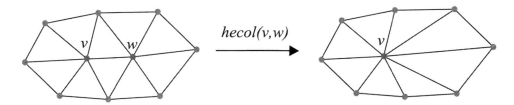

Figure 2.8.5   Half-edge collapse decimation operation.

Let $A(v)$ be the list of the ancestors of the vertex v. Initially, $A(v)$ is empty. At each operation $hecol(v,w)$ applied to the vertex v, the list $A(v)$ is updated as follows:

$$A(v) \leftarrow A(v) \cup A(w) \cup \{w\}   (1)$$

Simplification Strategy

The decimation process described in the previous section is guided by a cost function describing the concavity and the aspect ratio of the surface $S(v,w)$ resulting from the unification of the vertices v and w and their ancestors [Garland01]:

$$S(v,w) \leftarrow A(v) \cup A(w) \cup \{w,v\}   (2)$$

As in [Garland01], we define the aspect ratio $E_{shape}(v,w)$ of the surface $S(v,w)$ as follows:

$$E_{shape}(v,w) = \frac{\rho^2(S(v,w))}{4\pi\sigma(S(v,w))}   (3)$$

where $\rho(S(v,w))$ and $\sigma(S(v,w))$ represent the perimeter and the area of $S(v,w)$, respectively.

The cost $E_{Shape}(v,w)$ was introduced in order to favor the generation of compact clusters. In the case of a disk, the cost E_{Shape} equals one. The more irregular a surface, the higher its aspect ratio cost.

Inspired by [Lien08], we define the concavity $C(v,w)$ of $S(v,w)$, as follows (see Figure 2.8.6):

$$C(v,w) = \max_{M \in S(u,w)} \|M - P(M)\| (4)$$

where $P(M)$ represents the projection of the point M on the convex hull $CH(u,w)$ of $S(v,w)$, with respect to the half ray with origin M and direction normal to the surface $S(v,w)$ at M.

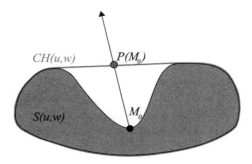

Figure 2.8.6 Concavity measure for a 3D mesh.

The global decimation cost $E(v,w)$ associated with the edge (v,w) is given by:

$$E(v,w) = \frac{C(v,w)}{D} + \alpha.E_{shape}(v,w) \quad (5)$$

where

- D is a normalization factor equal to the diagonal of the bounding box of S, and
- α is a parameter controlling the contribution of the shape factor $E_{Shape}(v,w)$ with respect to the concavity cost. (See the upcoming "Choice of the Parameter α" section.)

At each step of the decimation process, the $hecol\,(v,w)$ operation with the lowest decimation cost is applied, and a new partition $\Pi(i) = \{\pi_1(i), \pi_2(i), \cdots, \pi_K(i)\}$ is computed as follows:

$$\forall k \in \{1, 2, \cdots, K(i)\}, \quad \pi_k(i) = \{v_k(i)\} \cup A(v_k(i)) \quad (6)$$

where $(v_k(i))_{k \in \{1,2,\cdots,K(i)\}}$ represents the vertices of the dual graph S^* obtained after i half-edge collapse operations. This process is iterated until all the edges of S^* generating clusters with concavities lower than ε are decimated.

Choice of the Parameter α

The clusters detected during the early stages of the algorithm are composed of a low number of adjacent triangles with a concavity almost equal to zero. Therefore, the decimation cost E is dominated by the aspect ratio related cost E_{Shape}, which favors the generation of compact surfaces. This behavior is progressively inverted during the decimation process, since the clusters become more and more concave. To ensure that the cost $(\alpha.E_{Shape})$ has no influence on the choice of the later decimation operations, we have set the parameter α as follows:

$$\alpha = \frac{\varepsilon}{10 \times D} \quad (7)$$

This choice guarantees, for disk-shaped clusters, that the cost ($\alpha.E_{Shape}$) is 10 times lower than the concavity-related cost $\dfrac{C(v,w)}{D}$.

Experimental Results

To validate our approach, we have first compared its segmentation results to those of [Ratcliff06], which provides a simplified version of the original algorithm described in [Lien04] and [Lien08]. In Figure 2.8.7, we compare the ACDs generated by our approach to those obtained by using Ratcliff's method. Here, the accuracy of the generated piecewise convex approximations is objectively evaluated by using the root mean squares (RMS) and Hausdorff errors [Aspert02]. Let's recall that the RMS error measures the mean distance from the original mesh S to its piecewise convex approximation S'. It is defined as follows:

$$RMS(S,S') = \frac{100}{D} \times \sqrt{\frac{1}{\sigma(S)} \iint_{p\in S} d^2(p,S')ds} \qquad (8)$$

where D is the diagonal of the bounding box of S, $\alpha(S)$ is its area, and $d(p,S')$ is the distance from a point $p \in S$ to S'. The distance $d(p,S')$ is given by:

$$d(p,S') = \min_{p'\in S'}\|p - p'\| \qquad (9)$$

The Hausdorff error, denoted H, measures the maximal distance from S to S' and is defined as follows:

$$H(S,S') = \frac{100}{D} \times \max_{p\in S} d(p,S') \qquad (10)$$

The reported results show that the proposed HACD technique provides significantly (that is, from 20 percent to 80 percent) lower RMS and H errors, while detecting a lower number of clusters. Figures 2.8.7(j) through 2.8.7(r) clearly show the limitations of the plane-based bisection strategy and the aggregation post-processing procedure of Ratcliff, which generates over-segmentations and poor ACDs.

Color Plate 8 presents the segmentation results and the approximate convex decompositions generated by our approach for different 3D meshes. For all the models, the generated segmentations ensure a concavity lower than ε and guarantee that the maximal distance from S to S' is lower than 3 percent of D. Therefore, the generated piecewise convex approximations provide faithful approximations of the original meshes with a small number of clusters. Moreover, our technique successfully detects the convex parts and the anatomical structure of the analyzed 3D models.

For all of the models shown in Color Plate 8, the piecewise convex approximations were computed by considering an approximation of the clusters' convex hulls with a maximum of 32 vertices for each. The number of triangles composing the obtained convex surfaces is lower than 8 percent of T. Furthermore, the piecewise convexity property makes the generated approximations particularly well suited to collision detection.

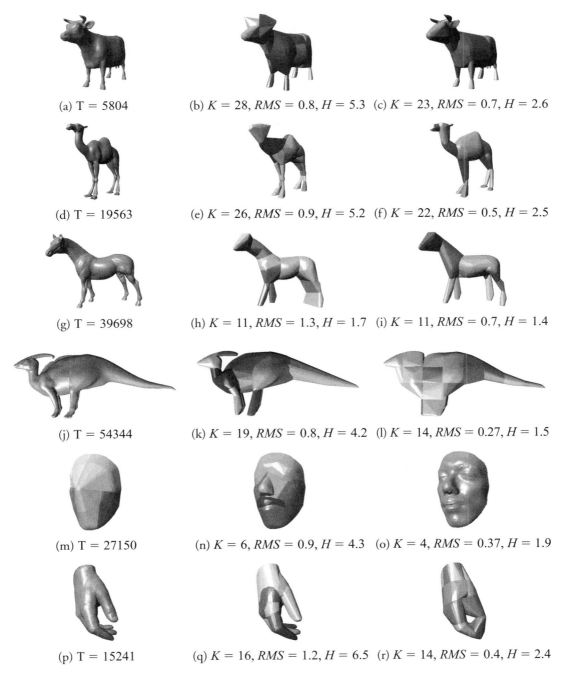

(a) T = 5804   (b) $K = 28$, $RMS = 0.8$, $H = 5.3$ (c) $K = 23$, $RMS = 0.7$, $H = 2.6$

(d) T = 19563   (e) $K = 26$, $RMS = 0.9$, $H = 5.2$ (f) $K = 22$, $RMS = 0.5$, $H = 2.5$

(g) T = 39698   (h) $K = 11$, $RMS = 1.3$, $H = 1.7$ (i) $K = 11$, $RMS = 0.7$, $H = 1.4$

(j) T = 54344   (k) $K = 19$, $RMS = 0.8$, $H = 4.2$ (l) $K = 14$, $RMS = 0.27$, $H = 1.5$

(m) T = 27150   (n) $K = 6$, $RMS = 0.9$, $H = 4.3$ (o) $K = 4$, $RMS = 0.37$, $H = 1.9$

(p) T = 15241   (q) $K = 16$, $RMS = 1.2$, $H = 6.5$ (r) $K = 14$, $RMS = 0.4$, $H = 2.4$

Figure 2.8.7   Comparative evaluation: (a,d,g,j,m,p) original meshes, (b,e,h,k,n,q) piecewise convex approximations generated by [Ratcliff06], and (c,f,i,l,o,r) piecewise convex approximations generated by the proposed HACD technique.

Conclusion

We have presented a hierarchical segmentation approach for approximate convex decomposition of 3D meshes. The generated segmentations are exploited to construct faithful approximations of the original mesh by a set of convex surfaces. This new representation is particularly well suited for collision detection. We have shown that our proposed technique efficiently decomposes a concave 3D model into a small set of nearly convex surfaces while automatically detecting its anatomical structure. This property makes the proposed HACD technique an ideal candidate for skeleton extraction and pattern recognition applications.

References

[Attene08] Attene, M., et al. "Hierarchical Convex Approximation of 3D Shapes for Fast Region Selection." *Computer Graphics Forum* 27.5 (2008): 503–522.

[Chazelle95] Chazelle, B., et al. "Strategies for Polyhedral Surface Decomposition: An Experimental Study." *Symposium on Computational Geometry* (1995): 297–305.

[Garland 01] Garland, M., et al. "Hierarchical Face Clustering on Polygonal Surfaces." *Symposium on Interactive 3D Graphics* (2001): 49–58.

[Hoppe96] Hoppe, H. "Progressive Meshes." *International Conference on Computer Graphics and Interactive Techniques* (1996): 99–108.

[Kraevoy07] Kraevoy, V., et al. "Model Composition from Interchangeable Components." *Pacific Conference on Computer Graphics and Applications* (2008): 129–138.

[Lien04] Lien, J.M., et al. "Approximate Convex Decomposition." *Symposium on Computational Geometry* (2004): 457–458.

[Lien08] Lien, J.M., et al. "Approximate Convex Decomposition of Polyhedra and Its Applications." *Computer Aided Geometric Design* (2008): 503–522.

[Aspert02] Aspert, N., et al. "MESH: Measuring Error Between Surfaces Using the Hausdorff Distance." *IEEE International Conference on Multimedia and Expo* 1 (2002): 705–708.

[Preparata77] Preparata, F. P., et al. "Convex Hulls of Finite Sets of Points in Two and Three Dimensions." *ACM Communication* 29.2 (1977): 87–93.

[Ratcliff06] Ratcliff, J. "Approximate Convex Decomposition." *John Ratcliff's Code Suppository*. April 2006. Bolgspot.com. n.d. <http://codesuppository.blogspot.com/2006/04/approximate-convex-decomposition.html>.

AI

Introduction

Borut Pfeifer

borut_p@yahoo.com

With recent advances in graphics and animation, AI is one of the areas of game programming with the most potential for growth. The techniques in this section address some of the most troublesome and encouraging future areas for game AI development. Advances in AI architecture, believable decision-making, more detailed character simulation, and player modeling all offer the possibility of creating new or improved aspects of gameplay, as well as enhancing our ability to actually build that gameplay more quickly.

AI architecture is crucial for effective development. A poor architecture can bring the development of new AI gameplay on a project to a halt. A good one can empower new features and new experiences. Cyril Brom, Tomáš Poch, and Ondřej Šerý discuss creating worlds with high numbers of NPCs in their gem, "AI Level of Detail for Really Large Worlds," managing multiple simulation levels for each area of the game world. Kevin Dill writes about using patterns in AI decision-making code in his gem "A Pattern-Based Approach to Modular AI for Games." The more effective an AI programmer is in creating reusable and scalable code, the more time there is to iterate on gameplay.

AI movement and pathfinding are always the earliest difficult problems an AI programmer has to solve on a project. "Automated Navigation Mesh Generation Using Advanced Growth-Based Techniques," by D. Hunter Hale and G. Michael Youngblood, details their research on new methods of creating navigation meshes using space-filling algorithms. Michael Ramsey covers the pathfinding used for a wide variety of animals and movement types in *World of Zoo* in his gem "A Practical Spatial Architecture for Animal and Agent Navigation." Brian Pickrell sheds some light on the often-overlooked area of control theory and how it can be applied to an agent's steering in "Applying Control Theory to Game AI and Physics."

Decision-making is the aspect of AI that affects players most directly. The challenge is finding meaningful decisions characters can make to appear intelligent, while also being understandable to the player. It is much easier to create decision-making that allows for an NPC's success than it is to balance understandable behavior with the complexity and depth required to appear intelligent. Thomas Hartley and Quasim Mehdi describe a method to allow NPCs to adapt better to players' combat behavior over time with their gem "Adaptive Tactic Selection in First-Person Shooter (FPS) Games." Dave Mark discusses how to use complexity in building AI decision-making models in "Embracing Chaos Theory: Generating Apparent Unpredictability through Deterministic Systems."

More detailed character simulation can also help create that depth and believability. Rob Zubek breaks down an AI decision-making approach used in games such as the Sims series in his gem, "Needs-Based AI." Phil Carlisle takes a look at how we can easily add emotional modeling to a behavior tree–based architecture in his gem, "A Framework for Emotional Digital Actors." Baylor Wetzel's gem, "Scalable Dialog Authoring," confronts the difficult problem of creating dialog for many NPCs by abstracting concepts, such as a cultural group an NPC belongs to, and describes how to empower designers to author more variety in dialog with these abstractions.

Player modeling is a burgeoning area of game AI. It can be used to help improve a player's experience, such as in *Left 4 Dead*. In the gem "Graph-Based Data Mining for Player Trace Analysis in MMORPGs," Nikhil Ketkar and G. Michael Youngblood write about their work modeling players in massively multiplayer games (MMOs). They've used MMO player data to determine models to detect gold farmers and bots as well to determine effective locations for in-game advertising. Such models and processes can be used to improve a wide variety of aspects of the player experience.

As game AI programmers, we are now in the spotlight to create the next level of innovative game experiences. People are no longer impressed by the same fancy normal maps and motion-captured animation; they want their characters to be more believable and more entertaining in how they act. It's up us to make this a reality, and I hope the gems in this section will help give you ideas to solve some of these problems.

AI Level of Detail
for Really Large Worlds

Cyril Brom, Charles University in Prague
brom@ksvi.mff.cuni.cz

Tomáš Poch
poch@dsrg.mff.cuni.cz

Ondřej Šerý
ondrej.sery@dsrg.mff.cuni.cz

One challenge for games featuring large worlds with many non-player characters (NPCs) is to find a good balance between the consumption of computational resources and simulation believability. On the one hand, the cost of simulation of a whole world, including all the NPCs, is enormous. On the other hand, if one simulates just the proximity of a player, one asks for plausibility troubles. For instance, when a player is supposed to return to a once left area, NPCs and objects in this area may not be in a believable state—the area has not changed since it was left, people have not moved, the ice cream left on the table has not melted, and so on. Additionally, this approach cannot handle NPCs that can move freely around the world.

To compromise between these two extremes, a number of level-of-detail AI techniques (LOD AI) have been invented. While LOD AI for a traffic simulation [Chenney01] and for enemies in an RPG [Brockington02] and an action game [Grinke04] has already been written about, less is known about how to vary simulation detail for general NPCs.

This gem presents a LOD AI technique tailored for simulations of large worlds featuring hundreds of commonplace NPCs with relatively complex behavior. These NPCs can perform tasks that include manipulation with several objects and require a variety of everyday behaviors, such as harvesting, merchandising, or watering a garden (as opposed to pure walking and fighting). The NPCs are interactive, and they can move around the world as the story dictates. The technique is gradual, which means that it allows for several levels of detail (LOD) based on the distance from the player or important places (Figure 3.1.1). The technique also considers the fact that whole locations containing objects and NPCs may cease to exist when the LOD decreases and need to be re-created when it increases again.

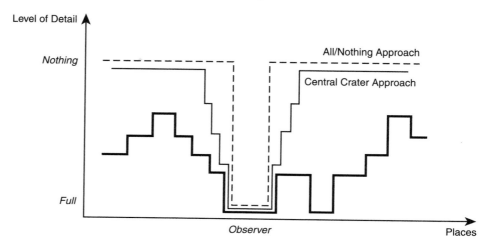

Figure 3.1.1   Three types of level-of-detail AI techniques. Places are projected on the X-axis.

Gradual LOD Example

Think of a classic fantasy RPG setting: a medieval county with many villages. There is a pub in one of them, where miners go to have some fun after their shift. A player can go there as well; she can leave and return any time. You want to avoid the situation in which she would realize that the miners were not being simulated properly when she was at the other end of the village, but you want to save the resources when she is out. You may define the following LODs ranging from the full simulation to almost no simulation.

- Detail 5: Full simulation—used when the player is in the pub or in its proximity.
- Detail 4: Every room from the pub is abstracted to a single point. The tables in the saloon are organized just in a list or an abstract graph; exact positions become unimportant. Miners (and other NPCs) are still sitting at the tables, but they are not drinking properly; they just empty the whole glass of beer in one go, say, every 20 to 40 minutes. The barman brings new beer, but now he is not walking as he would with LOD 5. Instead, he "jumps" from table to table. The beer still has to be paid for. A miner can jump to another table as well, or to a next room, or he can leave the pub. LOD 4 will be used typically if the player is, say, 100 to 300 meters from the pub.

- Detail 3: The glasses, the tables, and the pub's rooms cease to exist. The whole pub is abstracted to a single point. Yet the miners can still be there (we don't know where exactly, but we need not care, as will be detailed later). The beer level in the barrel will decrease a bit every half an hour or so based on the number of miners in the pub. The miners can leave the pub or enter. LOD 3 will be used if the player is at the other end of the village. Notice that when she is approaching the pub, the detail first jumps to 4 and only then to 5. Additionally, when it jumps to 4 from 3, the miners must be assigned to tables, and glasses must be generated properly (for example, at the tables).
- Detail 2: The whole village is abstracted to a single point. The barman is not simulated because his story, as specified by designers, never leads him out of the bar, while the miners still are; they may go from a village (meaning the pub or home) to the mine (in other words, to work). This detail is used when the player is not in the village but is in its proximity.
- Detail 1: The village and its surroundings are abstracted to a single point; no village's inhabitants are simulated, but a foreigner may pay a visit.

You can imagine that the foreigner is a story-important persona. His importance can demand that the area he is located in has an LOD of at least 4. Thus, as he moves, he redefines LOD similarly to the player. Alternatively, some events may be considered important. When miners—in the pub, at LOD 3—start a brawl, the brawl can level up the detail to 5 no matter where the user is.

Throughout, we will assume that LOD increases or decreases just by 1; larger changes can be done by repetition. We will assume one player in the simulation, but the technique can be used for multiplayer games as well.

The LOD technique introduced in this game has been implemented as a part of a general simulator of 2D virtual words, including the aforementioned example (with some modifications). The simulator and the example are included on the CD.

Graphical LOD versus LOD AI

Conceptually, it is often useful to think about a game's control mechanisms in terms of a two-layered architecture. While AI is the higher layer, physics and graphics are the lower layer. (See [Chenney01] for more on this point.) This is actually a simplified view, nevertheless useful for explanatory purposes. According to this metaphor, the player's direct experience is provided by the lower animation layer, which is only influenced by the higher layer. The LOD AI technique is only related to the higher layer.

Since the position of the player's avatar forces the maximum LOD AI in correctly designed worlds, only the areas (or their parts) simulated at the maximum detail may be visualized. The animation layer takes the outcome of the AI layer as an abstract prescription of what to show. The animation layer operates with several graphical levels of detail, and it may add additional complexity above the finest LOD AI detail. In our example, LOD AI Detail 5 takes care of whether a miner will drink a beer or whether he will go to the waypoint on the right or on the left, but the movement of his hand or walking smoothly will be dealt with by the animation engine.

Simulation at the Full Detail

This gem concerns itself only with the AI layer. Assume to start that our goal is to simulate the whole world at the full AI LOD and that we need not care about animation. A good way to think about what happens in the AI layer is in terms of a discrete-event simulation paradigm. According to this view, time is represented by a chronological sequence of simulation events, which are ordered in an event list. These simulation events are abstract entities that mark time instants in which the state of the game is modified. Additionally, every simulation event can generate a new simulation event to the event list or remove an existing event. Technically, every simulation event is associated with a piece of code. In a nutshell, after initialization, the whole system works in the following cycle:

1. Take the first simulation event from the event list and remove it from the list.
2. Process this event; that is, run the code associated with the event. As a part of this:
   a. Change the state variables of some entities.
   b. Insert new simulation events to the event list at appropriate places.
   c. Remove some simulation events from the event list.

When this paradigm is used, it is important to distinguish between real time, which is the time the user experiences, and simulation time, which is the time of the simulated world as represented by the event list. One processing cycle happens, by definition, in zero simulation time (though it cannot happen in zero real time). For real-time games, these two times must of course be synchronized. For more on discrete-event simulations and event handling, see [Channey01, Harvey02, Wiki09].

The simulation paradigm per se says nothing about how the simulation events relate to what really happens in the game. There are designers who specify this; they must create simulation events around those changes in the state of the game that the AI layer should be aware of. In a sense, the simulation events present the AI layer's window into the virtual world.

One class of simulation events is story-important events (for example, the dungeon's gate will open every day at midnight). These events typically will be pre-scheduled in the event list from the beginning or hooked into the event list by a trigger in run time (for example, from the moment the player enters the village, the neighboring dungeon will open every day at midnight). A different class of events is due to slow changes of objects' states (for example, increasing the rust level of a sword every week by one). But the most important class is due to changes caused by atomic actions of NPCs or the player; these actions must be represented by simulation events in the event list.

Because these actions are indivisible from the standpoint of the AI layer, it suffices to represent each of them by a start event and an end event. Typically, these two events will not be present in the event list simultaneously. During processing of a start event, first, other parts of the game are notified that the action starts, and second, it is estimated how long the action will last, and its end event is hooked to the event list at the appropriate place (Figure 3.1.2). When this time comes and the end event is processed, states of some objects are changed, and the NPC's AI controller is invoked to decide what the next action of this NPC is, hooking the start event of that action to the event list. In fact, because start events tend to be hooked at the beginning of the event list, it is often possible to skip their generation and to hook the respective end events directly. Note that this mechanism allows you to have atomic actions with various durations.

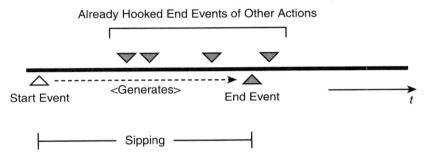

Figure 3.1.2 Atomic action of sipping a beer is represented in the event list by a start event and an end event.

Classic discrete-event simulations typically work only with simulation events hooked into the event list. However, for games, asynchronous events are also needed. That is, sometimes another part of the game can generate an event that has to be propagated to the AI layer and processed by it immediately. For instance, the collision detection may recognize that someone has nudged the sipping person with an elbow. This means that the atomic action of sipping a beer cannot be finished. Thus, the AI layer must delete its end event and generate the start event of spilling action instead.

Another issue is that the time of actions' ends (thus, the time of end events) is only estimated by the AI layer. This is fine when we simulate a part of the world that is not visualized: An estimate becomes the actual duration provided the action is not interrupted by an asynchronous event. However, for visualized parts, duration of some atomic actions will be determined by the animation engine. End events of these actions need to be synchronized with the actual end of the action.

Toward LOD AI: Hierarchical Behavior

The question of this gem is how to make the mechanism of start events and end events cheaper when the full detail is not required. Our solution will capitalize on the fact that behavior of NPCs can be represented hierarchically. This means, more or less, that the NPCs are conceived as having a list of behaviors that are decomposed to sub-behaviors, which are further refined until some atomic actions are reached. Figure 3.1.3 shows how this applies to a drinking miner.

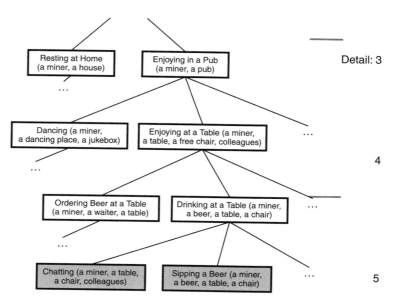

Figure 3.1.3   Hierarchical representation of a drinking miner's behavior.
Atomic actions are in gray. Other nodes represent tasks.
Note that one detail can be assigned to more levels.

Conceptually, this follows the Belief-Desire-Intention architecture [Bratman87]. This will most likely be implemented with behavior trees or hierarchical FSMs—for example [Fu&Houlette04, Isla05, Champandard08].

In academic literature, the decomposition of high-level behaviors to sub-behaviors is often more complicated. There, the distinction between goals and tasks is often made. While goals represent what shall be achieved, tasks represent how to achieve this. Every goal can be accomplished by several tasks, and every task can be achieved by adopting some sub-goals. Importantly, an NPC needs to perform only one task to achieve a goal, provided there is no failure, but it must fulfill all sub-goals, or most of them, to solve a task. Consequently, the behavioral decomposition is given by an AND-OR tree (AND levels for goals, OR levels for tasks). The CD examples feature such AND-OR trees; however, the LOD technique works well with any behavioral decomposition; the distinction between goals and tasks is unimportant for it. Thus, for explanatory purposes, we assume throughout that we have just ordinary sub-behaviors, and we call them *tasks*.

Whatever the exact representation is, the key is that a) the hierarchy can be constructed so that its highest level represents abstract behavior to which lower levels add more detail, and b) each level can be made executable. Thus:

1. In the design phase, construct the hierarchy in this way and manually assign LODs to its levels (refer to Figure 3.1.3).

2. During execution, determine what level of the behavioral hierarchy is the lowest that should be executed. This is the level of the LOD that corresponds to the detail of the simulation at the place where the NPCs are located (see Figure 3.1.4).
3. Execute this task as *atomic*, approximating what would happen when the simulation is run at a finer detail.

Unfortunately, these three points brings many problems. We will address them in turn.

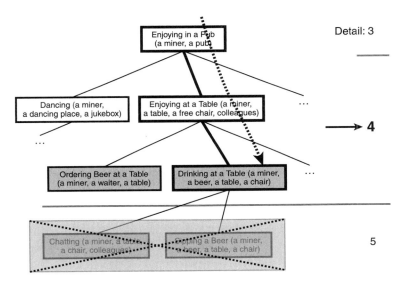

Figure 3.1.4   "Drinking at a table" is executed as atomic. Atomic tasks are in gray.

What Does It Mean to Execute a Task as Atomic?

Atomic execution means two things. First, every task to be executed atomically must be represented in the event list by a start event and an end event, similar to atomic actions. For instance, assume that there is LOD 4 in the pub. The corresponding behavioral level contains the task of drinking at a table. The event list will contain the end event of this act but not of atomic actions of sipping a beer or chatting.

Second, for every task, designers must specify a) its result, and b) its estimated duration. When a task is simulated in full detail, its particular runs can have different durations. Often, the exact duration of a run will be influenced by the animation layer (for example, an NPC walks from one room to another in a different amount of time based on the positions of objects the NPC has to avoid). Fortunately, with lower LODs, you need not worry about exactly how long the task would have lasted had the simulation run in the full detail. All you need is a plausible estimate of that time.

Based on this estimate, you place the task's end event in the event list. Note that you may generate this estimate from a probabilistic distribution given by designers.

When should the result (in other words, Point A) be revealed? There are three possibilities: 1) at the beginning of the task (that is, when the start event is processed); 2) at the end (in other words, when the end event is processed); or 3) during the task. For the drinking miner, (1) would mean drinking the glass at once and then doing nothing for 20 to 40 minutes, while (2) would be doing nothing for 20 to 40 minutes and then drinking the glass at once. Variant (3) is not consistent, and (1) changes the world sooner than it is known that the task is successfully finished. Thus, we recommend using (2).

However, designing the scenario at different levels presents extra work, and you have to consider in which situations these shortcuts are really needed. In extreme, you program the whole simulation from scratch at each LOD, though programming more abstract levels is much simpler than the full detail.

What to Do When the Detail Increases

Sadly, the detail can elevate in the middle of a task's atomic execution—in other words, between its start event and end event. For instance, the player may enter the pub while the miners are drinking at a table atomically. We call such situation a *task expansion* and the part of the task that has already been performed at the lower detail a *task stub* (see Figure 3.1.5). When this happens, you need to:

1. Remove the end event of the expanded task from the event list.
2. Compute the partial effect of the task stub, if needed.
3. Start the simulation at the higher detail.

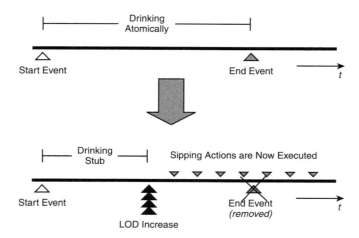

Figure 3.1.5   LOD has increased from 4 (up) to 5 (bottom), creating a stub from drinking atomically. The original end event must be removed.

The partial effect of a task stub should approximate the outcome of the stub's detailed simulation (in other words, as if the task was running from the beginning until the moment of expansion at the higher detail). You again need the designer's specification and the code for determining the partial effect, which is extra work.

Actually, it is necessary to perform Point 2 only if the user may notice the discrepancy; otherwise, it is sufficient to start execution of the expanded task at the lower detail from its beginning, pretending that the task stub has never happened. In other words, you specify that the partial effect is nothing. In our drinking example, this would mean that all the drinkers would start with a full glass at the time of the LOD increase, but this may be fine if you do not visualize how much beer is in the glasses. However, consider watering a garden: Here, the player may find it strange that the gardener is always just starting with the first garden bed at the time the player enters the garden. It may be necessary to decide that some fraction of the garden has already been watered at the time of expansion.

When you need to compute the partial effect of a task stub, what are the options? Often, it is desirable to avoid simulation of the task stub at the higher detail. This would give you an exact result, but at the cost of too much overhead. Instead, you need to consider which state variables the task changes predictably (see Figure 3.1.6, left and middle) and which it does not (see Figure 3.1.6, right). In the former case, the partial effect can be determined by a simple formula. In the latter case, a more sophisticated *ad hoc* mechanism has to be created.

For instance, think of the LOD increase from Detail 3 to 4 in the pub. On one hand, you can easily figure out how much beer has been drunk based on the number of miners in the pub. On the other hand, you also need to assign the miners to the tables. To do the latter, the designer has to come up with an *ad hoc* mechanism.

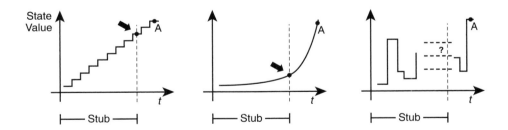

Figure 3.1.6 Although the final outcome of three tasks being executed atomically is the same (Point A), their details differ. At the finer LOD, the state variable may change in a predictable way (left, middle) or in an unpredictable way (right). The arrows denote the LOD increase.

What to Do When the Detail Decreases

Let us have a location in which detail n should be decreased to $n-1$. We say that tasks (or atomic actions) corresponding to detail n are being pruned away, whereas tasks corresponding to detail $n-1$ are being shrunk—that is, starting to be executed as atomic.

Since the LOD decrease must apply to a whole area, as detailed later, more tasks may need to be pruned away—for example, drinking tasks of all individual miners in the pub. These tasks may not end at the same moment. Thus, they should be stopped using the mechanism of partial effect described previously. Only then can you execute shrinking tasks as atomic. It is important to stop the tasks being pruned away at one instant; otherwise, the area will end up in an inconsistent state, with some tasks being simulated at detail n and others at $n-1$.

An important point of any LOD AI is that, by definition, some information is lost during a LOD decrease. This brings two problems. First, the partial effect of tasks and actions being pruned away should be partly forgotten but also partly exploited by the subsequent simulation at LOD $n-1$. Second, when the LOD increases again, the missing information should be reconstructed. This is similar to lossy compression.

The second problem was partly treated earlier (assigning miners to tables), and we will also return to it later. The first problem is exemplified now in Figure 3.1.7, showing a barman walking to a table while LOD goes from 5 to 4. In this example, we are concerned with the barman's position, but similar reasoning applies for any state of an object.

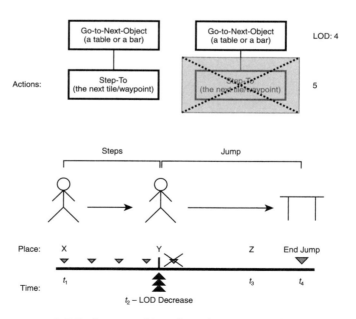

Figure 3.1.7   LOD decrease. "Steps" are being pruned away at t_2, while "go-to-next-object" task is being shrunk into the atomic "jump."

Recall that the saloon is a single point at LOD 4. Figure 3.1.7 shows that when the simulation runs on the LOD 4, the walking barman is engaged in the task "go-to-next-object," which makes the barman "jump" from one object to another. These objects are tables or the bar. If the saloon is not too oblong, we may further assume unitary distances (at LOD 4) between all pairs of these objects. At LOD 5, "go-to-next-object" breaks down into a sequence of "step-to" atomic actions.

Now, consider the LOD decrease from 5 to 4 at time t_2—that is, around the middle of the "go-to-next-object" from Object X to the table. Should the barman start his "jump" from Object X or Place Y, and how long should it take?

Because Place Y does not exist at LOD 4, it seems that the best option is to let the barman start his "jump" from X. However, since you cannot roll back what has already happened, the barman would walk from X to Y twice, and a clever user may notice this should the detail increase soon (say, at time t_3, when the barman is expected to be around Z).

The second option is to say that the barman is somewhere on the way and compute how long the rest of the "jump" (in other words, from Y to the table) will last. This is more accurate, but it creates an extra work. Additionally, this works well only when the object's state is updated in a predictable way at the finer detail (refer to Figure 3.1.6, left and middle).

The first method actually works acceptably if you manage to avoid an early LOD increase. The longer the period between a LOD decrease and the subsequent LOD increase, the more inconsistencies due to a simplified determination of the initial state of the simulation at LOD *n-1* are disguised. A simple mechanism for avoiding early LOD increase will be shown later.

Space Representation

So far, we have spoken about how to simplify behavior given a LOD, but we also need to know the value of the LOD and its radius, and we need these values for all parts of the virtual world. Perhaps the simplest way to get this information is to represent the world hierarchically, as you can examine on the CD example. The spatial hierarchy keeps information about children, parents, and neighbors of every location except for the leaves and the root, which lack children or has only them, respectively.

For simplification, assume now that the number of LODs equals the number of spatial levels. (This is not a strict requirement.) Now, a membrane metaphor can be used to describe which LOD is where. Imagine an elastic membrane cutting through the spatial hierarchy (see Figure 3.1.8), touching some locations. We say that every location or an atomic place that is at the membrane at a particular instant is simulated as an abstract point. No location "below" the membrane exists. Every NPC is simulated at the LOD equal to the level on which the membrane is touching the area in which that NPC is located; spatial LOD determines behavioral LOD.

Formally, the membrane is nothing more than a list of locations that are simulated as abstract points at a particular moment. The membrane can be reshaped in every time step.

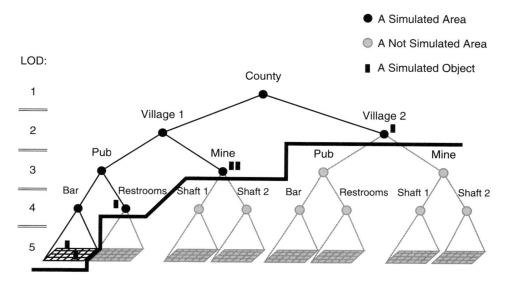

Figure 3.1.8 LOD membrane.

For the purposes of coherence, we enforce the following shaping rules:

1. If a location or an atomic place X is at the membrane, every location or atomic place with the same parent as X is at the membrane, too.

2. If a location Y is above the membrane, every location with the same parent as Y is above or at least at the membrane, too. For example, if an atomic place from the saloon is at the membrane, all the saloon's atomic places will be at the membrane, too (Rule 1). This ensures that when the simulation runs in the full detail somewhere in the saloon, it will run in the full detail everywhere here. Because the saloon itself is above the membrane in this case, all rooms from the pub must be simulated at least as abstract points (Rule 2). This ensures that almost always at least something happens in the locations near the center of attention.

   Because LODs of two adjacent locations can differ (that is, when they do not have the same parent), the visibility of a player should be limited to the location she is in. If this is not possible, such as in open spaces, another shaping rule must be settled.

3. The detail must be maximum in all locations the player can see at a given instant.

Limitations of Rules 1 through 3

Rules 1 through 3 work fine, but you should know that there is an exception in which they do not guarantee that something happens near the center of attention. The problem is that two neighboring locations may have different parents, thus their LODs can differ by more than 1. Think of a world with two kingdoms. There are two houses there next to each other, but the border goes right between them. Even though the first house is simulated in full detail, the second kingdom may still have just LOD 1; the houses do not have a common parent.

To deal with this, a mechanism of influences is needed. This would allow you to specify another shaping rule based on the influence a location has on its all neighboring locations. The trouble with this mechanism is that it may cause cascade effects during membrane reshaping, increasing the overhead. You can read more about this topic in the documentation on the CD.

Pathfinding

So far, we have been silent on pathfinding. With the spatial hierarchy, it is apparent that a hierarchical refinement of A^* can be used easily for simplifying pathfinding at a lower LOD.

Positions of Objects and NPCs

We know that the pub is abstracted to a single point at LOD 3. Assume there is one miner and one barman there. What happens with their positions during LOD changes?

Because the pub's rooms do not exist at LOD 3, both the barman and the miner are, so to speak, spread out in the whole pub as two uncollapsed quantum particles; they are at the membrane. Assume further that the LOD decreases to 2. While this lifts the miner a level up, spreading him out in the village, the barman becomes non-simulated because his story never leads him out of the pub (see Figure 3.1.9). This means that the barman "fell through" the membrane; his traces have been lost for the rest of the simulation.

The problem is that we need to narrow down object and NPC positions after the detail elevates. When the LOD goes from 2 to 3, we know that the barman has to be collapsed into the pub, but this is not the case of the miner. We do not know where to generate him; he can be collapsed into the pub or into his house or on the street, and so on. A similar problem arises for the LOD increase from Detail 3 to 4.

We now introduce a basic mechanism dealing with generation of positions of objects. The real case is actually more complex than this mechanism. Following, we will extend it and comment on how to use it for NPCs.

1. Objects in every location should be divided into two groups—those that are *location-native*, for objects owned by the location, and those that are *location-foreign*, for objects owned by other locations. (A glass is location-native in the pub, as opposed to a mine truck.) An object can be location-native in more locations. (A glass is location-native in the bar as well as in the kitchen.)

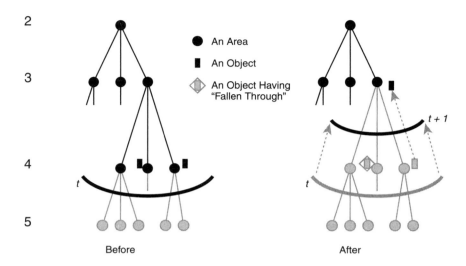

2

3

4

5

● An Area

■ An Object

◈ An Object Having "Fallen Through"

t + 1

Before   After

Figure 3.1.9   LOD increase. Some objects are "lifted up," while others are not.

2. Every location from the nth level of the spatial hierarchy should have a method implementing where to generate location-native objects if the detail elevates from n to $n+1$ (for example, during the Detail 3 to 4 transition, the pub "knows" where to generate the tables and glasses).

3. When LOD decreases in a particular location, the detailed positional information for all the location-foreign objects having been "lifted up" is memorized, but not for the location-native objects having been "lifted up" (due to Point 2).

4. When location-native objects "fall through" the membrane, only their total number in the area where they "fall though" is remembered (for example, after the 4-to-3 transition, it will be remembered that there are, say, 27 beer glasses in the pub). For location-foreign objects, the exact positions are remembered. (After the same transition, the watering can will become non-simulated, but two memory records will be kept: for the 5-to-4 and 4-to-3 transitions.)

5. When LOD increases, location-foreign objects are generated based on their stored positional information. In some rare situations, this information may not be available; this will be discussed in a moment.

The idea behind this is that during the design phase, one can specify relatively easily which objects are native in which locations and implement placing algorithms appropriately.

Storage of Positional Information

When a location-foreign object is simulated, it can hold its own positional information. The records about location-foreign non-simulated objects' positions and about numbers of location-native non-simulated objects can be kept by parent locations. (For example, the pub "knows" that it contains 27 glasses.)

Often, when the parent location ceases to exist, the player is so far away that the records held by this location can be happily forgotten. Nevertheless, should a piece of information survive destruction of the location to which it is attached, you can do the following. In the design phase, specify the information level denoting the LOD at which this particular kind of information can be forgotten. At run time, after the location "falls through" the membrane, attach your record to the upper location (in our case, the village) provided the new LOD is still higher than or equal to the information level of this record. (Mind the direction: A higher LOD is lower in the hierarchy!)

General Information and Expirations

The aforementioned mechanism can be generalized in two ways. First, one can store not only positional information, but any state information. Assume a player has broken a window in the pub. A clever player would not return soon, but if she does, she may expect the window to still be broken. The record about the broken window can be stored by the pub. Similarly, sometimes it may be beneficial to record the exact positional information for a location-native object. If the player moves a table a bit, and the pub's LOD goes to and fro, the basic aforementioned mechanism would generate the table incorrectly, on the original place. The extra record will remedy this problem.

After a while, this record may become useless; sooner or later, someone may repair the window and move the table back. If you need this feature, you can basically delete a record after a specified amount of time using a mechanism of expirations.

Initialization and Traveling Objects

There are two situations in which it is necessary to initialize objects' positions. The first one occurs after the simulation starts. Additionally, sometimes it is necessary to initialize objects' positions when the objects move between locations.

The first situation is trivial: You must have an implicit initialization procedure. Let us now elaborate on the second case. Assume the pub is simulated at LOD 4, meaning all the pub's rooms are single points. A miner puts down a watering can in the saloon, where the can is location-foreign. Now, the LOD elevates to 5. Where do you place the can? Sometimes, the procedure initializing positions at the beginning of the simulation can help. More often, you would find useful a general placing mechanism that groups objects based on their typical places of occurrence into floor-objects, table-objects, and so on, and that generates these objects randomly within constraints of the objects' categories. Consider now that LOD decreases later from 5 to 4, and the miner picks up the can in the pub and takes it out. If this happens, do not forget to delete the record about the can's detailed position.

NPCs

When the detail increases, we have to refine a) positions of NPCs, and b) tasks they are engaged in. For (a), we can treat NPCs as objects. For (b), the task expansion mechanism described earlier should be used.

Reshaping the Membrane

The final question is how to shape the membrane. A simple solution, adopted by the example on the CD, is to assign an existence level and a view level to every object. If the detail decreases below the existence level, the object ceases to exist; otherwise, it is to be simulated. The view level then determines the detail required by the object after it starts to be simulated. Hence, the view level is always equal to or higher than the existence level. For many common objects, these levels will be equal, but not for story-important objects or NPCs. Every user's avatar will have the existence level equal to 1 and the view level equal to the maximum.

Assume now a traveler with his view level set to 4 and his existence level to 2. He will not exist until the detail is at least 2, but when it elevates to this value, the traveler will demand that in the location to which he has been generated, the detail goes further to 4. Note that according to the shaping rules, this further determines increasing detail in some of the neighboring locations. Because this may create new objects demanding additional LOD increases, a cascade of changes may be triggered. The algorithm for doing this consistently is detailed in [Šerý06].

Sometimes, you may want to increase the detail even if no important object is around; for instance, think of a brawl being simulated in a village far away that is expected to grow into a local uprising. You may need to show the behavior of those NPCs to the player in a cut scene. To do this, you can simply put an invisible object into the simulation with the appropriate view level to ensure the player will see the AI behavior.

What Is the Radius of LODs?

Using this technique, all users and important objects/NPCs tend to automatically create a "simulation crater" around them due to the spatial hierarchy and the shaping rules. As they move, the detail elevates (typically) by one in locations at the edge of the crater, avoiding abrupt jumps of LOD. LODs are not specified in terms of metrical distances, but in terms of number of locations between the object/NPC and the edge of the crater.

This has two advantages. First, the LOD does not change all the time, as would be the case with pure metrical distances, helping to reduce the overhead. Further, the overhead is spread in time: If you go from 1 to 5, you do this in more steps. Figure 3.1.10 demonstrates that there is indeed a qualitative difference in overhead between the 4-to-5 increase (left) and 3-to-5 (right) in the pub in our CD example.

Second, by the time a person arrives at a location, that location typically has been simulated for a while, disguising inconsistencies caused due to lower LODs.

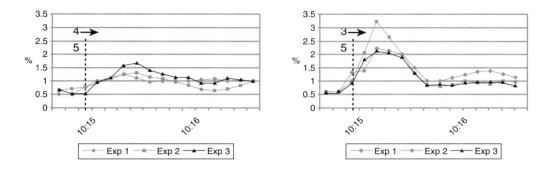

Figure 3.1.10 Processor consumption during the LOD increase.
The X-axis represents the time in the game. The LOD increases at 10:15 p.m.;
this time is arbitrary. This figure shows data from three particular runs.
Note that the data for the 3-to-4 increase resembles the data for the 4-to-5 increase.

When to Decrease the Detail

There is a problem with reshaping the LOD membrane when an object moves between two locations repeatedly. The LOD may start to oscillate, increasing the resources' consumption. You can do either of the following two things. First, you can have a larger crater determining when to decrease the LOD. This larger crater would embrace the smaller crater that enforces the LOD increase. Second, you can use, as we did, a garbage mechanism. With the garbage mechanism, you do not decrease LOD until the resources are needed for something else. This mimics the larger crater automatically. However, because the cleanup causes overhead, it is better to use the garbage mechanism a bit sooner than the resources are actually needed, letting the mechanism work over several time steps.

Creating the Structure of the World

In practice, it rarely makes sense to have more LODs than levels of the spatial hierarchy. In the spatial hierarchy, you should keep a reasonable number of sublocations for every parent—neither 1 nor 50. This is not a strict rule, but if you violate this principle too often, the hierarchy should be reconstructed. Even though higher numbers may make sense logically (a building with many small rooms), with respect to the technique presented here, this would increase the overhead for a LOD change.

Recall that LODs also have to be assigned to the behavioral hierarchy. You should do this consistently, meaning the degree of abstraction of two tasks from a particular level should be similar. For instance, if LOD 3 is assigned to watering a garden, it should also be assigned to cooking, but not peeling potatoes. For technical purposes, you may need more levels in behavioral hierarchy than LODs, as demonstrated on the CD example.

Another aspect to keep in mind is that after assigning LODs to tasks, objects required for these tasks must have their existence level set accordingly. Assume watering a garden has LOD 3, and the garden is an abstract point at LOD 3. If it is required by designers that watering a garden has to run with a watering can at this LOD, meaning the gardener has to pick up the can before he comes to the garden, the existence level of the can must be 3 or less. Watering a garden would then mean something like, "Stay there holding the can for a specified amount of time, after which the garden will become watered at one instant." Of course, designers might also specify that the gardener is able to water the garden without the can at LOD 3; the task's outcome would be the same, only the can would not be required. In the latter case, you would need to generate the can after the LOD increase.

Note that the technique does not allow for two existence levels for one object kind—for example, it is not possible that a knife for fighting has existence level 3, while a knife for cooking has 5. You must define either one object kind with the lower number or two different object kinds with two different existence levels.

Source Code Summary

The application included on the CD is a simulator of virtual worlds with LOD AI (in other words, it is not a game). The examples discussed in this chapter are based on the implemented demo world, which features five LODs and three kinds of NPCs: miners, barmen, and singers. The following behaviors have been implemented: walking home from a pub or a mine and vice versa, leisure time behavior (for pubs), and working behavior (for mines). The code is in Java, and the documentation that is included details the LOD technique further.

Conclusion

Level-of-detail techniques allow for compromising between the consumption of computational resources and simulation plausibility. However, every LOD technique presents extra work for designers and programmers. Thus, it should be contemplated carefully which LOD approach is needed and whether it is needed at all.

The technique introduced in this gem fits well for large worlds with many NPCs with everyday behavior. It capitalizes on the fact that both space and behavior of NPCs can be, and often already are, represented hierarchically. The different number of LODs helps not only with simulation plausibility, but also with keeping the overhead under control during LOD changes.

The technique is generic, which means that for specific domains, special-purpose mechanisms can outperform it—for example, for fighting behavior [Brockington02, Grinke04]. Even in complex worlds, any special-purpose mechanism can be augmented with some or all of this technique if needed.

Acknowledgements

This technique and the simulator on the CD were developed as a part of research projects 1ET100300517 of the Program Information Society and MSM0021620838 of the Ministry of Education of the Czech Republic. We want to thank several students who participated in the simulator development: Martin Juhász, Jan Kubr, Jiří Kulhánek, Pavel Šafrata, Zdeněk Šulc, Jiří Vorba, and Petr Zíta.

References

[Bratman87] Bratman, Michael E. *Intention, Plans, and Practical Reason.* Harvard University Press, 1987.

[Brockington02] Brockington, Mark. "Level-Of-Detail AI for a Large Role-Playing Game." *AI Game Programming Wisdom I.* Boston: Charles River Media, 2002. 419–425.

[Champandard08] Champandard, Alex J. "Getting Started with Decision Making and Control Systems." *AI Game Programming Wisdom IV.* Boston: Charles River Media, 2008. 257–264.

[Chenney01] Chenney, Stephen. "Simulation Level-Of-Detail." 2001. University of Wisconsin. n.d. <http://www.cs.wisc.edu/~schenney/research/culling/chenney-gdc2001.pdf>.

[Fu04] Fu, Dan, and Ryan Houlette. "The Ultimate Guide to FSMs in Games." *AI Game Programming Wisdom II.* Boston: Charles River Media, 2004. 283–302.

[Grinke04] Grinke, Sebastian. "Minimizing Agent Processing in 'Conflict: Desert Storm.'" *AI Game Programming Wisdom II.* Boston: Charles River Media, 2004. 373–378.

[Harvey02] Harvey, Michael, and Carl Marshall. "Scheduling Game Events." *Game Programming Gems 3.* Boston: Charles River Media, 2002. 5–14.

[Isla05] Isla, Damian. "Handling Complexity in Halo 2." 3 Nov. 2005. Gamasutra. n.d. <http://www.gamasutra.com/view/feature/2250/gdc_2005_proceeding_handling_php>.

[Šerý06] Šerý, Ondřej, et al. "Level-Of-Detail in Behaviour of Virtual Humans." *Proceedings of SOFSEM 2006: Theory and Practice of Computer Science* 3831 (2006): 565–574.

[Wiki09] Wikipedia, The Free Encyclopedia. "Discrete Event Simulation." 2009. Wikipedia. n.d. <http://en.wikipedia.org/wiki/Discrete_event_simulation>.

3.2

A Pattern-Based Approach to Modular AI for Games

Kevin Dill, Boston University
kdill4@gmail.com

A great deal of time and effort is spent developing the AI for the average modern game. Years ago, AI was often an afterthought for a single gameplay programmer, but these days most game projects employ at least one dedicated AI specialist, and entire AI teams are becoming increasingly common. At the same time, more and more developers are coming to realize that, even in multiplayer games, AI is not only a critical component for providing fun gameplay, but it is also essential if we are going to continue to increase the sense of realism and believability that were previously the domain of physics and rendering. It does no good to have a brilliantly rendered game with true-to-life physics if your characters feel like cardboard cutouts or zombie robots.

Given this increase in team size, the increasing prominence of AI in the success or failure of a game, and the inevitable balancing and feature creep that occur toward the end of every project, it behooves us to search for AI techniques that enable fast implementation, shared conventions between team members, and easy modification. Toward that end, this gem describes methods for applying patterns to our AI in such a way as to allow it to be built, tuned, and extended in a modular fashion.

The key insight that drives the entirety of this work is that the decisions made by the AI can typically be broken down into much smaller considerations, individual tests used in combination to make a single decision. The same considerations can apply to many different decisions. Furthermore, the evaluation of those considerations can be performed independent of the larger decision, and then the results can be combined as necessary into a final decision. Thus, we can implement the logic for each consideration once, test it extensively, and then reuse that logic throughout our AI.

None of the core principles described here are new. They can be found throughout software engineering and academic AI in a variety of forms. However, all too often we game programmers rush into building code, trying to solve our specific problem of the day and get the product out the door, without taking a step back and thinking about how to improve those systems. With some thought and organization, it could be easier to change, extend, and even reuse bits and pieces in future projects. Taking the time to do that would pay off both in the short run, making life easier (and thus improving the final result) for the current title, and in the long run, as more AI code is carried forward from game to game.

A Real-World Example: Apartment Shopping

Let's begin with a real-world example that illustrates the general ideas behind this work. Imagine that you have just taken a new job as an AI engineer at Middle of Nowhere Games, and you are in the process of searching for an apartment in some faraway city. You might visit a variety of candidates, write down a list of the advantages and disadvantages of each, and then use that list to guide your final decision.

For an apartment in a large complex near a busy shopping area, for example, your list might look something like this:

606 Automobile Way, Apt 316

Pros	Cons
Close to work	Great view...of a used car lot
Easy highway access	No off-street parking
Convenient shopping district	Highway noise

Another apartment, located in the attic of a kindly old lady's country house, might have a wholly different list:

10-B Placid Avenue

Pros	Cons
Low rent	45-minute commute
Nearby woods, biking trails	No shopping nearby
Electricity and water included	Thin walls, landlady downstairs

These lists clearly reflect the decision-maker's personal taste—in fact, it seems likely that if two people were to make lists for the same apartment, their lists would have little in common. It is not the actual decision being made that's important, but rather the process being used to arrive at that decision. That is to say, given a large decision (Where should I live for the next several years of my life?), this process breaks that decision down into a number of independent considerations, each of which can be evaluated in isolation. Only after each consideration has been properly evaluated do we tackle the larger decision.

There is a reasonably finite set of common considerations (such as the rent, ease of commute, size of the apartment, aesthetics of the apartment and surrounding environment, and so forth) that would commonly be taken into account by apartment shoppers.

From an AI point of view, if we can encode those considerations, we can then share the logic for them from actor to actor, and in some cases even from decision to decision.

As an example of the latter advantage, imagine that we wanted to select a location for a picnic. Several of the considerations used for apartments—such as overall cost, the aesthetics of the surrounding environment, and the length of the drive to get there—would also be used when picking a picnic spot. Again, if it were an NPC making this decision, then cleverly designed code could be shared in a modular way and could perhaps even be configured by a designer once the initial work of implementing the overall architecture and individual considerations was complete.

Another advantage of this type of approach is that it supports extensibility. For example, imagine that after visiting several apartments, we came across one that had a hot tub and pool or a tennis court. Previously, we had not even considered the availability of these features. However, we can now add this consideration to our list of pros and cons without disturbing the remainder of our logic.

At this point we have made a number of grandiose claims—hopefully sufficient to pique the reader's interest—but we clearly have some practical problems as well. What is described above is a wholly human approach to decision-making, not easily replicated in code. Our next step, then, should be to see whether we can apply a similar approach to making relatively simple decisions, such as those that rely on a single yes or no answer.

Boolean Decisions

Many common architectures rely on simple Boolean logic at their core. For example, from a functional point of view, finite state machines have a Boolean decision-maker attached to each transition, determining whether to take that transition given the current situation. Behavior trees navigate the tree through a series of Boolean decisions (take this branch or don't take this branch) until they arrive at an action they want to take. Rule-based architectures consist of a series of "rules," each of which is a Boolean decision stating whether or not to execute the associated action. And so forth.

Constructing Decisions

To build a pattern-based architecture for our AI, we first need to define a shared interface for our considerations and then decide how to combine the results of their evaluation into a final decision. For Boolean decisions, consider the following interface:

```
class IConsiderationBoolean
{
public:
    IConsiderationBoolean()              {}
    virtual ~IConsiderationBoolean()     {}

    // Evaluate this consideration
    bool Evaluate(const DecisionContext& context) = 0;
```

```
// Load the data that controls our decisions
void LoadData(const DataNode& node) = 0;
}
```

Every consideration will inherit from this interface and therefore will be required to specify the `Evaluate()` and `LoadData()` methods.

`Evaluate()` takes a `DecisionContext` as its only argument. The context contains whatever information might be needed to make a decision. For example, it might include the current game time, a pointer to the actor being controlled, a pointer to the game world, and so on. Alternatively, it might simply be a pointer to the actor's knowledge base, where beliefs about the world are stored. Regardless, `Evaluate()` processes the state of the world (as contained in the context) and then returns true if execution is approved or false otherwise.

The other mandatory function is `LoadData()`. The data being loaded specifies how the decision should be made. We will go into more detail on this issue later in this gem.

Games are rife with examples of considerations that can be encoded in this way. For example, we might have a health consideration that will only allow an action to be taken if a character's hit points are in a specified range. A time-of-day consideration might only allow an action to take place during the day (or at night or between noon and 1:00 p.m.). A cool-down consideration could prevent an action from being taken if it has been executed in the recent past.

The simplest approach for combining Boolean considerations into a final decision is to give each consideration veto power on the overall decision. That is, take the action being gated by the decision if and only if every consideration returns true. Obviously, more robust techniques can be implemented, up to and including full predicate logic, but this simple approach works well for a surprisingly large number of cases and has the advantage of being extremely simple to implement.

A Simple Example: First-Person Shooter AI

As an example of this approach in a game environment, consider the simple state machine in Figure 3.2.1, which is a simplified version of what might be found in a typical first-person shooter's combat AI (for example).

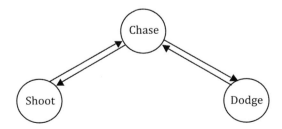

Figure 3.2.1   A simplified state machine for FPS combat AI.

In this AI, Chase is our default state. We exit it briefly to dodge or take a shot, but then return to it as soon as we're done with that action. Here are the considerations we might attach to each transition:

Chase ⇒ Shoot:
- We have a line of sight to the player.
- It has been at least two seconds since our last shot.
- It has been at least one second since we last dodged.
- The player's health is over 0 percent (that is, he's not dead yet).

Chase ⇒ Dodge:
- We have a line of sight to the player.
- The player is aiming at us.
- It has been at least one seconds since our last shot.
- It has been at least five seconds since we last dodged.
- Our health is below 60 percent. (As we take more damage, we become more cautious.)
- Our health is less than 1.2 times the player's health. (If we're winning, we become more aggressive.)

Shoot ⇒ Chase:
- We've completed the Shoot action.

Dodge ⇒ Chase:
- We've completed the Dodge action.

One advantage of breaking down our logic in this way is that we can encapsulate the shared logic from each decision in a single place. Here are the considerations used above:
- **Line of Sight Consideration.** Checks the line of sight from our actor to the player (or, more generally, from our actor to an arbitrary target that can be specified in the data or the `DecisionContext`).
- **Aiming at Consideration.** Checks whether the player's weapon is pointed toward our actor.
- **Cool-down Consideration.** Checks elapsed time since a specified type of action was last taken.
- **Absolute Health Consideration.** Checks whether the current health of our actor (or the player) is over (or under) a specified cutoff.
- **Health Comparison Consideration.** Checks the ratio between our actor's health and the player's health.
- **Completion Consideration.** Checks whether the current action is complete.

Each of those considerations represents a common pattern that can be found not only in this specific example, but also in a great many decisions in a great many games.

These patterns are not unique to these particular decisions or even this particular genre. In fact, many of them can be seen in one form or another in virtually every game that has ever been written. Line-of-sight checks, for example, or cool-downs to prevent abilities from being used too frequently…these are basic to game AI.

AI Specification

At this point we have all the pieces we need. We know what behaviors we plan to support (in this case, one behavior per state), we know all of the decisions that need to be made (represented by the transitions), and we know the considerations that go into each decision. However, there is still some work to do to put it all together.

Most of what needs to be done is straightforward. We can implement a character class that contains an AI. The AI contains a set of states. Each state contains a list of transitions, and each transition contains a list of considerations.

Keep in mind that the considerations don't always do the same thing. For example, both Chase ⇒ Shoot and Chase ⇒ Dodge contain an Absolute Health consideration, but those considerations are expected to return true under very different conditions. For Chase ⇒ Shoot, we return true if the health of the player is above 0 percent. For Chase ⇒ Dodge, on the other hand, we return true if the health of our actor is below 60 percent. More generally, each decision that includes this condition also needs to specify whether it should examine the health of the player or our actor, whether it should return true when that value is above or below the cutoff, and what cutoff it should use. The information used to specify how each instance of a consideration should evaluate the world is obtained through the LoadData() function:

```
void CsdrHealth::LoadData(const DataNode& node)
{
    // If true we check the player's health, otherwise
    //   we check our actor's health.
    m_CheckPlayer = node.GetBoolean("CheckPlayer");

    // The cutoff for our health check — may be the
    //   upper or lower limit, depending on the value
    //   of m_HighIsGood.
    m_Cutoff = node.GetFloat("Cutoff");

    // If true then we return true when our health is
    //   above the cutoff, otherwise we return true when
    //   our health is below the cutoff.
    m_HighIsGood = node.GetBoolean("HighIsGood");
}
```

As you can see, this is fairly straightforward. We simply acquire the three values the Evaluate() function will need from our data node. With that in mind, here is the Evaluate() function itself:

```
bool CsdrHealth::Evaluate(const DecisionContext& ctxt)
{
```

```
    // Get the health that we're checking — either ours
    //  or the player's.
    float health;
    if (m_CheckPlayer)
        health = ctxt.GetHealth(ctxt.GetPlayer());
    else
        health = ctxt.GetHealth(ctxt.GetMyActor());

    // Do the check.
    if (m_HighIsGood)
        return currentHealth >= m_Cutoff;
    else
        return currentHealth <= m_Cutoff;
    }
}
```

Again, there's nothing complicated here. We get the appropriate health value (either ours or the player's, depending on what LoadData() told us) from the context and compare it to the cutoff.

The simplicity of this code is in many ways the entire point. Each consideration is simple and easy to test in its own right, but combined they become powerfully expressive.

Extending the AI

Now that we have built a functional core AI for our shiny new FPS game, it's time to start iterating on that AI, finding ways in which it's less than perfect, and fixing them. As a first step, let's imagine that we wanted to add two new states: Flee and Search (as seen in Figure 3.2.2). Like all existing states, these new states transition to and from the Chase state. Here are the considerations for our new transitions:

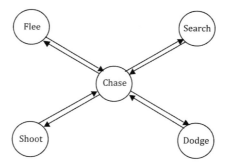

Figure 3.2.2   Our state machine with two new states.

Chase ⇒ Flee:
- Our health is below 15 percent.
- The player's health is above 10 percent. (If he's almost dead, finish him.)

Flee $\Rightarrow$ Chase:
* The player's health is below 10 percent.
* We have a line of sight to the player.

Chase $\Rightarrow$ Search:
* We don't have a line of sight to the player.

Search $\Rightarrow$ Chase:
* We have a line of sight to the player.

As you can see, adding these states should be fairly simple. We will need to implement the new behaviors, but all of the considerations needed to decide whether to execute those behaviors already exist.

Of course, not all changes can be made using existing considerations. For example, imagine that we want to make two further changes to our AI:

* QA complains that dodging is too predictable. Instead of always using a five-second cool-down, they want us to use a cool-down that varies randomly between three and seven seconds.
* The artists would like to add a really cool-looking animation for drawing your weapon. In order to support this, the designers have asked us to have the characters draw their weapons when they enter Chase and then holster them again if they go into Search.

The key is to find a way to modify our existing code so that we can support these new specifications without affecting any other portion of the AI. We certainly don't want to have to go through the entire AI for every character, find every place that these considerations are used, and change the data for all of them.

Implementing the variable cool-down is fairly straightforward. Previously the Cool-Down consideration took a single argument to specify the length of the cool-down. We'll modify it to optionally take minimum and maximum values instead. Thus, all the existing cases will continue to work (with an exact value specified), but our Cool-Down consideration will now have improved functionality that can be used to fix this bug and can also be used in the future as we continue to build the AI. We'll have to take some care in making sure that we check that exactly one type of cool-down is specified. In other words, the user needs to specify either an exact cool-down or a variable cool-down; he or she can't specify both. An Assert in `LoadData()` should be sufficient.

For the second change, we can make the Chase behavior automatically draw the weapon (if it's not drawn already), so that doesn't require a change to our decision logic. We do need to ensure that we don't start shooting until the weapon is fully drawn, however. In order to do that, we simply implement an Is Weapon Drawn consideration and add it to the transition from Chase to Shoot.

Data-Driven AI

One thing to notice is that all of the values required to specify our AI are selected at game design time. That is, we determine up front what decisions our AI needs to make, what considerations are necessary to support those decisions, and what tuning values we should specify for each consideration. Once the game is running, they are always the same. For example, our actor's hit points might go up or down, but if a decision uses an Absolute Health consideration, then the threshold at which we switch between true and false never changes during gameplay.

Since none of this changes during gameplay, nearly all of the decision-making logic can be specified in data. We can specify the AI for each character, where the AI contains a set of states, each state contains a list of transitions, each transition contains a list of considerations, and each consideration contains the tuning values used for that portion of the AI. This sort of hierarchical structure is something that XML does well, making it an excellent choice for our data specification.

As with all data-driven architectures, the big advantage is that if we want to change the way the decisions are made, we only have to change data, not code. No recompile is required. If you've implemented the ability to reload the data while the game is live, you don't even need to restart the game, which can save a lot of time when testing a situation that is tricky to re-create in-game. Of course, some changes, such as implementing an entirely new consideration, will require code changes, but much of the tuning and tweaking—and sometimes even more sizeable adjustments—will not.

One thing to consider when taking this approach is whether it's worth investing some time into the tools you use for data specification. Our experience has been that the time spent specifying and tuning behavior is significantly greater than the time spent writing the core reasoner. Good tools can not only make those adjustments quicker and easier (especially if they're integrated into the game so that adjustments can be made in real time), but they can also include error checking for common mistakes and help to avoid subtle behavioral bugs that might otherwise be hard to catch. Further, since many of these considerations are broadly applicable to a variety of games, not only the considerations but also the tools for specifying them could be carried from game to game as part of your engine (or even integrated into a new engine). Finally, it is often possible to allow designers and artists to specify AI logic if you create good tools for doing so, giving them more direct control over the look and feel of the game and freeing you up to focus on issues that require your technical expertise.

Meta-Considerations

One of the benefits of this approach is that it reduces the amount of duplicate code in your AI. For example, if there are seven different decisions that evaluate the player's hit points, instead of writing that evaluation code in seven places we write it once, in the form of the Absolute Health consideration.

As our work on the AI progresses, we might quickly find that we also have an Absolute Mana consideration, an Absolute Stamina consideration, a Time of Day consideration, a Cool-Down consideration, and a Distance to Player consideration.

Although each of these considers a different aspect of the situation in-game, under the covers they each do exactly the same thing. That is, they compare a floating-point value from the game (such as the player's hit points, the current time of day, the distance to the player, and so forth) to one or two static values that are specified in data.

With that in mind, it's worth looking for opportunities to further reduce duplicate code by building meta-considerations, which is to say high-level considerations that handle the implementation of more specific, low-level considerations, such as the ones given above. This has the advantage of not only further reducing the duplication of code, but also enforcing a uniform set of conventions for specifying data. In other words, if all of those considerations inherit from a Float Comparison consideration base class, then the data for them is likely to look remarkably similar, and a designer specifying data for one that he hasn't used before is likely to get the result he expects on his first try, because it works the same way as every other Float Comparison consideration that he's used before.

Float-Based Decisions

While nearly all decisions are ultimately Boolean (that is, an AI either takes an action or it doesn't), it is often useful to evaluate the suitability of a variety of options and then allow that evaluation to guide our decisions. As with Boolean approaches, there are a variety of approaches for doing this. Discussion of these approaches can be found throughout the AI literature. A few game-specific examples include [Dill06, Dill08, and Mark09]. For the purposes of this gem, however, the interesting question is not how and when to use a float-based approach, but rather how to build modular, pattern-based evaluation functions when we do.

An Example: Attack Goals

Imagine that we are responsible for building the opposing-player AI for a real-time strategy game. Such an AI would need to decide when and where to attack. In order to do this, we might periodically score several prospective targets. For each target we would consider a number of factors, including its economic value (that is, whether it generates revenue or costs money to maintain), its impact on the strategic situation (for example, would it allow you access to the enemy's territory, consolidate your defenses, or protect your lines of supply), and the overall military situation (in other words, whether you can win this fight).

Our next step should be to find a way for each of these considerations to evaluate the situation independently that enables us to easily combine the results of all of those evaluations into a single score, which can be used to make our final decision.

Creating an evaluation function is as much art as science, and in fact there is an entire book dedicated to this subject [Mark09]. However, just as with Boolean decisions, there are simple tricks that can be used to handle the vast majority of situations. Specifically, we can modify our Evaluate() function so that it returns two values: a base priority and a final multiplier. When every consideration has been evaluated, we first add all of the base priorities together and then multiply that total by the product of the final multipliers. This allows us to create considerations that are either additive or multiplicative in nature, which are two of the most common techniques for creating priority values.

Coming back to our example, the considerations for economic value and strategic value might both return base priorities between –500 and 500, generating an overall base priority between –1,000 and 1,000 for each target. They would return a negative value if, from their point of view, taking this action would be a bad idea. For example, capturing a building that has an ongoing upkeep cost might receive a negative value from the economic consideration (unless it had some economic benefit to offset that cost), because once you own it, you'll have to start paying its upkeep. Similarly, attacking a position that, if obtained, would leave you overextended and exposed would receive a negative value from the strategic consideration. These considerations could return a final multiplier of 1.

The consideration for the military situation, however, could be multiplicative in nature. That is, it would return a base priority of 0 but would return a final multiplier between 0 and 3. (For a better idea of how to generate that multiplier, see our previous work [Dill06].) Thus if the military situation is completely untenable (in other words, the defensive forces are much stronger than the units we would use to attack), then we could return a very small multiplier (such as 0.000001), making it unlikely that this target would be chosen no matter how attractive it is from an economic or strategic standpoint. On the other hand, if the military situation is very favorable, then we would strongly consider this target (by specifying a multiplier of 3), even if it is not tremendously important in an economic or strategic sense. If we have no military units to attack with, then this consideration might even return a multiplier of 0.

We do not execute an action whose overall priority is less than or equal to zero. Thus if all of the base priorities add up to a negative value, or if any consideration returns a final multiplier of zero, then the action will not be executed. Just as in the Boolean logic case, a single consideration can effectively veto an action by returning a final multiplier of zero.

As with the previous examples, the greatest value to be found is that these same considerations can be reused elsewhere in the AI. For example, the economic value might be used when selecting buildings to build or technologies to research. The strategic value might be used when selecting locations for military forts and other defensive structures. The military situation would be considered not only for attacks, but also when deciding where to defend, and perhaps even when deciding whether to build structures in contested areas of the map.

Alternate Approaches

One weakness of the aforementioned approach is that it only allows considerations to have additive or multiplicative effects on one another. Certainly there are many other ways to combine techniques—in fact, much of the field of mathematics addresses this topic!

One common trick, for example, is to use an exponent to change the shape of the curve when comparing two values. Certainly we can extend our architecture to include this, perhaps including an exponent to the set of values returned by our `Evaluate()` function and applying all of the exponents after the final multipliers. Doing so significantly increases the complexity of our AI, however, because this new value needs to be taken into account with every consideration we implement and every decision we make. This may not seem like a big deal, but it can make the task of specifying, tuning, and debugging the AI significantly harder than it would otherwise be—especially if it is to be done by non-technical folks who may not have the same intuitive sense of how the numbers combine as an experienced AI engineer would.

Along the same lines, in many cases even the final multiplier is overkill. For simpler decisions (such as those in an FPS game or an action game), we can often have the `Evaluate()` function return a base priority as before, but instead of returning a multiplier, it can simply return a Boolean value that specifies whether it wants to veto this action. If any consideration returns false, then the action is not taken (the score is set to 0); otherwise, the score is the sum of the base priorities.

Conclusion

This gem has presented a set of approaches for building modular, pattern-based architectures for game AI. All of these approaches function by breaking a decision into separate considerations and then encoding each consideration independently. There are several advantages to techniques of this type:

- Code duplication between decisions is dramatically reduced, because the code for each consideration goes in a single place.
- Considerations are reusable not only within a single project, but in some cases also between multiple projects. As a result, AI implementation will become easier as the library of considerations grows larger and more robust.
- Much of the AI can be specified in data, with all the advantages that implies.
- With proper tools and a good library of considerations, designers and artists can be enabled to specify AI logic directly, both getting them more directly involved in the game AI and freeing up the programmer for other tasks.

References

[Dill06] Dill, Kevin. "Prioritizing Actions in a Goal-Based AI." *AI Game Programming Wisdom 3*. Boston: Charles River Media Inc., 2006. 321–330.

[Dill08] Dill, Kevin. "Embracing Declarative AI with a Goal-Based Approach." *AI Game Programming Wisdom 4*. Boston: Charles River Media Inc., 2008. 229–238.

[Mark09] Mark, Dave. *Behavioral Mathematics for Game AI*. Course Technology PTR, 2009.

3.3

Automated Navigation Mesh Generation Using Advanced Growth-Based Techniques

D. Hunter Hale

G. Michael Youngblood

When implementing a navigation system for intelligent agents in a virtual environment, the agent's world representation is one of the most important decisions of the development process [Tozour04]. A good world representation provides the agent with a wealth of information about its environment and how to navigate through it. Conversely, a bad representation of the world can confuse or mislead an agent and become more of a hindrance than an aid. Currently, the most common type of world representation is the navigation mesh [McAnils08]. This mesh contains a complete listing of all of the navigable areas (negative space) and occupied areas (positive space) present in a level or area of a game.

Traditional methods of generating the navigation mesh focus on using the vertices of objects to generate series of triangles. These triangles then become the navigation mesh [Tozour02]. This does generate high-coverage navigation meshes, but the meshes tend to have areas that can cause problems for agents navigating through the world. These problem areas take the form of many separate triangular negative space areas coming together at a single point. Agents or other objects that are standing on or near this point are simultaneously in more than one region. The presence of objects in more than one region at once means that every region will have to be evaluated for events involving the overlapping objects instead of just a single region if objects were well localized.

Instead of using a triangulation-based navigation mesh generation technique, we approached the problem using the Space Filling Volume (SFV) algorithm [Tozour04] as a base. SFV is a growth-based technique that first seeds the empty areas of a game world with quads or cubes and then expands the objects in every direction until they hit an obstruction. The quads and the connections between them define the navigation mesh.

By using quads as the core shape in the algorithm, the problem of many regions coming together in a single point is dramatically reduced, since quads can only meet at most four corners. This basic approach works well for worlds composed of axis-aligned obstructions but produces low-coverage navigation meshes when applied to non-axis-aligned worlds or highly complex worlds. Our improved algorithms address these limitations, as well as provide several other benefits over traditional navigation mesh generation techniques.

The two algorithms described here are enhancements to the traditional implementations of 2D and 3D Space Filling Volumes. The first is a 2D algorithm called Planar Adaptive Space Filling Volumes (PASFV). PASFV consumes a representation of an arbitrary non-axis-aligned 3D environment, similar to a blueprint of a building, and then generates a high-quality decomposition. Our new decomposition algorithms seed the world with growing quads, which, when a collision with geometry occurs, dynamically increase their number of sides to better approximate the shape the growing region intersected. Using the ability to dynamically create higher-order polygons from quads along with a few other features not present in classic SFV, PASFV generates almost 100-percent coverage navigation meshes for levels where it is possible to generate planar splices of the obstructing geometry in the level.

The second algorithm, Volumetric Adaptive Space Filling Volumes (VASFV), is, as the name implies, a native 3D implementation of Adaptive Space Filling Volumes with several enhancements. The enhancements allow VASFV to grow cuboids that morph into complex shapes to better adapt to the geometry of the level they are decomposing, similar to the 2D version. This algorithm, like its 2D cousin, generates a high-coverage decomposition of the environment; however, the world does not need to be projected into a planar representation, and the native geometry can be decomposed without simplification. In addition, this algorithm has a speed/time advantage over the PASFV in post-processing because it can consume complex levels in a single run. PASFV generally has to decompose a level one floor at a time, and the generated navigation meshes must then be reconnected to be useful. VASFV will generate a single navigation mesh per level, removing a potentially expensive step from the process of generating a spatial decomposition.

The Algorithms

Both the PASFV and VASFV algorithms work off the common principle of expanding a grid of pre-seeded regions in a game environment to fill all of the available negative space. In practice, this filling effect looks somewhat similar to a marshmallow that has been heated in the microwave. Both of these algorithms use a similar approach, but the implementations are sufficiently different that each algorithm deserves a full explanation.

PASFV

The PASFV algorithm [Hale08] is an iterative algorithm that can be broken down into a series of simple steps. First, a set of invariants and starting conditions must be established and maintained. For our implementation of PASFV, all of the input geometry must be convex. This allows the use of the point-in-convex-object collision test [Schneider03] when determining whether a growing region has intruded into a positive space area. If the input geometry is not natively convex, it can be converted to be convex by using a triangular subdivision algorithm. While the algorithm is running, the following two conditions must be maintained to have a successful decomposition. First, at the end of every growth cycle, all the negative space regions in the world must be convex; otherwise, the collision detection tests, which are based on an assumption of convexity, will return invalid data. Second, if a region has ended a growth cycle covering an area of the level, it must continue to cover that area. If this restriction is not maintained, there will be gaps in the final decomposition.

Our algorithm begins in a state we refer to as the *initial seeding state*, where the world is "seeded" with a user-defined grid at specified intervals of negative space regions. These regions will grow and decompose the world. If the proposed seed placement falls within a positive space obstruction, it is discarded. Initial regions are unit squares (a unit square is a square with an edge length equal to one of the base units of the world) with four edges arranged in a counterclockwise direction from the point closest to the origin.

The initial placement of these regions in the world is such that they are axis-aligned. After being seeded in the world, each of the placed regions is iteratively provided a chance to grow. Growth is defined for a region as a chance to move each edge outward individually in the direction of each edge's normal. The decomposition of a level may take two general cases. The first case occurs when all of the positive space regions are axis-aligned. The more advanced decomposition case occurs if there is non-axis-aligned geometry.

First, we will examine the base case or axis-aligned case for a spatial decomposition in PASFV. Growth occurs in the direction of the normal for each of the edges of a region and is a single unit in length. After an edge has advanced, we verify the new regional coverage with three collision detection tests. We want to guarantee that no points from our newly expanded region have intruded into any of the other regions or any positive space obstructions. We also want to prove that no points from other regions or obstructions would be contained within the growing region. Finally, the region will perform a self-test to ensure that the region is still convex. This final check is not necessary for the base case of the axis-aligned world and can be omitted if there are no non-axis-aligned collision objects. Assuming all tests return results showing there are no collisions or violations of convexity, the region finalizes its current shape, and the next region grows.

If a collision is detected, several things must be done to correct it. First, the growing region must return to its previous shape. At this point, since both the region and the obstruction it collided with are axis-aligned, we know the region is parallel and adjacent to the object, as shown in Figure 3.3.1(a). Stopping growth here will provide an excellent representation of free space near the collided object. Finally, we set a flag on the edge of the region where the collision occurred. This flag indicates the edge should not attempt to grow again. The iterative growth proceeds until no region is able to grow. This method of growth is sufficient to deal with axis-aligned worlds and produces results similar to traditional SFV.

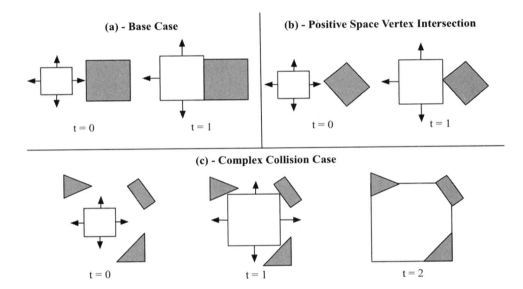

Figure 3.3.1 In this illustration we see all of the potential collision cases in PASFV. The growing negative space regions are shown as white boxes, and the direction of growth is marked with an arrow. Positive space regions are drawn in gray. In (a) we see the most basic axis-aligned collision case. Then (b) shows the collision case that occurs when a vertex of a positive space object intersects a growing negative space region. Finally, in (c) we illustrate the most complex case, where a negative space region is subdivided into a higher-order polygon to better adapt to world geometry.

The advanced case algorithm for PASFV is able to deal with a much wider variety of world environments. This case begins by building from the base case algorithm; however, because it needs to deal with non-axis-aligned positive space regions, it incorporates several new ways of dealing with potential collisions. When a collision with a positive space object occurs, one of three cases handles the collision. The first case occurs if the colliding edge of the positive space object is parallel to the edge of the growing negative space region. The particular obstruction is axis-aligned, so we revert to the base case.

The second case occurs when a single vertex of an obstruction collides with a growing edge, as shown in Figure 3.3.1(b). In this case, there is, unfortunately, nothing we can do to grow further in this direction. This occurs because unless we are willing to lose the convex property of the region or relinquish some of the area already covered by the region, doing either of these things would violate our invariants. This case reverts to the base case, and the negative space around the object will have to be covered by additional seeding passes, which are described at the end of this section.

The final, most complex, collision case occurs when a vertex of the growing region collides with a non-axis-aligned edge of a positive space obstruction, as shown in Figure 3.3.1(c). In this case, the colliding vertex must be split into a pair of new vertices and a new edge inserted between them. This increases the order of the polygon that collided with the obstruction. The directions of growth for these two newly created vertices are modified so they will follow the line equation for the edge that they collided with instead of the normal of the edge they were on.

In addition, potential expansions of these new vertices are limited to the extent of the positive space edge they collided with. In this manner, the original edges, which were adjacent to the collision point, grow outward. This outward movement expands the newly created edge, so that it is spread out along the obstruction. Limiting the growth of these vertices is important because they are creating a non-axis-aligned edge as they expand. As long as this newly generated non-axis-aligned edge is adjacent to positive space, no other region can interact with it, and we limit region-to-region collisions to the base case.

By using these three advanced case collision solutions, we are able to generate high-quality decompositions for non-axis-aligned worlds. As in the simple case with an axis-aligned world, the algorithm stops once all of the regions present in the world are unable to grow any further.

The aforementioned growth methods are not, by themselves, enough to ensure that the entirety of the world is covered by the resulting navigation mesh. In particular, the decompositions resulting from the second collision case are suboptimal. In order to deal with these issues, the second half of the PASFV algorithm comes into play. After all growth has terminated, the algorithm enters a new seeding phase. In this phase, each region places new regions (seeds) in any adjacent unclaimed free space, and then we flag the region as seeded so they will not be considered if there are any later seeding passes. If any seeds are placed, they are provided the opportunity for growth like the originally placed regions. This cycle of growth and seeding repeats until there are no new seeds placed in the world, as shown in Figure 3.3.2. At this point, the algorithm has fully decomposed the world and terminates.

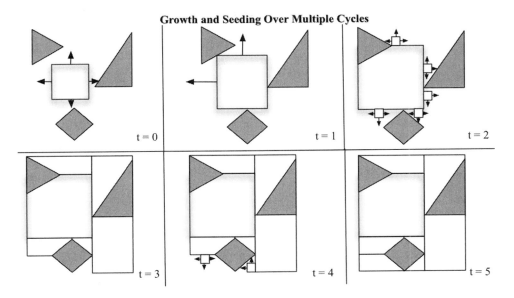

Figure 3.3.2   In this illustration we see several growth and seeding cycles in the PASFV algorithm to decompose an area. The growing negative space regions are shown as white boxes, and the direction of growth is marked with an arrow. Positive space regions are drawn in gray.

VASFV

The Volumetric Adaptive Space Filling Volume (VASFV) algorithm [Hale09] is a natural extension of the PASFV algorithm. Unlike PASFV, the VASFV algorithm works in native 3D and grows cubes and higher-order polyhedrons instead of quads. The initial constraint of convex input shapes is the same for both algorithms. In addition, the requirements that decomposed areas remain decomposed and that all regions always end a growth step in a convex state are still necessary.

The initial setup of VASFV is very similar to its predecessor. Both algorithms begin by seeding a grid of initial regions throughout the world. In VASFV, the grid extends upward along the Z-axis of the world as well as X-axis and Y-axis. Then, in the first of many departures from the previous algorithm, the seeds fall down in the direction of gravity until they come to rest on an object. Seeds that end in the same location are removed. This helps to prevent the formation of large, relatively useless regions that float above the level and allows the ground-based regions to grow up to the maximum allowable height. These seeds are initially spawned as unit cubes represented as regions with four faces listed in a counterclockwise order, starting with the closest to the origin followed by the bottom and top faces, respectively. At this point, the regions may grow and expand.

As with the planar version of this algorithm, there are two main cases to deal with: axis-aligned and non-axis-aligned worlds. The base case for the axis-aligned world proceeds in a manner almost identical to the planar algorithm. Each region is iteratively provided the opportunity to grow out each face one unit in the direction of the normal of each face. We then run the same three tests for error conditions as performed in the planar version of the algorithm. As a reminder, these three tests are checks to ensure that the growing region has not intersected an existing region or obstruction with one of its vertices, that no region's or object's vertices have intersected the newly expanded region with their vertices, and that the region is still convex. If any of these checks fail, the region will revert to its previous size and not attempt to grow again in that direction. These steps are identical to the planar case; however, the secondary algorithms required to implement them are more complex in 3D. As with the planar version of this algorithm, this base case will produce a very good decomposition of an axis-aligned world.

Like the planar version of the algorithm, the advanced growth case for dealing with collisions with non-axis-aligned geometry can be broken down into four cases (shown in Figure 3.3.3). The primary determining factor of which of the cases the algorithm will go into is determined by how many vertices are in collision and whether negative space vertices collide with positive space, or vice versa. The simplest case occurs when the growing cubic region has intersected one or more vertices of a positive space obstruction. Just like in 2D, since there is nothing that the growth algorithm can do to better approximate the free space around the object it has collided with, it returns to its previous valid shape, halting further growth in that direction.

The next three collision cases occur when vertices from a single face of the growing negative space region intersect positive space. The first and simplest of these cases occurs when three or more vertices of a negative space region intersect the same face of a positive space object. When this happens, it means that the growing face of the negative space object is parallel to and collinear with the face of the positive space obstruction it intersected. Therefore, these two faces are both axis-aligned. We know this because three points define a plane, so by sharing these three points, both of these faces are on the same plane. This tells us that since the negative space face is axis-aligned, the positive space face we collided with must be as well. We can thus revert to the base case for this collision.

The final two collision cases require the insertion of a new face into the negative space region so that it adapts to the face of the collided object. The first case occurs when a single vertex of the region intersects an obstruction. In this case, the vertex will be subdivided into three new vertices, and a new triangular face is inserted (which has the same plane equation as the face of the object it collided with). The normal of this new face will be the inverse of the normal of the face of the intersected obstruction. These new points are restricted to prevent them from growing beyond the face of the obstruction they collided with in order to not create more non-axis-aligned geometry.

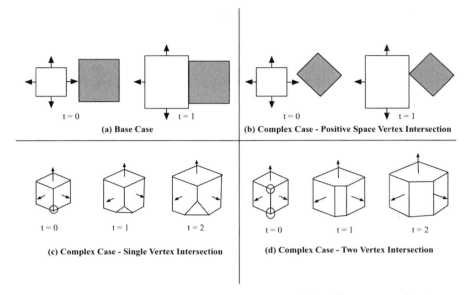

Figure 3.3.3 This illustration shows the possible collision cases for the VASFV algorithm. The growing negative space regions are shown in white. The positive space objects are shown in gray. Section (a) shows the base axis-aligned collision case from above. Section (b) shows the more complex positive space vertex collision case, again from above. Sections (c) and (d) are illustrated slightly differently. In order to clearly show how the negative space region reacts to a positive space collision, the positive space object is not drawn, and the colliding vertex is marked with a circle. Section (c) shows the single vertex collision case where a new triangular face is inserted into the negative space region. Section (d) shows the more complex two-vertex collision where a quadrilateral face is inserted into a negative space region to better approximate the object it collided with.

The final collision case occurs when exactly two vertices of a negative space region intersect another object. This means that a single edge of the region is in contact with the shape it collided with and that edge needs to be split. We split the edge by adding a new rectangular face to the region and by subdividing each colliding vertex into two vertices. This new face is once again created using the negation of the normal of the face it would intersect. The points involved in the collision are restricted to growing just along the collided obstruction. With the last two special collision cases, it is possible to generate navigation meshes with a degree of accuracy and fidelity to the underlying level that is not possible using previous growth-based techniques.

Like the planar version of this algorithm, VASFV also uses a seeding algorithm to ensure full coverage of a level. However, the volumetric seeding approach is slightly different from the planar version. Once each region has reached its maximum possible extents, the seeding algorithm iteratively provides each region a chance to create new seeds in adjacent negative space regions. However, instead of immediately growing the new regions, the newly placed seeds are subjected to a simulated gravity and projected downward until they hit something, and duplicate seeds that end up occupying the same space as already placed seeds are removed. At this point, the algorithm allows the newly placed seeds a chance to grow. This cycle of growth and seeding repeats until no new seeds are successfully placed, at which point the algorithm terminates.

The application of gravity to seeds might not be the most obvious approach to seeding in 3D, but it serves an important purpose in orienting region growth to better accommodate agent movement through the world. A good example of this occurs on staircases. First, consider the case where seeds do not drop due to gravity. As shown in Figure 3.3.4, a region that grows up adjacent to the bottom of the stairs will generate a single seed midway up the stairs, which will contain air space above the first several stairs and only land on one of the middle stairs. Then later seedings will result in a confusing mess of regions, none of which accurately models stair usage. Some of these regions require the agent to crawl through, while other regions require the agent to fly.

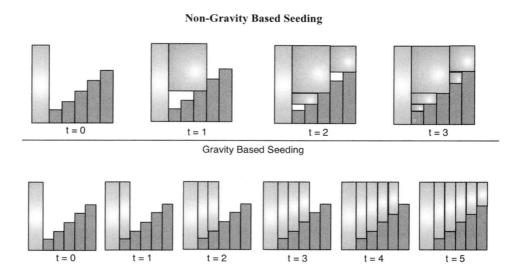

Figure 3.3.4   This figure serves to illustrate how gravity affects the seeding process for VASFV. In this figure, we see a staircase viewed from the side. Positive space regions are marked in white. Negative space regions in this illustration are marked with the light gray gradient. The upper set of four time steps shows what happens if the generated seeds are allowed to float freely and grow in midair. The lower six time steps show how the decomposition changes to better model the stair steps after the application of gravity to each generated seed.

Now consider the same staircase decomposed using a gravity-based seeding method. With gravity-assisted seeding, when a seed is generated from the initial region at the bottom of the stairs, it falls into the floor space of the first stair. The seed then grows outward to fully decompose the floor of that single stair and grows up into the airspace over the stair. In this manner, the seeds gradually climb the stairs, and each stair will become its own logical region, which makes sense given how stairs are typically traversed. This gravity-based seeding is also applicable to other methods of world space traversal, such as flight, because biasing the decomposition world in respect to the features present on the ground still makes sense.

Post-Processing

Decompositions generated using either of the algorithms presented here can be improved by the application of several simple post-processing steps. Most importantly, if any two regions are positioned such that they could be combined into a single region while maintaining convexity, these regions should combine into a single region. The same technique can be applied to compress three input regions into two convex regions. This technique can be extended to higher numbers of regions, but it becomes harder to implement and the returns generally decline, because larger combinations are less likely to yield new convex shapes. All of the negative space regions should be examined for zero-length edges or collinear vertices, which, if detected, should be removed.

A full navigation mesh can be constructed from the decomposition by linking adjacent negative space regions. Aside from which negative space regions connect to each other, each region can also store least-cost paths to every other region. Other navigation mesh quality metrics can be applied to the generated mesh to determine whether it is good enough for its intended purpose or if some of the input parameters for initial seeding should be adjusted and a better navigation mesh generated.

Conclusion

In this gem, we have presented two new growth-based methods of generating navigation meshes. Both of these new methods are derived from the classic Space Filling Volumes algorithm. These two methods each have areas where they specialize, and both generate excellent decompositions, as shown in Figure 3.3.5.

The PASFV technique works very well for levels that can be projected to a single 2D plane. It also can deal with levels that have more than one 2D representation, though these will require a touch more post-processing to combine all of the navigation meshes into a single mesh. The navigation meshes produced by this algorithm are very clean with few sharp points or narrow regions that taper off to a point. Such regions are problematic because they cannot contain all of an agent moving through the world, and an agent can end up in many different regions at the same time. This is not a problem for PASFV because at most four different negative space regions can come together at a point, since all negative-space-to-negative-space collisions will be axis-aligned, and the angles involved in these collisions tend to be around 90 degrees.

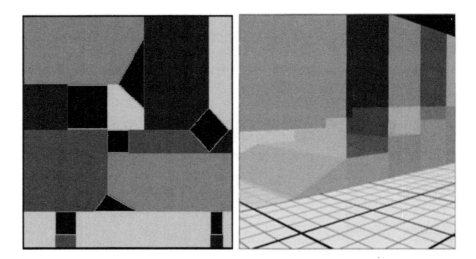

Figure 3.3.5   The first image shows the results of PASFV.
Black areas indicate obstructions, while the variously colored regions show
negative space. The second image shows a navigation mesh generated by
VASFV on a non-axis-aligned staircase and viewed from the side.

PASFV is also highly comparable to other navigation mesh generation algorithms in terms of speed, as it can be shown to run in $O(n1/x)$ with an upper bound of $O(n)$, where n is the number of square units of space to decompose and x is a function of how many seeds are placed in the world [Hale09b].

For more complex world environments that do not approximate to 2D very well or that would require multiple 2D approximations, Volumetric Adaptive Space Filling Volumes is a solution for navigation mesh generation, even though it is slightly harder to implement and takes longer to run due to the more complex collision calculations. VASFV will also provide good decompositions that have few narrow corners or poorly accessible regions. In addition, because of its gravity-based seeding, VASFV will better model how agents move, resulting in superior decompositions to traditional triangulation-based methods [Hale09a]. The run time for VASFV is algorithmically the same as PASFV; however, instead of n being the number of square units in the world, it is the number of cubic units.

By presenting both 2D and 3D algorithms for generating spatial decompositions, we are offering multiple options to move beyond traditional triangulation-based methods of producing a navigation mesh and into advanced growth-based techniques. The most current implementations of both of these algorithms can be found at http://gameintelligencegroup.org/projects/cgul/deaccon/, along with some other interesting tools and techniques for navigation mesh generation and evaluation.

References

[Hale08] Hale, D. H., G. M. Youngblood, and P. Dixit. "Automatically-Generated Convex Region Decomposition for Real-time Spatial Agent Navigation in Virtual Worlds." *Artificial Intelligence and Interactive Digital Entertainment (AIIDE)*. Stanford University, Stanford, CA. 2008.

[Hale09a] Hale, D. H., and G. M. Youngblood. "Full 3D Spatial Decomposition for the Generation of Navigation Meshes." *Artificial Intelligence and Interactive Digital Entertainment (AIIDE)*. Stanford University, Stanford, CA. 2009.

[Hale09b] Hale, D. H., and G. M. Youngblood. "Dynamic Updating of Navigation Meshes in Response to Changes in a GameWorld." *Florida Artificial Intelligence Research Society (FLAIRS)*. The Shores Resort and Spa, Daytona Beach, FL. 2009.

[McAnils08] McAnils, C., and J. Stewart. "Intrinsic Detail in Navigation Mesh Generation." *AI Game Programming Wisdom 4*. Boston: Charles River Media, 2008. 95–112.

[Touzor02] Tozour, P. "Building a Near-Optimal Navigation Mesh." *AI Game Programming Wisdom*. Boston: Charles River Media, 2002. 171–185.

[Tozour04] Tozour, P. "Search Space Representations." *AI Game Programming Wisdom 2*. Boston: Charles River Media, 2004. 85–102.

[Schneider03] Schneider, P. and D. Eberly. "Point in Polygon/Polyhedron." *Geometric Tools for Computer Graphics*. Morgan Kaufmann Publishers, 2003. 695–713.

3.4

A Practical Spatial Architecture for Animal and Agent Navigation

Michael Ramsey—Blue Fang Games, LLC.
miker@masterempire.com

> *"Not so many years ago, the word 'space' had a strictly geometrical meaning: the idea evoked was simply that of an empty area."*
>
> —Henri Lefebvre

Game literature is inundated with various techniques to facilitate navigation in an environment. However, many of them fail to take into account the primary unifying medium that animals and agents use as locomotion in the real world. And that unifying medium is *space* [Lefebvre97]. The architectonics[1] of space relative to an animal's or agent's motion in a game environment is the motivation for this gem. Traditional game development focuses on modeling what is physically in the environment, so it may seem counterintuitive to model what is not there, but one of the primary reasons for modeling the empty space of an environment is that it is this *spatial vacuum* that frames our interactions (be they locomotion or a simple idle animation) within that environment. Space is the associative system between objects in our environments.

This article will discuss this spatial paradigm and the techniques that we used during the development of a multi-platform game, entitled *World of Zoo* (WOZ). WOZ was a challenging project not only by any standard definition of game development, but also because we desired our animals' motion to be credible.

An important aspect of any animal's believability is that they are not only aware of their surroundings, but that they also move *through* a dynamic environment (Color Plates 1 and 2 contain examples of WOZ's environment) in a spatially appropriate

---

[1]A unifying structure is commonly referred to as an architectonic, as it is used to describe and associate elements that are separated into a perceived whole.

and consistent manner. This maxim had to hold true whether the animal was locomoting over land, over water, or even through air! To help facilitate the representation of our spatial environments, we used several old tools in new ways, and in conjunction with a few inventions of our own, we believe we accomplished our goals.

Fundamental Components of the Spatial Representation System

The primary element for constructing a spatial representation in WOZ was the sphere, termed a *navsphere*. Figure 3.4.1 shows a subset of a navsphere layout from an exhibit. The navsphere is fundamentally important because not only is it used to generate the navigable representation of the world (see below), but more importantly, it defines the interactable spatial dimensions of the world. What this means is that we define in 3D space where an animal can go, not just where it cannot. To keep animals from going places, we rely not only upon the tried-and-true techniques of collision detection [Bergen04], but also on collision determination.

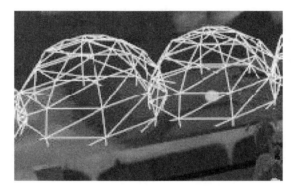

Figure 3.4.1 Two navspheres in a level. Connectivity information between neighboring navspheres is accomplished by having a slight overlap.

Collision determination is a technique of knowing ahead of time that a collision may occur (similar to how the majority of physics packages handle contact points). This determination of a potential collision is implicit when using navspheres, because we are able to determine that an animal is nearing the edge of navigable representation. These edges are termed *spatial boundaries*, and in this specific example, it defines the implicit relationship between the navspheres and the outer lying geometry [Gibson86]. Because of this knowledge, we can augment the animal's behavior to slow down, start to turn away, or skid to a stop.

It should be noted that the navsphere is an approximation of space, and it is not an exact spatial inverse of the placed geometry. A spatial system that is modeled from constructive solid geometry (CSG) principles would definitely be ideal, but the dynamic nature of WOZ's environments made this unfeasible. However, we did invest some initial time into investigating and utilizing various CSG techniques. The primary aspect of CSG that we discovered to be applicable for a spatially accurate representation of an environment was the Boolean intersection operator, which is the overlap of two objects merged into a convex component. The cumulative Boolean intersections would form the space through which our animals would move. The complexity and cost would come from the determination of an agent's occupancy within that environment's CSG representation, as they are not primitives but complex convex objects. This approach would definitely be more accurate than spheres, but at the cost of not being usable on current-generation consoles or the typical desktop PC (mainly due to the arbitrary manner in which WOZ's environments were modeled).

As an animal moves through an environment, there need to be mechanisms in place to help control an animal's interaction with navspheres—we do this by assigning properties to the navsphere that define how certain interactions will occur. Some of these properties include defining the type of animal locomotion allowed in that navshape (whether it be land, water, or air) and spatial parameters for certain animal sizes.

Having a system that is spatially centric requires a single enabling component that allows it to be easily accessed by other game systems. By allowing navspheres to overlap, we are capable of generating a navigable representation—a *navrep*—of the environment. A similar system is the circle-based waypoint graph [Tozour03]. For a visual example of this process, compare Figure 3.4.2 and Figure 3.4.3. Figure 3.4.2 shows the overlapping navspheres for one of WOZ's nursery levels. Figure 3.4.3 shows the type of connectivity information generated from that navsphere layout. You can think of the navrep generated as the walkable surface for the world; however, note that the navrep is in 3D space and can wrap around other geometry as well as other navreps.

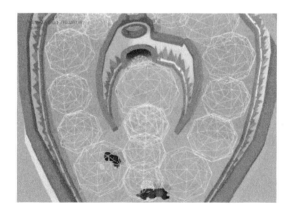

Figure 3.4.2 A navsphere layout for the bear nursery.

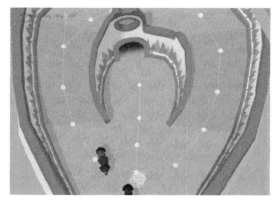

Figure 3.4.3 This figure shows how the connectivity information is generated from the overlapping navspheres in Figure 3.4.2.

The primary reason to construct a connectivity graph from the spatial representation is that we need to execute potentially expensive operations on the game world, such as pathing queries, reachability tests, and visibility queries. The basic algorithm for generating the navrep is to iterate over the navspheres, searching for overlap with any other navspheres. If we find any overlap, we establish a bidirectional link between the navspheres. Later on in the development of WOZ, we also found that we could use the same mechanism for one-way links by embedding directed connectivity information in the navsphere itself; this manifested itself in game objects such as one-way teleport doors.

Navigation System Architecture

As we move on to discussing the spatial aspects of the WOZ navigation system, it will help to understand the basic structure and components of the system as a whole (see Figure 3.4.4). The primary interface between the navigation system and the other components of the WOZ game is the navigation manager. The navigation manager facilitates access to the planner. The planner contains the navigable representation of the environment—both the spatial vacuum and the generated connectivity graph. The pathfinder uses the A* algorithm, which provides support for both spatial and routing biases [Hart68, Stout00].

Also provided is a general utilities object that contains general navigation code. When an animal (noted as an entity in Figure 3.4.4) needs to route through an environment, it will issue a call through the animal planner into the navigation manager. The navigation manager will then access its own world planner, and using the navrep it generates a coarse route through the environment. This coarse route is then returned to the animal's planner for use. As you'll notice in Figure 3.4.4, WOZ has two planners: the navigation planner and the animal planner. The animal planner handles any immediate spatial or interanimal tasks, while the navigation planner handles the more rudimentary routing operations (for example, path biasing) as well as handling the interactions with the navsphere reservation system.

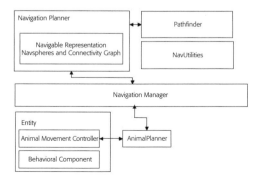

Figure 3.4.4　The navigation system.

Navrep Continuity and Stitching

Navreps are not necessarily continuous. What this means is that the level designers can author disparate navreps based upon differing navrep types (for example, land or water), as well as navreps that represent differing levels of elevation in a zoo exhibit, such as the ledges on a cliff face. Linking multiple, non-overlapping navreps in the navigation system requires the creation of navfeelers. Figure 3.4.5 (left) contains an example of two navreps that were authored as disconnected. There is a navrep on the ledge and also a navrep on the base of the exhibit. The navfeeler is the fishing pole–like extrusion from the top navsphere to one of the bottom navspheres.

Navfeelers allow the level authors to link these navreps together. It attempts to find any navsphere below; if it finds a navsphere below itself, we then establish a bidirectional link between the two. The analogy that we used during development to help explain this was to think of a fisherman at the end of pier, with his fishing pole sticking out over the water at roughly 45 degrees. His line would dangle into the water, which effectively links land and water for the navigation system. If the navfeeler finds a navsphere below it, we then establish a bidirectional link between the two navspheres. Once these navreps are linked together (refer to Figure 3.4.5, right), the navigation system can then pathfind over the multiple navreps. Although this example is shown for a land-to-land navrep, the same mechanism is used for land-to-water bridges, which allows the penguins to dive into and jump out of water.

Figure 3.4.5   On the left is an example of a navfeeler
authored in level to connect two disparate navreps
with the final result, on the right, of a navigable navrep.

Handling Locomotion and Turning

Locomotion in WOZ is executed by root accumulation of multiple animations that form a final pose. By root accumulation, we mean that the animators author with full displacement; any movement of the root of the animal's skeleton is contained in the animation. This allows the animations to retain all the inherent tweaks, such as deceleration, that might otherwise be lost in the typical engineer-centric approach, where the animators are required to author animations on the spot. While root motion is very necessary for exhibiting animator-envisaged motion, it also does not mesh well with traditional navigation paradigms.

Turning was handled independently of locomotion, which was advantageous because it allowed the animators to avoid generating a host of different turn animations. To generate a turn angle, an animal selects a target point, such as the next point along a route or a game object. This target point is then turned into a turn angle (by doing a dot product between the target point and the heading of the animal and then solving for theta), which is then used to twist the spine of an animal in the desired direction. If we had an animal with a four-bone spine and a turn angle of 40 degrees, we would simply apply 10 degrees of twist to each of the bones. In this section I'll talk about how we handled two central components of progression through our navigation system: locomotion and turning.

While the navigation system plans through the world using the connectivity graph (which was generated from the navspheres), we turn to the spatial representation of the world in order to facilitate locomotion and turning validation. Each animal has associated with itself an occupancy shape (see Figure 3.4.6). This occupancy shape is used to control progression through the suggested route. The occupancy shape is not static; it can grow in size, as well as placement, according to the current animation. A fast-galloping zebra will have its occupancy shape projected out in front, whereas a slow-moving zebra would have the occupancy shape centered more on itself.

One key differentiation in the navigation system implemented for WOZ versus other games is that during normal locomotion an animation could and generally would deviate from the proposed path through the environment. A combination of root motion, behavioral prodding, and turn speeds that vary based upon the state in the behavior graph makes following an exact route impossible without adversely affecting the quality of an animal's movement. This is not dissimilar to how real animals or humans move through the world. Humans don't plan exact motions; we don't plan our exact muscle contractions—we move in accordance with our understanding of the space made available to us. It's this space that allows us to identify boundaries and make use of the relationships between the space and objects we are afforded [Gibson86]. So it made sense to ensure that WOZ's animals respect the spatial relationships of the environment accordingly.

Figure 3.4.6   Each animal has an occupancy shape.
This variable occupancy shape is used to denote the rough
spatial representation relative to the navigation system.

To help influence the turning of an animal, we implemented a system that uses a series of spheres projected around an animal in order to determine the suggested turn angles. We accomplished this by determining whether the projected spheres were inside the navrep. If one of the projected spheres was completely outside the navrep, we would execute a turn in the opposite direction. For example, if an animal's motion wanted to move it into a wall, we could execute a tight turn in the opposite direction simply by altering the blend weights of the current animation. The blend weights would effectively bias the animal away from obstructions. It is important to remember that we modeled the world not only geometrically, but also its spatial representation, so this type of *inside* or *outside* test would be possible. By projecting these spheres around the animal, we could make turns that would take the animal away from objects according to their spatial proximity to the navrep boundaries. Another positive side effect of this approach is that we avoided doing costly and potentially numerous ray-casts for this operation.

Conclusion

While there are many navigable representations that can be used in a game, very few of them concern themselves with the spatial vacuum that exists in between the static geometry. This gem has shown you how to represent this space using several common tools, in conjunction with some new approaches to modeling locomotion. While modeling locomotion based on a desired sense of progression through the environment is different than most locomotion models, it also opens the door to modeling the actual motion of an animal or agent as it occurs in the real world. Animals or agents don't follow exact routes; they alter their movement according to an understanding of not only the static objects in the world, but also the available space in which to exhibit their behaviors.

Hopefully, the presentation of a few old ideas intermixed with a few new ones will help you rethink an animal's or agent's interactions inside an environment. By considering the space in between physical aspects of an environment, we now have the capability to make decisions about our environment that are not purely reactive by nature. We are afforded the mechanisms to forecast environmental interactions, which is perhaps one of the first steps toward a credible motion management system.

Acknowledgements

I wish to thank the following team members for their contributive efforts to the WOZ AI system: Bruce Blumberg, Steve Gargolinksi, Ralph Hebb, and Natalia Murray.

References

[Bergen04] Bergen, Gino Van Den. *Collision Detection in Interactive 3D Environments.* Morgan Kaufmann, 2004.

[Ericson05] Ericson, Christer. *Real-Time Collision Detection.* Morgan Kaufmann, 2005.

[Gibson86] Gibson, James J. *The Ecological Approach to Visual Perception.* LEA, 1986.

[Hart68] Hart, P. E., N. J. Nilsson, and B. Raphael. "A Formal Basis for the Heuristic Determination of Minimum Cost Paths." *IEEE Transactions on Systems Science and Cybernetics* 4.2 (1968): 100–107.

[Lefebvre97] Lefebvre, Henri. *The Production of Space.* Blackwell Publishing, 1997.

[Richenbach58] Reichenbach, Hans. *The Philosophy of Space and Time.* Dover, 1958.

[Stout00] Stout, Bryan. "The Basics of A* for Path Planning." *Game Programming Gems.* Boston: Charles River Media, 2000. 254–263.

[Tozour03] Tozour, P. "Search Space Representations." *AI Game Programming Wisdom 2.* Boston: Charles River Media, 2003. 85–102.

[Week01] Week, Jeffrey. *The Shaping of Space.* Marcel Dekker, Inc., 2001.

3.5

Applying Control Theory to Game AI and Physics

Brian Pickrell

bobthrollop@brandx.net

Control theory is the engineering study of dynamic systems, such as airplanes and other machines. The name is a bit misleading, since designing controls (in other words, airplane autopilots or missile guidance systems) is only one application of the theory. Control theory is actually the analysis of equations to extract some fundamental information about how entire classes of systems act in all possible circumstances.

Control theory is something of a sister science to simulation. A simulation looks at a specific situation and predicts what the system will do in great detail, but it doesn't explain how the system behaves in general. Control theory, on the other hand, doesn't predict anything at all, but it gives general information in the form of quantifiable measurements that are true for any situation or inputs. In other words, it tells you what the system can and cannot do. These measures are mathematical and quite abstract, but they are important, and for the most part, they are things that simulation engines just do not provide. Some of the ideas described in this gem may seem like shortcuts to avoid doing proper simulation, but in fact they have just as much scientific validity. It is better to think of controls analysis as complementary to simulation, and as a way to do some things that your physics engine was not designed for.

One task for which control theory is better suited is designing the steering and motion of physics objects in games. To give a specific example, how would you depict the motion of an in-game car making a sudden turn? We all know that a simple, abrupt change of direction is not realistic and doesn't look believable—the vehicle should swerve and sway a little bit while turning. If you just program a motion curve by guessing, the results will not be much more believable. If you use a high-fidelity physics engine to simulate the turn, you will likely have to work out the forces and other parameters required to make it sway convincingly by trial and error, and the results of this tweaking cannot be reused for other cars in other turns.

Our first formula describes the family of functions that you can use for this situation. An object such as a moving vehicle must obey these functions in its motions. If your game object doesn't move like this, it's not physically realistic. Conversely, you can create a plausible motion curve at very little cost in physics analysis by following this formula and using some common-sense rules of thumb.

Here is that result: Any unforced dynamic system moving under a set of linear differential equations has an output motion of the form:

$$y(t) = \sum_n A_n e^{-\zeta_n t} \cos(\omega_n t) \quad (1)$$

This is a set of harmonic oscillators, each of the form:

$$y(t) = A e^{-\zeta t} \cos(\omega t) \quad (2)$$

$$\omega = \text{natural frequency}$$

$$\zeta = \text{damping coefficient}$$

This is a sinusoidal wave where A is the amplitude and ω (omega) is the frequency, and the oscillations die out (or grow) exponentially according to a damping coefficient ζ (zeta). A single harmonic oscillator looks something like Figure 3.5.1.

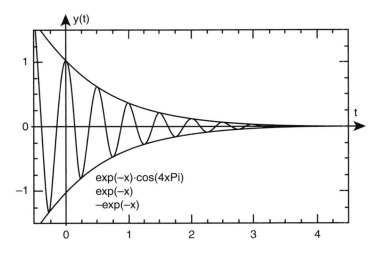

Figure 3.5.1 Simple damped harmonic oscillator.

Several harmonic modes added together, each with its own amplitude, frequency, and damping coefficient, as in Equation (1), look like Figure 3.5.2.

We will spend most of the rest of this gem defining the concepts behind Equation (1) and showing how they were derived.

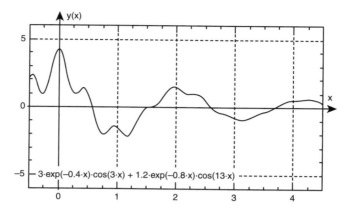

Figure 3.5.2   Oscillator with two harmonic modes.

Dynamic Systems

The concept of a dynamic system in control theory is the same as that used in simulation; that is, a system is any set of parts that act on each other in some quantifiable way and change over time. The underlying mathematics applies equally to all different sorts of systems, using any units of measurement that are appropriate and any scientific laws that produce linear equations. The "parts" themselves may be conceptual rather than physical, as when measuring the concentrations of different reagents in a chemical reaction. The "output" can be any measurable quantity at some point in the system, measured in whatever units are appropriate. In this gem, we will mostly refer to objects moving under the physical laws of mass, force, and so on, but with the understanding that other dynamic systems work the same way.

We did not say what the units of Equation (1) are or how you should implement the result. This is up to the game programmer to decide. Your output $y(t)$ can be distance measurements (xyz coordinates) or velocities or angular units, such as steering heading, as long as your system is linear in the units you choose. This explains how an airplane flying in a circle (which doesn't look like Equation (1) at all) is consistent with linear control theory: because in angular units, its heading changes at a constant rate, which does fit the template of Equation (1). This should be good news to programmers of cockpit view–style games. Everything we tell you here can be implemented directly in angular units, without requiring messy polar coordinate conversions.

Linear Systems

We have already stated the requirement that a system be linear. What does this mean? A linear dynamic system is one whose defining equations of motion follow the form:

$$A_1 y(t) + A_2 \frac{dy}{dt} + A_3 \frac{d^2 y}{dt^2} + \ldots + A_n \frac{d_n y}{dt^n} = 0 \quad (3)$$

where all of the coefficients A_n are constants. The reason that we could say with such certainty that all linear systems follow the form of Equation (1) is that the result is a necessary mathematical consequence of Equation (3). If you don't make that assumption, then the results don't look like those sinusoidal functions. Engineers talk all the time about non-linearities in their systems; this usually means that the coefficients A in the equations of motion are not constant. They are functions of some other value, or they change over time. (It can also mean that something else is being done with the derivatives—for example, $\sin \dfrac{dy}{dt}$ is not linear.) When engineers try to apply linear control theory to systems with non-linearities (and they always do; a good part of controls engineering consists of finding ways to approximate non-linear reality with linear equations), the results often look similar to Equation (1) but the ω, ζ, and A values of the different modes keep changing, or the poles and frequency responses in the charts we'll soon see keep moving around.

All that said, it is safe in an in-game world to define all physical responses as being always linear. Then we can go ahead and use our linear results without worry.

Feedback, Damping, and Stability

Systems oscillate the way they do because of internal feedback among components. Sometimes unexpected feedback effects can cause a system to oscillate more rather than less; in fact, the 19th-century origins of control theory lie in explanations of why a steam engine's mechanical governor couldn't keep it running at a steady speed. One of the primary questions that controls engineers analyze is whether the system is stable. If any of the damping coefficients ζ in Equation (1) is negative, then the entire system is unstable (in other words, the equation does not converge as $t \to \infty$). Notice that in such a case, the exponential part of the equation is positive, so the sinusoidal oscillations expand correspondingly. Fortunately, instability is never a surprise in the game world, since we have the luxury of declaring positive ζ's for all of our systems. However, you will see this effect in physics simulations that drift out of limits and in game object movements that go wild because of player overcontrolling.

Most programmers know a little bit about feedback and use it occasionally but do not have a way to quantify the system stability or instability that results. Here are some different types of damping:

$\zeta > 2\,\omega$	Overdamped (stable, no oscillations)
$\zeta = 2\,\omega$	Critical damping (stable)
$0 < \zeta < 2\,\omega$	Underdamped (stable)
$\zeta = 0$	Undamped (oscillates)
$\zeta < 0$	Unstable

Second-Order Linear Differential Equations

Let's look at how Equation (2) is derived for a couple of simple harmonic oscillators. Equation (2) is the general solution of the second-order linear differential equation (LDE); that is, one where the differential terms go as high as the second derivative $\dfrac{d^2 y}{dt^2}$ but no higher. Each of these examples, then, can form a single component of a more complicated system that has multiple oscillatory modes.

Both of these examples are basic textbook cases. You can see from them how the same control theory applies in so many different scientific fields; it is because many natural laws (in these cases, Coulomb's law and Newton's second law) express themselves as similar first- and second-order differential equations.

Example 1: Mass and Spring

Figure 3.5.3 shows a heavy object M bouncing up and down on a spring K, obeying Newton's laws of motion. The "output" value being measured is x_2, the position of the object measured in units of distance. We'll pretend that all of the friction in the system occurs at dashpot B. (A dashpot is the working part of a shock absorber.) The equations show that the weight moves under the forces of the spring and friction. The spring force changes as the object moves, a built-in feedback. The friction force depends on velocity (which is the derivative of the position). Newton's second law converts force to acceleration, which is the second derivative of position. Outside forces pushing on the system are represented by $x_1(t)$. (We'll get to that later; for now, assume it is zero.)

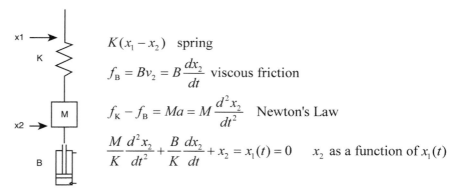

$$K(x_1 - x_2) \quad \text{spring}$$

$$f_B = Bv_2 = B\frac{dx_2}{dt} \quad \text{viscous friction}$$

$$f_K - f_B = Ma = M\frac{d^2 x_2}{dt^2} \quad \text{Newton's Law}$$

$$\frac{M}{K}\frac{d^2 x_2}{dt^2} + \frac{B}{K}\frac{dx_2}{dt} + x_2 = x_1(t) = 0 \quad x_2 \text{ as a function of } x_1(t)$$

Figure 3.5.3   Mass and spring.

Example 2: RCL Circuit

Figure 3.5.4 shows a very simple electronic circuit with a resistor R, a capacitor C, an inductor L, and a voltage input E. The inductor tends to keep current i flowing once started, while the capacitor builds up a charge that fights against the current. The interaction of these two causes the current (and voltage) in the circuit to oscillate back and forth. Either voltage or current can be read as the output value; in this case, we're using current.

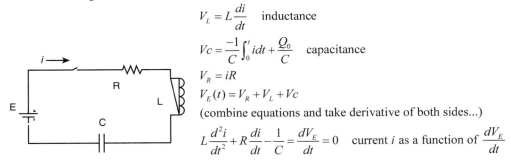

$$V_L = L\frac{di}{dt} \quad \text{inductance}$$

$$Vc = \frac{-1}{C}\int_0^t idt + \frac{Q_0}{C} \quad \text{capacitance}$$

$$V_R = iR$$

$$V_E(t) = V_R + V_L + Vc$$

(combine equations and take derivative of both sides...)

$$L\frac{d^2i}{dt^2} + R\frac{di}{dt} - \frac{1}{C} = \frac{dV_E}{dt} = 0 \quad \text{current } i \text{ as a function of } \frac{dV_E}{dt}$$

Figure 3.5.4   RCL circuit.

Some Math Formulae

We are almost ready to give the solution to the general second-order LDE, but let's review two fundamental mathematical formulae we will use.

Euler's Formula

$$e^{i\theta} = \cos\theta + i\sin\theta \quad \text{Euler's Formula} \quad (4)$$

This is a fundamental identity from complex mathematics that relates exponentials to trigonometric functions. It says that *e* to any power that is a pure imaginary number lies on the unit circle in the complex plane, and that for an exponential with a complex exponent, the imaginary part of the result oscillates in a sine-like way while the real part either grows or diminishes exponentially (depending on whether the real part is positive or negative), as shown in Figure 3.5.5.

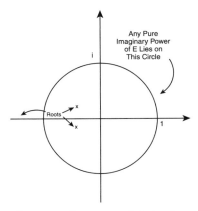

Figure 3.5.5   Roots and exponentials in the complex plane.

Fundamental Theorem of Algebra

A real polynomial of degree n:

$$a_0 x^0 + a_1 x^1 + \ldots + a_n x^n = 0 \quad (5)$$

has n roots (including complex and multiple roots). Complex roots always come in conjugate pairs $a+bi$, $a-bi$.

Between them, these two formulae mean that, in the complex number domain, sine and exponential functions are the same thing!

Harmonic Oscillator—Derivation

Now for the solution to the equation resulting from Examples 1 and 2:

Find all equations y(t) that obey the differential relation

$$Ay''(t) + By'(t) + Cy(t) = 0 \quad (6)$$

The derivation of the result is interesting because it shows how imaginary numbers keep coming up in control theory. Solving a differential equation, solving an exponential equation, and finding roots of a polynomial are tantamount to the same thing. Also, we'll see how a complex exponential can be separated into two parts: an exponential (ζ) and a sinusoidal component (ω). Control engineers tend to talk lightly of complex "roots" as damping ratios and frequencies, an abstraction that can be weird and confusing for outsiders. This is where that equivalency comes from.

The solution starts by assuming that all solutions are variations on the basic form $y = e^{rt}$ where r is a complex number.

$y = e^{rt}$ r a complex number

$e^{rt}\left(Ar^2 + Br + C\right) = 0$ Apply derivatives

$Ar^2 + Br + C = 0$ (e^{rt} can never be 0)

$r = \dfrac{-B \pm \sqrt{B^2 - 4AC}}{2A}$ Quadratic Formula

complex roots $p + qi$, $p - qi$

Any linear combination of these roots is a solution

$y = a_1 e^{(p+qi)t} + a_2 e^{(p-qi)t}$ arbitrary constants a_1, a_2

$y = e^{pt}\left(a_1 e^{qit} + a_2 e^{-qit}\right)$

$y = e^{pt}\left(a_1\left(\cos(qt) + \sin(qt)i\right) + a_2\left(\cos(-qt) + \sin(-qt)i\right)\right)$ Euler's Formula

$y = e^{pt}\left(\left(a_1 + a_2\right)\cos(qt) + \left(a_1 - a_2\right)\sin(qt)i\right)$

$\zeta = -p, \omega = q, c_1 = a_1 + a_2, c_2 = a_1 - a_2$ substitute variables   (7)

The general solution, then, is:

$$y = e^{-\zeta t}\left(c_1 \cos(\omega t) + c_2 \sin(\omega t)i\right)$$

$$\zeta = \frac{B}{2\sqrt{AC}}, \omega = \sqrt{\frac{C}{A}} \qquad (8)$$

General solution of second-order LDE (unforced) [1]

where ζ and ω can be derived directly from the coefficients A, B, and C once you know the solution. c_1 and c_2 are arbitrary constants—any values are valid, and the values for a particular case depend on the initial conditions. You can find the system's frequency and damping ratio directly from the system constants (such as inductance and capacitance) without going back through the differential equation. Here is another formulation that is handy to have:

$$\frac{1}{\omega^2}\frac{d^2 y}{dt^2} + 2\frac{\zeta}{\omega}\frac{dy}{dt} + y = 0 \qquad (9)$$

Block Diagrams

What about a system that has more parts than our examples? When an analysis extends to multiple equations of motion, the interrelationships quickly become much harder to sort out. A block diagram analysis is one way to manage this. Making a suitable block diagram to represent a complex system is a matter of engineering judgment, much like designing a system model for a simulation. We do not want to explain all the ins and outs of block diagramming, but a block diagram can help explain how control inputs apply to the equations we've done so far.

We said that Equations (1) and (2) applied to unforced systems—that is, ones with no inputs. In the case of modeling a car's steering, that would mean that there was no one at the wheel. What use is a model like that? One answer is that we can include the steering inside the block being modeled.

Equations (1) and (2) are what are called *transfer functions*. In a block diagram, you can represent an entire subsystem as a single box with an input and an output, and the transfer function is the conversion between input and output. Figure 3.5.6 shows a diagram that demonstrates "closing the loop"—that is, converting an open-loop (uncontrolled) equation into one that accounts for the effects of steering or other control inputs.

---

[1] It would be a fair question to ask what the meaning is of the imaginary part of the equation, since you can't have imaginary distances or voltages. An (evasive) answer is that the imaginary part is required to be zero as a constraint condition in an analysis, which we're skipping over. The reader may just ignore the imaginary part and read only the real part of the equation.

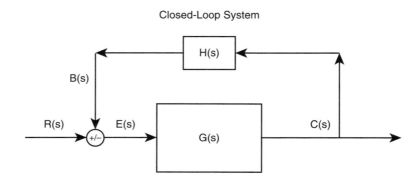

Figure 3.5.6 Closed-loop block diagram.

G(s) is our original transfer function. R(s) is an external input (steering), and G(s) converts the input to the final output value C(s). H(s) is a feedback control system that reads the output, transforms it in a certain way, and uses it to modify the command input.

The following is important if you want to model autonomously steered (NPC) vehicles in a game: H(s), which represents the internal dynamics of the steering system, is modeled as a linear system of components exactly like the main system G(s). H(s) could be a collection of levers, springs, hydraulics, electronics, and so forth—it is just another linear system and is conceptually no different than G(s). Furthermore, the entire diagram that results, including controls, is also linear and can be redrawn as a single "black box" transfer function. Therefore, you can legitimately represent a vehicle and its driver as a single, complicated transfer function where the input is the desired course and the output is the actual motions of the vehicle. This does not work for a real person but can represent any linear controls, including a simple autopilot, a smart or dumb robot driver, or a human non-player character (NPC) whose driving style is a linear function.

The caveat to this is that you would be simulating the steering behavior of a control system without actually doing the steering. Only in extremely simple cases is it possible to extract the implied control responses from a system transfer function. The demo on the CD shows an example of this.

Laplace Transform

The block diagram of Figure 3.5.6 replaces differential equations with Laplace transforms. For our examples, G(s) is the Laplacian L of Equation (6), which is $As^2 + Bs + C$. The Laplace transform is a clever mathematical trick that converts differential equations to more manageable polynomial functions.

$$\mathcal{L}\left[f\left(t\right)\right] = F\left(s\right) \equiv \int_{0}^{\infty} f\left(t\right) e^{-st} dt \tag{10}$$

Definition of Laplace Transform[2]

Laplace transforms are written as capital letters in the block diagrams, and the original function parameter—time t—becomes s, which is not a measurable value but an abstract complex number. Laplace transforms have several useful properties. First of all, the transforms of the most common functions are all polynomials. Also, they are linear and can be added and multiplied by constants. They support integration and differentiation; they convert step inputs and other discontinuous functions into continuous functions. And, function composition is the same as multiplying in the Laplacian domain—in other words:

$$\mathcal{L}\big[f(g(t))\big] = F(s)G(s) \quad \text{function composition} \quad (11)$$

Yet another handy property of the Laplacian is that it is units-independent. Since all units of measurement transform to the same s, it is possible to mix transfer functions whose outputs are in different units in the same block diagram. Using the properties of the Laplace transform, Figure 3.5.6 leads to the following relationships:

$$E(s) = R(s) - B(s)$$
$$C(s) = G(s)E(s)$$
$$B(s) = H(s)C(s)$$
$$\frac{C(s)}{R(s)} = \frac{G(s)}{1 + G(s)H(s)} \quad \text{control ratio} \quad (12)$$

The denominator of the last function is called the *characteristic equation*[3] of the system.

$$1 + G(s)H(s) = 0 \quad \text{characteristic equation} \quad (13)$$

From Characteristic Equation to Equations of Motion

The next step is simple but powerful. The Laplace transform implicitly does the same conversion to exponentials that was done in the derivation of Equation (8). Therefore, the roots of the characteristic equation of the system correspond to the n harmonic modes in Equation (1), with $-\zeta$ as the real part and ω as the imaginary part.[4] If you can factor a system's characteristic equation into the form:

$$\big[s - (\zeta_1 + \omega_1 i)\big]\big[s - (\zeta_2 + \omega_2 i)\big]\ldots\big[s - (\zeta_n + \omega_n i)\big] = 0 \quad (14)$$

roots of characteristic equation

---

[2] By convention, a lowercase letter denotes an original function and a capital letter denotes a Laplace transform with the parameter s. It is important to notice which is which throughout this article.

[3] This is the same as the characteristic equations found in linear algebra, if you represent the underlying system of differential equations as a matrix.

[4] Note the $-$ sign in front of ζ. A positive real part of a root means a negative damping coefficient.

then any function matching Equation (1) with any constants A_n is a possible motion of this system.[5]

If you're not allowed to make up an answer, characteristic equations are hard to solve! The transfer function from our examples was easy, but in general both $G(s)$ and $H(s)$ may be polynomial fractions (one polynomial divided by another) that require numerical methods to factor. But for game simulations, you may invent a characteristic equation in already-factored form! If you do so, you are implicitly stating that the physics of the system are unknown, the internal logic of the controls is unknown, the roots were found in an unknown way, but the overall response of the entire system including controls is just what the designer specified.

Root-Locus Plots

Root-locus plots are a bit of a digression, but they give a measure of insight into how one would choose the invented roots mentioned earlier. Aeronautical engineers found that in many cases, control systems included an electronic amplifier or the equivalent, and the amplification, or gain, came out as a constant multiplier in $H(s)$ in Figure 3.5.6 and that furthermore, the stability or instability of the entire system depended in hard-to-anticipate ways on what gain (K) was chosen. The original root-locus method[6] used some extremely clever pencil-and-ruler methods to replace the computation-intensive factoring of Equation (13) into Equation (14); the plots are still useful even though we're doing them by computer now[7]. A root-locus plot is a plot of all possible roots of the characteristic equation for values of K from zero to ∞. Here are some examples:

In a root-locus plot, circles represent roots of the numerator of the characteristic equation, called *zeroes*. X's represent roots of the denominator, called *poles* because the function is infinite at the poles. The actual roots begin at the poles when gain K=0 and move toward the zeroes as K increases. The graph is drawn in complex s-space, where the real (X-axis) component is damping coefficient $-\zeta$ and the imaginary (vertical axis) component is frequency ω. Again, each root corresponds to one of the modes of Equation (1), so you can draw an output function directly if you know what the roots are.

As mentioned, if any mode of a system has a negative damping ratio, the entire system is unstable. In a root-locus plot, this means that if any root lies on the right of the Y-axis, the system is unstable. This happens in Figure 3.5.7(c)—the system is stable at low gain, but if you turn up the gain past a certain point, it becomes unstable.

---

[5] Phase offsets of the various modes, which we have neglected in this gem, are also allowable and in fact are very important in matching Equation (1) to real motion curves.

[6] The root-locus method is also known as the *Evans* method. It was developed in 1948 by Walter R. Evans, a graduate student at UCLA.

[7] For instance, Matlab's `rlocus()` function, or [El-Dawy03], a freeware root-locus plotting program.

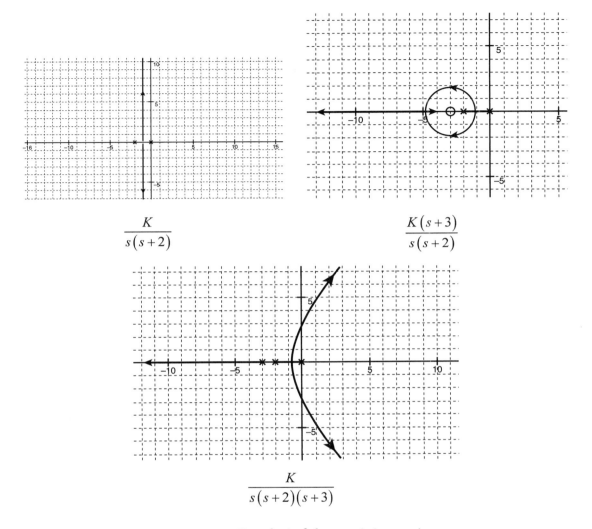

$$\frac{K}{s(s+2)}$$

$$\frac{K(s+3)}{s(s+2)}$$

$$\frac{K}{s(s+2)(s+3)}$$

Figure 3.5.7 Root loci of characteristic equations.

In this example, notice that (b) and (c) are modifications of (a) made by adding a zero and a pole, respectively, to the characteristic equation. This represents adding components (such as resistors and capacitors) to the control system. The shape of the plot and the stability of the system changed dramatically each time. Controls engineers make it their business to know what to add to a circuit to shape the root locus the way they want. Fortunately for the game designer, we can usually just place roots where we like and pretend that a root-locus analysis has been done. A root close to the vertical axis represents underdamping and an oscillation that takes a long time to die out; roots far to the left represent great stability and rapid response.

Frequency Analysis[8]

This gem has completely skipped over a branch of control theory that is actually of equal importance. This is frequency analysis. It is based on the idea that a system's behavior can be broken down into its responses to sine-wave inputs at different frequencies.

If the input to a linear system is a pure sinusoidal function—in other words, $\sin(\phi t)$, where ϕ is any frequency (not necessarily ω)—the output will always be a sinusoidal wave at the same frequency ϕ, but with a different amplitude A. It will also be delayed from the input wave by a time offset that is expressed as a phase angle θ. A and θ are different for every input frequency ϕ, and a graph of frequency response $A(\phi)$ and phase delay $\theta(\phi)$ is a frequency analysis. The best-known plot types are the Bode plot and the Nyquist plot[9].

Any input function can be broken down into a sum of a (possibly infinite) set of sinusoidal functions and can usually be approximated by just a few. (This is the basis of Fourier theory.) Therefore, a frequency analysis can be used to break down a system's motions into a few harmonic modes based on A and θ rather than ζ and ω. The demo on the book's CD has chosen not to follow this route, for simplicity.

Code Example: Control Law Racers

The demo program on the book's CD shows one way to apply the ideas behind a root-locus analysis in a game. Rather than modeling a real system and then analyzing it, the demo goes the other way by asking what behavior a system ought to have and then displaying it without actually doing a model.

The demo shows several slot cars moving down a track. The simulation uses a side-scrolling format, so there is just one degree of freedom: y position. When the player tells them to change lanes, the cars swerve abruptly and then maneuver into the new lane. Their steering is a bit weak compared to the weight of the cars, so they weave back and forth before finding their target. What is interesting is that every car is a little bit different and steers differently. The steering behavior of the cars is encapsulated in the mode structure, which contains the frequencies and damping rates of their motions.

```
struct mode {
  float zeta;  // damping coefficient
  float omega; // frequency
  float A;     // Initial amplitude of wave
};
```

---

[8] See [D'Azzo60], chapters 8–10, and [Thaler60], §4.8, 7.5.

[9] Developed by Hendrik Bode and Harry Nyquist, respectively, who were both engineers at Bell Laboratories in the 1930s.

Each mode supplies one of the terms in Equation (1). Each car can have any number of modes. There is no steering or simulation loop in this demo; the control law models both the physics of the car itself and the actions of its driver. Since a car with only one mode is no more complex than the weight and spring of Example 1, this may be a simple autopilot indeed.

To design your car's control law, add modes. Imagine a root-locus plot like Figure 3.5.7. But instead of plotting a real function, just draw one or more X's for the roots. Think about how well you want your car to handle and how quickly you want it to sway. A real car weaving back and forth on the road may move with a period of one to five seconds or so; that is, an omega of 0.2–1.0. As for damping, if you want your car to keep shimmying for a long time, then give it a zeta close to 0; if you want it to handle well and accurately, then give it a large zeta. A critical damping ratio of zeta = 2 * omega will produce fastest settling.

The in-code comments explain how to add modes to your car. The step after that, giving an actual steering command by setting the A for each mode, is handled arbitrarily by the demo. The next step of interest is the navigation step. This is where the values in the car's modes are applied to Equation (1).

```
vector<driver>::iterator drivIt;

// <for-each> car
for( drivIt = driverList.begin();
     drivIt != driverList.end();
     drivIt++ )
{
    // Sum of all the oscillatory modes

    // measuring distance from target lane implicitly commands the
    // car to go there when all oscillations have settled
    drivIt->driverPos.y = targetLane + Y_BASE;

    modeList::iterator theModeIter;
    // <for-each> mode
    for( theModeIter = drivIt->modes.begin();
         theModeIter != drivIt->modes.end();
         theModeIter++ )
    {
        // Add this mode's contribution to position
        float zeta = theModeIter->zeta;
        float omega = theModeIter->omega;
        float A = theModeIter->A;
        // Time conversion from dimensionless units (radians and
        // rad/sec) to full cycles per second
        float t = 2.0 * PI * resetTime;
        drivIt->driverPos.y += A * exp(-zeta * t) * cos(omega * t);
    }
}
```

The last statement computes the output position `driverPos.y` directly, without going through a simulation step.

You will have to go into source code to change the cars. Try adding more cars and changing modes. See what happens when a car's modes include both large and small damping coefficients.

Conclusion

The control theory presented in this gem is the so-called classical control theory, based on linear systems, that was current practice in the aerospace and electronics industries from roughly the 1930s through the 1960s and has been eclipsed by the rise of computers but has certainly not gone away. It's a bit surprising that such a well-established body of knowledge is so forgotten in the game industry. This gem is meant to introduce programmers and designers to the concepts of control theory as well as to present one way to simulate and direct physical objects. Other applications of these ideas provide a virtually unexplored field for the industry.

References

[D'Azzo60] D'Azzo, John J., and Constantine H. Houpis. *Feedback Control System Analysis and Synthesis*. McGraw-Hill Book Company, Inc., 1960.

[El-Dawy03] El-Dawy, Ahmed Saad. "RootLocus." n.d. Geocities. n.d. <http://www.geocities.com/aseldawy/root_locus.html>.

[Graham61] Graham, Dunstan, and Duane McRuer. *Analysis of Nonlinear Control Systems*. John Wiley & Sons, Inc., 1960.

[Thaler60] Thaler, George J., and Robert G. Brown. *Analysis and Design of Feedback Control Systems*. McGraw-Hill Book Company, Inc., 1960.

3.6

Adaptive Tactic Selection in First-Person Shooter (FPS) Games

Thomas Hartley, Institute of Gaming and Animation (IGA), University of Wolverhampton

tom.hartley5@googlemail.com

and

Quasim Mehdi, Institute of Gaming and Animation (IGA), University of Wolverhampton

One of the key capabilities of human game players that is not typically employed by non-player characters (NPCs) in commercial first-person shooter (FPS) games is in-game learning and adaptation. The ability of a human player to adapt to opponents' tactics is an important skill and one that separates an expert game player from a novice. NPCs that incorporate in-game learning and adaptation are more responsive to human players' actions and are therefore more capable opponents. This gem presents a practical in-game approach to adapting an NPC's selection of combat tactics.

A Dynamic Approach to Adaptive Tactic Selection

To achieve successful in-game (that is, run-time) tactic selection in FPS games, we proposed to adapt the online adaptation algorithm dynamic scripting [Spronck06, Spronck05]. The reinforcement learning–inspired dynamic scripting algorithm has been designed specifically for use in online learning scenarios and has previously shown significant promise in other genres of scripted games, such as role playing and strategy games. Consequently, the approach offers an interesting augmentation to the traditionally scripted tactic selection techniques used in commercial FPS games. However, the approach does need to be adapted to make it suitable for use in an FPS environment.

The FPS version of the dynamic scripting algorithm presented in this gem has been adapted to the selection of tactics rather than rules for scripts, so it has a number of differences from previously implemented versions. First, the library of tactics in the developed system is organized in groups according to a dual-layered state representation. Previous implementations organize the dynamic scripting rulebases according to NPC type and high-level game states [Ponsen and Spronck04]. However this limited state representation is not suited to FPS games, as the selection of player-versus-player tactics greatly depends on the current state of the NPC [Thurau06]. The second contribution is the development of fitness functions to evaluate the success of a tactic and the encounter with an opponent. The third contribution is the development of a tactic selection process that makes use of a prioritized list approach in combination with the K-Nearest Neighbor algorithm (K-NN) [Mitchell97]. The goal of this approach is to organize the tactics so that the most successful ones are more likely to be selected first.

Overview of the Adaptive Tactic Selection Architecture

Tactics in the system are organized into tactic libraries, which in turn are organized according to a dual-layered representation of the game environment. As illustrated in Figure 3.6.1, the upper layer determines which tactic library should be selected according to an abstract state representation and/or rules, which are typically described in terms of a behavior type or goal. For example, an "engage enemy" library of tactics could be defined by health above 50 percent and the possession of a high-powered weapon. This process can be performed manually using a game developer's domain knowledge and traditional game development techniques, such as finite state machines (FSM), decision trees, or rules. For example, the abstract state space in Figure 3.6.2 is based on the hierarchical FSM/prioritized list approach used to control NPC behavior in *Halo 2* [Isla05]. The highest priority state (arranged right to left) that matches the current game state is selected. This approach should allow the tactic selection architecture to be easily integrated with existing game AI techniques.

As illustrated in Figure 3.6.2, the lower state space contains instances of a library's tactics at points in an n-dimensional feature space. The feature space and the number of tactic instances within a tactic library are kept relatively small in order to maintain performance. Once the upper layer has determined the current tactic library, the K closest library instance(s) to the current game state are selected and used to determine the NPC's current list of tactics. The following procedure outlines how an instance of the lower state space is selected. If the closest library instance to the query state (in other words, the NPC's current state) is equal or below a predefined threshold, it is used to determine a prioritized tactic list. If the closest library instance is above a predefined query threshold, the K closest tactic instances to the current environment state are used for tactic selection. This multi-layered approach to selection allows tactics to be associated with detailed game states, while also being efficient in retrieving from the library.

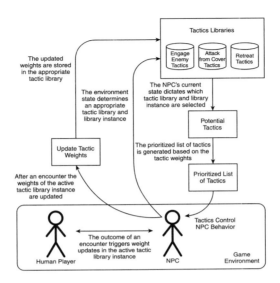

Figure 3.6.1   High-level overview of the tactic selection architecture.

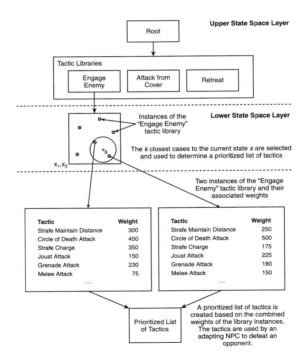

Figure 3.6.2   Overview of the tactic selection process and the state organization. The K closest library instances are selected. The weights of each tactic are combined using distance weighting and are used to determine a prioritized list.

All tactics have an associated weight that influences the order in which they are selected in a given state. The weights reflect the success or failure of a tactic during previous encounters with an opponent. Learning only occurs between the tactics in each library instance, and one library does not affect the learning in another, even if the same tactic is found in both libraries. Tactic selection is achieved through a prioritized list [Isla05], which is adapted to support online list generation.

First, the procedure outlined above is used to determine the K library instance(s) closest to the current game state. If K > 1 and the closest tactic instance is above a query threshold, the tactic's weights are combined using the distance-weighted K-NN algorithm. The individual or combined tactic library instance is used to create the prioritized list. The K-NN algorithm classifies an unlabeled instance (for example, s in Figure 3.6.2) by comparing its n-dimensional feature vector to stored instances. The K-Nearest Neighbors to the query instance are found and used to determine a combined weight for a tactic. This is achieved through a weighted average that reflects a stored instance's distance to the query instance.

The position of a tactic within the prioritized list is determined by ordering tactics according to their weight. (For example, the tactics with the largest weights have the highest priority of selection.) A new prioritized list of tactics is generated whenever an upper layer state change occurs or when the library instance changes. If a distance-weighted prioritized list has been created, a predefined distance threshold is used to determine whether a new list should be generated. The distance threshold is based on the distance from the current list's query state to the NPC's present world state.

Once a list of tactics is generated, the tactic that has the highest priority and is capable of running is selected as the current behavior. If higher-priority tactics become available, they can interrupt the current tactic on the next game loop. To avoid repetitive behavior, the tactic selection process can also include a check to prevent the same variant of tactic from following each other. (For example, "strafe a short distance" would not follow "strafe a long distance.") Therefore, if the next tactic is a similar variant to the current tactic, it is skipped, and the subsequent tactic is evaluated. This rule doesn't apply to tactic interrupts, which occur regardless of tactic variation.

When a tactic is complete, is no longer capable of running, or a fixed amount of time has elapsed, the next tactic in the list that is capable of running is selected. When a tactic is interrupted, is completed, or times out; a library change occurs; or a library instance change occurs, the tactic has its weight updated according to a weight-update and fitness function (outlined in the next section). If the query instance was above a distance threshold, the weight update is applied to the tactics in each K close library instance according to the instance's distance from the initial query point.

Fitness and Weight-Update Functions

The weight-update function alters the weights associated with tactics in response to a reinforcement signal that is supplied by tactic and encounter fitness functions. The aim of the fitness function is to reward tactics that defeated an opponent or improved the NPC's chance of defeating the opponent. The fitness functions for the tactic and the encounter are defined below. Each function returns a value in the range of [-1,1].

$$f(t) = \frac{1}{10}(7A(t) + 3S(t)) \quad (1)$$

The equation above evaluates the fitness of a tactic and contains two components. In the equation, f refers to the fitness of the tactic t that is being evaluated. The first component $A(t) \in [-1,1]$ determines the difference in life caused by the tactic [Andrade04]. That is the life lost from the opponent minus the life lost from the NPC. The difference in life lost represents a key metric in measuring the performance of a tactic, as removing all an opponent's life is the ultimate goal of FPS combat.

The second component of the fitness function $S(t) \in [-1,1]$ evaluates the surprise of the tactic. A surprise is the anticipation of an experience that the actual experience does not fulfil [Saunders02]. In the tactic selection architecture, the experience is the average value of the difference in life lost from previous encounters, and the actual experience is the current difference in life lost.

Each component of the tactic fitness function is weighted according to its contribution as in the standard dynamic scripting approach [Spronck05]. The selection of the fitness function's contribution is based on game goals. (For example, an NPC places high value on its health.) The two components of the tactic fitness function are determined using Equations (2) and (3). The function $hl(NPC)$ in Equations (2) and (3) refers to the health (in other words, life) lost from the adapting NPC, and $hl(opp)$ refers to the health lost from an opponent (in other words, the damage caused by the adapting NPC). $AvghLifeLost_n$ in Equation (3) contains the average difference in life caused by the tactic from the previous n weight updates.

$$A(t) = \frac{hl(opp) - hl(NPC)}{100} \quad (2)$$

$$S(t) = \frac{(hl(opp) - hl(NPC)) - AvgLifeLost_n}{200} \quad (3)$$

Equation (4) evaluates the fitness of an encounter, that is, the tactics used by the adapting NPC during a combat to reach a winning or losing state. When an NPC reaches a terminal state, the tactics used during the encounter are updated according to whether the NPC won or lost. In Equation 4, f refers to the fitness of the encounter e that is being evaluated. $hl_t(NPC)$ refers to the health (in other words, life) lost from the adapting NPC during the performance of tactic t. $hl_t(opp)$ refers to the health lost from an opponent during the performance of tactic t.

$$f(e) = \begin{cases} 1 - (hl_t(NPC)/125) & \{\text{NPC Won}\} \\ -1 + (hl_t(OPP)/125) & \{\text{NPC Lost}\} \end{cases} \quad (4)$$

Equations (2), (3), and (4) assume that the life lost or damage is in the range of 0 to 100. Equation (3) divides surprise by 200 so that the returned value will be in the range of −1 to 1. Equation (4) divides health lost by 125 in order to give the tactic a guaranteed reward or punishment depending on whether the encounter was winning or losing. The scale of the reward or punishment can be set according to game requirements.

The weight update function uses the tactic and encounter fitness functions to generate a weight adaptation for the library tactics (i.e. an amount to adjust the current weight of a tactic). The function is based on the standard dynamic scripting technique, where weights are bound by a range $[W_{min}, W_{max}]$ and surplus weights (that is, weight adjustments that result in a remainder outside the minimum and maximum range) are shared between all other weights [Spronck05]. However the fitness functions outlined in Equations (1) and (4) return a value between $[−1, 1]$, where a negative fitness value indicates a losing tactic, while a positive fitness value indicates a winning tactic. Therefore a simplified weight update function is used in this approach. In Equation (5), P_{max} is the maximum penalty, R_{max} is the maximum reward, F is the fitness of the tactic, and b is set to 0 and is the break-even point for the tactic's fitness. Above this point, the tactic's fitness is considered to be winning, while below this point the tactic is considered to be losing. In this simplified weight update function, the break-even point is built into the function itself. A fitness of 0 means the weights are unchanged.

$$\Delta w = \begin{cases} P_{max}F & \{F < b\} \\ R_{max}F & \{F \geq b\} \end{cases} \quad (5)$$

When multiple tactic library instances are used to create a combined prioritized list, the weight update is shared between the K instances according to their distance to the initial query state (in other words, the point that resulted in the library instances being retrieved). The sharing of the weight update is performed using Equation (6), where Δw_i is the weight update for a library instance, d_i is the distance to the library instance from the query state, and d is the total weight.

$$\Delta w_i = \frac{d\Delta w}{d_i^2} \qquad \text{Where:} \qquad d = \frac{1}{\sum \frac{1}{d_i^2}} \quad (6)$$

Adapting Tactic Selection

To illustrate the tactic selection architecture, we describe the example of an NPC learning to adapt its selection of combat tactics. In this example, the adapting NPC is endowed with an "Attack" library of tactics that could include melee attack, charge attack, strafe charge attack, circle strafe attack, and attack from cover. Tactics are manually coded and comprise multiple lines of logic that define the behavior to be performed (for example, movement and weapon handling code). In addition to behavior logic, there should also be code to determine whether a tactic is capable of running. For example, the circle strafe tactic may not be capable of running in a narrow corridor.

For clarity, only one tactic library is used in this example. The upper state space controls the selection of tactic libraries using conventional techniques, and adaptation occurs independently within each tactic library instance; therefore, additional tactic libraries can be easily added. After a library has been defined, the default weight of the tactics needs to be set. Tactics can be given the same initial weight, or a weight can be selected based on domain knowledge. In this example, all the tactic weights are initially set to the same default weight; therefore, the position of tactics within the initial prioritized list is randomly determined.

Once a tactic library has been defined, the next step is to determine the instances of the library. This involves defining the state space, the number of instances, the position of the instances within the state space, and how the state space is organized. In this example, the lower state space is defined as the relative distance between the adapting NPC and the targeted opponent. This simple feature vector was selected because distance is a prominent factor in the selection of FPS tactics. In most cases the requirements of the game can be used to determine the most appropriate state space representation.

The number of library instances is determined by the size of the state space. In this example, the state space is compact; therefore, only a few instances are needed. The requisite number of instances is also affected by their position in the state space and how the state space is organized. The position of tactic instances in the state space can be manually managed using domain knowledge or automatically added using a distance metric, such as: if $s > r$, then create a new instance of the tactic library, where s is the distance between the current state and the closest tactic instance and r is a predefined distance threshold. If the distance is below the threshold, then the closest tactic cases are used. Figure 3.6.3 illustrates an example of tactic library instances and state space organization.

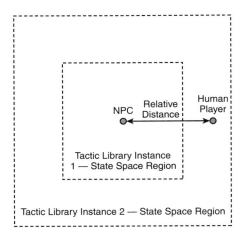

Figure 3.6.3   Example arrangement of the lower state space.

At the start of a combat encounter, the tactic selection architecture generates a list of tactics that are ordered by their associated weight. The NPC attempts to defeat the opponent by executing the first tactic in the list. If the tactic is not capable of running, the next tactic in the list is selected. This is repeated until a tactic capable of running is found. The list of tactics is generated by determining the closest K library instances to the NPC's position in the lower state space. Once a tactic and encounter are complete, the weight of the tactics used are updated using Equations (1) and (4). In this example, K is set to 1, and the initial weights of tactics are the same; therefore, only the closest library instance is used, and the order of the tactics is initially random. The process of an NPC selecting and adjusting its weights is summarized below:

- A prioritized list of tactics is generated, and the melee attack tactic is selected for execution. The tactic performs poorly during the encounter and results in 100-percent health loss for the adapting NPC and 5-percent health loss for the opponent.

- The encounter finishes with the death of the adapting NPC; therefore, the tactic and encounter fitness are determined. The tactic's weight is updated based on its success. The first step in the process is to determine a tactic's fitness—in this example, `hl_npc` equals 100 and `hl_opp` equals 5.

```
int hl_npc = botDamage()
int hl_opp = playerDamage()
float a = (hl_opp - hl_npc) / 100
float s = ( (hl_opp - hl_npc) - avgDiffInLifeLost ) / 200
float fitness = 1 / 10 * (7 * a + 3 * s)
```

- Once the fitness of the tactic has been determined, the weights of all the tactics in the library instance are updated. If the number of library instances equals 1, as in this example, the weight adjustment for the performed tactic is determined as follows:

```
if (fitness < 0)
    weightAdjustment = tacticPenaltyMax * fitness
else
    weightAdjustment = tacticRewardMax * fitness
```

- Next, the encounter weight update is performed. This process involves the algorithm looping through the tactics used during the encounter, determining their encounter fitness, weight adjustment, and weight update. The calculation of the encounter fitness is shown below. The `tacticResults` array contains information on each tactic used during the encounter and its performance.

```
if (hasWon == true)
    fitness = 1 - (tacticResults[i].getHl_npc() / 125)
else
    fitness = -1 + (tacticResults[i].getHl_opp() / 125)
```

- After the tactic weights have been updated, the adapting NPC can generate a new prioritized list. In this example, the melee attack tactic will be at the end of the list due to its poor performance.

Conclusion

This gem has outlined an approach to the in-game adaptation of scripted tactical behavior in FPS computer games. The technique enables NPCs in these games to adapt their selection of tactics in a given state based on their experience of the tactics' success. Less successful tactics are not selected or are only selected when more preferred tactics are not available.

References

[Andrade04] Andrade, G. D., H. P. Santana, A. W. B. Furtado, A. R. G. A. Leitão, and G. L. Ramalho. "Online Adaptation of Computer Games Agents: A Reinforcement Learning Approach." *1st Brazilian Symposium on Computer Games and Digital Entertainment* (SBGames2004).

[Isla05] Isla, D. "Handling Complexity in the *Halo 2* AI." *GDC 2005 Proceedings*. 2005. Gamasutra. n.d. <http://www.gamasutra.com/gdc2005/features /20050311/isla_01.shtml>.

[Mitchell97] Mitchell, T. *Machine Learning*. McGraw-Hill, 1997.

[Ponsen and Spronck04] Ponsen, M. and P. Spronck. "Improving Adaptive Game AI with Evolutionary Learning." *Computer Games: Artificial Intelligence, Design and Education* (CGAIDE 2004): 389–396.

[Saunders02] Saunders, R. "Curious Design Agents and Artificial Creativity: A Synthetic Approach to the Study of Creative Behaviour." Ph.D. thesis. University of Sydney, Sydney. 2002.

[Spronck05] Spronck, P. "Adaptive Game AI." Ph.D. Thesis. Universiteit Maastricht, Maastricht. 2005.

[Spronck06] Spronck, P. "Dynamic Scripting." *AI Game Programming Wisdom 3*. Ed. S. Rabin. Boston: Charles River Media, 2006. 661–675.

[Thurau06] Thurau, C. "Behavior Acquisition in Artificial Agents." Ph.D. thesis. Bielefeld University, Bielefeld. 2006.

3.7

Embracing Chaos Theory: Generating Apparent Unpredictability through Deterministic Systems

Dave Mark, Intrinsic Algorithm LLC
dave@intrinsicalgorithm.com

One of the challenges of creating deep, interesting behaviors in games and simulations is to enable our agents to select from a wide variety of actions while not abandoning completely deterministic systems. On the one hand, we want to step away from having very obvious if/then triggers or monotonous sequences of actions for our agents. On the other hand, the need for simple testing and debugging necessitates the avoidance of introducing random selection to our algorithms.

This gem shows how, through embracing the concept and deterministic techniques of chaos theory, we can achieve complex-looking behaviors that are reasonable yet not immediately predictable by the viewer. By citing examples from nature and science (such as weather) as well as the simple artificial simulations of cellular automation, the gem explains what causes chaotic-looking systems through purely deterministic rules. The gem then presents some sample, purely deterministic behavior systems that exhibit complex, observably unpredictable sequences of behavior. The gem concludes by explaining how these sorts of algorithms can be easily integrated into game AI and simulation models to generate deeper, more immersive behavior.

The Need for Predictability

The game development industry often finds itself in a curious predicament with regard to randomness in games. Game developers rely heavily on deterministic systems. Programming is inherently a deterministic environment. Even looking only at the lowly if/then statement, it is obvious that computers themselves are most "comfortable" in a realm where there is a hard-coded relationship between cause and effect. Even non-binary systems, such as fuzzy state machines and response curves, could theoretically be reduced to a potentially infinite sequence of statements that state, "Given the value x, the one and only result is y."

Game designers, programmers, and testers also feel comfortable with this technological bedrock. After all, in the course of designing, developing, and observing the complex algorithms and behaviors, they often have the need to be able to say, with certainty, "Given this set of parameters, this is what should happen." Often the only metric of the success or failure of the development process we have is the question, "Is this action what we expected? If not, what went wrong?"

Shaking Things Up

Game players, on the other hand, have a different perspective on the situation. The very factor that comforts the programmer—the knowledge that his program is doing exactly what he predicts—is the factor that can annoy the player...the program is doing exactly what he predicts. From the standpoint of the player, predictability in game characters can lead to repetitive, and therefore monotonous, gameplay.

The inclusion of randomness can be a powerful and effective tool to simulate the wide variety of choices that intelligent agents are inclined to make [Mark09]. Used correctly and limiting the application to the selection of behaviors that are reasonable for the NPC's archetype, randomness can create deeper, more believable characters [Ellinger08]. While this approach provides a realistic depth of behavior that can be attractive to the game player, it is this same abandonment of a predictable environment that makes the analysis, testing, and debugging of behaviors more complicated. Complete unpredictability can also lead to player frustration, as they are unable to progress in the game by learning complex agent behavior. The only recourse that a programming staff has in controlling random behaviors is through tight selection of random seeds. In a dynamic environment, however, the juxtaposition of random selection of AI with the unpredictable nature of the player's actions can lead to a combinatorial explosion of possible scenario-to-reaction mappings. This is often a situation that is an unwanted—or even unacceptable—risk or burden for a development staff.

The solution lies in questioning one of the premises in the above analysis—that is, that the experience of the players is improved through the inclusion of randomness in the decision models of the agent AI. While that statement may well be true, the premise in question is that the experience that the player has is based on the actual random number call in the code. The random number generation in the agent AI is merely a tool in a greater process. What is important is that the player cannot perceive excessive predictable regularity in the actions of the agent. As we shall discuss in this article, accomplishing the goal of unpredictability can exist without sacrificing the moment-by-moment logical determinism that developers need in order to confidently craft their agent code.

A Brief History of Chaos

The central point of how and why this approach is viable can be illustrated simply by analyzing the term *chaos theory*. The word *chaos* is defined as "a state of utter confusion or disorder; a total lack of organization or order." This is also how we tend to use it in general speech. By stating that there is no organization or order to a system, we imply randomness. However, chaos theory deals entirely within the realm of purely deterministic systems; there is no randomness involved. In this sense, the idea of chaos is more aligned with the idea of "extremely complex information" than with the absence of order. To the point of this article, because the information is so complex, we observers are unable to adequately perceive the complexity of the interactions. Given a momentary initial state (the input), we fail to determine the rule set that was in effect that led to the next momentary state (the output).

Our inability to perceive order falls into two general categories. First, we are often limited by flawed perception of information. This occurs by not perceiving the existence of relevant information and not perceiving relevant information with great enough accuracy to determine the ultimate effect of the information on the system.

The second failure is to adequately perceive and understand the relationships that define the systems. Even with perfect perception of information, if we are not aware of how that information interacts, we will not be able to understand the dynamics of the system. We may not perceive a relationship in its entirety or we may not be clear on the exact magnitude that a relationship has. For example, while we may realize that A and B are related in some way, we may not know exactly what the details of that relationship are.

Perceiving Error

Chaos theory is based largely on the first of these two categories—the inability to perceive the accuracy of the information. In 1873, the Scottish theoretical physicist and mathematician James Clerk Maxwell hypothesized that there are classes of phenomena affected by "influences whose physical magnitude is too small to be taken account of by a finite being, [but which] may produce results of the highest importance."

As prophetic as this speculation is, it was the French mathematician Henri Poincaré, considered by some to be the father of chaos theory, who put it to more formal study in his examination of the "three-body problem" in 1887. Despite inventing an entirely new branch of mathematics, algebraic topology, to tackle the problem, he never completely succeeded. What he found in the process, however, was profound in its own right. He summed up his findings as follows:

> If we knew exactly the laws of nature and the situation of the universe at the initial moment, we could predict exactly the situation of the same universe at a succeeding moment. But even if it were the case that the natural laws had no longer any secret for us, we could still know the situation approximately. If that enabled us to predict the succeeding situation with the same approximation, that is all we require, and we should say that the phenomenon had been predicted, that it is governed by the laws. But [it] is not always so; it may happen that small differences in the initial conditions produce very great ones in the final phenomena. A small error in the former will produce an enormous error in the later. Prediction becomes impossible....[Wikipedia09]

This concept eventually led to what is popularly referred to as the *butterfly effect*. The origin of the term is somewhat nebulous, but it is most often linked to the work of Edward Lorenz. In 1961, Lorenz was working on the issue of weather prediction using a large computer. Due to logistics, he had to terminate a particularly long run of processing midway through. In order to resume the calculations at a later time, he made a note of all the relevant variables in the registers. When it was time to continue the process, he re-entered the values that he had recorded previously. Rather than re-enter one value as 0.506127, he simply entered 0.506. Eventually, the complex simulation diverged significantly from what he had predicted. He later determined that the removal of 0.000127 from the data was what had dramatically changed the course of the dynamic system—in this case, resulting in a dramatically different weather system. In 1963, he wrote of his findings in a paper for the New York Academy of Sciences, noting that, "One meteorologist remarked that if the theory were correct, one flap of a seagull's wings could change the course of weather forever." (He later substituted "butterfly" for "seagull" for poetic effect.)

Despite being an inherently deterministic environment, much of the problem with predicting weather lies in the size of the scope. Certainly, it is too much to ask scientists to predict on which city blocks rain will fall and on which it will not during an isolated shower. However, even predicting the single broad path of a large, seemingly well-organized storm system, such as a hurricane, baffles current technology. Even without accounting for the intensity of the storm as a whole, much less the individual bands of rain and wind, the various forecasts of simply the path of the eye of the hurricane that the different prediction algorithms churn out lay out like the strings of a discarded tassel. That these mathematical models all process the same information in such widely divergent ways speaks to the complexity of the problem.

Thankfully, the mathematical error issue is not much of a factor in the closed system of a computer game. We do not have to worry about errors in initial observations of the world, because our modeling system is actually a part of the world. If we restart the model from the same initial point, we can guarantee that, unlike Lorenz' misfortune, we won't have an error of 0.000127 to send our calculations spinning off wildly into the solar system. (Interestingly, in our quest for randomness, we can build a system that relies on a truly random seed to provide interesting variation—the player.) Additionally, we don't have to worry about differences in mathematical calculation on any given run. All other things being equal (for example, processor type), a given combination of formula and input will always yield the same output. These two factors are important in constructing a reliable deterministic system that is entirely under our control.

Brownian Motion

As mentioned earlier, the second reason why people mistake deterministic chaos for randomness is that we often lack the ability to perceive or realize the relationships between entities in a system. In fact, we often are not aware of some of the entities at all.

This was the case with the discovery of a phenomenon that eventually became known as *Brownian motion*. Although there had been observations of the seemingly random movement of particles before, the accepted genesis of this idea is the work of botanist Robert Brown in 1827. As he watched the microscopic inner workings of pollen grains, he observed minute "jittery" movement by vacuoles. Over time, the vacuoles would even seem to travel around their neighborhood in an "alive-looking" manner. Not having a convenient explanation for this motion, he assumed that pollen was "alive" and was, after the way of living things, moving of its own accord. He later repeated the experiments with dust, which ruled out the "alive" theory but did nothing to explain the motion of the particles.

The real reason for the motion of the vacuoles was due to the molecular and atomic level vibrations due to heat. Each atom in the neighborhood of the target vibrates on its own pattern and schedule, with each vibration nudging both the target and other adjacent atoms slightly. The combination of many atoms doing so in myriad directions and amounts provides a staggering level of complexity. While completely deterministic from one moment to the next—that is, "A will nudge B n distance in d direction"—the combinatorial explosion of interconnected factors goes well beyond the paltry scope of Poincaré's three-body problem.

The problem that Brown had was that he could not perceive the existence of the atoms buffeting the visible grains. What's more, even when the existence of those atoms is known (and more to the point, once the heat-induced vibration of molecules is understood), there is no way that anyone can know what that relationship between cause and effect is from moment to moment. We only know that there will be an effect.

This speaks to the second of the reasons we listed earlier—that we often lack the ability to perceive or realize the relationships between entities in a system. This effect is easier for us to take advantage of in order to accomplish our goal. By incorporating connections between agents and world data that are beyond the ability of the player to adequately perceive, we can generate purely deterministic cause/effect chains that look either random or at least reasonably unpredictable.

Exploring Cellular Automata

One well-known example bed for purely deterministic environments is the world of cellular automata. Accordingly, one of the most well-known examples of cellular automata is Conway's Game of Life. Conway's creation (because the term "game" is probably pushing things a little) started as an attempt to boil down John von Neumann's theories of self-replicating Turing machines. What spilled out of his project was an interesting vantage point on emergent behavior and, more to the point of this gem, the appearance of seemingly coordinated, logical behavior. Using Conway's Life as an example, we will show how applying simple, deterministic rules produce this seemingly random behavior.

The environment for Life is a square grid of cells. A cell can be either on or off. Its state in any given time slice is based on the states of the eight cells in its immediate neighborhood. The number of possible combinations of the cells in the local neighborhood is 28 or 256. (If you account for mirroring or rotation of the state space, the actual number of unique arrangements is somewhat smaller.) The reason that the Game of Life is easy for us to digest is its brevity and simplicity, however. We do not care about the orientation of the live neighbors, but only a sum of how many are alive at that moment. The only rules that are in effect are:

1. Any live cell with two or three live neighbors lives on to the next generation.
2. Any live cell with fewer than two live neighbors dies (loneliness/starvation).
3. Any live cell with more than three live neighbors dies (overcrowding).
4. Any dead cell with exactly three live neighbors becomes a live cell (birth).

Figure 3.7.1 shows a very simple example of these rules in action. In the initial grid, there are three "live" cells shown in black. Additionally, each cell contains a number showing how many neighbors that cell currently has. Note that two of the "dead" cells (shown in gray) have three neighbors, which, according to Rule 4 above, means they will become alive in the next iteration. The other dead cells have zero, one, or two neighbors, meaning they will remain at a status quo (in other words, dead) for the next round. The center "live" cell has two neighbors, which, according to Rule 1 above, allows it to continue living. On the other hand, the two end cells have only a single live neighbor (the center cell) and will therefore die of starvation the next round. The results are shown on the right of Figure 3.7.1. Two of the prior cells are now dead (shown in gray), and two new cells have been born to join the single surviving cell.

Interestingly, this pattern repeats such that the next iteration will be identical to the first (a horizontal line), and so on. This is one of the many stable or tightly repeating patterns that can be found in Life. Specifically, this one is commonly called a *blinker*.

Figure 3.7.2 shows another, slightly more involved example. The numbers in the initial frame make it easier to understand why the results are there. Even without the numbers, however, the relationships between the initial state and the subsequent one are relatively easy to discern on this small scale.

While the rule set seems simple and intuitive enough, when placed on a larger scale and run over time, the "behavior" of the entire "colony" of cells starts to look random. This is due to the overwhelming number of interactions that we perceive at any one moment. Looking at the four panels of Figure 3.7.3, it is difficult for us to intuitively predict what would have happened next except for either in the most general sense (for example, that solid blob in the middle is too crowded and will likely collapse) or in regard to very specific subsets of the whole (for example, that is a blinker in the lower-left corner).

Interestingly, it is this very combination of "reasonable" expectations with not knowing *exactly* what is going to appear next that gives depth to Conway's simulation. Over time, one develops a sense of familiarity with the generalized feel of the simulation.

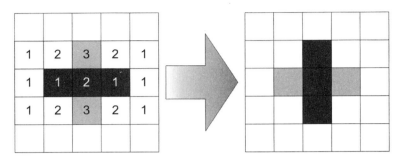

Figure 3.7.1   A simple example of the rule set in Conway's Game of Life. In this case, a two-step repeating figure called a *blinker* is generated by the three boxes.

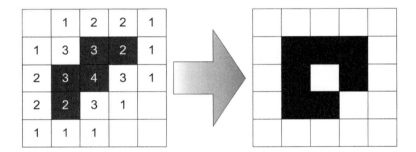

Figure 3.7.2   The dynamic nature of the cells acting together.

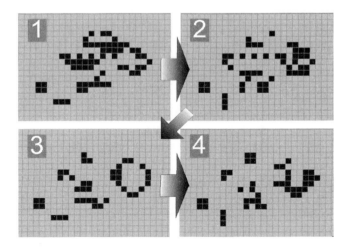

Figure 3.7.3   When taken as a whole, the simple cells in Life take on a variety of complex-looking behaviors. While each cell's state is purely deterministic, it is difficult for the human mind to quickly predict what the next overall image will look like.

For example, we can expect that overcrowded sections will collapse under their own weight, and isolated pockets will die off or stagnate. We also recognize how certain static or repeating features will persist until they are interfered with—even slightly—by an outside influence. Still, the casual observer will still perceive the unfolding (and seemingly complex) action as being somewhat random…or at least undirected. Short of pausing to analyze every cell on every frame, the underlying strictly rule-based engine goes unnoticed.

On the other hand, from the standpoint of the designer and tester, this simulation model is elegantly simplistic. The very fact that you *can* pause the simulation and confirm that each cell is behaving properly is a boon. For any given cell at any stage, it is a trivial problem to confirm that the resulting state change is performing exactly as designed.

Leveraging Chaos Theory in Games

What sets Conway's Life apart from many game scenarios is not the complexity of the rule set, but rather the depth of it. On its own, the process of passing the sum of eight binary inputs through four rules to receive a new binary state does not seem terribly complex. When we compare it to what a typical AI entity in a game may use as its decision model, we realize that it is actually a relatively robust model.

For instance, imagine a very simple AI agent in a first-person shooter game (see Figure 3.7.4). It may take into account the distance to the player and the direction in which the player lies. When the player enters a specified range, the NPC "wakes up," turns, and moves toward the player. There is one input state—distance—and two output states: "idle" and "move toward player." While this seems extraordinarily simple, as recently as 10 to 15 years ago, this was still common for enemy AI. Needless to say, the threshold and resultant behavior were easy to discern over time. Players could perceive both the cause and the effect with very little difficulty. Likewise, designers and programmers could test this behavior with something as simple as an onscreen distance counter. At this point, there is very little divergence between the simplicity for the player and the simplicity for the programmer.

Adding a Second Factor

If we were to add a second criterion to the decision, the situation does not necessarily become much more complicated. For example, we could add a criterion stating that the agent will only attack the player when he is in range and carrying a weapon. This is an intuitively sound addition and is likely something that the player will quickly understand. On the other hand, this also means that the enemy is again rigidly predictable.

Other factors can be added to a decision model, however, which could obscure the point at which a behavior change should occur. Even the addition of other binary factors (such as the states of the cells in Life) can complicate things quickly for the observer if they aren't intuitively obvious. For instance, imagine that the rule for attacking the player was no longer "if the distance from player to enemy < n" but rather "if the player's distance to two enemies < n" (see Figure 3.7.5). As the player approaches the first enemy, there would be no reaction from that first enemy until a second enemy is within range as well. While this may seem like a contrived rule, it stresses an important point. The player will most certainly be interested in the actions of the first enemy and will not easily recognize that its reaction was ultimately based on the distance to the *second* enemy.

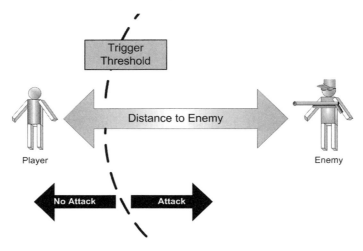

Figure 3.7.4   If there is only one criterion in a decision model, it is relatively simple for the player to determine not only what the criterion is, but what the critical threshold value is for that criterion to trigger the behavior.

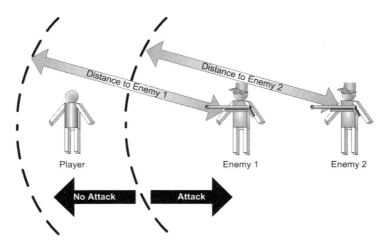

Figure 3.7.5   The inclusion of a second criterion can obscure the threshold value for—or even the existence of—the first criterion. In this case, because the second enemy is included, the player is not attacked as he enters the normal decision radius of the first enemy.

The player may not be able to adequately determine what the trigger conditions are because we have masked the existence of the second criterion from the player. People assume that causes and effects are linked in some fashion. In this example, because there is no intuitive link between the player's distance to the second enemy and the actions of the first, the player will be at a loss to determine when the first enemy will attack. The benefit of this approach is that the enemy no longer seems like it is acting strictly on the whims of the player. That is, the player is no longer deciding when *he* wants the enemy to attack—it is seemingly attacking on its own. This imparts an aura of unpredictability on the enemy, which, in essence, makes it seem more autonomous.

Of course, we programmers know that the agent is not truly autonomous but merely acting as a result of second criterion. In fact, this new rule set is almost as simple to monitor and test as it is to program in the first place. We have the benefit of knowing what the two rules are and how they interact—something that is somewhat opaque to the player.

Selecting the Right Factors

As mentioned, the inclusion of the player's distance to the second agent as a criterion for the decisions of the first agent is a little contrived. In fact, it has the potential for embarrassing error. If the second agent was far away, it is possible that the player could walk right up to the first one and not be inside the threshold radius of the second. In this case, the first agent would check his decision criteria and determine that the player was not in range of two people and, as a result, would not attack the player. This does not mean that there is a flaw in the use of more than one criterion for the decision—simply that there is a flaw in which criteria are being used in conjunction. In this case, the criterion that was based on the position of the second agent—and, more specifically, the player's proximity to the second agent—was arbitrary. It was not directly related to the decision that the agent is making.

The solution to this is to include factors on which it is reasonable for an agent to base his decisions. In this example, the factors may include items such as:

- Distance to player
- Perceived threat (for example, visible weapon)
- Agent's health
- Agent's ammo
- Agent's alertness level
- Player's distance to sensitive location

We already covered the first two. The others are simply examples of information that could be considered relevant. For the last one, we could use the distance measurement from the player to a location such as a bomb detonator. If the player is too close to it, the agent will attack. This is different than the example with two agents above in that the distance to a detonator is presumably more relevant to the agent's job than the player's proximity to two separate agents.

While a number of the criteria listed previously could be expressed as continuous values, such as the agent's health ranging from 0 to 100, for the sake of simplicity, they can also be reduced to Boolean values. We could rephrase "agent's health" as "agent has low health," for instance. If we define "low health" as a value below 25, we are now able to reduce that criterion to a Boolean value. The same could be done with "agent's ammo." This, of course, is very similar to what we did with the distance. We could assert that "if agent has less than 10 shots remaining," then "agent has low ammo."

What we have achieved with the above list could be summed up with the following pseudo-code query:

```
If   PlayerTooCloseToMe()
     or PlayerCloseToTarget()
     and WeaponVisible()
     and IAmHealthy()
     and IHaveEnoughAmmo()
     and IAmAlert())
     then Attack()
```

Even with these criteria, the number of possible configurations is 2^7 or 128. (Incidentally, the number of configurations of cells in Life is 2^8 or 256.) In our initial example, it would take only a short amount of time to determine the distance threshold at which the agent attacks. By the inclusion of so many relevant factors into the agent's behavior model, the only way that any one threshold can be ascertained is with the inclusion of the caveat "all other things being equal." Certainly in a dynamic environment, it is a difficult prospect to control for all variables simultaneously.

While having 128 possible configurations seems like a lot, it is not necessarily the number of possible configurations of data that will obscure the agent's possible selection from the player. Much of the difficulty that a player would have in knowing exactly what reaction the agent will have is due to the fact that the player cannot perceive all the data. This is similar to the impasse at which Robert Brown found himself. He could not detect the actual underlying cause of the jitteriness of the pollen grains and dust particles. His observation, therefore, was that the motion was random yet reasonable; he perceived lifelike motion where there was no life.

A good way of illustrating this point is by working backward—that is, looking at the situation from the point of the player. If the agent's behavior changes from one moment to the next, the player may not be able to determine which of the aforementioned factors crossed one of the defined thresholds to trigger the change. In some cases, this would be easy. For example, if the player draws his weapon and the agent attacks, the player can make the assertion that the weapon was the deciding factor. However, if the agent does not attack and, for instance, runs away instead, the player may not be able to determine whether it was due to the agent having low health or low ammo.

Similarly, if the player is moving near the agent with his weapon drawn, and the agent begins to attack, the player may not be able to ascertain whether it was his proximity to the agent, a secondary point (for example, a detonator), or a change in the agent's alertness status that caused the transition to occur. Once combat is engaged and values such as health and ammo are changing regularly, the number of possible reasons for a change in behavior increases significantly.

Of course, this is the reason why it is important to use relevant information as part of your decision. If you use rational bases for your decisions, it makes it more likely that the decision can at least be understood after it happens. There is a big difference between predictability and understandability. The player may not know exactly when the agent is going to change behaviors, but he should be able to offer a reasonable guess as to why it happened.

From a development and testing standpoint, the important issue to note here is that this is still purely deterministic. There is no randomness included at all. A simple code trace or onscreen debug information would confirm the status of all seven of these criteria. When compared against the decision code, the developer can confirm whether the agents are operating as planned or, in the case that they are not, determine which of the criteria needs to be adjusted.

Beyond Booleans

We can extend the aforementioned ideas to go beyond purely Boolean flags, however. By incorporating fuzzy values and appropriate systems to handle them, we could have more than one threshold value on any of the previous criteria. For instance, we could use the seven aforementioned factors to select from a variety of behaviors. Rather than simply determining whether the agent will attack the player, for example, we could include actions such as finding cover, running away, reloading, or calling for help. In order to do this, we could partition one or many of the factors into multiple zones.

For example, if we were to arrange two factors on two axes and determine a threshold across each, we would arrive at four distinct "zones" (see Figure 3.7.6, Panel 1). Each of these zones can be assigned to a behavior. In this case, using only two factors and two threshold values, we can arrive at four distinct behaviors. The more thresholds we insert, the more zones are created. Using our two-axis example, by increasing the threshold values from 1 to 3 in each direction, we increase the number of result spaces from 4 to 16 (see Figure 3.7.6, Panel 2).

We can visualize how this would affect behaviors if we imagine the values of our two factors moving independently along their respective axes. For example, imagine a data point located in Behavior G in Panel 2. If Factor 1's value were to change, we could expect to see Behaviors F and H—and even E—depending on the amount of change in Factor 1. If Factor 2 were the only one changing, we could expect to see changes to Behaviors C, K, and O. If changes were occurring in only Factor 1 or 2, by observing the changes in behavior that occurred, we could eventually determine where those thresholds between behaviors are. However, if both factors were continually changing independent of each other, we now could possibly see any one of the 16 behaviors. This would make it significantly more difficult to exactly predict the cause-and-effect chain between factors and behaviors.

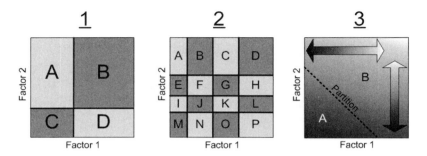

Figure 3.7.6 As the number of logical partitions through axes is increased, the number of potential results increases exponentially as a factor of the number of axes involved. By combining the factors *prior* to partitioning (Panel 3), thresholds can be made more expressive.

For instance, assume once again that we start with the data point in G. If we were witnessing a reduction in Factor 1, we may see a state change to B, C, F, J, or K. All of those states can be reached from G if Factor 1 is decreasing. What we would have to realize is that the ultimate state is decided by Factor 2 as well—for example, G→C could happen if Factor 1 was decreasing slowly and Factor 2 was increasing. Correspondingly, G→K could happen if Factor 1 was decreasing slowly and Factor 2 was decreasing. Naturally, similar extensions of logic apply to result states of B and J. The conclusion is, while we can make a general statement about where our data point may end up while Factor 1 is decreasing, we can't know the eventual result state without also knowing the behavior of Factor 2.

The examples shown in Figure 3.7.6 only show two dimensions due the limitations of what can be shown on paper. Our decision model does not share those limitations, however. By using each potential factor in our decision model and defining one or more thresholds of meaning, we can create a complex state space of potential results.

As a measurement of how this expands the potential number of actions, we can compare the number of possible outcomes. When the system was composed of 7 Boolean values, we had 128 possible combinations of data. Even by simply partitioning each of the 7 inputs into 3 ranges rather than 2, the number of combinations becomes 37 or 2,187. These results could then be mapped to a startling array of behaviors. Of course, not all the result zones need to represent individual behaviors. Imagine mapping the 2,187 possible result spaces onto 30 different behaviors, for instance.

To further leverage the power of this system, we can step beyond the mentality of mapping a single value onto a series of states. Instead, we can use systems that can take multiple inputs in conjunction and select a state that is dependant on values of those multiple inputs.

For example, we may want our agent to consider a combination of its distance to the player and their own health. That is, the state of their own health becomes more important if the player is closer. The two endpoints of the "relevancy vector" of this decision would be between ("player far" + "perfect health") and ("player near" + "zero health"). As either of those factors moves from one end to the other, it has less effect on the outcome than if both of these factors were moving simultaneously.

Figure 3.7.6, Panel 3 shows a two-dimensional visualization of this effect. In this case, the factors themselves are not partitioned. Instead, they remain continuous variables. When combined, however, they create a new directed axis in the state space—in this case shown by the combined shading. We can set a threshold across that new axis (dotted line) that can be used to determine where the behavior changes. Now, from the point of view of the player, he cannot determine at what point on Factor 1 the behavior changes without taking into account changes in Factor 2 as well.

Just as we did with single-axis-based thresholds, by determining one or more multi-axis threshold lines in an *n*-dimensional space, we partition our space into a variety of zones. By analyzing in which sections of the resulting partitioned space our current input data falls, we can select from multiple potential outputs. By combining values in this way, we can potentially arrive at more expressive outputs at any stage of our decision model.

Specific techniques for accomplishing and managing this sort of decision complexity can be found elsewhere [Mark08]. The methods that we use to arrive at the resulting values are not the focus here, however. The important part is that we are doing all of this in a purely deterministic fashion—that is, we could verify that any given combination of factors is mapped to the appropriate action. While there is still no random factor being included in these calculations, the dizzying number of potential combinations provides for reasonable-looking, yet not inherently predictable results.

Conclusion

To sum up, while our desire as game developers may be to express a variety of reasonable-looking but slightly unpredictable behaviors, we do not have to resort to randomness in order to generate that effect. By including more than one or two simple, easily perceivable criteria in our decision models, we can begin to obscure the workings of that model from the player, yet leave it perfectly exposed and understandable to the programmer and even the design team. However, in order to avoid the potential for arbitrary-looking decisions by our agents, we must be careful to select criteria that are relevant to the decision being made. In this way we are also providing deeper, more realistic-looking, and potentially more immersive behaviors for our agents.

References

[Ellinger08] Ellinger, Benjamin. "Artificial Personality: A Personal Approach to AI." *AI Game Programming Wisdom 4*. Boston: Charles River Media, 2008.

[Mark08] Mark, Dave. "Multi-Axial, Dynamic Threshold Fuzzy State Machine." *AI Game Programming Wisdom 4*. Boston: Charles River Media, 2008.

[Mark09] Mark, Dave. *Behavioral Mathematics for Game AI*. Boston: Charles River Media, 2009.

[Wikipedia09] "Henri Poincaré." n.d. Wikipedia. n.d. <http://en.wikipedia.org/wiki/Henri_Poincaré>.

3.8

Needs-Based AI

Robert Zubek

Needs-based AI is a general term for action selection based on attempting to fulfill a set of mutually competing needs. An artificial agent is modeled as having a set of conflicting motivations, such as the need to eat or sleep, and the world is modeled as full of objects that can satisfy those needs at some cost.

The core of the AI is an action selection algorithm that weighs those various possible actions against each other, trying to find the best one given the agent's needs at the given moment. The result is a very flexible and intuitive method for building moderately complex autonomous agents, which are nevertheless efficient and easy to understand.

This gem presents some technical details of needs-based AI. We begin with a general overview and then dive directly into technical implementation, presenting both general information and some specific hints born out of experience implementing this AI. Finally, we finish with an overview of some design consequences of using this style of AI.

Background

In terms of its historical context, the needs-based AI approach is related to the family of behavior-with-activation-level action selection methods common in autonomous robotics. (For an overview, see [Arkin98], page 141.) In game development, it was also independently rediscovered by *The Sims*, where it has been enjoyed by millions of game players. *The Sims* also contributed a very useful innovation on knowledge representation, where behaviors and their advertisements are literally distributed "in the world" in the game, and therefore are very easily configurable.

My own interest in this style of AI was mainly driven by working with *The Sims* (at Northwestern University and later at EA/Maxis). I have since reimplemented variations on this approach in two other games: *Roller Coaster Kingdom*, a web business simulation game, and an unpublished RPG from the *Lord of the Rings* franchise. I found the technique to be extremely useful, even across such a range of genres and platforms.

Unfortunately, very few resources about the original Sims AI remain available; of those, only a set of course notes by Ken Forbus and Will Wright, plus a *Sims 2* presentation by Jake Simpson are freely downloadable on the web at this point. (Links can be found in the "References" section at the end of this gem.) My goal here is to present some of this knowledge to a wider audience, based on what I've gained from robotics and *The Sims*, as well as personal experience building such agents in other games.

Needs-Based AI Overview

There are many ways to drive an artificial agent; some games use finite state machines, others use behavior trees, and so on. Needs-based AI is an alternative with an exciting benefit: The smarts for picking the next action configure themselves automatically, based on the agent's situation as well as internal state; yet the entire algorithm remains easy to understand and implement.

Each agent has some set of ever-changing needs that demand to be satisfied. When deciding what to do, the agent looks around the world and figures out what can be done based on what's in the area. Then it scores all those possibilities, based on how beneficial they are in satisfying its internal needs. Finally, it picks an appropriate one based on the score, finds what concrete sequence of actions it requires, and pushes those onto its action queue.

The highest-level AI loop looks like this:

- While there are *actions* in the queue, pop the next one off, perform it, and maybe get a reward.
- If you run out of actions, perform *action selection*, based on current needs, to find more actions.
- If you still have nothing to do, do some *fallback* actions.

That second step, the action selection point, is where the actual choice happens. It decomposes as follows:

1. Examine objects around you and find out what they advertise.
2. Score each advertisement based on your current needs.
3. Pick the best advertisement and get its action sequence.
4. Push the action sequence on your queue.

The next sections will delve more deeply into each of these steps.

Needs

Needs correspond to individual motivations—for example, the need to eat, drink, or rest. The choice of needs depends very much on the game. *The Sims*, being a simulator of everyday people, borrowed heavily from Maslow's hierarchy (a theory of human behavior based on increasingly important psychological needs) and ended up with a mix of basic biological and emotional drivers. A different game should include a more specific set of motivations, based on what the agents should care about in their context.

Inside the engine, needs are routinely represented as an array of numeric values, which decay over time. In this discussion we use the range of [0, 100]. Depending on the context, we use the term "need" to describe both the motivation itself (written in boldface—for example, **hunger**) and its numeric value (for example, 50).

Needs routinely have the semantics of "lower is worse and more urgent," so that hunger=30 means "I'm pretty hungry," while hunger=90 means "I'm satiated." Need values should decay over time to simulate unattended needs getting increasingly worse and more urgent. Performing an appropriate action then refills the need, raising it back to a higher value.

For example, we simulate agents getting hungry if they don't eat by decaying the hunger value over time. Performing the "eat" action would then refill it, causing it to become less urgent (for a while).

Advertisements and Action Selection

When the time comes to pick a new set of actions, the agent looks at what can be done in the environment around them and evaluates the effect of the available actions.

Each object in the world advertises a set of action/reward tuples—some actions to be taken with a promise that they will refill some needs by some amount. For example, a fridge might advertise a "prepare food" action with a reward of +30 hunger and "clean" with the reward of +10 environment.

To pick an action, the agent examines the various objects around them and finds out what they advertise. Once we know what advertisements are available, each of them gets scored, as described in the next section. The agent then picks the best advertisement using the score and adds its actions to their pending action queue.

Advertisement Decoupling

Please notice that the discovery of what actions are available is decoupled from choosing among them: The agent "asks" each object what it advertises, and only then scores what's available. The object completely controls what it advertises, so it's easy to enable or disable actions based on object state. This provides great flexibility. For example, a working fridge might advertise "prepare food" by default; once it's been used several times, it also starts advertising "clean me"; finally, once it breaks, it stops advertising anything other than "fix me" until it's repaired.

Without this decoupling, imagine coding all those choices and possibilities into the agent itself, not just for the fridge but also for all the possible objects in the world—it would be a disaster and impossible to maintain.

On the other side of the responsibility divide, the agent can also be selective about what kinds of advertisements it accepts. We can use this to build different agent subtypes or personalities. For example, in a later section we will describe how to use advertisement filtering to implement child agents with different abilities and opportunities than adults.

Advertisement Scoring

Once we have an object's advertisements, we need to score them and stack them against all the other advertisements from other objects. We score each advertisement separately, based on the reward it promises (for example, +10 environment) and the agent's current needs. Of course it's not strictly necessary that those rewards actually be granted as promised; this is known as false advertising, and it can be used with some interesting effects, as described later.

Here are some common scoring functions, from the simplest to the more sophisticated:

A. Trivial scoring

$$\text{future value}_{need} = \text{current value}_{need} + \text{advertised delta}_{need}$$

$$\text{score} = \sum\nolimits_{\text{all needs}} (\text{future value}_{need})$$

Under this model, we go through each need, look up the promised future need value, and add them up. For example, if the agent's hunger is at 70, an advertisement of +20 hunger means the future value of hunger will be 90; the final score is the sum of all future values.

This model is trivially easy and has significant drawbacks: It's only sensitive to the magnitude of changes, and it doesn't differentiate between urgent and non-urgent needs. So increasing hunger from 70 to 90 has the same score as increasing thirst from 10 to 30—but the latter should be much more important, considering the agent is very thirsty!

B. Attenuated need scoring

Needs at low levels should be much more urgent than those at high levels. To model this, we introduce a non-linear attenuation function for each need. So the score becomes:

$$\text{score} = \sum\nolimits_{\text{all needs}} A_{need} (\text{future value}_{need})$$

where A_{need} is the attenuation function, mapping from a need value to some numeric value. The attenuation function is commonly non-linear and non-increasing: It starts out high when the need level is low and then drops quickly as the need level increases.

For example, consider the attenuation function $A(x) = 10/x$. An action that increases hunger to 90 will have a score of 1/9, while an action that increases thirst to 30 will have a score of 1/3, so three times higher, because low thirst is much more important to fulfill. These attenuation functions are a major tuning knob in needs-based AI.

You might also notice one drawback: Under this scheme, improving hunger from 30 to 90 would have the same score as improving it from 50 to 90. Worse yet, worsening hunger from 100 to 90 would have the same score as well! This detail may not be noticeable in a running system, but it's easy to fix by examining the need delta as well.

C. Attenuated need-delta scoring

It's better to eat a filling meal than a snack, especially when you're hungry, and it's worse to eat something that leaves you hungrier than before. To model this, we can score based on need level difference:

$$\text{score} = \sum\nolimits_{\text{all needs}} (A_{\text{need}} (\text{current value}_{\text{need}}) - A_{\text{need}} (\text{future value}_{\text{need}}))$$

For example, let's consider our attenuation function $A(x) = 10/x$ again. Increasing hunger from 30 to 90 will now score $1/3 - 1/9 = 2/9$, while increasing it from 60 to 90 will score $1/6 - 1/9 = 1/18$, so only a quarter as high. Also, decreasing hunger from 100 to 90 will have a negative score, so it will not be selected unless there is nothing else to do.

Action Selection

Once we know the scores, it's easy to pick the best one. Several approaches for arbitration are standard:

- Winner-takes-all: The highest-scoring action always gets picked.
- Weighted-random: Do a random selection from the top *n* (for example, top three) high-scoring advertisements, with probability proportional to score.
- Other approaches are easy to imagine, such as a priority-based behavior stack.

In everyday implementation, weighted-random is a good compromise between having some predictability about what will happen and not having the agent look unpleasantly deterministic.

Action Selection Additions

The model described earlier can be extended in many directions to add more flexibility or nuance. Here are a few additions, along with their advantages and disadvantages:

A. Attenuating score based on distance

Given two objects with identical advertisements, an agent should tend to pick the one closer to them. We can do this by attenuating each object's score based on distance or containment:

$$\text{score} = D \left(\sum\nolimits_{\text{all needs}} (\dots) \right)$$

where D is some distance-based attenuation function, commonly a non-increasing one, such as the physically inspired $D(x) = x \,/\, \text{distance}^2$. However, distance attenuation can be difficult to tune, because a distant object's advertisement will be lowered not just compared to other objects of this type, but also compared to all other advertisements. This may lead to a "bird in hand" kind of behavior, where the agent always prefers a much worse action nearby rather than a better one farther away.

B. Filtering advertisements before scoring

It's useful to add prerequisites to advertisements. For example, kids should not be able to operate stoves, so the stove should not advertise the "cook" action to them. This can be implemented in several ways, from simple attribute tests to a full language for expressing predicates.

It's often best to start with a simple filter mechanism, because complex prerequisites are more difficult to debug when there are many agents running around. An easy prerequisites system could be as simple as setting Boolean attributes on characters (for example, is-adult, and so on) and adding an attribute mask on each advertisement; action selection would only consider advertisements whose mask matches up against the agent's attributes.

C. Tuning need decay

Agents' need levels should decay over time. This causes agents to change their priorities as they go through the game. We can tune this system by modifying need decay rates individually. For example, if an agent's hunger doesn't decay as quickly, they will not need to eat as often and will have more time for other pursuits.

We can use this to model a bare-bones personality profile—for example, whether someone needs to eat/drink/entertain themselves more or less often. It can also be used for difficulty tuning—agents whose needs decay more quickly are harder to please.

D. Tuning advertisement scores

The scoring function can also simulate simple personality types directly, by tuning down particular advertisement scores. To do this, we would have each agent contain a set of tuning parameters, one for each need, that modify that need's score:

$$\text{new score}_{\text{agent,need}} = \text{old score}_{\text{agent,need}} * \text{tuning}_{\text{agent,need}}$$

For example, by tuning down the +hunger advertisement's score, we'll get an agent that has a stronger preference for highly fulfilling food; tuning up a +thirst advertisement will produce an agent that will happily opt for less satisfying drinks, and so on.

E. Attenuation function tuning

Attenuation functions map from low need levels to high scores. Each need can be attenuated differently, since some needs are more urgent than others. As such, they are a major tuning knob in games, but a delicate one because their effects are global, affecting all agents. This requires good design iterations, but analytic functions (for example, $A(x) = 10/x$) are not easy for designers to tweak or reason about.

A happy medium can be found by defining attenuation functions using piecewise-linear functions (in other words, point pairs that define individual straight-line segments, rather than continuous, analytic formulas). These can be stored and graphed in a spreadsheet file and loaded during the game.

Action Performance

Having chosen something to do, we push the advertisement's actions on the agent's action queue, to be performed in order. Each action would routinely be a complete mini-script. For example, the stove's "clean" action might be small script that:

- Animates the agent getting out a sponge and scrubbing the stove
- Runs the animation loop and an animated stove condition meter
- Grants the promised reward

It's important that the actual reward be granted manually as part of the action, and not be awarded automatically. This gives us two benefits:

- Interrupted actions will not be rewarded.
- Objects can falsely advertise and not actually grant the rewards they promised.

False advertisement is an especially powerful but dangerous option. For example, suppose that we have a food item that advertises a hunger reward but doesn't actually award it. A hungry agent would be likely to pick that action—but since they got no reward, at the next selection point they would again likely pick, and then again, and again. This quickly leads to very intriguing "addictive" behaviors.

This may seem like a useful way to force agents to perform an action. But it's just as hard to make them stop once they've started. False advertisements create action loops that are very difficult to tune. In practice, forcing an action is easier done by just pushing the desired action on the agent's action queue.

Action Chaining

Performing a complex action, such as cooking a meal, usually involves several steps (such as preparing and cooking) and several objects (a fridge, a cutting board, a stove). This sequence must not be atomic—steps can be interrupted, or they can fail due to some external factors.

Complex sequences are implemented by chaining multiple actions together. For example, eating dinner might decompose into several separate actions:

- Take a food item from the fridge.
- Prepare the food item on a counter.
- Cook the food item on the stove.
- Sit down and eat, thereby getting a hunger reward.

It would be suboptimal to implement this as a single action; there is too much variability in the world for it to always work out perfectly.

We can create action sequences in two ways. The simpler way is to just manufacture the entire sequence of actions right away and push the whole thing on the agent's queue. Of course, these steps can fail, in which case the remaining actions should also be aborted. For some interesting side effects, aborting an action chain could create new actions in its place. For example, a failed "cook food" action sequence could create a new "burned food" object that needs to be cleaned up.

The second method, more powerful but more difficult, is to implement action chaining by "lazy evaluation." In this approach, only one action step is created and run at a time, and when it ends, it knows how to create the next action and front-loads it on the queue.

For an example of how that might look, consider eating dinner again. The refrigerator's advertisement would specify only one action: "take food." That action, toward the end, would then find the nearest kitchen counter object, ask it for the "prepare food" action, and load that on the queue. Once "prepare food" was done, it would find the nearest stove, ask it for a new "cook food" action, and so on.

Lazy action chaining makes it possible to modify the chain based on what objects are available to the agent. For example, a microwave oven might create a different "cook food" action than a stove would, providing more variety and surprise for the player. Second, it makes interesting failures easier. For example, the stove can look up some internal variable (for example, repair level) to determine failure and randomly push a "create a kitchen fire" action instead.

In either case, using an action queue provides nice modularity. Sequences of smaller action components are more loosely coupled and arguably more maintainable than standard state machines.

Action Chain State Saving

When an action chain is interrupted, we might want to be able to save its state somehow so that it gets picked up later.

Since all actions are done on objects, one way to do this is to mutate the state of the object in question. For example, the progress of "cleaning" can be stored as a separate numeric cleanness value on an object, which gets continuously increased while the action is running.

But sometimes actions involve multiple objects, or the state is more complicated. Another way to implement this is by creating new state objects. An intuitive example is food from the original *Sims*: The action of prepping food creates a "prepped food" object, cooking then turns it into a pot of "cooked food," which can be plated and turned into a "dinner plate." The state of preparation is then embedded right in the world; if the agent is interrupted while prepping, the cut-up food will just sit there until the agent picks it up later and puts it on the stove.

Design Consequences of Needs-Based AI

With the technical details of needs-based AI behind us, let's also consider some of the design implications of this style of development, since it's different from more traditional techniques.

First of all, the player's experience with this AI really benefits from adding some feedback to the agents. Developers can just look at the internal variables and immediately see "the agent is doing this because it's hungry, or sleepy, or other such." But the player will have no such access and is likely to build an entirely different mental model of what the agent is doing. Little bits of feedback, like thought bubbles about what needs are being fulfilled, are easy to implement and go a long way toward making the system comprehensible to the player.

A second point is about tuning. Some of the tunable parameters have global effect and are therefore very difficult to tune after the game has grown past a certain size. The set of needs, their decay rates, score attenuation functions, and other such elements will apply to all characters in the game equally, so tuning them globally requires a lot of testing and a delicate touch.

If a lot of variety is desired between different parts of the game, it might be a good idea to split the game into a number of smaller logical partitions (levels, and so on) and have a different set of those tunable parameters, one for each partition. Ideally, there would be a set of global tuning defaults, which work for the entire game, and each partition could specifically override some of them as needed. Partitioning and overriding tuning values buys us greater flexibility, although at the cost of having to tune each partition separately.

Third, this AI approach tends heavily toward simulation and makes it hard to do scripted scenes or other triggered actions. Imagine implementing some actions on a trigger, such as having the agent approach the player when he comes into view. One might be tempted to try to implement that using just needs and advertisements, but the result will be brittle.

If particular one-off scripted behaviors are desired, it would be better to just manually manufacture appropriate action sequences and forcibly push them on the agent's action queue. But in general, this overall approach is not very good for games that need a lot of triggered, scripted sequences (for example, shooter level designs). Needs-based AI works better for simulated worlds than for scripted ones.

Conclusion

Needs-based AI is computationally very efficient; only a trivial amount of the CPU is required to pick what to do and to handle the resulting action sequence. The system's internals are very easy to understand; by just inspecting the agent's internal needs values, you can get a good idea of why it does what it does. And by externalizing the set of possible actions into the world, the system also achieves great modularity—the AI can be "reconfigured" literally by adding or removing objects around the agent.

In spite of unusual design consequences, the needs-based approach is very capable, easy to implement, and effective at creating good characters. It's a powerful tool for many situations.

Acknowledgements

Thanks to Ken Forbus and Richard Evans, from whom I've learned most of what I know about this style of AI.

References

[Arkin98] Arkin, R. *Behavior Based Robotics*. MIT Press, 1998.

[Forbus02] Forbus, Ken, and Will Wright. "Simulation and Modeling: Under the Hood of The Sims." 2002. Northwestern University. n.d. <http://www.cs.northwestern.edu/~forbus/c95-gd/lectures/The_Sims_Under_the_Hood_files/frame.htm>.

[Simpson] Simpson, Jake. "Making The Sims the Sims." n.d. <https://www.cmpevents.com/Sessions/GD/ScriptingAndSims2.ppt>.

3.9

A Framework for Emotional Digital Actors

Phil Carlisle

zoombapup@gmail.com

In this gem, we will describe a framework that may be used to endow game characters with some level of emotional behavior. Using a simple behavior tree implementation augmented with supporting appraisal and blackboard implementations, we will demonstrate that emotions can be easily implemented and can enhance the behavior and expression of game characters. We use the term "digital actor" because although the emotional system we present is based on sound academic research in psychology and cognitive science, the intention is to produce the "illusion" of emotion, rather than specifically trying to model emotion itself. However, the reader is advised to read [Oatley06] as an accessible introduction to emotional psychology, which is a useful starting point for anyone trying to add more emotion to their games.

The first section of this gem will describe models of personality, mood, and emotion derived from academic literature in the area. The second section will describe how these models are incorporated into an emotional framework. The third section will describe how the framework is used in a number of game scenarios. In conclusion, we will offer some ideas for further work.

Models of Emotion, Mood, and Personality

In addition to emotion, we need to represent both personality and mood in order to have a complete emotional framework. It is useful to consider these elements in terms of the timescale required for change.

Typically, our personality changes very slowly, if at all. It can take many years for our personalities to alter. Mood, on the other hand, tends to change in a relatively shorter period of days or weeks. Finally, we have emotions, which are frequently expressed minute to minute and can often only be portrayed for fleeting seconds. For instance, it is not unusual to hear someone described as having a "quick temper."

Emotion

There are many theories of emotion and models of personality associated with them. For example, [Eyesenck65] describes models of personality and emotion often cited in academic literature. One model of emotion used in a large volume of academic literature is the OCC model [Ortony88] created by Ortony, Chlore, and Collins. This model is discussed very well in [Bartneck02], and, as is the case with many academic implementations, we are going to use a subset of the OCC model for our emotional representation.

The OCC model typically represents 22 discrete emotional categories. In practice, this is probably too complex a model for most video games; thus, the model should be simplified based on the requirements for a particular game. The OCC model, broadly speaking, breaks down emotions into three categories: emotional reaction to objects, events, and agents. Each category is then broken down further depending on whether the emotion is related to self or other and whether the emotion is considered a good thing or a bad thing. The complexity arises because we have to account for the consequences for others and our relationship with them. Consider the following case:

- Agent A likes apples.
- Agent B likes apples *and* Agent A.
- Agent C likes apples *but not* Agent A.

In a simulation with all three agents and one apple, assuming that Agent A acquires the apple, we then have the following emotional reactions:

- Agent A is happy (due to acquiring the apple).
- Agent B is unhappy at not acquiring the apple but happy at Agent A acquiring the apple.
- Agent C is unhappy at not acquiring the apple and is even less happy at seeing Agent A acquire the apple.

These are relatively simple direct relationships between goal (acquire apple, self/friend) and emotion (happy, sad). But human emotion is a little more complicated. In this case, Agent C may immediately feel unhappy, but that feeling may then cause him to feel ashamed that he was made to feel unhappy by the actions of A. Clearly, we are going to have to simplify the model somewhat to be useful in a video-game context, but be aware that sometimes the most interesting emotional expression comes from the feelings created by social situations exactly like this.

Mood

Mood is generally more changeable than personality. However it is often represented very simply. A useful paper that represents mood simply is [Egges04], which maps mood to a single floating-point number in the range of $-1..1$ to represent negative or positive moods, respectively. Typically, mood changes over weeks or months and acts as an overall bias that changes as different emotional events occur.

Interestingly, mood can color our perception of emotional events. For instance, people in a negative mood may view all emotional events as negative, even if the event is generally to their advantage. In the case of the earlier example, a negative mood might be used within the behavior tree to disable certain actions. For instance, if Agent A is in a highly negative mood, even the perception of an apple may not trigger the behavior tree action required to seek attainment of the apple. This can be accomplished only by adding knowledge of the available apple to the agent's blackboard when it has a mood that is higher than a given threshold, although care must be taken to allow the desire to maintain the agent's health (by acquiring food, for example) to override this behavior. See the description of the appraisal class later in this gem for further information.

Personality

Personality is often represented in the academic literature via the OCEAN model of [McRae96]. This personality model represents a person's personality across five dimensions representing:

- Openness
- Conscientiousness
- Agreeability
- Extroversion
- Neuroticism

The values portrayed for each of the five dimensions are typically in the range of 0..1, where, for example, 0 for openness means that the person is fully closed off and +1 means the person is fully open. Essentially, the model of personality provides a default biasing mechanism for further formulas and allows us to represent different personality types by simply configuring each dimension with different default floating-point values.

Personality is the least changeable part of our emotional makeup, so it is reasonable to simply store personality as a series of fixed values. Personality provides bias toward a particular set of possible actions within the behavior tree. Referring to the earlier example scenario for Agent B, given the choice of two potential actions of either trying to obtain the apple for oneself or allowing Agent A to obtain the apple, the personality model can be used to select from the two choices. An agent with high agreeability would choose to allow Agent A to obtain the apple, whereas the converse would simply try to obtain the apple for itself. Thus, the personality model allows us to create unique behavior for each agent without the need for per-agent behavior trees.

The Emotional Framework

Given the emotional model described in the previous section, we need to be able to incorporate code that represents the model within an architecture that enables it to affect our characters' behavior. In this example, we will incorporate the emotional model by implementing an appraisal class, which modifies values within a character's blackboard.

(See [Isla02] for information concerning blackboards.) The blackboard will be inspected by a simple behavior tree in order to incorporate the emotional values within the characters' update logic, and the same mechanism can also be used to incorporate the emotional values with the characters' movement logic—for example, animating with a sullen walk cycle if the emotional mood is negative. A very good reference concerning the use of behavior trees and emotional models is the work of the Oz project group at Carnegie Mellon University [Reilly96], which went on to be used in the game *Façade*.

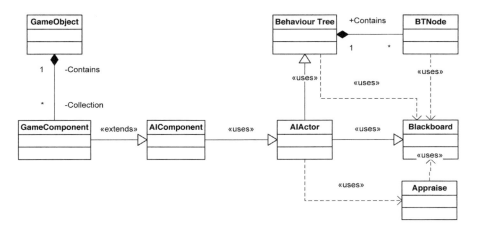

Figure 3.9.1   The emotional framework architecture.

Appraisal/Arousal

Typically, emotion is broken up into appraisal, where goals are created and events and objects are classified, and arousal, where the magnitude of the reaction to the sensory input is processed. The purpose of the appraisal class is to map any sensory input to changes in the agent's emotional variables and blackboard data. In our framework, for convenience this class handles both appraisal and arousal. During appraisal, sensory input and event data are fed to the appraisal class, which then determines the appropriate changes in blackboard data. During the appraisal, data may be added to the knowledge representation, changes may be made to the emotional variables, and in certain cases input may be ignored. Similarly, the appraisal class is responsible for determining the changes occurring from the success or failure of the agent's goals, which may again alter the agent's blackboard or emotional variables.

Knowledge Representation

There is a choice to be made with regard to the appraisal class relating to its usage of memory and dynamic data structures. In a human context, we are capable of learning about new objects we have not encountered before, new events that happen, or new agents (human or otherwise) that we meet. This implies that we are able to store information as we build up an emotional picture relating to these objects, events, and agents. In a game context, we may or may not be able to spare the memory to process previously unknown information.

The easiest case for implementation and perhaps the more robust case for design is that we explicitly determine all possible known objects/events/agents *a priori* and simply load that information at run time. This is the method chosen for the example implementation. An easy method of expanding on this simple implementation is to incorporate a classifier system such that instead of storing a reaction to an individual object/event/agent, we classify them and store a reaction to the "class" rather than a specific instance of the class. An alternative method is to simply place an upper limit on the number of memories stored dynamically, allowing new memories to be created. These memories would then expire over time to allow further memories to be formed. In addition, this scheme may be extended with different limits on the amount of memories stored for each type of event, thus allowing for more "important" memories to be stored. The use of a blackboard allows us to store all per-agent data in a generic structure that allows access from all of our actor's systems. Typically, this is used to store agent goals or attributes, such as the currently selected target enemy. However, the blackboard is a useful storage mechanism to employ for the creation of emotional agents.

It is worth bearing in mind that the most common case of retrieval from the blackboard—to retrieve a particular value associated with a new sensed object/agent/event—must be as efficient as possible. An alternative structure, such as a semantic network [Sowa92], may prove to be a far better solution, if slightly more complex in terms of code.

For convenience, each agent's blackboard and behavior tree configurations are parsed from XML data. This allows for run-time configuration of each agent, using a unique blackboard, a unique behavior tree, or both.

XML data for an example blackboard:

```
<BB>
<Personality O="0.1" C="0.6" E="0.1" A="0.9" N="0.2"></Personality>
<Mood default="1.0"></Mood>
<Event name="PickupApple"        valence="1.0">    </Event>
<Event name="PickupOrange"       valence="-1.0">   </Event>
<Event name="PickupGrenade"      valence="-10.0">  </Event>
<Object name="Apple"             valence="1.0">    </Object>
<Object name="Orange"            valence="-1.0">   </Object>
<Object name="Grenade"           valence="-10.0">  </Object>
<Agent name="Fred"               valence="2.0">    </Agent>
<Agent name="Wilma"              valence="3.0">    </Agent>
<Agent name="Betty"              valence="30.0">   </Agent>
</BB>
```

Here we can see a simple blackboard specification for an agent. Each sub-element with a tag of `<agent>`, `< object>`, or `<event>` defines a unique structure that is stored within the blackboard. Each element is stored internally as a simple `stl::vector` of the appropriate type.

The Appraisal Process

To modify our behavior based on the emotional framework, we need to consider the steps that occur when new emotional responses are required.

Sensing a New Object

An agent's perception system typically responds to queries instigated by its behavior tree (which we will refer to as a *BT* for brevity's sake). For example, the BT may have executed a sequence of nodes that resulted in a query for the availability of nearby food. Our goal in this case is to determine the agent's emotional reaction to each sensed object—specifically, the more useful case of allowing the agent to determine the selection of which food object to try to obtain based on the emotional reward associated with those available.

Consider the case where a query returns three different food items within the query radius. In the simplest case, we can simply determine our like/dislike of the available food items based on a simple classification, such as whether the item is fruit or vegetable or whether the item is sweet or sour. In the ideal case, we need to consider our past experiences either with the unique object or with objects with a similar classification. It is beyond the scope of this gem to discuss the intricacies of human memory and its method of classification. Another aspect of this pattern of memory is that the relative novelty of an object can greatly alter the intensity of the reaction to the object. An agent who is unused to seeing guns may react significantly to the sight of an armed friend, whereas a gangster would be less likely to have a similar reaction. The final aspect we should consider when dealing with objects is the penalty or reward associated with interactions. For example, an agent may have a strong liking for apples, but if the agent consumes an apple that is sour, it should have some effect on the subsequent desire for more apples.

In practical terms, in the case of our object queries, we first use the appraisal class to return preference values for each object in turn. We then simply choose the object with the highest appraisal value for interaction. Once an object has been selected, we store that object as a goal within the blackboard as an object to obtain. It is important to constrain our memory usage at this point, as new objects may be perceived quite often and marked for attainment. We can achieve this by attaching an expiration value to each new object attainment goal. The blackboard then removes all expired goals within its update loop.

Once an object is attained (typically via another node in the behavior tree), we then consider any attainment goals relating to the object. If a specific attainment goal is found within the blackboard, we then consider the arousal value of achieving the specific goal. This arousal processing takes into account the goals for attainment of the object. There are two major reactions to consider here. The first is that the agent must consider his own reaction to the object. Typically, we would try to obtain objects we like, but if the game allows attaining of objects by other means—for example, by allowing agents to simply give objects to each other—there may be negative consequences.

An agent who obtains a ticking time bomb should definitely not be happy about its attainment. The second reaction to the attainment of an object is with respect to other agents. An agent who obtains an object that is highly desired by another agent, depending on whether the other agent is liked or disliked, may feel guilty or happy for acquiring the item, respectively.

Alternatively, if no specific attainment goals are stored in the blackboard, we can simply consider the attainment goals of other agents for the object, or we can consider the general valence of the object and react based on our positive or negative feelings about it. For example, an object that is attained may allow us to accomplish a goal for another agent if we give it to him. In this case, we may simply decide to create a goal to pass on the object if it achieves a goal of an agent we have positive affect towards, or we may decide to keep or dispose of the object if it denies a goal of an agent we have negative affect towards.

Sensing a New Agent

The term "agent" in the OCC model does not describe an AI agent, but instead describes an agent of change. Typically, these are often other characters in a game context. However, this is not always the case, and an agent in OCC terms may be some other external force that has an effect on the world. In the most common case, the agents in our emotional framework will actually describe characters within the game world. With this in mind, we will use the term "agent" to mean both the OCC model of an agent and the AI game character agent.

Modeling of inter-agent affect affords us some unique social interactions, such as the seemingly altruistic act of passing on an object. The most obvious use of agent knowledge when considering emotion is for a like/dislike evaluation. This can be simply stored as a positive or negative value associated with a unique identifier. In the example framework, agents are stored by name with a valence value associated with them within the blackboard. This value is useful for when any opportunities are presented to the agent, such as denying another agent a resource or being able to give another agent something they require.

This brings up an important point about agent-to-agent interactions. Typically, when humans interact, they create mental models of the motivations of the interacting agent in order to determine how to proceed with the interaction. For instance, when a human considers giving a gift to another, they try and imagine the reaction to the gift the other person will have, using this as a method of deciding whether to proceed with the interaction. This agent mental modeling is important for social interactions; however, it is problematic for games because of the amount of memory and processing time required for implementation. The problem is compounded by the notion that humans often model other humans' models of themselves (in other words, how does this person feel about us?). In the example framework, we have decided to leave this mental modeling unimplemented for the sake of brevity and for practical purposes. However, for a truly deep social simulation, this modeling is a highly desirable feature.

Sensing an Event

A great deal of an agent's behavior will generally stem from sensing some event that occurs within the world. This event could be an object attainment event, for self or for other. It might also be an important event that requires immediate action, such as hearing a grenade drop at the agent's feet. In this situation, the appraisal class uses its understanding of available events to create the associated knowledge within the agent's blackboard.

In the case of the grenade event, the appraisal class simply adds a threat object with a high reaction value to the blackboard. This will then allow the BT that has a branch "respond to threat" to take the appropriate actions. The reason why it is useful to pass events via the appraisal class is that the importance of an event can change over time as an agent responds to more of the same event. Consider the case of the grenade event. There is a radius within which we can expect to take damage, but outside of that radius, the reaction to the grenade can change depending on how many times we have seen grenades explode.

If we know from experience that outside of a certain radius we may sustain injury but that the injury is entirely random, then we may, over time, be conditioned to simply block the grenade from thought. This effect can happen in any stressful situation where our emotions allow us to regulate our reactions, essentially becoming "numb" to what would normally be highly stressful situations over time. This change in attitude toward events is due to the appraisal/arousal process. Essentially, this is a feedback loop that changes an agent's response over time as the agent adds positive or negative arousal to the event depending on the event's outcome; in addition, this effect is subject to some decay in the dulling of the arousal. In essence, this means that events that occur frequently become less arousing emotionally, but that if the event has not occurred for some time, the arousal may once again be relatively high. In the example framework, this dulling of arousal values for events happens by a simple scaling factor being applied to the arousal value for the event. Over time, the scaling factor is reset to 1.0, with any events of that type causing the scale factor to reduce slightly. Thus, over time, the arousal associated with the event can move between 0..1 depending on the frequency of the event.

Another aspect to the appraisal class is the incorporation of personality and mood into the emotional outcomes expressed in the blackboard. In effect, personality and mood modulate the intensity of the emotional reaction to any given stimulus. For a good introduction to why this is important, see [Eckman04]. To correctly simulate the effect of personality, mood, varying arousal, and decay, we therefore apply different functions for calculating the effect of any given emotional stimulus and then apply the results of these functions to the agent's blackboard. For event stimulus, the first role of the appraisal is to determine whether to respond to the event at all. Some events can simply be ignored, especially when in a state of high overall arousal. For instance, if a grenade event is perceived, any subsequent event is blocked from being perceived until the agent has dealt with the response. This simulates the effect of our emotions, which act as regulatory systems allowing for rapid response to dangerous threats. Given a relatively low state of overall arousal, we can often respond to relatively minor events.

The personality model acts to bias available choices within the behavior tree. Given two possible outcomes for any sensory input, we can use a scale factor based on the personality variable associated with a given choice to determine which outcome has a higher priority. For example, when given the choice to interact in a conversation with another agent or to obtain a required item, an agent with an introverted personality would choose the latter. The mechanism for this choice involves classifying each behavior tree selection with respect to personality and then using this as a scaling value when doing priority selection, each choice essentially scaling its priority up or down based on the personality trait variable value.

The model of mood, although simplistic in nature, allows us to further apply some filtering on the selection of available behavior tree choices. The mood value is initially used in the input phase of the appraisal class. This simply scales the emotional valence of input senses, which may cause some sensory input to be ignored when it otherwise may have been acted upon. For example, if we perceive an object that is beneficial to another agent, we calculate a valence for the goal of attaining the apple for the other agent. Normally, we would then create the goal for the attainment of the apple by adding the apple to the blackboard. However, when the mood is negative, the positive affect generated by attaining the apple for the other agent is cancelled out, and we simply never add the apple to the blackboard.

Given the framework described thus far, what does a typical update loop look like for the agent? See Figure 3.9.2.

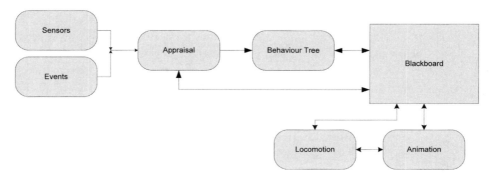

Figure 3.9.2   Agent update loop.

The update loop begins with sensory input. In practical usage, the event input can happen at any point in time, but it follows a very similar cyclic pattern represented by the sensory update loop represented in Figure 3.9.2. Input is fed into the appraisal class for processing. This appraisal class is used to then map the input into changes in the agent blackboard. The appraisal may add or remove goals within the blackboard depending on the input. It also may affect the emotional values associated with agents, objects, or events stored within the blackboard, which in turn may affect the processing within the appraisal class during the next update cycle. Then the behavior tree responds to new knowledge within its blackboard and in turn effects changes in the game world.

The cycle is then repeated continually. This reactive framework simply represents a sense > think > act cycle that is enhanced with emotion to become a sense > feel > think > act cycle. The blackboard may also be interrogated by animation and locomotion systems. For example, to alter walk-cycle blending to allow for a display of mood, an agent with a negative mood value may blend in more of a labored walk cycle. In comparison, an agent with a positive mood may blend more of a bouncy walk cycle.

Conclusion

Emotion is a very complex subject, and there are many academic theories that attempt to describe how emotions work and how they might be classified. Video games are unlikely to ever completely simulate the entire spectrum of emotional responses, even if it were desirable to do so. As game designers and developers, we can incorporate simple models of emotion in order to add some personality to individual agents.

Non-verbal communication is an important part of human social interaction [Mehrabian72], and emotional values modify this communication. For instance, we tend to hold gaze on agents we are attracted to for a lot longer. A large part of the motivation for the incorporation of emotion into video games is that we can start to add non-verbal communication signals to our agents. This helps to create agents that feel more realistic and alive. Emotions can be used to modify things such as posture, gesture, gaze, gait, behavior, and memory. Imagine a world where agents remember your actions and are positively brimming with joy when you come to visit them! Imagine a world where you can understand simply from the posture of an agent whether it is happy to see you or intends to do you harm. To learn more about non-verbal communication and how it works in humans, see [Argyle75].

As more memory and processing time become available on newer platforms, we may begin to consider deeper models of agent emotion and memory, which in turn should lead to a more effective display of an agent's emotional state. This emotional display should lead to more engaging and believable characters—agents that can express themselves and their emotions non-verbally and engage the emotions of players at a deeper level.

References

[Argyle75] Argyle, M. *Bodily Communication*. Methuen & Co Ltd., 1975.

[Bartneck02] Bartneck, C. "Integrating the OCC Model of Emotions in Embodied Characters." *Workshop on Virtual Conversational Characters*, 2002.

[Eckman04] Ekman, P. *Emotions Revealed*. UK: Phoenix Books, 2004.

[Egges2004] Egges, Arjan, Sumedha Kshirsagar, and Nadia Magnenat-Thalmann. "Generic Personality and Emotion Simulation for Conversational Agents." *Computer Animation and Virtual Worlds* 15.1 (2004): 1–13.

[Eysenck65] Eysenck, H. J. *Fact and Fiction in Psychology*. Harmondsworth: Penguin, 1965.

[Isla02] Isla, D., and B. Blumburg. "Blackboard Architecture." *AI Game Programming Wisdom 1*. Boston: Charles River Media, 2002. 333–344.

[McRae96] McCrae, R., and P. T. Costa Jr. "Toward a New Generation of Personality Theories: Theoretical Contexts for the Five-Factor Model." *The Five-Factor Model of Personality: Theoretical Perspectives*. Guilford Press, 1996. 51–87.

[Mehrabian72] Mehrabian, A. *Non-Verbal Communication*. Transaction Publishing, 1972.

[Oatley06] Oatley K., D. Keltner, and J. Jenkins. *Understanding Emotions* (2nd edition). Blackwell Publishers Inc., 2006.

[Ortony88] Ortony, A., G. Clore, and A. Collins. *The Cognitive Structure of Emotions*. Cambridge University Press, 1988.

[Reilly96] Reilly, W. S. "Believable Social and Emotional Agents." PhD Thesis. School of Computer Science, Carnegie Melon University, Pittsburgh. 1996.

[Sowa92] Sowa, J. "Semantic Networks." n.d. John F. Sowa. 15 Sept. 2009. <http://www.jfsowa.com/pubs/semnet.htm>.

3.10

Scalable Dialog Authoring

Baylor Wetzel, Shikigami Games
baylorw@ShikigamiGames.com

It has been a goal of many a game to create a large city filled with people you can talk to. Not an inn or castle or a small town, but a city. A big city filled with hundreds (or thousands, or more!) of agents, each of which acts like an individual. But there's a reason we fill shopping malls with zombies and countrysides with monsters but not cities with people—creating hundreds of people, each with their own personality, takes a lot of time…a cost-prohibitively long time. There won't be games with large spaces truly filled with intelligent, conversational non-player characters (NPCs) until we find a way to create these agents more efficiently. Although the techniques in this gem don't try to tackle every problem and bottleneck that you'll encounter in building a dialog system, hopefully they will help you create large groups of agents much faster.

Conversational Agents Today

Games are filled with characters that talk. Although not every game and every character needs to be able to answer questions or carry on a conversation, conversational ability is important to a wide variety of games. Dialog varies from the "select a topic" approach used in the *Elder Scroll* series (where one scenario involves convincing a love-addled stalker to give back the item he stole from a woman who would not go out with him), to the deep conversational trees of the original *Fallout*, to the multi-way conversations of *Planescape: Torment*, to the jury trials in *Jade Empire*. NPCs in these games are normally more complex than NPCs in other games. They might refuse to discuss a given topic with someone they don't know, ignore someone they previously argued with, insult someone from a rival group, or yell at someone trying to strike up a conversation in the ladies' bathroom. Conversations can lead characters to give up their evil plans, join the player's team, or reveal the secret of their miniature giant space hamster.

The work described here is part of research done at Alelo, which makes "serious games" designed to teach foreign languages and cultures. Many (though not all) of these games are used to train soldiers how to perform tasks overseas. These tasks range from manning checkpoints and conducting house-to-house searches to negotiating with local leaders and helping set up clinics. Success often depends on showing the proper level of politeness and professionalism, earning trust through culturally appropriate small talk and asking the correct questions in the correct way. In this gem, we'll use the example of a U.S. soldier in Iraq to explain the techniques.

Typical Methods for Building Conversational Agents

There are a few ways to make conversational agents, one of the more common (and painful) ways being to build them manually in script (`if (1==option) bobDialog42() else…`). An easier approach is to use a dialog editor to build a tree, where one node is what the NPC says, the nodes under that are things the player can say in response, the nodes under those are the NPC's response, and so on. Each node typically contains the exact text the agent will say. You say, "Do you like football?" and the NPC will reply "Sure, who doesn't?" An NPC might have several responses based on whether they like you, if you have fulfilled a quest for them, if you are both at a bar, and so on. In *Neverwinter Nights*, this is done by calling the `TextAppearsWhen` script, and in the *Elder Scrolls* editors (including *Fallout 3*'s G.E.C.K. editor), it's done by checking the `Conditions` field, but the idea is the same—for every possible dialog option, the designer writes the input text (player choice), the output text (from the NPC), and for each possible output writes a script (either by hand in *NWN* or using a spreadsheet-like tool in *Elder Scrolls*) to determine whether that particular output should be used. If not, the game checks the next output in the list. The results can be very good, but it takes a lot of time, thought, and planning to build.

The Scalability Problem

Let's start with a positive—the range of dialog that can be created by current techniques is essentially perfect. If you want an NPC's response to change based on the player's shoes, intelligence, the last enemy they fought, the health of the NPC's dog, and the phase of the moon, you can do that. The problem is that it's going to take you a long time.

This isn't the only problem. Because of the sheer volume of data, designers face the problem of covering the whole possibility space—you handled a lot of the possible variable combinations, but did you get all of them? In *Fallout*, NPCs asked about quests that have long since been completed. In *Mass Effect*, the person sitting next to you will calmly inform you that they've picked up a communications signal right rather than ask why you've just driven off a bridge into a bottomless chasm. In *Neverwinter Nights*, you can rescue a girl from a giant, go to the girl's farm, kill her family, then talk to her, and she'll thank you and ask you to visit again soon.

Finding and correcting problems like this isn't hard, it just takes time. How much time? To build a professional dialog tree, you not only have to decide which topics an agent can discuss, the words to use, and the flow of the conversation, you need to think about all the factors (NPC personality, NPC culture, NPC state, world state, player state, conversational history, history with player, and so on) that should affect a conversation and make sure the NPC reacts appropriately. For one of the games I worked on in 2009, creating the full dialog tree for an important NPC took two to three weeks. Even then, the agent had the standard lapses in awareness and limited conversational ability that you find in any game. That particular game was a bit more complex than most, but creating a decent conversational agent in any game is still measured in days and weeks, not minutes or hours.

The required effort influences how games are made. It would take a small team of designers working on nothing but conversations a full year to make 100 individual (non-cloned) NPCs, and those NPCs would still suffer from limited conversational ability and situational awareness. Assuming one wishes to at least break even on their game, it is essentially impossible to make large worlds filled with unique, believable agents using current techniques. As a result, time and money force those worlds to be filled with a handful of high-quality NPCs (those that drive the plot) and dozens to hundreds of generic NPCs with no or almost no conversational abilities at all.

Unique Personalities and Other Things We Might Want

Our primary goal is to reduce the time it takes to create a conversational agent. The associated goal is to reduce the cost to create a single agent, allowing us to reduce the cost of making the game or to create significantly more agents for the same cost. (This gem focuses on the latter.)

We have already said we want agents with better conversational breadth and situational awareness. (In other words, responses are based on the NPC's personality, state, job, culture, feelings toward the player, and so on.) Another desirable trait is realistic uniqueness—characters in the game are roughly as diverse as people in the real world. Which highlights the problems of a common technique—making a few high-quality NPCs (or dialog trees) and cloning them. Using templates ("Hi, my name is %this.name; I live here in %this.city"), you could fill a world with hundreds of agents who knew some basic information about themselves but who all acted the same (or behaved like one of a handful of personality types). What we want are people who are realistically unique—based on who they are, two agents will give different answers when it makes sense and the same answer when it makes sense.

Another desirable feature (already present in some games) is for the player to be able to change an agent's attitude and behavior toward them. Scenarios often require the player to earn the trust of an NPC. Likewise, bad behavior on the player's part should have consequences. Being able to win an agent's trust is often the key to a mission, and being able to make someone hopping mad is simply fun.

Culture describes how a group of people behave in certain circumstances. For example, it might be considered rude to ask an Afghani man about his wife, refuse a cup of tea in Iraq, or ask a first-level character about their flying mount. If you're dealing with a large number of cultures (groups, roles, character types, and so on), the sheer volume of dialog data makes it hard to verify that agents behave consistently or behave the way the lead designer requested. For serious games, where the behavior often has to be evaluated by an educational expert and/or people from the culture being modeled, unless those people are also game programmers, this is a serious problem.

Format is also a problem. All of the behavioral information can be captured in the standard script and tree structure of most dialog systems, but if the knowledge is explicit (say, a spreadsheet that focuses on behavior rather than wording), it's easier for an expert to review (and author) the information. It's much harder to bring in a group of people from that culture and ask them to review the information if the information is scattered across hundreds of script files. So another desirable feature is the ability to explicitly describe a culture or group of people.

A benefit of an explicit cultural representation is that it allows another desirable feature—plug-and-play cultures. If the culture of the NPCs could be swapped out with other cultures, making a new city filled with conversational agents would be as easy as cloning an existing city and swapping the culture, which meets both the goal of being fast (and cheap) and the goal of the NPCs being realistically different.

Editing dialog must entail an easy-to-understand workflow (not requiring a Ph.D. to use it). It needs to be data driven in a way that makes it quick to create easy-to-use tools, as well as quick to write unit tests for the system.

A final thing is something we don't want—the tool should not preclude designers from being able to do things they can do now. An example is a tool that uses psychological data to generate realistic behavior but doesn't allow the designer to override that behavior. While realism is often nice, it is more important that designers be able to achieve the behavior they want. In entertainment games, realism must sometimes be sacrificed to fun or moving the plot along. In educational games, characters must sometimes do things to further the educational goal, such as a character correcting rather than overlooking an error, or leading the player to the correct behavior rather than harshly punishing them.

What We Won't Cover

It likely comes as no surprise that a gem of this length will not cover every aspect of conversational agents. The focus of this gem is on intention planning, which means deciding how you want to respond to a topic. We'll use topics, concept trees, response types, trust levels, rapport modifiers, temperament stats, explicitly modeled cultural groups, sets of sparse culture wrappers, and a bit of memory to help decide when we should answer a question, feign ignorance, or insult the speaker's mother.

What this gem doesn't cover is realization, the actual words that come out of the NPC's mouth. In the old days, this was a simple problem—if the designer decides the NPC should insult the player, the response type Insult would map to one or more insults. If the NPC's intent is Answer, the response type and topic can be used to look up a specific answer, which might be specific to that character or used by the entire world. Using the techniques presented here, if the designer decides halfway through the project that all 300 guards in the game need to be able to discuss bunnies or Pre-Raphaelite poetry with complete strangers (but still act stuffy around people they actively dislike), the change can be made in a few minutes or less.

Being able to add entirely new responses or whole topics to hundreds of NPCs in a matter of minutes is a nice feature and offers all sorts of dreams of large, expansive dialog-filled worlds. Unfortunately, these days, things are a little more difficult. Most high-end games now use voice actors, meaning each statement a designer adds to an NPC must be recorded, a slow and expensive process. In these situations, voice recording, rather than designer creativity or predicting variable combinations, becomes the bottleneck. The topic of faster, cheaper speech won't be covered in this gem, but it is worth noting that even when the set of lines an NPC can say are fixed, considerable time must still be spent mapping the player's input to the NPC's output. The techniques presented here can help you more intelligently (and quickly) build those mappings.

Overview

The goal of this gem is to describe a way to scale how one authors conversational agents. Current systems typically use hard-coded input-output mappings annotated with gateway scripts to decide which of the hard-coded responses to use. The system described here uses a variety of techniques, but at the core, it tries to break the hard-coded links and replace them with abstractions. Rather than linking the player's input directly to the NPC's output, we use the player's input to determine the NPC's intention and then use the intention to select the NPC's behavior.

All inputs are mapped to a `Topic`. The `Topic` is checked against the NPC's `CulturalGroup` and current level of `Trust` toward the player to determine a `ResponseType`. Topics belong to a topic hierarchy, so if there is no match on the `Topic` in the NPC's dialog specification, the system moves up a level and checks for a `ResponseType` to the parent `Topic`.

`CulturalGroup` is a sparse set of `{Trust-Topic-ResponseType}` mappings. Culture represents not just nationality, but any group membership that affects how the agent will respond to a topic. An agent can (and almost certainly will) belong to multiple groups. Groups are prioritized, and conflicts are resolved by selecting the highest-priority matching group.

Throughout this gem, we'll use the example of a U.S. soldier (the player) in an Iraqi city. Table 3.10.1 lists seven NPCs the player might interact with—a typical civilian, a policeman, a policeman secretly working for the insurgents, another U.S. soldier, an insurgent (although the player doesn't know this), and two doctors.

TABLE 3.10.1 NPCs in an Iraqi City

Name:	Nori	Anwar	Zuhair	Scott	Shakir	Suha	Halema
Bio:	Iraqi Man	Policeman	Policeman	U.S. Soldier	Insurgent	Doctor	Doctor
Roles:	Iraqi	Policeman	Zuhair	Scott	SoccerFan	AidWorker	GovRep
	SoccerFan	GovRep	GovRep	Soldier	Insurgent	GovRep	AidWorker
	Person	Iraqi	Insurgent	USCitizen	Iraqi	IraqiFemale	IraqiFemale
		Person	Policeman	Person	Person	Iraqi	Iraqi
			Person			Person	Person
Trust:	0	0	−2	2	−6	0	0

Intention Modeling

Imagine a game in which there are 100 NPCs, and the player can insult any of them. How will they react? Most will return the insult in a dozen different ways, based on their personality, intelligence, culture, and preferred insult. Many will ignore the player. A few will attack. There are potentially 100 actual actions or phrases that might be used, but (in our example) there are only three intentions (insult, ignore, attack). In most games, the player's action (the input) is hard-coded directly to the NPC's behavior (the output). The result is that the designer must write thousands of pairings, such as `{input:Hear("Do you like films about gladiators?"), output:Say("Get away from me, weirdo.")}`. Much of this work is redundant—the same output is used for multiple inputs, and the same pairings are used in dozens of NPCs. If it is decided that this behavior is no longer desired (say, if designers decide late in the process that elves, unlike dwarves and humans, never insult others), the dialog pairings must be tracked down across dozens or hundreds of scripts or dialog files and changed.

Doing duplicate work is not only inefficient and hard to maintain, it's not fun. To make the designer's life easier, we'll have them map inputs to intentions (a much easier task) and separately map intentions to behaviors.

Topics, Response Types, and Trust

In our approach, for a given culture (which we'll discuss a little later), a `Topic` and `Trust` level are used to select `ResponseType`. `Topic` is the subject the player is asking about (swords, rumors, dragons, and so on). In this gem, we'll assume that `Topic` is the only input. While this is sufficient for most current video games, more demanding games will likely use a more complex input consisting of an action (asking a question, demanding, greeting, complimenting, insulting, and so on), a topic, and possibly some metadata (vigor, politeness, and so on). The type of input is irrelevant to the rest of the system, so we'll keep things simple and assume `Topic` is the sole input.

The `ResponseType` represents the responding NPC's intention. Possible values include `Answer` (give the player the information they're looking for, if possible), `Refuse`, `Evade`, `ChangeTopic`, `VagueAnswer`, `Lie`, `Ignore`, `Insult`, `Threaten`, `Correct` (if the player has made a mistake in what they asked for; this is more useful in educational games), `PositiveLie` (say something is great, regardless of whether it is), `NegativeLie`, and `Custom` (e.g., attack). More complicated (and academically respectable) schemes exist, but this works well for our purposes.

The actual words spoken by the NPC are based on the `ResponseType`. Suppose the player has been told that a bomb has been placed in the market. The player stops a person on the street and asks for directions. Table 3.10.2 shows how the NPCs defined in Table 3.10.1 might react. Five of the seven will attempt to answer the question (although one, Scott, does not know the answer). Shakir, an insurgent, will insult the player, while Zuhair, a corrupt cop, will lie to the player, sending him away from the market. (Note that the policeman does not necessarily know there is a bomb and wants it to explode, he merely dislikes the player; if the policeman knew about the bomb, he could be made to respond differently using a context modifier, but that is outside of the scope of this gem.)

TABLE 3.10.2   What an NPC Says Depends on Their Intention

Player asks: Where is the market?						lying
Name:	Nori	Anwar	Zuhair	Scott	Shakir	Suha	Halema
Role:	Iraqi	Iraqi	Iraqi	USCitizen	Insurgent	Iraqi	Iraqi
Intent:	Answer	Answer	**Lie**	Answer	**Insult**	Answer	Answer
Say:	*Left*	*Left*	***Right***	***Not sure***	***Pig***	*Left*	*Left*

`Trust` is the amount of trust the NPC has in the player. It's what ties the `Topic` to the `ResponseType` for that cultural group. This attribute does not have to be `Trust`—it could be rapport or some combination of other attributes, although trust as a single value works well in most instances. The important thing is that there is an attitudinal value that unambiguously ties an input to a `ResponseType`.

Using the example in Table 3.10.1, let's assume that the player has insulted Anwar the policeman. Let's measure trust from −10 (distrust) to 10 (full trust). `Topic=insult`, `Culture=Police`, and `Trust=0`. We have the rules (evaluated in order):

```
{Trust >=  5, Ignore}
{Trust >=  0, Insult}
{Trust >= -7, Threaten}
{Trust <  -7, Custom:Attack}
```

When the player insults Anwar, Anwar will decide to insult the player. Assuming an insult lowers `Trust` by 1, if the player insults Anwar again, Anwar will threaten him. If the player keeps it up, Anwar will eventually attack.

Knowing that an NPC will insult the player does not automatically determine what the NPC will do. The behavior generation system might be as simple as mapping `ResponseType=Insult` to `Say("Oh yeah, your momma.")`. The intent is mapped at the group level (all policemen), but the behavior could be different for each individual policeman. Each NPC could have his own favorite insult. Insults could be chosen based on that NPC's intelligence. They could be based on the player's class, how they're dressed, or their location (sports arena, store, and so on). This decision is made independent of the intention system.

Separating intention from behavior has several important implications. First, separate designers can be assigned to intent (say, someone familiar with personality or social psychology) and realization (for example, a writer). Second, because it's a smaller set of data and explicit in its goals, it is easier for one person to view and correct the data (important when striving for consistency across agents and designers).

Third, the smaller set of options (which presumably will be chosen from a list rather than entered as free text) means the intent portion can be built faster and more easily. By removing duplicate data (in the behavior system, you only have to map behaviors to a small set of intents, not the much larger set of inputs), the overall amount of work should be reduced. Fourth, it makes it easier for designers to tweak dialog later in the development process without editing (and possibly adding bugs to) individual NPC dialog trees. Fifth, having a separate intention layer makes it easier to write unit tests, in part because there's less data to test and in part because the tests aren't dependent on free text (important both because text is often changed and because of internationalization). Sixth, the explicit ResponseType and Trust levels help designers remember which conditions they need to handle. (Note that this is not required: One can create a group Person that returns Answer for all topics at all Trust levels.)

A final, and important, reason why separating intention from behavior is important is because it allows for design by composition, as seen in the next section.

Concept Hierarchies

To enhance conversational breadth, topics belong to a topic hierarchy. If the player asked about murders and the NPC's group didn't have an entry for Murder, the system would check the parent topic (say, Problems). If that was missing, it would check the next level until it had reached the root topic. There are several advantages to this, but two are worth mentioning. First, by placing a ResponseType on the root node, the agent has a default answer to anything the player asks. This helps cover errors when a mapping has been forgotten. Second, it allows a designer to add new topics through extension, which is normally lower risk than edits. If the designer decides that some characters need special behaviors when discussing Pre-Raphaelite poetry, they can add it to the topic hierarchy. The groups configured to discuss obscure Victorian poetry will do so, and everyone else will respond to the general topic of poetry, writing, or something more general.

It should also be noted that the {Topic-Trust-ResponseType} mappings do not have to be completely specified. An NPC can be set up to talk about local crime when Trust is eight or better and have no other mapping for that topic. If Trust was below that value, the system would then use the parent topic. This comes in handy when a person belongs to multiple groups, as described in the next section.

Cultural Wrappers

When designers specify intent, they do so at the group level, not for individual NPCs. We will refer to these groups as CulturalGroups. A CulturalGroup can represent race, nationality, occupation, political affiliation, or any group membership that affects how one reacts to something. Examples include Thai, Rural, Soldier, FootballFan, PunkRocker, AngryLoner, and Parent. Designers can also use the cultural group concept to model personality traits, such as Paranoid and Bully.

TABLE 3.10.3 Questions about Football Can Be Answered as Questions about Either Football or Sports

Do you like football? rapport building, concept abstraction

Name:	Nori	Anwar	Zuhair	Scott	Shakir	Suha	Halema
Topic:	Football	Sports	Sports	Sports	Football	Sports	Sports
Role:	**SoccerFan**	Iraqi	Iraqi	USCitizen	**SoccerFan**	Iraqi	Iraqi
Intent:	Answer	Answer	Answer	Answer	**Evasive**	Answer	Answer
Say:	*Yes*	*Yes*	*Yes*	*No*	*Maybe*	*Not really*	*Yes*
Trust:	+1	+1	+1	+1	+1	+1	+1

TABLE 3.10.4 U.S. and Iraqi Cultures Differ in Their Willingness to Discuss Their Spouse with a Stranger

Tell me about your spouse.

Name:	Nori	Anwar	Zuhair	Scott	Shakir	Suha	Halema
Topic:	Spouse	Spouse	Spouse	Spouse	Spouse	Spouse	Spouse
Role:	Iraqi	Iraqi	Iraqi	**USCitizen**	Iraqi	Iraqi	Iraqi
Intent:	Refuse	Refuse	Refuse	**Answer**	Insult	Refuse	Refuse
Say:	*How rude!*	*I refuse*	*No*	*Chevy's nice*	*You're a pig!*	*No*	*No*
Trust:	−1	−1	−1	+1	−1	−1	−1

A cultural group contains one or more {Topic-Trust-ResponseType} mapping. These mappings are typically sparse—most doctors have a predictable reaction to medical questions but not to questions about books, movies, or enchanted swords.

Agents belong to one or more groups. Typically, one of those groups will be Person, which will contain default mappings. Other groups specialize the agent. Some, such as Iraqi, will be fairly broad and dense, containing a lot of mappings, while others, such as FootballFan, will be small and focused. The agent can have an unlimited number of groups.

When designing agents, two design principles are used: design by composition and design by exception.

Design by composition says that the designer should build the agent by selecting pieces (cultural groups) rather than writing the agent from scratch. The process is simple and fast—Agent A is a Doctor, GovernmentRepresentative, Iraqi, IraqiFemale, and Person, and Agent B is a GovernmentRepresentative, Insurgent, Policeman, Iraqi, and Person. It takes only a few seconds to select the groups from a list, and assigning the groups fully specifies how the agents will react to any dialog option in the game.

(Note that if per-agent behavior is used, that work will still need to be done, although it should still be less work than in a traditional system.) Design by composition speeds up the authoring process for a single agent.

Design by exception speeds up the group authoring process. Following the principle of design by exception, default values should be set up in the base group (in our example, `Person`), and only those values that differ from the default should be placed in new groups. For example, you could have the group `LittleGirl` love to talk to complete strangers about any type of animal, the group `DemonEnthusiast` love to discuss demons, and the group `RabbitPhobe` be too terrified to discuss rabbits with anyone but their closest friends. Assigning those three groups to an agent produces an agent that will gladly talk about animals and demons yet refuse to discuss bunnies. The group `RabbitPhobe` does not contain mappings for any `Topic` other than `Rabbit`, making it fast to create, and the designer is not forced to create hundreds of combination groups, such as `PeopleWhoLoveAnimalsAndDemonsButNotRabbits`.

Although it won't be frequent, conflicts between `CulturalGroups` can occur. Consider a doctor who runs a government clinic in a war zone. Although the clinic is trying its best, there are still rampant health problems in the area. If you ask the agent about the problems, the `Doctor` in her wants to complain that they aren't doing enough, while the `GovernmentRepresentative` in her wants to say that the clinic is doing just fine.

The dialog system we describe here works more generally for any problem of determining an agent's reaction to an event. How one handles the cultural group conflicts depends on the domain. For the dialog system, we decided to use a first-chance event handler with a prioritized group list (referred to as *Cultural Wrappers*). When setting up the agent, the designer must select the order of the groups. In Table 3.10.1, Suha has `Doctor` prioritized over `GovernmentRepresentative`, while Halema has the same groups but in a different order. When asked about problems (Table 3.10.5), Suha complains about healthcare, while Halema says there are no problems.

TABLE 3.10.5 An NPC's Answer Is Based on the Order (Prioritization) of Their Groups

Are there any problems here?

Name:	Nori	Anwar	Zuhair	Scott	Shakir	Suha	Halema
Role:	Iraqi	Iraqi	**GovRep**	USCitizen	Insurgent	Iraqi	**GovRep**
Intent:	Answer	Answer	**Deny**	Answer	Insult	Answer	**Deny**
Say:	*Yes*	*Crime*	*It's very safe*	*I don't know*	*You!*	*Healthcare*	*No*

In a very small number of cases, there is no acceptable ordering of groups—sometimes Group A supersedes Group B, and other times B supersedes A. As an example, in Table 3.10.1, Zuhair is both a policeman and (secretly) an insurgent. He wants to help the terrorists, but not at the risk of blowing his cover. He might voice support for the terrorists around people he trusts (as a terrorist) but be polite to the player (as a policeman). In these instances, a simple solution is to create a new group that contains only those Topics and Trust levels needed to resolve conflicts. This new group might be an actual general-purpose group, such as UndercoverInsurgent, but it can also represent that specific individual (in this case, Zuhair). Individuals have their personal quirks that can't be captured by any group, so modeling the things that are truly specific to an individual is okay, but the "individual group" should only contain the exceptions. Unless the agent is truly, eccentrically unique, most of his responses should be specified in the more general groups.

Earlier it was mentioned that Topics belong to a topic hierarchy. When determining the agent's intent, if a match on the Topic isn't found, the parent Topic is used, moving up the tree until a match is found. When multiple groups are used, preference is given to Topic specificity. Consider the Topic TableTennis, child of Sports, and the ordered group list [USCitizen, PingPongFan]. USCitizen does not have a mapping for TableTennis but does for Sports, while PingPongFan matches on TableTennis. Assuming a Trust level of 0, the program first checks for a match on {USCitizen, TableTennis, 0} and fails to find a match. It then checks {PingPongFan, TableTennis, 0}, where it finds a match. Had it failed, it would have then checked {USCitizen, Sports, 0} and then {PingPongFan, Sports, 0}. This gives greater freedom in arranging groups and allows for a greater number of groups to be used. If the system moved up the topic heirarchy before checking the next group, any group with a value high in the tree (for example, at the root node, which matches everything) would prevent any other group from having an influence.

Creating Unique Individuals

Each combination (and ordering) of groups results in an individual who is unique. It does not mean that he will behave differently than every other agent under all circumstances at all times. We could design them to do so, but the agents wouldn't appear realistic, they'd appear insane. It doesn't matter whether someone loves kittens, is a doctor, or grew up in a small town; if you ask him whether a particular neighborhood is dangerous or whether a given restaurant is good, there are only a limited number of responses you should get. Responding to the question "where is the train station" by juggling cats might be unique, but it isn't helpful. That said, there's nothing preventing the designer from adding that reaction.

The number of unique individuals you can create by combining groups grows quickly with the number of groups. With three groups, 15 unique individuals can be made. With five groups, the number is 325. With 10 groups, the number is 9,864,100, a number larger than most cities in the world. Add one more group, and you can cover all cities and most countries.

The process of assigning and ordering groups is not the only way to create unique NPCs. Intent can be tweaked at the NPC level using the TrustModifier property. This represents how trusting someone is and how quick they are to change their trust level.

It is multiplied against `Trust` to produce a modified trust score used in `Trust` checks. The default `TrustModifier` is 1. An agent with a `TrustModifier` of 1.5 is 50 percent more trusting than normal—the agent needs only a `Trust` of four to trigger responses that other agents with the same group list require a six for.

Circumstantial modifiers can be used to modify `Trust` scores. For example, if the agent has been arrested or has a gun pointed at him, the threshold for giving an answer could be lowered. It seems likely that this would need to vary by NPC somehow (perhaps by a willpower property).

Although beyond the scope of this article, uniqueness can also be created in the behavior generation system. A single {`Topic`, `ResponseType`} pairing (where `Topic` can be a wildcard when topic is irrelevant, such as when insulting or ignoring the player) can map to a set of realizations, one of which is selected at random (preferably using an intelligent random system that filters out long repeated sequences). Behaviors can also be chosen based on attributes of the agent. For example, if the `ResponseType` was `Compliment`, an agent with a high intelligence or charisma might say something clever, while someone with low intelligence might stumble badly and say something offensive.

Conclusion

One of the biggest obstacles to creating games filled with hundreds of intelligent, conversational agents is the sheer amount of work (and therefore cost) required to create them. It's not that it's hard work (although designing interesting characters and dialog can certainly be difficult); it's that any kind of work done several hundred times is a lot of work. And sometimes, quantity is as important as quality—you can't make a living, breathing, realistic city with just three characters. One of the keys to improving AI is to improve its authoring scalability; there needs to be processes and tools that make it easier to populate virtual worlds. Hopefully, the ideas presented in this gem will be a big step toward helping you fill your own worlds with intelligent, interesting, unique characters.

3.11

Graph-Based Data Mining for Player Trace Analysis in MMORPGs

Nikhil S. Ketkar and
G. Michael Youngblood

In this gem we will present techniques for analyzing player trace data in massively multiplayer role-playing games (MMORPGs). As MMORPGs become increasingly popular, with the number of subscribers going into the millions, an MMORPG provider is faced with a number of technical and business questions. For instance, how do you place an advertisement in MMORPGs, or how do you detect cheating in the form of bots and gold farmers? We observe that these and a lot of other such questions can be answered by analyzing player traces (graph representations of the player's movement in the world), but most traditional approaches in machine learning and data mining fall short when applied to the task due to the inherent structural nature of player trace data. We claim that the application of techniques in the area of graph-based data mining that are designed to work with structured data are most suitable for the analysis of player traces.

Data Logging and Preprocessing

Typically, player movements in the world can be logged as the location of the player in 3D space at discrete intervals in time. Thus, the logged data for a single player is a sequence of the form $\{(x_0, y_0, z_0, t_0), (x_2, y_2, z_2, t_2)...\}$. The player spawns in the world at time t_0 (which is 0) and (x_0, y_0, z_0) refers to the position where the player spawns. Subsequently, the player moves in the world, and assuming that we are logging data at every second, (x_1, y_1, z_1, t_1) refers to the position the player is at $t_1 = 1$. Similarly, we have a number of positions with the corresponding time for the player movements until the player exits the world.

We refer to this sequence as a *walk*. Our overall dataset consists of a set of such walks, where each walk corresponds to one session of a single player in the game.

Figure 3.11.1 presents a visual representation of three walks. This data was collected in a world shown in Figures 3.11.2 and 3.11.3. This world is a part of the Urban MMO Testbed (UMMOT). UMMOT is an experimental environment designed to study human interactions in virtual worlds and is an extension of the Urban Combat Testbed [Cook07, Youngblood08].

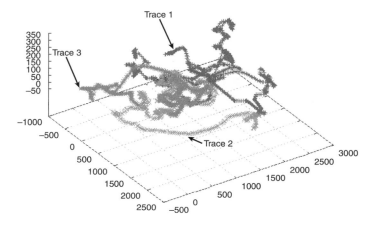

Figure 3.11.1 A visual representation of three walks in a world.

Figure 3.11.2 Urban MMO Testbed: Birds-eye view.

Figure 3.11.3 Urban MMO Testbed: Screenshot.

While data in such raw form is easy to log, for the purposes of analysis it needs to be preprocessed to a more suitable form. Dealing with data at this level of granularity (locations in 3D coordinate space) is computationally intensive and leads to poor results. Hence, we convert the 3D locations to a discrete form by superimposing a grid on the world. Figure 3.11.4 illustrates this process. Once such a grid is superimposed, all points inside one grid cube are assigned to the same discrete location. Once data is preprocessed in this manner, it consists of a set of walks of the form $W = \{(l_1, t_1), (l_2, t_2)...\}$, which is a sequence of discrete grid locations for the corresponding time instance.

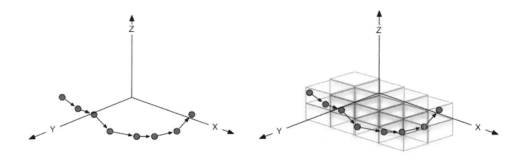

Figure 3.11.4 Superimposing a grid to get discrete locations.

Selecting a proper granularity for the grid (the size of a single cube) is important. Too small a cube size will lead to too many locations, and too large will lead to too few locations. It is recommended that the cube size be equal to, or a small multiple of, the bounding box of the character model.

Advertisement Placement in MMORPGs

Placing advertisements in MMORPGs can provide host companies with an additional source of revenue. However, in order to capitalize on this business opportunity, companies hosting the MMORPGs need to provide coverage guarantees to their clients who would pay for placing advertisements. The notion of advertisement coverage is central to all marketing and is loosely defined as the estimated number of prospects reached by an advertisement. A lot of value is placed on advertisement coverage, as the clients placing the advertisement are solely interested in reaching as many prospects as possible and would be willing to pay a higher amount of money for higher coverage. An advertisement in the *New York Times* costs significantly more than an advertisement in the *Charlotte Observer* precisely because an advertisement in the *New York Times* will achieve higher coverage.

In the case of MMORPGs, estimating and providing guarantees on coverage is challenging for a number of reasons. Players typically spawn in different locations, moving around the world performing tasks, and this is quite different from a reader reading a newspaper or visiting a webpage. Advertisements can be placed in different locations in the world, but where should they be placed? Furthermore, can some guarantees on coverage be provided?

Given a set of preprocessed walks, as described in the previous section, advertisements could be placed at any of the locations in the walks. We define coverage for a set of locations as the number of walks that contain the specified locations divided by the total number of walks. Intuitively, coverage captures the number of players that will get quite close to and most likely see an advertisement. Note that it is quite possible, although unlikely, that a player will get close to a location but not see the advertisement because he or she is looking in a different direction. In our setting, we do not explicitly model where the player is looking. Such an approach has been tried before and has been found to be quite computationally expensive [Dixit08].

Figure 3.11.5 illustrates examples of how the coverage is computed. Note that there are four distinct walks, as illustrated in the large graph on the left. Subfigures (a), (b), (c), and (d) illustrate four different location selections for this graph. For location selection as illustrated in Subfigure (a), two locations are selected, which cover Walks 2, 3, and 4. Because there are a total of four walks, this amounts to coverage of 75 percent. For (b), two locations are selected, which covers all four walks, which amounts to coverage of 100 percent. Similarly for (c) and (d) we have 50-percent and 100-percent coverage, respectively.

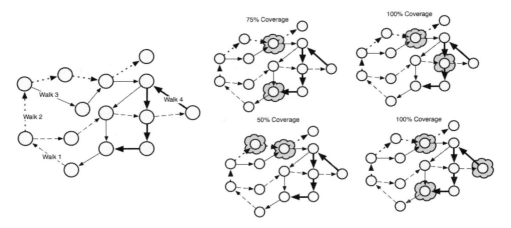

Figure 3.11.5   Coverage computation.

In such a setting, our task is to maximize the coverage while minimizing the number of advertisements placed. This task is equivalent to the set-cover problem, which is NP-Complete. Thus, optimal solutions are not feasible, and it is necessary to develop approaches that can produce near-optimal solutions at moderate computation cost.

An important, additional dimension in the task of advertisement placement is that of generalization to future player behavior (in terms of walks). Given a certain amount of training data, suppose that we select a set of locations that maximize coverage on this data. Then, our selected set of locations should achieve the required level of coverage on future walks. Assuming that training data is a good reflection of the entire population, maximizing coverage on training data will most likely achieve high coverage on unseen data. The important question here is how large of a sample is required to get a good generalization on unseen data.

Another factor to consider is the cost of collecting and logging data. Clearly, in order to have training sets on which to base advertisement placement, some data needs to be collected. The most expensive case is where actual positions (3D locations) are logged. The space required for such logging grows linearly with the number of walks and may not be feasible. Another approach is to simply log the number of players that visit a particular location, which is constant in the number of walks. There is an inherent tradeoff in the amount of logged data and the quality of the solution.

We now present a set of approaches for these tasks and discuss their strengths and weaknesses.

Frequency Maximizing Approach

Frequency-based placement is a relatively simple approach that selects locations based on the number of walks passing through a particular location. Walks in the training data are processed sequentially to count the number of walks passing through each location, and these counts are used to select the topmost locations. Note that this approach only requires the logging of frequencies of visits to each position, which requires space constant with respect to the number of walks. Another important thing to note is that this approach might produce suboptimal solutions in many cases, because it does not consider the overlap between walks. Figure 3.11.6 illustrates an example of such a case. Assuming that Position B has already been selected, the frequency maximizing approach will select Location A over Location C. This is because, individually, A covers four walks and C covers two. This is clearly suboptimal, as there is an overlap of three walks between A and B (Walks 1, 2, and 3).

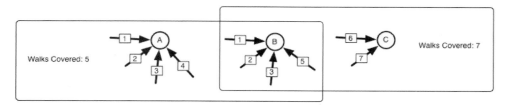

Figure 3.11.6   Suboptimal selection by frequency maximizing approach.

Markov Steady-State Probability-Based Approach

The Markov steady-state probability-based placement approach is based on computing the probability of a player visiting a particular location based on the transition probabilities. The first step in this approach is to process the walks to generate a transition probability matrix. The transition probability matrix stores probabilities of transitions from a location to any other location and is computed by counting the transitions and dividing by the total number of outgoing transitions. Once this matrix is generated, which we will refer to as M, the steady-state probabilities can be computed by solving $xM = x$. There are several exact and iterative approaches to solve such a system of linear equations. Based on the steady-state probabilities, advertisements can be placed by selecting locations with the highest probabilities.

Figure 3.11.7 illustrates an example of this. Note that this approach requires the logging of transitions and requires space constant with respect to the number of walks.

Greedy, Marginal Gain Maximizing Approach

This approach is based on selecting locations in a greedy manner, maximizing the marginal gain with each added location. Initially, the location with the highest frequency (or coverage) is selected. This is followed by considering each location (not already selected) and evaluating the coverage of the newly formed set of locations (previously selected locations with the current location). After evaluating each location in this manner, the location that maximizes the coverage is added to the set.

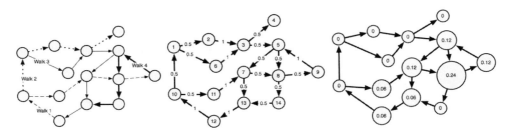

Figure 3.11.7   Computation of steady-state probabilities.

This is illustrated in Figure 3.11.8. Note that this approach considers the marginal coverage while considering a new location to add and therefore would produce solutions that are more optimal as compared to the frequency-based approach. Another important point is that this approach requires logging the actual walks—that is, the space required to log the necessary data grows linearly with the length of the walk as well as the number of walks.

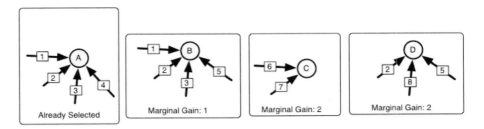

Figure 3.11.8   Computing the marginal coverage.

Experimental Comparison

We experimentally compared the three approaches to advertisement placement on a dataset of 2,436 walks. More details on the dataset can be found in [Cook07] and [Youngblood08]. Experiments were conducted for various sizes of training sets, ranging from 0.25 percent to 50 percent of the entire dataset, while the remaining data was used for testing. (Advertisement placements were selected based on the walks in the training set, and these placements were evaluated on the test set.)

Figure 3.11.9 shows the coverage achieved by each of the three approaches for different numbers of advertisements, with 5 percent of the data used for training, on the training set. Figure 3.11.10 shows coverage on the test set. As a baseline, we also include a random placement approach in the experimentation. Each result is an average over five runs of different samples of training and test sets. Results indicate that the greedy marginal gain maximizing approach significantly outperforms both the frequency-based and the Markov steady-state probability-based approaches. The frequency-based approach is comparable to the Markov steady-state probability-based approach. Similar results are observed on various other training sizes greater than 5 percent. An interesting observation is that we get diminishing returns with an increased number of advertisements placed. That is, a lot of coverage is achieved due to the initial advertisements, but after about seven or eight advertisements are placed, there is very little improvement in coverage.

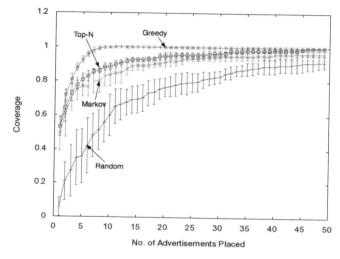

Figure 3.11.9 Comparison of approaches to advertisement placement. Five percent of the data used for training, coverage on the training set.

The closeness between the coverage on the training sets and the coverage on the test sets implies that our advertisement placement generalizes well to unseen data. However, this is not the case for very small training sizes. Figure 3.11.11 shows the coverage achieved by each of the three approaches for various budgets on the number of advertisements placed with 0.25 percent of the data used for training, on the training set. Figure 3.11.12 shows coverage on the test set. For such a small size of training set, 100-percent coverage is achieved for very few advertisements, but these results do not carry over to the unseen data. For very small training sizes, we see that the performance of each of the three approaches is no better than random. The important point to take home is to have a sufficiently large sample size. Unfortunately, our present work does not include a theoretical bound on the sample size, and we advise users to partition their datasets (into training and testing sets) to determine the appropriate size experimentally. In general, the size of the training set depends on the size of the world and the variability in the walks, and we are working toward proving an upper bound on the training set size.

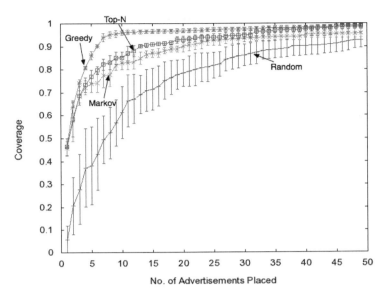

Figure 3.11.10 Comparison of approaches to advertisement placement. Five percent of the data used for training, coverage on the test set.

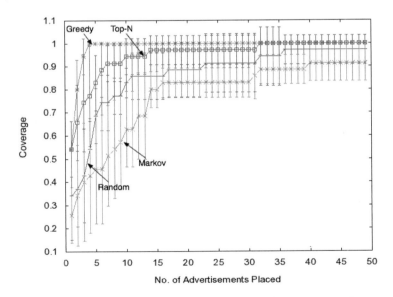

Figure 3.11.11 Comparison of approaches to advertisement placement. 0.25 percent of the data used for training, coverage on the training set.

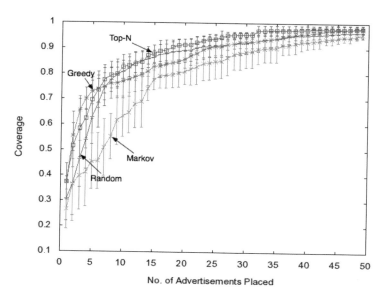

Figure 3.11.12   Comparison of approaches to advertisement placement. 0.25 percent of the data used for training, coverage on the test set.

Each of the three approaches generalizes well to future data given a sufficient size of the training data. In our experimentation, the greedy marginal gain maximizing approach significantly outperforms the frequency-based and Markov steady-state probability-based approaches. However, it should be noted that for a large-scale implementation, the greedy marginal gain maximizing approach requires the logging of the actual walks, which can consume space that grows linearly with the number of walks as well as the length of walks. The other approaches require the logging of visits to particular locations or transition probabilities, which is constant with respect to the number of walks.

Building Player Profiles with Clustering

The idea behind clustering is partitioning a given set of examples into subsets (referred to as *clusters*) such that examples in each subset are similar to other examples in the subset by some measure. Cluster analysis is an unsupervised learning technique that allows us to categorize data such that trends in the data are identified. A good introduction to cluster analysis can be found in [Jain99].

In the case of player trace analysis, we are interested in building player profiles that group players into categories such that players in a group have similar behaviors. Figure 3.11.13 shows player traces for six different players. Although visualizing such information can lead to important insight, this is only possible for small datasets.

When player traces become long or there are too many player traces, analyzing them visually becomes a tedious process. Clustering player traces serves as an important step in analyzing traces because it reduces the data from individual player traces to groups of player traces. Since there are far fewer groups than individual traces, it becomes possible to perform a visual analysis of these groups instead of individual traces.

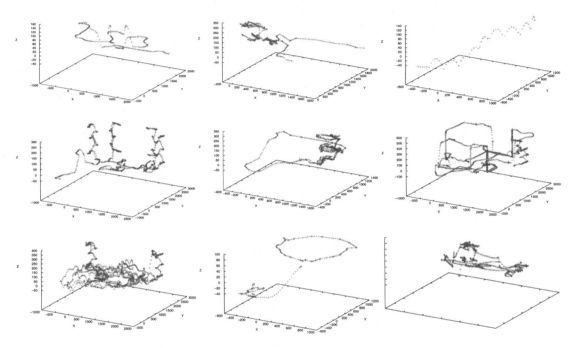

Figure 3.11.13   Visualizing player traces in 3D space.

The key challenge in applying clustering algorithms to player trace data is that typically clustering algorithms are designed for attribute-valued data (data represented as a single table), and player trace data is structured and cannot be represented as a single table without losing important information. A simple example of such data can be a table representing information about customers where each row represents a customer and each column represents a specific attribute, such as age or yearly income.

To produce such a grouping, a similarity measure between two examples (in this case, customers) is required. There are several distances measured for attribute-valued data—for instance, Euclidean distance, which can be used to achieve good results. Contrast this customer data (represented as a table) with player trace data introduced earlier, which cannot be represented as a table. The notion of Euclidean distance cannot be used to measure the similarity between two player traces. This is because

Euclidean distance can only be used on data points represented as *n*-dimensional vectors of equal length, and walks in the world are a sequence of points with variable length.

To address this difficulty, we introduce a similarity measure between two player walks in the world. Using this similarity measure, any of the standard clustering algorithms can be applied to clustering player trace data.

Distance Measure

The largest common subsequence (LCS) is used to measure the similarity between two walks. An illustration of longest common subsequence can be found in Figure 3.11.14. Using LCS accounts for fragments of similarity between two walks. For example, suppose that some walks consist of an important set of behaviors that are sequentially repeated in each of the walks. However, these repeating behaviors are interlaced with other actions that are not common to all the walks.

1: ABCBDAB

2: BDCABA

LCS: BCBA

ABCBDAB

BDCABA

Figure 3.11.14   Longest common subsequence.

Such a case is illustrated in Figure 3.11.15. Here we have four walks, where Walks 1 and 2 have two behaviors in common. Walks 3 and 4 also have two behaviors in common. The uncommon actions represent the variability or the noise in the data and should be ignored. What should be considered are the sequentially repeating, common aspects of the walks, which are in fact captured by the LCS. If we group the walks in Figure 3.11.15 based on LCS, we will have two groups—the first with Walks 1 and 2 and the second with Walks 3 and 4. However, the LCS by itself does not take into account what fraction of two traces is similar. For example, in Figure 3.11.15, Walks 3 and 4 have much longer chunks of portions in common (with respect to the length of the entire walk) as compared to Walks 1 and 2. Hence, Walks 3 and 4 are much more similar to each other than Walks 1 and 2.

To take this into consideration, we define the similarity measure as:

$$\frac{\left(LCS(A,B)\right)^2}{Length(A) \times Length(B)},$$

where A and B are the two walks under consideration. Note that this similarity measure is typically a number between 0 and 1. Identical walks will have a similarity measure of 1, while completely dissimilar walks will have a similarity measure of 0.

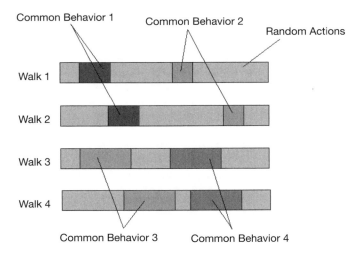

Figure 3.11.15   Longest common subsequence captures common behavior.

The LCS problem is quite well studied in literature, with numerous applications in bioinformatics. An $O(mn)$ time algorithm (where m and n are the lengths of the input sequences) for LCS can be found in [Wagner74].

Applying Standard Clustering Algorithms

Using the distance measure for player trace walks specified earlier, it is now possible to extend any of the standard clustering algorithms for the task of clustering player traces. The general idea is to replace the distance computation (which is typically Euclidian distance) by the distance measure based on LCS. Alternatively, for a given set of walks, we can precompute a similarity matrix, which is basically a triangular matrix where each entry indicates the similarity between the example in the row and the example in the column (illustrated in Figure 3.11.16). Many clustering algorithms can operate on such a similarity matrix to produce clusters that can be used for subsequent analysis.

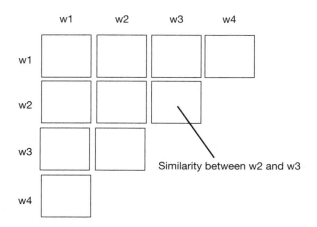

Figure 3.11.16   Similarity matrix.

A common way to visualize clustering results is a dendrogram, which is a treelike structure that depicts the similarity between the examples. We illustrate a dendrogram on the first five walks (due to space limitations) in our datasets in Figure 3.11.17.

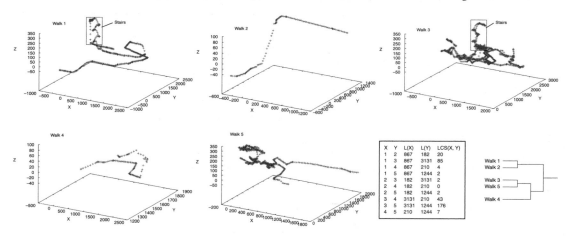

Figure 3.11.17   Results of clustering (on a very small subset).

The overall procedure for cluster analysis is to first generate a dendrogram (source code for generating a dendrogram has been provided on CD, and more details can be found in [Jain99]) for the entire dataset, as depicted in Figure 3.11.17, and then focus on specific clusters to understand their common elements. The dendrogram is an extremely effective tool for visual data analysis because it allows the user to focus on specific samples in the data rather than the entire dataset. The LCS procedure can also be used to produce the common subsequence thereby identifying such common elements. For example, in Figure 3.11.17, the common element between Walks 1 and 3 is the walk up the stairs. Following such a procedure (looking at clusters and identifying common elements) can allow the identification of several important behaviors.

Detecting Bots and Gold Farmers with Classification Models

The basic task underlying the detection of bots and gold farmers is that of learning a binary classification model. This task is quite well studied in the field of machine learning and is commonly referred to as *supervised learning*. In supervised learning, we are given a set of examples labeled as positive or negative (positive and negative are the two classes or categories), and a supervised learning algorithm induces a function that can classify unseen examples into these two categories. A good introduction to supervised learning can be found in [Mitchell97]. While the supervised learning problem is quite well studied, most algorithms for supervised learning only deal with attribute valued data. As mentioned earlier, player traces cannot be represented as attribute valued data, and hence applying existing algorithms to the task can be quite challenging.

An important class of supervised learning algorithms is support vector machines (SVMs), which have been successfully applied to many application domains. A good introduction to SVMs can be found in [Cristianini00]. While SVMs also typically deal with attribute valued data, they can be extended to operate with structured data by specifying a kernel function. A kernel function basically computes a similarity measure between two examples. The LCS-based similarity measure used for clustering can also be used as a kernel function, allowing us to apply SVMs to classify player traces.

Using an LCS-Based Similarity Measure with K-NN

We begin by discussing the use of the LCS-based similarity measure with the K-Nearest Neighbor (K-NN) algorithm, which is a relatively simple classification algorithm and would allow the reader to develop an intuition for the task of player trace classification. The K-NN algorithm is a simple lazy algorithm that stores all the input examples, and when a prediction is to be made on an unseen example, it first computes the K nearest neighbors using some measure of similarity and predicts the class of the unseen example as the majority of its neighbors. Typically, in the case of attribute valued data, Euclidian distance is used to measure the similarity between two examples. Although simple, the K-NN algorithm can produce good classification models.

To extend the K-NN algorithm to operate on player trace data, we use the LCS-based measure to calculate neighbor distance. To predict whether a given player trace is a bot trace or a human trace, we detect K nearest neighbors of the trace under consideration and predict its class (bot or human) based on the majority of the neighbors.

To see why the LCS similarity measure serves the purpose of distinguishing between bots and humans, consider the following observations. First, bots (or gold farmers) constantly repeat a set of actions. While these actions may be interlaced by random movements, in order to achieve their objective (for example, killing boars in *World of Warcraft* (WoW) to gain experience points), they have to repeat some sequence of actions. Second, the areas on the world where these actions can be performed are specific. (For example, there are particular locations in WoW that are intended for neophyte players to kill boars and gain experience points.) A set of player traces that represent bots (or gold farmers) will have specific repeating locations easily captured by the LCS.

While K-NN is conceptually simple, it is computationally unfeasible for the task of player trace analysis on large datasets. This is because in order to identify the K nearest neighbors, we have to compute the LCS similarity measure of the unseen examples with all the other examples in the training set. The LCS-similarity measure can be computed in $O(mn)$. (m and n are lengths of the input sequences.) This is sufficiently fast for batch processing (offline classification and analysis of player traces); however, when bot detection needs to be performed in real time, this is too slow. To address this issue, we need a more sophisticated technique, namely SVMs.

Using an LCS-Based Similarity Measure with SVMs

The LCS-based similarity measure can also be used in conjunction with SVMs. SVMs typically operate on attribute valued data and, given a set of training examples (categorized into two categories), produce a hyperplane (a higher dimensional plane) that separates examples into the two categories. In order to classify an unseen example, its distance and orientation with the hyperplane are computed, and based on this, we can make a prediction about its category. Figure 3.11.18 illustrates this process.

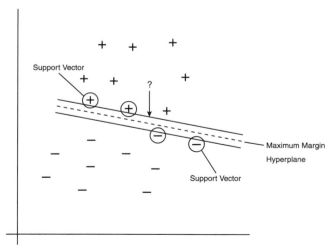

Figure 3.11.18 Support vector machines.

The hyperplane, more correctly referred to as the *maximum margin hyperplane*, is a plane that puts the maximum distance between the positive and negative examples. The maximum margin hyperplane is defined by the examples, which, in a sense, lie on the boundary of the positive and negative regions and are referred to as the *support vectors*. The key point to note here is that in order to classify an unseen example, the LCS measure only needs to be computed against the support vectors, and not the entire set of examples. This significantly speeds up the process of prediction.

Conclusion

We presented a number of techniques to analyze data in MMORPGs, dealing with specific problems such as advertisement placement, profile building, and bot detection. In conclusion, the most important point we would like to convey to the community is the added value of logging player data. Understanding interaction and behavior in virtual worlds can help us design better virtual worlds, and this is only possible through the collection and analysis of such data. In most cases, the cost of collecting such data is a small price to pay compared to the insight received by analyzing the data.

References

[Cook07] Cook, D. J., L. B. Holder, and G. M. Youngblood. "Graph-Based Analysis of Human Transfer Learning Using a Game Testbed." *IEEE Transactions on Knowledge and Data Engineering* 19.11 (2007): 1465–478.

[Cristianini00] Cristianini, N. and J. Shawe-Taylor. *An Introduction to Support Vector Machines and Other Kernel-based Learning Methods.* Cambridge University Press, 2000.

[Dixit08] Dixit, Priyesh N., and G. Michael Youngblood. "Understanding Information Observation in Interactive 3D Environments." *Sandbox '08: Proceedings of the 2008 ACM SIGGRAPH Symposium on Video Games.* 2008. 163–170.

[Jain99] Jain, A. K., M. N. Murty, and P. J. Flynn. "Data Clustering: A Review." *ACM Computing Surveys* 31.3 (1999): 264–323.

[Mitchell97] Mitchell, T. *Machine Learning.* WCB McGraw Hill, 1997.

[Wagner74] Wagner, R. A., and M. J. Fischer. "The String-to-String Correction Problem." *Journal of the ACM (JACM)* 21.1 (1974): 168–173.

[Youngblood08] Youngblood, G. M. and P. N. Dixit. "Understanding Intelligence in Games Using Player Traces and Interactive Player Graphs." *Game Programming Gems 7.* Boston: Charles River Media, 2008. 265–280.

GENERAL PROGRAMMING

Introduction

Doug Binks, Intel Semiconductors AG

doug.binks@googlemail.com

Game programming, like many disciplines, is becoming increasingly specialized. The steady trend of technical innovation, along with the broadening requirements of game development, force us to focus our finite mental resources on an ever-narrowing section of the field. Yet the very basis of the programming endeavor is the ability to coerce the computational architecture into performing to our will. Most of the gems in this section deal with this—the fundamental art of game programming.

Performance is a critical aspect of most game software, and so several gems deal with this issue, either directly, by showcasing solutions for common tasks with enhanced performance, or indirectly, by providing a better understanding of some aspect of performance programming. Multi-threading is an increasingly important area for programmers looking for more cycles to execute their instructions, and suitably, a pair of articles targets this. Several articles deal with memory issues, from allocation to optimization and profiling.

A good part of getting a system to do what we want is ensuring that it actually does. In this vein, a couple of articles deal with error logging and enabling the QA process. The solutions presented require minimal effort to implement, so they stand a good chance of being widely used if included in a code base.

Other articles deal with functionality. It's here that the gems cover the widest area, partly through addressing general approaches to adding functionality and partly through describing specific but different types of functionality. Continuing the trend of many previous editions, there's a bias toward tools—rightly so, as tools play an ever-important role in game development.

Whether you're a jack of all trades, a master of one, or new to game programming, you'll find a good deal of useful innovation, information, and experience within this section.

4.1

Fast-IsA

Joshua Grass, PhD
joshua.grass@gmail.com

Many advanced scripting languages have notions of class hierarchies similar to those in programming languages such as C++, C#, or Java. Scripts written in these languages often need to perform safe casts or IsA checks on objects. In our game, *This Is Vegas*, we found that the amount of time spent performing the IsA check was not insignificant. This gem describes a method for processing class hierarchy data to change the IsA operation from O(N) to O(1). In our case, this resulted in a performance improvement of more than one percent for the cost of adding one DWORD for each class (depending on your platform; if the platform does not have the BitScanReverse operator, you will need to store the location of the most significant bit along with the index). The algorithm is also an interesting study in combining several well-known data structures that we often see in school but rarely get to use to achieve some tangible results.

Problem Definition

Given a class hierarchy, we need to be able to determine whether Class A is a subclass of Class B. A typical class hierarchy might look like Figure 4.1.1.

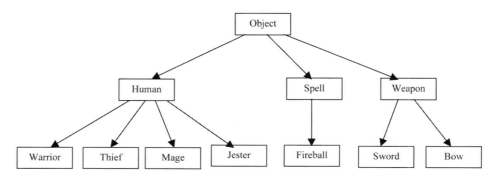

Figure 4.1.1 An example class hierarchy.

Our first implementation of an IsA() function would be as follows:

```
bool IsA(Class *pA, Class *pB)
{
    while (*pA != NULL)
    {
        if (pA == pB)
        {
            return true;
        }
        pA = pA->GetParentClass();
    }
    return false;
}
```

This algorithm has two major problems: The worst-case scenario requires a traversal from leaf to root of the class tree, which can be very expensive if you are frequently doing IsA tests on leaf nodes (for example, we have an array of humans, and we want to process only thieves). The second problem is one of cache issues. The class metadata may be loaded anywhere in memory, and if one of the classes we traverse is not currently in the cache, this operation can result in cache thrashing and low performance.

Balanced Class Hierarchies

While a graph with a variable number of branches at each node gives the system a huge amount of flexibility, it also means that there is no regular way in which we can store or access the hierarchy. Let's imagine that we were incredibly lucky in our class hierarchy, and at the very end of the project, we had a uniform graph in which each node branched exactly twice, such as in the class hierarchy displayed in Figure 4.1.2.

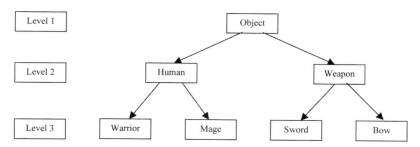

Figure 4.1.2   A balanced binary class hierarchy.

This graph has many useful properties, the main advantage being that there is a simple way of laying out the classes such that they can fit in one contiguous array of memory. Programmers writing A* algorithms use this structure (a heap) all the time because it eliminates the need for storing pointers and it makes memory management of an open list extremely easy.

NULL	Object	Human	Weapon	Warrior	Mage	Sword	Bow
0	1	2	3	4	5	6	7
Level 0	Level 1	Level 2	Level 2	Level 3	Level 3	Level 3	Level 3

Each level we add to the tree adds $2^{(N-1)}$ new nodes to the storage array, where N is the new level. So if we were to add Level 4 in our aforementioned example, we would need to add eight additional items to our array. Adding Level 5 would add 16 new nodes, and so on. We start our table at Entry 1 instead of Entry 0 for reasons that will be discussed later in the gem.

What we're really interested in here is the index of the nodes and their relationship to their parents. I will refer to this index as the *class index* for the rest of the gem. In the above table, the class index is the second row. It is important to note that we do not actually create a heap or store the classes in it. We use the heap structure purely to create a useful ordering for the classes.

The function for getting the parent's class index of a node is trivial:

```
int parentIndex(int nIndex)
{
    return nIndex >> 1;
}
```

If we take the class index of Sword (6) and right shift it by 1, we get the result 3, which is the class index of the parent node, Weapon. We can do this again and determine that the parent node of Weapon (3) is, in fact, Object (1).

Given this perfectly balanced tree, we can easily rewrite our IsA function to use the class indices in the storage array to determine whether a class is a subclass of another.

```
bool IsA_Balanced2Tree(Class *pA, Class *pB)
{
    int nAIndex = pA->GetClassIndex();
    int nBIndex = pB->GetClassIndex();

    while (nAIndex != 0)
    {
        if (nAIndex == nBIndex)
        {
            return true;
        }
        nAIndex = nAIndex >> 1;
    }
    return false;
}
```

So while this function doesn't look that much better initially, it does have one huge advantage over our previous algorithm. It doesn't depend on any information from the parent classes of A. It only retrieves information from Class A and from Class B, which are very likely to already be in the cache. So we have eliminated the possibility of any unnecessary cache misses for intermediary classes between A or B or, in the worst-case scenario where A is not a child of B, all of the parent classes of A.

We can further improve this algorithm by realizing that once the index for a parent of A is less than the index for B, there is no way that they are ever going to be equal.

```
bool IsA_Balanced2Tree_V2(Class *pA, Class *pB)
{
    int nAIndex = pA->GetClassIndex();
    int nBIndex = pB->GetClassIndex();

    while (nAIndex >= nBIndex)
    {
        if (nAIndex == nBIndex)
        {
            return true;
        }
        nAIndex = nAIndex >> 1;
    }
    return false;
}
```

This has just reduced our worst-case scenario drastically. In the case where we are testing a list of Humans to see whether they are Mages, we can halt immediately if they are Warriors, because the index of Warrior (4) is less than the index for Mage (5). Even in the case where we were searching for Warriors, we would only need to do one right shift before we could halt the function and return false.

Eliminating the Tree Traversal

The class indices have an additional property that allows us to remove the while loop from our function. Here is the child function for our nodes in our class tree:

```
int childIndex(int nIndex, bool bRight)
{
    if (bRight)
        return (nIndex << 1) + 1;
    else
        return (nIndex << 1);
}
```

Any child of Node A has an index equal to the index Node A left-shifted a number of times plus a number defining the child's position in the sub-tree. The usefulness of this observation becomes much more apparent if we write out the indices in binary (see Figure 4.1.3).

This observation allows us to make the following rule:

If Class A is a child of Class B, then the leftmost N bits of B will match A where N is the highest bit set in A.

This works because we started our class hierarchy at Index 1, so we know that all indices are 1 followed by an arbitrary number of bits.

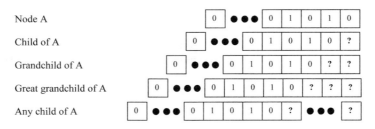

Figure 4.1.3   Binary representation of indices of a node and its children.

Using this rule we can write our IsA function one more time without the use of the `while` loop. (Non-constant bit-shift operators are emulated on the PS3, but this is implemented in microcode, so it is still much faster than a `while` loop.)

```
bool IsA_Balanced2Tree_V3(Class *pA, Class *pB)
{
    int nAIndex = pA->GetClassIndex();
    int nBIndex = pB->GetClassIndex();

    if (nAIndex <= nBIndex)
        return nAIndex == nBIndex;

    nAIndex = nAIndex >>
            (BSR(nAIndex) - BSR(nBIndex));

    return nAIndex == nBIndex;
}
```

The BSR function in our case is a wrapper for an inline assembly function that uses the BSR assembly instruction (`BitScanReverse`). This instruction returns the index of the leftmost set bit/most significant bit, which is exactly what we need for this algorithm. If a platform does not have the BSR assembly instruction, we can easily pre-calculate this value and store it in the `Class` object along with the array index (`GetArrayIndexMSB()`). This was our first implementation of the function before we found out about the BSR instruction.

Finally, we can take advantage of one further property of the right-shift operator. If the amount to shift is negative, then the result is 0. And since we start our class hierarchy with an index of 1, no class will match 0. This leads to our final implementation of Fast-Isa.

```
bool FastIsA(Class *pA, Class *pB)
{
    int nAIndex = pA->GetClassIndex();
    int nBIndex = pB->GetClassIndex();

    return nBIndex ==
        (nAIndex >> (BSR(nAIndex) - BSR(nBIndex)));
}
```

Building a Balanced Tree

All of the previous work has been built upon the notion that our class hierarchy is a perfectly balanced binary tree. In practice, this is rarely the case. Luckily, what we want out of the IsA function isn't any notion of depth between nodes, but only if they are in fact ancestors. Because of this, there is no reason why we cannot insert phantom classes to balance our tree. Figure 4.1.4 displays an example of the transformation from an unbalanced to a balanced hierarchy.

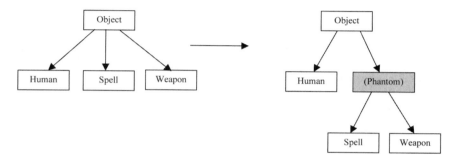

Figure 4.1.4   Converting a three-child node into a binary hierarchy.

In the case of these two class trees, every possible IsA relationship is maintained.

In any situation where we have more than two direct children of a class, we can insert a number of phantom class nodes between the parent and the children to ensure that the IsA tree is a balanced binary tree.

It is important to realize that while we are using the notion of a heap to generate the indices, we are not actually storing anything in this structure. It is purely virtual, so adding large numbers of phantom nodes to balance the tree does nothing except use up our index space. For most games, a 32-bit DWORD will contain more than enough space for the class hierarchy.

The simplest implementation for building the class tree is the following algorithm. I recommend implementing this and determining whether you are close to running out of index space before moving to a more complicated algorithm.

```
void BuildTree(Class *pA)
{
    int nCurrentClassIndex = pA->GetClassIndex();
    int nNumChildClasses = pA->GetNumberOfChildClasses();
    int nNumLevels = BSR(nNumChildClasses) + 1;
    int nChildIndexStart =
            nCurrentClassIndex << nNumLevels;
    for (int i = 0; i < nNumChildClasses; ++i)
    {
```

```
        Class *pChild = pA->GetChildClass(i);
        pChild->SetClassIndex(nChildIndexStart + i);
        BuildTree(pChild);
    }
}
```

The heart of implementing a more complicated class tree construction algorithm is realizing that in most cases we have a fair amount of play in how we actually lay out the phantom nodes. Take the four-child case (see Figure 4.1.5).

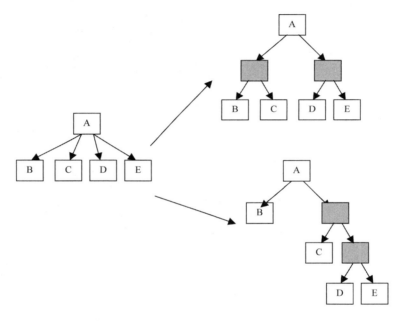

Figure 4.1.5   Alternate ways of decomposing a four-child node into a binary hierarchy.

Both of these class trees have the exact same IsA relationship, so to the Fast-IsA algorithm there is no distinction. If our class tree was very complex (or deep), we could balance the tree based on the number of subclasses or the maximum depth of any subclass of a class. This leads to an algorithm similar to Huffman encoding to optimize the class tree such that the maximum depth of any leaf is minimized. With more than 3,700 script classes in *This Is Vegas*, we never encountered a problem with our hierarchy depth.

If your class tree is greater than 32 levels deep, there is no reason why you cannot simply change your class index from a DWORD to a QWORD. The memory costs are minimal (since we only pay per class and not per instance), and 64-bit processors will be able to perform these operations at the same speed.

Conclusion

Moving to the Fast-IsA algorithm had a large impact on the performance of our game for the cost of only one additional DWORD per class. In our case, it was a performance improvement of more than one percent for the entire game and far greater in specific portions of the code. Given how simple the implementation is and how little it costs, this was an easy optimization win for us. We also found the Fast-IsA function to impact performance in our pipeline's baking process, which uses a large number of IsA checks.

4.2

Registered Variables

Peter Dalton, Smart Bomb Interactive
pdalton@madprog.com

Inter-system communication is a critical consideration in a game engine, often dictating the broad architecture of the code base. In practice, sacrifices are often made to allow one system to know about the internal workings of another in order to accommodate better communication. Although sometimes this can be appropriate, it often results in a loss of modularity. These compromised systems lose their "black box" characteristics and become harder to maintain and replace. This gem will present a solution to this problem by demonstrating a technique for linking up shared variables across disparate systems. This allows systems to define a set of inputs or control variables that can be seamlessly linked to variables in other systems.

It is important to recognize that this is not a messaging system, nor is it meant to replace one. Rather, it is a system that allows a programmer to control communication across various systems without requiring blind casts, global variables, or a flat class hierarchy. This technique allows for basic variable types, such as integers and floats, as well as complex data types, such as arrays, classes, and other user-defined types. This technique has been successfully utilized to facilitate the necessary communication required to control animation systems, user interface parameters, display shader parameters, and various other systems where variable manipulation is required.

Getting Started

The basic idea is to create a wrapper for a variable and then allow these wrapped variables to be linked together. The code that is dependent upon the variables can be implemented without any special considerations. Rather than just accessing the value that has been wrapped, the registered variable will walk the chain of linked variables and provide access to the appropriate variable. When building registered variables, there are several key goals to keep in mind.

- **Keep the registered variable seamless.** To make a registered variable truly useful, it needs to be easy to work with. The goal is to make it transparent to the programmer whether they are using a regular integer or our newly created integer registered variable. Operator overloading will be the key here.

- **Allow one registered variable to be linked to another.** We are going to allow registered variables to set redirectors, or in other words, allow registered variables to be chained together.
- **Tracking of a "dirty state."** To enhance the usefulness of a registered variable, we will include a dirty state in the variable. This provides users with knowledge of when the variable has actually changed, which is useful for run-time optimizations.
- **Custom run-time type information.** This will become necessary when we start registering variables together. It allows us to confidently cast to a specific type without the need for blind casts.
- **Provide a way to link registered variables directly.** We will provide an initial, explicit method for linking variables together. This method is important when dealing with specific situations where the control variables are well defined.
- **Provide a way to link registered variables indirectly.** As our systems grow in complexity, we want to allow for variables to be generically linked together without either system knowing the internal details of the other. This indirect method will become the key to dealing with complex situations where all control variables are not well defined or are ambiguous.

Assumptions

The code we will present is taken from a commercial Xbox 360 engine. It utilizes several routines and data structures provided by the base engine that are beyond the scope of this gem. These dependencies are minimal; however, we need to explicitly mention them in order to avoid confusion. A basic implementation of these data structures has been included on the accompanying CD-ROM.

TArrays

The TArray class is a templated array holder. It is used to hold links to other registered variables.

FNames

This class implements a string token system. It is a holder for all of the strings that exist within the game engine. Each string is assigned a unique identifier by which it can then be referenced and compared against other FNames with a constant cost of $O(1)$. This functionality is the key to implementing the required run-time type information and the means by which registered variables are given unique names for linking.

The Base Class: RegisteredVar

The base class from which all registered variables will be derived is the RegisteredVar class. This class provides all of the support for linking registered variables together and tracking the dirty state. Here only key portions of the RegisteredVar class are shown; a complete implementation can be found on the accompanying CD-ROM.

```
class RegisteredVar
{
public:
    // Provides IsA<>() and GetClassType() routines, described later.
    DECLARE_BASEREGISTERED_VARIABLE( RegisteredVar );

    RegisteredVar() : m_bDirty(false), m_pRedirector(null) {}
    virtual ~RegisteredVar()
    {
        if (m_pRedirector)
            m_pRedirector->m_References.RemoveItem( this );
        while (m_References.Num())
            m_References[0]->SetRedirector( null, false );
    }
    void SetRedirector( RegisteredVar* InRedir )
    {
        if (InRedir!=this && (!InRedir || (InRedir->IsA( GetClassType() )
            && !InRedir->IsRegistered( this ))))
        {
            if (m_pRedirector)
                m_pRedirector->m_References.RemoveItem( this );
            m_pRedirector = InRedir;
            if (m_pRedirector)
                m_pRedirector->m_References.AddItem( this );
        }
    }
    void SetDirty( bool InDirty, bool InRecurse=false );
    bool IsDirty() const;
    void SetFName( FName InName ) { m_Name = InName; }
    FName GetFName() const { return m_Name; }
protected:
    template<class T> T* GetBaseVariable() const
    {
        return m_pRedirector ?
            m_pRedirector->GetBaseVariable<T>() : (T*)this;
    }
    FName m_Name;
    bool m_bDirty;
    RegisteredVar* m_pRedirector;
    TArray<RegisteredVar*> m_References;
};
```

There are two key elements to getting this class correct. The first is preventing dangling pointers in the destructor. The important consideration here is that since we are going to be linking up registered variables blindly between systems, we do not want to end up pointing to a registered variable that has been deleted. This scenario would result in dangling pointers to invalid memory addresses and severe headaches. To prevent this, we create a link back to the referencing registered variable so that we can clean it up when the referenced registered variable is deleted. This would normally create a doubly linked list; however, in our case it is common for multiple registered variables to redirect to a single registered variable, thus creating the need for an array of pointers as illustrated in Figure 4.2.1.

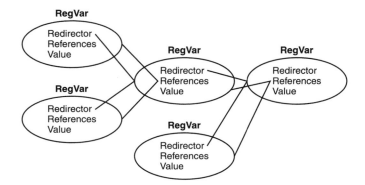

Figure 4.2.1   This diagram illustrates how registered variables will be linked together and how we will also be tracking referencing registered variables to avoid dangling pointers.

The second key to keep in mind is that anytime you access a registered variable, you need to ask yourself an important question: Should I be working with "this" copy of the registered variable or should I forward the request to the redirected registered variable? If you decide that the correct answer is to work on the redirected registered variable, the GetBaseVariable() routine will retrieve the base registered variable that should be used.

Single Variable Values versus Array Variable Values

The next step is to divide all the variables into two distinct classifications: single value types and arrays. The first classification, single value types, encompasses integers, floats, user-defined types, and so on and will be the focus of the examples provided. The second, array types, will encompass arrays of integers, floats, user-defined types, and so on. The implementation of array types is very similar to single values types with just a few minor alterations. The implementation of array types has been provided on the accompanying CD-ROM. Having made this distinction, we will now create a templated base class that provides 99 percent of the functionality required by any variable type.

```
template<class T, class RegVar>
class RegisteredVarType : public RegisteredVar
{
public:
    RegisteredVarType();

    T Get() { return GetBaseVariable<RegVar>()->m_Value; }
    const T& Get() const { return GetBaseVariable<RegVar>()->m_Value; }
    void Set( const T& InV )
    { GetBaseVariable<RegVar>()->SetDirectly( InV ); }
```

```
        operator T() const { return GetBaseVariable<RegVar>()->m_Value; }
        operator T&() { return GetBaseVariable<RegVar>()->m_Value; }

        void operator=( const RegVar& InV ) { Set( InV.Get() ); }

        // Implement comparison operators >,<,>=,<=,==,!=, see CD-ROM.
        bool operator>( const T& InV ) { return Get() > InV; }

        // Implement mathematic operators /,*,+,-, see CD-ROM.
        T operator/( const T& InV ) const { return Get() / InV; }

        // Implement assignment operators /=,*=,+=,-=, see CD-ROM.
        RegVar& operator/=( const T& InV )
        { Set( Get() / InV ); return *(RegVar*)this; }
    protected:
        void SetDirectly( const T& InValue )
        {
            if (m_Value != InValue)
            {
                m_Value = InValue;
                SetDirty( true );
            }
            for (int ii = 0; ii < m_Parents.Num(); ++ii)
                ((RegVar*)m_References[ii])->SetDirectly( InValue );
        }
        T m_Value;
};
```

Examining the code should illustrate the emphasis placed on providing the appropriate overloaded operators to allow the programmer to seamlessly use registered variables. The programmer should not have to change the code whether they are using a standard variable or a registered variable. This ensures that the registered variable is used correctly and seamlessly. It also makes it easy to add and remove registered variables from a system since only the variable definition and linking code needs to be updated.

Another important consideration is the SetDirectly() routine used by the Set() method. The SetDirectly() routine first determines whether the value is actually different than the current value and sets the dirty flag if appropriate. This dirty flag allows the owner of the variable to effectively track when the state of the variable has truly changed, thus allowing for run-time optimizations.

A common optimization, when dealing with shader parameter blocks within DirectX, is to prevent the blocks from being invalidated and rebuilt unless absolutely necessary. Thus, if you have a variable controlling the state of a shader, you will want to make sure that the variable has actually changed before processing it. You should also notice that there is no automatic means by which the dirty flag is cleared. To clear the flag, the owner of the variable will need to explicitly call the SetDirty(false) routine when the owner is done dealing with the change. Since the dirty flag is stored in each variable, the owner of the variable can deal with the flag in its own way. In the case of a variable controlling a shader parameter, we would not want to handle the variable change and rebuild the state block until the material is required by the renderer.

However, another variable might also be linked to this state and want to handle the change immediately. It is also safe for the owner to choose to ignore the dirty flag if it isn't required.

The SetDirectly() routine also has the task of copying the value to the entire chain of linked registered variables. This feature is important to retain the most recent value in the event that a registered variable clears its redirector either explicitly or if the redirector is deleted. If the value was not copied, we would see a pop from the old value to whatever value is currently stored. While this might not be a critical issue, it can cause undesired behavior, as the variable might appear un-initialized. Copying the value is also useful when debugging, allowing for the value to be easily shown in the watch window without digging through a list of linked variables.

Type-Specific Registered Variable

At this point we have built all the base classes required, and creating registered variables is now straightforward.

```
class RegisteredVarBOOL
    : public RegisteredVarType<bool, RegisteredVarBOOL>
{
DECLARE_REGISTERED_VARIABLE( RegisteredVarBOOL, RegisteredVarType );
    RegisteredVarBOOL& operator=( const bool& InValue )
    { Set( InValue ); return *this; }
};

class RegisteredVarFLOAT
    : public RegisteredVarType<float, RegisteredVarFLOAT>
{
DECLARE_REGISTERED_VARIABLE(RegisteredVarFLOAT, RegisteredVarType );
    RegisteredVarFLOAT & operator=( const float& InValue )
    { Set( InValue ); return *this; }
};
```

The listings above add support for both the standard Boolean and float types. Implementing additional types is as simple as duplicating the provided code and updating the names and types appropriately. Note that the operator=() was not specified within the templated base class RegisteredVarType in order to resolve conflicts when using the Visual Studio 2008 C++ compiler.

Setting a Registered Variable Directly

We'll now look at a simple example to illustrate what registered variables can do. We have a weapon class attached to a vehicle class, and the vehicle needs to tell the weapon when to fire. If we create a Boolean registered variable within the vehicle and link it to the weapon, we can then just manipulate the variable within the vehicle and control the state of the weapon. Also, if we have multiple components that need to know about the weapon firing, such as AI logic, user interfaces, or game code, we now only have one variable that needs to be updated to keep everyone in sync. In contrast, without using registered variables we would need to create a `Fire()` function within the weapon and call it to start and stop firing. We would also need to manually notify all other systems that the weapon is firing. The registered variable approach has the advantage that once the variables are correctly registered, it is much easier to control communication.

```
class Weapon
{
    void SetFireRegVar( RegisteredVar* InVar )
    {
        m_Fire.SetRedirector( InVar );
    }
    void HeartBeat( float InDeltaTime )
    {
        if (m_Fire) FireWeapon();
    }
    RegisteredVarBOOL m_Fire;
};
class Vehicle
{
    void Initialize()
    {
        m_MyWeapon.SetFireRegVar( &m_FireWeapon );
    }
    void HeartBeat( float InDeltaTime )
    {
        m_FireWeapon = DoWeWantToFire();
    }
    bool DoWeWantToFire();
    RegisteredVarBOOL m_FireWeapon;
    Weapon m_MyWeapon;
};
```

IsA Functionality

The `DECLARE_REGISTERED_VARIABLE` macro requires further explanation to assist in understanding the implementation. The purpose of this macro is to provide type information for the registered variable. It ensures that we do not link two registered variables together that are not of the same basic type. It also allows us to determine the type of register variable that we have given only a pointer to the base class `RegisteredVar`.

```
#define DECLARE_REGISTERED_VARIABLE( InClass, InBaseClass )         \
  protected:                                                        \
      typedef InClass ThisClass;                                    \
      typedef InBaseClass Super;                                    \
  public:                                                           \
      virtual FName GetSuperClassType( FName InComponentType ) const \
      {                                                             \
          FName SuperType = NAME_None;                              \
          if (InClass::StaticGetClassType() == InComponentType)     \
              SuperType = Super::StaticGetClassType();              \
```

```
            else if (InComponentType != NAME_None)                       \
                SuperType = Super::GetSuperClassType( InComponentType ); \
            return SuperType == InComponentType ? NAME_None : SuperType; \
    }                                                                    \
    virtual FName GetClassType() const                                   \
    {                                                                    \
        return InClass::StaticGetClassType();                            \
    }                                                                    \
    static FName StaticGetClassType()                                    \
    {                                                                    \
        static FName TypeName = FName( STRING( InClass ) );              \
        return TypeName;                                                 \
    }
#define DECLARE_BASEREGISTERED_VARIABLE( InClass )                       \
    DECLARE_REGISTERED_VARIABLE( InClass, InClass )                      \
    template<class T> bool IsA() const                                   \
    {                                                                    \
         return IsA( T::StaticGetClassType() );                          \
    }                                                                    \
    bool IsA( const FName& InTypeName ) const                            \
    {                                                                    \
        for (FName Type = GetClassType(); Type != NAME_None;             \
            Type = GetSuperClassType( Type ))                            \
        {                                                                \
            if (Type == InTypeName)                                      \
                return true;                                             \
        }                                                                \
        return false;                                                    \
    }
```

While this code is being utilized here to provide IsA functionality for registered variables, it is generic in nature and can be used to provide RTTI functionality to any class or structure. The code is written in the form of a macro to prevent the code from being duplicated due to it being required at every level of the inheritance chain. An important consideration is to recognize that this implementation does not support multiple inheritance but could be extended to do so.

Setting a Registered Variable Indirectly

Now that we have basic RTTI information, we can safely link registered variables together without knowing the internals of other systems. Let's examine another example.

Suppose we have a material used for rendering that has a parameter we can adjust to change its damage state. The damage state is defined within the material and used to determine how the material is rendered. In this example we would like to create a generic system in which a high-level object can register a variable with another object and have it correctly link to a control variable. We want a vehicle class to provide a variable to control the damage state of the material, and then the vehicle can drive the material's control variable by simply modifying its own variable. In this example, adding a function or parameter to the Material class would not be desirable because it would lead to bloat and would not be applicable to all materials.

```
class RegisterVariableHolder
{
    virtual void RegisterVariable( RegisterVar& InVar ) {}
};
class BaseClass : public RegisteredVariableHolder
{
    virtual void RegisterVariables(RegisterVariableHolder& InHolder) {}
};
class Material : public BaseClass
{};
class DamageStateMaterial : public Material
{
    void Initialize()
    {
        m_DamageState.SetFName( "DamageState" );
    }
    virtual void RegisterVariable( RegisteredVar& InVar )
    {
        if (InVar.IsA<RegisteredVarFLOAT>() &&
            InVar.GetFName() == m_Trans.GetFName())
        {
            m_DamageState.SetRedirector( &InVar );
        }
    }
    RegisteredVarFLOAT m_DamageState;
};
class Vehicle : public BaseClass
{
    void Initialize()
    {
        m_VehicleDamageState.SetFName( "DamageState" );
        m_Fire.SetFName( "Fire" );
        RegisterVariables( *m_pMaterial );
    }
    virtual void RegisterVariables( RegisterVariableHolder& InHolder )
    {
        InHolder.RegisterVariable( m_VehicleDamageState );
        InHolder.RegisterVariable( m_Fire );
    }
    RegisteredVarFLOAT m_VehicleDamageState;
    RegisteredVarBOOL m_Fire;
    Material* m_pMaterial;
};
```

Now, whenever the vehicle changes `m_VehicleDamageState`, the material class's `m_DamageState` variable will be automatically updated without the material being required to provide accessor routines or the vehicle knowing the type of material it has been assigned. The vehicle can also ignore the material since the only thing it needs to do is update its own registered variable. While the example is fairly simple, the principle can be applied to solve many more problems.

Conclusion

Within our game engine we have found registered variables to be an essential part of inter-system communication because they abstract the communication layer and minimize system dependencies. Registered variables are utilized to control the state of animation flow systems, expose data to user interfaces, such as hit points and ammo counts, and control material parameters, such as damage states and special rendering stages. We provide tools within the game's editor to allow artists and level designers to specify exactly which registered variables should be linked together within the game. Systems have been designed to allow users to dynamically create new registered variables within the game editor and link them to any other appropriate registered variable. For us, this has opened the door for content builders to access any set of data within the game engine and gives them the necessary controls to manipulate gameplay.

We hope that you will have fun experimenting with the concept of registered variables and that you will find them useful in improving your code. You will find an implementation of the techniques presented on the CD-ROM.

4.3

Efficient and Scalable Multi-Core Programming

Jean-François Dubé, Ubisoft Montreal
jfdube75@gmail.com

Nowadays, multi-core computers (and game consoles such as the Microsoft Xbox 360 and Sony PlayStation 3) are very common. Programmers are faced with the challenges of writing multi-threaded code: data sharing, synchronization, deadlocks, efficiency, and scalability. Adding multi-threading to an existing game engine is an enormous effort and might give an initial speed gain, but will it run twice as fast if you double the number of cores? What if you run it on a 16+ cores system, such as Intel's Larrabee architecture? Will it be able to run on platforms with co-processors, such as Sony's PlayStation 3?

In this gem, we'll see how to write efficient and scalable multi-threaded code. The first section will deal with the "efficiency" part of the problem, while the second part will deal with the "scalability" part.

Efficient Multi-Threaded Programming

Multi-threaded programming introduces a variety of issues the programmer must be aware of in order to produce code that performs the required operations correctly. Additionally, certain operations can lead to additional overheads in a multi-threaded program. In this section we'll look at high-performance methods for resolving these issues.

Shared Data

The main problem with multi-threaded programming is concurrent access to the same memory locations. Consider this simple example:

```
uint32 IncrementCount()
{
    static uint32 Count=0;
    return Count++;
}
```

This is commonly translated into three operations: a load, an addition, and a store. Now, if two threads execute this function slightly at the same time, what will happen? Here's an example:

```
Thread 1 read Count and store it into register R1
Thread 1 increment R1
Thread 2 read Count and store it into register R1
Thread 2 increment R1
Thread 1 store the value of R1 into Count
Thread 2 store the value of R1 into Count
```

If Count was originally 5 before this sequence of events, what will be the result afterward? While the expected value is 7, the resulting value would be 6, because each thread has a copy of Count in its register R1 before it was actually updated to memory. This example is very simple, but with more complex interactions this could lead to data corruption or invalid object states. This can be fixed by using atomic operations or by using synchronization primitives.

Atomic Operations

Atomic operations are special instructions that perform operations on a memory location in an atomic manner; that is, when executed by more than one core on the same memory location, it is guaranteed to be done atomically. For example, the InterlockedIncrement function could be used in the previous example to make it thread-safe and lock-free.

A very useful atomic operation is the Compare And Swap (CAS) function, implemented as InterlockedCompareExchange on Windows. Essentially, it compares a value with another and exchanges it with a third value based on the outcome of the comparison, atomically. It then returns the original value before the swap. Here's how it can be represented in pseudocode:

```
uint32 CAS(uint32* Ptr, uint32 Value, uint32 Comperand)
{
    if(*Ptr == Comperand)
    {
        *Ptr = Value;
        return Comperand;
    }
    return *Ptr;
}
```

This atomic operation is very powerful when used correctly and can be used to perform almost any type of operation atomically. Here's an example of its usage:

```
uint32 AtomicAND(volatile uint32* Value, uint32 Op)
{
    while(1)
    {
        uint32 CurValue = *Value;
        uint32 NewValue = (CurValue & Op);
```

```
            if(CAS(Value, NewValue, CurValue) == CurValue)
            {
                return NewValue;
            }
        }
    }
```

In this example, we read the current value and try to exchange it with the new value. If the result of the CAS returns the old value, we know that it wasn't changed during the operation and that the operation succeeded. (It was swapped with the new value.) On the other hand, if the result is not equal to the old value, we must retry, since it was changed by another thread during the operation. This is the basic operation on which almost all lock-free algorithms are based.

Synchronization Primitives

Sometimes, atomic operations are not enough, and we need to be able to ensure that only a single thread is executing a certain piece of code. The most common synchronization primitives are mutexes, semaphores, and critical sections. Although in essence they all do the same thing—prevent execution of code from multiple threads—their performance varies significantly. They are kernel objects, which means that the operating system is aware when they are locked. Therefore, they will generate a costly context switch if already locked by another thread. On the other hand, most operating systems will make sure the thread that has a critical section locked will not be preempted by another thread while it holds the lock. So using those primitives depends on a lot of factors: the time span of the lock, the frequency of locking, and so on.

When locking is required very frequently and for a very low amount of time, we want to avoid the overhead from operating system process rescheduling or context switching. This can be achieved by using a spin lock. A spin lock is simply a lock that will actively wait for a resource to be freed, as seen in this simplified implementation:

```
while(CAS(&Lock, 1, 0)) {}
```

What it does is simple: It uses the CAS function to try to gain access to the lock variable. When the function returns 0, it means we acquired the lock. Releasing the lock is simply assigning 0 to the Lock variable.

A real implementation of a spin lock usually should contain another waiting loop that doesn't use atomic functions to reduce inter-CPU bus traffic. Also, on some architectures, memory barriers are required to make sure that the state of the Lock variable is not reordered in some ways, as seen in the next section. The complete implementation is available on the CD.

On architectures that don't change a thread's affinity (in other words, that don't reschedule threads on different processors, such as Xbox 360), running several threads on the same core competing for a shared resource using a spin lock is a very bad idea.

If the lock is held by a thread when it gets interrupted by the operating system scheduler, other threads will be left spinning trying to acquire the lock, while the thread holding it is not making progress toward releasing it. This results in worse performance than using a critical section, as shown in Figures 4.3.1 and 4.3.2.

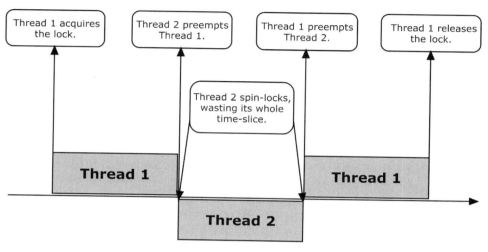

Figure 4.3.1   Wasting cycles when using spin locks for a long time.

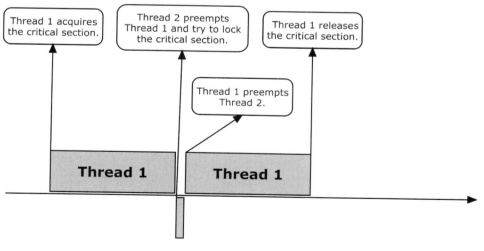

Figure 4.3.2   Efficient locking when using critical sections.

Memory Ordering

Memory can be read and written in a different order than written in your code for two main reasons: compiler optimizations and hardware CPU reordering. The latter differs a lot depending on the hardware, so knowing your architecture is important. See [McKenney07] for a detailed look at this problem.

Consider the following pieces of code running simultaneously:

Thread 1	**Thread 2**
`GlobalValue = 50;`	`while(!ValueIsReady) {}`
`ValueIsReady = true;`	`LocalValue = GlobalValue;`

While this looks completely fine and will almost always work when running on a single core depending on the compiler optimizations, it will probably fail when running on different cores. Why? First, the compiler will most likely optimize the `while` loop and keep `ValueIsReady` in a register; therefore, declaring it as volatile should fix the problem on most compilers. Second, due to out-of-order memory accesses, `ValueIsReady` might get written first; therefore, Thread 2 can read `GlobalValue` before it is actually written by Thread 1. Debugging this kind of bug without knowing that memory reordering exists can be long and painful.

Three types of memory barriers exist: read, write, and full barriers. A read memory barrier forces reads from memory to complete, while a write memory barrier forces writes from memory to complete, so other threads can access the memory safely. A full memory barrier is simply forcing both reads and writes to complete. Some compilers will also correctly handle reads and writes of volatile variables by treating them as memory barriers (Visual Studio 2005 for instance, as described in [MSDN]). Also, some of the Interlocked functions come with the Acquire and Release semantics, which behave like read and write barriers, respectfully.

The previous example can be solved by using a write memory barrier before setting `ValueIsReady` to ensure that the write to `GlobalValue` actually gets written before `ValueIsReady`, ensuring that other threads will see the new `GlobalValue` before `ValueIsReady` is written.

False Sharing

Most multi-core architectures have a per-core cache, which is generally organized as an array of memory blocks, each with a power of two size (128 bytes, for example), called *cache lines*. When a core performs a memory access, the whole line is copied into the cache to hide the memory latency and maximize speed. False sharing occurs when two cores operate on different data that resides in the same cache line. In order to keep memory coherency, the system has to transfer the whole cache line across the bus for every write, wasting bandwidth and memory cycles. The solution to this problem is to make sure that the data is structured in a way that avoids this problem.

Memory Allocator Contention

Memory allocators can rapidly become a bottleneck in multi-threaded applications. Standard memory allocator implementations provided in the C run time (malloc/free) or even optimized and widely used allocators, such as Doug Lea's dlmalloc [Lea00], aren't designed to be used concurrently; they need a global lock to protect all calls, which inherently leads to false sharing. The design of a multi-processor's optimized memory allocator is beyond the scope of this gem, but a good comparison of available multi-processor allocators can be found in [Intel07].

Idle Thread State

When a thread is idle, it is important that it doesn't waste CPU cycles. Here's some code we often see from a person writing multi-threaded code for the first time:

```
while(!HasWork())
{
    Sleep(0);
}
```

The Sleep(0) will make the thread give up the remainder of its time slice for other threads, which is fine. But, when it gets rescheduled, it will loop back, unnecessarily wasting CPU time (and multiple context switches) until it has work to do. A better solution is to put the thread in sleep mode, waiting for an event. This is achieved by using the CreateEvent and WaitForSingleObject functions. Waiting for an event essentially tells the operating system scheduler that the thread is waiting and shouldn't get any CPU time until the event is triggered.

Thread Local Storage

It is possible to declare per-thread global variables using Thread Local Storage (TLS). The declaration differs from compiler to compiler, but here's how it works under Visual Studio:

```
__declspec(thread) int GlobalVar;
```

Each thread now has its own GlobalVar variable copy. This can be especially useful for per-thread debugging information (such as the thread name, its profiling stats, and so on) or for custom memory allocators that can operate on a per-thread basis, effectively removing the need for locking.

Lock-Free Algorithms

A good introduction to such things is discussed in detail in [Jones05] and [Herlihy08]. Essentially, these algorithms are pieces of code that can be executed by multiple threads without locking. This can lead to enormous speed gain for some algorithms, such as memory allocators and data containers. For example, a lock-free queue could need to be safe when multiple threads push data into it, while multiple threads also pop data at the same time. This is normally implemented using CAS functions. A complete implementation is available on the CD.

Scalable Multi-Threaded Programming

The most common way to rapidly thread an existing application is to take large and independent parts of the code and run them in their own thread (for example, rendering or artificial intelligence). While this leads to an immediate speed gain and lots of synchronization problems, it is not scalable. For example, if we run an application using three threads on an eight-core system, then five cores will sit idle. On the other hand, if the application is designed from the start to use small and independent tasks, then perfect scalability can be achieved. To accomplish this, several options already exist, such as the Cilk language [CILK], which is a multi-threaded parallel programming language based on ANSI C, or Intel's Threading Building Blocks [TBB]. An implementation of a simple task scheduler is presented next.

Task Scheduler Requirements

The required properties of our scheduler are:

1. Handle task dependencies.
2. Keep worker threads' idle time at a minimum.
3. Keep CPU usage low for internal task scheduling.
4. Have extensibility to allow executing tasks remotely and on co-processors.

The scheduler is lock-free, which means that it will never block the worker threads or the threads that push tasks to it. This is achieved by using fixed-size lock-free queues and a custom spin lock and by never allocating memory for its internal execution.

Tasks

A task is the base unit of the scheduler; this is what gets scheduled and executed. In order to achieve good performance and scalability, the tasks need to be small and independent. The (simplified) interface looks like this:

```
class Task
{
    volatile sint* ExecCounter;
    volatile sint SyncCounter;
public:
    virtual void Execute()=0;
    virtual sint GetDependencies(Task**& Deps);
    virtual void OnExecuted() {}
}
```

A task needs to implement the Execute function, which is what gets called when it is ready to be executed (in other words, no more dependencies).

To expose dependencies to the scheduler, the GetDependencies() function can be overloaded to return the addresses and the number of dependent tasks. A base implementation that returns no dependencies is implemented by default.

A task is considered as fully executed when its Execute function has been called and when its internal SyncCounter becomes zero. The ExecCounter is an optional counter that gets atomically decremented when the Execute function is called. For tasks that spawn sub-tasks, setting the sub-task's ExecCounter pointer to the parent's SyncCounter ensures that their OnExecuted functions will only be called when all sub-tasks have been executed.

Worker Threads

The scheduler automatically creates one worker thread per logical core. Figure 4.3.3 illustrates how the worker threads behave: Each worker thread is initially pushed in a lock-free queue of idle threads and waits for a wakeup event. When a new task is assigned to a worker thread by the scheduler, it wakes up and executes the task. Once the task is done, the worker thread does several things. First, it tries to execute a scheduling slice (which will be explained in the next section) by checking whether the scheduler lock is already acquired by another thread. Then, it tries to pop a waiting task from the scheduler. If a task is available, it executes it, and the cycle restarts. On the other hand, if no tasks are available, it pushes itself in the lock-free queue of idle threads and waits for the wakeup event again.

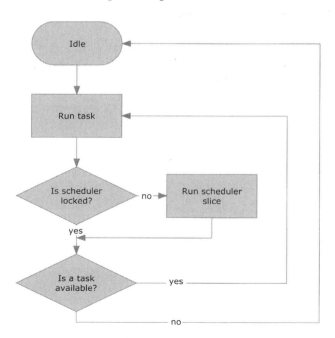

Figure 4.3.3 Worker thread logic.

Scheduler

The scheduler is responsible for assigning tasks to the worker threads and performing tidying of its internal task queues. To schedule a task, any thread simply needs to call a function that will push the task pointer in the lock-free queue of unscheduled tasks. This triggers a scheduling slice, which is explained next.

Scheduling Slice

At this point, pending tasks are simply queued in a lock-free queue, waiting to be scheduled by the scheduler. This is done in the scheduling slice, which does the following, as described in Figure 4.3.4:

1. Register pending tasks.
2. Schedule ready tasks.
3. Delete executed tasks.

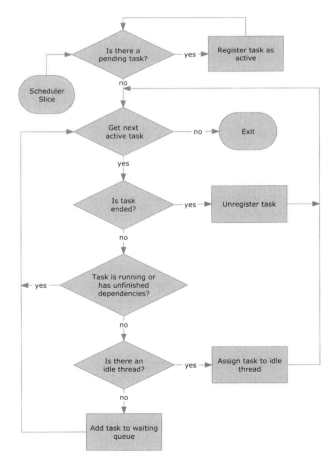

Figure 4.3.4   Scheduler slice logic.

Registering Pending Tasks

During this phase, the scheduler pops the pending tasks and registers them internally. Then, it needs to handle dependencies. If a task is dependent on previously scheduled tasks, it goes through the dependencies and checks to see whether they have been executed. If that's the case, the task is ready to execute and is marked as ready. Otherwise, the task is kept as pending until the next scheduling slice.

Scheduling Ready Tasks

The second phase of the scheduling slice is to assign tasks that are ready to be executed to worker threads. The scheduler first tries to pop an idle thread from a lock-free queue of idle threads. If it succeeds, the task is directly assigned to that thread, and the thread waiting event is signaled. If all threads are working, the task is queued in the lock-free queue of waiting tasks. The scheduler then repeats the process until there are no more tasks to assign.

Deleting Executed Tasks

The last phase of the scheduling slice handles the tasks that are considered fully executed by calling the OnExecuted function on them and by deleting them if they are marked as auto-destroy; some tasks may need to be manually deleted by their owner, as they might contain results, and so on.

Future Work

Since tasks are usually independent from each other, the scheduler can be extended to support execution of tasks on remote computers or on architectures with co-processors. To achieve this, each task would have a way to package all the data it needs to execute. Then, the scheduler would dispatch the task to other computers or co-processors though a simple protocol. Compilation of the Execute function might be required to target the co-processor's architecture. When a completed task message arrives, the task would then receive and unpackage the resulting data. This could be used as a distributed system (such as static lighting/normal map computations, distribution of the load of a game server to clients, and so on) or as a way to distribute work on the PlayStation 3 SPUs automatically.

Optimizations

The single task queue could become a bottleneck on systems with a large number of cores or ones that have no shared cache between all cores. Here, using per-worker thread task queues along with task stealing could prove advantageous. Furthermore, the scheduling could be made more cache friendly through a policy of inserting newly created tasks into the front of the worker thread's queue that generated the task, as these are likely to be consuming the data generated by the task that created them. All of these optimizations depend on the target architecture details.

Conclusion

As we have just seen, the scheduler is completely lock-free; its internal CPU usage is kept to a minimum, the worker threads are either executing a task or waiting for one, and most of all, it scales with the number of cores. The complete source code on the CD comes with several sample tasks that have been tested on a Intel Core 2 Quad CPU running at 2.83 GHz, with the following results (also see Figure 4.3.5):

	Fibonacci Sequence	**Perlin Noise**	**QuickSort**
1 thread	1.05ms	9.06s	9.30s
2 threads	0.29ms	4.55s	4.84s
3 threads	0.22ms	3.03s	3.44s
4 threads	0.15ms	2.29s	2.74s
5 threads	0.14ms	2.21s	2.81s
6 threads	0.12ms	2.31s	2.86s

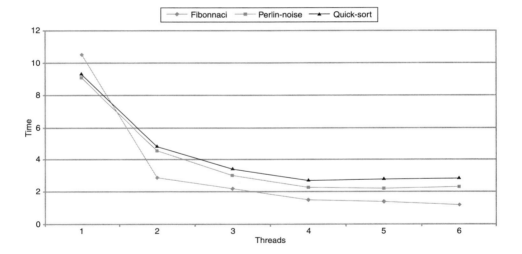

Figure 4.3.5 Test results.

The Fibonacci sequence test has been created to see how dependencies are handled. The Perlin noise test, on the other hand, has been implemented to see how performance and scalability can be achieved; the test consists of computing a 2048×2048 Perlin noise grayscale image with 16 octaves. The QuickSort test consists of sorting 65 million random integers. As we can see, the expected scalability is achieved for all of these tests.

References

[CILK] "The Cilk Project." Massachusetts Institute of Technology. n.d. <http://supertech.csail.mit.edu/cilk>.

[Lea00] Lea, Doug. "A Memory Allocator." 2000. State University of New York, Oswego. n.d. <http://gee.cs.oswego.edu/dl/html/malloc.html>.

[Herlihy08] Herlihy, Maurice and Nir Shavit. *The Art of Multiprocessor Programming.* Morgan Kaufmann Publisher, 2008.

[Intel07] "The Foundations for Scalable Multi-Core Software in Intel® Threading Building Blocks." 2007. Intel. n.d. <http://download.intel.com/technology/itj/2007/v11i4/5-foundations/5-Foundations_for_Scalable_Multi-core_Software.pdf>.

[Jones05] Jones, Toby. "Lock-Free Algorithms." *Game Programming Gems 6.* Ed. Mark Deloura. Boston: Charles River Media, 2005.

[McKenney07] MeKenney, Paul E. "Memory Ordering in Modern Microprocessors." 2007. Raindrop Laboratories. n.d. <http://www.rdrop.com/users/paulmck/scalability/paper/ordering.2007.09.19a.pdf>.

[MSDN] "Synchronization and Multiprocessor Issues." n.d. Microsoft. n.d. <http://msdn.microsoft.com/en-us/library/ms686355(VS.85).aspx>.

[TBB] "Intel Threading Building Blocks." n.d. Intel. n.d. <http://www.threadingbuildingblocks.org>.

4.4

Game Optimization through the Lens of Memory and Data Access

Steve Rabin, Nintendo of America Inc.
steve.rabin@gmail.com

As modern processors have become faster and faster, memory access has failed to keep pace. This is such a pressing issue on current console hardware that experts advise developers to treat memory as if it were as slow as hard drive access [Isensee06]. As a result of this vast disparity between CPU and memory speed, a great deal of horsepower goes to waste as CPUs wait for data to work on. Thus, a key aspect to optimizing games is keeping the CPU well fed with data.

But isn't the cache supposed to alleviate this problem? While the cache is indispensible to any complex computer architecture, it isn't a panacea. To its benefit, cache is brilliantly transparent to the code, but if we want to truly optimize our game, we'll have to pull back the curtains and understand how the cache works in order to help it out.

Once we better understand the cache and the memory architecture, it will become apparent that we need to respect the cache by shrinking the size of data and keeping it better organized. These will be our two guiding principles for most of our optimizations.

Understand the Cache

Main memory is extremely slow relative to the CPU. It's slow because it's typically far away from the CPU (on another chip) and made with fewer transistors per bit (which requires the bits to be refreshed so they don't fade away—which takes extra time). However, it's possible to make more expensive memory that is closer to the CPU (directly on the same chip) and faster by using more chip real estate per bit (so it doesn't need to be refreshed). However, this more expensive memory can't be as large as main memory because it simply won't fit on the silicon die next to the CPU. So what is a computer architect to do?

The solution is to keep copies of the most recently used main memory bits in the ultra-fast cache memory that sits on the CPU die. In fact, this strategy works so well that modern computer architectures have multiple levels of cache, usually referred to as level 1, level 2, and level 3 (L1, L2 and L3, respectively).

L1 cache is the smallest and fastest. Because of different access patterns between data and instructions, it's commonly split into an L1 data cache and an L1 instruction cache (typically 32 KB each). L2 cache is slightly slower and is usually shared between data and instructions (typically 256 KB to 6 MB, larger if shared among cores). L3 cache is a relatively new development in consumer hardware and appears on Intel's i7. On the i7, each core has a dedicated L1 and L2, but the 8-MB L3 is shared among the four cores. Table 4.4.1 shows cache sizes for various platforms [AMD09, Bell08, Lanterman07, Shimpi09, Wikipedia09].

TABLE 4.4.1   Cache Sizes for Various Platforms

Platform	L1 Instruction/Data Cache	L2 Cache	L3 Cache	Cache Line Size
iPhone 3GS	32 KB/32 KB	256 KB	N/A	64 bytes
Wii	32 KB/32 KB	256 KB	N/A	32 bytes
PS3	32 KB/32 KB	512 KB	N/A	128 bytes
Xbox 360	32 KB/32KB	1 MB	N/A	128 bytes
AMD Athlon X2	64 KB/64 KB	512 KB to 1 MB	N/A	64 bytes
Intel Core 2	32 KB/32 KB	1 MB to 6 MB	N/A	64 bytes
Intel i7	32 KB/32 KB	256 KB	8 MB	64 bytes

But how do these multiple levels of cache work? If the CPU needs to load a word from memory, it will first ask the L1 cache. If the data is there, it's a hit in the L1 cache, and the data will be delivered very quickly to the CPU. If the data isn't in the L1 cache, then it is a miss in the L1 cache, and then the L2 cache is checked. If the data is in the L2 cache, it is a hit, and the data is delivered to the L1 cache and the CPU. If it is a miss in the L2 cache, then the next level must be checked. If the next level is main memory, then the requested data will be delivered to the L2, the L1, and the CPU.

However, there is one more twist to how cache works. Memory isn't just copied to different levels of cache in bytes or words. It's copied in chunks known as *cache lines*, which are aligned sequential pieces of memory (for example, 128 bytes on the PS3 and Xbox 360, which is 32 words of 4 bytes each). So when the CPU asks for a 4-byte word and it misses in each cache, the entire cache line is copied from main memory into each cache level. This cache line copy is the reason why spatial coherency is so important for the working data set. Table 4.4.1 shows cache line sizes for various platforms.

Knowing that main memory is slow and the cache is fast, our goal will be to keep data and instructions in the cache as long as possible. The worst thing that can happen is cache thrashing, where the working set of data and instructions can't fit inside the cache at the same time. In this case, memory is brought into the cache only to be thrown out because there isn't enough room for the next needed piece of data. Imagine a tight loop that continually operates on 512 KB of data when the L2 cache size is only 256 KB.

With the limited size of cache and the importance of our data being in the cache, it becomes clear why we must keep data small and well organized.

Pinpoint Problem Areas

If we were to optimize every system in our game, we would waste a lot of time and effort. For example, if we double the speed of a function that only takes 0.01 percent of the frame time, then we have effectively done nothing toward speeding up our game. It's a hard truth to face since doubling the speed of a function sounds so satisfying, but the overall improvement is too small to make a difference.

Profiling our game is the only true way to pinpoint which areas are worth spending time to improve. Unless you can prove that a system or section of code is a bottleneck, you shouldn't waste your effort even thinking about optimizing it.

Once you identify code that takes a significant amount of time, how can you tell whether the CPU is waiting for data? The answer is performance counters. Performance counters are measurement tools built directly into the CPU that can count events and help identify problems during code execution. Many profilers can record performance counters, or you can usually turn them on and record the results directly in your code.

Using the performance counters, there are two key metrics to measure in order to identify when the CPU is spinning, waiting for data. The first is instructions per cycle (IPC), which gives a rough measure of how much work gets done per CPU cycle. If you measure an IPC of 0.8, then on average 0.8 instructions are completing per CPU cycle. The second key performance counter is the percentage of loads or stores that resulted in an L2 cache miss (which means a load from main memory). If the IPC is low and the percentage of L2 cache misses is high, then the cache isn't working well for this piece of code, perhaps because of cache thrashing.

Once you know which code or data needs to be optimized, you can go to work with the following suggestions.

Avoid Waste

The key to being efficient is avoiding waste. One source of wasted CPU cycles comes from reading memory that you don't use. Since the cache copies memory in cache line chunks, it's critical to use everything you read, in order to be efficient. For example, if you have an array of structs and only need to operate on one element in each struct, then you might be wasting a majority of the data you're bringing in from main memory.

For example, if you only operate on 30 percent of the struct, then as much as 70 percent of the data you're bringing in from main memory is wasted. Solutions to this problem are presented in the "Organize the Data" section.

Another source of waste comes from reading or writing memory that is not contiguous. Again, since memory is copied in cache line chunks, it is important to read and write sequentially to avoid waste.

Lastly, waste can arise from redundancy. It would be wasteful to read the same data multiple times a frame. Instead, batch operations together and try to optimize for a single pass through the data per frame.

Shrink the Data

Our first main strategy is simple: If your data is smaller, more of it will fit in the cache. This is as easy as carefully managing your data type sizes. If you're working with integers that won't get very large, consider using a short (2-byte integer) or just a single byte to represent the value. Instead of using 64-bit doubles, consider using 32-bit floats. However, one of the biggest wins is with Booleans. Typically, a Boolean takes up 4 bytes, but this is a huge waste of space since ideally it should be represented as a single bit.

Packed Structures

An easy way to manage your data type sizes is by defining them inside a structure. The following code is an example of an inefficient structure for a billboard particle, followed by an efficiently packed one. Notice the use of reduced ranges, bitfields, and indices, as well as how types are reordered by size to reduce padding. The result is a 1/3 savings in space, or about 7 K saved for 500 particles.

```
struct InefficientParticle //total size 44 bytes
{
    bool visible;          //31 bits of padding
    Texture *texture;      //pointer to texture
    int alpha;             //only needs 0 to 255
    float rotation;        //too much precision
    int type;              //enumeration - 4 possible types
    Vec3 position;
    Vec3 velocity;
};

struct EfficientParticle    //total size 30 bytes
{
    Vec3 position;
    Vec3 velocity;
    unsigned char alpha;    //saved 3 bytes (0-255)
    unsigned char rotation; //saved 3 bytes (0-255 degrees)
    unsigned texture:4;     //saved 28 bits (texture index)
    unsigned type:2;        //saved 29 bits (enumeration)
    unsigned visible:1;     //saved 31 bits (single bit)
};
```

To emphasize the importance of ordering struct variables from largest to smallest (which reduces padding and results in smaller structs), consider the following two examples of the same data:

```
struct WastedPadding          //20 bytes total
{
    char      var1;           //1 byte
    float     var2;           //4 bytes
    char      var3;           //1 byte
    int       var4;           //4 bytes
    char      var5;           //1 byte
};

struct OptimalPadding         //12 bytes total
{
    float     var2;           //4 bytes
    int       var4;           //4 bytes
    char      var1;           //1 byte
    char      var3;           //1 byte
    char      var5;           //1 byte
};
```

The following is a struct packing checklist for quick reference:

- Are numbers represented as the smallest reasonable data type?
  - Use a float instead of a double?
  - Use an 8-bit or 16-bit integer instead of an int?
  - Use an 8-bit or 16-bit integer instead of a float (lose some precision)?
  - Use the minimal bits necessary to represent the highest number?
- Can a char array be converted to a pointer and the string stored elsewhere?
- Can a pointer be converted to an index?
- Are all Booleans converted to a single bit?
- Are all enumerations converted to the range of numbers needed?
- Are the data types ordered from largest to smallest to reduce padding?

Compile for Size

Code is data! The smaller your code is, the more code will persist in the L1 instruction cache and in the shared instruction/data L2 cache. Since both code and data compete for L2 cache, smaller code also helps keep data in the cache.

All compilers offer the ability to optimize the compiled code for either speed or size. By compiling for speed, small functions will be inlined, and loops will be unrolled (which will bloat the size of the code). If you compile for size, then compact code will be favored. Since it's not clear which option will make your game run the fastest, you'll need to profile each option. It also may be the case that you want to compile some parts for speed and others for size.

Organize the Data

The second main strategy is to better organize your data to be *cache-conscious*. This means creating contiguous data structures (rather than scattered around memory) and grouping frequently used data together, away from infrequently used data.

Prefer Compact Contiguous Containers

Node-based containers, such as linked lists, hurt cache performance in two ways. The first is that they waste space by storing pointers to the next node, thus bloating the data structure. The second is that they allow the container nodes to be scattered around memory, hurting spatial locality [Isensee06]. A much more efficient data structure is either an array, an STL vector, or an STL deque, where the data is stored sequentially without the use of pointers. If you are using STL node–based containers, be sure to allocate new nodes from a dedicated heap to maintain spatial locality.

Separate Hot and Cold Data

While object-oriented programming and encapsulation lead to effective organization and comprehension, they can also lead to inefficient cache use. Within each struct or class, some members are referenced often by the code, and others are referenced infrequently. Ideally, all of the hot data (data that is used often) is placed together and is separate from the cold data (data that is seldom used) [Ericson03, Kaeli01, Franz98]. This would result in better cache utilization since the hot data is adjacent and more likely to be in the cache.

However, it's not enough to just separate hot and cold data within a struct or class. Consider what happens with an array of structs that have both hot and cold data. The problem that arises is that the cold data causes gaps between the groups of hot data, as in the left side of Figure 4.4.1.

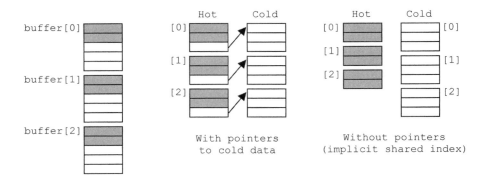

Figure 4.4.1 On the left, an array of structs containing a mix of hot and cold data. The middle image shows splitting the hot and cold data for each struct, with a pointer linking data from the same struct. The right image is slightly more efficient since the pointers are eliminated and struct correspondence is implicit in the array index.

Clearly, we need to further distill the hot and cold data even between structs or classes. In order to preserve encapsulation, one solution is to keep the hot data within the data structure, but then reference the cold data with a pointer (with the cold data living in some other part of memory). This is shown in the middle image of Figure 4.4.1.

The most cache-efficient solution would be to further weaken encapsulation and eliminate the extra pointer. In this scheme, there are two corresponding arrays: one holding the hot data and another holding the cold data. The link between the hot and cold data is maintained implicitly by the array index. For example, if a particular struct was originally stored in buffer[2], then the hot data is now stored in hot[2], and the cold data is stored in cold[2]. This is shown in the right image of Figure 4.4.1.

Manipulate the Cache

So far the optimizations have been centered around being cache-conscious and playing nice with the cache. The following two optimizations are more direct and attempt to directly manipulate the cache to our benefit.

Prefetch Data

Since the CPU will spin while waiting for data, it can be advantageous to prefetch data so that it's in the cache when the CPU is ready to use it. Some CPUs have specific prefetch instructions, but if these aren't available, you might have to cleverly prefetch the data yourself. The following code performs software prefetching for the next four array elements in a loop [Ericson03].

```
for (int i = 0; i < 4 * n; i += 4)
{
   Touch(array[i + 4]);     //Forces prefetch of memory
   Process(array[i + 0]);
   Process(array[i + 1]);
   Process(array[i + 2]);
   Process(array[i + 3]);
}
```

When prefetching data, timing is of the essence. You must not get the data too early, since it could be evicted from the cache before it's ever used. Conversely, you must not do it too late, since it might not be ready in time. Verifying with a profiler is the only surefire way to confirm that prefetching is having an effect.

Lock the Cache

To maximally use the cache, some consoles, such as the Wii, allow a portion of the cache to be locked and directly managed by the game. (Data must be manually moved in and out.) This can be extremely effective, since you are guaranteed to have particular data in the cache. However, this is console dependent, so check with your target platform to see whether this is available. General-purpose computers, such as PCs, do not allow the cache to be locked, because this would interfere with other processes.

Conclusion

Optimization in games is about eliminating wasted cycles. With CPUs chronically waiting on memory access, waste comes in several forms: from waiting for bloated data structures from main memory, not using everything that is read into the cache, and redundantly pulling the same data into the cache. These things can be avoided by shrinking your data structures and organizing them better to be cache-conscious. Lastly, you can manipulate the cache through prefetching and potentially locking the cache.

However, as with any optimization work, ensure that you're spending time improving actual bottlenecks. Only a profiler and performance counters can give you a good idea of where to concentrate your efforts. Finally, measure and compare improvements with a profiler to ensure that you're making a tangible difference, resulting in the entire game running faster and not just the code you modified.

References

[AMD09] AMD. "Key Architectural Features AMD Athlon™ X2 Dual-Core Processors." 2009. Advanced Micro Devices. n.d. <http://www.amd.com/us/products/desktop/processors/athlon-x2/Pages/amd-athlon-x2-dual-core-processors-key-architectural-features.aspx>.

[Bell08] Bell, Brandon. "Intel Core i7 (Nehalem) Performance Preview." 2008. Firing Squad. n.d. <http://www.firingsquad.com/hardware/intel_core_i7_nehalem_performance_preview/>.

[Ericson03] Ericson, Christer. "Memory Optimization." Game Developers Conference. 2003. Sony Computer Entertainment. n.d. <http://www.research.scea.com/research/pdfs/GDC2003_Memory_Optimization_18Mar03.pdf>.

[Franz98] Franz, Michael and Thomas Kister. "Splitting Data Objects to Increase Cache Utilization." 1998. Technical Report – University of California-Department of Information and Computer Science. n.d. <http://www.ics.uci.edu/~franz/Site/pubs-pdf/ICS-TR-98-34.pdf>.

[Isensee06] Isensee, Pete. "C++ on Next-Gen Consoles: Effective Code for New Architectures." 2006. Game Developers Conference. n.d. <https://www.cmpevents.com/sessions/GD/S1549i1.ppt>.

[Kaeli01] Kaeli, David. "Profile-Guided Instruction and Data Memory Layout." 2001. Northeastern University Computer Architecture Research Laboratory. n.d. <http://www.ece.neu.edu/groups/nucar/publications/Tufts.pdf>.

[Lanterman07] Lanterman, Aaron. "Architectural Comparison: Xbox 360 vs. PlayStation 3." 2007. Georgia Institute of Technology. n.d. <http://users.ece.gatech.edu/~lanterma/mpg/ece4893_xbox360_vs_ps3_4up.pdf>.

[Shimpi09] Shimpi, Anand. "The iPhone 3GS Hardware Exposed & Analyzed." 2009. AnandTech. n.d. <http://www.anandtech.com/gadgets/showdoc.aspx?i=3579>.

[Wikipedia09] Wikipedia. "Broadway (microprocessor)." 2009. Wikipedia. n.d. <http://en.wikipedia.org/wiki/Broadway_microprocessor>.

4.5

Stack Allocation

Michael Dailly
mike@dailly.org

Performance in games has always been important—and fun! Indeed, it's what brings many people into our profession in the first place, and it's always fun looking for simple new ways of speeding up our code. One of the best places to optimize has always been in the center of a tight loop, where every cycle counts. Although this doesn't happen as much as it used to, if you're dealing with anything that allocates, speed is almost always important. This gem describes a method of allocation that allows you to shave valuable cycles off of your allocator, yet is frighteningly simple to follow and implement.

Overview

The standard way of doing rapid allocation is to use a linked list of sorts, either single or doubly linked. This allows you to get the next free element quickly, and all you need to do is maintain the links. However, when dealing with linked lists (particularly doubly linked lists), you can end up touching more memory than you want, and thus incur cache misses and delays. The code is also longer than we'd all like, and in these days of 64-bit address pointers, you can end up burning more memory than you really need to. So what's the answer? Well, you could use indices instead of pointers to do your linked list with, but they can be even slower if you're not careful.

So, in steps the stack allocator. This system uses a pre-allocated list of items, with arbitrary-sized indices—be that pointers, INTs, WORDs, BYTEs, or even BITs! But unlike a normal list, we use a simple stack concept and position the stack pointer (SP) at the end. We can then pop the next free item off the stack and return it with minimal fuss or code, while we push items onto the list to free them.

Figure 4.5.1 illustrates a typical sequence where several objects are allocated and freed (where SP is the current stack pointer).

The ability to easily use varying sizes of indices, bits, pointers, or even POD types directly without having to really change the implementation is very powerful. But before looking at some examples, let's look at how we would implement the code.

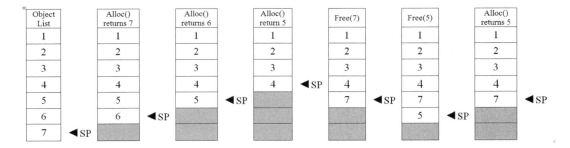

Figure 4.5.1 Object allocation in action.

Example Implementation

We'll start with a simple example implementation using a stack. But unlike a normal stack, you pre-fill it with your object's pointers, indexes (INTs, SHORTs, BYTEs, or even bits), or any other kind of object handle. First, we need to create and initialize the array. In this example we'll use basic pointer allocation.

```
#define     MAX_OBJECT          10000

Particle*   Stack[MAX_OBJECT];              // Our object stack
int         SP;                             // The Stack Pointer
Particle    ParticleArray[MAX_OBJECT];      // The object pool

// ####################################################################
//   Inititialise the stack with object indexes from 0 to MAX_OBJECT-1
// ####################################################################
void InitStack( void )
{
     // Create our object list
     // Pre-Fill stack with indexes (or pointers)
     for(int i=0;i<MAX_OBJECT;i++){
          Stack[i] = &ParticleArray[i];
     }

     // Initialise the stack pointer
     SP = MAX_OBJECT;
}
```

As you can see, creation is simply a matter of filling the array with object pointers and then setting up a stack pointer. Next, allocation and releasing of a particle object:

```
// ####################################################################
//   Pop a particle from the free pool.
//   -1 is returned if there are no free particles left.
// ####################################################################
Particle*   Pop(void)
{
```

```
        ASSERT( SP>=0, " Error: Stack pointer has gone negative!");
        if( SP==0 ) return -1;
        return pStack[-SP];
}


// ####################################################################
//  Push a used particle back onto the free pool
// ####################################################################
void Push(Particle* _pParticle )
{
        ASSERT( SP>=0, "Error: Stack pointer has gone negative");
        ASSERT( SP!= MAX_OBJECT, " Error: Not enough space in stack. Object
freed twice?");
        pStack[SP++] = _pParticle;
}
```

Allocating a particle is simply a matter of calling Pop(), while releasing it only requires you to call Push(). Again, not rocket science. Of course, these functions could just as well be called Alloc() and Free(), but for the sake of clarity when dealing with a stack method, we'll stick with Push() and Pop().

You can find code for a template based on this method on the accompanying CD (TemplateExample_V1).

Index-Based Implementation

Let's now look at another couple of possible uses. The most obvious one is to allocate an index as a handle to an object rather than a pointer to the object. In this example, we have 256 sprites that we wish to allocate from, and rather than allocating an object and returning a whole pointer, we'll simply allocate and return the BYTE index, thereby saving memory.

```
#define           MAX_SPRITES          256

unsigned char     Stack[MAX_SPRITES];
Sprite            SpritePool[MAX_SPRITES];

// ####################################################################
//  Inititialise the stack with object indexes from 0 to MAX_OBJECT-1
// ####################################################################
void InitStack( void )
{
        // Pre-Fill stack with ready to use particles.
        for(int i=0;i<MAX_SPRITES;i++){
                Stack[i] = (unsigned char) i;
        }

        // Initialise the stack pointer
        SP = MAX_ SPRITES;
}
```

Here you can see that by simply replacing the `Particle*` with a sprite index, we've changed the allocation type. This is important because it opens up all manner of interesting tricks. In the above example, we knew that we were only ever going to have 256 sprites, so we were able to allocate an index and keep our memory footprint down. The calling class can then store the index and use it as a handle directly, or at the very least take the address of `&SpritePool[index]` just before using it. This obviously saves more storage with only minimal effort on the coder's part.

The CD holds code for another example (TemplateExample_V2), based on the index method.

How about taking an extreme case of 16 million objects (a full 24-bit number). This would normally be hard to allocate, as you would normally either opt for a full INT index or use a 1D linked list. However, using the stack method, you can easily store 3 bytes per entry, either by working out the byte offset yourself or by storing two tables of a byte and a short, thereby saving you 16 MB of data. So instead of 64 MB of memory required for rapid allocation, you can quickly and easily reduce it down to 48 MB.

Taking this further, there's nothing to stop you from doing bit allocation. That is allocation of (say) 18 bits of information. Normally, you would again have to round this up to an INT so that you can easily deal with the number, but in this case you can easily deal with multiple tables, one holding a short and another holding the leftover bits. Due to the nature of the Push/Pop, bit allocation can be processed fairly simply, either by masking and shifting down or by assuming the next 2 bits are the lowest two in the INT and shifting them off as needed.

Let's see how this could be achieved. First, we need to allocate the arrays and create the index list.

```
const int             MAX_OBJ = 0x40000;
unsigned short        Stack_short[MAX_OBJ];
unsigned int          Stack_bits[MAX_OBJ/16];
int                   SP;

// ###################################################################
/// Function:<summary>
///             Initialise the free list
///          </summary>
// ###################################################################
void  Init( void )
{
        // Create and fill our 18bit table.
        // Use Push to build the table as it's easier in this case.
        SP = 0;
        for(int i=0;i<MAX_OBJ; i++){
                Push(i);
        }
}
```

In this case, we'll use Push to actually create the buffer, as it's far easier. This will create a list of indices from 0 right up to 0x3ffff (262,143).

Next we need to create the Push command itself.

```
// ########################################################################
/// Function:<summary>
///             Push an 18bit index onto the object stack
///           </summary>
///
/// In:       <param name="_value">18Bit number to store</param>
// ########################################################################
void Push( int _value)
{
    assert(_value>=0);
    assert(_value<0x40000);
    assert(SP<MAX_OBJ);

    Stack_short[SP] = (unsigned short)_value&0xffff;

    // Clear the bits we're about to OR into.
    int shift = (SP&0xf)<<1;
    int index = SP>>4;
    Stack_bits[index] &= ~(3<<shift);
    Stack_bits[index] |= ((_value>>16)&0x3) << shift;
    SP++;
}
```

While much slower than a linked list or using the stack with a straight array of pointers, it's obviously written for storage efficiency, in this case saving around 458 K compared to storing the whole 32-bit pointer. Next, allocation...

```
// ########################################################################
/// Function:<summary>
///             Return the next free index (an 18bit number)
///           </summary>
///
/// Out:      <returns>
///             Return the next free 18bit index, or -1 for an error.
///           </returns>
// ########################################################################
int   Pop( void )
{
    // If none left, then return an error
    if( SP==0)  return -1;

    // Get the main 16bits
    int val = Stack_short[-SP];

    // Now OR in the extra bits we need to make up the 18bit index.
    val |= (  (Stack_bits[SP>>4]>>((SP&0xf)<<1)) &0x3)<<16;

    return val;
}
```

The ease and speed at which you can adapt the stack allocation system to your needs is a real strength, and the ability to rapidly allocate not only pointers, BYTEs, SHORTs, and INTs, but also groups of bits efficiently is always going to be a winner.

Using this system, you can compress your data right down into as few bits as required without sacrificing all your speed. There are always better ways to compress data down, but this method often allows you to strike a middle ground in a matter of minutes, not days.

These are obviously extreme cases, but when trying to save memory, these types of options aren't usually open to you, so you usually end up either not bothering or wasting valuable time on far more complex methods; after all, how else could you easily allocate using 18-bit indices? It's normally not such a straightforward problem.

The example 18BitAlloc can also be found on the CD.

POD Types

Lastly, we'll show how to use POD types for more complex indexing requirements. For those who don't know, POD stands for *Plain Old Data*. POD types can store whole structures as long as they fit inside a standard native type, such as an INT, SHORT, or BYTE. Here's an example of a simple POD type.

```
struct STileCoordinate
{
        unsigned char    X;     // 64x64 X tile coordinate
        unsigned char    Y;     // 64x64 Y tile coordinate
        short            page;  // Texture page to use. (also padding)
};
```

This POD stores several pieces of pre-generated information—in this case, a 64×64 tile coordinate inside multiple 4096×4096 texture pages. First, let's see how you would normally deal with them.

```
class TileCoordinate
{
        STileCoordinate*  m_pNext;   // Next in the list
        unsigned char     m_X;       // 64x64 X tile coordinate
        unsigned char     m_Y;       // 64x64 Y tile coordinate
        short             m_page;    // Texture page to use.
};
```

If we had 10 texture pages, this would mean 40,960 tiles we need to allocate from. At 8 bytes per tile (the m_page member is padded for better alignment), this makes 327,680 bytes. Calling a standard allocator would then return a pointer to this structure, allowing us to use it as an origin for copying tile data into the free space.

So how can we do better? First, let's remove the pointer, as we know the stack system doesn't need that (or rather stores it outside the object itself). This leaves us with a 4-byte structure, and while we could use the very first example to allocate using a pointer to the structure (and saving no extra memory), we can do better.

Since this data fits inside 4 bytes, we can actually allocate and return the whole structure's data directly without the need for pointers. Taking the STileCoordinate type, we can actually make an array of these that is the same amount of memory as an array of INTs (since the whole structure is 4 bytes long). Now modern compilers will recognize this and allow us to pass around this data inside a register; that is, the whole structure is copied around without the need for pointers or expensive `memcpy()` operations. In fact, this is copied around at the same speed as a standard integer number.

Now our `Pop()` command doesn't return a pointer, but a structure, like so:

```
// ######################################################################
/// Function:<summary>
///                 Return the a free tile structure
///             </summary>
///
/// Out:        <returns>
///                 Return the next free tile structure, or an error tile.
///             </returns>
// ######################################################################
STileCoordinate    Pop( void )
{
    // If none left, then return an error
    if( SP==0)  return EmptyTile;

    // Get the main 16bits
    return TileStack[-SP];
}
```

We need to pre-define what an empty tile is (probably just –1 for X,Y and page), but aside from that, we get the data passed to us directly. You can then store this as an `STileCoordinate` (without the need for a pointer) and save yourself 163,840 bytes of memory in the process.

The beauty of the stack allocator is that it doesn't care what it returns; it will return pretty much anything to you, and it's up to you to decide what that anything is. You could just as easily define the type as plain UNSIGNED INT and mask out bits of information as you need to, rather than relying on bytes or shorts to make things fit.

For example, we could have assigned 12 bits for the X and Y coordinates and 8 for the page number, which would allow us to specify an actual pixel coordinate inside the 4096×4096 texture if we really wanted to. The important thing to remember is that the stack system returns data quickly, and that data doesn't have to be a pointer to some data or even a handle to data! In fact, it can be an entire structure if you wanted it to be. POD types are best because there's no special copying as they fit inside a register, but any type could be used.

You can find the POD example on the CD in the PODAlloc folder.

Known Issues

One of the few drawbacks to the stack allocation method is that you currently can't do it atomically, and so it's not automatically thread-safe. This means you must manage multiple-thread access yourself using all the standard lock methods normally at your disposal or use per-thread stacks.

You also can't put any limits on the allocation; that is, you can't search through the whole list and allocate one that better suits your needs—not without manually compacting the remain elements in the list, that is. If this is exceptional, then it might be worth occasionally compressing the list, but chances are if you need to do this, then you shouldn't use this method.

The only other real disadvantage is that there's no easy way to keep a used list. In a doubly linked list, you can move an item from the free to the used list, and this can help you debug things because it's easy to see what's in use. In this system, it's very much a free-only list. This doesn't mean you can't maintain debug tables or lists, but it does mean it's not a natural part of the system.

Advantages and Disadvantages

First, the advantages:

1. The code is microscopic, so small it can easily be placed inline. The compiler will often do this anyway.
2. Since all the objects' pointers or indices are gathered next to each other, they are very cache-friendly. In fact, you'll get multiple items per cache line, reducing cache misses to a bare minimum, particularly if you're allocating one after the other.
3. You can allocate a number of any type and of any bit size, from only a few bits to longer, more complex streams, and you can do so almost as easily as any other value or item.
4. You can allocate POD types (or bit-packed data) directly and rapidly. This saves on having to wrap simple types or include pointers through them, thereby increasing their size.
5. You don't have to modify any object to put links through it or have wrapper objects or templates to link things together. This simplifies your code.
6. It requires either the same or less memory than a 1D linked list system.
7. Allocation time is constant no matter how many elements you're allocating from.
8. Block allocation is not only possible, but very simple and quick. Depending on use, you could even return a pointer into the stack that holds the allocated block so you don't even have to allocate an array to return.
9. It's fast and easy to implement, even on severely restricted CPUs, and in any language. It works just as well on an old 6502 as it does on a modern PC.
10. It's very simple to debug, since you don't have to follow links all over the place.

Next, the disadvantages:

1. You can't easily remove items from the middle of the stack. This means it's hard to keep an allocated list as well as a free list.
2. It's not automatically thread-safe.
3. You can't easily place any restrictions on allocation without severely affecting performance.

Conclusion

This system has been used to allocate a single bullet from 20, sprites for rendering, scripting slots, blocks of memory, particles—you name it. The ease in setting up and using, not to mention the fact that debugging is simply a matter of viewing the stack, makes it simple for any level of ability to implement. Also, on modern hardware, with its relatively slow memory and cache lines, the cache coherency is an added bonus that's particularly useful when dealing with thousands (or even tens of thousands) of allocations in a single game cycle. Memory bandwidth is the ultimate enemy when dealing with large numbers of objects in a game, and being able to reduce the size of an object handle to an index and group them into the same cache line can be a big win. Finally, it's fast, simple, easy to implement, usually uses less memory than most other methods, and is very easy to adapt as your needs change!

4.6

Design and Implementation of an In-Game Memory Profiler

Ricky Lung

mtlung@gmail.com

This gem introduces an architecture and implementation for a low-overhead in-game memory profiler with multi-threading support. With this profiler, one can examine the memory allocation distribution of a running game in a call-stack-style table in real time. These statistics can be extremely valuable for performing memory usage optimization and memory leak tracking.

Introduction

Memory consumption management is one of the cornerstones of technical quality for games. Developers try their best to fit as much content as possible into a finite memory resource. We all know that choosing the right tool to do any kind of performance tuning is crucial, as it provides solid data instead of guesswork. Strangely, there is only a very limited number of memory profiling tools available for C++ in both the open-source and commercial worlds. This gem tries to narrow this gap by providing a lightweight memory profiling library. Now, let us have a look at what it will provide.

The profiler can generate a call graph at a given time interval, as shown in Figure 4.6.1. Each column of the table reveals useful information:

- **Name.** Mimics the program structure as a call stack, where the name of the function comes from the user-supplied string literal.
- **TCount.** Total number of allocations currently made in the calling function and its child call.
- **SCount.** Number of allocations currently made in the calling function without counting its child call.
- **TkBytes.** Total amount of memory currently allocated in the calling function and its child call, in units of kilobytes.

- **SkBytes.** Amount of memory currently allocated in the calling function. If you are looking for the memory eater, this column might be the first place to look.
- **SCount / F.** Number of allocations performed by this function per frame. You might want to reduce this number such that less run-time overhead of your game is spent on memory allocation/deallocation.
- **Call / F.** Tells you how many times a function is invoked in a single rendering frame.

Callstack	TCount	SCount	TkBytes	SkBytes	SCount/F	Call/F
⊟ root	278	0	33.9814	0	0	0
⊟ MAIN THREAD	270	193	33.6221	28.2803	0.0004820	0
⊟ functionA	7	2	0.328125	0.09375	5	1
⊟ functionB	5	2	0.234375	0.09375	1	1
⊟ functionC	2	2	0.09375	0.09375	0	1
recurse	0	0	0	0	11	11
⊟ recurse1	1	1	0.046875	0.046875	5	11
recurse2	0	0	0	0	6	11
system("cls")	70	70	5.01367	5.01367	0.0090777	8.03342E-05
⊟ WORKER THREAD	9	1	0.421875	0.046875	0	0
⊟ LoopRunnable::run	8	1	0.375	0.046875	0	1.25964
⊟ functionA	7	2	0.328125	0.09375	6.29836	1.25964
⊟ functionB	5	2	0.234375	0.09375	1.25964	1.25964
⊟ functionC	2	2	0.09375	0.09375	0	1.25964
recurse	0	0	0	0	13.856	13.856
⊟ recurse1	1	1	0.046875	0.046875	6.2982	13.856
recurse2	0	0	0	0	7.55784	13.856

Figure 4.6.1   A view of the memory profiling remote client.

Memory Profiling Basics

The memory profiling mechanism can be divided into three main parts: *collect* memory allocation information, *relate* the collected information with the program structure, and, finally, *present* the results. At first glance, the technique we use in CPU profiling can be applied: taking a measure at the beginning of a code block of interest and again at the end, minus their difference. But the challenge is yet to come, because memory allocated within a code block can be deallocated somewhere else. Therefore, instead of collecting information for a single code block at a time, we turn the problem into asking which corresponding code block the current memory operation is related to by intercepting every memory allocation operation.

The remaining sections of this gem will discuss how to utilize function hooking to intercept allocation operations and how to get their corresponding call-stack information and statistics. Of course, in this multi-core era, we will add support for multi-threaded applications.

Function Hooking

One simple way of intercepting memory allocation is defining your own new/delete operator in C++, but it has the limitation of not being able to intercept code that you don't have source code access to. Instead, we use a more low-level approach called *function hooking*, which is extremely powerful.

The term "hooking" in computer programming covers a range of techniques used to alter or augment the behavior of an application. Some applications, such as DirectX/OpenGL debuggers and profilers, use such a technique. Although it can be very complicated to hook other processes' functions as those standalone profiling applications do, in this memory profiler we only need to do some patching on the memory that a function is resident in. After the patching is done on a function—for example, the `malloc` function—whenever anywhere else in the program tries to invoke it, a proxy function `myHookedMalloc` is invoked instead of the original one. The patching process needs a few assembly tricks, so let's get our hands dirty and examine what the assembly of the `malloc` function looks like under x86 first.

```
void * __cdecl malloc(size_t size) {
    78583D3F   mov      edi,edi
    78583D41   push     ebp
    78583D42   mov      ebp,esp
    78583D44   push     esi
    ...
```

The above assembly shows the first four assembly instructions of the `malloc` function, which prepare the stack and register for use with that function, commonly called the *function prologue*. We will replace the first instruction with a jump instruction.

```
    void * __cdecl malloc(size_t size) {
    78583D3F   jmp      myHookedMalloc
    78583D41   push     ebp
    78583D42   mov      ebp,esp
    78583D44   push     esi
    ...
```

With the unconditional jump instruction added to the very beginning of the `malloc` function, all control flow will be directly transferred to our proxy function.

```
    void* myHookedMalloc(size_t size) {
        void* p = (*originalMalloc)(size);
        logMallocUsage(p, size);
        return p;
    }
```

What the proxy function does is simple: It invokes the original `malloc` function to perform the actual allocation and log the memory size along with the allocated memory pointer for further processing. We then need to resolve the problem of how we can invoke the original `malloc` function. To get back the original function, we need to back up the first assembly instruction before we perform the patching and store it in an executable memory location. (Note that you can make a block of memory executable on the Windows platform using `VirtualProtect`.) Following that memory location, put a jump instruction pointing to the second instruction of the original function.

```
mov     edi,edi
jmp     &malloc + sizeof(mov edi,edi) = 78583D41
```

We give this block of executable memory a meaningful name, `originalMalloc`, with the same function signature as `malloc` does. These backup instructions can also be utilized for restoring the patched function when the memory profile gets shut down. One particular issue that we haven't addressed is how to get the size of a binary assembly instruction, which is necessary to perform the replace and copy operations correctly. A easy way to tackle this problem is to simply hardcode the instruction size, but this will create maintenance problems because different C run times may have different compiled binary code, even for the same function. A better solution is to calculate it at run time. Luckily, there are free libraries that can do the task, such as `libdasm`.

All the aforementioned details of function hooking are encapsulated into a single class with only three functions, which can be found on the CD-ROM.

```
class FunctionPatcher {
    void* copyPrologue(void* func, int givenPrologueSize);
    void patch(void* func, void* replacement);
    void unPatchAll();
}
```

Again, using `malloc` as the example, the usage of the class is as follows.

```
void (*origianlMalloc)(size_t);
FunctionPatcher functionPatcher;
origianlMalloc = functionPatcher.copyPrologue(&::malloc, 5);
funcitonPatcher.patch(&malloc, &myMalloc);
```

Although all the source code and example here only work under x86, the same concept should be able to be applied to other platforms, including game consoles.

Call-Stack Generation

In the current generation of software architecture, most programs are built on a command and control scheme: One method calls another method and instructs it to perform some action. The place that stores the nested method call information is the *call stack*. From a low-level point of view, it is just a simple memory block with some integer offsets giving the stack size; while at a higher-level point of view, we can use a graph structure to represent the call stack. (The terms *call graph* and *call stack* can be used interchangeably.)

To collect the full call stack of a running program, a stack-walker [Gaurav08] with debug symbol information can be used. However, generating a full call stack is not only time consuming, but it also clutters the profiling results. Thus, a custom function call annotation scheme inspired by the previous *Gems* articles [Rabin00] and [Hjeistrom02] is used instead, which gives users a more flexible way to collect statistics for their most important functions. Those applications that already use similar profiling tools can easily integrate with this memory profiler by combining the scope variable/macro.

We use a tree-like structure in C++ to mimic the actual call-graph structure. A tree is used instead of a graph because we will accumulate the profiling data recursively instead of making more general node connections. This tree structure contains a number of nodes, while each of these nodes contains the necessary memory profiling statistic and the link to its sub-nodes. Obviously, the root node of the tree represents the entry point of the program, usually the main function. More nodes can be added to the tree on user's request, through declaring a scope variable.

```
void createMesh() {
    ProfilingScope scope("createMesh");
...
}
```

Suppose Function A calls Function B, and both functions have a scope variable declared. Then a node named B will be inserted as a child of the node named A. The next time Function A invokes B, a linear search for all the child nodes under A with the name B is performed. This implementation assumes that the name argument of the scope variable must be a string literal; therefore, we can use a simple pointer comparison instead of a full-blown string comparison during searching. Provided that the average number of child node is around the order of 10, the call-stack generation process is reasonably fast.

For the hooked memory allocation function to make use of the call-stack information, the call tree will store a variable that points to the current call-stack node. Thus, a connection between the current allocation and the current call stack is made.

Collecting Statistics

Once we have the call-stack data structure on hand, we can start to collect statistics. Only a handful of statistics need to be stored in each node:

- Invocation count
- Exclusive allocation count
- Exclusive allocation size

The exclusive allocation count and size will be updated whenever the hooked functions are invoked. Apart from simply updating the statistics, the hooked functions need to perform some bookkeeping in order to retrieve the corresponding call-stack node for a particular allocated memory block during the deallocation operation.

The mapping between the two can be established using an STL map, but this results in a high run time and memory overhead; therefore, we use the approach of embedding the call-stack node pointer with the allocated memory block.

```
void* myHookedMalloc(size_t size) {
    void* p = (*originalMalloc)(sizeof(Node*)+sizeof(int)+size);
     (Node*)p = currentCallStackNode;
    *(int*)((char*)p + sizeof(Node*)) = size;
    currentCallStackNode->allocCount++;
    currentCallStackNode->byte += size;
    return (char*)p+sizeof(Node*)+sizeof(int);
}
void myHookedFree(void* p) {
    int allocSize = *(int*)((char*)p-sizeof(int));
    p = ((char*)p-sizeof(Node*)-sizeof(int));
    Node* n = (Node*)p;
    n->allocCount--;
    n->byte -= allocSize;
     (*originalFree)(p);
}
```

Other statistics that take into account the child function calls can be calculated on the fly during profile report generation, because this step needs to traverse the call tree anyway.

Multi-Thread Issues

By definition, each executing thread should have its own call stack. This means every call of myHookMalloc can access the per-thread call-stack data structure freely without any problem. Thread Local Storage (TLS) comes to assistance here. For each thread, we store the pointer to its corresponding call-stack root node and another pointer to the current node using the win32 API TlsSetValue. This data will be retrieved by myHookedMalloc using TlsGetValue. Care has to be taken in implementing myHookedFree because it may operate on a call-stack node that doesn't belong to the current thread.

To protect the deallocation routine from race conditions, each thread's root node is assigned a critical section, and all its ancestor nodes will keep a reference to it. When myHookedMalloc or myHookedFree is invoked, the critical section of that node will be locked before any statistic information update. Such a design keeps the number of critical sections to a minimum while preserving a very low lock contention level; moreover, it does not create a locking hierarchy, so it should be free from dead-lock.

The Source Code

The source code on the CD comes with Microsoft Visual Studio solutions that allow you to compile and execute several demo programs related to the memory profiler. Although the code snippets in this gem are simplified for illustration purposes, the code on the CD is carefully crafted for maximum correctness and robustness. A client-to-server architecture is also employed in one of the demos, which shows you how to make an external tool to monitor the memory usage of your application.

A CPU profiler based on the same code base as the memory profiler is also supplied as a reference.

Conclusion

By moving a step forward, our in-game CPU profiling techniques can be extended to measure memory usage as well. This gem also demonstrated how to modify the profiler to cope with the multi-core era. We hope you will utilize this profiler to develop a greater understanding of your program, locate memory hotspots, and improve your memory consumption and performance.

References

[Gaurav08] Kumar, Gaurav. "Authoring Stack Walker for X86." 6 Jan. 2008. WinToolZone. n.d. <http://www.wintoolzone.com/PermaLink.aspx?ID=141>.

[Rabin00] Rabin, Steve. *Game Programming Gems*. Boston: Charles River Media, 2000.

[Hjeistrom02] Hjeistrom, Greg, and Byon Garrabrant. *Game Programming Gems*. Boston: Charles River Media, 2002.

4.7

A More Informative Error Log Generator

J.L. Raza and Peter Iliev Jr.

jraza@versus-software.com, pete.iliev@gmail.com

Programmers commonly create error logging functions to aid in debugging during development. Usually, these functions print out error messages onscreen or to a log file. Although it is functional, the error message is only as good as the programmer's insight into how the problem could have occurred. In other words, a one-line message is not always enough to help fix the bug. You may need to know which function passed in bad data or how the program got into this bad state, and that is what this gem seeks to help with.

In this gem, we'll present a new error logging function that automatically generates useful information for the programmer and/or tester via what is known as *retrieving the Run-Time Stack Information* (RTSI).

Definition of RTSI

Retrieving the RTSI is a debugging tool conventionally used to aid in software development. During debugging, *stack walking* is the act of pausing the program and taking a glimpse into the program's function stack at run time. For example, given the following code:

```
void C()
{
      int i = 0;//set a breakpoint here
}

void B()
{
      C() ;
}

void A()
{
```

```
        B() ;
}

int main()
{
        A() ;
        ...
        return 1 ;
}
```

When the compiler reaches the breakpoint in function C(), and the programmer requests the program's run-time stack information, it would return something like this:

```
        C
        B
        A
        Main
        ...
```

The bottom of the stack shows the program's entry point. For simplicity, the operating system functions called have been omitted from this example. In this case, the entry point is main(). It then details what function main() called, A(), and recursively what function A() called, and so on until it reaches the current function where the breakpoint was set. As the flow of execution on the program continues, retrieving the RTSI again will return a different result based on where the program's execution is paused.

Potential Uses

RTSI is a normal component in many commercial and open-source compilers. It can be useful for tracking stack-overflow bugs, as well as taking a snapshot of the program's current execution status once it hits a breakpoint.

Most often, programmers will only use the RTSI inside their compiler. But when working in game development teams, there are more people around than just programmers. There are artists, level designers, and testers. All of these people will be playing the game. Yet, not everyone may have access to a compiler or a debug development kit, and anyone can run into a crash bug. Having the program dump out as much info as possible during these situations is vital, and dumping out the RTSI can be a big help.

The RTSI's usefulness extends beyond just the work environment, too. Online games, such as MMORPGs or RTS games, do beta testing where they release the game to a select few people in their homes and let them play the game before it's out. The main intent is balancing and getting feedback. Beta testing is also valuable time that can be used for bulletproofing the game. So as not to waste the testing time, whenever bad data is encountered or a crash occurs, the RTSI can be sent from the tester's machine to a developer-owned server for use later.

C/C++ does not have a standard function to call to print the program's RTSI, so it's up to the operating system and hardware vendors to distribute a set of functions in an API to accomplish this job. In this gem, we'll explore the API functions on the Windows XP platform for gathering the RTSI on an x86 processor. The example will also work on x64 processors, but some of the assembly code will need to change to reference the correct registers.

Setting Up the Code

So you have decided that the RTSI is a resource that's going to be used in your game. Henceforth, it needs to go through the three basic steps any resource goes through: loading, usage, and unloading.

Loading

Since the RTSI resource will probably be used in several different spots in the game code, we have the issue of when to load it, when to unload it, and how to handle access to it. All these issues can be solved by setting it up as a singleton resource. For reference on singletons, see [Bilas00]. To load our RTSI API function calls, we use the following code:

```
//load the dbghelp.dll which is the windows library used
//for crawling up the stack
m_dllHandle = LoadLibrary( "dbghelp.dll" );

//sets up which processes symbols
//we are going to look at
m_pSymInitialize = (SymInitialize) GetProcAddress(
     m_dllHandle, "SymInitialize" );

//used to crawl up the stack
//and look at each function call
m_pStackWalk64 = (StackWalk64) GetProcAddress(
     m_dllHandle, "StackWalk64" );

//used to retrieve the line number in each file the
//function was called from
m_pSymGetLineFromAddr64 = (SymGetLineFromAddr64) GetProcAddress( m_dllHandle,
"SymGetLineFromAddr64" );

//used to get the name of each function in string form
m_pSymGetSymFromAddr64 =
     (SymGetSymFromAddr64)GetProcAddress(
          m_dllHandle, "SymGetSymFromAddr64" );

//get and set for the options of what information we want
//to retrieve.
//this example only cares for line numbers and
//function names.
m_pSymGetOptions = (SymGetOptions) GetProcAddress(
     m_dllHandle, "SymGetOptions" );

m_pSymSetOptions = (SymSetOptions) GetProcAddress(
     m_dllHandle, "SymSetOptions" );
```

Usage

We need to set up an access point to the RTSI with the required function pointers. We only need to activate it when something is about to go wrong; this is what the ASSERT() call is for. For reference on how to use that and a few handy tricks, see [Rabin00].

This access point can be created as such:

```
#if DEBUG
    #define ASSERT( expression ) \
        if ( !expression ) \
        { \
            printf( "ASSERT[" #expression "]\n" ); \
            AssertWrapper::a.PrintStack(); \
            printf( "\n\nPress enter to continue:\n" );\
            getchar(); \
        }

#else
    //If we aren't in a debug configuration then just compile out
    //Asserts
    #define ASSERT( expression )
#endif
```

Now, when we call the ASSERT() macro and the result is false, we'll print out the RTSI. Notice that it's the PrintStack function inside the Assert class that does the interesting work. There are a couple of important pieces of code in that function. The first is how we fill the CONTEXT data structure:

```
CONTEXT context;
memset( &context, 0, sizeof(CONTEXT));
context.ContextFlags = CONTEXT_FULL;

__asm    call x
__asm    x: pop eax
__asm    mov context.Eip, eax
__asm    mov context.Ebp, ebp
__asm    mov context.Esp, esp
```

Here we are copying the instruction, frame, and stack pointers into Context. This will let the StackWalk function know where to look for all the debugging info we need. Normally, you would copy the instruction pointer directly (EIP), but on x86 processors there is no direct way to access that pointer, so we use a trick. This section of code is processor family–specific, so the register will probably be named differently for the different companies. For example, x64 (AMD) uses Rip, Rbp, and Rsp.

The other important aspect of the PrintStack function is the loop that displays the functions on the run-time stack.

```
unsigned int i = 0;
do
{
```

```
                 //get the next stack frame info
                 this->m_pStackWalk64(    IMAGE_FILE_MACHINE_I386,
                                          process,
                                          thread,
                                          &frame,
                                          (void*)&context,
                                          NULL,
                                          SymFunctionTableAccess64,
                                          SymGetModuleBase64,
                                          NULL );

                 //now we try to print the current frame's info
                 if ( frame.AddrReturn.Offset != 0 && i != 0 )
                 {
                         char line1[32];
                         char line2[32];
                         memset( line1, '\0', 32 );
                         memset( line2, '\0', 32 );
                         PrintLineNumber( process, frame.AddrPC.Offset, line2 );
                         PrintFuncName( process, frame.AddrPC.Offset, line1 );
                         printf( "%-32s || %s\n", line1, line2 );
                 }
                 i++;
         } while( frame.AddrReturn.Offset != 0 );
```

Thus, if we want to integrate the RTSI to a game GUI, then that is where we would make our changes.

Unloading

To unload it, we perform the reverse of the loading steps.

```
FreeLibrary( m_dllHandle );

m_pSymInitialize = NULL;
m_pStackWalk64 = NULL;
m_pSymGetLineFromAddr64 = NULL;
m_pSymGetSymFromAddr64 = NULL;
m_pSymGetOptions = NULL;
m_pSymSetOptions = NULL;
```

Error Logs Redundancy Problem versus Using RTSI

Having explained the RTSI and how to implement it in a non-compiler environment, we can now begin to exemplify scenarios in which this feature could be quite useful. It is common for programmers to create a set of functions that display an error message when something goes wrong during testing. The problem with a generic error log function is that the programmer has to keep track of where he is in the code in order for the error message to create any useful information. Following is an example of this common scenario.

```
int A()
{
     if ( did_an_error_occur() )
     {
          assert( ! "Problem with function A()" ) ;
          return 0 ;
     }
     else
     {
          ...
          return 1 ; // All went well
     }
}


int B()
{
     if ( did_an_error_occur () )
     {
          assert( ! "Problem with function B()" ) ;
          return 0 ;
     }
     else
     {
          ...
          return 1 ; // All went well
     }
}

int C()
{
     if( A() && B() )
          return 1 ;

     return 0 ;
}

...
```

The problem with this design is that as the software evolves, so will its function calls and the context in which these functions are called. Keeping track of those error messages adds extra overhead to the development of the game. This could be solved if the error log function could "know" its current context and report accordingly, which is exactly what RTSI can do.

With the given code sample, the programmer could then bind the error log to the in-game GUI. This means that once an error log function gets triggered, a tester can report to the programmer a wider span of technical information (since the log is intrinsically related to the game's code) as well as not have to resort to an error check table.

Conclusion

It's important for there to be a continuous flow of information among the staff on a game development team. Unfortunately, quantitative data regarding when a game hits an error in a non-compiler environment is not an easy thing to capture. With tools like the RTSI, these potential problems can be smoothed out. One could even bind the RTSI entry point to a script that fills a form in a bug database with this kind of information so that it could be later analyzed by the programming team.

References

[Bilas00] Bilas, Scott. "An Automatic Singleton Utility." *Game Programming Gems*. Boston: Charles River Media, 2000. 36–40.

[Rabin00] Rabin, Steve. "Squeezing More Out of Assert." *Game Programming Gems*. Boston: Charles River Media, 2000. 109–114.

4.8

Code Coverage for QA

Matthew Jack
mtj22@cantab.net

When working on a rapidly developing code base, a good QA team is a highly versatile resource that no automated testing can replace. However, actually playing the game is such a high-level form of testing that it can be hard to relate it to low-level changes in the code.

First, changes that a programmer has made may only be executed in certain situations depending on the player's actions, which can be hard to give a procedure to re-create. For a given piece of low-level code, a programmer may have little idea where and when in the games it is actually used! Further, even when we can give clear instructions for testing, we are rarely absolutely sure whether they worked and the code was actually executed; in some cases there will be a clear visible indication, but in many others the effect of the code is subtle. Often, it is simplest in the end to throw up our hands, give no details, and just ask QA to "be thorough"—which is time-consuming for them and still provides no guarantees about the result.

This gem describes a framework that combines code coverage analysis and conventional QA by using real-time feedback. It addresses these issues and improves the testing process for both QA and programmers. It can bring rigor and repeatability to testing and yield valuable insight to the low-level programmer about where the code is actually used.

Common Approaches

Before examining the approach of this gem, let's consider some of the established testing methodologies.

- **Unit testing.** Especially for localized, pure refactoring, unit testing can be rigorous and fast. However, to be pragmatic, most games are developed without comprehensive unit testing. One reason for this, at least for rapidly changing game code, may be that unit testing is considered to add too much development overhead. If unit tests are not present in the original code, then restructuring to add them is likely to be an enormous task that could itself introduce bugs.

- **Automated functional testing.** For instance, a repeatable play-through using an input recorder. This is very convenient for detecting crashes; however, an experienced eye is still required to watch for changes in behavior, and it in no way addresses the thoroughness of the original play-through. Furthermore, if the game you are testing is currently under development, it may change so quickly that a recording has a very short lifespan.
- **QA testing.** Plain old QA is essentially a manual form of functional testing. A good QA team can adapt rapidly to a changing specification, report changes in behavior, and benefit from human intuition when something looks wrong. These are valuable qualities to build upon.

In all of these approaches, we might ask: How complete is their testing? One way of assessing this is through code coverage analysis. This measures how rigorously a given test exercises source code, allowing this to be quantified and improved. Fundamental to this gem, we will examine it in detail.

An Analogy: Breakpoint Testing

There is a rough-and-ready version of this gem that I have often employed, and it turns out it is already available in your IDE. We might call it *breakpoint testing*.

In refactoring a function/class/file/blob, one systematic approach to testing on the developer's machine is to place a breakpoint on every statement that represents a relevant code path and then run the game, removing each breakpoint as it is hit. When all breakpoints have been removed, without any crashes or unexpected behavior, testing is complete.

This can be a good minimal test of changes, as it ensures the developer has executed all the code he changed and has observed the overall results. However, playing through takes time, and it must be done on that computer, so this cannot easily be delegated. Furthermore, it is not repeatable: Future regression tests would require re-creating all of the breakpoints.

However, note that breakpoint testing works for new code as well as refactored code and that it directly couples high-level functional tests to low-level details in the source.

This gem is a framework that formalizes and expands that ad hoc hybrid of code coverage and manual testing.

Code Coverage

Conventional code coverage analysis is used to quantify how completely a testing procedure (usually automatic) exercises source code [Cornett96]. It works by monitoring at run time the number of unique lines (or functions, branches, code paths, and so on) that have been executed by the test, compared to the number theoretically possible. This basic principle of discovering which code we have actually run is attractive, but there are several questions we must address when applying this to games.

The first is what kind of testing procedure we should use, since code coverage is only useful in analyzing tests. Unit testing is the standard in the wider software industry, but for games we propose QA testing of real levels. This is simple and flexible, and chances are your company is already doing it every day. It also better represents the end product, where code and assets intertwine to determine final quality.

Next, we have to consider granularity. Instrumenting every line will cause a significant slowdown that may make the game unplayable—especially on consoles—and the increased executable size may prevent it from loading at all. Furthermore, this is sheer data overload: Such a glut of information would take further processing to make any sense to us. Monitoring every function is too arbitrary—some functions are trivial and/or speed-critical, while others may, for instance, contain large switch statements. Tracking all branches may again generate too much data.

Also, we must consider the final output, which is related to the granularity. A list of all the numbers of all the lines executed would be meaningless in itself—and rendered useless as soon as the source code changes. Function names would be instantly recognizable, but what if we change them?

The result most commonly quoted from code coverage is a single figure: a percentage representing the completeness of testing, where targets are commonly 90- to 100-percent coverage [Cornett96, Obermeit06]. Note that if we use real levels as tests, in most games we will see much lower coverage, as each level usually employs only a subset of the features. If we accept that we will only test a fraction of our code, we have an ambiguity: Was a given feature left unexercised because testing was insufficient or because it is not used in this level? It may also beg the question: Much of the code may have been tested, but was this piece of code tested?

Finally, if we use human testers to perform the tests, our results may vary wildly with different play-throughs. Can we guide them toward comprehensive, repeatable testing?

There are various code coverage packages already available, but without addressing these issues, their value in practical games development is limited.

Implementation

Key to our approach is that, rather than use any automatic instrumentation, the programmer places his own markers into the code using a simple macro. This allows us to solve the problems of granularity and meaningful output and leads us to solutions for the remaining issues.

By using manual markers, we can keep them to a manageable number, applied only where required and omitted from performance-critical or trivial code. This—and careful implementation of the marker code—avoids slowdown and code-bloat.

We use a unique string to label each marker. You could base these on the class and method name—for example, `CCoverBehaviour_ThrowGrenade_A`—or use a pure feature descriptor—for example, `ThrowGrenadeFromCover_A`. The labels make the output meaningful, while still allowing the programmer to add markers to individual if/else branches, cases of a switch statement, loop bodies, or anywhere else he thinks they may be useful.

The Markers

The following macro expands to code that constructs a static object with a trivial constructor and calls its `Hit()` function:

```
#define CCMARKER( label ) \
  { \
    static CCodeCoverageMarker ccMarker_##label( #label ); \
    ccMarker_##label.Hit(); \
  }
```

where `Hit()` registers the marker with a singleton [Alexandrescu01] for tracking the first time it is executed. Keeping this method separate allows for a reset feature.

```
inline void Hit()
{
  if (!m_bHit)
  {
    m_bHit = true;
    CCodeCoverageTracker::GetInstance().Register(this);
  }
}
```

Some of the advantages of this approach include:

- Macros are easily compiled out, ensuring zero performance impact in the release.
- Using a static object allows a fast check for whether this is the first time hit.
- Functions can be renamed or moved into a different class or file, but while marker labels are preserved, code coverage results remain undisrupted. This is helpful as we build up a history. (See the upcoming "Collecting Results" section.)
- Descriptive labels immediately provide hints for real-time feedback to QA. When wondering how to hit that last one percent of markers, a tester will really appreciate the onscreen text "`ThrowGrenadeFromCover_A`".

C++ compilers include predefined macros that could generate marker labels automatically, based on function names, line numbers, and so on. Note, however, that for this saving of a few moments, we lose much of the advantage of a manually defined label.

If labels are not unique, our results will of course be misleading. This would usually occur if someone copied and pasted code somewhere else, but it could also occur if a single marker declaration was instantiated multiple times in the binary. This could happen through use within macros or templates. Functions inlined as an optimization are not a problem, as the C++ standard defines that all inlined copies of a function must share one copy of any local static variables [ISO/IEC14882-98]. Note that some older compilers did not handle this properly.

The best way to avoid the more common copy/paste problem would be to write a simple script to scan the source code for duplicate labels. All types of duplicates can also be detected by the framework itself at run time—the example implementation includes such a check.

In my own experience, there have been no problems with duplicates.

Examples: Applying Markers

Markers are commonly embedded at the start of methods:

```
void BrainClass::Update()
{
  CCMARKER("Brain_Update");
  UpdateVision();
  UpdateBlackboard();
  ...
}
```

while, if the method includes various early-out checks, it is most effective to place the marker at the end, where the "meat" of the code has already been used:

```
void Brain::SendSignal( const char * signal, int targetID )
{
  if (targetID == m_myTargetID) // Am I the target?
    return;
  if (GetDistanceToTarget(targetId) > 20.0f) // Is it too far?
    return;
  ...
  CCMARKER("Brain_SendSignal");
}
```

Here I've used a structured name, confident that sending signals will always be a responsibility of my Brain class, or perhaps distinguishing it from other places where signals are sent—but in many cases you may prefer a totally pure name, as below. Where you only describe the feature, you can freely move the code and preserve the label without it becoming misleading.

You can also include multiple markers at different points in the same scope if desired, in loops (if not speed-critical):

```
for (int i=0; i<nSignalsToSend; ++i)
{
  CCMARKER(SignalSent);
  SendSignal(i);
}
```

or in branches of switch statements:

```
CObject * pObj = NULL;
switch (n)
{
  case 0: CCMARKER(FetchedLeader);
          pObj = m_pLeader;
          break;
  case 1: CCMARKER(FetchedCompanion);
          pObj = m_pCompanion;
          break;
  ...
}
```

The Tracker

As earlier, each marker registers with the tracker the first time it is hit, which maintains the set of all markers hit thus far. In the example implementation, the tracker adds the marker to an STL vector and does nothing more; all other work is put off to help avoid disrupting caches and skewing profiling results.

The markers are completely unknown to the program until they are hit, because their scope is local to function bodies. A simple script could extract the complete set from the source, but usually we are only interested in the subset used by a given level.

Per-Level Coverage Input File

Since we have established that real levels only use a subset of features, we keep a separate list of expected marker labels for each level. Once loaded, this defines the 100-percent coverage that testers will aim for. After the testing process, these files are updated using the results from code coverage—in particular, adding any "unexpected" markers that were hit.

We can form the initial set of input files in the same way, employing "blind" testing to find most of the markers without guidance. We can then improve upon them in subsequent runs as testers find any remaining markers, gradually raising the bar for test quality.

This also smoothly assimilates new code: The markers will appear in results as "unexpected," confirming to the programmer where they were used, and will be expected in that level from then on.

Maintenance of these per-level coverage files should obviously be automated by a processing script, but summaries of their changes are informative. (See the upcoming "Collecting Results" section.)

The Manager

The manager class loads the per-level input file containing the set of "expected" marker labels for the level being tested. It also monitors which of these have actually been hit, which are still remaining, and whether any "unexpected" markers have been hit. The class exposes a simple interface to this data, allowing progress to be checked and results to be output.

The same interface makes it easy to write a GUI for real-time feedback. We describe this in the next section.

QA Interface and Workflow

Getting the most out of this approach requires real-time feedback, guiding testers toward 100-percent coverage while making the smallest changes possible to workflow. One-hundred percent is often a realistic target. Markers have been deliberately placed and so should be reachable. They must have been hit in this level before to be "expected," and we provide guidance in reaching the last few percent. However, in branching levels it may be necessary to combine multiple runs. (See the upcoming "Collecting Results" section.)

The GUI

The implementation within *CryENGINE*, as shown in Figure 4.8.1, uses a simple onscreen display comprising:

- Progress bar (0 to 100 percent "expected" markers hit)
- Indication whenever a marker is hit for the first time
- List of the remaining marker labels as hints

Figure 4.8.1   Code coverage GUI implementation within *CryENGINE*, including progress bar, hit indicators, and a list of markers hit within the last few seconds.

The list of expected markers for each level is stored as a separate file in the level folder itself, loaded automatically when the code coverage display is activated.

To avoid clutter, it is best to only display marker labels when few remain. Normal testing should easily hit 90 percent of markers reachable in a given level, but guidance on the last few is important if high coverage scores are to be reliably reached.

Labels as Hints

It would be a fair criticism that in some cases the "meaningful" labels given by programmers may be useless when appearing out of context on a tester's screen. However, they form the vocabulary of a common language between testers and programmers, allowing testers to find out how they might hit that specific marker and to communicate that knowledge to others.

For example, while "Throw_Grenade" might be helpful, "Reorganise_Brain_E" is less intuitive, but for the programmer still only a moment's string search away—hence, it can be clarified by a quick email from tester to programmer. Also, should a tester discover how to hit this infamous marker through trial and error, he can easily relate that to others on the QA team. A Wiki or similar maintained by QA would be a good repository for details of any tricky markers.

We make it simple for programmers to help QA achieve high coverage, but we also give QA the means to be self-sufficient in this regard, so in practice little or no programmer time should be required.

Figure 4.8.2 Code coverage within *CryENGINE*, when 93 percent of markers for the level have already been hit and the remainder are displayed as hints to the tester.

Output of Results

Results are output as a list of labels of the markers hit, either dumped to a log file or sent automatically over the network.

The use of log files is simple and quite robust. Since it is common for testers to send logs with their bug reports, it may be best for workflow to add them to the existing log file in an easily extracted format. This can be as the complete status of known labels in one block, or dumped periodically or manually, or you could also write individual labels as their markers are hit. The latter has the advantages of forming a record of when they were hit and losing no results should the game crash, although it does add clutter to the log. Log files must be collected by testers and delivered to the programming team.

Sending results over the network is potentially much more elegant, with no impact on QA workflow and coping easily with crashes. However, it requires more work to set up and some thought in its deployment. (See the upcoming "Possible Expansions" section.)

QA Workflow

Final instructions to QA are simply:

- Load the level, activate coverage, and test as normal.
- Try to reach 100-percent coverage, using the textual hints to help if need be.
- Send the logs as usual when you're finished (if you use a log-based approach).

You may also ask testers to quit and restart the game between levels—this is to reset the coverage state and thus avoid mixing results. However, in the example code provided with this gem, the state can be reset at any time and so chain-loading levels may be practical, depending on how much state your game carries over.

As a final note on presentation: It may already have occurred to the reader that testing with code coverage feedback is rather like playing a mini-game. An example of screen output while testing is shown in Color Plate 11.

Collecting Results

Output from a code-coverage testing run should contain at least the following data:

- Level tested
- Markers hit (as text labels)

It may be useful to include:

- Build identifier
- Date/time
- Tester's name
- Specifications of test platform
- Separate list of unexpected markers hit
- Expected markers that were not hit

Some of this may be found already in your log file and so, as above, you may choose to simply add your code coverage results there.

You might find that on a small scale, this information is already enough. Your QA testing will benefit from being guided to cover all markers, and by examining the logs you can now check that good coverage was achieved, check that specific code was tested, and look out for code that should be run that isn't or code that needn't be run but is!

However, you can get much more from the system by going further:

- **Merge.** Merge the results from multiple runs of the same level to reach a higher combined coverage and to confirm unusual results. In many cases, branching player choices may even make it impossible to reach 100-percent coverage in a single play-through. Further, merge the results of all your levels, looking for code that is not used anywhere.
- **Update.** Update your lists of expected checkpoints. After making changes to the code and addressing any anomalies in the code coverage results, extract the list of markers hit to form a new list of expected markers for subsequent runs of the level.
- **History.** Build a history of results for each level over time. You can achieve this by simply checking in the list of expected checkpoints for each level—which may in any case be the best way to include them in the build. You can then leverage your existing diff tools to analyze changes in results over time. For programmers, this can help with diagnosing bugs or tracking changes in levels under active development. With a very large marker set, this could also be helpful in test planning to track when a feature was last tested.

All of this can be done automatically. We use a simple text-processing tool that takes any collection of log files and digests them into final results: sorting by level, merging separate runs, highlighting anything unusual, and outputting updated lists of expected checkpoints for the next run.

Possible Expansions

There is potential for getting more out of the framework:

- **Collecting results over the network.** Rather than using log files and extracting their results offline, it may be better to send results directly over the network to a database server. This assumes that all builds tested can be reliably distinguished. If programmers often send their own local builds to QA, a simple build number may not be enough. This approach simplifies the workflow for collecting and processing results.
- **Automated testing.** As described, the core testing method recommended for use with this gem is a good QA team. However, the automated methods discussed, such as recorded play-throughs, are also compatible with this framework and would complement the QA process well. (Refer to the "Common Approaches" section earlier in this gem.) In particular, code coverage reports from any automated tests performed by your build machine would provide very fast feedback.
- **Categorized markers.** While the original implementation was applied to just AI system code, were it deployed more widely, it could make sense to divide the markers by module and/or feature. The ability to only consider a certain group of markers could then become useful, focusing testing on, say, the sound system, game code, HUD features, and so on.

- **Prioritized markers.** Assigning priority levels to markers could help with test planning, especially in times of fast turnaround. A simple high/medium/low scheme would ensure the most important code is tested first. This would be most effective if integrated into the GUI and if programmers had a simple way to promote/demote marker priority in the builds.
- **Activity display for markers.** Flagging a group of markers to give a visual indication every time they are executed could be useful for better understanding the activity of code or for guided stress-testing of a particular feature.
- **Hit counts.** Rather than a hit flag, keeping a count for each marker could be useful as part of built-in performance tracking or monitoring the relative frequency of branches, loop counts, and so on.
- **Recentness tracking.** Add a global counter that is advanced every time a marker is hit, writing the current counter value to that marker. This could be useful for tricky crash bugs, to find out what code ran in the preceding moments.
- **Custom levels for testing.** This framework could be used to guide the creation of levels for testing specific features, or indeed a single level that includes all features! This offers the potential for very fast turnaround.

A Post-Mortem

This framework was developed in order to safely make a particularly major refactor to our AI system, replacing a fundamental aspect of the system and involving around 25 percent of the code. The AI system is in constant use by developers, so full confidence in the result was required before finally merging the branch. Milestones could not be disrupted, and no one enjoys an endless bug-hunt.

As we have actively maintained our last major title as a test platform—which QA knows inside out—the levels of *Crysis* formed the subject of code coverage tests. In the process we formed a list of the features used—in other words, markers hit—in each level. Before this, various programmers and designers had different pieces of the puzzle, but no one had a complete, verified record of what was used and where—which is an invaluable reference for future maintenance.

The GUI proved useful to developers as well as QA testers, making it easy to observe when and where markers were first hit during their own testing, and with this information allowing QA time to be better targeted. By merging results from all levels, we were also able to find redundant code that would escape other forms of analysis—for example, minor features that were not used in the released title.

Reception in the QA team was enthusiastic: They appreciated the feedback of the new tool and would like to see its use expanded. They also found no measurable impact on frame rate.

Having a text-processing tool to form the reports was essential in dealing with results from multiple testers and many different levels. The tool processes entire folders of log files (one or more tests of each level of the game) in one pass, merging results, updating the label data files in each level folder, and outputting a summary of changes to the console. After that, it is easy to check the updated label files into source control.

When investigating a bug, it was often useful to look through the history of the per-level label files and verify that this was the first test of that code, or to see that the code really had been running successfully for some time, implying the problem must lie elsewhere.

Use of the framework was focused on this refactor and testing in the following weeks. Greater automation would be instrumental in realizing its potential as an everyday maintenance tool—in particular, a network-based collection of results to a central server, emailed summaries of results, and combination with automated tests.

Code coverage helped inform the refactor, helped discover bugs quickly, and gave a new measure of confidence in the result. Some months after the final merge, we've found only two bugs.

Conclusion

This gem presented an adaptation of the code coverage methodology specifically for practical games development, employing QA testing guided by real-time feedback. It can be added to existing code and workflows to augment your existing testing procedures, improving their rigor. It also provides programmers with more information about the usage of their code and greater confidence in their changes.

Included on the CD is an efficient implementation of the framework, complete except for a GUI. This also forms a suitable basis for the various possible extensions of the framework that have been discussed.

References

[Alexandrescu01] Alexandrescu, Andrei. "Modern C++ Design." 2001.

[Cornett96] Cornett, Steve. "Code Coverage Analysis." 1996. Bullseye Testing Technology. n.d. <http://www.bullseye.com/coverage.html.>

[ISO/IEC14882-98] "Standard for Programming Language C++." dcl.fct.spec/4. 1998.

[Obermeit06] Obermeit, Tony. "Code Coverage Lessons." 2006. Mobile Me. n.d. <http://homepage.mac.com/hey.you/lessons.html>.

4.9

Domain-Specific Languages in Game Engines

Gabriel Ware

gabrielware@free.fr

Domain-specific languages, DSLs for short, are computer languages used to solve problems within the explicit boundaries of the problem domain. The benefits of DSLs are multiple: They help by separating domain-related code from application code; they let domain experts solve problems using a language they understand; they can have multiple outputs, and users can easily shift from one to another; and last but not least, designing domain-specific languages usually tighten relations between programmers and experts. This gem will dig into domain-specific languages, answering the following questions: What is a DSL? When should I use a DSL? How do I build a DSL?

Domain-Specific Languages in Depth

In this section we'll explore DSLs and their uses, concluding with some guidance on when to use them.

Domain-Specific Languages: Definitions and Examples

Several definitions have been proposed for domain-specific languages. DSLs can be defined as artificial languages expressing instructions to a machine while working on a narrow field of expertise, a specific domain. These computer languages are sometimes referred to as *little languages* or *micro-languages* because of the limited expressivity of their syntaxes. Their syntaxes are restricted to the problem domain they are modeling, including only what is relevant to the problems. Languages such as C, C++, or Java, which are labeled *general programming languages*, or *GPLs*, provide generic solutions to a broad range of problems and, as such, can be opposed to DSLs that provide more tailored solutions to a restricted set of problems.

Domain-specific languages have existed for a long time, and their use in computer science is widespread. Successful examples include Lex and Yacc, programming languages intended to create lexers and parsers to help in building compilers; SQL, a computer language targeted at relational databases; and LaTeX, a document markup language providing a high-level abstraction of TeX. DSLs have several characteristics emerging from their form and the process used to build them. The main characteristic of DSLs is their syntaxes, which provide appropriate notations to the domain model and a very limited set of instructions. This limits what problems users can solve but at the same time allows the language to be learned quickly. DSLs are also usually declarative. They can sometimes be viewed as specification languages, providing domain experts with the capability of writing specifications that will become new tools, solve problems, and encode domain knowledge. Because they encode domain knowledge as perceived by domain experts, DSLs are usually built from a user perspective. Such a user-centric process tries not to take into account external factors, such as compiler capabilities, and prefers focusing on user experience.

Data mining is a domain that could be used as an example illustrating how domain-specific languages help. Code to search for persons matching certain criteria in tables can be written in any GPL, but it is much easier to write with a language that is appropriate to the domain. Listings 4.9.1 and 4.9.2 show SQL and C++ code snippets that provide the same feature to an application. Even if C++ is more adequate on a general basis, it does not focus on the domain and thus is harder to use in this specific case than SQL.

LISTING 4.9.1   Mining a table for persons named Paul in SQL

```
Select users from table where name='Paul'
```

LISTING 4.9.2   Mining a table for persons named Paul in C++—relying on the STL to handle allocations and strings manipulation

```
std::list<CUser>::const_iterator const table_end = table.end();
    std::string SearchedName("Paul");
    for(std::list<CUser>::iterator it = table.begin();
        it != table_end;
         ++it)
    {
        if (it->Name == SearchedName)
        {
            users.push_back(*it);
        }
    }
```

Another interesting feature these two listings exhibit is the differences in term of interface. While GPLs provide a satisfying interface for programmers, some DSLs provide very light syntaxes nearly exempt from notations that do not translate into everyday language, dropping parentheses, braces, and any other artifact as much as possible. These notations are referred to as *language noise*, and programming interfaces that minimize this noise are called *fluent interfaces*. Domain-specific languages do not always provide a fluent interface to their users, but this can be a useful feature to provide when end users do not have a programming background.

The Different Types of Domain-Specific Languages

While GPLs are usually classified by their programming paradigm and the type of output produced by their compilers, domain-specific languages are distinguished by the methods used to build them. As such, two main categories are emerging—internal DSLs, sometimes referred to as *embedded DSL*, and external DSLs.

When a DSL provides a custom syntax and relies on a custom-made lexer, parser, and compiler, it is categorized as an external DSL. Building an external DSL is the same process as building a new general-purpose language: Programmers have to design the language and implement it as well as any needed tools, such as editors, parsers, compilers, and debuggers. On the other hand, internal DSLs are built from general programming languages that offer syntaxes malleable enough to build new language from them. This greatly reduces the amount of work needed to implement the language as programmers rely on the existing tool chain and language's features. On the down side, internal DSLs' syntaxes usually include language noise from their host language.

In addition to these two categories, DSLs are also often classified by the type of interface they provide to end users. While some DSLs are created by programmers to be used by other programmers, others are designed to be used by domain experts who do not have programming experience. Thus, some DSLs provide textual interfaces, but other DSLs adopt graphical front ends in order to ease programming. An example of a successful visual domain-specific language is Unreal Engine's Kismet, which allows designers to control actions and handle events by connecting boxes using the graphical user interface provided by Unreal Editor.

Advantages of DSLs

Domain experts may not be able to write code but are usually able to review code written using domain-focused syntaxes. DSL code can sometimes even be written directly by domain experts, achieving end user programming. DSLs concentrate on domain knowledge, and thus it is important that coders creating new DSLs deeply understand the problem domain. As a side effect, this usually tightens relations between programmers and domain experts, resulting in more accurate solutions.

The limited expressiveness of DSLs limits user input and, as such, can help to reduce user errors. DSLs are easier to master, and as interfaces become more fluent, the code starts to be self documenting.

Through these characteristics, DSLs are able to express important information while hiding implementation details. Just like good APIs, DSLs provide users the ability to program at a higher level of abstraction. This leads to a clear separation between domain knowledge and implementation that allows for better conservation and reuse of this knowledge.

Finally, DSLs provide new opportunities to do error checking, statistical analysis, or any other transformation of the domain knowledge.

Disadvantages of DSLs

There are also several drawbacks to using domain-specific languages. The most problematic is the cost of building and maintaining a new language. While building external DSLs still requires quite a bit of effort, new tools and new techniques have been used to reduce these costs. Another alternative is to embed the DSL in a host language. As the language evolves and requirements change, language maintenance can become a burden. It can be very tempting to grow the problem domain by adding new keywords and notations, but this usually leads to building general-purpose languages with some domain-specific keywords. This is a very costly approach and should be avoided unless it is desired. Another drawback of using multiple languages to build an application is that programmers need to learn more than a few languages to control the whole pipeline, and thus they need to quickly learn and adapt. One last problematic aspect of using domain-specific languages is that it introduces an extra layer of complexity, which can slow the debugging process.

Relations between DSL and Game Development

Game development provides a wide variety of challenges in many different domains. To take up these challenges, programmers usually use a few general-purpose languages and build frameworks that will help resolve domain-related issues. DSLs appear to be a good fit to this environment. Typical examples of problem domains related to video games are game logic, navigation, animation, locomotion, data modeling, serialization, and transport. Thinking in terms of modeling problem domains and user experience helps to define what solutions are needed.

When to Create a New Language

Creating new languages is a difficult and time-consuming task, so deciding when to use a DSL is a very important process. The need for a domain-specific language usually arises when a common pattern is detected from several problems. Those patterns can occur at code level, in programs, subroutines, or data, as well as at the application level, building similar tools or architecture several times. The problem domain can usually be identified from these patterns, and the boundaries of the domain can then be determined. Domain-specific languages stress staying domain-focused, so it is important to deeply understand the domain's definition. If the boundaries are blurry and users can't anticipate requirements, then it may be impossible to design the language. It is important to carefully choose the bounds because if they are too narrow, the DSL won't be used to encode enough domain language, whereas if they are too broad, the language may lose its focus. Boundaries also influence the language interface by defining which variants are to be exposed to the user. Exposing too many variants will slow language learning, while not exposing enough will render it less usable. Domain experts, documentations, and specifications can help determine such boundaries.

Lastly, because creating a new language is a difficult task, it is important to know whether such a language will be reused. If the problem domain is too narrow and domain knowledge should be encoded only once, it may be better to build a framework over a general-purpose language, but if domain knowledge needs to be encoded multiple times, solve multiple issues, or requires a lot of effort to be encoded using a GPL, then creating a new domain-specific language may be a good option.

Figure 4.9.1 depicts part of the decision process.

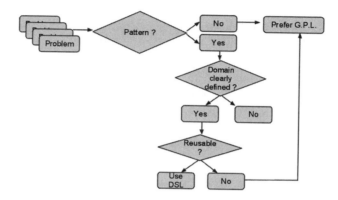

Figure 4.9.1   DSL decision process.

Creating a DSL

The process applied when creating a domain-specific language can be summed in six steps, as illustrated by Figure 4.9.2.

We start with the problems that must be solved to meet our goals. As stressed earlier, it is important to be able to detect recurrent patterns coming from different problems because it will lead to the identification of a problem domain. If patterns are detected soon enough, the domain can be examined, and new problems may be anticipated. The second step is to acquire as much knowledge about the domain as possible. Documentation and domain experts are the best sources of domain knowledge and will be able to explain what users expect from the domain. This leads to a user-centric approach and designing the language from a user perspective. The last step before designing the language is to choose between internal and external DSLs and the type of interface the language will provide to the end user. Interfaces are usually driven by the domain model to represent end user ability to use graphical and textual interfaces. In the language design phase, the specifications of the language are laid down. Notations and keywords needed to model the domain are chosen, and variants—what the interface will show—and invariants—what assumptions about the model will be hidden in the implementation—are identified. Lastly, all tools required to implement the language are created.

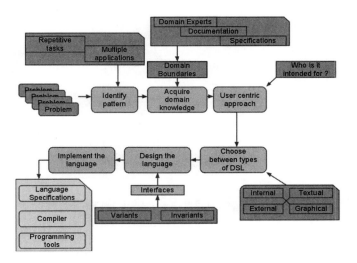

Figure 4.9.2 DSL creation process.

Choosing between Types of DSLs

Determining the user interface of a new language is a decisive factor for its adoption as a new tool. By understanding what users are expecting from the tool, programmers will be able to refine the required features.

If the domain can be modeled using text, then both internal and external DSLs can satisfy the needs, and choosing between them is a matter of understanding their constraints along with the programming proficiencies of the end user. Internal DSLs rely on the availability of a host language that is malleable enough to let a DSL emerge from its own syntax. When such a language is available, its syntax and tool chain will influence the look and feel of the DSL. If those constraints are acceptable, then building an internal DSL is the quickest way to create a new textual DSL, as it will provide needed tools for the language. On the other hand, external DSLs do not rely on another language, allowing for a better customization of their syntaxes. But they also require that programmers build tools such as parsers, interpreters, or compilers to support the new language. If no host language that satisfies syntax needs is available, then external DSLs are the way to go.

While some domains are very easy to model using words, other domains cannot be modeled, or at least are difficult to model, using text. In this case, the domain-specific language can rely on a graphical interface to help end users encode their knowledge. Another factor for building a graphical front end to the DSLs is the programming background of their users. Some DSLs are intended for non-programmers, and if the domain is too complex and thus requires exposing too many variants and keywords, it will then probably be easier for the user to represent the domain knowledge using graphical tools. Although graphical DSLs are usually built from scratch, some tools do exist that help in creating them.

Figure 4.9.3 synthesizes the whole process.

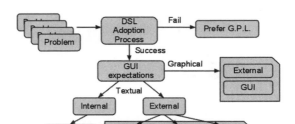

Figure 4.9.3 DSL type decision process.

Common Programming Techniques for Building Internal DSLs

As domain-specific languages become more and more popular, several programming patterns used to build them emerge. Luckily, most programming tips used to build domain-specific languages are easy to understand and use, but some may not be available from all host languages.

The first, and probably oldest, technique is the use of macros. It has been widely used by C and C++ developers to pre-process source code. It uses the preprocessor capabilities to build fluent interfaces that generate complex code at pre-processing time.

Another old and widely available technique is called *function sequencing*. Domain knowledge is encoded using sequences of function calls. The implementation of this method relies heavily on the side effects of each function to affect the execution context of each subsequent call. While this method provides a potentially acceptable solution in terms of interface, relying on side effects can be dangerous and hard to debug as sequences become more and more complex. Listing 4.9.3 shows an example of function sequencing.

LISTING 4.9.3 Function sequencing

```
animation_engine();
    character_controller();
        playanimation("run_fast");
            easing_in_using(LINEAR_EASE_FUNCTION);
                during(10_MSEC);
```

An evolution of function sequencing is called *method chaining*. It uses objects to pass the context between calls without adding noise to the language. With this technique, each method call returns an object that provides a part of the language interface. This helps to fragment the interface across multiple types of objects. Rewriting the previous example using method chaining leads to Listing 4.9.4.

LISTING 4.9.4 Method chaining

```
animation_engine().
    character_controller().
        playanimation("run_fast").
            easing_in_using(LINEAR_EASE_FUNCTION).
                during(10_MSEC);
```

Nested functions are another way to call functions while removing language noise as much as possible. When using this method, all calls are nested, as presented in Listing 4.9.5. The main characteristic of nested functions is the order in which functions get called. It can be very useful when domain knowledge can be expressed as a sum of properties and containers.

LISTING 4.9.5 Nested functions

```
character_controller(
    playanimation(
        "run_fast",
        easing_in_using(LINEAR_EASE_FUNCTION),
        during(10_MSEC) ) )
```

Another frequently used technique for building domain-specific languages on top of an existing framework is to separate the fluent interface from the existing API. Fluent interfaces are usually created using assumptions about the calling context of their routines. Although this helps naming methods that chain efficiently and produce nearly fluent code, this way of writing an API violates what is considered good programming practices. Thus, it may be interesting to get the best of both worlds by adding a fluent interface on top of a more standard framework.

Lambda functions, sometimes named *blocks*, *anonymous methods*, or *closures*, are a feature that only recently became widespread in many mainstream languages. They have been successfully applied to creating DSLs because they offer the key characteristic of evaluating code, with minimal language noise, in a predetermined context. Lambda functions are very similar to a standard method definition but do not require the same textual overhead as functions: They do not need to have names, complete parameter lists, and return types and are simply associated to standard variables that can be passed across functions.

The *dynamic handling of missing methods* is another widespread technique to create domain-specific languages. It is a popular feature of languages such as Smalltalk and Ruby, where you can override doesNotUnderstand and method_missing, respectively. Other languages, such as Python, can provide similar features using other internal mechanisms. Handling missing keywords can be very convenient when the language has to deal with unknown keywords and unknown function names. This technique allows the user to create keywords as needed. It allows creating new modeling languages with very little noise very easily.

LISTING 4.9.6   Animation DSL relying on `method_missing`, nested function, and closures

```
 1: animset = define_animation_set( :terrestrial_locomotion) {
 2:     idle(from_file("tm_idle"))
 3:     run_forward from_file "tm_run_fwrd"
 4:     walk_forward from_file "tm_wlk_fwrd"
 5:     turn_90degsLeft from_file "tm_trn_90deg"
 6:
 7:     jump_forward from_file "tm_jmp_fwrd"
 8:     jump_forward { can_blend_with all_from("terrestrial_locomotion") }
 9:     jump_forward { can_blend_with transitions_from("aerial_locomotion")
10: }
```

Listing 4.9.6 shows a domain-specific language where animation identifiers are keywords chosen by the user and thus impossible to predict. It demonstrates usage of blocks and nested functions using the Ruby programming language. The code block is written between brackets and, in our example, it is given to the `define_animation_set` function. In this domain-specific language, `define_animation_set` creates an animation set object and asks Ruby to evaluate the given block in the context of this object. The animation set object interface will provide functions such as `from_file`, which is used to load an animation from a given filename. In order to reduce language noise, the language relies on the ability of Ruby to deduce parentheses placement. Lines 2 and 3 are similar and interpreted the same way by the Ruby language, the only difference coming from parentheses' presence. Lastly, Ruby handles function calls such as `idle` or `run_forward` as missing calls that are handled by our implementation to identify new animations. A sample demonstrating how Listing 4.9.6 is implemented using the Ruby programming language is provided on the accompanying CD-ROM.

Another easy and very powerful technique to add meaning to code is called *literals extension* and is usually available from object-oriented languages. Extending literals helps readers by allowing modifiers, which may or may not do anything useful, to be used on literals in order to add fluency to the code. It requires the language to handle everything, including literals, as objects that can call methods. Literal extension also relies on the ability of the language to reopen and extend class definitions.

LISTING 4.9.7   Literal extension

```
run if distance_to(nearest_enemy) < 10.meters
```

One last technique worth mentioning is *abstract syntax tree and parse tree manipulations*. It is a rare feature allowing programmers to access the parse tree or the abstract syntax tree after the code has been parsed by the host-language parser. Ruby's ParseTree and C# 3.0 both work in a similar function; a library call is used to parse a code fragment and return a data structure representing the code expressions. This feature is useful when translating code from one language to another or when the DSL needs to rely on a wider range of expression than happens to be available in the host language and thus needs to be transformed before use.

Tools Easing Language Construction

External domain-specific languages have fewer constraints than internal ones but need slightly more effort to create because of the time required to build parsers and compilers. Luckily, tools have been created to ease this process and reduce this overhead.

Lexical analyzers and parser generators, such as Lex and Yacc, have been around for a long time and are still a great help to build languages, but they tend to be replaced by new tools, such as ANTLRWorks or Microsoft's DSL tools, which are both providing powerful development environments focused on creating domain-specific languages. ANTLRWorks is an integrated development environment for creating languages using ANTLR V3 grammars. It offers rapid iteration cycles by providing a full-featured editor, embedding an interpreter, and providing a debugger and a lot of other tools to ease the development process. While ANTLRWorks uses textual grammars to create external textual DSLs, Microsoft's DSL tools provide a way to create visual domain-specific languages to be integrated into Microsoft Visual Studio. The Microsoft DSL tools help design the language and its graphical interface by providing wizards and tools easing domain modeling, specifying classes and relationships, and binding designers' shapes to the model concepts. Although Microsoft's tools for domain-specific languages can't be used for building run-time DSLs, they offer opportunities for integrating a custom visual domain-specific language inside Visual Studio.

Multi-Language Game Engine Development

This section presents domain-specific languages for two domains related to low-level engine programming. Other examples of DSLs for game engines are shading and rendering passes, sound logic encoding emitters, occluders and propagation logic, behaviors of artificial agents, and locomotion rules for animation systems.

The first example of a domain-specific language in a game engine relates to data structure modeling. Data management issues occur in many places, such as a pipeline's applications intercommunication, engine working set, multi-threading and performance issues, and network replication. A common problem is the need to write data manipulation and serialization code multiple times. Thus, it may be interesting to encode as much knowledge about data structures as possible using a domain-specific language that handles tasks such as generating code for serializing and accessing data in all languages used in the pipeline. Such a DSL could also allow for statistical analysis of working sets, which would help profile the engine's need in terms of data.

Acquiring knowledge about the domain of data management is easy because programmers are the domain experts. This type of DSL should solve data-related problems by providing a simple syntax to encode the data structures' layout. The language will encode structures and should provide end users with a way to control fields' identification, alignment properties, and serialization requirements. Lastly, this domain-specific language will be used by programmers, and thus it is acceptable to use a textual interface with low language noise. Listing 4.9.8 shows a sample of such data management DSL using Ruby as its host language. You can find an implementation of this DSL on the CD-ROM.

LISTING 4.9.8   Simple structure layout using a domain-specific language

```
struct (:PlayerInfos) {
  required string :name, replicate_over_network!
  required key :race
  required boolean :is_male
  required int32 :level
  required int32 :exp_points
  required vector3f :position, replicate_over_network!, 16.bytes.alignment
  required quaternion :orientation, replicate_over_network!
  optional int32 :money
  optional float :reputation
}
```

The second use case for domain-specific languages targets the engine's threading model. Scalability of the engine's performance over machine generations has become a very active field of research. Console engines usually take advantage of running on fixed hardware with known specifications, but good engines must allow evolution of hardware. A recurring pattern when changing hardware is to rewrite the threading model to reflect new hardware and get better performance. Another pattern related to threading models happens during development when programmers try to offload heavy tasks from one processor to another, thus changing how tasks update. Again, a language focused on task dependencies and hardware specifications can help handling modifications of the threading model. Such a language has to expose to the user variants such as number of cores, number of threads per core, or preferred number of software threads. It can also expose tasks that are run by the engine and their dependencies in order to help scheduling given the hardware constraints. The output of such a language can be either code or data that would drive current engine's threading framework. Like the previous domain-specific language presented, this language is targeted at programmers, and an internal DSL's properties satisfy our requirements. Listing 4.9.9 shows what such a DSL could look like, and its implementation is provided on the accompanying CD-ROM.

LISTING 4.9.9   Threading a domain-specific language

```
hardware {
     has 3.cores.each { |core| core.have 2.hardware_threads }
}

software do
     instanciate 6.software_threads
     instanciate :camera.module
     instanciate :player.module, :bots.module, :sound.module
     instanciate :physics.module, :graphics.module

     camera.depends_on(:player)
     bots.depends_on(:player)
     graphics.is_bound_to(thread(0))
end
```

Integrating DSLs into the Pipeline

We will now focus on how DSLs integrate in the production pipeline.

Engine Integration through Embedding

The quickest and easiest way to integrate a domain-specific language into an engine is to directly embed it. As such, creating an internal DSL that relies on the engine's main language seems to be an evident way to provide domain-specific languages from the game engine. But, with C++ being the preferred language for building game engines, it is difficult to provide a domain-specific language that allows for rapid iterations. C++ provides a very strict syntax, and most of the advanced features used to build DSLs are difficult, if not impossible, to use. Another problem of relying on C++ to build an internal DSL is the compilation process that may disturb domain experts without any programming background. However, C++ provides macros, nested functions, method chaining, and templates that are powerful tools for building fluent interfaces.

Developers who create DSLs using C++ as a host language must be careful about build times, ease of debugging, and code bloat, as many of the aforementioned techniques can lead to these problems if not used properly.

Engine Integration through Code Generation

Integrating a DSL that relies on a language other than the one used by the engine is made possible by using DSLs as application generators. In this case, the domain-specific language is used to input domain knowledge and transform these high-level specifications to low-level code that will be included in the engine. This approach provides the same advantages as any other code generation technique: End users can easily input data without worrying about the implementation, programmers can modify an implementation without the user noticing, and code need only be optimized once per code generator.

Although this technique has the advantage of separating the domain-specific language from the language used to implement the engine, it has the major drawback of increasing the complexity of the build process.

An example of DSL relying on code generation is Unreal Script, as it binds scripts to native classes by generating C++ headers. Although this is very convenient for debugging and for very tight integration into the engine, it requires script programmers to be really careful when modifying scripts, because it may trigger a full rebuild of the engine. When using this code generation technique, developers must try to reduce compilation and link time as much as possible.

Engine Integration through Interpretation

DSLs can also be integrated into the engine by using a virtual machine that will read and execute domain-specific code at run time. Embedding virtual machines for languages such as Lua or Python has been a popular method for years, and it is possible to build internal DSLs on top of such languages. Another path is to create an external DSL and embed its virtual machine inside the engine, like [Gregory09] and [Sweeney06]. This integration method has the advantage of removing any constraint previously imposed by the engine's language and also helping reduce iteration cycles, but it sacrifices run-time performances.

Independent of building your own virtual machine or using a preexisting one, it is crucial to provide tools that will assist the debugging phase, since this new language will add an extra layer of complexity.

Engine Integration through a Hybrid Approach

An interesting way to integrate DSLs in an engine is a hybrid approach where DSL code can be either compiled to machine code or interpreted by a virtual machine. Although such an approach requires substantial effort to write compilers and interpreters, it would provide the best of both worlds, allowing for fast iteration during development and maximizing release build performance.

Tools are crucial to overcome debugging issues, but developers need to also care about the execution environment of scripts, as it will change when going from interpreted to compiled. The quickest way to set up this hybrid approach for game engines is to create an internal DSL using an already available interpreter, such as Lua, Python, Lisp, or Ruby, and bind it to the native engine's framework. Code generation routines should be written in the host language and used to translate DSL code to native code relying on the engine's framework.

Pipeline Integration through Data Generation

Tools that help domain experts input their knowledge into the pipeline usually provide an interface relying on domain-specific languages. Tools providing DSLs integrated into game pipelines are very common. Unreal Engine provides Kismet for scripting game events [Unreal05], Crytek's CryENGINE offers Flow Graph—a visual editing system allowing designers to script game logic [Crytek09]. Other examples exist in the field of artificial intelligence [Borovikov08].

Pipeline Integration through Centralization

DSLs let users encode domain knowledge using custom syntax and usually help centralize this knowledge. As a side effect, it can be very interesting to use DSLs not only to encode domain knowledge, but also to distribute it to any application of the production pipeline, easing knowledge transfer across multiple languages and applications. For example, tools such as Google's protocol buffers or Facebook's thrift provide domain-specific languages that ease data transfer across complex application architectures, which are very similar to game pipelines.

Conclusion

Domain-specific languages have been around for a long time and are successfully employed to solve a wide variety of problems throughout the software industry. They offer tailored solutions, are easy to learn and manipulate, enable various opportunities to mine the knowledge they encode, and focus on end user experience. It is still difficult to reduce the costs associated with creating and learning several languages, but because video game development addresses such a wide range of problem domains, it seems to be a perfect fit for domain-specific languages.

References

[Borovikov08] Borovikov, Igor, and Aleksey Kadukin. "Building a Behavior Editor for Abstract State Machines." *AI Game Programming Wisdom 4*. Boston: Charles River Media, 2008.

[Crytek09] CryEngine Team, Crytek. "CryEngine3 specifications." 11 March 2009.

[Gregory09] Gregory, Jason. "State-Based Scripting in Uncharted2." Game Developers Conference. 2009.

[Sweeney06] Sweeney, Tim. "The Next Mainstream Programming Language: A Game Developer's Perspective." Symposium on Principles of Programming Languages. 2006.

[Unreal05] Unreal Engine Team, Epic. "Unreal Kismet, the Visual Scripting System." 2005-2008. <http://www.unrealtechnology.com/features.php?ref=kismet>.

4.10

A Flexible User Interface Layout System for Divergent Environments

Gero Gerber, Electronic Arts (EA Phenomic)

kontakt@gerogerber.de

The more people you want to address with your game, the more divergent system environments you have to support and take into account. The differences are not only different CPUs and/or GPUs, but also displays. So what you want and need to develop is software that scales with its environment and makes efficient use of it in all aspects.

In this gem, we highlight an approach to efficient resource usage, especially the available screen size, from the perspective of the user interface (UI) layout. We show how you can keep the UI layout system sufficiently flexible so that, once in place, you can achieve optimal layout results without the need to handle special cases in the source code.

The Problem

The more UI elements (widgets) you have in your game, and the smaller the screen size of your minimum supported system requirements, the more important it is to have efficient and flexible UI layouts. In addition to the fact that there's a wide range of screen resolutions out there, you also have to take into account the fact that there are different aspect ratios. For example, many current laptops make use of previously unusual aspect ratios. So when designing the UI layout, you may need to consider more than the widget's size, position, and font size. In most cases, where the difference between minimum supported system requirements and high end is large, you also have to make use of different assets—for example, textures, which you put on the widgets in order to have a crisply rendered widget. Finding an algorithmic solution for making optimal use of screen space and giving a useful layout is difficult and may, if done in code, not always result in solutions UI designers or artists want.

Some Cheap Solutions

There are some solutions that solve this problem in a cheap and sometimes acceptable way.

The first solution makes use of virtual screen coordinates (see Figure 4.10.1). Here the space the UI works with is always the same (for example, 1024x768). All widgets are positioned in this virtual space. When the physical screen resolution differs from the virtual space, all widgets are then scaled automatically. This effectively projects the virtual screen coordinates onto the physical screen resolution. As long as the two spaces do not differ that much in size or aspect ratio, everything can look acceptable. But if the difference in size or aspect ratio becomes too large, you get non-uniform-scaled widgets with blurred textures.

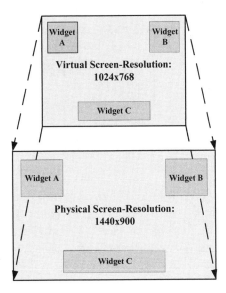

Figure 4.10.1   Virtual screen coordinates.

The second solution works for designs with only a few widgets. Here, all widgets are bound to a combination of screen borders or are centered. So when, for example, you define a widget that is bound to the lower and right screen borders, the widget will stick to the lower-right part of the screen when the screen resolution increases in width or height. You can see border linking as a form of alignment (see Figure 4.10.2). (.Net users may know border linking under the name of *anchoring*.) The difference is that with border linking, in contrast to simple alignment, you can define multiple borders to link to, and you can define a specific number of pixels the widget has to stay away from the borders. This way, you can make use of a large number of screen resolutions without non-uniform-scaled widgets or blurred textures. The drawback here is that with increasing screen resolutions, the widgets make use of a smaller part of the screen and so become harder to read. At the other end, below a given screen resolution the widgets may start overlapping each other, which may not be the desired behavior. But for some designs, this may be the way to go.

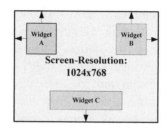

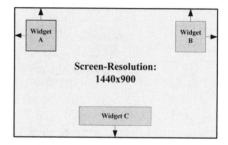

Figure 4.10.2　Border linking.

However, both solutions may not work optimally when additional constraints exist. For example, when you develop for consoles such as Xbox 360, you have to take into account the fact that on some TVs, only 80 to 90 percent of the picture may be visible. This area is called the *title-safe region*. Parts of the display outside this region may not be visible and should not be occupied by any widget or other important game elements. This case has to be considered in the UI layout when running in this special environment.

Another solution would be to do multiple UI layouts and check inside the source code for which layout to use (see Figure 4.10.3). This results in significant extra work for the UI artist, and you have many duplicate layout definitions that need to be kept in sync. Adding, removing, or editing existing widgets in multiple layouts can become complicated and error prone.

Things become worse for the software engineer in a multi-layout scenario when, at run time, widgets have to be created (for example, adding new widgets to a list box), widget textures have to be exchanged, or UI effects have to be started (for example, you want to use different scaled UI effects for different screen resolutions). In these cases there would have to be a check in the source code that decides which asset to load in order to fit into the current UI layout. When, later during development, new layouts are added or removed, all these code sections have to be adjusted in order to make use of this new layout.

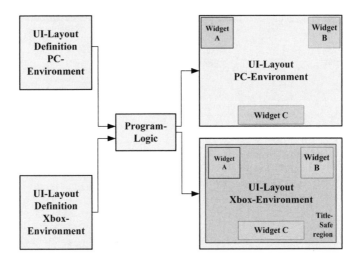

Figure 4.10.3 Multi UI layout scenario.

A More Flexible Solution

Widgets are defined by a set of properties (position, size, texture, font style, and so on) that can be seen as key-value pairs. Many applications make use of XML to define widgets. Using a binary format would result in faster loading times, but for the sake of readability, we will stick to plain text XML in the examples. The following is a sample XML definition for a widget that defines the widget's name, position, and size.

```
<Widget
    name = "player_name"
    x = "10"
    y = "15"
    width = "20"
    height = "30"
/>
```

This example is static and may not suit all environments. It could be better to have a larger widget in larger screen resolutions. A more flexible solution we have already used in a simpler form in our last project is the use of conditional modifiers (CM). A conditional modifier is a node in a widget's XML definition that contains an additional set of widget properties. You can attach a CM to any widget. A CM always contains a set of conditions connected with condition operators, which, when evaluated to true, enable the properties defined inside the CM. An example of a CM inside a widget's XML definition is presented here:

```
<Widget
    name = "player_name"
    x = "15"
    y = "15"
```

```
      width = "20"
      height = "30"
>
    <CM
       cm_name = "xbox360"
       x = "30"
       y = "30"
       width = "40"
       height = "50"
    >
       <Conditions>
          <Condition_Platform
             value = "xbox360"
          />
       </Conditions>
    </CM>
</Widget>
```

In this example the widget is created with the properties defined in the `Widget` node. As a child node of the widget, we added a `CM` node. As a child node of the CM, there is a condition that evaluates to true when the current platform is equal to `xbox360`. The CM is loaded into memory when the corresponding condition is fulfilled. After the widget is fully created, we iterate over all loaded CMs attached to the widget (in the order defined in the XML). For each CM whose conditions evaluate to true, we apply the specified properties to the outer widget. The property `cm_name` inside the `CM` node is just cosmetic and shall help to give the CM construct a meaning. So in the example above on a PC, the widget would be placed at position (15, 15) with a size of (20, 30), and on the Xbox 360 its position would be (30, 30) with a width of (40, 50). Of course, you do not have to re-specify all widget properties inside a CM, but only those will be applied when the CM evaluates to true. So in this example, you could, for example, only change the size of the widget if needed.

It is also possible to combine the previously discussed border-linking solution with the CM system.

Concatenate Conditional Modifiers and Conditions

Using only a single CM or a single condition inside a CM is not that useful. So to further improve the flexibility of CMs, you can chain together multiple conditions and CMs to form a more complex set of conditions. In the following example you can see how this works:

```
<Widget
   name = "player_name"
   x = "15"
   y = "15"
   width = "20"
   height = "30"
   texture = "high_res_texture.tga"
>
```

```
<CM
    cm_name = "above_minspec_screen_size_pc"
    x = "30"
    y = "30"
>
    <Conditions>
        <Condition_ScreenWidth
            operator = "greater_than"
            value = "1024"
        />
        <Condition_Operator_And/>
        <Condition_ScreenHeight
            operator = "greater_than"
            value = "768"
        />
        <Condition_Operator_And/>
        <Condition_ Platform
            negate = "true"
            value = "xbox360"
        />
    </Conditions>
</CM>
<CM
    cm_name = "low_res_gfx"
    texture = "low_res_texture.tga"
>
    <Condition_MinSpec/>
</CM>
</Widget>
```

Here we apply the properties inside the CM only in the case that screen width is greater than 1024, screen height is greater than 768, and if the current platform is not Xbox 360. In this case we change the widget's position. As you can see in this example, there's a second CM that changes the widget's texture to a low-resolution variant when Condition_MinSpec evaluates to true. Both CMs are independent from each other and change different properties of the widget in a different environment. It is also possible for two different CMs to change the same widget property in different cases. The number of different conditions only depends on the needs you have to obtain the desired UI layout for a specific environment.

Implementation Details of the CM System

Implementing the CM system is straightforward. In order to keep the creation of CMs and their corresponding conditions in one place in the code, you can use the well-known Factory Method Pattern [Gamma94] for creating conditions. Figure 4.10.4 shows the class diagram for the CM system.

What you can see from the UML diagram is that a widget can contain an arbitrary number of CMs and that each CM contains at least one condition. Two conditions with a condition operator in between form a condition pair that can be evaluated.

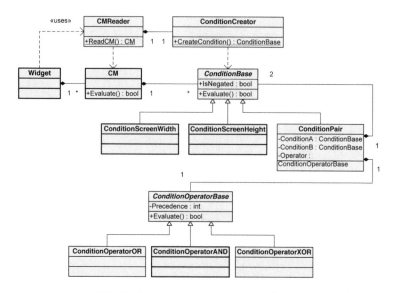

Figure 4.10.4   UML class diagram for the conditional modifier system.

Of course, you have to consider operator precedence in these cases. For the sake of simplicity, we show only two custom conditions in the diagram (`ConditionScreenWidth` and `ConditionScreenHeight`). Additional condition types can be added, depending on your needs. You can also add custom condition operators derived from `Condition-OperatorBase`.

Conditional Modifier Condition References

As you may have noticed, a non-trivial CM definition adds a good deal of potentially redundant data to each widget definition. This redundancy can be resolved by adding a CM-specific property (`cm_conditions_reference`) to the CM definition that references an XML file containing all the relevant conditions and condition operators. The advantage of this is that when you have to modify this set of conditions, you only need to touch one single file, and all referring CMs will work with the new definition. Here's an example:

```
<Widget
    name = "player_name"
    x = "15"
    y = "15"
    width = "20"
    height = "30"
>
    <CM
        cm_name = "xbox360"
        x = "30"
        y = "30"
```

```
        width = "40"
        height = "50"
        cm_conditions_reference = "conditions_xbox360.xml"
    />
</Widget>
```

Following are the corresponding definitions from `conditions_xbox360.xml`.

```
<Conditions>
    <Condition_ScreenWidth
        operator = "greater_than"
        value = "1024"
    />
    <Condition_Operator_And/>
    <Condition_ScreenHeight
        operator = "greater_than"
        value = "768"
    />
    <Condition_Operator_And/>
    <Condition_ Platform
        value = "xbox360"
    />
</Conditions>
```

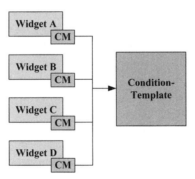

Figure 4.10.5   Conditional modifier condition references.

Widget Templates

We can further improve the way we define widgets, especially if we make use of many similar widget definitions. A good example for this is the definition for a default button style in a game. Default buttons may share many properties that are equal in all instances. For example, the default button's size, texture states, sounds, and so on would be the same for each instance of a default button. It would not make much sense if at each place where you define some sort of default button, you have to specify all the properties by which a default button is defined. For these cases you can make use of widget templates (see Figure 4.10.6).

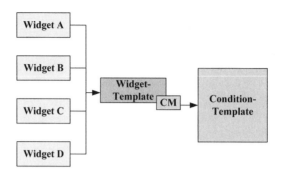

Figure 4.10.6 Defining widgets with widget template files.

A widget template defines a widget with a default set of properties. A widget template is an additional XML widget definition file. A concrete widget definition can refer to widget templates via the additional property `template_filename`. The widget template can contain CMs and conditions. From the implementation point of view, you create a widget instance from the specified template XML definition, apply all properties found in the widget template, then apply all CMs defined in the template, and at the end you set the instance-specific properties for the concrete widget instance. If we stay with the default button example instance, specific properties would be the text shown on the button or the event that gets fired when clicking the button. This way you can save a lot of data inside the widget definitions, and you can make changes quickly because you only have to change the widget template itself. This feature is particularly useful for global styles. The following example shows how you can make use of widget templates.

```
<Widget
   name = "player_name"
   x = "15"
   y = "15"
   template_filename="default_widget.xml"
/>
```

The property `template_filename` refers to the widget template and contains all default properties and CMs including conditions. So in this example, the only custom properties for this widget instance are its position and its name.

Proxy Assets

Many situations require assets such as textures or UI effects to be loaded at run time. One example would be that you want to exchange a texture or show some UI effects to highlight some widget. This requires the specific UI effects that fit the current widget shape and size to be loaded. At this point, when using CMs, you don't know which asset to load, because on different widget sizes you may want to apply textures with different resolutions, and on different widget shapes and widget sizes you have to use different UI effects. In order to decouple these problems from the source code, you can make use of proxy assets. A proxy asset is an XML file that contains the asset information itself (for example, the path to some texture or some UI effects file) and some CMs that control which asset to use in which environment. This is similar to the use of CMs in conjunction with widgets. Here is an example of a proxy asset for a texture:

```
<Texture
   filename = "high_res_texture.tga"
>
   <CM
      cm_name = "minspec"
      filename = "low_res_texture.tga"
   >
      <Conditions>
         <Condition_MinSpec/>
      </Conditions>
   </CM>
</Texture>
```

This example by default uses the texture `high_res_texture.tga`. Only when `Condition_MinSpec` evaluates to true do we actually load `low_res_texture.tga`. So in the source code you would reference the proxy asset's XML definition instead of a concrete texture filename. This way, we have decoupled the asset from the source code. Because we use the same CM system here as described in conjunction with widgets, we can make use of the same factory as well. So when adding new conditions, you can use them automatically for proxy assets, too. See Figure 4.10.7.

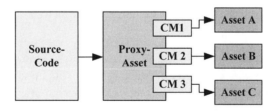

Figure 4.10.7   Proxy assets decouple assets from the source code.

Performance

Of course, all this parsing of CMs takes time. The conditions need only be evaluated once, so it would make sense to keep the conditions in memory and query the result when needed. This is, of course, only valid in cases where you do not create conditions that can change during run time. The same is true for widget templates. If your engine supports the cloning of widgets, you can keep a copy of the widget template in memory and clone it when you create a new widget instance of it. Proxy assets can be optimized by loading and evaluating them only once and reusing the results from memory.

Problems

When using CMs, the definition of widgets becomes a more complex task, and additional work is required to configure all CMs and their corresponding conditions. We recommend tool support for adding, removing, and modifying CMs. In our last project, we had effectively three different UI layouts we used for all different screen resolutions. We defined a minimum screen resolution of 1024×768 (4:3), a medium one of 1280×1024 (5:4), and a large one defined by 1680×1050 (16:10). Screen resolutions greater in width and height than the ones defined use the large screen resolution layout. Screen resolutions in between use the next smaller layout. UI elements positioned relative to a screen border keep the correct position via their border linking property. Because of this, it is possible to scale the UI layout to higher screen resolutions. This way, we covered the most common screen resolutions used by our customers. We also disabled some laptop screen resolutions in order to save time. Of course, when running the game with extremely large screen resolutions, you run into the problem described earlier (widgets become small in relation to screen size). Fortunately, screen sizes do not grow at such a pace that this should become a problem. The UI Editor we used in house was capable of generating CMs recursively regarding the position and size of the widgets. Therefore, we created our base UI layout for the smallest supported screen resolution of 1024×768 and let the UI Editor create CMs with a corresponding scale factor for the higher resolutions.

Another aspect you have to consider is the additional amount of testing you need when you have different UI layouts. Therefore, you should plan early which UI layouts you need and by which conditions these layouts are being controlled. This way, your QA can check out the different UI layouts with a defined checklist.

Conclusion

The CM system described in this gem gives you a good deal of flexibility in defining your UI layout. It offers UI designers and UI artists many options to define the UI layout without requiring corresponding source code changes. On the other hand, you have to invest some work to integrate this system into your engine, and testing the UI layouts is more work compared to just testing a single simple UI layout. But from experience with this system, the advantages outweigh the additional amount of work.

References

[Gamma94] Gamma, E., et. al. *Design Patterns: Elements of Reusable Object-Oriented Software*. Addison-Wesley Professional, 1994.

4.11

Road Creation for Projectable Terrain Meshes

Igor Borovikov, Aleksey Kadukin

igor.borovikov@gmail.com,
akadukin@gmail.com

Roads are becoming an increasingly important part of large environments in modern games. They play a significant role for both the aesthetics and the functionality of the environment. In this gem, we explore several techniques that are useful for modeling roads in a large game environment like that of *The Sims 3* by Electronic Arts [EA:Sims3]. The techniques discussed are general, and for simplicity we limit our discussion to the case of projectable terrain meshes. Some of our inspiration was drawn from earlier works, such as Digital Element World Builder [DEWB], a package for modeling and rendering natural scenes.

We start by building a trajectory for a road on a projectable mesh using elements of variational calculus and describe an algorithm for creating optimal paths on the terrain surface. Next, we move to building a mesh for the terrain while satisfying a number of natural design requirements for the local road geometry.

Roads as Geodesic Curves

Many roads in the real world exhibit certain optimal properties in a sense that they were built to minimize the cost of connecting one location to another. As a trivial example, consider an ideal road between two points A and B on a horizontal plane, which is a straight line and is the shortest length curve connecting the points.

When placing roads between two locations on a terrain model, we can use the same principle and require that a certain cost function is minimized on the curve representing the road. Variational calculus provides a framework for describing such curves. An introduction to variational calculus can be found in any good book on differential geometry, for example [DNF91]. We will limit the formal part of our presentation here to the bare minimum, skipping details that are not important for the algorithm we propose.

Variation Problem for Roads

We will represent a road between points A and B on a terrain with a smooth curve $\gamma(t)$ parameterized with the natural parameter $t \in [0, L]$ (in other words, the curve is parameterized by the arc length), where $\gamma(0)$=A, $\gamma(L)$=B, and L is the length of the curve. Then we can define the cost of moving from A to B along such curve as the length of the curve:

$$L = \int_0^L \ell(t)\, dt \quad (1)$$

where $\ell(t)$ is the cost function:

$$\ell^2(t) = \left| d\gamma / dt \right|^2 = x_t(t)^2 + y_t(t)^2 + z_t(t)^2 \quad (2)$$

This cost function is calculated based on a Euclidian metric in 3D space. The cost function (2) restricted to the terrain surface induces the so-called Riemannian metric on the terrain (which still directly corresponds to our intuitive geometric notions of distance). Shortest length curves on such a Riemannian space are called *geodesics*.

For terrain modeled as a height map $z = f(x,y)$, we have:

$$\ell^2(t) = x_t(t)^2 + y_t(t)^2 + z_t(t)^2 = x_t(t)^2 + y_t(t)^2 + (f_x x_t(t) + f_y y_t(t))^2 \quad (3)$$

Geodesics for such a cost function are similar to a rubber band stretched across the terrain along the shortest trajectory between destination points while keeping contact with the surface across their entire length. Such curves provide the shortest path but do not correspond to our desire to provide natural-looking roads, and in particular they ignore the role of gravity.

An important observation is that actual roads also minimize variation of altitude along the trajectory. This is true for both foot trails and automobile roads. Instead of going along the shortest path across a hill, roads tend to bend around while trying to maintain the same altitude. The altitude variation element along a path is:

$$h^2(t) = z_t(t)^2 = (f_x(x(t), y(t)) + f_y(x(t), y(t)))^2 \quad (4)$$

We can define a new length element as follows:

$$\tilde{\ell}^2 = \ell^2 + \lambda h^2 \quad (5)$$

with $\lambda \geq 0$. For larger values of λ, we expect the geodesics to be "flatter" in the z direction. Using in (1) the new cost function (5) will give us:

$$L = \int_0^L \tilde{\ell}(t)\, dt = \int_0^L \sqrt{\ell^2 + \lambda h^2}\, dt \quad (6)$$

which will provide a better approximation to the behavior of actual roads. The parameter λ corresponds to the tradeoff between the desire to reach the destination point as soon as possible versus the desire to save on climbing up and down any slopes along the pathway.

Solutions for the variational problem (1) can be found among the solutions of Euler-Lagrange equations:

$$\frac{d}{dt}\frac{\partial \ell}{\partial x_t} - \frac{\partial \ell}{\partial x} = 0, \qquad \frac{d}{dt}\frac{\partial \ell}{\partial y_t} - \frac{\partial \ell}{\partial y} = 0 \qquad (7)$$

When solving the equations (3), we need to also satisfy the boundary conditions $\gamma(0)=A$ and $\gamma(L)=B$. However, solving the boundary condition problem for the equations (7) is not a simple task. Instead, in the next section, we will obtain a numeric solution by directly optimizing a discrete version of (6).

Numerical Solution for Geodesics

Here we will look for the minimum of the cost functional (6) directly by approximating the smooth curve γ with a piecewise linear curve on the surface. The following procedure converges to the solution of the original continuous problem in a wide range of conditions; however, in the interest of brevity, we will leave out the proof.

A piecewise linear representation of the curve $\gamma(t)$ requires n+1 nodes: $\{\gamma_i, i=0,\ldots,n\}$ or, in coordinates, $\gamma_i=(x_i, y_i, f(x_i, y_i))$. For such a curve, there will be n line cuts between nodes: $c_i=[\gamma_i, \gamma_i+1]$. The length of the line cut c_i is denoted as $|c_i|$. Obviously,

$$|c_i| = \sqrt{(x_i - x_{i+1})^2 + (y_i - y_{i+1})^2 + (f(x_i,y_i) - f(x_{i+1},y_{i+1}))^2} \qquad (8)$$

The discrete approximation of the cost along a curve for the variational problem (7) is the following sum instead of an integral:

$$G = \sum_{i=0,\ldots,n-1} g_i = \sum_{i=0,\ldots,n-1} \lambda |f_i - f_{i+1}| + (1-\lambda)|c_i| \qquad (9)$$

For a fixed number of nodes, the following iterative optimization process allows us to find local minimum for (9).

G := calculate the cost using (9)
CostChange := G
While cost change is greater than threshold do:
　　For each node 0<i<n do:
　　　　$\gamma_i := \arg \min_{\gamma \in M_i}(g_{i-1} + g_i)$ // optimize node i
　　NewG := calculate using (9)
　　CostChange: = G − NewG
　　G := NewG

where M_i is the line equidistant from the current nodes γ_{i-1} and γ_{i+1}. In other words, for each three neighbor nodes, we optimize the location of the middle node by finding the minimum cost local to the two-segment part of the path by varying the location of the middle node on the middle line M_i between the two other nodes. See Figure 4.11.1.

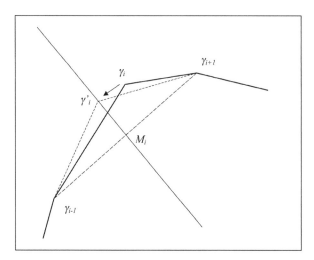

Figure 4.11.1   Optimization of the middle node.

Such a choice of the per-node optimization domain ensures that the spacing between nodes will remain relatively uniform, thus adding to the method's stability. Also, single-parameter optimization is much cheaper computationally than the two-parameter optimization case, which searches for an optimal location in an area between two nodes. Another advantage is that such an optimization is in direct correspondence with the variations used in the proof, such that we get the correct continuous limit for our procedure when the number of nodes approaches infinity. Note that we optimize the location of every node except the first and last nodes of the curve. The iterations stop when the cumulative change of cost is less than a given threshold, which is input as a parameter for the method.

The method can be relatively expensive for a detailed representation of a road curve with many nodes. This can be addressed by starting with a less detailed representation with fewer nodes and subdividing it when the iterations on this curve stop. Subdivision stops when the length of the road segment reaches a minimal allowed length. This minimal length depends on the design requirements but can be naturally set comparable to the distance between vertices for the regular mesh built from the height field.

A Python-based version of the algorithm is provided on the CD for your experimentation. This takes the file ridge.png as input and generates ridge_path.png as output. These are shown in the left and right sides, respectively, of Figure 4.11.2. Note that the Python code requires Python 2.4 or later along with a matching version of the Python Imaging Library (PIL).

A final touch for the created curve could be node resolution optimization. We can eliminate nodes where the angle between adjoined segments is sufficiently small. Again, a cost function and angle can provide criteria for optimization so that nodes are not removed too aggressively.

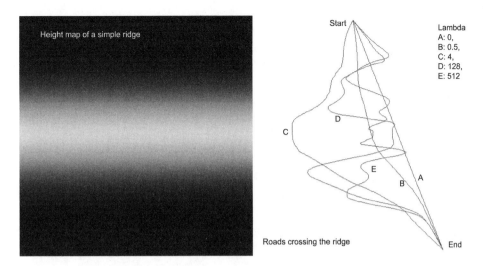

Figure 4.11.2 Sample paths built with the proposed algorithm.

The branching of roads requires a little extra work. The problem of connecting Point C to one of the Points A or B in the presence of an already-built road from A to B can be reduced to the same variational problem with any movement along the existing road being negligibly small in comparison to the movement across terrain without roads. This simplification may be used to reduce the problem to a similar variational problem but with a slightly different boundary condition: The end point D of the new curve will belong to the existing road rather than being fixed to A or B. The required modification to the algorithm is very simple: We include D in the optimization by allowing it to move freely between the nodes of the existing road.

Road Grading Techniques for The Sims 3 Worlds

After creating a trajectory for a road, we need to deliver a road mesh that is consistent with the terrain—this means the terrain mesh also needs to be locally modified around the road. This produced a number of challenges during *The Sims 3* [EA:Sims3] development.

Blending Roads with Terrain in The Sims 3

The Sims 3 worlds were designed without grid-based placement restrictions for roads. The roads could be placed anywhere with respect to the mesh, and the road segments were not limited to straight lines and simple intersections.

Road segments were the spline-based curves connected to each other by connection ports. The intersections have fixed (prebuilt) geometry. The world designer could place and edit roads in an in-house build tool. *The Sims 3* world terrain is a 3D mesh generated from a 2D image height map, which played a critical role in road network construction algorithms.

The road mesh is generated using a base spline and world terrain geometry that is covered by the road segment. This provides a relatively easy and intuitive way to lay down the road network. However, as shown in Figure 4.11.3, the road surface generated in such way follows the terrain surface exactly and may not be smooth enough.

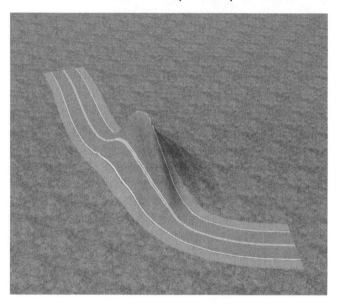

Figure 4.11.3   The road segment placed on the uneven terrain.

Road Grade and Road Slope

The road surface must satisfy a number of conditions enforced by the road-grading tool. The most important characteristics controlled by this tool are road grade and road slope. A road slope is defined as a road surface tilt (the gradient perpendicular to the road), and a road grade is defined as steepness of the road (the gradient parallel to the road) [Wiest98].

The tool allows designers to set up the road grade and slope limits and automatically modify the road surface to create a realistic look and improve the routable functionality of roads. The algorithm adjusts individual or connected road segments' tilt and steepness using height map grid cells. We describe a technique that deals with the slope and grade limits separately.

Flattening Road Slope

The purpose of the road slope flattening algorithm is to set to zero the slope across a road segment. The same technique can be applied to the connected road segments.

The actual road mesh modification is accomplished by a world terrain height map data modification. The advantage of this method is a smooth coupling of road surface with the surrounding terrain. The disadvantage is that the road surface geometry will become imprinted to the terrain geometry. Moving the graded road will leave a modified terrain behind, and this may lead to visual artifacts.

Alternatively, the road network surface could be managed by a separate height map, and terrain generation code should support multiple height map layers to combine the original terrain data and road network maps.

The road segment spline defines a road profile. At the first step, we divide a road segment by sub-dividers, as shown in Figure 4.11.4.

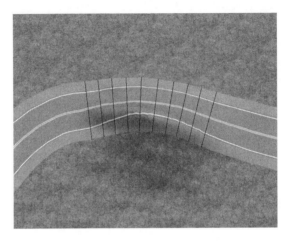

Figure 4.11.4   The road segment divided by sub-dividers.

The distance between sub-dividers depends on the terrain height map resolution and the road edges' lengths. For example, if each height map point represents a 1×1 unit in world coordinates, then the sub-divider distance could be an average value between maximum and minimum road edge lengths.

The second step is determining a height for sub-divider end points. The height of sub-divider end points should match the height of the sub-divider center point (a height at the intersection between the sub-divider and a road spline) to set zero road slope.

The third step is applying a new height to each height map point inside of a sub-quad formed by a pair of sub-dividers. Since there is no guarantee that the four points defining the sub-quad corners belong to the same plane, we need to triangulate each sub-quad and flatten the inner height map points for each triangle, as shown in Figure 4.11.5. We use the plane equation to calculate the new height of height map points inside the triangle.

The fourth and final step is to create a smooth road surface. The results of the previous step can leave visual artifacts between road sub-quads. To fix the surface, we use a bilinear interpolation between neighboring height map points across the entire road segment. In the case of connected road segments, the bilinear interpolation should be performed across the entire road network. Figure 4.11.6 shows the result.

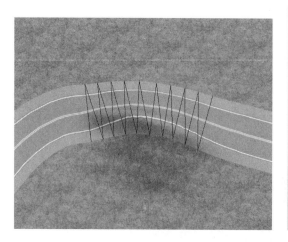

Figure 4.11.5 Triangulated road segment.

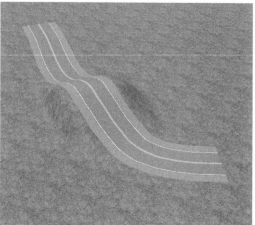

Figure 4.11.6 Smoothed road segment.

Limiting Road Grade Angle

To limit a road segment grade, we use a modified road slope flattening technique. After the road segment subdivision, we calculate an inclination angle for each sub-quad. Then we adjust the angle by raising or lowering sub-quad dividers. The challenge here is to determine which road direction should be used for raising or lowering each end. Figure 4.11.7 shows the difference.

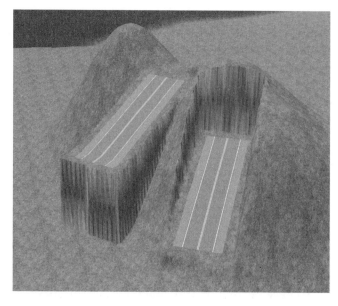

Figure 4.11.7 The road grade limit difference for opposed road directions.

Results and Possible Generalizations

These algorithms were very useful during *The Sims 3* development and saved a significant amount of world designers' time by automating mesh modifications. The in-game routing system also benefited from flattened road slopes and reasonably limited road grades.

The same algorithms could also be applied to the flattening of water surfaces (such as rivers) or can be modified to achieve more complex road surfaces, such as road banking on curves. However, using such an algorithm on non-height map–based terrain meshes may require different approaches for sub-quad height calculation, surface triangle flattening, and surrounding geometry transitions.

Conclusion

These techniques cover a relatively complete set of road creation tasks for large environments. An abstract definition of a road as a geodesic curve may not be sufficient to deliver fully automated road creation, but it can provide a good starting point for the world designers, from which they can tweak road layout to their liking. The road-grading tool proved to be so versatile that very few (if any) manual adjustments of the meshes were required after the road was created and imprinted into the terrain.

References

[EA:Sims3] The Sims 3, PC/Mac. Electronic Arts, 2009.

[DEWB] "Digital Element WorldBuilder, PC." n.d. Digital Element Inc. n.d. <http://www.digi-element.com/wb/index.htm>.

[DNF91] Dubrovin, B. A., A. T. Fomenko, and S. P. Novikov. *Modern Geometry—Methods and Applications: Part I: The Geometry of Surfaces, Transformation Groups, and Fields.* Springer, 1991.

[Wiest98] Wiest, Richard L. "A Landowner's Guide to Building Forest Access Roads." July 1998. National Forest Service. n.d. <http://www.na.fs.fed.us/SPFO/pubs/stewardship/accessroads/accessroads.htm>.

4.12

Developing for Digital Drawing Tablets

Neil Gower

neilg@vertexblast.com

A walk though the art department in almost any game studio will reveal a wide selection of digital drawing tablets. In their most basic form, tablets replace the mouse with a stylus for pointer input. However, treating a tablet as merely a mouse substitute greatly underutilizes its potential. Most tablets offer a rich set of inputs, including pressure and tilt sensitivity as well as a variety of buttons.

In this gem, we look at ways to harness the full potential of the drawing tablet as an input device, first by surveying the research on pen-based interfaces and then by developing an interface layer in C++ to conveniently access tablet functionality.

Equipped with this knowledge, you will be able to make full use of tablet features directly in your tools. Along the way, we also note best practices to follow when developing for tablets.

Background

The pen-based interface devices we find in game development are typically digitizer tablets, tablet PCs, or displays with built-in tablet functionality. Standard tablets provide a form of indirect interaction—the user moves the pen on a tablet on their desk to move the pointer on the screen. Tablet PCs and tablet displays provide direct interaction by allowing the user to place the pen directly on the display. Direct interaction can be very empowering, although it is not yet commonplace. The majority of the pen-based devices we work with today are indirect tablet interfaces.

Building a Better Mouse

If you and your users are already proficient with the mouse (usually a safe assumption in a game studio), you might wonder why you should bother with tablets.

Low-level studies, such as [MacKenzie91], have shown that pen tablets perform as well as the mouse for pointing tasks and even slightly better for dragging tasks.

Considering more complex tasks, such as drawing, we find that mouse users have trouble reproducing strokes more complex than straight lines [Kurtenbach93]. This is an intuitive result when you consider the difficulty of signing your name with a mouse versus with a pen.

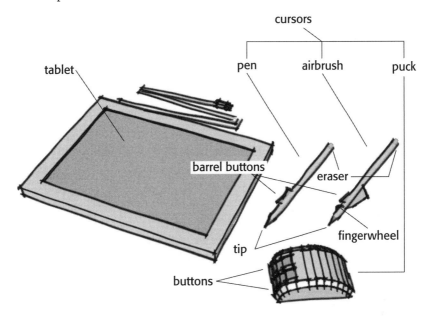

Figure 4.12.1 Tablet terminology.

In addition to pen position and touch detection, a modern tablet offers features a mouse cannot match, such as reporting the amount of pressure on the pen tip, the tilt and orientation of the pen, and even which end of the pen is being used. These input channels can be combined with keyboard modifiers to create a huge, expressive palette of inputs to your application. Recently, tablets and touch-based devices have begun to offer the ability to detect multiple points of contact as well, which opens up opportunities for more advanced gestures and for interfaces that support multiple users working together on a single device.

Applications

Two-dimensional drawing is one of the archetypal applications of pen tablets. Another class of application is digitizing, which involves precisely transcribing real-world data (such as schematics) into digital form. In most drawing and creative applications, precision is less important than expressiveness and convenience. Pressure is commonly used to vary brush parameters, such as width or opacity. Using keyboard shortcuts and extra buttons on the tablet, we can enable quick tool changes with minimal interruptions to the creative process.

The same principles from drawing can be transferred directly to game development applications. For example, terrain height-map editing—tip pressure can control height changes or foliage density, and the eraser can be used to reverse the height changes or thin out foliage. Of course, with a modern tablet this is only the beginning. For example, additional parameters, such as the normal direction of the foliage, can be taken from the pen's tilt values.

Another important area of pen-based applications is sketch-based interfaces. This includes sketch-based modeling, which involves taking 2D pen strokes and transforming them into 3D modeling operations, and sketch-based design tools. Sketch-based design tools can be used for everything from game logic state diagrams, to UI design and layout, to even UML or box-and-arrow software design.

Researchers have found that pen-based interfaces are good for encouraging users to focus on quick design iterations. (For example, see the discussion in [Kimura93].) This is in part because for most users, drawing with a pen is a familiar way to brainstorm. Other factors include the low level of detail and consequent low level of commitment to sketched content. Kimura, et al. also discuss evidence that users of fully featured 3D programs get easily distracted by style issues rather than focusing on substance during the design process, and even that tools that present content in a "sketchy" style encourage faster iteration. By stripping our early design tools down to little more than the pen and the user, removing complex menus and tool palettes, we can potentially create situations where users just draw what they think, which would be the ideal design tool.

Tablet Theory

Before we jump into coding tablet-enabled tools, we will take a look at the research and theory related to pen-based interfaces. The field of human-computer interaction (HCI) is rich with innovative ideas and empirical studies to help you make informed design decisions about your tablet-enabled tools.

Since most tools will not be designed exclusively for tablets, a comparison to the mouse is a good place to start. Although low-level speed and accuracy are comparable, there are some subtle differences between these devices. For example, users tend to produce larger gestures with the stylus than with the mouse [Moyle02], which may require you to scale the user's input to compensate if you use a gesture-recognition system. There is also a tendency for right-handed users to err upward when moving the pointer to the right and downward when moving left. The reverse is true of left-handed users. This horizontal error effect is less noticeable in mouse users; however, they tend to have more difficulty with accurate vertical motions compared to pen users. These differences imply that we should try to make decisions early on about whether to design our interfaces to favor one device type or to provide customized modes for each.

Another issue to consider is accuracy. When targets are only a few pixels wide, accurate selection can become an issue in pen-based systems. This is a common scenario in 3D editing applications—for example, when selecting vertices. Remember, too, that if the user must hold the pen over a location before touching the tablet, he has to steady his hand while doing so. This is more difficult than with a mouse, which sits perfectly still on the desk when at rest. Direct-input setups, such as tablet PCs, introduce additional challenges for precise selections, caused by the parallax between the display and its protective surface.

One solution to precision selection problems is presented in [Ramos07], which describes a pressure-activated zoom lens. They found this interface effective at increasing both speed and accuracy, and it was well received by users. In pressure-activated systems, it is good practice to provide feedback to the user about how much pressure is required to activate the system. In the case of the zoom lens, as the user approaches the pressure threshold, the lens becomes more opaque to indicate its readiness.

Working in 3D

Manipulating 3D objects viewed with 2D displays using 2D input devices is always a challenge. [Chen88] contains a good discussion of techniques for three-axis rotation techniques that work with tablets. Their paper provides a good implementation-level description of their "Virtual Sphere Controller."

The virtual sphere essentially places a bounding sphere around the object to be rotated. Dragging the stylus up and down or left and right rotates around X (forward) and Y (up), respectively. To rotate around Z (out of page), the user moves the stylus around the circumference of the sphere.

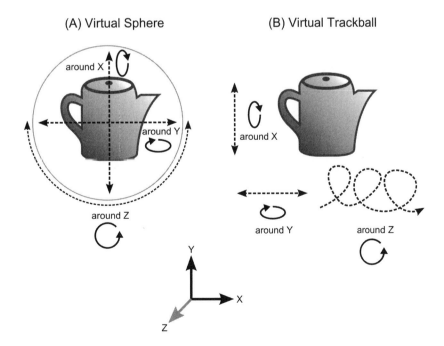

Figure 4.12.2 3D rotation controllers.

Another interesting stylus technique is the "stirrer," introduced by [Evan81]. For this tool, users make small circular motions, analogous to stirring, to modify a single axis value. The stirrer has several nice properties. It can be used anywhere on the tablet, so it doesn't require the user to pay attention to pen location. Instead, users can focus on the object being manipulated. Users can also vary the rate of change by varying the size of the circles, with larger circles changing the value more slowly. Evans uses the stirrer to create a virtual three-axis trackball, which maps x and y stylus movement to rotation around X and Y and a stirrer to rotation around Z.

Shortcuts and Gestural Interfaces

As users become more proficient with software tools, they seek ways to optimize their workflow and focus their efforts on the creative aspects of their work. A typical optimization is the use of shortcut keys to directly invoke commands. In practice, however, studies have shown that many users fail to make the transition to using shortcut keys. Gestural shortcuts have been shown to be easier to learn while still providing the same level of performance to expert users. In [Appert09], there is a good discussion of the performance and implementation of a gesture-recognition system for this purpose, including references to a variety of alterative approaches as well.

A general principle of UI design is to make the functions of the system self-revealing, which just means that users should be exposed to the functions through normal interaction with the system. For example, listing shortcut keys with their menu items makes the shortcuts self-revealing. You can similarly show gesture marks next to menu items or draw the gestures on the screen briefly when the user invokes the command. This concept of self-revealing gestural shortcuts has also evolved into an elegant menu solution—marking menus.

Gestures and Pie Menus: Marking Menus

Marking menus evolved out of pie menus. Pie menus are menus arranged in a circular layout, rather than the traditional linear box arrangement. The user touches the pen down to open the menu and then drags the pointer into the pie slice corresponding to the command he wants. Once the correct command is highlighted, the user lifts the pen to invoke the command. Different menus can be triggered by opening the menu in different areas of the workspace, similar to right-click context menus in mouse interfaces.

Pie menus present several advantages to tablet users. The circular layout means different menu options are accessed by moving the pointer in different directions, rather than just varying the magnitude in a single direction. This requires less precision and effort to make correct menu selections. Another useful property is that due to the widening of the slices as the pointer moves away from the center of the pie, the user is able to dynamically increase the effective size of the menu items, simply by making larger gestures.

The circular layout can also be used to represent logical relationships between menu options—for example, placing logically opposite commands such as cut and paste spatially opposite each other in the menu. This helps users remember where commands are in the menus. Studies show that even numbers of pie slices facilitate the best performance, especially 4, 8, and 12. There is also evidence that right-handed users access the upper-right and lower-left quadrants of the pie most quickly (see [Hancock04]), so you may want to place your most frequently used commands in these spots. Since the effect is related to the handedness of the user, it's also a good idea to provide an option to flip the menu layout for left-handed users.

Marking menus take pie menus and combine them with gestural shortcuts to create a highly efficient interface [Kurtenbach93]. The basic marking menu implementation is very similar to a pie menu. The menu is pressure activated, and the user's pen motions are shown as a trail on the screen. There is also a delay before the pie menu appears. The user can move the pen in the anticipated direction of their selection and lift the pen to complete the selection during this delay before the menu appears. In this case, they have "marked" their selection. See Figure 4.12.3.

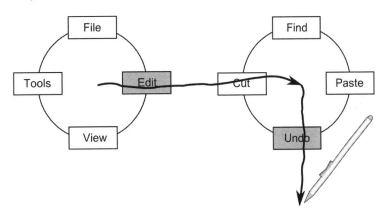

Figure 4.12.3   Marking menus.

What makes marking menus so effective is that using the pie-menu interface is also a rehearsal of the shortcut marking gesture, so learning the shortcuts does not require any additional effort from the user. Since the gestures created by the marking menus are all sequences of linear motions, marking menus can be combined with other gesture-recognition systems that use non-linear gestures. This concept can be extended to hierarchical marking menus as well.

Tablet Programming

A high-level point about adding tablet support to your tools is that it's highly advisable to package your tablet code into a reusable toolkit. Your toolkit can include things such as a gesture-recognition system, custom UI widgets, and low-level tablet interface code.

This helps provide consistency across applications and makes it easier and therefore more likely that other tool developers will add gesture support to their projects.

For Windows applications, Wintab is the industry-standard API for accessing tablet devices. For Mac OS X, we have a choice between the older Carbon (C) API and the newer Cocoa (Objective C) API. On Linux, we use the XFree86 input extension and XFree86 event queue. On the CD-ROM, you will find an example program that uses Wintab to read and display the various types of tablet data discussed in this gem.

Tablets generally have a wide variety of device capabilities, much like PC joysticks. It's important to query the capabilities of the device at run time and make the necessary adjustments in your code. A few of these capabilities can even change at run time, such as the type of stylus being used.

Getting Started with Wintab

To get things started, let's take a look at what's needed to initialize Wintab.

```
#define PACKETDATA (PK_X | PK_Y | PK_BUTTONS)
#define PACKETMODE PK_BUTTONS
#include "pktdefs.h"

if ( !WTInfo(0, 0, NULL) ) {
    // Wintab is not available on this system
    return -1;
}

// start with a default context...
LOGCONTEXT contextParams;
WTInfo( WTI_DEFCONTEXT, 0, &contextParams );

// customize it for your application...
contextParams.lcOptions  |= CXO_MESSAGES | CXO_SYSTEM;
contextParams.lcPktData   = PACKETDATA;
contextParams.lcPktMode   = PACKETMODE;
contextParams.lcBtnUpMask = contextParams.lcBtnDnMask;

// then get a context handle and we're ready to go!
HCTX hContext = WTOpen( hWnd, &contextParams, TRUE );
```

At the top, we have some macro magic that enables `pktdefs.h` to generate the PACKET struct that matches the values you set in `lcPktData` further on. The second `WTInfo()` call initializes our context parameters struct with reasonable defaults for most applications. Then we just tweak the parts we need before giving it to `WTOpen()` to initialize the tablet context and generate a handle for it.

Now that we're up and running, let's see how to get position data from the tablet. With Wintab, we get data from the tablet via packets in a message queue. When we configured the context parameters, we had to set CXO_MESSAGES in `lcOptions`. This tells Wintab to send our application WT_PACKET messages through the standard Windows messaging system. WT_PACKET signals our code when the tablet has data queued up for the application. In the handler for this message, we use `WTPacket()` to extract the data.

```
case WT_PACKET:
    PACKET pkt;
    WTPacket( hContext, wParam, &pkt );
    cursorX = pkt.pkX;
    cursorY = pkt.pkY;
    break;
```

It's important to stay on top of the packet queue, because if it overflows we'll stop getting WT_PACKET messages, and the tablet will stop sending state information. Practically speaking, this means we'll usually use WTPacketsGet() to retrieve all of the packets currently in the queue and then process each one (demonstrated in the example code on the CD-ROM).

As shown in the previous code listing, each packet contains the state information we requested in PACKETDATA during initialization. In this case, pkX and pkY are the cursor coordinates.

Note that when we set up the context, we also set CXO_SYSTEM in lcOptions. This tells Wintab to move the system cursor, rather than depending on our code to do it. This is the simplest way to handle tablet versus mouse positioning. Clearing CXO_SYSTEM allows you to track mouse and tablet positions separately. This can get tricky and is potentially confusing to the user. If you are rendering your own pointer, hiding the system cursor is a good solution that still leverages Wintab to manage the pointer location.

By default, the tablet will deliver position information in tablet units (in other words, at the resolution of the tablet). With Wintab, you can specify a different range. For example, you can have it scale positions to screen units by setting lcOutExtX/Y to the screen dimensions. Keep in mind that the origin of the default tablet coordinate system is in the lower-left corner of the tablet. You can change this by supplying negative extents to the context. If you also want to translate the tablet origin—for example, to match the origin of your application's drawing area—you can do so with lcOutOrgX/Y.

The pen tip and eraser post standard Windows button up/down messages. This provides compatibility with non-tablet-aware applications, since pen-down is usually equivalent to left-click. Our code is tablet aware, though, so it can ignore the button messages and instead process the tablet's button and pressure values directly from the packet queue.

```
case WT_PACKET:
    PACKET pkt;
    WTPacket( hContext, wParam, &pkt );
    DWORD buttonNum    = LOWORD( pkt.pkButtons );
    DWORD buttonChange = HIWORD( pkt.pkButtons );
    // buttonChange is one of TBN_UP, TBN_DOWN, TBN_NONE
```

This code listing extracts the button number and button state from the packet. This is based on the button reporting being in relative mode, which we configured by including PK_BUTTONS in our PACKETDATA and setting PK_BUTTONS in our context's lcPktMode.

Being a Good Neighbor

Remember that more than one application can be running that uses the tablet for input. With Wintab, tablet contexts are layered so that usually only the application with the top-most context receives tablet events. It's up to you to make sure your context's stacking position is in sync with the application's window position. When your window loses focus or gets minimized, you should push your tablet context to the bottom of the context stack with WTOverlap().

Cursor Proximity

We have a basic level of functionality now, but really this only gets us to the same level as a mouse. Let's start adding some more advanced tablet features to the application.

A key part of the tablet system is the cursor. The cursor is the physical device that the user uses to interact with the tablet surface. There are a variety of cursor types in addition to the pen, including the eraser (usually the opposite end of the pen), airbrush, and puck.

The cursor does not have to be touching the tablet surface for it to be detected. Most tablets sense the cursor from about half a centimeter above the actual surface. Depending on how general you want your application to be, you can request WT_CSR-CHANGE events when a cursor comes within proximity of the tablet by setting CXO_CSRMESSAGES in lcOptions. If you're not interested in the details of the cursor being used with the tablet, you can just do everything with WT_PROXIMITY, which you'll get whenever any cursor enters or leaves the range of the tablet. WT_CSRCHANGE is an extra message that you get only when the cursor enters proximity, which is the ideal time to update your cursor capabilities and options.

```
case WT_PROXIMITY:
    bIsInProximity = LOWORD(lParam);
    break;

case WT_CSRCHANGE:
    WTPacket( hContext, wParam, &pkt );
    // use pkt.pkCursor with WTInfo() to get properties of the
    // active cursor...
    break;
```

Additional Input Axes

Pressure is a common and very useful pen feature. This data is relatively straightforward to access. When querying the device capabilities, you can get the parameters for the "normal pressure axis," which tells you how many levels of pressure the device reports. This can then be used to scale the pressure values you get from pkt.pkNormalPressure when you have PK_NORMAL_PRESSURE set in your PACKET struct. Users can customize thresholds and response curves for pressure sensitivity at the system level, but as long as you access the pressure data this way, this will all be transparent to your application.

If you're looking at the pressure information in the Wintab spec, you'll also see there is a tangent pressure property. This is pressure parallel to the tablet surface, which can come from special cursors like the airbrush, which has a finger wheel that produces tangent pressure values.

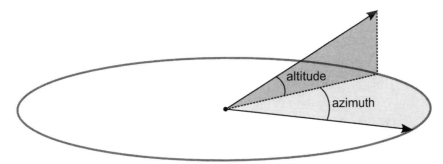

Figure 4.12.4   Azimuth and altitude representation of orientation.

Another useful feature is tilt sensing. This allows you to detect the angle that the stylus is being held at relative to the tablet surface. Wintab exposes this as pkt.pkOrientation, which represents the orientation as an azimuth and altitude angle (see Figure 4.12.4). Like the pressure values, the orientation values should be scaled based on the device capabilities. We can convert the orientation angles into a unit vector with a little trigonometry:

```
float azimuthRads  = 2.0f * PI * pkt.pkOrientation.orAzimuth
                        * azimuthScale;
float altitudeRads = PI * pkt.pkOrientation.orAltitude
                        * altitudeScale;
float lengthXY = cos( altitudeRads );
float tiltX = sin( azimuthRads ) * lengthXY;
float tiltY = cos( azimuthRads ) * lengthXY;
float tiltZ = sin( altitudeRads );
```

Buttons

Besides the tip, most pens have buttons on the barrel as well. The states of these buttons are given to your application through pkt.pkButtons, just like the tip. Some tablets have additional buttons on the tablet itself. These are not usually part of the main Wintab specification, so they must be accessed through vendor-specific extensions. Vendors such as Wacom supply documentation and examples of how to access these extended features.

Conclusion

We've looked at a variety of topics and techniques from the human-computer interaction research community and learned how to use the Wintab API to interact with tablets. The example code on the CD-ROM can serve as a starting point for creating your own tablet-enabled software. The papers listed in the "References" section (and the many papers they reference) provide much more detail than could be included here about the design and implementation of the various pen-based solutions we touched on. They are an invaluable resource when you decide to tackle one of these projects yourself.

With the recent popularity of touch-based devices, touch- and pen-based computing has become an active and exciting area of research. Hopefully, this gem will inspire you to add rich and powerful tablet functionality to your next game tool project.

References

[Appert09] Appert, C., and S. Zhai. "Using Strokes as Command Shortcuts: Cognitive Benefits and Toolkit Support." *Proceedings of the 27th International Conference on Human Factors in Computing Systems* (2009): 2289–2298.

[Chen88] Chen, M., S. Mountford, and A. Sellen. "A Study in Interactive 3-D Rotation Using 2-D Control Devices." *Proceedings of the 15th Annual Conference on Computer Graphics and Interactive Techniques* (1988): 121–129.

[Evans81] Evans, K. B., P. P. Tanner, and M. Wein. "Tablet-Based Valuators That Provide One, Two, or Three Degrees of Freedom." *Proceedings of the 8th Annual Conference on Computer Graphics and Interactive Techniques* (1981): 91–97.

[Hancock04] Hancock, M., and K. S. Booth. "Improving Menu Placement Strategies for Pen Input." *Proceedings of Graphics Interface* (2004): 221–230.

[Kimura93] Kimura, T. D., W. Citrin, D. Halbert, C. Hewitt, N. Meyrowitz, and B. Shneiderman. "Potentials and Limitations of Pen-Based Computers." *Proceedings of the 1993 ACM Conference on Computer Science* (1993): 536–539.

[Kurtenbach93] Kurtenbach, G., A. Sellen, and W. Buxton. "An Empirical Evaluation of Some Articulatory and Cognitive Aspects of Marking Menus." *Journal of Human Computer Interaction* 8 (1993): 1–23.

[MacKenzie91] MacKenzie, S., A. Sellen, and W. Buxton. "A Comparison of Input Devices in Elemental Pointing and Dragging Tasks." *Proceedings of the CHI '91 Conference on Human Factors in Computing Systems* (1991): 161–166.

[Moyle02] Moyle, M., and A. Cockburn. "Analysing Mouse and Pen Flick Gestures." *CHI'02.* (2002): 19–24.

[Ramos07] Ramos, G., A. Cockburn, R. Balakrishnan, and M. Beaudouin-Lafon. "Pointing Lenses: Facilitating Stylus Input through Visual- and Motor-Space Magnification." *Proceedings of the SIGCHI Conference on Human Factors in Computing Systems* (2007): 757–766.

[Wacom09] "Wacom Software Developer Support." n.d. Wacom Technology. 1 Sept. 2009. <http://www.wacomeng.com/devsupport/index.html>.

Creating a Multi-Threaded Actor-Based Architecture Using Intel® Threading Building Blocks

Robert Jay Gould, Square-Enix

robert.jay.gould@gmail.com

With the next generation of consoles and personal computers having dozens of smaller processing cores, developers will have to redesign the architecture of their game engines to take advantage of this processing power. In some areas, such as graphics and physics, various methods to achieve higher performance already exist. In general, there has been less success in adapting higher-level AI- and gameplay-related systems to massively multi-cored environments.

This gem presents one architecture and implementation that can be used for AI and gameplay systems capable of scaling through high concurrency. The proposed architecture is a multi-threaded message passing actor architecture, which uses engineering tradeoffs similar to those of the Erlang language in order to achieve its concurrency and scalability. The implementation is in C++, using Intel's Threading Building Blocks (TBB) for high-performance concurrency and Lua to create a friendly programming interface that hides the typical complexity associated with message-passing systems so that designers and gameplay programmers can get their work done productively.

Introduction

When striving for performance in multi-cored environments, the only solution is to increase the concurrency (amount of work that can be done in parallel) to leverage the system's processing power. Thus, finding concurrency patterns in gameplay systems should be the first goal when designing scalable architectures.

Finding Concurrency in Games

Games are composed of several systems, and although each system might have its own peculiarities, they can be broadly grouped together by considering what kind of concurrency, or parallel, programming patterns [Mattson04] best suit them. For example, systems like graphics and physics that are almost entirely data-driven can be easily parallelized by applying data decomposition patterns and using implicit parallelization and referential transparency techniques. On the other hand, gameplay systems are primarily event-driven. If one looks at event handling as creating tasks to process events, task decomposition patterns can be applied to gameplay systems to increase their concurrency.

Task Decomposition

In simple terms, task decomposition is about breaking down the useful work of a system into atomic tasks that can be processed concurrently, without compromising the state of the system. In games, we usually have no problem in dividing work into tasks, as this is something that is already part of most game architectures today. Instead, fulfilling the "without compromising the state" part is the tricky part in game development. So finding ways in which state can be effectively divided and can be protected is the key to achieving task decomposition in the event-driven parts of our game engines.

State Protection Strategies

Perhaps the most familiar way to protect the state of a system, for game programmers, is through lock-based synchronization. As most programmers also know, lock-based systems can grow in complexity quite easily, and avoiding dead locks, live locks, data races, and convoying can consume a large chunk of precious development time. Besides the complexity and instruction overhead, lock-based synchronization also forces a non-negligible degree of serialization on processing, meaning that as the number of processing cores increases, scalability levels out, and it provides decreasing returns. Of course, the ideal alternative to lock-based synchronization is to use lock-free algorithms, but besides implementations being devilishly difficult even for algorithm experts, in many cases there are simply no known lock-free algorithms for some problems.

Other common techniques involve attacking the problem by using memory policies as opposed to processing policies, as the previous two alternatives do. One of these techniques, generally applicable to any sort of system, is to use immutable data like pure functional languages have decided to do. The benefit of immutable data is that state cannot be compromised; instead, state changes are implemented through data copying and garbage collection. Unfortunately, in systems that require lots of data and have rather tight memory constraints, such as games, all this redundancy can become an issue in itself. One solution to reduce this redundancy is called *transactional memory*. It consists of maintaining metadata of the protected state, so it is possible to determine when conflicts arise and roll back and retry conflicting operations.

The strength of transactional memory is that unlike locks, it provides increasing returns as concurrency increases, so one day transactional memory may be the easiest solution for high throughput systems, such as games [Sweeney08]. However, we are limited to software transactional memory (STM), as there is no hardware support for these features. STM's current downsides are mostly due to its experimental nature, which requires experimental compiler extensions and proprietary run-time libraries. It also has a large memory and instruction overhead due to the current bookkeeping algorithms, meaning that its performance penalties typically outweigh its benefits when shared state contention levels are low [Cascaval08], as they typically are in games.

Finally, one more solution—and the one used by the architecture presented in this gem—is the *shared nothing* [Stonebraker86] approach, where state cannot be compromised because it is not shared. This is typically achieved by having each concurrent process be completely responsible for modifying its own data through strong encapsulation. For this approach to scale on multi-cored environments, implementing lightweight processing units that can work concurrently is the way to go, and these techniques can be found in actor-based programming.

Actor-Based Programming

Actor-based programming is a programming paradigm in which the basic programming and processing unit is the actor. Actors are similar to objects in that they encapsulate state, but unlike typical objects they are also capable of processing information on their own, sort of like a cross between an object and a thread. Another difference between C++ style objects and actors is that instead of relying on method invocation for interaction, actors use message passing for communication.

Unfortunately, many game programmers relate message passing to the typical centralized message-pump design commonly used in games (as if the entire game were a single actor). Message passing is also associated with lots of the boilerplate code necessary to define and handle all these messages, but these are just the artifacts of a poor interface design and C++'s syntax. In fact, message-passing interfaces can be quite elegant without any tedious boilerplate code, with Smalltalk and Objective-C being good examples of elegant message-passing interfaces.

The actor-based architecture in this gem is in great part inspired by the Erlang language, which is the most successful actor-oriented language in use and also one of the most scalable languages in general. Erlang is a mature language that was designed by Joe Armstrong while working at Ericsson in 1986 to develop robust and scalable applications to handle telecommunications systems [Armstrong07]. Nowadays, Erlang is used by many telecoms around the world to power their telephony systems, and recently Erlang has been gaining ground in scalable commercial web applications, such as Amazon's EC2 and SimpleDB platforms and Facebook's chat system. Erlang's younger sibling and close competitor, Scala, which runs on the Java Virtual Machine, is used to provide the scalability behind services such as Twitter, demonstrating the power of actor-based designs.

One critical diverging engineering point between Erlang and the architecture in this gem is that Erlang is optimized for scaling in highly distributed environments, meaning that it has efficient IO handling as one of its central pillars. The actor-based architecture in this gem is optimized for running in highly multi-cored environments, focusing on efficient use of a single machine's multiple cores, foregoing IO-based considerations almost entirely.

Implementing an Actor Engine

The first concern of implementing an actor engine is to fulfill the need to support the ability of each actor to process its own work individually and concurrently. The simplest, yet least scalable solution to this is to provide an individual physical thread (or even OS-level process) for each actor. Unfortunately, that means that as the number of actors increases, the memory and processing overhead due to context switches increases, and scalability will level off and even decrease. The better solution is to use something lighter than threads, as Erlang does, so we can support thousands of concurrent actors with near linear scalability. In Erlang, this primitive processing unit is simply called a *process*, which is a lightweight context similar in nature to a green thread or a coroutine in implementation. The actor engine herein utilizes Intel's TBB library to provide the parallel processing needs of its actors, based on task-processing algorithms.

Intel's TBB is an open-source threading library that provides a platform- and compiler-independent production-ready foundation for building multi-threaded applications that only require standard C++ support from the compiler. It includes several high-level tools such as concurrent algorithms like `tbb::parallel_for` and several thread-safe containers like `tbb::concurrent_hash` and `tbb::concurrent_queue`. There are also lower-level tools, such as scalable memory allocators, and a scalable task scheduler, `tbb::task_scheduler`, that is used to power all of TBB's higher-level concurrent algorithms. It is these lower-level task scheduler components that are used to construct the processing workhorse for the actor engine of this gem.

The Task Scheduler

The task scheduler's main job is to effectively map its task-based workload onto the resources available to it in a way that avoids unnecessary context switching, thus providing a scalable solution for task-based concurrency. Yet its performance benefits don't stop there. Unlike most simple schedulers, the `tbb::task_scheduler` it isn't a fair scheduler that uses a round-robin-like algorithm. Instead, it is implemented as a finely tuned work-stealing scheduler [Intel09] that schedules tasks in a fashion that decreases cache misses and memory thrashing. It does this by first working on tasks that are hot in the cache and then working its way onto colder tasks as necessary. This cache-friendly scheduling also means that the task scheduler actually resembles a LIFO-like processor more than a typical FIFO-like processor.

What this means to our architecture, besides high performance processing, is that it doesn't impose any ordering restrictions on message processing. Although this might sound strange at first, allowing messages to be handled out of order is just what Erlang's message passing algorithm does, because this is an important area that is best left open for scalability optimizations.

The Message Class

With the processing implementation decided, we'll quickly look at the messages that will be used to allow actors to interact. This, however, is actually just a simple implementation detail, and the precise type of a message is probably best left for each system to define based on the system's other requirements. For this reason, the message type that actors handle is simply defined as a template argument in our implementation.

The Actor Class

In implementing the actor class, we can divide its functionality into four fundamental parts—its internal state, a message queue, a message processor, and the message handling. The message queue and message processing are the critical core features that are in the domain of the system programmer to implement efficiently to provide good scalability with little overhead, and as such, they are implemented in the base actor class. The internal state and the message handling are the extensible features of the actor, so they are derived by subclasses of the base actor class.

The Message Queue

As one of the core features of the actor class, the message queue is important because it is the only contention point in the actor's architecture where several threads may interact on the same data. This implies that its performance directly affects the overall performance of the actor and the scalability of system at large. The obvious candidate as a container for our message queue is `tbb::concurrent_queue`. It provides a thread-safe queue that allows several actors to add messages to it concurrently, with a relatively low overhead when compared to a `std::queue` with a big lock around it.

On this subject, an optimization not present in the sample code but likely of interest to system programmers is that the `tbb::concurrent_queue` is what is called a *thread-safe multi-producer multi-consumer (MPMC) queue*, which is safe when several producers and consumers push and pop on the queue concurrently. However, our actors only need a multi-producer single-consumer (MPSC) queue, because the only consumer of the queue is the actor itself. So we are paying for more than we need by using `tbb::concurrent_queue`. While doing tests and benchmarks using an excellent lock-free MPSC queue algorithm [V'jukov08], the system's performance increased as much as 10 percent under a heavy load with high contention rates, showing just how important the performance of the message queue is to the actor engine.

Actor Hierarchies

In this architecture, any number of root actors can be spawned, and all actors are allowed to spawn children, which become their responsibility. This means there can typically be many trees of actors (a forest) running concurrently. This is useful because it allows any particular actor hierarchies to be spawned or shut down independently, allowing particular subsystems to be restarted without affecting others. As long as two actors can understand each other's messages, they can communicate, even if they belong to different hierarchies; however, actors within a single hierarchy will likely be processed in closer temporal proximity.

LISTING 4.13.1 Actor construction

```
Actor::Actor( Actor* parent ) :pParent(parent)
{
    if (pParent)
    {
        //Get root processing unit/task
        pRootTask = pParent->pRootTask;
    }
    else
    {
        //Become a new root processing unit/task
        pRootTask = new (
            tbb::task::allocate_root())tbb::empty_task();
        pRootTask->set_ref_count(++childrenCounter);
    }
}
```

As seen in Listing 4.13.1, root actors keep circular references to their own TBB processing root task. This prevents the scheduler from cleaning up the task associated with each processing hierarchy when no work is left, allowing us to reuse the same root task for each actor tree indefinitely. Also of note is TBB's use of in-place object allocation using `new(tbb::task::allocate_root())`. This idiom has the purpose of avoiding the overhead of creating tasks by recycling tasks from object pools behind the scene. Both features serve to avoid memory management bottlenecks due to the large number of tasks that will be spawned during the engine's lifetime.

Message Processing

The message processing cycle is the heart of the actor engine, and most of the important implementation details are located in this section. Things will get a bit grittier from here on.

As in Erlang, message passing between actors in our design is totally asynchronous. The interactions among actors are entirely one-way affairs, not requiring any sort of handshake between actors. This allows the sender to continue on with its own processing without having to wait on the recipient to handle the message sent. If we forced interactions to be synchronous by requiring handshakes, message passing would not be scalable as Erlang's message passing is, and instead it would be similar to the message passing found in Objective-C or Smalltalk.

By decoupling actor interactions, the message handling can be decomposed into a great number of very finely grained discrete tasks. Theoretically, this allows the system to scale linearly as long as actors outnumber the number of processing cores. However, in reality, the creation and processing of tasks by the task scheduler has an overhead in itself. Because of this, TBB's documentation recommends that the grain size of a task be between 100 and 100,000 instructions for the best performance [Intel09]. So unless most message handling is quite heavy, assigning one task per message can become quite wasteful. This issue requires optimizations to increase the total throughput of the system.

When an actor places a message into another actor's inbox, the processing thread kick-starts the recipient actor, as shown in Listing 4.13.2. In situations where the sender will be waiting for a reply from the recipient, this optimization allows for reduced latency as the recipient's task will be hot in the cache and favored by the task scheduler for being processed next. More importantly, this design also removes the need for having actors wastefully poll for work, making processing entirely event-driven.

LISTING 4.13.2 Message passing

```
void Actor::inbox(Actor* sender, const MESSAGE_TYPE& msg)
{
    this->messageQueue..push(msg);
    this->tryProcessing(sender->GetProcessingTask());
}
void Actor::tryProcessing(tbb::task* processing_unit)
{
    if( !messageQueue.empty() &&
        isProcessingNow.compare_and_swap(true,false))
    {
        //use a continuation task
        tbb::empty_task* continuation = new(
            root->allocate_continuation())tbb::empty task;
        this->pMessageProcessorTask = new(
            continuation.allocate_child())MsgProcessor(this);
        continuation.set_ref_count(1);
        this->root->spawn( this->pMessageProcessorTask );
    }
}
```

Also in Listing 4.13.2, you can see that TBB continuations are utilized. This allows more freedom to the scheduler for optimizing its own workflow by decoupling execution order. A detailed explanation of continuation-style programming can be found in [Dybvig03].

As mentioned earlier, to increase the workload of a single task over 100 instructions, an actor will consume the entirety of its message queue, as well as any messages that arrive while it is processing within the execution of a single task, as seen in Listing 4.13.3. This design dynamically eases the task-processing overhead as work increases.

LISTING 4.13.3   Message consumption loop

```
void Actor::processAllMessages()
{
    isProcessingNow = true;
    Msg_t msg;
    while(messageQueue.trypop(msg))
    {
        try
        {
            if(!this->receive(msg))
            {
                throw(messageHandlingError);
            }
        }
        catch(tbb::exception e)
        {
            sendException(pParent, e, msg);
        }
    }

    isProcessingNow = false;
}
```

Also of note is the error handling logic employed for message processing. In an actor-based architecture, when an actor encounters an exception or error it cannot handle, it doesn't make sense for the error to bubble up through the call stack. Instead, it needs to bubble up through its actor hierarchy, forwarding the exception to its parent. Generally, when a parent receives an error from a child, it has few options because it can't query or fix the child's state directly. Typical error handling includes ignoring the message altogether, reporting the error to another actor, or as is common in Erlang, creating a fresh new child actor to replace the actor having problems. The functionality of the failing actor is thereby automatically reset to a clean state.

Message Handling

Like actors in Erlang, our actors have a `receive` method, which can be seen in Listing 4.13.3. The `receive` method is called whenever a message needs handling; the actual implementation of this method is the responsibility of the derived actor classes. Typical implementations of `receive` consist of matching message signatures to specific message handling routines. This can be done in many ways, from something like a `switch`/`case` construct or a series of `if`/`else` statements to something more complex, such as recognizing message signatures, regular expression matching, hierarchical state-machines, or even neural networks. A couple of implementation prototypes that might serve as inspiration can be found on the CD, but the one design that will be the focus for the rest of this gem is that of a scripted actor, which matches message signatures directly to Lua functions registered to the actor. This straightforward design provides a simple and generic, boilerplate-free solution that can be easily extended by gameplay programmers and designers using Lua alone to build whatever class hierarchies or aggregations they need to get their work done, without having to touch any of the library code directly.

As promised earlier in this gem, message-passing APIs can be friendly and don't have to involve lots of boilerplate, as the Lua code in Listing 4.13.4 demonstrates. In fact, it looks pretty much like any ordinary Lua API.

LISTING 4.13.4 Lua-based actor API

```
class "Player":inherit "Character"
{
    attack=function(target)
        target:mod_hp(math.random(5,10))
    end,
}
—Example use case
local player = getActor("player1","Player")
local enemy = getActor("goblin01")
player:attack(enemy)
```

To provide a clean, scriptable API, getActor takes an actor name and returns an actor proxy, not an actual actor reference. Using the proxy's metatable's index logic, it is capable of responding to any sort of function call. The proxy then converts these object-oriented function calls and its arguments into a message that gets sent to the C++ actor. Of course, simply allowing game code to call any method on the proxy with no error checking could make debugging quite complicated, but typically an unhandled message log combined with some class-based checking makes most debugging reasonable. To add the class-based message checking feature to a proxy, an optional second argument is passed in—the class name of the class that should be used for verifying message calls, seen in Listing 4.13.5.

LISTING 4.13.5 Lua actor proxies

```
function getActor(address,classname)
    local class = findClass(classname)
    return setmetatable({__address=address,__class=class},mt_actor)
end

mt_actor.__index = function(self,message,...)
    if rawget(self,"class") and not self.class[message] then
        error(("class [%s] can't handle message [%s]"):format(
            self._class.name,message))
    else
        self._message = message
        return send(self) —> a C-function connected to the actor engine
    end
end
```

Message-Passing Patterns

When working with asynchronous actors and message passing, some issues may appear. As with other styles of programming, there are already several useful and tested programming patterns that can be applied to resolve most of these problems.

Querying for State and Promises

At times an actor may need to query the state of another actor, not just send it a message. Because actor message passing is asynchronous, this can be an issue. One solution is to add a way to force a synchronous message passing when required, but that adds coupling to the system that could compromise its concurrency. Another solution, and the one commonly used by actor-based architectures, is to handle this scenario using a future or promise. Promises are implemented by sending along with the message the address of the calling actor and a continuation context, to which the recipient will respond back to, resuming the context of the sender, or in this implementation by use of TBB continuations [Werth09]. In the proposed API, this is handled as seen in Listing 4.13.6, by calling the promise to block until the value is returned.

LISTING 4.13.6   Using promises to query an actor for state

```
promiseHp = enemy:get_hp()
if promiseHp() > 50 then --invoking the promise returns its value
    player:run()
end
```

Another type of promise is to obtain an actor reference from another actor, as in Listing 4.13.7. This style of promise is accomplished by chaining proxy promises.

LISTING 4.13.7   Using promises to obtain actors in second degree

```
player.healClosest = function(self)
    local map = getActor("map")
    local closestActor =
        map:findClosestActor(self:get_position())
    closestActor:heal(100)
end
```

Sequential Message Processing

Another special case that requires consideration because the actor-based system is asynchronous is how to handle messages when they only make sense in a certain order. For example, when opening a door, it is required to first insert a key and then push it open. However, there is no assurance that the "insert key" message will actually arrive before the "push door" message, even if they were sent in the correct order. The typical actor-based solution is to use a sequencer actor that works in conjunction with the door. The job of the sequencer is to queue and sort messages according to some internal logic and then forward them in an appropriate order as they become available. In our example, the sequencer would not send the "push door" message to the door before it has received the "insert key" message. Although sequencers tend to be more effective than direct coupling, they do introduce a degree of serialization to the code, so they should be used only where truly necessary.

Message Epochs

One more common scenario is that it is possible for an actor to receive a message that, say, lowers its HP below 0, although a heal message had actually been sent before the damage message was issued. In most cases within a single atomic gameplay frame, the actual production order of messages should not be important, making this sort of issue actually more like a quantum physics conundrum than a real gameplay issue. This means that generally, this sort of event can be ignored with no detriment to the game. Nevertheless, when disambiguation is required, an easy solution is to use epochs [Solworth92] or timestamps to determine which message was sent first.

Conclusion

This gem reviewed the requirements and alternatives to build a highly scalable architecture and went into the details of implementing one viable alternative, based on the actor model and a shared nothing policy using Intel's Threading Building Blocks. On the CD there is a reference implementation in the form of an actor-based Lua console, along with sample scripts for experimentation with the concepts presented in this gem.

References

[Armstrong07] Armstrong, Joe. *Programming Erlang: Software for a Concurrent World.* Pragmatic Bookshelf, 2007.

[Cascaval08] Cascaval, Calin. "Software Transactional Memory: Why Is It Only a Research Toy?" *ACM QUEUE* (October 2008): n.p.

[Dybvig03] Dybvig, Kent R. "The Scheme Programming Language." Sept. 2009. Cadence Research Systems. n.d. <http://scheme.com/tspl3/further.html#./further:h4>.

[Intel09] Intel. "Intel(R) Threading Building Blocks, Reference Manual." Sept. 2009. Intel. n.d. <http://www.threadingbuildingblocks.org/documentation.php>.

[Mattson04] Mattson, Timothy G. *Patterns for Parallel Programming.* Addison-Wesley Professional, 2004.

[Solworth92] Solworth , Jon. *ACM Transactions on Programming Languages and Systems* 14.1 (Jan. 1992): n.p.

[Stonebraker86] Stonebraker, Michael. "The Case for Shared Nothing Architecture." *Database Engineering* 9.1 (1986): n.p.

[Sweeney08] Sweeney, Tim. "The End of the GPU Roadmap." Sept. 2009. Williams College. n.d. <http://graphics.cs.williams.edu/archive/SweeneyHPG2009/TimHPG2009.pdf>.

[V'jukov08] V'jukov, Dmitriy. "Scalable Synchronization Algorithms, low-overhead mpsc queue." 13 May 2008. Google. n.d. <http://groups.google.com/group/lock-free/browse_thread/thread/55df71b87acb8201>.

[Werth09] Werth, Bradley. "Sponsored Feature: Optimizing Game Architectures with Intel Threading Building Blocks." 30 March 2009. Gamasutra. n.d. <http://www.gamasutra.com/view/feature/3970/sponsored_feature_optimizing_game_.ph>.

5

NETWORKING AND MULTIPLAYER

Introduction

Craig Tiller and Adam Lake

The current generation of consoles all possess the capability to create a networked, multiplayer experience. In effect, multiplayer networked gameplay has gone mainstream. On the Xbox 360, there are 771,476 people playing *Call of Duty: Modern Warfare 2* online this very minute (4:37 p.m. on 11/28/2009). Several portable devices, such as the Nintendo DS and Apple's iPhone, enable multiplayer networked experiences. Significant numbers of men, women, and children now spend their entertainment dollars and time socializing through online games.

Each of the authors in this section addresses critical components in the networked multiplayer architecture: security, scalability, social network harvesting, and streaming. First, in the gem "Secure Channel Communication," we discuss the issues related to creating and maintaining secure communication and the various attacks and responses posed in a networked gaming environment. Next, leveraging social network APIs to obtain player data is discussed in the gem "Social Networks in Games: Playing with Your Facebook Friends." This allows a game developer, with the user's permission, to gain access to a player's Facebook friends list to be leveraged to create a multiplayer experience. The third gem, "Asynchronous I/O for Scalable Game Servers," deals with the issues of scaling the I/O system architecture to handle the large number of requests generated in networked multiplayer scenarios. Finally, the gem "Introduction to 3D Streaming Technology in Massively Multiplayer Online Games," was written by Kevin He at Blizzard and includes source code to a terrain streaming application. This article is longer than a typical gem but contains many details useful for those creating such a large system.

It is our hope that you will find these gems useful in your own applications and that you will contribute your own innovations to this exciting and important area of game development.

5.1

Secure Channel Communication

Chris Lomont
chris@lomont.org

This gem is an overview of creating secure networking protocols. There is not enough space to detail all pieces, so instead a checklist of items is presented that covers necessary points.

Online games must prevent cheaters from using tools and hacks to their advantage, often to the detriment of other players' enjoyment. Cheating can be done through software add-ons or changes, often making the cheater too powerful for other players or performing denial-of-service attacks, making the game unresponsive for others' requests, such as gold, items, services, and accounts. Since any code running on the client can be disassembled, studied, and modified, security decisions must be made assuming the cheater has access to game source code. Any system should be designed with the twin goals of making it difficult to cheat and making it easy to detect cheaters.

The main reason game and network security is often broken is that security designers must protect against every possible avenue of attack, while a cheater only needs one hole for an exploit. This asymmetric warfare makes doing it right very hard and a continual arms race.

The goal of this gem is to supply a checklist of items to consider when designing and implementing secure networking protocols. The ordering of topics is designed to be top down, which is a good way to think through security design. Many related security features are mentioned, such as copy protection and code obfuscation, which, although not exactly networking, do play a role in an overall security of game networking by making it harder to change assets.

Architecture

The most important decision when designing a gaming networking protocol is to decide how the architecture is going to work before any programming is started. This architecture choice has profound effects on later choices; making a significant change to the networking component will have costly ripple effects throughout the rest of your game components. Three aspects of game engine design need up-front thought: multi-threading design, networking architecture, and code security. None of these can be bolted onto an existing engine without severe problems and bugs, resulting in poor quality for all components. So fix these three design decisions up front, document them as gospel, and build the rest of the game around these choices.

Code Security

Code security is based on using secure coding practices. Without having this lowest layer done well, it is impossible to get networking secure. Many games are written in C/C++. Three good references are [Seacord05, Howard03, and Graff03].

Peer to Peer

The main choice in architecture is whether to be peer to peer or client/server. In a peer-to-peer architecture, it is up to peers to detect cheaters, and of course such mechanisms can be subverted by a cheating client. For example, if there is a "feature" that allows a client to kick a suspected cheater off a network, then cheaters will subvert this to kick off legitimate players. In this case, a secure and anonymous voting protocol should be used, so numerous clients need to agree on a cheater before a ban occurs.

Client/Server

Most online games are a client/server architecture, where a central server is the authority on game state, and clients send player input to and receive game state back from the server. The main benefit of this architecture from a security point of view is the server can be assumed to be a trusted, central authority on the game state. Unless your server is compromised or there are fake servers for players to log onto, the server can be trusted to detect cheaters and ban them and their accounts.

The Unreal Engine [Sweeny99] uses what Tim Sweeny calls *generalized client-server*, where the server contains the definitive game state, and clients work on approximate and limited knowledge of the world. This information is synced at appropriate intervals. The limited game state supports the security principle of least privilege, covered later.

Protocol

The next big networking decision is selecting protocols to use and how to use them. A common tradeoff is between using slower TCP/IP for guaranteed delivery or faster UDP for speed. Ensure selected security methods work with the protocol chosen. For example, if your packets are encrypted in a manner requiring that all packets get delivered, then UDP will cause you headaches. Good encryption needs an appropriate block-chaining method, as covered later, but it will cause problems if some packets in a chain are not delivered.

A recommendation is to use TCP/IP for login and authentication to guarantee communication, and then use UDP if needed for speed or bandwidth with symmetric key encryption during gameplay.

Network Security

In this section we discuss the components related to basic security principles, including encryption, hash generation, login best practices, and authentication. Any secure channel architecture should include details of how your system will respond to each of the issues discussed in this section.

Basic Security Principles

Follow basic security principles. Find the person on your team who is best versed in these areas, preferably someone who has experience cracking/hacking games, and have that person teach the team how various techniques are insecure and how to create secure code. Have the team read a few books on code security, hacking, and network security.

Design security into every interface—your web portal, your UI, your message handlers. For example, don't assume packets coming into your server are from valid clients. Allowing buffer overflows and other malware into your server will definitely compromise the system. Assume all inputs to the system (whether client or server side) are malicious and validate them all. Have periodic security reviews with competent staff members to review input code. Definitely walk through interface code before shipping.

Use best security practices. Design what data is given to which game sessions in a least privileges manner—that is, do not give data to a session unless it is absolutely needed by that device to do some computation. For example, in an online first-person shooter, you don't need to send actors to a given player that cannot affect that actor. Prevent hacked clients from having more information than needed.

Expect common attacks on networking, such as:

- **Packet sniffing.** Here, a cheater on a network can see all packets, allowing reading and sometimes injecting other packets into the flow. Unencrpyted data, such as login and passwords, can be seen if in plain text.
- **Man-in-the-middle (MITM) attacks.** Here, another cheater sits between the client and the server, pretending to be the server to the client and vice versa. The MITM may be an employee at an ISP, a university network, and so on and can steal user information from poorly designed protocols. This can be defeated using proper protocols, described later.
- **Denial of service.** Here, a network is flooded with packets, making it unresponsive. The game should detect such activity and not penalize innocent players.

Finally, be sure to observe these basic security principles:

- **Confidentiality.** Make sure system assets cannot be read by those who absolutely do not need to.
- **Integrity.** Assets should not be modifiable or deleted by those who do not need to.
- **Availability.** Assets must be accessible to those who need them in a timely manner. Failure of this leads to denial of service.

Encryption

Encryption of some or all data is needed for a good network protocol, so here are a few key points and common errors.

The first rule of encryption is never invent your own encryption methods. Always use ones created and implemented by professionals. Programmers like to invent and implement algorithms, but security has a history of bad decisions made by developers, and it is even hard for security professionals to get right. It is very hard to create good implementations of popular algorithms. Knowledgeable crackers will break your implementations using a variety of tricks—poor random number generation, cache and timing attacks, and simple buffer overflows.

At this point, make sure to use cryptographically secure random number generation where needed, such as salts for passwords, user key generation, and so on. These are much slower than standard pseudo-random number generators (PRNGs) but don't suffer from allowing crackers to shrink your keyspaces for attacks. For non-secure PRNGs, basically a bit of the seed is given to a cracker per bit of decision he can see from the PRNG. Once he knows the seed (or part of it), he knows the future PRNG values (or some smaller subset).

Next, you have to choose appropriate encryption methods for things you want encrypted. The two main classes are public key and private key encryption. Public key is slower, but it is useful for setting up connections to players and then agreeing on a (secure) random private key.

Private key AES is currently pretty secure, although recent attacks have some worried.

Most common private key methods are block ciphers—that is, they encrypt a block at a time. How these blocks are linked together is called a *mode of operation*. Encrypting one block at a time (called *Electronic CodeBook* mode, or *ECB* for short) independently is inherently weak and should be avoided unless absolutely necessary. [WikiCipher09] has a good example of how this leaks information. Almost any other chaining method on this page is acceptable, and Cipher Block Chaining (CPC) is recommended for simplicity and security.

Even with encryption, to prevent attacks by man in the middle, a Message Authentication Code (MAC) must be used to ensure data integrity. This is left to the reader to pursue further.

Finally, a good method for exchanging data over insecure channels to agree on encryption keys is the Diffie-Hellman key exchange, which allows two parties without prior communication to jointly establish a shared secret key over an insecure communications channel. The rough idea is as follows, using a lockbox metaphor. Alice and Bob want to share a message by sending a box through the mail. The box, if unlocked, can be opened and the message copied. So, Alice puts the message in the box and locks it with a lock for which only she has the key. Bob receives the box and puts another lock on it for which only he has the key and then returns the box to Alice. Alice removes her lock and sends it once again to Bob. Bob removes his lock and reads the message. At no point was the box mailed in an unlocked state.

In practice, the messages are numbers, and locks are based on modular arithmetic and the hardness of factoring.

Finally, the downside of encryption is it slows down performance, so methods must be selected carefully.

Excellent references are [Ferguson03] and [Schneier96].

Hashes

Many secure operations use hashes to reduce some large set of data into a smaller hash value, often 128, 256, or 512 bits. The purpose is to guarantee that the original data has not been tampered with; otherwise, the hash would be an incorrect value. This can be used to check game assets, network packets, identities, and more.

Be sure to select a hash that is considered secure by the security community. For example, many still use MD5 as a hash algorithm in secure settings, even though it has been broken for that use for many years. SHA-1 is also falling out of favor, with some attacks coming close to breaking it. SHA-2 is acceptable. Currently WHIRLPOOL, based on AES, is considered secure, and NIST has competition for a SHA replacement, and the competitors are currently unbroken. (Skein seems to be a good one, designed by some very good researchers.) Note MD6 is broken. So make hash function choices modular, versioned, and changeable, since they might be changed over the life of your game.

Complete Secure Protocols

A final choice for a lot of secure protocols is to use an industry standard, such as SSH-2 (not SSH-1, vulnerable to man in the middle) or SSL, to perform encrypted networking.

Login

After connecting to a server or other players, the player usually has to log in. Never send the username or password across the network unencrypted; this prevents man-in-the-middle attacks. Having to guess a username and password is more work than just guessing a password. Never send the password, and definitely never store the password unhashed directly on the server. Generate a secure random salt, prefix the password, and then send/store a hash and the salt. The salt prevents pre-computed dictionary attacks, such as rainbow tables. If you have never heard of password salting or rainbow tables, and you are implementing a login system, then you should read up on them.

Require the username to be visible characters, and enforce this to prevent players from using names that cannot be seen on some screens or names that allow security breaches. Otherwise, a player can choose a name consisting of non-printable or non-ASCII symbols, preventing, for example, discussion about the player online or voting for a ban. You may go so far as preventing a player from typing their password into any user interface portion except the login box, preventing phishing attacks where players are tricked into entering their login/password in game chat windows.

Once a login and password have been transmitted to the server, in future logins a challenge hash [Watte08] can be used, thereby avoiding sending passwords ever again over the network.

Make sure players choose secure passwords—for example, by forcing them to be 10 or more characters and use uppercase, lowercase, numeric, and/or non-alphanumeric characters. A brief Internet search gives good guidelines.

Use a per-session secure key to prevent packet playback attacks.

Authentication

Authentication is the process of making sure a player is who they claim to be and not an imposter. The *Game Programming Gems 7* article [Watte08] has good coverage of this topic. A couple ideas are using an IP address or a token stored on the player computer to authenticate and performing some authentication questioning if this changes.

Gaming

The network needs the highest performance during game play, so encryption and security methods are usually kept to a minimum. The right balance must be determined on a case-by-case basis.

Attacks

The level of attack sophistication against your game is directly proportional to popularity and longevity. Hence, more security is needed for a triple-A title than for a casual game. For example, *World of Warcraft* (WoW) uses the Warden, a sophisticated kernel mode anti-cheat tool described in [Hoglund07, Messner09, and WikiWarden09].

Reverse Engineering

Using tools such as IDA Pro and OllyDbg and a little skill, one can disassemble game executables into assembly code for any platform, and there are plug-ins that reverse the code into C/C++ with good results. It only takes one cracker skilled in reverse engineering to remove or break weak security measures, and he then distributes the tool/crack to everyone. Assume crackers have access to your code and algorithms.

Kernel Mode

Kernel mode is the security layer that operating system code runs in (for the Windows PC and many other protected OSes), and most games run in user mode. WoW's Warden and copy protection schemes such as SecuROM run as kernel mode processes, giving them access to all processes and memory. However, even kernel mode software can be subverted by other kernel mode software. Using kernel mode tricks like those used in rootkits and other malware, a sophisticated cracker can run tools that hide under any snooping you might do and can watch/record/modify run-time structures. This is done to circumvent Warden and many of the CD-ROM and DVD protection schemes. To detect and prevent kernel mode attacks on your code, you need kernel mode services, likely your own driver or a commercial product, to do the work for you.

Lagging

Also known as *tapping*, this is when a player attaches a physical device called a *lag switch* to an Ethernet cable, slowing down communication to the server and slowing down the game for all involved. However, the player with the lag switch can still run around and act, sending updates to the server. From the opponent's view, the player with the lag switch may jump around, teleport, have super speed, and generally be able to kill opponents with ease.

In peer-to-peer network architecture, this can also be achieved with packet flooding the opponents since each client sees other IP addresses.

Other Attacks

- **Internal misuse.** A game must protect against employee cheating. For example, an online poker site was implicated in using inside information for some individual to win an online tournament using full knowledge of other player hands [Levitt07]. When these prizes reach tens or hundreds of thousands of dollars, there is a lot of incentive for employee cheating.
- **Client hacking.** Client hacks are changes made to a local executable, such as making wall textures transparent to see things a player should not (called *wallhacking*).
- **Packet sniffing.** To reverse network protocol, looking for weaknesses such as playback attacks, DDoS, usernames/passwords, chat packet stealing. Some networks allow some users to see others' packets, such as colleges and others on the same LAN, making packet sniffing attractive.
- **Bots.** Numerous bots help by using auto aiming and auto firing and collecting goods such as gold and other items. Several years ago, this author created an (unnamed) word game-playing bot that was very successful, climbing to the top of the ranks during the course of the experiment.
- **Aids.** Aids assist a player, such as auto aiming, auto firing when aimed well, back-door communication, poker stats, poker playing games, and so on. Imagine how easy it is to cheat online for chess, checkers, Scrabble, and similar games where computers are better than humans. Other tools give multiple camera angles, better camera angles, player highlighting, and so on.

- **Design flaws.** Game design can be exploited. For example, on a game with scoring, it would be a design flaw if a player about to record a bad score can quit before the score gets recorded and not be penalized.

Responses

In response to all the attack methods, here are some methods to help defeat cheaters.

Code Integrity

First of all, write secure code. Then key code assets can be further hardened using methods from the malware community, such as code packing, encryption, and polymorphism. These all slow the code down but could still be used for infrequent actions, such as logging on or periodic cheat detection. Further tools and methods along these lines should be researched on the Internet, starting at sites such as www.openrce.com and www.rootkit.com.

One way to check code integrity is to integrate a small integrity scripting system and have the server (or perhaps other clients in a peer-to-peer setting) send snippets of script code to execute. These snippets perform integrity checks such as hashing game assets, checking game process memory for problems, and so on, returning the answer to the server for verification. The queries are generated randomly from a large space of possible code snippets to send. To defeat this technique, a cheater has to answer each query correctly. This requires keeping correct answers on hand, keeping a copy of modified game assets and remapping the scripting system, or something similar. Although doable, this adds another level of complexity for a cracker to work with since the script language is not built into existing reversing tools. A variant of this takes it further and randomizes the language per run and updates the client side as needed.

A final method of code protection is integrated into commercial copy protection schemes, such as SecuROM, Steam, and PunkBuster.

An interesting attack on PunkBuster (which likely would work on other anti-cheat tools) was the introduction of false positives getting players banned from games. The false positives were caused by malicious users transmitting text fragments from known cheat programs into popular IRC channels, and PunkBuster's aggressive memory scanning would see the fragments and [Punk08] ban players. This is likely to be fixed by the time this gem reaches print.

Again, any code will eventually be reverse engineered given a determined cracker. A good place to start reading is [Eliam05]. [Guilfanov09] shows some advanced code obfuscation techniques from the creator of IDA Pro.

Kernel Mode Help

As mentioned earlier, this gives the highest level of computer control but also can crash a computer. An operating system may ban access to kernel mode code for gaming in the future, making kernel mode code a short-term solution. Kernel code mistakes often crash the computer, not just the game process, so code must be extremely well tested before shipping.

Cheat Detection

Having the server detect cheaters through statistics is a powerful technique. Statistics from players should be kept and logged by username, including time online and game stats such as kills, deaths, scores, gold, character growth, kill rate, speed, and so on. An automated system or moderator should investigate any players with stats too many standard deviations outside the norm. A rating system could be implemented behind the scenes like ELO scores in chess, and players who suddenly show profound skills can be detected and watched.

Continued Vigilance

Every current solution requires vigilance from the game creators to patch games, update cheat lists, and evolve the game as cheats evolve. So far there is no one-shot method for preventing cheating in online games. However, following all the advice and reading deeper into each topic will make protecting the game much easier by making cheats much harder to implement. Game creators should monitor common cheat sites, such as www.gamexploits.com, and per-game forums looking for cheats and techniques.

Backups/Restore

To prevent worst-case damage to a game environment, have a regularly scheduled backup in case of server hacking.

Disciplinary Measures

When a cheater is caught, the game has to have a well-defined punishment system. Most games and anti-cheat systems currently ban accounts either temporarily, permanently, or with some resolution process.

Examples

Here are two examples of current online game security features.

WoW

World of Warcraft uses a module called the Warden to ensure client integrity. From [Hoglund07, Messner09, and WikiWarden09], the following is found:

- It checks the system once about every 15 seconds.
- It dumps all DLLs to see what is running.
- It reads the text of all Windows title bars.
- The DLL names and title bars are hashed and compared to banned item hashes.

- It hashes 10 to 20 bytes for each running process and compares these to known cheat program hashes, such as WoW Glider.
- It looks for API hooks.
- It looks for exploitative model edits.
- It looks for known cheating drivers and rootkits.

Unreal Tournament

Sweeny [Sweeny99] lists the following network cheats that have been seen in *Unreal Tournament*:

- Speedhack. Exploits the client's clock for movement updates. Fixed by verifying client and server clock stay nearly synced.
- Aimbots. UnrealScript and external versions.
- Wall hacks and radars. UnrealScript and external versions.

Conclusion

To develop a secure networking protocol for gaming, securing all game assets from code to art and networking data is important. Performance versus security tradeoffs must be designed into encryption and message protocols from the beginning.

Securing an online game is a constantly evolving war, and whatever methods are used today may fail tomorrow. Developers must constantly monitor the servers and communities to detect, mitigate, and prevent cheating. This involves tools to update clients, protocols, servers, and assets as needed to provide an enjoyable, level playing field for all customers.

Finally, throughout the game development process, keep a list of security checkpoints and follow them religiously.

References

[Eliam05] Eliam, Eldad. *Reversing: Secrets of Reverse Engineering*. Wiley, 2005.

[Ferguson03] Ferguson, Neils, and Bruce Schneier. *Practical Cryptography*. Wiley, 2003.

[Graff03] Graff, Mark, and Kenneth Van Wyk. *Secure Coding: Principles and Practices*. O'Reilly Media, 2003.

[Guilfanov09] Guilfanov, Ilfak. "IDA and Obfuscated Code." 2009. Hex-Rays. n.d. <http://www.hex-rays.com/idapro/ppt/caro_obfuscation.ppt>.

[Hoglund07] Hoglund, Greg. "4.5 Million Copies of EULA-Compliant Spyware." 2009. Rootkit. n.d. <http://www.rootkit.com/blog.php?newsid=358>.

[Howard03] Howard, Michael, and David LeBlanc. *Writing Secure Code, 2nd Edition*. Microsoft Press, 2003.

[Levitt07] Levitt, Steven D. "The Absolute Poker Cheating Scandal Blown Wide Open." 2007. The New York Times. n.d. <http://freakonomics.blogs.nytimes.com/2007/10/17/the-absolute-poker-cheating-scandal-blown-wide-open/>.

[Messner09] Messner, James. "Under the Surface of Azeroth: A Network Baseline and Security Analysis of Blizzard's World of Warcraft." 2009. Network Uptime. n.d. <http://www.networkuptime.com/wow/>.

[Punk08] "netCoders vs. PunkBuster." 26 March 2008. Bashandslash.com. n.d. <http://bashandslash.com/index.php?Itemid=78&id=297&option=com_content&task=view>.

[Schneier96] Schneier, Bruce. *Applied Cryptography: Protocols, Algorithms, and Source Code in C, 2nd Edition*. Wiley, 1996.

[Seacord05] Seacord, Robert. *Secure Coding in C and C++*. Addison-Wesley, 2005.

[Sweeny99] Sweeny, Tim. "Unreal Networking Architecture." 2009. Epic Games, Inc. n.d. <http://udn.epicgames.com/Three/NetworkingOverview.html>.

[Watte08] Watte, Jon. "Authentication for Online Games." *Games Programming Gems 7* Boston: Charles River Media, 2008.

[WikiCipher09] "Block Cipher Modes of Operation." 2009. Wikipedia. n.d. <http://en.wikipedia.org/wiki/Block_cipher_modes_of_operation>.

[WikiWarden09] "Warden (software)." 2009. Wikipedia. n.d. <http://en.wikipedia.org/wiki/Warden_(software)>.

5.2

Social Networks in Games: Playing with Your Facebook Friends

Claus Höfele, Team Bondi
claus@claushoefele.com

While multiplayer features are now commonplace, games often pit anonymous Internet users against each other. This is a step backward from the enjoyment of playing split-screen games with a friend sitting right next to you. In order to re-create this friendly atmosphere in online games, developers have to understand more about a player's ties with people, which is the domain of social networks such as Facebook, MySpace, and Twitter.

This gem describes how to access the web services of social networks from your game. As an example of how this might be put to use, the application developed in this gem will demonstrate how your game can get access to a player's friends on Facebook.

The explanations in this gem describe Facebook integration from the point of view of a standalone, desktop-style game as opposed to a game executed in a web browser. Standalone applications pose unique challenges because web services are primarily designed to be good web citizens but do not necessarily integrate well with desktop applications.

RESTful Web Services

Representational State Transfer (REST) is the predominant architecture for offering programmatic access to data stored on the web.

A RESTful service is composed of a collection of resources, which are identified by a web address, such as http://example.com/resource. Clients gain access to data through a set of well-defined operations that can be used on these resources. Because RESTful services are based on stateless operations (any state information is held in the client), a service can scale to a large number of clients—ideal for web services, which might have millions of accesses each day.

REST does not demand any specific technologies in its implementation, which means every web service has a similar but slightly different way of offering access to its resources. Also, web services comply with pure RESTful design principles to varying degrees.

In practice, a RESTful service means that you'll send HTTP requests to send and receive data. The most common HTTP operations are `HTTP GET` to retrieve data and `HTTP POST` to create new data on the server.

Requesting Data

As an example of accessing data from a social network, consider the following request that uses Twitter's RESTful API [Twitter09]:

```
curl http://search.twitter.com/trends/current.json
```

cURL [cURL09] is a tool that allows you to issue network requests on the command line. The previous example sends an `HTTP GET` request to Twitter's servers to retrieve the most popular topics currently being discussed on Twitter.

In this simple example, you could have pasted the web address mentioned in the cURL command into the address field of your web browser. Because a web browser issues `HTTP GET` requests by default, you would have achieved the same result. When developing access to web services, however, it's a good idea to learn how to use cURL because it has many options that allow you to assemble more complex requests. For example, cURL also allows you to send `HTTP POST` requests and use HTTP's basic access authentication scheme.

The cURL command presented previously will result in a response similar to the following output (formatted for easier reading):

```
{"trends":{"2009-08-23 04:00:47":[
  {"query":"\"Best love song?\"","name":"Best love song?"},
  {"query":"#fact","name":"#fact"},
  {"query":"#shoutout","name":"#shoutout"},
  {"query":"#HappyBDayHowieD","name":"#HappyBDayHowieD"},
  {"query":"\"District 9\"","name":"District 9"},
  {"query":"\"Inglourious Basterds\"","name":"Inglourious Basterds"},
  {"query":"\"Hurricane Bill\"","name":"Hurricane Bill"},
  {"query":"#peacebetweenjbfans","name":"#peacebetweenjbfans"},
  {"query":"#Nascar","name":"#Nascar"},
  {"query":"Raiders","name":"Raiders"}
]},"as_of":1251000047}
```

Here, the output from the Twitter API is in JavaScript Object Notation (JSON) format [JSON09]. JSON is a lightweight data format that is becoming popular because it is less verbose and easier to parse than XML.

Depending on the request, Twitter—like most web services—can be configured to produce either XML- or JSON-formatted output. I find that my applications often need an XML parser anyway because of other application requirements. For this reason, I tend to use XML more often because it is convenient to have a single data format in your application.

A quick glance at the JSON data should give you a good idea of the information returned in the request: Each line that starts with the word "query" contains the name of a trending topic as well as the search query that can be used to find all Twitter messages relating to this topic.

Authenticating a User

The data received from the previous example represents public information that everyone has access to. To gain access to private data, such as contact details and friends, you have to confirm a user's identity.

People are understandably cautious to give applications access to their private data. For this reason, social networks have developed a variety of authentication mechanisms to cope with different situations and technical limitations. Because these mechanisms vary wildly from service to service, authentication is often the most time-consuming request to implement.

The most basic authentication mechanism requires users to enter a user name and password, which your application sends to the web service. Entering authentication data into your application requires users to trust your application not to collect passwords and abuse them for other purposes. This fear might stop users from trying out new applications because they don't want to risk their accounts being hijacked by malicious applications.

Applications on the web have answered this need by offering authentication mechanisms based on forwarding. The basic principle is that when logging in to a website, you are forwarded to the login page of the account provider and enter your user name and password there. The application will never see your credentials, but will only receive a confirmation of whether the login was successful.

Identifying Your Application

Apart from authenticating the user on whose behalf your application signs in to the service, most websites also require a unique identifier that represents your application. Facebook, for example, requires this. Twitter, on the other hand, doesn't use an application identifier.

Application identifiers allow for application-specific configurations on the service provider's website but are also used to enforce service agreements between the developer and the service provider. A social network might, for example, restrict what you are allowed to do with the data received from the network. The service provider can choose to disable your application if you violate the service agreement.

Debugging RESTful Requests

When developing my applications, I find it useful to see the data that is sent and received in the requests to a web service. There are a number of good HTTP debug proxies [Fiddler09, Charles09] that act as middlemen between your application and a website. They often contain special support to display and format XML and JSON data.

HTTP proxies require a system-specific configuration so that the debugged application uses the proxy instead of accessing the Internet directly.

For example:

```
curl —proxy localhost:8080 http://search.twitter.com/trends/current.json
```

will send the Twitter request from the previous example to a proxy on the local machine (localhost) using port 8080. An HTTP proxy installed on this port will then forward the request to the real server at search.twitter.com and record all data that goes back and forth between your computer and Twitter's server.

Another possibility is a network protocol analyzer, such as Wireshark [Wireshark09]. Network protocol analyzers work by listening to network packets going through your network adapter. Because Wireshark works on a lower level than HTTP proxies, the application is not aware of the fact that it is being debugged and thus doesn't need to change its configuration. This is a more generic solution to monitor network traffic, but HTTP proxies are often easier to use because they specialize in HTTP traffic and automatically filter out unnecessary information.

The Facebook API

As an example of how to integrate social networks into your game, this gem demonstrates how to use Facebook's REST interfaces.

Setting Up a Facebook Application

Before starting with your Facebook application, you have to register as a developer with Facebook. You do this by creating a Facebook user account and adding the Facebook Developer Application to your profile [Facebook09].

Within the Developer Application, you'll find a link to set up your own Facebook application. Finishing this process will give you an API key that identifies your application when exchanging data with Facebook and a configuration page that contains your application's setup.

One parameter you have to configure is the Canvas Callback URL, which determines from where Facebook pulls the content of your application if you were to display a page within Facebook. Since the demo application described in this gem is a desktop application, this URL is not used at all, but it is required nevertheless.

More importantly, you have to switch the Application Type from Web to Desktop. This changes the authentication process when accessing Facebook's REST server to better suit desktop applications.

Facebook's REST Server

Facebook runs a RESTful service at the URL http://api.facebook.com/restserver.php. In order to exchange data with this server, you have to send an HTTP POST request with at least the following parameters:

- **api_key.** This is the API key you get when registering your application with Facebook.
- **call_id.** A number that increases with every request.
- **session_key.** The session key obtained from the login process or empty if the request doesn't require a session.
- **method.** The API endpoint name that identifies the request.
- **v.** A version identifier, currently 1.0.

Some requests have additional parameters, which are then appended to this list.

For Facebook's server to accept a request, you also have to send a signature that identifies your application. To create the signature, you concatenate all input parameters to a string, append a secret key, and build an MD5 hash out of this data. Since both Facebook and your application know the secret key, Facebook's server can create the same signature and check that the request is indeed coming from your application.

The secret key that's used for the signature is obtained by establishing a session. The secret is then called a *session secret*. Requests that are sent without a session context use the application secret that you can look up in your application's configuration page on Facebook.

The handling of the secret key depends on the way you authenticate the user, so I'll have to talk a bit more about authentication methods first.

Authenticating Facebook Users

As part of their terms of service—which must be agreed to in order to get an API key—Facebook forbids you to receive user names and passwords directly in your applications. Instead, users have to go through Facebook's website to log in. The reasoning is that users are more likely to trust the application because the same login screen is used that people are already familiar with from logging into Facebook on the web. In addition, it makes it less likely, but not impossible, that applications will capture and hijack the user's password because the credentials are entered into a separate application (the browser).

Obviously, displaying a website for login purposes is easy for web applications. For desktop applications, on the other hand, you essentially have two choices: You can use the browser that's installed on the user's system, or you can integrate a web browser, such as WebKit, into your application.

Authentication with an External Browser

Loading Facebook's login page in a browser separate from your application means that the user has to leave your application until the Facebook login is complete. After the login, the user returns to your application and confirms the authentication. Figure 5.2.1 illustrates this process.

To start with, your application has to request an authentication token from Facebook. (The method name of this request is auth.createToken.) Since you haven't established a session yet, you use the application secret to sign this request.

Next, you launch the external browser with a login page hosted by Facebook and pass the token to this website as part of the URL. The user can now log in to Facebook to establish a session for your application.

Finally, the user returns to your application and confirms the login process, whereupon your application sends an auth.getSession request to Facebook. If the login was successful, you will get a session key and a secret. The session key has to be used as part of the input parameters, and the session secret replaces the application secret in subsequent requests.

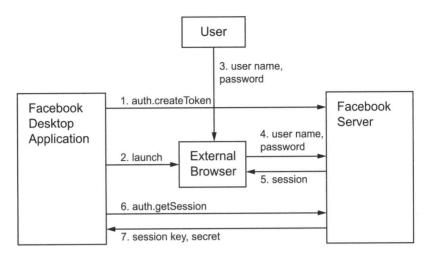

Figure 5.2.1   Authenticating a Facebook user through an external web browser.

The demo application that comes on the CD for this gem contains an implementation of this login process, so you can see exactly what data needs to be sent to Facebook.

Authentication with an Application-Integrated Browser

You can achieve a better user experience by integrating a browser into your application. Again, you have to load Facebook's login page to start the process. But this time, the web page is displayed as part of your application. Figure 5.2.2 shows the application flow.

When loading Facebook's login page, you pass in a parameter to configure a URL that gets displayed when the login is successful. This way, your application can figure out whether the user has successfully logged in to Facebook by checking the URL that's currently being displayed in the browser.

This tight integration is only possible if you have complete control over the browser, for example, by embedding WebKit [WebKit09] into your application. WebKit is an open-source web browser layout engine that's also used as the basis of Apple's Safari and Google's Chrome browsers.

Instead of using WebKit directly, the demo for this gem uses the WebKit version that comes with the Qt application framework [Qt09]. This makes it easy to display the browser component as part of a dialog. For games, however, it might be better to render a web page's content to an image, which could then be displayed as a texture. (Have a look at the `QWebFrame::render()` API.)

Because the process starts off with Facebook's website when using an integrated browser, your application never needs the application secret. This is a big advantage compared to the authentication process with an external browser because it means the application secret can never be compromised.

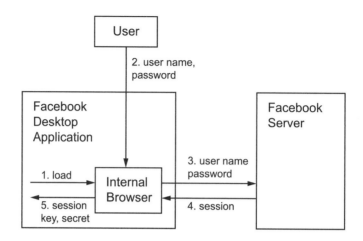

Figure 5.2.2   Authenticating a Facebook user through
an application-integrated web browser.

Persisting a User Session

By default, a session is valid only for a limited time. To avoid going though the authentication procedure every time the session expires, you can ask the user for offline access. This permission can be requested during the login process by appending a parameter to the login URL (authentication with integrated browser only) or by displaying a website with a permission form hosted by Facebook (works with both integrated and external browser authentication).

   To skip the authentication, you store the session key and secret on the user's computer and use these two values again the next time your application needs it. You have to check that the permission is still valid because the user can revoke the authorization on Facebook's website at any time. The demo application on the CD does this by sending a confirmation request to Facebook every time you start the application.

   Apart from the session information, you should avoid storing data locally because it might become out of sync with the information on Facebook's website.

Retrieving the Friends List

Once you have obtained a session, getting information about the user's friends is straightforward: You send a request with the name `friends.get`, which will return a list of user IDs. Alternatively, you can query only those friends that already have used your application by using `friends.getAppUsers`.

   You could match these IDs to a database of high scores, for example, to realize a high score table that only contains friends of the user. Also, if a friend hasn't played the game yet, your application could send out invitations to try out the game.

Posting Messages

Another often-used request is `stream.publish`, which posts a message to the user's Facebook page. Similar to the offline access, this requires that the user grant special permission to your application.

Publishing messages could be used to post status updates about the user's progress in your game.

Conclusion

In this gem, I have shown you how Facebook can provide social context to your game. By integrating a player's friends network, you can make your games a more personal experience, which avoids the anonymity often associated with multiplayer games played over the Internet.

While the majority of this gem has focused on Facebook, the information in this article should provide enough information to extend your games with features from other web services. Here are some ideas you might want to try:

- Record a player's gameplay as a video and upload it to YouTube so it can be viewed by others.
- Send status updates to Twitter when someone achieves a new high score.
- Send messages to a player's Facebook friends to invite them for a game.
- Record the location of the player and create high score lists of people in your neighborhood.

References

[Charles09] "Charles: Web Debugging Proxy Application." n.d. Karl von Randow. n.d. <http://www.charlesproxy.com/>.

[cURL09] "cURL." n.d. <http://curl.haxx.se/>.

[Facebook09] Website of Facebook's developer application. <http://www.facebook.com/developers>

[Fiddler09] "Fiddler Web Debugging Proxy." n.d. Microsoft. n.d. <http://www.fiddler2.com/>.

[JSON09] "Introducing JSON." n.d. JSON. n.d. <http://json.org/>.

[Qt09] "Qt Cross-Platform Application and UI Framework." n.d. Nokia Corporation. n.d. <http://qt.nokia.com/>.

[Twitter09] "Twitter API Documentation." n.d. Twitter. n.d. <http://apiwiki.twitter.com/>.

[WebKit09] "The WebKit Open Source Project." n.d. WebKit. n.d. <http://webkit.org/>.

[Wireshark09] "Wireshark." n.d. Wirehsark. n.d. <http://www.wireshark.org/>.

5.3

Asynchronous I/O for Scalable Game Servers

Neil Gower

neilg@vertexblast.com

Scalability is a critical concern in today's online gaming market. The small-scale networking of 8- to 32-player LAN games has given way to massively multiplayer Internet games and centralized game-hosting services. Even if a single game instance supports only a small number of players, the ability to run additional game instances on a single server has serious repercussions for the cost of operating a game service. Every physical server incurs ongoing space, power, and cooling costs on top of the initial hardware purchases and software license fees.

This gem explores asynchronous I/O as a technique for improving the scalability of multiplayer game servers. We first review traditional synchronous I/O techniques and their implications for server architecture. Then we take a look at the asynchronous alternatives for Windows and POSIX and demonstrate their use in a sample game server. We conclude with an analysis of asynchronous I/O and its applicability to building scalable game servers.

Background

Input/output (I/O) operations have always posed a challenge to game developers and to network programmers in particular. I/O operations are often among the most time consuming and unpredictable functions that game code will use. In part, this is because the actual I/O systems reside deep in the operating system. Making system calls and crossing the user-space to kernel-space boundary takes time, both in terms of CPU state changes and in terms of data transfers between user space and kernel space. Furthermore, I/O operations deal with physical devices that don't always behave the way they should in principle. Physical devices such as DVD drives have to cope with things like discs covered in real-world fingerprints and scratches, and network cards have to contend with the real-world tangle of wires and devices that makes up our LANs and the Internet.

Some of this chaos is hidden from our code by OS buffers. For example, when we call a write function, the data is rarely written directly to the device. Instead, the OS places the data in an internal buffer, which it will then use to write to the physical device when it is ready. While this is usually effective at protecting user code from the underlying complexity of the device, buffers still get full under heavy loads and traffic spikes. When that occurs, the real world ripples back up to the application code in the form of failed operations and unexpected delays.

Aside from the impact of these delays on the performance of our game code, the other problem we encounter with I/O operations is that our process sits idle while synchronous I/O operations execute. When there is plenty of processing left to do, we can't afford to waste CPU cycles doing nothing.

Blocking and Non-Blocking Synchronous I/O

Most standard I/O APIs operate synchronously. They keep us synchronized with the I/O system by blocking further execution of our code until the current I/O operation is complete. This is the model you'll encounter when using functions such as `fread()` and `fwrite()`, or `send()` and `recv()` for sockets. For applications whose main function is I/O, such as an FTP client, these APIs can be perfectly adequate. If there's nothing else for the app to do, blocking on I/O may be fine.

However, for real-time games, we generally have a game-world simulation running at 30 to 60 updates per second. Some game architectures may be more event-driven on the server side, but to maintain responsiveness within any architecture, we can't waste time waiting on I/O. The biggest delay we want to avoid is making blocking I/O requests when the OS is not ready to handle them. For example, this occurs if we call `recv()` when there is nothing to read or `send()` when the OS's send buffer is full.

One way to address this is the socket API's non-blocking mode. However non-blocking sockets are not quite as great as they sound. In non-blocking mode, when the operation is not possible (for example, the send buffer is full), the function will return immediately with an error code telling us to try again later. This "try again later" cycle is polling, and we have to be careful that it doesn't get out of hand. It is easy with non-blocking sockets to waste many CPU cycles polling for I/O readiness. Non-blocking sockets help us avoid our initial obstacle of getting hung up on I/O calls when the OS is not ready, but they don't necessarily improve the execution efficiency of our program overall.

Handling Multiple Clients

A game server must handle multiple connections, and a scalable server must handle many connections. One simple server design is to iterate over the set of all client connections and perform non-blocking I/O operations for each client in turn. However, this can involve a lot of polling, especially when the majority of the connections are idle, as is often the case when reading data from clients. As the number of connections increases, so does the length of the iterations, which in turn degrades the server's responsiveness to each client.

Rather than polling one socket at a time, an alternative approach is to use an I/O multiplexer, such as `select()` or `WaitForMultipleObjects()` (or one of the many platform-specific variants of these functions). This allows our code to block on a whole set of sockets and unblock with a set of sockets ready for I/O, which we can then process sequentially.

This addresses two issues. First, we don't have to worry about getting blocked on sockets that aren't ready, because in principle the multiplexer only returns ready sockets—although in practice a socket's state can still change between when the multiplexer returns and our code performs I/O with it. Second, the OS monitors the whole set of sockets for readiness, so we don't have to explicitly iterate over them in our code, making numerous system calls on sockets whose state hasn't changed since the last iteration.

However, we can't block the main game loop on a multiplexer call, because even with a long list of clients, it's still impossible to know how long we'll have to wait. Putting a timeout on the call is one way around this, but now we're turning the I/O multiplexer into a (potentially very) expensive polling system. We need to decouple the I/O processing from the rest of the code.

Thread Carefully

To allow the main game loop to execute while I/O operations are being processed and to take advantage of the OS's ability to handle many parallel I/O streams, we could introduce additional threads to the server.

The obvious one-thread-per-client approach, while relatively easy to implement, scales very poorly. This is due to several factors. For one, the cost of synchronization primitives such as mutexes generally scales relative to the number of threads involved. Threads also consume limited OS resources and waste cycles as they get swapped in and out of execution focus. The ideal number of threads to minimize context switching is proportional to the number of instruction streams the CPU can process in parallel. On present-day hardware, this means we should really only have a small number of threads, so for any significant number of clients it is simply not an option to spawn a thread for each.

A more practical approach is to dedicate one thread (or a pool of threads) to I/O operations, allowing the main thread to proceed while the new thread deals with the I/O operations.

By introducing more than one thread into our application, we have also introduced synchronization overhead (mutexes, critical sections, and so on) and some overhead for the thread-safe run-time environment and libraries. On the upside, this approach also has a well-defined interface point between threads—the queues used to store I/O requests and results. The synchronization code still requires some careful programming to avoid deadlock and race conditions, but this is a textbook application of multi-threading.

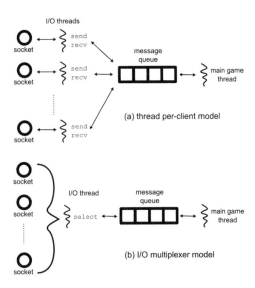

Figure 5.3.1   (a) Thread per-client versus (b) I/O thread with multiplexing.

The solution we've devised so far is very common in network server implementations. It essentially emulates asynchronous I/O—the main thread (or threads) submit I/O requests to a queue for the I/O thread, which processes the requests and then notifies the callers of the results via an event queue or similar mechanism.

Asynchronous I/O uses native OS services to deliver similar functionality without crossing the system call boundary as often and without introducing additional I/O threads. It also enables the OS to take maximum advantage of its own internal scheduling systems to optimize I/O.

Asynchronous I/O APIs

The two main APIs for asynchronous I/O are Windows Overlapped I/O and the AIO API in the POSIX real-time extensions. Overlapped I/O is supported on Windows 2000 and later. POSIX AIO is available on most UNIX-like operating systems, though the capabilities of the implementations can vary considerably, so look before you leap.

Working with either the Windows or the POSIX API is quite similar. AIO requests are associated with a control struct when they are made, which the OS uses to track the request and return the results to our code. These structs contain hidden internal fields for the OS, so they have to be explicitly zeroed out before each request. Once a request has been made, the struct is off limits to our code until we have been notified that the operation is complete. It is important to realize that the data you pass into the asynchronous API must be valid for at least as long as the asynchronous operation and also must be exclusively accessible to the OS during that time. In particular, this means we can't pass local variables into AIO calls, and we can't read from or write to the buffers until the operation completes.

After the AIO operation has been initiated, there are several ways to get completion notifications. The simplest option is usually to use a callback function. Both POSIX and the Windows API provide mechanisms to include an application-defined pointer in the callback's context. This pointer can be used to refer to our own data structures (such as the object that initiated the request), containing any additional information required from the game code's perspective to handle the completion event.

As you would expect, there are also functions for cancelling active I/O operations and for querying their current status. One thing to watch out for when cancelling asynchronous operations is that they are not guaranteed to be done when the cancel function returns—the cancel operation itself is asynchronous! This means we have to be a little bit careful in the shutdown process of our game, so as not to free any control structs or buffers in use by active operations.

Implementation

The code accompanying this gem on the CD-ROM includes a sample asynchronous game server implemented with both POSIX AIO and Windows Overlapped I/O. The code models a simple game server that runs multiple `GameInstance` objects, each with a collection of `Socket` objects for the clients connected to that instance. The `Socket` class is a wrapper around a `SocketImpl` object, which provides access to the platform's socket API.

For portability, the server uses synchronous I/O to accept incoming connections. Once the preconfigured number of connections is made, the server begins running each session's main game loop.

In `GameInstance::tick()`, the server looks for input from the clients, as seen in Figure 5.3.2. Using an asynchronous read call, `tick()` keeps a read operation open for each client. The `SocketImpl` code has some logic in it to ignore new read requests if one is already in progress. This is an improvement over a non-blocking read, because the check looks at a simple Boolean flag rather than making any calls into the actual I/O system.

The socket code also contains logic for the case when we send or receive less than the expected amount of data in a single I/O call. The `SocketImpl` initiates additional asynchronous reads and writes until the expected data arrives. The synchronous implementation of this functionality requires polling and some additional bookkeeping code.

After the game sessions are updated, the server calls `GameInstance::update-Clients()` on up to one game instance per iteration. This models game instances that send regular state updates to the clients at a rate that is less than the game's main loop frequency. By updating sessions in a round-robin fashion, the load is spread out to avoid I/O spikes caused by all of the sessions updating all of their clients at once.

As mentioned earlier, we have to be careful to make sure that the AIO control structs are valid for the entire duration of the I/O operations. In the sample code, the `ReadRequest` and `WriteRequest` structs are used for this purpose. They contain the control struct, buffers, and other I/O request-related information and are stored in the `SocketImpl` instance, so they will be valid at least as long as the socket handle. `SocketImpl::close()` contains logic for ensuring that outstanding operations are complete before the socket is destroyed.

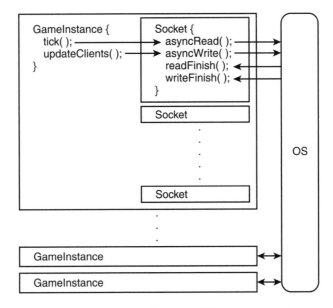

Figure 5.3.2 Asynchronous I/O server overview.

Results and Analysis

Running the sample server on a supported platform, such as Windows XP or Open-Solaris, we find that as the amount of "would block" time on the sockets increases, the efficiency (in terms of time spent executing application code) of asynchronous I/O over synchronous sockets grows. Small transfers, combined with clients that read and write continuously as fast as the server, give synchronous I/O an advantage. However, these are not conditions that are found in real-world applications. There will always be times when clients have no data to send or are not ready to receive more data from the server, and this is where asynchronous I/O excels.

To summarize, the main advantages of asynchronous I/O for game server design are:

- It eliminates idleness due to blocking.
- It eliminates system call overhead due to polling.
- It eliminates the need for multi-threading to handle I/O.
- It leverages the OS for tricky subsystems that handle concurrent I/O processing and notification dispatching.
- It creates opportunities for internal I/O optimizations in the OS kernel.

The main disadvantages of asynchronous I/O are:

- It has greater overhead per system call.
- I/O-related code may be harder to understand and debug.
- Asynchronous I/O capabilities can vary across platforms.

The greater overhead of asynchronous system calls is a consequence of their more complex functionality. In addition to the functionality equivalent to their synchronous peers, they must also register the operations for asynchronous processing and configure the pending notifications. Due to this overhead, it is best to avoid many small requests and make fewer, larger I/O requests when working with asynchronous I/O.

Asynchronous I/O code can be more difficult to understand, particularly when the underlying logic is naturally I/O driven. For example, consider a protocol exchange like the following pseudocode:

```
recv( playerName )
send( loginChallenge )
recv( loginResponse )
if ( loginResponse is valid ) startGameLoop()
else close()
```

Implemented using synchronous I/O, the code for this exchange could read almost exactly like the pseudocode (with suitable error checking added, of course). However, as shown in Figure 5.3.3, when implemented using asynchronous I/O, it is necessary to store various pieces of state information so that we can resume the process at the appropriate stage after each operation completes.

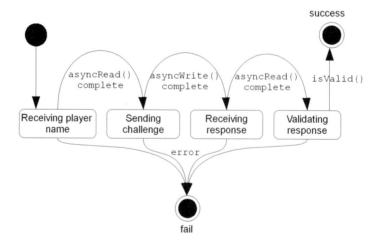

Figure 5.3.3   A simple network protocol state machine.

Whether we represent this information with ad hoc flags and status variables or with a formal state machine, we now need a state machine to manage the protocol, instead of having the protocol state maintained implicitly by the game's execution stack. How applicable this is to real-world game servers is highly design-dependent. In the case of the model server code, asynchronous I/O actually simplifies the implementation, because the main protocol between the clients and the server is stateless.

Asynchronous code is often more difficult to debug because of the flow issues just described and because of the non-deterministic behavior of the I/O notifications. On the other hand, a multi-threaded server will contain comparable levels of complexity in both the code and debugging techniques required. Which approach is more difficult to work with may be largely a matter of preference.

The variability in platforms' asynchronous I/O support is a concern for the long-term maintainability of a code base. If we want to port our game server to a new platform, we may get markedly different results, or we may be stopped altogether by lack of support for asynchronous I/O. Subtle differences in behavior can also complicate porting efforts.

Conclusion

Asynchronous I/O is a tool for network programmers to use to improve scalability. It is best planned for from the outset when building a game server, but some server architectures emulate similar functionality already using threads, so asynchronous I/O can be a reasonable retrofit in some code bases. The sample code included on the CD-ROM can serve as a starting point for evaluating the applicability of asynchronous I/O to your project.

Whether we choose to use it for network I/O or even for other server I/O tasks, such as writing log files, asynchronous I/O can offer significant benefits to the scalability of our servers. By adopting this approach, we can also hope to see asynchronous I/O implementations mature on game server platforms and someday perhaps become the *de facto* standard for network server programming.

References

[Schmidt00] Schmidt, D., M. Stal, H. Rohnert, and F. Buschmann. *Pattern-Oriented Software Architecture, Volume 2: Patterns for Concurrent and Networked Objects.* John Wiley & Sons, Ltd, 2000.

[Schmidt02] Schmidt, D., and S. Huston. *C++ Network Programming, Volume 1: Mastering Complexity with ACE and Patterns.* Addison-Wesley, 2002.

[Schmidt03] Schimdt, D., and S. Huston. *C++ Network Programming, Volume 2: Systematic Reuse with ACE and Frameworks.* Addison-Wesley, 2003.

[Silberschatz02] Silberschatz, A., P. B. Galvin, and G. Gagne. *Operating System Concepts.* John Wiley and Sons, Inc., 2002.

[Wright94] Wright, G., and R. Stevens. *TCP/IP Illustrated, Volume 2: The Implementation.* Addison-Wesley, 1994.

5.4

Introduction to 3D Streaming Technology in Massively Multiplayer Online Games

Kevin Kaichuan He
khe@blizzard.com

Massively multiplayer online games (MMOGs) have become very popular all over the world. With millions of players and tens of gigabytes of game content, popular MMOGs such as *World of Warcraft* face challenges when trying to satisfy players' increasing demand for content. Delivering content efficiently and economically will have more and more impact on an MMO game's success. Today, game content is distributed primarily through retail DVDs or downloads, which are expensive and slow.

In the future, it should be possible to deliver game content disc-free and wait-free through streaming technology. Game streaming will deliver the game world incrementally and on demand to players. Any update of the game world on the developer side will be immediately available to players. Sending only the portion of the game world that players are interacting with will save us significant bandwidth. As a result, 3D game streaming will give MMOG developers the edge of lower delivery cost, real-time content updates, and design for more dynamic gameplay.

This gem will give an introduction to the 3D game streaming technology and its challenges. It will also dive into the key components of a 3D streaming engine, including the renderer, the transport layer, the predictive loading algorithm, and client/server architecture. Various techniques to partition, stream, and re-integrate the 3D world data, including the terrain height map, alpha blending texture, shadow texture, and static objects, will be revealed. A real implementation of a 3D terrain streaming engine will be provided to serve the purpose of an illustrative demo. Source code is available and written in Visual C++/DirectX.

The Problem

Delivering a large amount of content from one point to the other over the network is not a new problem. Since the inception of the Internet, various file transport tools such as FTP, HTTP, and BitTorrent have been designed to deliver content. We could argue that these protocols are sufficient if all of the content we delivered could be perceived as an opaque, undividable, monolithic pile of binary numbers and if we had an infinite amount of bandwidth to ship this content from one place to another. In reality, we have only limited bandwidth, and latency matters. Also, it's not only the final result that we care to deliver for games, it is the experience the end user receives at the other end of the network that matters. There are two goals to reach in order to deliver a great gaming experience to the users:

- Low wait time
- High-quality content

Unfortunately, the two goals conflict with each other using traditional download technology because the higher the quality of the content, the larger the size of the content, and the longer the delivery time. How do we solve this dilemma?

The Solution

The conflict between the goals of low wait time and high quality leads us to consider new representations that enable intelligent partitioning of the data into smaller data units, sending the units in a continuous stream over the network, then re-integrating the units at the receiving end. This is the fundamental process of 3D game streaming technology. To understand how to stream game content, let's quickly review how video is streamed over the Internet.

Video Streaming

Video is the progressive representation of images. Streaming video is naturally represented by a sequence of frames. Loss cannot be tolerated within a frame, but each of these frames is an independent entity that allows video streaming to tolerate the loss of some frames. To leverage the temporal dependency among video frames, MPEG is designed to delta-encode frames within the same temporal group. MPEG divides the entire sequence of frames into multiple GOFs (groups of frames) and for each GOF, it encodes the key frame (I frame) with a JPEG algorithm and delta-encodes the B/P frames based on the I frames. At the client side, the GOFs can be rendered progressively as soon as the I frame is delivered. There are strict playback deadlines associated with each frame. Delayed frames are supposed to be dropped; otherwise, the user would experience out-of-order display of the frames.

The RTP transport protocol is based on unreliable UDP and is designed to ship media content in the unit of frames, as well as being aware of time sensitivity of the video/audio stream and doing smart packet loss handling.

To meet the goal of low wait time, linear playback order of the video frames is leveraged. Most of today's video streaming clients and servers employ prefetching optimization at various stages of the streaming pipeline to load video frames seconds or even minutes ahead of the time when they are rendered. This way, enough buffer is created for decoding and rendering the frames. As a result, users will enjoy a very smooth playback experience at the client side.

Game Streaming

MMORPG 3D content has a different nature when compared to video. First, it is not consumed linearly unless we de-generate the 3D content to one dimension and force players to watch it from beginning to end—which defeats the purpose of creating a 3D environment in the first place. Second, unlike video, 3D content has no intrinsic temporal locality. With video, the frame we play is directly tied to the clock on the wall. In 3D, an immersed gamer can choose to navigate through the content in an unpredictable way. He can park his avatar at a vista point to watch a magnificent view of a valley for minutes, and there is no deadline that forces him to move. He can also move in an arbitrary direction at full speed to explore the unseen. Thus, we cannot prefetch 3D content according to the time the content is supposed to be played back because there is no such time associated with the content. On the other hand, just like wandering in the real world, avatars in the virtual world tend to move continuously in the 3D space, and there is a continuity in the subset of the content falling in the avatar's view frustum, thus we should leverage the spatial locality instead of temporal locality when streaming 3D content. As a result, 3D world streaming generally involves the following steps:

1. Partition the world geographically into independently renderable pieces.
2. Prefetch the right pieces of world at the right time ahead of when the avatar will interact with the pieces.
3. Send the pieces from server to client.
4. Re-integrate the pieces and render them at the client side.

Throughout this gem, we will discuss these technologies in more detail, as well as how to integrate them to build a fully functional 3D streaming demo, the 3DStreamer. The full source code and data of 3DStreamer is included on the CD-ROM. Please make sure to check out the code and experiment with it to fully understand how 3D streaming works.

The World

Before we can stream a 3D world from an MMO content server to the clients, we have to build it. In this section we discuss the basic 3D terrain rendering components and how they are generated and prepared for streaming.

What Constitutes a 3D World

In this gem we will focus on streaming the artistic content of a 3D world, because artistic content easily constitutes 90 percent of the entire content set of today's MMO, and it is the part being patched most aggressively to renew players' interest in the game.

Typical artistic content of a MMORPG includes:

- Terrain
  - Mesh (height map, normal map)
  - Textures (multiple layers)
  - Alpha blending map (for blending textures)
  - Shadow map (for drawing shadows)
- Terrain objects (stationary objects)
  - Mesh/textures
- Animated objects (characters, NPCs, creatures)
  - Mesh/textures/animations
- Sound

It is beyond the scope of a single gem to cover them all, and we will focus on terrain and terrain objects in this gem because they form the foundation of a 3D world streaming engine.

Slice the Land

This section discusses the details of breaking up the world into tiles for rendering and streaming.

Patches of Land

I always wondered why my house was bought as Parcel #1234 in the grant deed until I ran into the need of slicing 3D terrain data in a virtual world. Today's MMORPG has a huge world that can easily overwhelm a top-of-the-line computer if we want to render it all at once. Similarly, it takes forever to download the entire MMO terrain data. Thus, to prepare the world for streaming, the first step is slicing it into pieces that we can progressively send over and render.

As shown in Figure 5.4.1, in 3DStreamer, we divide the world into 32×32 patches so that each patch can be stored, downloaded, and rendered independently. The terrain information for each patch is stored in its own data file, Terrain_y_x.dat, including all the data needed to render the patch, such as the height map, normal map, alpha blending textures, shadow map, terrain object information, and so on.

Tiles and Height Map

To generate the mesh for each terrain patch using the height map, we need to further divide each patch into tiles. As shown in Figure 5.4.2, each patch is divided into 32×32 tiles. A tile has four vertices, thus we have 33×33 vertices per patch. To render a terrain with varying heights, we assign each vertex of a patch a height. Altogether, we will have 33×33 height values, which constitute the height map of the patch.

To build a mesh for each patch, we simply render each tile with two triangles, as shown in Figure 5.4.3.

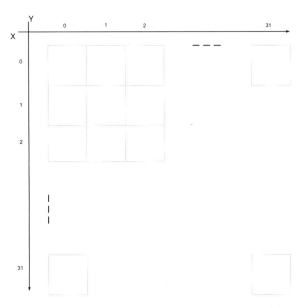

Figure 5.4.1   World consisting of 32×32 patches.

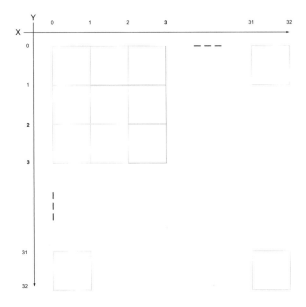

Figure 5.4.2   Patch consisting of 32×32 tiles.

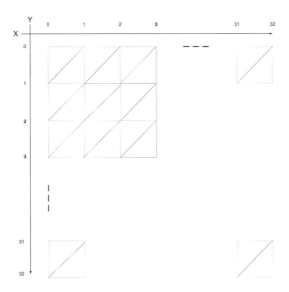

Figure 5.4.3 Patch consisting of 32×32 tiles.

To build a 3D height map, we need to map the above 2D mesh to 3D space. Here is the mapping between the 2D coordinate (x', y') we used above and its 3D world coordinates (x, y, z):

$$\{x, y, z\} \ ç \ \{x', \text{height}, -y'\}$$

As shown in Figure 5.4.4, the x' axis of the 2D coordinates becomes the X-axis of the 3D world coordinate. The opposite of y' axis of the 2D coordinates becomes the Z-axis of the 3D world coordinate. The 3D y-coordinate is given by the height of the vertices from the height map.

Figure 5.4.4 shows a few terrain patches rendered by 3DStreamer. Note that the entire terrain (32×32 patches) is located between the X-axis (x' axis of 2D space) and −Z-axis (y' axis of 2D space). This makes the traversal of tiles and patches very easy: Both start from zero.

To stitch the patches together seamlessly, the 33rd column of vertices of the patch (x', y') is replicated to the first column of vertices of the patch (x'+1, y'). Similarly, the 33rd row of patch (x', y') is replicated to the first row of patch (x', y'+1).

The following constants define the scale of the terrain and reveal the relationship among patches, tiles, and vertices.

```
#define TILES_PER_PATCH_X 32
#define TILES_PER_PATCH_Y 32
#define PATCHES_PER_TERRAIN_X 32
#define PATCHES_PER_TERRAIN_Y 32
#define TILES_PER_TERRAIN_X (TILES_PER_PATCH_X * PATCHES_PER_TERRAIN_X)
#define TILES_PER_TERRAIN_Y (TILES_PER_PATCH_Y * PATCHES_PER_TERRAIN_Y)
#define VERTICES_PER_TERRAIN_X (TILES_PER_TERRAIN_X + 1)
#define VERTICES_PER_TERRAIN_Y (TILES_PER_TERRAIN_Y + 1)
```

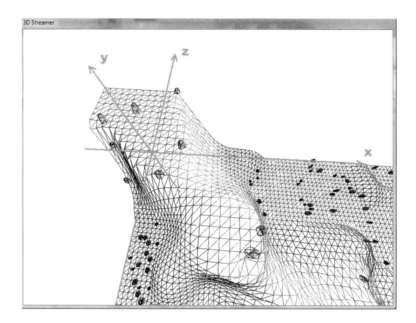

Figure 5.4.4   A rendered patch consisting of 32×32 tiles.

Terrain Generation

3DStreamer has a random terrain generator that will generate random terrain data and store it into two types of output files.

```
Terrain_y_x.dat: The terrain patch (x,y)
Terrain_BB.dat:  The bounding boxes for all patches
```

The reason that we need Terrain_BB.dat is for collision detection before the patches are loaded. To keep the avatar on the ground, even for patches not loaded, we need to be able to perform a rough collision detection using the patch's bounding box (BB). Also, the BB enables us to perform a rough view frustum culling before the detailed mesh information of the patches is streamed over.

In a commercial MMO, the terrain data is usually handcrafted by a designer and artist to create a visually appealing environment. For demo and research purposes, though, it is convenient to generate an arbitrary large terrain procedurally and use it to stress the streaming engine.

Here is the process of how to generate random terrain data and deploy it using 3DStreamer.

1. Run 3DStreamer with "-g" on the command line. Alternatively, copy the pre-generated data from the 3Dstreamer source folder on the CD-ROM to skip this step.
2. Upload the terrain data to an HTTP server (such as Apache).

Now we can run 3DStreamer in client mode to stream the above data from the HTTP server and render the terrain incrementally based on a user's input. In production projects, though, you probably won't use procedurally generated terrain with streaming because it's much cheaper to send the seed parameters of the procedure instead of the output data of the procedure.

The Rendering

This section introduces the basic rendering features of terrain and how they are integrated with streaming.

Terrain Mesh

As described earlier, we will have a per-patch height map. From the height map, we'll build the mesh for each patch as in the following code.

```
CreateMesh(int patch_x, int patch_y)
{
 TERRAINVertex* vertex = 0;
   D3DXCreateMeshFVF ( nrTri, nrVert, D3DXMESH_MANAGED,
                   TERRAINVertex::FVF, m_pDevice, &m_pMesh);
   m_pMesh->LockVertexBuffer(0,(void**)&vertex);
     for(int y = patch_y * TILES_PER_PATCH_Y, y0 = 0;
             y <= (patch_y+1) * TILES_PER_PATCH_Y;
             y++, y0++)
     for(int x = patch_x * TILES_PER_PATCH_X, x0 = 0;
             x<= (patch_x+1) * TILES_PER_PATCH_X;
             x++, x0++)
     {
        int height = GetHeight(x, y);
        D3DXVECTOR3 pos = D3DXVECTOR3(x, height, -y);
        // Alpha UV stretches across the entire terrain in range [0, 1)
        D3DXVECTOR2 alphaUV = D3DXVECTOR2(x / VERTICES_PER_TERRAIN_X,
                                  y / VERTICES_PER_TERRAIN_Y);
        // Color UV repeats every 10 tiles
        D3DXVECTOR2 colorUV = alphaUV * TILES_PER_TERRAIN_X / 10.0f;
        vertex[z0 * (width + 1) + x0] =
                TERRAINVertex(pos, GetNormal(x, z), alphaUV, colorUV);
        // Update BBox of the patch
     }
     m_pMesh->UnlockVertexBuffer();
     ...
}
```

First, we create a D3D mesh using the D3DXCreateMeshFVF API. Then we lock the mesh's vertex buffer and fill it up with vertex information. For each tile (x,y) of the patch (patch_x, patch_y), we retrieve its height from the height map and build the position vector as (x, height, -y).

Next, we set up two sets of texture coordinates—colorUV for sampling texels from the terrain textures and alphaUV for sampling the alpha blending values of the terrain textures. We'll discuss more about alpha blending in the next section. Then we calculate the normals of each vertex based on the height map. Note that we don't want to only store the position vectors at the server and re-generate normals at the client, because normals on the patch border depend on the height from multiple patches. Since we need each patch to be independently renderable, it's better that we store pre-computed normals with the patch data itself. During the process of adding vertices, we update the BBox of the patch and store it in the patch as well. The total size of vertex data of our demo terrain is about 40 bytes $* (32 * 32) ^\wedge 2 = 40$ MB.

Multi-Texture and Alpha Blending

With the mesh set up for each patch, we'll be able to render a wireframe terrain as shown in Figure 5.4.4. To give the terrain a more realistic look, we need to draw multiple types of textures on top of the mesh to represent different terrain features (for example, dirt, grass, and stone). Three common methods exist for multi-texturing terrain.

Single Texture

The simplest way to texture the terrain is to manually bake multiple textures into one huge image that covers the entire terrain. This method gives us total control over the texture details, but the cost of doing so can be prohibitive for large terrains.

Per-Tile Texturing

A more common method is to create multiple small textures at sizes from 128×128 to 512×512 and then tile them across the terrain. For example, we can create a dirt texture, a grass texture, and a stone texture, and then based on the height of each tile, we can procedurally assign one of the textures to the tile. In a D3D environment, we can divide the mesh of a patch into three subsets, assign each subset a unique texture, and render the three subsets in three iterations. However, this method has drawbacks. First, it's slow because it needs to render each mesh in three iterations for three subsets. Second, the border between two areas with different textures will have a zigzag-shaped contour and abrupt change in tone of color. This is because our tile is square-shaped, and we can only draw the entire tile using the same texture. Unless we apply special treatment to the textures at the borders, the zigzag-shaped texture divider looks ugly.

Alpha Blending Multi-Layer Textures

A better way to do this is to assign each texture to its own layer, create an alpha channel for each layer, and use a pixel shader to blend the textures. For example, we have three texture layers (dirt, grass, stone) in 3DStreamer and one alpha texture with three channels corresponding to the three layers. For each vertex, we can independently control whether it's dirt, grass, or stone. This way, we will not have the obvious zigzag border between different textures because textures are assigned at the vertex level, not at the tile level. With per-tile texturing, two triangles of the same tiles are always assigned to the same texture, thus we'll have the shape of the tile show up at the border between different texture areas. With alpha-blended multi-textures, the triangle that crosses the border of different textures will have different textures assigned to different vertices. Thus, the color of pixels inside the triangle will be interpolated based on samples from different textures.

As a result, we will have a tile-wide blending zone between different textures, which eliminates the clear zigzag border line. To further smooth the texture transition, we can broaden the blending zone by assigning partial textures to the vertex at the border. For example, instead of assigning a vertex with entirely dirt, grass, or stone, we can assign a vertex with 50 percent dirt and 50 percent grass if it is at the border.

The following code shows how we create a single alpha texture with three channels used to blend three layers of textures. We assign each vertex a texture type (dirt, grass, or stone) procedurally. We also apply a smoothing filter to the alpha texture so that alpha at the border transitions slower.

```
D3DXCreateTexture(pDevice, VERTICES_PER_TERRAIN_X, VERTICES_PER_TERRAIN_Y,
1, D3DUSAGE_DYNAMIC, D3DFMT_A8R8G8B8, D3DPOOL_DEFAULT, pAlphaMap);

 D3DLOCKED_RECT sRect;
(*pAlphaMap)->LockRect(0, &sRect, NULL, NULL);
BYTE *bytes = (BYTE*)sRect.pBits;

for(int i = 0;i < numOfTextures; i++)
  for(int y = 0; y < VERTICES_PER_TERRAIN_Y; y++)
  {
    for(int x = 0; x < VERTICES_PER_TERRAIN_X; x++)
    {
        TerrainTile *tile = GetTile(x,y);
        // Apply a filter to smooth the border among different tile types
        int intensity = 0;
        // tile->m_type has procedually generated texture types
        if(tile->m_type == i) ++intensity;
        tile = GetTile(x - 1, y);
        if(tile->m_type == i) ++intensity;
        tile = GetTile(x , y - 1);
        if(tile->m_type == i) ++intensity;
        tile = GetTile(x + 1, y);
        if(tile->m_type == i) ++intensity;
         tile = GetTile(x , y + 1);
         if(tile->m_type == i) ++intensity;
         bytes[y * sRect.Pitch + x * 4 + i] = 255 * intensity / 5;
    }
  }
(*pAlphaMap)->UnlockRect(0);
```

Figure 5.4.5 shows the effect of alpha blending of three different textures (dirt, grass, stone) rendered by 3DStreamer. As you can see, the transition from one to another is smooth. The total size of our terrain's alpha-blending data is about 3 bytes * $(32 * 32) \wedge 2 = 3$ MB.

Static Shadow

To create a dynamic 3D terrain, we need to draw shadows of the mountains. We can either calculate the shadow dynamically based on the direction of the light source or pre-calculate a shadow map based on a preset light source. The latter approach is much faster because it does not require CPU cycles at run time. Basically, we build a per-vertex shadow texture that covers the entire terrain. Each shadow texel represents whether the vertex is in shadow. We can determine whether a vertex is in shadow by creating a ray from the terrain vertex to the light source and test whether the ray intersects with the terrain mesh. If there is intersection, the vertex is in shadow, and it will have a texel value of 128 in the shadow map. Otherwise, it is outside shadow and has a texel value 255. We can then use a pixel shader to blend in the shadow by multiplying the shadow texel with the original pixel.

Figure 5.4.6 shows the effect of static shadow when the light source is preset at the left-hand side. The cost of storing the shadow texture of our terrain is not much—only 1 byte * (32 * 32) ^ 2 = 1 MB for the entire terrain.

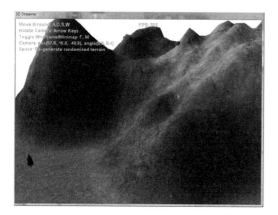

Figure 5.4.5   Multi-texturing.

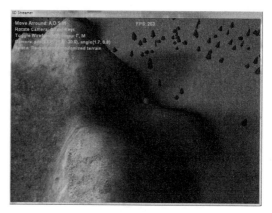

Figure 5.4.6   Shadow.

Terrain Objects

Without any objects, the terrain looks boring. Thus, 3DStreamer adds two types of terrain objects (stones and trees) to the terrain. The mesh of each terrain object is stored in a .X file and loaded during startup. We are not streaming the .X files in 3DStreamer because there are only two of them. In a game where a lot of unique terrain objects are used, we should stream the model files of terrain objects as well.

To place terrain objects on top of terrain, we can use the terrain generator to randomly pick one of the object types and place it at a random tile with random orientation with a random size. We need to save the terrain objects' placement information with the per-patch terrain data in order to redraw the objects at the client side. The following code fragment is an example of writing terrain object placement information to the disk for each tile during terrain generation.

```
OBJECT *object = tile->m_pObject;
If (object)
{
  out.write((char*)&object->m_type, sizeof(object->m_type));
  out.write((char*)&object->m_meshInstance.m_pos,
sizeof(object->m_meshInstance.m_pos));
  out.write((char*)&object->m_meshInstance.m_rot,
sizeof(object->m_meshInstance.m_rot));
  out.write((char*)&object->m_meshInstance.m_sca,
sizeof(object->m_meshInstance.m_sca));
} else
{
      OBJECTTYPE otype = OBJ_NONE;
      out.write((char*)&otype, sizeof(otype)
}
```

Assuming 20 percent of tiles have objects on them, the disk space taken by terrain objects' placement information is about (4 B+12 B * 3) * (32 * 32)^2 * 20% = 8 MB.

Divide and Conquer

Based on discussion in previous sections, our experiment terrain used in 3DStreamer consists of 32×32 patches and about one million tiles. Altogether, this takes about 60 MB of disk space to store. Here is a rough breakdown of the sizes of various components of the terrain data.

Component	Data Size
Terrain mesh	40 MB
Terrain object	8 MB
Alpha blending	3 MB
Shadow map	1 MB
Other	8 MB

As shown in the Figure 5.4.7, it is a big terrain that takes a broadband user of 1-Mbps bandwidth 480 seconds (8 minutes) to download the complete data set. Thus, without streaming we cannot start rendering the terrain for eight minutes! With streaming we can start rendering the terrain in just a few seconds, and we will continuously stream the terrain patches the avatar interacts with over the network to the client.

The Transport

To this point we have generated our terrain, partitioned it into patches, and stored the patches in Terrain_y_x.dat and the bounding boxes of all the patches in Terrain_BB.dat. We also know how to render the terrain based on these patches of data. The question left is how to store the streaming data and send it over to the client from its data source.

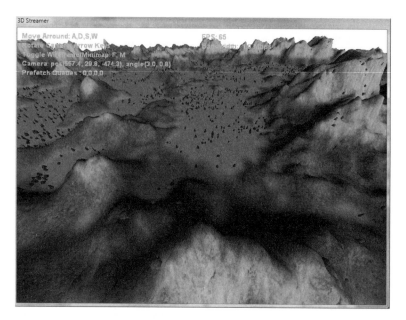

Figure 5.4.7   Big terrain.

Data Source and File Object

Streaming is a progressive data transfer and rendering technology that enables a "short wait" and "high-quality" content experience. The 3D streaming discussed here targets streaming over the network. However, the basic concepts and technique works for streaming from the disk as well. Disk streaming can be very convenient for debugging or research purposes (for example, if you don't have an HTTP server set up, you can run 3DStreamer with data stored on a local disk, too). We want to build a data storage abstraction layer that allows us to source 3D terrain data from both the local disk and a remote file server. 3DStreamer defined a `FileObject` class for this purpose.

```
// Asynchronous File Read Interface for local disk read and remote HTTP read
class FileObject
{
public:
        FileObject(const char* path, int bufSize);
        ~FileObject();
        // Schedule the file object to be loaded
        void Enqueue(FileQueue::QueueType priority);
        // Wait until the file object is loaded
        void Wait();
        // Read data sequentially out of an object after it is loaded
        void Read(char* buf, int bytesToRead);
        virtual void Load(LeakyBucket* bucket) = 0;
};
```

FileObject provides an asynchronous file-loading interface consisting of the following public methods:

- **Enqueue.** Schedule a file object to be loaded according to a specified priority.
- **Wait.** Wait for a file object to be completely loaded.
- **Read.** Stream data out of the file after it is loaded to memory.

This is the main interface between the game's prefetching algorithm and the underlying multi-queue asynchronous file read engine. The preloading algorithm will Enqueue() to queue a file object for downloading at the specified priority. The render will call Wait() to wait for critical data if necessary. We should avoid blocking the render thread as much as possible to avoid visual lag. Currently 3DStreamer only calls Wait() for loading the BB data at the beginning. The design goal of the prefetching algorithm is to minimize the wait time for the render loop. Ideally, the prefetching algorithm should have requested the right piece of content in advance, and the renderer will always have the data it needs and never need to block. When a file object is downloaded to the client, the render loop calls Read() to de-serialize the content from the file buffer to the 3D rendering buffers for rendering.

Behind the scene, the FileObject will interact with the FileQueueManager to add itself to one of the four queues with different priorities, as shown in Figure 5.4.8. The FileQueueReadThread will continuously dequeue FileObjects from the FileQueues according to the priority of the queues and invoke the FileObject::Load() virtual method to perform the actual download from the data source. We define the pure virtual method Load() as an interface to source specific downloading algorithms.

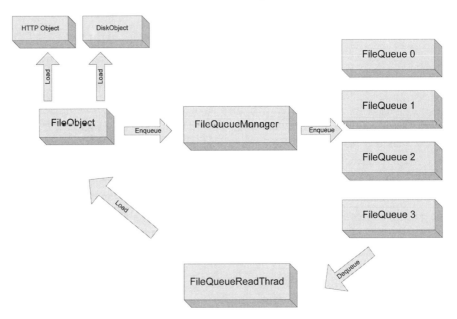

Figure 5.4.8 FileObject and FileQueue.

Both `HTTPObject` and `DiskObject` are derived from `FileObject`, and they encapsulate details of downloading a file object from the specific data source. They both implement the `FileObject::Load()` interface. So when `FileQueueThread` invokes the `FileObject::Load()`, the corresponding `Load` method of `HTTPObject` or `DiskObject` will take care of the data source–specific file downloading. Thus, `FileObject` hides the data source (protocol)–specific downloading details from the remainder of the system, which makes the asynchronous loading design agnostic to data source.

Asynchronous Loading with Multi-Priority Queues

To fulfill the "low wait time" goal of game streaming, we need to achieve the following as much as possible:

The render loop does not block for streaming.

This translates into two requirements:

* When we request the loading of a file object, such as a terrain patch, the request needs to be fulfilled asynchronously outside the render thread.
* We only render the patches when they are available and skip the patches not loaded or being loaded.

To fulfill the "high quality" goal for game streaming, we need to achieve the following requirements:

* Dynamically adjust the prefetching order of content in response to the player's input.
* Optimize the predictive loading algorithm so that the patches needed for rendering are always loaded in advance.

We will discuss the first three requirements here and leave the last requirement to later in this gem.

To support asynchronous loading (the first requirement), the render thread only enqueues a loading request to one of the prefetching queues via `FileQueueManager` and never blocks on loading. The `FileQueueReadThread` is a dedicated file download thread, and it dequeues a request from one of the four queues and executes it. `FileQueueReadThread` follows a strict priority model when walking through the priority queues. It starts with priority 0 and only moves to the next priority when the queue for the current priority is empty. After it dequeues a request, it will invoke the transport protocol–specific `Load` method to download the `FileObject` from the corresponding data source. (Refer to the "Transport Protocol" section for transport details.) At the end of the `Load` function, when data is read into memory of the client, the `FileObject::m_Loaded` is marked as true.

The third requirement is to react to players' input promptly. Our multi-priority asynchronous queueing system supports on-the-fly cancel and requeue. At each frame, we will reevaluate the player's area of interest, adjust the priorities of download requests, and move them across queues if necessary. To support the second requirement, the render loop will do the following: For patches in the viewing frustum and already submitted to DirectX (p->m_loaded is TRUE), we render them directly. For patches not submitted yet but already loaded to the file buffer (p->m_fileObject->m_loaded is TRUE), we call PuntPatchToGPU() to fill vertex/index/texture buffers with the data and then render the patches.

```
void TERRAIN::Render(CAMERA &camera)
{
  …
  for (int y = 0; y < m_numPatches.y; y++)
   for (int x = 0; x < m_numPatches.x; x++)
   {
     PATCH* p = m_patches[y * m_numPatches.x + x];
     if(!camera.Cull(p->m_BBox))
      {
        if (p->m_loaded)
          p->Render();
        if (p->m_fileObject && p->m_fileObject->m_loaded)
        {
          PuntPatchToGPU(p);
          p->Render();
        }
      }
    }
  }
  …
}
```

With the above multi-priority asynchronous queueing system, we can load patches asynchronously with differentiated priority. The dedicated FileQueueReadThread thread decouples the file downloading from the video rendering in the main thread. As a result, video will never be frozen due to the lag in the streaming system. The worst case that could happen here is we walk onto a patch that is still being downloaded. This should rarely happen if our predictive loading algorithm works properly and we are within our tested and expected bandwidth amount. We did have a safety net designed in this case, which is the per-patch bounding box data we loaded during startup. We will simply use the BB of the patch for collision detection between the avatar and the terrain. So even in the worst case, the avatar will not fall under the terrain and die—phew!

Transport Protocol

We will use HTTP 1.1 as the transport protocol that supports persistent connections. Thus, all the requests from the same 3DStreamer client will be sent to the server via the same TCP connection. This saves us connection establishment and teardown overhead for downloading each patch. Also, HTTP gives us the following benefits:

- HTTP is a reliable protocol, necessary for 3D streaming.
- HTTP is a well-known protocol with stable support. So we can directly use a mature HTTP server, such as Apache, to serve our game content.

- HTTP is feature-rich. A lot of features useful to 3D streaming, such as caching, compression, and encryption, come for free with HTTP.
- The implementation is easy, since most platforms provides a ready-to-use HTTP library.

As described in the "Transport Protocol" section, the HTTP transport is supported via HTTPObject, whose primary work is to implement the FileObject::Load() interface. The framework is very easy to extend to support other protocols as well, when such need arises.

HTTP Compression

Compression is very useful to reduce bandwidth of streaming. With HTTP, we can enable the deflate/zlib transport encoding for general compression.

HTTP Caching

We will not discuss caching in detail. For what it's worth, we can easily enable client-side HTTP caching by not giving INTERNET_FLAG_NO_CACHE_WRITE to the HttpOpenRequest() in the HttpObject::Load() method.

Leaky Bucket

A leaky bucket–based bandwidth rate limiter becomes handy when we need to evaluate the performance of a game streaming engine. Say we want to see how the terrain rendering works at different bandwidth caps—2 Mbps, 1 Mbps, and 100 Kbps—and tune our predictive loading algorithms accordingly, or we want to use the local hard disk as a data source to simulate a 1-Mbps connection, but the real hard disk runs at 300 Mbps—how do we do this?

Leaky bucket is a widely used algorithm for implementing a rate limiter for any I/O channel, including disk and network.

The following function implements a simple leaky bucket model. m_fillRate is how fast download credits (1 byte per unit) are filled into the bucket and is essentially the bandwidth cap we want to enforce. The m_burstSize is the depth of the bucket and is essentially the maximum burst size the bucket can tolerate. Every time the bucket is negative on credits, it returns a positive value, which is how many milliseconds the caller needs to wait to regain the minimum credit level.

```
int LeakyBucket::Update( int bytesRcvd )
{
   ULONGLONG tick = GetTickCount64();
 int deltaMs = (int)(tick - m_tick);
 if (deltaMs > 0)
 {
 // Update the running average of the rate
  m_rate = 0.5*m_rate + 0.5*bytesRcvd*8/1024/deltaMs;
  m_tick = tick;
 }
```

```
   // Refill the bucket
   m_credits += m_fillRate * deltaMs * 1024 * 1024 / 1000 / 8;
   if (m_credits > m_burstSize)
     m_credits = m_burstSize;
    // Leak the bucket
   m_credits -= bytesRcvd;
  if (m_credits >= 0)
    return 0;
  else
    return (-m_credits) * 8 * 1000 / (1024 * 1024) / m_fillRate;
}
```

This is the HTTP downloading code that invokes the leaky bucket for rate limiting.

```
void HttpObject::Load(LeakyBucket* bucket)
{
  …
  InternetReadFile(hRequest, buffer, m_bufferSize, &bytesRead);
  int ms = bucket->Update(bytesRead);
  if (ms)
    Sleep(ms);
  …
}
```

Figure 5.4.9 shows a scenario where we set the rate limiter to 1 Mbps to run a terrain walking test in 3DStreamer. The bandwidth we displayed is the actual bandwidth the 3DStreamer used, and it should be governed under 1 Mbps within the burst tolerance. Also, it shows how many file objects are in each priority queue. Since we are running fast with a relatively low bandwidth cap, there are some patches being downloaded in the four queues, including one critical patch close to the camera.

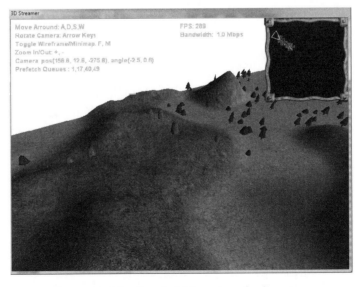

Figure 5.4.9   Bandwidth and prefetch queues.

Predictive Loading

The predictive loading algorithm is at the heart of a 3D streaming engine because it impacts performance and user experience directly. A poorly designed predictive loading algorithm will prefetch the wrong data at the wrong time and result in severe rendering lag caused by lack of critical data. A well-designed predictive algorithm will load the right piece of content at the right time and generate a pleasant user experience. The following are general guidelines to design a good prefetching algorithm:

- Do not prefetch a piece of content too early (wasting memory and bandwidth).
- Do not prefetch a piece of content too late (causing game lag).
- Understand the dependency among data files and prefetch dependent data first.
- React to user input promptly. (I turned away from the castle, stop loading it.)
- Utilize bandwidth effectively. (I have an 8-Mbps fat idle connection; use it all, even for faraway terrain patches.)
- Use differentiated priority for different types of content.

We designed a very simple prefetching algorithm for 3DStreamer following the guidelines. To understand how it works, let's take a look at the camera control first.

Camera Control

The camera controls what the players see in the virtual world and how they see it. To minimize visual lag caused by streaming, it is crucial that the prefetching algorithm understands camera controls and synchronizes with the camera state.

A camera in the 3D rendering pipeline is defined by three vectors:

- The "eye" vector that defines the position of the camera (a.k.a. "eye").
- The "LookAt" vector that defines the direction the eye is looking.
- The "Up" or "Right" vector that defines the "up" or "right" direction of the camera.

Some common camera controls supported by 3D games are:

- **Shift.** Forward/backward/left-shift/right-shift four-direction movement of the camera in the Z-O-X horizontal plane (no Y-axis movement).
- **Rotate.** Rotate the "LookAt" vector horizontally or vertically.
- **Terrain following.** Automatic update of the y-coordinate (height) of the eye.

3DStreamer supports all three controls. And the way we control the camera impacts the implementation of the predictive loading algorithm, as you can see next.

Distance Function

When do we need a patch of terrain to be loaded? When it is needed. We will present a few ways to calculate when the patches are needed in the following sections and compare them.

Viewing Frustum-Based Preloading

We should preload a patch before it is needed for rendering. As we know, the camera's view frustum is used by the terrain renderer to cull invisible patches, so it's natural to preload every patch that falls in the viewing frustum. With some experiments, we can easily find the dynamic range of that viewing frustum is so huge that it's hardly a good measure of what to load and when.

Sometimes the scope is so small (for example, when we are looking directly at the ground) that there is no patch except the current patch we are standing on in the frustum. Does this mean we need to preload nothing except the current patch in this case? What if we suddenly raise our heads and see 10 patches ahead?

Sometimes the scope is too big (for example, when you are looking straight at the horizon and the line of sight is parallel to the ground) and there are hundreds of patches falling in the frustum. Does this mean we should preload all of the patches up to the ones very far away, sitting on the edge of the horizon? What about the patches immediately to our left shoulder? We could turn to them anytime and only see blanks if we don't preload them. Also, we don't really care if a small patch far away is rendered or not even if it may be in the viewing frustum.

Distance Function–Based Preloading

To answer the question of when a patch is needed more precisely, we need to define a distance function:

$$D(p) = \text{distance of patch p to the camera}$$

Intuitively, the farther away the patch is from the camera, the less likely the avatar will interact with the patch shortly. Thus, we can calculate the distance of each patch to the avatar and prefetch the ones in the ascending order of their distances. The only thing left is to define exactly how the distance function is calculated.

Straight Line Distance Function

The simplest distance function we can define is:

$$D(p) = \text{sqrt}((x0 - x1) * (x0 - x1) + (z0 - z1) * (z0 - z1))$$

$(x0, z0)$ are the coordinates of the center of the patch projected to the XZ plane, and $(x1, z1)$ are the coordinates of the camera projected to the XZ plane. Then we can divide distance into several ranges and preload the patches in the following order:

- Critical-priority queue: Prefetch $D(p) < 1 * \text{size of a patch}$
- High-priority queue: Prefetch $D(p) < 2 * \text{size of a patch}$
- Medium-priority queue: Prefetch $D(p) < 4 * \text{size of a patch}$
- Low-priority queue: Prefetch $D(p) < 8 * \text{size of a patch}$

In other words, we will divide the entire terrain into multiple circular bands and assign the circular bands to different priority queues according to their distance from the camera.

This is a prefetching algorithm commonly used in many games. However, this algorithm does not take into consideration the orientation of the avatar. The patch immediately in front of the avatar and the patch immediately behind the avatar are treated the same as long as they have equal distances to the avatar. In reality, the character has a higher probability moving forward than moving backward, and most games give slower backward-moving speed than forward moving, thus it's unfair to prefetch the patch in front of a camera at the same priority as the patch behind it.

Probability-Based Distance Function

An avatar can move from its current location to the destination patch in different ways. For example:

1. Walk forward one patch and left shift one patch.
2. Turn left 45 degrees and walk forward 1.4 patch.
3. Turn right 45 degrees and left-shift 1.4 patch.
4. Take a portal connected to the patch directly.
5. Take a mount, turn left 45 degrees, and ride forward 1.4 patch.

I intentionally chose the word "way" instead of "path." In order to use a length of the path as a distance function, the avatar must walk to the destination on the terrain at a constant speed. In reality, there are different ways and different speeds for the avatar to get to the patch, and they may or may not involve walking on the terrain. Also, the distance cannot be measured by the physical length of the route the avatar takes to get to the patch in some cases (such as teleporting). A more universal unit to measure the distance of different ways is the time it takes the avatar to get there. With the above example, the time it takes the avatar to get to the destination is:

1. Assuming forward speed is 0.2 patch/second and left-shift speed is 0.1 patch/second, it takes the avatar 5 + 10 = 15 seconds to get there.
2. Assuming the turning speed is 45 degrees/second, it takes the avatar 1 + 7 = 8 seconds to get there.
3. It takes 1 + 14 = 15 seconds to get there.
4. Assuming the portal takes 5 seconds to start and 5 seconds in transit, it takes 10 seconds to get there.
5. Assuming the mount turns and moves two times as fast, it takes 8 / 2 = 4 seconds to get there.

Let's say we know that the probabilities of the avatar to use the aforementioned ways to get to patch p are: 0.2, 0.6, 0.0 (it's kind of brain-dead to do 3), 0.1, and 0.1, respectively.

The probability-based distance $D(p)$ will then be given by: 15 * 0.2 + 8 * 0.6 + 10 * 0.1 + 4 * 0.1 = 3 + 4.8 + 1 + 0.4 = 9.2 seconds.

Thus, the probability-based distance function can be written as:

$$D(p) = \sum_i p(i)t(i)$$

where *p(i)* is the probability of the avatar taking way *i* to get to patch *p*, and *t(i)* is the time it takes to get to *p* using way *i*.

As you can see, the power of this probability-based distance function is that it can be expanded to an extent as sophisticated as we want depending on how many factors we want to include to guide the predictive loading algorithm. For a game where we want to consider all kinds of combinations of moving options for an avatar, we can model the moving behavior of the avatar statistically in real time and feed statistics back to the above formula to have very accurate predictive loading. At the same time, we can simplify the above formula as much as we can to have a simple but still reasonably accurate predictive loading algorithm. In the 3DStreamer demo, we simplify the distance function as the following.

First, 3DStreamer does not support teleporting or mount, so options 4 and 5 are out of consideration. Second, as in most games, 3DStreamer defines the speeds for left/right shifting and moving backward at a much lower value than the speed of moving forward. From the user experience point of view, it's more intuitive for the player to move forward anyway. So in 3DStreamer, we assume that the probability of an avatar using the "turn and go forward" way is 100 percent. With this assumption, the distance function is reduced to:

$$D(p) = \text{rotation time} + \text{moving time} = \text{alpha} / w + d / v.$$

Alpha is the horizontal angle the camera needs to rotate to look at the center of *p* directly. *w* is the angular velocity for rotating the camera. *d* is the straight-line distance between the center of *p* and the camera. *v* is the forward-moving speed of the avatar.

The following code fragment shows the implementation of the predictive loading in 3DStreamer based on the simplified distance function.

```
D3DXVECTOR2 patchPos(((float)mr.left + mr.right) / 2, ((float)mr.top +
mr.bottom) / 2);
D3DXVECTOR2 eyePos(camera.Eye().x, - camera.Eye().z);
D3DXVECTOR2 eyeToPatch = patchPos - eyePos;
float patchAngle = atan2f(eyeToPatch.y, eyeToPatch.x); // [-Pi, +Pi]

// Calculate rotation distance and rotation time
float angleDelta = abs(patchAngle - camera.Alpha());
if (angleDelta > D3DX_PI)
    angleDelta = 2 * D3DX_PI - angleDelta;

float rotationTime = angleDelta / camera.AngularVelocity();

// Calculate linear distance and movement time
float distance = D3DXVec2Length(&eyeToPatch);
float linearTime = distance / camera.Velocity();

float totalTime = rotationTime + linearTime;
```

```
float patchTraverseTime = TILES_PER_PATCH_X / camera.Velocity();
if (totalTime < 2 * patchTraverseTime)
    RequestTerrainPatch(patch_x, patch_y, FileQueue::QUEUE_CRITICAL);
else if (totalTime < 4 * patchTraverseTime)
    RequestTerrainPatch(patch_x, patch_y, FileQueue::QUEUE_HIGH);
else if (totalTime < 6 * patchTraverseTime)
    RequestTerrainPatch(patch_x, patch_y, FileQueue::QUEUE_MEDIUM);
else if (totalTime < 8 * patchTraverseTime)
    RequestTerrainPatch(patch_x, patch_y, FileQueue::QUEUE_LOW);
  else
  {
      If (patch->m_loaded)
          patch->Unload();
      else if (patch->m_fileObject->GetQueue() != FileQueue::QUEUE_NONE)
        CancelTerrainPatch(patch);
  }
```

For each frame, we reevaluate the distance function of each patch and move the patch to the proper priority queue accordingly. The ability to dynamically move file prefetching requests across priorities is important. This will handle the case where an avatar makes a sharp turn and the high-priority patch in front of the avatar suddenly becomes less important. In an extreme case, a patch earlier in one of the priority queues could be downgraded so much that it's canceled from the prefetching queues entirely.

Note that in the last case, where D(p) >= 8 * patchTraverseTime, we will process it differently depending on its current state.

- **Already loaded.** Unload the patch and free memory for mesh and terrain objects.
- **Already in queue.** Cancel it from the queue.

With this predictive loading algorithm, 3DStreamer can render a terrain of one million tiles at 800×600 resolution under 1-Mbps bandwidth pretty decently. At a speed of 15 tiles/second, we still get enough time to prefetch most nearby patches in the avatar's viewing frustum, even though we make sharp turns.

Figure 5.4.10 shows what it looks like when we run the avatar around at 15 tiles/s with only 1-Mbps bandwidth to the HTTP streaming server. The mini-map shows which patches of the entire terrain have been preloaded, and the white box in the mini-map is the intersection of the viewing frustum with the ground. As you can see, the avatar is moving toward the upper-left corner of the map. As shown by "Prefetch Queues," all the critical- and high-priority patches are loaded already, which corresponds to all the nearby patches in the viewing frustum plus patches to the side of and behind the player. The medium- and low-priority queues have 80 patches to download, which are mostly the faraway patches in front of the player.

Also note that the non-black area in the mini-map shows the current memory footprint of the terrain data. It is important that when we move the avatar around, we unload faraway patches from memory to create space for new patches. This way, we will maintain a constant memory footprint regardless of the size of the entire terrain, which is a tremendously important feature of a 3D streaming engine in order to scale up to an infinitely large virtual world.

Figure 5.4.10 Predictive loading under 1-Mbps bandwidth at 15 tiles/s.

3DStreamer: Putting Everything Together

3DStreamer is a demo 3D terrain walker that implements most of the concepts and techniques discussed in this gem. It implements a user-controllable first-person camera that follows the multi-textured, shadow-mapped large terrain surface. A mini-map is rendered in real time to show the current active area of interest and the viewing frustum. Various keyboard controls are provided for navigation through the terrain as if in the game. (See the onscreen menu for the key bindings.) Here is the one-page manual to set it up.

Compile the Source

3DStreamer.sln can be loaded and compiled with Visual Studio 2008 with DirectX November 2008 or newer. The data is staged to the Debug folder for debug build by default. In order to run a release build, you need to manually copy the data (data, models, shaders, textures) from the Debug folder to the Release folder.

Terrain Generation

Running the 3DStreamer with the following command will generate a random 32×32-patch terrain and save the data in the executable's folder. It will take a while to complete. Alternatively, just use the pre-generated data in the Debug\Data folder on the CD-ROM.

```
3DStreamer -g
```

Staging the Data

For HTTP streaming, upload the data (terrain_XX_YY.dat and terrain_BB.dat) to your HTTP server and use the `-s=` command line argument to specify the server's host name and the `-p=` argument to specify the location of the data on the server.

For DISK streaming, simply give the data's path as the `-p=` argument.

Run

To run it in VS, please make sure to add `$(OutDir)` to the Working Directory of the project properties. Alternatively, you can run the executable from the executable folder directly. By default, 3DStreamer runs in DISK streaming mode with a default data path pointing to the executable folder.

To run it in HTTP streaming mode, you need to give the `-s` argument for the host name. For example, to stream the data from a server URL http://192.168.11.11/3dstreamer/32x32, just run it with the following command line:

```
3DStreamer -h -s=192.168.11.11 -p=3dstreamer\32x32\
```

Note that the trailing slash \ in the path is important. Otherwise, the client cannot construct the proper server URL.

You can also adjust the bandwidth cap (the default is 1 Mbps) with the `-b=` argument. For example, to run it in DISK streaming mode simulating a 2-Mbps link, just enter:

```
3DStreamer —b=2
```

Conclusion

In this gem we described a fundamental problem—delivering game content in a short time interval at high quality. We then discussed a 3D streaming solution. We presented a three-step method to build a 3D streaming engine: Decompose the world into independent components at the server, transfer the components with guidance from a predictive loading algorithm over the network, and reintegrate the components and render the world at the client. In the process, we defined the distance function–based predictive loading algorithm that is the heart of a 3D streaming engine. Finally, we integrated all the components to build a 3DStreamer demo that streams a large terrain of a million tiles that has multiple layers of textures blended to the client in real time with a remote HTTP server hosting the data. Now, the reader of this gem has everything he or she needs to apply 3D streaming technology to a next-generation MMO design!

6

AUDIO

Introduction

Brian Schmidt, Founder and Executive Director, GameSoundCon; President, Brian Schmidt Studios
brian@brianschmidtstudios.com

For a good deal of its lifetime, advances in game audio have been focused on creating more advanced audio chips and synthesis capabilities using dedicated pieces of hardware for audio processing. From the SID and NES chips through Yamaha chips, Sony SPUs, and the original Xbox audio chip, the trend has been toward more voices, higher fidelity, and greater audio signal processing capabilities in a never-ending goal to create realistic video game sounds. With the current generation and the movement toward a more easily C-programmable audio system, the emphasis has expanded somewhat—rather than focusing solely on driving more mathematics into the audio signal path, an effort has been made to make those (quite simple) technologies that are available easier to use and manipulate by the composer and the sound designer.

Game audio development, from a programming perspective, has therefore focused on two quite different areas: the very high and the very low level.

At the very high level, game audio development was radicalized by the introduction of high-level authoring tools and matching game audio engines. Prior to the creation of these tools, it was clear that one of the largest obstacles to great game audio was the ability for sound designers and composers (the people with the "ears") to bring their vision to fruition, rather than a lack of cutting-edge sound-processing technology. Often the ideas composers and sound designers had were well within the existing capabilities of common custom or third-party game audio engines. Indeed, creating cooler game audio technology was of limited value, because even if new technologies were available, it was difficult (and programmer intensive) to effectively use those technologies. Composers and sound designers weren't even able to use simple existing technologies effectively, because even the simplest creative notion required creating a detailed description of what they wanted and then going to the programmer in the hopes that it could be programmed without too much trouble. Such code-driven workflow was not conducive to creativity, because it relied both on programmer time (scarce in any project) and on the ability for the sound designer/composer to adequately describe what he or she wanted in a language the programmers could understand.

High-level tools were introduced broadly around 2002, with the introduction of XACT (*Xbox Audio Creation Tool*) for Xbox and SCREAM for Sony platforms. In these tools—and later in platform-independent tools, such as WWise and FMOD Designer—the sound designer or composer could use a graphical interface to create game audio content that was then playable by the matching high-level game audio engine. The key element of these *content-driven* tools was that they allowed, for the first time, highly desirable features to be used in a way that the composer or sound designer could try, modify, tweak, and otherwise experiment without needing to bother the programmer.

So, ironically, audio quality dramatically increased not in response to cool, cutting-edge low-level audio capabilities, but simply by packaging up the *existing* technologies into a format/tool chain that could be easily used by the creative audio professional. In essence, better game audio came from programming better tools with better workflows and better UIs.

The gem by Mat Noguchi of Bungie describes the content-driven system used in the *Halo* series of games across Xbox and Xbox 360. Note the UIs created for the sound designer. Also, pay particular attention to the mixing portion; game audio mixing and post-production represent some of the biggest issues in current-day game development.

The emphasis on high-level tools and content-driven audio systems notwithstanding, the cutting edge of game programming has no shortage of low-level problems to be solved. Audio signal processing down at the sample level still provides many challenges for great game audio. Growing in popularity in game development is the use of customized digital signal processing (DSP) algorithms to achieve specific effects.

Audio DSP in games is sometimes compared to pixel shaders in graphics; in fact, the term "sound shader" is occasionally used. Although game engines have for some time supported somewhat fixed-function DSP in the form of hard-coded resonant filters, occlusion/obstruction filtering, and environmental reverb, the advent of CPU-based audio systems has greatly lowered the bar for custom-written DSP tailored for a specific audio effect. The DSP effects are sometimes used to take a sound and modify it for a certain environment/circumstance (such as a reverb or voice effect), or it may be integral to creation of the sound itself (as in a pitch shifter used to create a low dinosaur roar from a recording of an elephant). Audio DSP is also used to process the final output of the audio engine using special DSP effects called *mastering effects*, which are used in virtually every other audio/visual medium to put final polish on the sound. The gem by Ian Lewis on creating a run-time radioization effect describes the creation of custom DSP for a particular voice effect used in a popular Xbox title.

In addition to audio DSP designed to process existing audio data, further low-level audio programming challenges lie in creating audio from pure mathematics. Physical modeling is such a system, where the vibrations that result from the collision of objects are modeled and treated as audio data and fed into the audio mix. Further, savvy game programmers recognize the treasure trove of data within the physics simulation code that can be used to either create audio or drive parameters of a sophisticated audio engine. The gem by Zhimin Ren describes such a system, deriving modal synthesis control parameters from the physics engine to create tightly correlated audio matching the visual images for impacting and rolling interactions.

So there remains no shortage of high-level and low-level challenges for game audio programmers. Better tools that enable composers and sound designers to work more efficiently and take advantage of existing technologies in unique and creative ways are continually undergoing development and improvement. Low-level signal processing in the form of off-the-shelf or custom-written DSP provides greater variety and tighter interaction with the visuals. And physical modeling, together with other procedurally generated audio, is beginning to show promise in real-world applications. In John Carmack's GDC 2004 keynote address, he postulated that, but for a bit more CPU, game audio was "basically done." We would challenge that assertion as... premature.

6.1

A Practical DSP Radio Effect

Ian Ni-Lewis
Singlemalt71@gmail.com

et's say you're making a squad-oriented first-person shooter and you want it to
have great immersive audio. So you carefully place all of the sound effects in the
world, making sure they have realistic distance-based roll-off curves. You calculate the
geometry of the game map and make sure each sound gets filtered for obstruction and
occlusion. And you set up zones for reverberation and get them all carefully cross-
faded. Everything sounds realistic.

But there's a problem, says your lead designer: The gameplay design requires that
you be able to hear messages from your squadmates. If the squad gets separated, that
dialog gets rolled off or occluded, and the player can't hear what's going on. You
explain that this is realistic, that people can't hear each other when they're hundreds
of yards away or separated by thick concrete walls, and that changing that would
break the immersiveness of the game. The designer is unmoved—and your dialog guy
is on his side for once. The dialog needs to be audible everywhere.

Assuming your FPS isn't set too far in the past, a great way to solve this problem
is with a radio effect. Keep all of the work you did on distance, obstruction, and
occlusion for each dialog source, because that still sounds great when the source is
nearby. But as the direct sound from the source gets fainter, you cross-fade in a version
of the dialog that is band-limited and distorted (see Figure 6.1.1).

This is a great effect—when the source is close by, you get the full environmental
audio; but when it's far away, it sounds like it's coming to you over the airwaves.

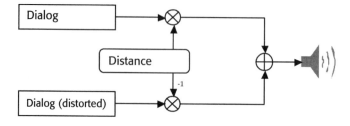

Figure 6.1.1 Cross-fading of original and distorted dialog based on distance.

The next question, and the topic of this gem, is: How do we get the distorted dialog? One easy solution is to just apply a radio effect offline in your favorite audio editing application. But taking the easy way out in this case is going to double your storage budget for audio, not to mention doubling the bandwidth required to render each line of dialog. Plus, it's no fun. It'd be a lot more interesting if we could apply the effect in real time. Fortunately, it's not too hard to do.

The Effect

I'm not going to try to explain exactly how signals are affected by radio transmission, because I can't. But we can come up with a pretty convincing approximation by making the signal sound tinny and distorted, with maybe a little static thrown in for good measure.

Cranking Up the Distortion

Distortion is the most interesting part of the effect from the programmer's point of view. We want to emulate clipping, which happens when the signal volume is too high for the output device to handle. This is insanely easy to do if you don't care about quality—just raise the volume and saturate. That lops off the top and bottom of each wave, as you see in Figure 6.1.2.

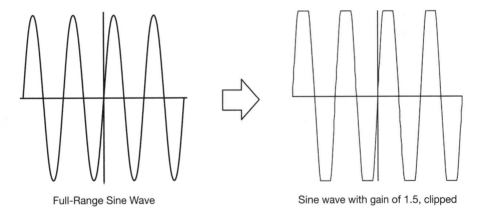

Full-Range Sine Wave   Sine wave with gain of 1.5, clipped

Figure 6.1.2 Distortion of a sine wave due to digital saturation.

With just a little extra gain, this doesn't sound all that bad—but it doesn't sound right, either. It's a little harsher and more "digital" than what we really want. We're getting noise and distortion, but it's not the good kind. It's the bad kind that makes you think maybe you need to go back and change all your sound levels. This is unsurprising, since all we've done so far is digital clipping—the same thing your digital-to-analog converter is going to end up doing if your levels are too hot.

What we really want is something that sounds grungy, but warm—something that won't irritate our ears or make us think something is wrong with the game. Something that sounds nice and warm and analog.... How do we do that?

To understand how we go about making nice-sounding distortion, let's start by taking a look at why our naïve distortion technique sounds so bad. Figure 6.1.3 shows a spectral plot of a clean, full-range sine wave with a frequency of just under 1/8 Nyquist.

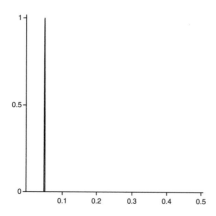

Figure 6.1.3   Spectral (frequency) plot of a clean sine wave.

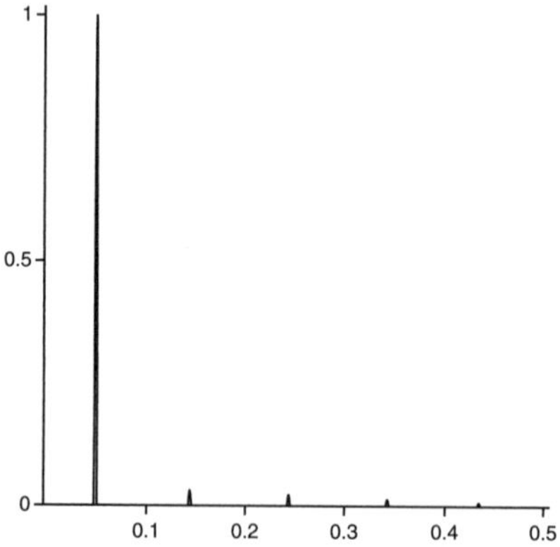

Figure 6.1.4   Spectral (frequency) plot of a clipped sine wave with gain = 1.1.

Figure 6.1.4 shows the same sine wave with the gain turned up to 1.1. Notice the little bumps that start appearing to the right of the original frequency? There's the grunge we're hearing. It's harmonic distortion—"distortion" because we're getting additional frequencies that weren't in the source, and "harmonic" because the new frequencies happen to be multiples of the frequency of the original sine wave. Normally, harmonic distortion is exactly what we want. But there's a problem here. It's hard to see in the previous graph, but watch what happens when we crank the gain up to 11 (see Figure 6.1.5).

It's a classic aliasing pattern: New frequencies are generated above Nyquist, so they wrap back over the top of the original frequencies. In the previous graph, only three of the frequencies—the original sine and the largest two harmonics—are below the Nyquist frequency. These three get smaller as you go from left to right. The next longest bars in the graph are between 2× and 3× Nyquist, so they're reflected. You can see that they get smaller from right to left. After that, the magnitudes get pretty small and hard to see, but at the resolution of this graph, there are still a couple of harmonics that bounced off zero and started decreasing from right to left again.

So there's where the harshness is coming from. The distortion is producing frequencies that aren't band-limited, and that's turning into aliasing, and it sounds awful. Let's see if we can fix that and add some warmth while we're at it.

What we've been talking about so far is hard clipping, which boils down to just throwing away any sample with a magnitude larger than some threshold value and replacing it with a sample at that threshold value (or a negative threshold value). If we plotted a graph of input sample values versus output values for a hard-clipping algorithm, it would look something like the graph in Figure 6.1.6, with input values on the X-axis and corresponding outputs on the Y-axis. This graph is called the *transfer function*.

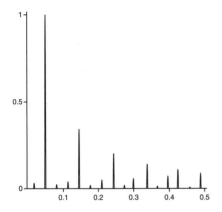

Figure 6.1.5 Spectral (frequency) plot of a clipped sine wave with gain = 11.

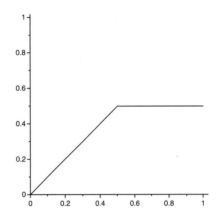

Figure 6.1.6 Transfer function for hard-clipping algorithm.

One easy way to improve on this is to gently reduce the values, rather than chopping them off entirely. We'll start by choosing a lower threshold than the one we used for hard clipping, so we have some headroom to work with. Our new soft-clipping code looks more like this:

```
if( input > threshold )
     output = ( ( input – threshold ) * ratio ) + threshold;
else
     output = input;
```

Or, simplifying some:

```
offset = ( 1.0f – ratio ) * threshold;
if( input > threshold )
     output = ( input * ratio ) + offset;
else
     output = input;
```

Graphing the transfer function of the soft clipper gives us something like what you see in Figure 6.1.7.

If you're familiar with studio production tools, you might recognize this as the transfer function for a hard-knee compressor. It's a common tool used to implement soft clipping. And it works, as you can see from the spectrum of our turned-to-11 sine wave run through the soft clipper (see Figure 6.1.8).

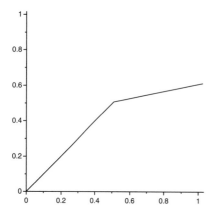

Figure 6.1.7 Transfer function for softened clipping algorithm.

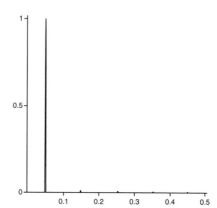

Figure 6.1.8 Spectral plot of hard-knee compressed sine, gain = 11, t = 0.2, r= 0.4.

It almost works too well, in fact—the aliasing has almost disappeared, but so has much of the harmonic distortion we were after in the first place. Well, maybe we can combine these two techniques. We could start out by implementing a hard-knee compressor, but instead of keeping the ratio constant, we could make the ratio also vary with the magnitude of the input sample. But now we're starting to do some expensive math. If we're going to go that far, let's not play around. Let's go straight for the power tools and use a higher-order polynomial.

Polynomials show up in games occasionally. They're sometimes used for audio sample rate conversion, for instance. In graphics and animation, they show up frequently in the guise of parametric splines. The polynomial we need is very similar to a spline, and we'll derive it in much the same way.

Unfortunately for us, the splines used in graphics are all parameterized on the single variable t, which is usually interpreted as a distance along the spline from the starting point. So we'll do this the old-fashioned way, by solving a system of linear equations based on a set of constraints. Here's what we want our function to look like:

1. The value of the function at $x=0$ is 0, and the slope of the function is 1 to begin with. Things don't get interesting until x is greater than or equal to a threshold value, which we'll call t. That means that the value of the function at $x=t$ is t.
2. The slope at t is still 1.
3. At $x=1$, the slope of the function is the compression ratio, which we'll call r.
4. We probably want the slope to reach r before $x=1$. Let's define a point k (for *knee*) where the slope of the function is r.

That's four constraints, which means we need a fourth-order polynomial to satisfy them. So let's start by defining that function:

$$f = ax^4 + bx^3 + cx^2 + dx$$

That's the function we'll run on each input value (x) to get the output value we're looking for. The function itself is pretty simple. The complicated question is, what are the values of the coefficients a, b, c, and d? We get those by solving a system of equations that represent our constraints. So let's restate those constraints as linear equations in a, b, c, and d, by substituting x, r, t, and k into our basic equation $f(x)$. The system of equations looks like this:

$$(t, k, r) \rightarrow \left[g\left(\left. \frac{d}{dx} f(x) \right|_{x=1}, r \right), g\left(\left. \frac{d}{dx} f(x) \right|_{x=t}, 1 \right), g\left(\left. \frac{d}{dx} f(x) \right|_{x=k}, r \right), g(f(t), t) \right]$$

At this point, we'll stop pretending to be good at math and turn things over to a symbolic solver (in this case, Maplesoft's Maple 13) and ask it to solve for a, b, c, and d in terms of t, k, and r. The results are:

$$a = -\left(\frac{1}{2}\right) \frac{3r + 4t - 4tr - 3k - 3 + 3kr}{-8tk^2 - 3kt^3 - 8kt + 2k^2t^2 + 11kt^2 + 2t^2 - 3t^3 + 6k^2 + t^4}$$

$$b = \frac{-2k^2 + 2k^2r - 2k + 2kr - 3t^2r + 3t^2 - 2 + 2r}{-8tk^2 - 3kt^3 - 8kt + 2k^2t^2 + 11kt^2 + 2t^2 - 3t^3 + 6k^2 + t^4}$$

$$c = -\left(\frac{1}{2}\right) \frac{t(8k^2r - 8k^2r + 9kt - 9ktr + 8kr - 8k + 9t - 9tr + 8r - 8)}{-8tk^2 - 3kt^3 - 8kt + 2k^2t^2 + 11kt^2 + 2t^2 - 3t^3 + 6k^2 + t^4}$$

$$d = \frac{2t^2k^2r - 8tk^2 + 6k^2 - 3t^3kr + 2kt^2r + 9kt^2 - 8kt + t^{4r} - 3t^3r + 2t^2r}{-8tk^2 - 3kt^3 - 8kt + 2k^2t^2 + 11kt^2 + 2t^2 - 3t^3 + 6k^2 + t^4}$$

Yes, it really is that ugly. Fortunately, we only have to calculate the coefficients when t, k, or r actually changes, which shouldn't be too often.

One last thing before we call the distortion finished. It turns out that if we set the parameters so that the function sounds nice for normal-range audio, it starts to behave badly when the amplitude is less than t or greater than k. We'll solve this by switching to a normal hard-knee compressor function when the input is higher than $t + k$ and ignoring the distortion function completely when the input is less than t.

Now we can start to play with this function—or rather, the piecewise function defined by our spline, the compressor ratio, and the inflection points t and k:

$$\begin{cases} f(x) & t < |x| < k \\ r(x - k) + k & |x| \geq k \\ x & \textit{otherwise} \end{cases}$$

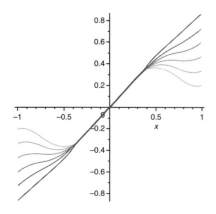 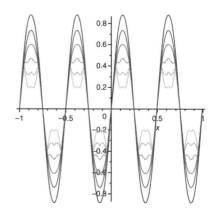

Figure 6.1.9a Transfer function with t = 0.2, k = 0.4, r varying from 0.9 to 0.4.

Figure 6.1.9b Transfer function with t = 0.2, k = 0.4, [0.9,0.4] applied to full-scale sine wave.

In Figure 6.1.9, notice how as the ratio decreases, the tops of the waves begin to look more squared off—but instead of being completely flat, they get rounded off to the point of turning inside out. Visually, this effect seems a little odd. But in the audio domain, where a wave's frequency content is far more important than its shape, it sounds much better. Why? Take a look at the spectrum of our turned-up-to-11 sine wave, once we've run its output through our new function (see Figure 6.1.10).

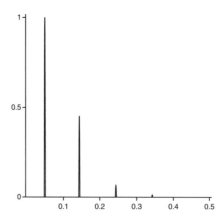

Figure 6.1.10 Spectral plot of distorted sine, gain = 11, t = 0.2, k = 0.4, r = 0.4.

The new harmonics are loud and strong, but the aliased frequencies have all but disappeared. (The aliased frequencies are in fact still present, but at such a low volume that they don't show up at the resolution of this graph. For our purposes, they've ceased to exist.)

Automatic Gain Control

So we've got a decent-sounding distortion, but it has one major downside: The quality of the distortion is heavily dependent on the volume of the input. That might not seem like a drawback at first—after all, that's how distortion works in the real world. But it's a significant problem for game dialog. It's not always possible to normalize the volume across all dialog samples, so some lines of dialog will sound more distorted than others. Sadly, the loudest lines of dialog are invariably the most important or emotional lines—exactly the ones you don't want to get lost in distortion.

There are a few different ways of dealing with this problem, but the one I've had the most success with is to fiddle with the volume before and after distortion. Decide on an ideal average volume of samples to feed into the distortion effect. Then measure the actual volume (or RMS, which we'll discuss in a moment) of your incoming samples. If the incoming RMS is lower than the ideal, then crank up the volume. If the incoming RMS is higher, then turn it down. On the way out of the distortion effect, just apply the reverse of whatever you did on the way in, so that the output volume stays about the same.

Fiddling with the volume like this is called *automatic gain control*, or AGC. It's a simple effect that's very popular in consumer recording devices. It's easy to implement.

First, we calculate the root mean square (RMS) of the incoming samples. In theory, this is the square root of the average of the square of all samples, or $rms(x)_n = \sqrt{\frac{\sum_{i=0}^{n} x_i^2}{n}}$. In practice, we don't average all samples, because that would give too much weight to past values and not enough to more recent ones. Instead, we calculate a windowed RMS, which is the root mean square of a subset of samples, from the current sample n back to some previous sample $n\text{-}m$: $rms(x, m)_n = \sqrt{\frac{\sum_{i=n-m}^{n} x_i^2}{m}}$. Of course, we don't need to calculate the complete sum for every sample—we just keep a running total. The C code for each sample looks something like this:

```
float* rms, *y;

const int m; // window length
float window[m];

float MS; // mean square

float current = (y[n] * y[n]) / m;
MS += current;             // add current value
MS -= window[n % m];       // subtract oldest previous value
window[n % m] = current;   // replace oldest value with current value

rms[n] = sqrt(MS); // voila, root-mean-square
```

This gives an accurate RMS measurement, but if you're in a hurry, you can leave out the square and square root (thus calculating a windowed mean rather than a windowed RMS) and still get decent results. The important part is the moving average, which is effectively a low-pass filter on our AGC inputs.

Once you've calculated the input RMS, the rest of the AGC is simple. Let T be the target volume. The AGC output is $y_n = x_n \frac{T}{rms\,(x,m)_n}$. In other words, we calculate the RMS as a percentage of the target and multiply each incoming sample by that percentage.

On the way out of the distortion effect, we want to readjust the volume to where it was before. We could just reverse our previous calculation and multiply by $\frac{rms\,(x,m)_n}{T}$, but that turns out to be a bad idea. The problem is that the distortion effect has a large and not always predictable effect on output volume. The volume of the output is a nonlinear function of the inputs. In non-mathematical terms, that means the output volume will be different in ways that won't be easy to understand or correct. And in practical terms, that means your sound guy will not be happy with you.

Fortunately, we already have the tools we need to fix this problem. All we need is yet another AGC. This time, instead of using a constant value for the target, we'll use the incoming RMS that we calculated before. The block diagram looks like Figure 6.1.11.

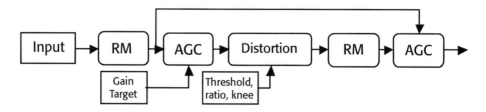

Figure 6.1.11   Volume compensation by pre- and post-distortion AGC.

One last note on the AGC: As with anything involving division, there are numerical instabilities in this formula. In particular, there's a singularity when the input volume is near zero. I've dealt with this in two ways: either always adding an epsilon or clamping the input volume to an arbitrary minimum. Both methods work equally well, in my opinion. The clamping method gives a little more headroom, so that's what I've used in the code that accompanies this article.

Adding Static

A little bit of snap, crackle, and pop is the finishing touch on this effect. Static should be subtle, so you can take some shortcuts here. Blending in a prerecorded noise sound is fine, but unless it's a long wave, the loop points will become obvious. Depending on exactly what your sound designer wants, it can be cheaper and more effective just to create your own. One technique that works well: Take your floating-point input value, cast it to an int, invert the bits, and divide by INT_MAX, like so:

```
float noise = (float)(~(*(int*)&input)) / (float)INT_MAX;
```

Drop that down to about –24 dB below the main outputs, and it sounds like a mixture of static and crosstalk. I personally love this effect, but it's not for everyone. It has a definite digital-age sound to it, so I wouldn't suggest it for games set much earlier than 1990.

Making It Tinny

The finishing touch that really sells this effect is band-pass filtering. The sound has to be thin, like it's coming from a very small and not very well-made speaker. It's a simple effect to achieve. You'll want to make the exact parameters configurable, but a band-pass filter with a 24-dB/octave roll off set at about 1 kHz makes a good starting point.

Designing this sort of filter is actually quite difficult. Fortunately, the heavy lifting has all been done long in the past. There is any number of excellent digital filter designs on the Internet, free for the taking. I recommend Robert Bristow-Johnson's excellent design, which is available at www.musicdsp.org/files/EQ-Coefficients.pdf. Try Bristow-Johnson's band-pass EQ, set to a center frequency of 1 kHz and a Q of 4.5.

Putting It All Together

Figure 6.1.12 shows the block diagram as implemented in the code accompanying this article.

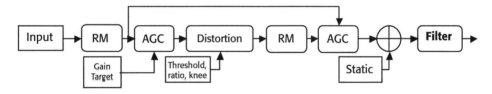

Figure 6.1.12   Complete block diagram of radio effect.

This configuration puts the band-pass filter at the end, so that the sound is easier to fit into a busy mix. You may want to try other configurations. For instance, if the radio is the main or the only sound playing, you'll get a fuller sound by putting the filter directly after the distortion instead of at the end. Or you can double the filter for that extra-tinny sound.

Finally, don't forget to add a limiter at the end of your mix.

Parameter Animation

The best part about applying a radio effect in-game, rather than baking it into your audio beforehand, is that it gives you an opportunity to animate the parameters. Varying the settings of your radio effect, either cyclically over time or dynamically in response to in-game parameters, makes the audio much more organic and unpredictable. For instance:

- **Increase the distortion AGC's gain target as the sound source gets further from the receiver.** The effect is to add another distance/occlusion cue to the sound.
- **Link the center frequency of the band-pass filter to a low-frequency oscillator.** This is a cheap way to get a phasing effect similar to an out-of-tune AM radio station.
- **Animate the ratio and knee of the distortion effect.** I love this technique because it adds motion to the sound in a subtle and non-obvious way. Be careful, though: A little of this goes a long way.

Sinusoidal low-frequency oscillators—LFOs—are extremely cheap to run. They require only two fused multiply-adds per sample and have no real storage needs, which means they can be easily interleaved with other processing. The technique takes advantage of the fact that the cosine and sine functions are derivatives of each other: $\sin(x)\frac{d}{dx} = \cos(x)$ and $\cos(x)\frac{d}{dx} = -\sin(x)$. As long as the frequency is low enough, you can just:

1. Scale the previous frame's sine and cosine values by the per-frame step (2π *frequency).
2. Increment the sine by the scaled cosine value.
3. Decrement the cosine by the scaled sine value.

That's all there is to it. This method falls apart at audio frequencies, but for LFOs it's remarkably stable.

Conclusion

The effect presented here isn't an accurate simulation of real-world electronics. But it's practical, relatively low cost, and effective. Most important, it's configurable and easy to use. The polynomial waveshaper gives it a unique sound, and the dual AGCs make it easy to drop into the mix. It's shipped in two triple-A titles that I know of, and I hope to see it ship in many more.

6.2

Empowering Your Audio Team with a Great Engine

Mat Noguchi, Bungie
matthewn@bungie.com

Making award-winning game audio at Bungie isn't just about the using best technology or having the best composers (although that doesn't hurt). The best technology will ring flat given poor audio, and the best music will sound out of place given poor technology. If you really want your game to sing, you need to put audio in the control of your audio team.

For the past nine years, with a core set of principles, a lot of code, and even more content, Bungie has empowered its audio team to make masterpieces. This gem will explore the audio engine that drives *Halo*, from the basic building blocks the sound designers use to the interesting ways the rest of the game interacts with audio. We will also take a peek at the post-production process to see how everything comes together.

Audio Code Building Blocks

The sound engine starts with the s_sound_source.

```
enum e_sound_spatialization_mode
{
    _sound_spatialization_mode_none,
    _sound_spatialization_mode_absolute,
    _sound_spatialization_mode_relative
};

struct s_sound_source
{
    e_sound_spatialization_mode spatialization_mode;
    float scale;

    // only valid if spatialization_mode is absolute.
    point3d position;
    quaternion orientation;
    vector3d translational_velocity;
};
```

This structure encompasses all the code-driven behavior of sound. You have your typical positional audio parameters, a fade on top of the default volume, some stereo parameters, and a single value called *scale*. What is scale?

The scale value is used to parameterize data from the game engine to the audio engine. It is normalized to lie within [0, 1], making it simple to use as an input into a function or linear range. Everything that can play a sound in our game exports at least one scale value, if not more. As a simple example, sounds that get generated from particle impacts receive a scale normalized between 0.5 and 1.5 world units/second. A more complex example would be the sounds that play when a Banshee banks sharply and forms contrails at the wing. The actual scale that gets exported is shown in Figure 6.2.1 in our object editor.

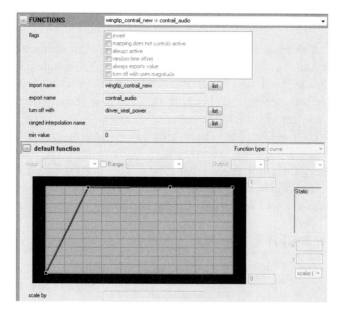

Figure 6.2.1 An object function from the Warthog for the engine sound.

This is an example of an object function; it takes various properties exported by an object and combines them into a single value that can be sent to the sound system. Incidentally, we drive our shaders in a similar way, although shaders can use more than one input.

In general, simple things such as impacts and effects export a single scale. Objects such as the Warthog and Brute can export a combination of multiple scales.

Parameterizing audio with a single value may seem a bit simplistic. However, as we'll explore later, we tend to parameterize only a few properties of a sound based on scale, and in almost all cases it makes sense to parameterize multiple properties in a coupled fashion. For spatialized audio, we have a separate distance envelope that we'll describe in the next section.

Sound Parameterization

Given that we can send the audio engine interesting data from the game, we need to author content to use this data (that is, the scale and distance). The audio designers export .AIFF files, which get converted into the native platform format (XBADPCM for Xbox and XMA2 for Xbox 360), and they attach in-game metadata through our custom game content files called *tags*. Sound content breaks down into one of two categories: impulse sounds and looping sounds.

Impulse Sounds

For impulse sounds, such as impacts, gunshots, and footsteps, we allow the audio designers to adjust gain and pitch with the scale shown in Figure 6.2.2.

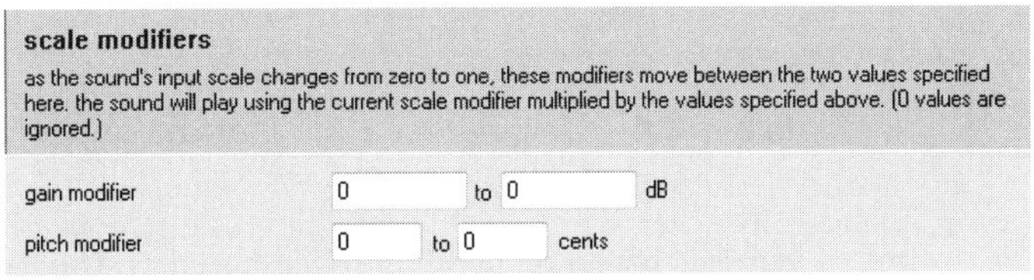

Figure 6.2.2   Scale parameter editor.

(Side note: Having your data use units that the audio team understands goes a long way to making them feel at home with the data they have to work with!)

For spatialized audio, we also can specify a distance envelope, as shown in Figure 6.2.3.

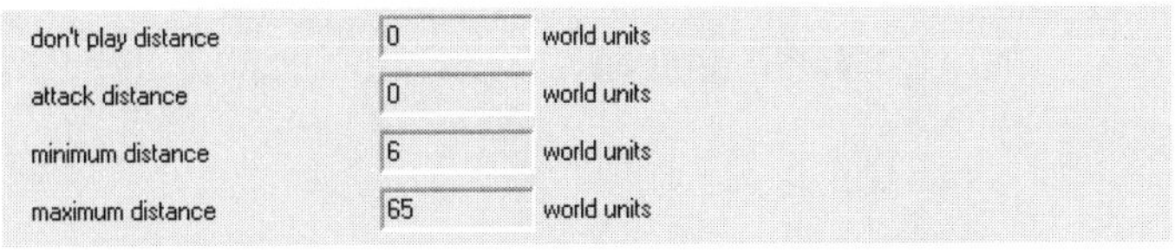

Figure 6.2.3   Distance envelope editor.

From the sound source origin to the "don't play distance," the sound is silent. From "don't play" to "attack distance," the sound scales from silence to full volume. Between "attack distance" and "minimum distance," the sound plays at full volume. And from "minimum distance" to "maximum distance," the sound scales from full volume back to silence.

The audio designers use the attack distance primarily for sound LODs. You can hear this for yourself in any *Halo 3* level: A sniper rifle firing far away sounds like a muffled echo, while the sniper rifle firing up close has the crisp report of a death machine. See Figure 6.2.4.

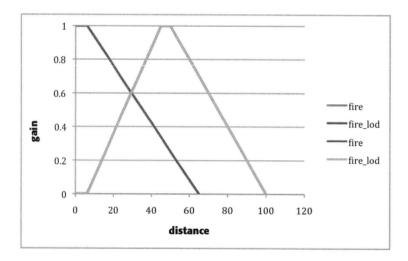

Figure 6.2.4 Distance envelopes for the sniper rifle gunshot.

Impulse sounds can also be parameterized based on the total number of instances of that sound playing. For example, when glass breaks, it can form a few or a lot of broken glass particles. A lot of glass hitting a concrete floor sounds much different than a little; attempting to replicate that sound by playing a lot of the same glass impact sound does not work without a prohibitively large variety of sounds.

To combat this, we allow sounds to "cascade" into other sounds as the total number of sounds hits a certain threshold. For glass, the sound tag can specify a set of *promotion rules* (see Figure 6.2.5).

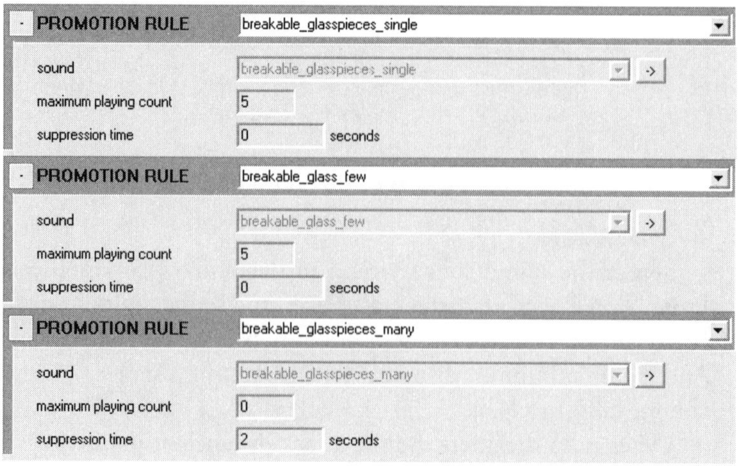

Figure 6.2.5 Broken glass particle promotion rules.

These promotion rules are defined in the order that they should play at run time. For each rule, you can specify which kind of sound to play (for example, few glass pieces, many glass pieces) as well as how many instances of that kind can play before you start the next rule. Each rule can also contain a timeout to suppress all sounds from previous rules.

Using the rules from Figure 6.2.5, if we played five glass sounds at once, we would play four instances of the `breakable_glasspieces_single` sounds. When the fifth sound played, we would play a `breakable_glass_few` sound and stop the previous four `breakable_glasspieces_single` sounds. If we then managed to play four more `breakable_glass_few` sounds in the same way (such that they were all playing at once), we would play a `breakable_glass_many` sound, stop the previous `breakable_glass_few` sounds, and then suppress any future glass sound for two seconds.

Cascading sounds allow us to have an expansive soundscape for particle impacts without playing a prohibitive number of sounds at once.

Looping Sounds

A sound that does not have a fixed lifetime (such as engine sounds, dynamic music, or ambience) is created using looping sounds. Because looping sounds are dynamic, we allow their playback to be controlled with a set of events: start, stop, enter alternate state, and exit alternate state. (More on alternate state in a bit.) Since these events are really just state transitions, we need just two more bits for playing looping sounds: one bit for whether the loop should be playing and one bit for whether it should be in the alternate state. For each event, as well as the steady state of normal playing and alternate playing, the audio designers can specify a sound. In the steady state when a looping sound is playing, we simply keep playing the loop sound. It's usually authored such that it can play forever without popping. For transition events (start, stop, enter alternate, exit alternate, and stop during alternate), those sounds either can be queued up to play after the loop or can play on top of the currently playing loop.

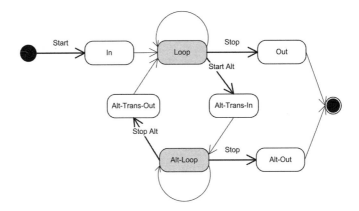

Figure 6.2.6 Looping sound state diagram.

("Alternate" is really a way of saying "cool." During the development of *Halo 1*, the audio director Marty O'Donnell asked for a way to have a cool track for music, so we added the alternate loop.)

Dynamic music is implemented with just a few script commands: start, stop, and set alternate <on/off>.

Vehicle engines are implemented with looping sounds; however, in order to capture more intricacies with how engines sound under various loads (in other words, cruising at a low speed sounds much different than flooring the accelerator), we use something similar to the cascade system to select different sounds to play based on scale: the pitch range. (In fact, as an implementation note, cascades are implemented referencing pitch ranges.)

As the name implies, a pitch range specifies a certain range of pitches to play in (for example, only play this pitch range when the sound is playing from –1200 cents to 1200 cents). There are many playback parameters for that pitch range, such as distance envelopes and relative bend. Relative bend is the bend applied to the permutation playing from this pitch range based on a reference pitch. In the example in Figure 6.2.7, if we were playing the sound with a scale-based pitch of 55 cents, the idle pitch range sounds would play with an actual pitch of –110 cents (pitch – reference pitch). The "playback bends bounds" simply clamps the pitch to those bounds before calculating the actual pitch.

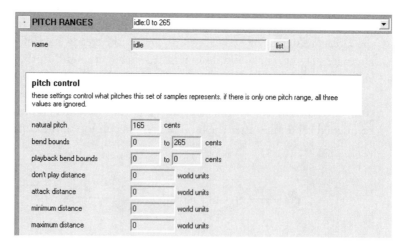

Figure 6.2.7   Pitch range editor.

This is probably more complicated than it needs to be, since we are basically parameterizing the pitch, then using that to select a pitch range, then converting that back into a relative bend to play sounds from that pitch range. But that's more a historical artifact than anything else, and now the audio designers are used to it.

At run time, you can have multiple pitch ranges from a single loop playing at once (see Figure 6.2.8).

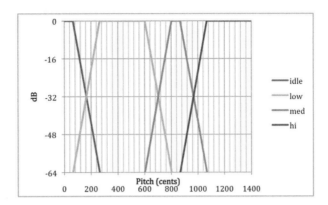

Figure 6.2.8 Warthog pitch ranges. Actual gain is displayed as power (gain^2).

This allows for smooth cross-fading between multiple pitch ranges based on the input scale.

The looping sound system has been powerful enough to add novel uses of sound without additional modifications. For example, in *Halo 2*, we added support for continuous collisions (for example, the sound a boulder makes rolling or sliding down a hill) from Havok by generating a looping sound at run time whenever we registered an object rolling or sliding; we mapped the normal loop to rolling and the alternate loop to sliding so that a single object transitioning between rolling and sliding would have a smooth audio transition between those states.

This kind of flexibility makes it very easy for the audio designers to collaborate with other programmers without necessarily having to involve an audio programmer. If you can export a scale value, you can easily add either an impulse or a looping sound to whatever it may be.

Mixing

One powerful aspect of Bungie's audio engine is how well it is integrated into the overall game engine; everything that should make a sound can make a sound, from weapons firing, to objects rolling and bouncing, to the various sounds in the HUD based on in-game events. One daunting aspect of the *Halo* audio engine is that almost everything makes a sound in some way, which means the audio designers have to make a lot of audio content.

To make it easier to manage sound across the entirety of a game, we assign every sound a sound class, essentially a label we use to define a set of default sound properties, such as distance envelope, Doppler effect multiplier, and so on. The properties in the sound class will be applied to all sounds with that sound class by default, so the audio designers only have to tweak a few sounds here and there.

LISTING 6.2.1   A non-exhaustive listing of sound classes

```
projectile_impact
projectile_detonation
projectile_flyby
projectile_detonation_lod

weapon_fire
weapon_ready
weapon_reload
weapon_empty

object_impacts
particle_impacts
weapon_fire_lod

unit_footsteps
unit_dialog
unit_animation

vehicle_collision
vehicle_engine
vehicle_animation
vehicle_engine_lod

music
ambient_nature
ambient_machinery
ambient_stationary
huge_ass

mission_dialog
cinematic_dialog
scripted_cinematic_foley
```

We also use sound classes to control the mix dynamically at run time. For each sound class, we store an additional attenuation to apply at run time—essentially, a sound class mix. These values can be script-driven; for example, during cinematics, we always turn down the ambience sound classes to silence with the following script call:

```
(sound_class_set_gain "amb" 0 0)
```

We use a simple LISP-like scripting language. With the sound_class script commands, we use the string as a sound class substring match, so this script command would affect the gain (in amplitude) for all sounds that have "amb" in them. If we had a sound class called "lambchop" it would also affect that, but we don't.

In addition to manually setting the mix, under certain gameplay conditions, we can activate a predefined sound class mix. For example, if we have Cortana saying something important to you over the radio, we'll activate the spoken dialog mix. These mixes, which are automatically activated, fade in and out over time so that the change in volume doesn't pop. The scripted mix and dynamic mix are cumulative; it's simple, but that tends to match the expected behavior anyway.

Post-Production

The bulk of audio production is spent in creating and refining audio content. This is a lot of work, but it's fairly straightforward: Create some sound in [insert sound application here], play it in game, tweak it, repeat. However, as the project gets closer to finishing, the audio team has two major tasks left: scoring the game and finalizing the overall mix.

Scoring any particular level is a collaborative process between the composer and the level designer. The composer works with the level designer to determine music triggers based on gameplay, progression, or anything else that can be scripted. (The endgame driving sequence of *Halo 3* has three triggers: one when you start driving on the collapsing ring, one after Cortana says "Charging to 50 percent!", and one when you make the final Warthog jump into the ship.) Each trigger can specify what looping sound to play, whether to use the regular or alternate loop, and when to start and stop. The composer can then work alone to determine the appropriate music to use for the entire level. This collaborative effort allows the composer to remain in creative control of the overall score for a level while allowing the level designer to provide the necessary hooks in his script to help create a dynamic musical score.

There is also a chunk of time set aside at the end of production for the audio team to work with finalized content. At this point all the graphics, cinematics, scripts, levels, animations, and so on, are locked down; this allows the audio team to polish without needing to worry about further content changes invalidating their work. Once all the sound is finally in place, the audio team then plays through the entire game in a reference 5.1 studio to adjust the final mix and make sure everything sounds great.

Conclusion

Bungie's audio engine isn't just a powerful engine; it's a powerful engine that has continued to evolve over time. Many of the concepts and features presented in this gem have been around since the first *Halo* game. Having a mature audio engine means that the entire audio team can iterate the process of making game audio instead of having to reinvent technology from scratch. Many of the innovations in Bungie's audio engine have come from the audio designers, not just the programmers. In *Halo 2*, they came up with coupling the environment ambience loops with the state of the weather so that when a level transitioned to rain, so would the ambience. In *Halo 3*, they suggested the attack portion of the distance envelope to support sound LODs.

In other words, Bungie's audio engine is not just about technology; it's about enabling everyone who works on audio to do great things. Any programmer who wants to add sound to their feature just needs to use the s_sound_source. Any audio designer can custom tailor the playback of any sound with a huge amount of flexibility and functionality. And with our mature and proven audio engine, an audio programmer has the framework to add functionality that can be used right away, in infinite variety.

The trifecta of lots of content, a fully integrated sound engine, and an effective audio production process, combined with Bungie's talented audio team, forms an award-winning game audio experience. The numerous accolades Bungie has received for audio for the entire *Halo* series show that our approach to game audio works—and works well.

Color Plate 1: Final results of the SSAO technique presented in Gem 1.2. The top-left pane shows lighting without the ambient occlusion, while the top-right pane shows lighting with the SSAO component mixed in. The final colored result is shown in the bottom image. Here the SSAO samples are very wide, bathing the background area with an effect that would otherwise only be obtained with a thorough global illumination algorithm. The SSAO term adds depth to the scene and helps anchor the characters within the environment.

Color Plate 2: Comparison of large- versus small-area SSAO samples from Gem 1.2. The images show the contrast between the large-area, low-contrast SSAO sampling component on the bar surface and background in the image on the left and the tighter, higher-contrast SSAO samples apparent within the helmet and nooks and crannies found on the character's space suit in the middle image. Final output is on the right.

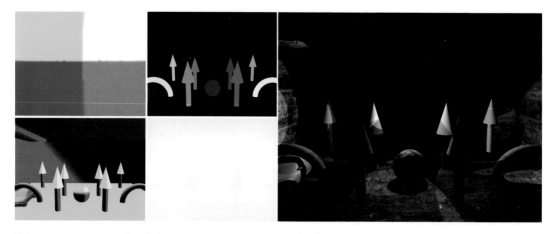

Color Plate 3: Output of rendering stages and final image from the deferred rendering technique described in Gem 1.3. Position and material ID (top left), normal and depth G-buffers (bottom left), and a resultant image (right).

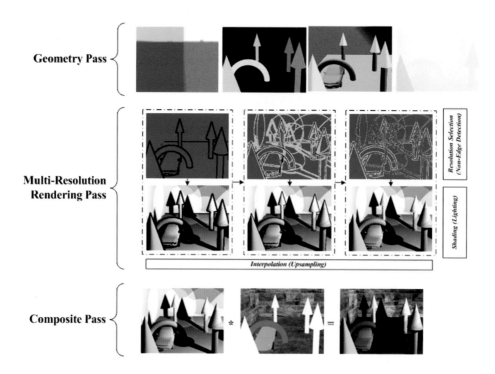

Color Plate 4: The deferred shading technique presented in Gem 1.2 has three steps: geometry pass, multi-resolution rendering pass, and composite pass.

Color Plate 5: A screenshot of *Blur*. The SPUs are used to compute position and normal offsets to deform the car as it takes damage. More details are in Gem 1.8.

Color Plate 6: A screenshot of *Blur*, showing a final result of the SPU-based lighting system presented in Gem 1.8.

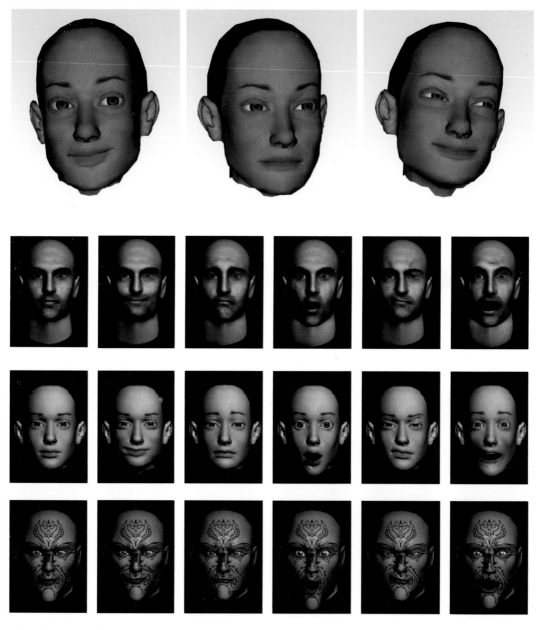

Color Plate 7: Test face models while performing basic expressions from the anatomical human face model presented in Gem 2.1. From left to right: neutral, joy, sadness, surprise, disgust, and fear.

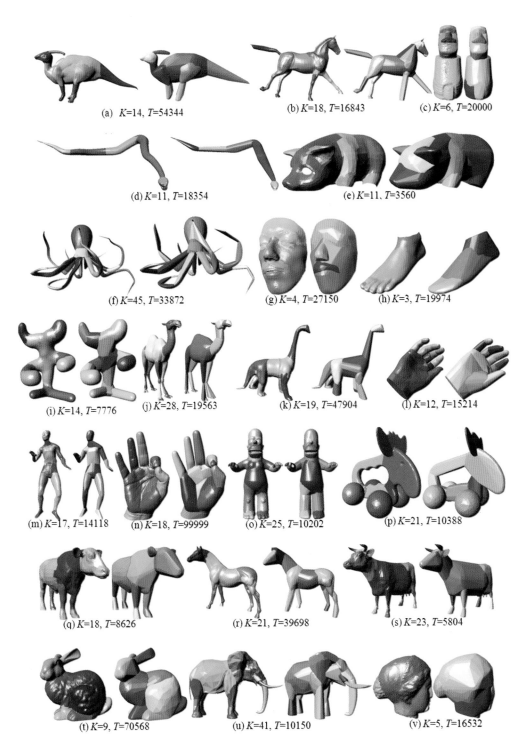

(a) K=14, T=54344

(b) K=18, T=16843

(c) K=6, T=20000

(d) K=11, T=18354

(e) K=11, T=3560

(f) K=45, T=33872

(g) K=4, T=27150

(h) K=3, T=19974

(i) K=14, T=7776

(j) K=28, T=19563

(k) K=19, T=47904

(l) K=12, T=15214

(m) K=17, T=14118

(n) K=18, T=99999

(o) K=25, T=10202

(p) K=21, T=10388

(q) K=18, T=8626

(r) K=21, T=39698

(s) K=23, T=5804

(t) K=9, T=70568

(u) K=41, T=10150

(v) K=5, T=16532

Color Plate 8: Segmentation results and piecewise convex approximations of different 3D meshes presented in Gem 2.8. (T number of triangles of the original mesh, D length of the diagonal of its bounding box, $\alpha = 0.03 \times D$ and the K number of the ACD clusters.)

Color Plates 9 and 10: From Gem 3.4, examples of characters in *World of Zoo*'s (WOZ's) environment. Characters move through the environment in a spatially appropriate and consistent manner when using the technique presented in this gem.

Color Plate 11: Example output from Gem 4.8 demonstrating an approach to testing code coverage. © Courtesy of Crytek GmbH and Electronic Arts, Inc.

Color Plate 12: Destructible wall section being placed into *Batman* in Unreal Editor from Gem 7.2.

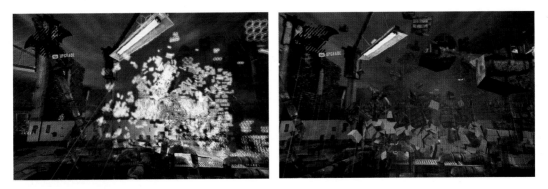

Color Plates 13 and 14: Destruction showing sphere representation of rigid bodies and rendered geometry from Gem 7.2.

Color Plate 15: *Batman: Arkham Asylum* with interactive PhysX SPH ground smoke, as described in Gem 7.3.

Color Plate 16: A close-up of screen-space fluid rendering with depth smoothing via Gaussian blur (left) and curvature flow (right) from Gem 7.3. The rendering on the right also uses surface Perlin noise to add visual detail.

6.3

Real-Time Sound Synthesis for Rigid Bodies

Zhimin Ren and Ming Lin

zren@cs.unc.edu

In recent 3D games, complex interactions among rigid bodies are ubiquitous. Objects collide with one another, slide on various surfaces, bounce, and roll. The rigid-body dynamic simulation considerably increases the engagement and excitation levels of games. Such examples are shown in Figure 6.3.1. However, without sound induced by these interactions, the synthesized interaction and virtual world are not as realistic, immersive, or convincing as they could be.

Figure 6.3.1 Complicated interactions among rigid bodies are shown in the two scenes above. In this gem, we introduce how to automatically synthesize sound that closely correlates to these interactions: impact, rolling, and sliding.

Although automatically playing back pre-recorded audio is an effective way for developers to add realistic sound that corresponds well to some specified interactions (for example, collision), it is not practical to pre-record sounds for all the potential complicated interactions that are controlled by players and triggered at run time.

Sound that is synthesized in real time and based on the ongoing physics simulation can provide a much richer variety of audio effects that correspond much more closely to complex interactions.

In this gem, we explore an approach to synthesize contact sounds induced by different types of interactions among rigid bodies in real time. We take advantage of common content resources in games, such as triangle meshes and normal maps, to generate sound that is coherent and consistent with the visual simulation. During the pre-processing stage, for each arbitrary triangle mesh of any sounding object given as an input, we use a *modal analysis* technique to pre-compute the vibration modes of each object. At run time, we classify contact events reported from physics engines and transform them into an impulse or sequence of impulses, which act as excitation to the modal model we obtained during pre-processing. The impulse generation process takes into consideration visual cues retrieved from normal maps. As a result, sound that closely corresponds to the visual rendering is automatically generated as the audio hardware mixes the impulse responses of the important modes.

Modal Analysis and Impulse Responses

In this section, we give a brief overview on the core sound synthesis processes: modal analysis and modal synthesis. Both of them have been covered in previous *Game Programming Gems*. More details on modal analysis can be found in *Game Programming Gems 4* [O'Brien04], and the impulse response to sound calculation (modal synthesis) is described in *Game Programming Gems 6* [Singer06].

Figure 6.3.2 shows the pipeline of the sound synthesis module.

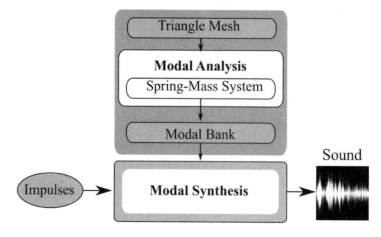

Figure 6.3.2   In pre-processing, a triangle mesh is converted into a spring-mass system. Then modal analysis is performed to obtain a bank of vibration modes for the spring-mass system. During run time, impulses are fed to excite the modal bank, and sound is generated as a linear combination of the modes. This is the modal synthesis process.

Spring-Mass System Construction

In the content creation process for games, triangle meshes are often used to represent the 3D objects. In pre-processing, we take these triangle meshes and convert them into spring-mass representations that are used for sound synthesis. We consider each vertex of the triangle mesh as a mass particle and the edge between any two vertices as a damped spring. The physical properties of the sounding objects are expressed in the spring constants of the edges and the masses of the particles. This conversion is shown in Equation (1), where k is the spring constant, Y is the Young's Modulus that indicates the elasticity of the material, t is the thickness of the object, m_i is the mass of particle i, p is the density, and a_i is the area covered by particle i.

$$k = Yt$$
$$m_i = \rho t a_i \quad (1)$$

For more details on the spring-mass system construction, we refer our readers to [Raghuvanshi07].

Since this spring-mass representation is only used in audio rendering and not graphics rendering, the triangle meshes used in this conversion do not necessarily have to be the same as the ones used for graphics rendering. For example, when a large plane can be represented with two triangles for visual rendering, these two triangles do not carry detailed information for approximating the sound of a large plane. (This will be explained later.) In this case, we can subdivide this triangle mesh before the spring-mass conversion and use the detailed mesh for further sound computation. On the contrary, sometimes high-complexity triangle meshes are required to represent some visual details, but we are not necessarily able to hear them. In this scenario, we can simplify the meshes first and then continue with sound synthesis–related computation.

Modal Analysis

Now that we have a discretized spring-mass representation for an arbitrary triangle mesh, we can perform modal analysis on this representation and pre-compute the vibration modes for this mesh. Vibration of the spring-mass system created from the input mesh can be described with an ordinary differential equation (ODE) system as in Equation (2).

$$\boldsymbol{M}\frac{d^2\boldsymbol{r}}{dt^2} + \boldsymbol{C}\frac{d\boldsymbol{r}}{dt} + \boldsymbol{K}\boldsymbol{r} = \boldsymbol{f} \quad (2)$$

where M, C, and K are the mass, damping, and stiffness matrix, respectively. If there are N vertices in the triangle mesh, r in Equation (1) is a vector of dimension N, and it represents the displacement of each mass particle from its rest position. Each diagonal element in M represents the mass of each particle. In our implementation, C adopts Rayleigh damping approximation, so it is a linear combination of M and K. The element at row i and column j in K represents the spring constant between particle i and particle j. f is the external force vector. The resulting ODE system turns into Equation (3).

$$M \frac{d^2 r}{dt^2} + (\gamma M + \mu K) \frac{dr}{dt} + Kr = f \quad (3)$$

where M is diagonal and K is real symmetric. Therefore, Equation (3) can be simplified into a decoupled system after diagonalizing K with $K = GDG^{-1}$, where D is a diagonal matrix containing the Eigenvalues of K.

The diagonal ODE system that we eventually need to solve is Equation (4).

$$M \frac{d^2 z}{dt^2} + (\gamma M + \mu D) \frac{dz}{dt} + Dz = G^{-1} f \quad (4)$$

where $Z = G^{-1} r$, a linear combination of the original vertex displacement. The general solution to Equation (4) is Equation (5).

$$z_i(t) = c_i e^{\omega_i^+ t} + \bar{c}_i e^{\omega_i^- t}$$
$$\omega_i^\pm = \frac{-(\gamma \lambda_i + \mu) \pm \sqrt{(\gamma \lambda_i + \mu)^2 - 4\lambda_i}}{2} \quad (5)$$

where λ is the ith Eigenvalue of D. With particular initial conditions, we can solve for the coefficient c_i and its complex conjugate, $\bar{c}_i$. The absolute value of ω_i's imaginary part is the frequency of that mode. Therefore, the vibration of the original triangle mesh is now approximated with the linear combination of the mode shapes z_i. This linear combination is directly played out as the synthesized sound. Since only frequencies between 20 Hz to 20 kHz are audible to human beings, we discard the modes that are outside this frequency range.

Impulse Response Calculation

When an object experiences a sudden external force f that lasts for a small duration of time, Δt, we say that there is an impulse $f \Delta t$ applied to the object. f is a vector that contains forces on each particle of the spring-mass system. This impulse either causes a resting object to oscillate or changes the way it oscillates; we say that the impulse *excites* the oscillation. Mathematically, since the right-hand side of Equation (4) changes, the solution of coefficients c_i and $\bar{c}_i$ also changes in response. This is called the *impulse response* of the model.

The impulse response, or the update rule of c_i and $\bar{c}_i$, for an impulse $f \Delta t$, follows the rule expressed in Equation (6):

$$c_{i,t_0 + \Delta t} = c_{i,t_0} e^{\omega^+ t_0} + \frac{g_i}{m_i(\omega_i^+ + \omega_i^-)}$$
$$\bar{c}_{i,t_0 + \Delta t} = \bar{c}_{i,t_0} e^{\omega^+ t_0} + \frac{g_i}{m_i(\omega_i^+ + \omega_i^-)} \quad (6)$$

where g_i is the ith element in vector $G^{-1} f$. Whenever an impulse acts on an object, we can quickly compute the summation of weighted mode shapes of the sounding object at any time instance onward by plugging Equation (6) into Equation (5). This linear combination is what we hear directly. With this approach, we generate sound that depends on the sounding objects' shape and material, and also the contact position.

In conclusion, we can synthesize sound caused by applying impulses on pre-processed 3D objects. In the following section, we show how to convert different contact events in physics simulation into a sequence of impulses that can be used as the excitation for our modal model.

From Physics Engine to Contact Sounds

When any two rigid bodies come into contact during a physics simulation, the physics engine is able to detect the collision and provide developers with information pertaining to the contact events. However, directly applying this information as excitation to a sound synthesis module does not generate good-quality sound. We describe a simple yet effective scheme that integrates the contact information and data from normal maps to generate impulses that produce sound that closely correlates with visual rendering in games.

Event Classification: Transient or Lasting Contacts?

We can imagine that transient contacts can be easily approximated with single impulses, while lasting contacts are more difficult to represent with impulses. Therefore, we handle them differently, and the very first step is to distinguish between a transient and a lasting contact. The way we distinguish the two is very similar to the one covered in [Sreng07].

Two objects are said to be contacting if their models overlap in space at a certain point p, and if $v_p \bullet n_p < 0$, where v_p and n_p are their relative velocity and contact normal at point p. Two contacting objects are said to be in lasting contact if $v_t \neq 0$, where v_t is their relative tangential velocity. Otherwise, they are in transient contact.

From Transient Contacts to Impulses

When our classifier detects that there are only transient contacts, corresponding single instances of impulses are added to the modal model. The impulse magnitude is scaled with the contact force at the contact point. Developers can specify the scale to control transient contact sound's volume. The direction of the impulse is the same as that of the contact force, and it is applied to the nearest neighboring mass particle (in other words, vertex of the original triangle mesh) of the contact point. We keep a k-d tree for fast nearest neighbor searches.

The following pseudocode gives some more details of this process.

```
IF a transient contact takes place THEN
        COMPUTE the local coordinates of the contact point
        FIND the nearest neighbor of the contact in local frame
        CREATE impulse = contactForce * scale
        CLEAR the buffer that stores impulse information
        ADD the new impulse to the nearest neighbor vertex
        UPDATE the coefficients of mode shapes
    ENDIF
```

From Lasting Contacts to Impulses: Using Normal Maps

When our classfier sees a lasting contact (for example, sliding, scraping, and so on), the contact reports from common real-time physics engines fall short for directly providing us with the contact forces for simulating the sliding sound. If we directly add impulses modulated with the contact force, we would not hear continuous sound that corresponds to the continuous sliding motion. Instead, we would "hear" all the discrete impulses that are applied to the object to maintain the sliding. One of the problems is the significant gap between physics simulation rate (about 100 Hz) and audio sampling rate (44,100 Hz).

We solve this problem with the use of normal maps, which exist in the majority of 3D games. We generate audio from this commonly used image representation for sound rendering as well as by noting the following observations:

- Normal maps can add very detailed visual rendering to games, while the underlying geometries are usually simple. However, common physics engines do not see any information from normal maps for simulation. Therefore, by only using contact information from physics engines, we miss all the important visual cues that are often apparent to players.
- Normal maps give us per-pixel normal perturbation data. With normal maps of common resolutions, a pixel is usually a lot smaller than a triangle of the 3D mesh. This pixel-level information allows us to generate impulses that correspond closely to visual rendering at a much higher sampling rate. This effect would have been impossible to achieve with common 3D meshes even if the physics engine were to calculate the contact force faithfully.
- Normal maps are easy to create and exist in almost every 3D game.

Figure 6.3.3 shows a pen scraping against three normal-mapped flat surfaces. The flat planes no longer sound flat after we take the normal map information as input to our impulse generation for sound synthesis.

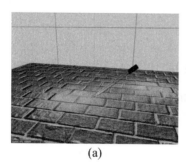 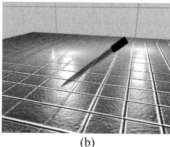 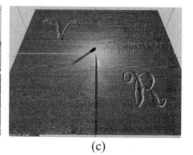

(a)   (b)   (c)

Figure 6.3.3   A pen scraping on three different materials: brick, porcelain, and wood.
The underlying geometries of the surfaces are all flat planes composed of triangles.
With normal maps applied on the surface, the plane looks bumpy.
And it also sounds bumpy when we scrape the pen on the surfaces!

We take the normal maps and calculate impulses in the following way.

Imagine an object in sliding contact with another object, whose surface F is shown in Figure 6.3.4; the contact point traverses the path P within a time step. We look up the normal map associated to F and collect those normals around P. The normals suggest that the high-resolution surface looks like f in Figure 6.3.4 and that the contact point is expected to traverse a path P on f. Therefore, besides the momentum along the tangential direction of F, the object must also have a time-varying momentum along the normal direction of F, namely p_N, where N is the normal vector of F. From simple geometry, we compute its value with Equation (7).

$$p_N = mv_N = mv_N N = m\left(-\frac{v_T \cdot n}{N \cdot n}\right) N \quad (7)$$

where m is the object's mass and v_T is the tangential velocity of the object relative to F. The impulse along the normal direction J_N that applies on the object is just the change of its normal momentum expressed in Equation (8)

$$J_N = p_N(i) - p_n(j) \quad (8)$$

when the object moves from pixel i to pixel j on the normal map. With this formulation, the impulses actually model the force applied by the normal variation on the surface of one object to another, generating sound that naturally correlates with the visual appearance of bumps from textures.

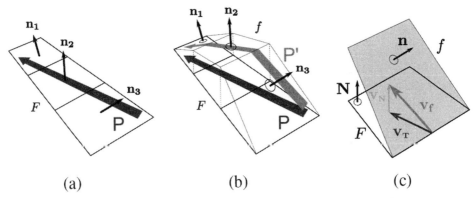

(a)   (b)   (c)

Figure 6.3.4   Impulse calculation. (a) The path P traced by an object sliding against another object within one physics simulation time step. Each square is a pixel of the normal map bound to the surface. n_i are the normals stored in the normal map around the path. The path lies on the surface F, which is represented coarsely with a low-resolution mesh (here a flat plane). (b) The normal map suggests that the high-resolution surface looks like f, and the object is expected to traverse the path P. (c) The impulse along the normal direction can be recovered from the geometry configuration of n, N, and V_T.

At the end of each time step, we collect impulses that should have taken place in this time step by tracing back the path the object took. We make up these impulses in the immediate following time step by adding them into our impulse queue at the end of this time step. The function for doing this is shown below.

```
/**
 * \param[in] endX the x coordinate of ending position
 * \param[in] endY the y coordinate of ending position
 * \param[in] endTime time stamp of the end of this time step
 * \param[in] elapsedTime time elapsed from last time step
 * \param[in] tangentialVelocity tagential velocity of the object
 * \param impulseEventQueue gets updated with the new impulses
 */
void CollectImpulses(float endX, float endY,
float endTime, float elapsedTime, Vec3f tangentialVelocity,
ImpulseEventQueue& impulseEventQueue)
{
      float speed = tangentialVelocity.Length();
      float traveledDistance = elapsedTime * speed;

// dx is the width of each pixel
// We assume pixels are square shaped, so dx = dy
// +1 to ensure nGridTraveled >= 1
      int nGridTraveled = int(traveledDistance / dx) + 1;

// Approximate the time used for going through one pixel
// Divided by 2 to be conservative on not missing a pixel
      // This can be loosen if performance is an issue
      float dtBump = ( elapsedTime / nGridTraveled ) / 2;
      float vX = tangentialVelocity.x, vY = tangentialVelocity.y;

// Trace back to the starting point
      float x = endX - vX * elapsedTime, y = endY - vY * elapsedTime;
      float startTime = endTime - elapsedTime;
      float dxTraveled = vX * dtBump, dyTraveled = vY * dtBump;

// Sample along the line segment traveled in the elapsedTime
      for(float t = startTime; t <= endTime; t += dtBump)
{
            ImpulseEvent impulseEvent;

            // Compute the impulse from the normal map value
            impulseEvent.impulse =
GetImpulseAt(x, y, tangentialVelocity);
            if (impulseEvent.Impulse.Length() == 0)
                  continue;

            // Update impulseEvent and
// add this impulse to impulse queue
            impulseEvent.Time = t;
            impulseEvent.x = x;
impulseEvent.y = y;
            impulseEventQueue.push_back(impulseEvent);
            x += dxTraveled;
y += dyTraveled;
      }
}
```

Notice that we are assuming the object has constant velocity in one time step when we trace back its path. The impulses in the impulse queue updated here are taken out of the queue and added sequentially to the modal model in the next time step. When we "play back" these impulses, we look at their time stamps (the variable shown in the code as impulseEvent.Time) and add the excitation exactly the same time in the next time step. Although there will be a delay of one time step, humans are not able to detect it according to [Guski03]. However, humans are able to detect the impression of all the impulses played at different time in one time step. This approach gives a finer approximation of the sound responses to the visual cues.

We refer our readers to [Ren10] for more details on contact sound synthesis for normal-mapped models.

Putting It Together

The complete pipeline (as shown in Figure 6.3.5) is composed of the interaction handling and sound synthesis modules. The sound synthesis module consists of the modal analysis and modal synthesis processes and the interaction handling, which converts a contact event into impulses. The sound synthesis module calculates the mode shapes at audio sampling rate (44.1 kHz), while interaction handling runs at the same rate as the physics engine (about 100 Hz). However, the impulses generated from normal maps are played back at a higher frequency than the physics engine.

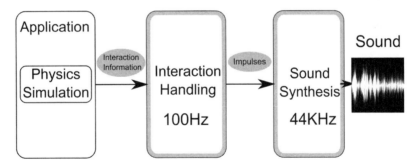

Figure 6.3.5 The complete pipeline for the sound synthesis algorithm discussed in this gem.

Conclusion

This gem describes a pipeline for automatically synthesizing sounds that correspond well to the visual rendering in games. This method utilizes graphics resources such as triangle meshes and normal maps to produce sound for different kinds of interactions. It renders audio effects that are tightly related to the visual cues, which otherwise cannot be captured at all. The method is general, works well with most game engines, and runs in real time.

References

[Guski03] Guski, Troje. "Audiovisual Phenomenal Causality." *Perception and Psychophysics* 65.5 (2003): 789–800.

[O'Brien04] O'Brien, James F. "Modal Analysis for Fast, Stable Deformation." *Game Programming Gems 4*. Boston: Charles River Media, 2004. 287-298.

[Raghuvanshi07] Raghuvanshi, Lin. "Physically Based Sound Synthesis for Large-Scale Virtual Environments." *IEEE Computer Graphics and Applications* 27.1 (2007): 14–18.

[Ren10] Ren, Z., H. Yeh, and Lin. "Synthesizing Contact Sounds Between Textured Models." *IEEE Virtual Reality*. 2010.

[Singer06] Singer, Marq. "Real-Time Sound Generation from Deformable Meshes." *Game Programming Gems 6*. Boston: Charles River Media, 2006. 541–547.

[Sreng07] Sreng, J., F. Bergez, J. Legarrec, A. L ecuyer, and C. Andriot. "Using an Event-Based Approach to Improve the Multimodal Rendering of 6dof Virtual Contact." *Proceedings of the 2007 ACM Symposium on Virtual Reality Software and Technology*. 165–173.

GENERAL PURPOSE COMPUTING ON GPUs

Introduction

Adam Lake, Sr. Graphics Software Architect,
Advanced Visual Computing, Intel
adam_t_lake@yahoo.com

This is a new chapter for the *Game Programming Gems* series. For the past decade we've seen academic literature filled with papers about using GPUs for various non-graphics tasks, in particular those that have a high ratio of compute-to-memory-bandwidth density. I believe we are at a new stage of this development, a time when this work migrates from the academic literature to use in production software. This hypothesis is validated by the exciting developments in both hardware and industry APIs supporting development on GPUs. The new gold rush is throughput computing, and GPUs will be at the forefront. Graphics and gaming will play a critical role in putting this computational horsepower into the hands of researchers, developers, and consumers at a cost that will create new industries, ecosystems, and value for society as a whole.

The first article in this section discusses OpenCL, an industry standard for harnessing the computational horsepower of both CPUs and GPUs in today's heterogeneous computing environment. OpenCL contains APIs and a programming model that allows developers to express both task and data parallelism in their applications in a cross-platform API. The author summarizes the basic principles of OpenCL and uses examples to discuss how to use OpenCL in a performant way. I'd expect to see this standard evolve over the next few years and to be leveraged for areas of both the game development process and in the game engines we ship in the not-too-distant future.

We've also included two articles on PhysX, one focused on rigid bodies and the other on fluid simulation used in the game *Batman: Arkham Asylum*. Fluid simulation was used to add smoke and fog, and the rigid body simulation was used to destroy the wall panels in the Scarecrow levels. The fluid simulation was done by leveraging the CPU to implement a particle system and simulate the fluid with Smoothed Particle Hydrodynamics (SPH). Rigid body simulation is performed using a rigid body simulation implemented on the GPU.

I hope these gems inspire game developers to think about other interesting ways to exploit the computational resources available in the coming decade of computing!

7.1

Using Heterogeneous Parallel Architectures with OpenCL

Udeepta Bordoloi, Benedict R. Gaster, and Marc Romankewicz, Advanced Micro Devices

Open Compute Language (OpenCL) [Munshi09] is an open standard for data- and task-parallel programming on CPUs and GPUs. It is developed by the Khronos Group, which is part of the Compute Working Group and includes members from AMD, Apple, Electronic Arts, IBM, Intel, NVIDIA, Qualcomm, and others. OpenCL is a standard to enable parallel programming on heterogeneous compute platforms. It can provide access to all the machine's compute resources, including CPUs and GPUs.

In this gem, we give a primer on OpenCL and then introduce a set of general techniques for using it to optimize games. Two examples are used: convolution and histogram. The former highlights many of the techniques for optimizing nested loop data parallelism; the latter showcases methods for accessing memory effectively.

Convolution is a technique in the field of image processing; it calculates an output pixel as a function of its corresponding input pixel and the values of the neighboring pixels. This technique, however, is expensive to compute. Its run time is proportional to the width and height of the image. If W and H are the width and height, respectively, the run time is $O(W^2H^2)$. The highly data-parallel nature of convolution makes it an excellent candidate for leveraging OpenCL optimizations.

In game programming, histograms improve the dynamic range of rendered frames through tone mapping. Fast on-GPU histogram computation is essential, since the image data originates on the GPU. Historically, histogram computation has been difficult to do on GPU, as typical algorithms become limited by the scatter (random write-access) performance. However, with the advent of large on-chip, user-controlled memories and related atomic operations, performance can be dramatically improved.

Efficient implementations for convolution and histogram calculations broaden the set of possibilities for game developers to exploit emerging heterogeneous parallel architectures; both PCs and game consoles have many-core CPUs and GPUs. They also highlight the difficulties that must be overcome to achieve anything like peak performance.

In this gem, we discuss a step-by-step optimization toolkit for game developers using OpenCL. These optimizations can be used together or individually, but their overall effect depends on the application; there is no magic wand for an algorithm with little parallelism or a dataset so small that there is little chance to amortize the associated run-time cost.

OpenCL Primer

OpenCL is based on the notion of a host API, which consists of a platform and run-time layer and a C-like language (OpenCL C) for programming compute devices; these devices can range from CPUs to GPUs and other kinds of accelerators. Figure 7.1.1 illustrates this model, with queues of commands, reading/writing data, and executing kernels for specific devices. The overall system is called a *platform*. There can be any number of platforms from different vendors within a particular system, but only devices within a single platform can share data within what OpenCL calls a *context*.

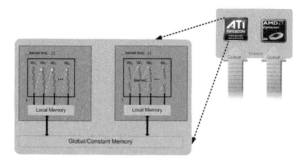

Figure 7.1.1　OpenCL host/device architecture.

The devices are capable of running data- and task-parallel work; a kernel can be executed as a function of multidimensional domains of indices. Each element is called a *work-item*; the total number of indices is defined as the *global work-size*. The global work-size can be divided into sub-domains, called *work-groups*, and individual work-items within a group can communicate through global or locally shared memory. Work-items are synchronized through barrier or fence operations. Figure 7.1.1 is a representation of the host/device architecture with a single platform, consisting of a GPU and a CPU.

Given an enumeration of platforms, we choose one, select a device or devices to create a context, allocate memory, create device-specific command queues used to submit work to a specific device, and perform computations. Essentially, the platform layer is the gateway to accessing specific devices. Given these devices and a corresponding context, the application is unlikely to have to refer to the platform layer again. It is the context that drives communication with, and between, specific devices. A context generally is created from one or more devices. A context allows us to:

- Create a command queue.
- Create programs to run on one or more associated devices.
- Create kernels within those programs.
- Allocate memory buffers or images, either on the host or on the device(s). (Memory can be copied between the host and device.)
- Write data to the device.
- Submit the kernel (with appropriate arguments) to the command queue for execution.
- Read data back to the host from the device.

The relationship between context(s), device(s), buffer(s), program(s), kernel(s), and command queue(s) is best seen by looking at sample code. The following program adds the elements of two input buffers, a and b, and stores the results in a single output buffer, o. While trivial in its application, the sample program is the foundational pattern of all OpenCL programs.

```cpp
#include <CL/cl.hpp>
#include <iostream>
static char kernelSourceCode[] =
"__kernel void\n"
"hello(__global int * inA, __global int * inB, __global int * out)\n"
"{\n"
"    size_t i =  get_global_id(0);\n"
"    out[i] = inA[i] + inB[i];\n"
"}\n";
int main(void) {
    int a[10] = {1,2,3,4,5,6,7,8,9,10};
    int b[10] = {1,2,3,4,5,6,7,8,9,10};
    int o[10] = {0,0,0,0,0,0,0,0,0,0};
    cl::Context context(CL_DEVICE_TYPE_ALL);
    std::vector<cl::Device> devices = context.getInfo<CL_CONTEXT_DEVICES>();
    cl::CommandQueue queue(context, devices[0]);
    cl::Program::Sources sources(1, std::make_pair(kernelSourceCode, 0));
    cl::Program program(context, sources);
    program.build(devices);
    cl::Kernel kernel(program, "hello");
    cl::Buffer inA(context,CL_MEM_READ_ONLY,10 * sizeof(int));
    cl::Buffer inB(context,CL_MEM_READ_ONLY,10 * sizeof(int));
    cl::Buffer out(context,CL_MEM_WRITE_ONLY,10 * sizeof(int));
    queue.enqueueWriteBuffer(inA,CL_TRUE,0,10 * sizeof(int),a);
    queue.enqueueWriteBuffer(inB,CL_TRUE,0,10 * sizeof(int),b);
    kernel.setArg(0,inA); kernel.setArg(1,inB); kernel.setArg(2,out);
    queue.enqueueNDRangeKernel(
```

```
                kernel, cl::NullRange, cl::NDRange(10), cl::NDRange(2)
        );
        queue.enqueueReadBuffer(out,CL_TRUE,0,10 * sizeof(int),o);
        std::cout << "{" ;
        for (int i = 0; i < 10; i++) {
            std::cout << o[i] << (i!=9 ? ", " : "") ;
        }
        std::cout << "}" << std::endl;
}
```

Because it is not possible to provide a full introduction to OpenCL in the limited amount of space allocated to this gem, we advise readers new to OpenCL to read through the references given at the end of the article. For example, many introductory samples are shipped with particular implementations, and readers might also like to work though a tutorial such as "hello world" [Gaster09].

Tips for Optimizing OpenCL C Kernels

Two-dimensional convolution is used to illustrate techniques that can be used to optimize OpenCL kernels.

Convolution Kernel

The OpenCL C kernel for convolution is given below. It is almost a replica of a corresponding C code for convolution; the only difference is that the C code uses two for loops that iterate over the output image to initialize the variables xOut and yOut, instead of using the get_global_id call. The output image dimensions are width by height, the input image width is inWidth (equals width+filterWidth-1), and the input height equals (height+filterWidth-1).

```
__kernel void Convolve(__global float * input,
                    __constant float * filter, __global  float * output,
                    int inWidth, int width, int height, int filterWidth)
{
    int yOut = get_global_id(1);//for (int yOut = 0; yOut < height; yOut++)
    int xOut = get_global_id(0);//for (int xOut = 0; xOut < width; xOut++)
    int xInTopLeft = xOut; int yInTopLeft = yOut;
    float sum = 0;
    for (int r = 0; r < filterWidth; r++) {
        int idxFtmp = r * filterWidth;
        int yIn = yInTopLeft + r;
        int idxIntmp = yIn * inWidth + xInTopLeft;
        for (int c = 0; c < filterWidth; c++)
            sum += filter[idxFtmp+c]*input[idxIntmp+c];
    } //for (int r = 0...
    int idxOut = yOut * width + xOut;
    output[idxOut] = sum;
}
```

Figure 7.1.2 shows the computation time for an output image of size 8192×8192. The test computer is an AMD Phenom X4 9950 Black Edition with 8 GB RAM. For a filter width of 2, the input image size is 8193×8193; for a filter of width 32, the input image is 8223×8223. For each pixel, the loop runs for (filterWidth)^2 times. The computation time increases approximately as a function of the square of the filter width. It takes about 14.54 seconds for a 20×20 filter and 3.73 seconds for a 10×10 filter. We first consider unrolling loops to improve performance of this workload.

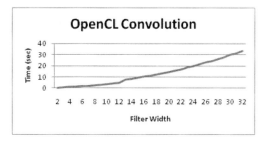

Figure 7.1.2 Computation time for various filter widths for an 8192×8192 output image

Loop Unrolling

Having loops in the code comes at a performance cost. For example, consider a 32×32 filter. For each pixel in the output image, the statements in the innermost loop are run 32×32 = 1024 times. This cost is negligible for small filters, but it becomes significant as the filter width increases. The solution is to reduce the loop count.

The following kernel has four iterations of the innermost loop unrolled. A second loop is added to handle the remainder of iterations when filter width is not an even multiple of four.

```
__kernel void ConvolveUnroll(...)
{
    ...
    for (int r = 0; r < filterWidth; r++){
        ...
        int c = 0;
        while (c <= filterWidth-4) {
            sum += filter[idxFtmp+c]  *input[idxIntmp+c];
            sum += filter[idxFtmp+c+1]*input[idxIntmp+c+1];
            sum += filter[idxFtmp+c+2]*input[idxIntmp+c+2];
            sum += filter[idxFtmp+c+3]*input[idxIntmp+c+3];
            c += 4;
        }
        for (int c1 = c; c1 < filterWidth; c1++)
            sum += filter[idxFtmp+c1]*input[idxIntmp+c1];
    } //for (int r = 0...
    ...
}
```

Figure 7.1.3 shows the results of the unrolled kernel. For larger filters, unrolling helps improve speed by as much as 20 percent. The sawtooth kind of behavior that we see in the graph is due to the iterations that are left over after unrolling and is easily handled by unrolling the second inner loop (and substituting it with an `if-else` statement).

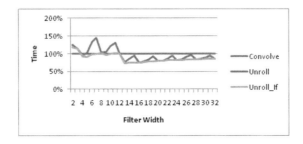

Figure 7.1.3   Loop unrolling. Unrolling the inner loop (`Unroll`) and the second inner loop (`Unroll_If`).

Invariants

For the aforementioned kernels, filter widths were passed as an argument. Consider an application where the filter size is constant (for example, 5×5). In this case, the inner loop can be unrolled five times, and the loop condition can be removed.

```
__kernel void DefConvolve(...)
{
    ...
    for (int r = 0; r < FILTER_WIDTH; r++) {
        int idxFtmp = r * FILTER_WIDTH;
        ...
        for (int c = 0; c < FILTER_WIDTH; c++)
    ...
}
```

As the filter width is static, `FILTER_WIDTH`, it can be defined when building the OpenCL program. The following code shows how to pass in the value of the invariant.

```
std::string  sourceStr = FileToString(kernelFileName);
cl::Program::Sources sources(1, std::make_pair(sourceStr.c_str(),
                                             sourceStr.length())));
program = cl::Program(context, sources);
char options[128];
sprintf(options, "-DFILTER_WIDTH=%d", param.filterWidth);
program.build(devices, options);
cl::Kernel kernel = cl::Kernel(program, kernelName.c_str());
```

Figure 7.1.4 shows that defining the filter width as an invariant helps the DefConvolve kernel gain about 20 percent performance over the Convolve kernel, particularly for small kernel sizes.

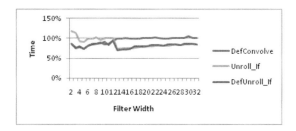

Figure 7.1.4   Using the filter width as an invariant
in the Convolve and the Unroll_If kernels.

Vectorization

Since the inner loop of the unrolled kernel has four products and four additions, it is possible to use one vector (SSE or GPU) packed-multiply and one packed-add to achieve the same results. But how do we use vectors in an OpenCL kernel? AMD's OpenCL implementation will try to use "packed-arithmetic" instructions whenever it encounters a vector data type in the kernel. The following kernel body uses the vector type float4. Note the additional loop at the end to handle any remaining iterations when filter width is not an even multiple of four.

```
__kernel void ConvolveFloat4(…) {
    ...
    float4 sum4 = 0;
    for (int r = 0; r < filterWidth; r++) {
        ...
        int c = 0; int c4 = 0;
        while (c <= filterWidth-4) {
            float4 filter4 = vload4(c4, filter+idxFtmp);
            float4 in4     = vload4(c4, input +idxIntmp);
            sum4 += in4 ^ filter4;
            c += 4; c4++;
        }
        for (int c1 = c; c1 < filterWidth; c1++)
            sum4.x += filter[idxFtmp+c1]*input[idxIntmp+c1];
    } //for (int r = 0...
    int idxOut = yOut * width + xOut;
    output[idxOut] = sum4.x + sum4.y + sum4.z + sum4.w;
}
```

The second inner loop can be unrolled (kernel ConvolveFloat4_If), and invariants can be used for further speedups (kernels DefFloat4 and DefFloat4_If). Figure 7.1.5 shows the results for the vectorized kernel.

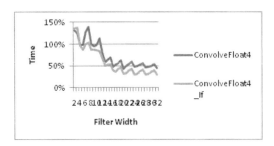 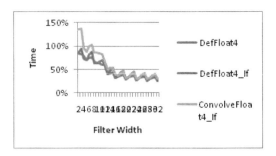

Figure 7.1.5   The effect of vectorization. `ConvolveFloat4` is the `float4`
version of `Convolve`; `ConvolveFloat4_If` has the second inner loop unrolled.
`DefFloat4` and `DefFloat4_If` use the filter width as an invariant.

Optimizing Memory-Bound OpenCL Kernels

So far, our optimizations have focused on how to maximize ALU throughput. In the
following section, we use a histogram calculation to address techniques for optimizing
kernels limited by memory performance.

For simplicity, we assume that a histogram consists of 32-bit-per-pixel images with
256 32-bit bins. The algorithm parallelizes the computation over a number of work-
groups, each of which uses a number of sub-histograms stored in on-chip `__local`
memory.

Number of Work-Groups

When choosing the optimal number of work-items and work-groups, some constraints
follow automatically from the algorithm, the device architecture, and the size of `__local`
memory.

`__local` memory is shared within a single work-group. For the histogram algorithm, it is desirable to have fewer, larger work-groups. This allows many successive
threads to contribute to the same `__local` memory area. Conversely, using more and
smaller work-groups would require costly flushing of `__local` sub-histograms to `__global`
memory more frequently, since the lifetime of a work-group is shorter.

To maximize the use of `__local` memory, the number of work-groups should be
as close as possible to the number of compute units. Each compute unit typically has
a dedicated block of `__local` memory, and using as many of them concurrently as
possible is advantageous.

The actual number of compute units, typically in the tens per GPU, can be
queried at run time using:

```
clGetDeviceInfo( …, CL_DEVICE_MAX_COMPUTE_UNITS, … );
```

Work-Group Size

A work-group should be at least as big as the basic hardware unit for scheduling. On AMD GPUs, a wavefront is a hardware unit of work-items executing concurrently on a given compute unit. OpenCL work-groups are executed as a collection of wavefronts. Wavefront size cannot be queried via OpenCL—on current high-end AMD GPUs, it is 64 work-items. Also, a total of two wavefronts can be scheduled to run on a single compute unit at a time.

This sets an absolute minimum for the total work-item number: Multiply two times the wavefront size with the number of work-groups. An integer multiple of that number is often advisable, as it will allow more flexibility for run-time scheduling—hiding memory latency, allocating register use, and so on. On the other hand, the upper limit of the number of threads is given by the maximum work-group size times the chosen number of work-groups. The maximum work-group size can be queried using:

```
clGetDeviceInfo( …, CL_DEVICE_MAX_WORK_GROUP_SIZE, … );
```

Within this range, fine-tuning remains an algorithm- and kernel-specific matter. Kernels can request a particular set of resources. For example, they can request the number of registers, the size of the __local buffer, and the number of instructions. These parameters influence how the kernel is scheduled on the GPU at run time. Possible tuning knobs include the number of groups, the group size, and the number of work-items. The upcoming section on optimal read patterns gives an example.

__global Read/Write Access Patterns

For any implementation of either a parallel or a serial histogram, very few arithmetic operations are required. This implies that the first limiting factor for histogram performance is the read bandwidth from __global memory, as the input image originates from there. Fortunately, because the histogram read is order-independent, it is possible to optimize each work-item's read pattern to that which is best supported by the GPU or CPU.

The CPU/GPU memory subsystem and the compiler tool chain are optimized for 128-bit quantities—the common shader pixel size of four 32-bit floats. On the GPU, multiples of these quantities are advantageous to allow the memory subsystem to take advantage of the wide (typically hundreds of bits) data path to memory. Ideally, all simultaneously executing work-items read adjacent 128-bit quantities, so that these can be combined to larger quantities.

This leads to the following access pattern: Each thread reads unsigned integer quantities packed into four-wide vectors (uint4) quantities, starting at its global work-item index and continuing with a stride equal to the number of threads, until it reaches the end. For a total work-item number of NT, the resulting pattern is:

uint4 addr	0	1	2	3	...	N_T-4	N_T-3	N_T-2	N_T-1
Thread	0	1	2	3	...	N_T-4	N_T-3	N_T-2	N_T-1
uint4 addr	N_T	N_T+1	N_T+2	N_T+3	...	$2N_T$-4	$2N_T$-3	$2N_T$-2	$2N_T$-1
Thread	0	1	2	3	...	N_T-4	N_T-3	N_T-2	N_T-1

As many of the work-items execute this step at the same time, it results in a large number of simultaneous, adjacent read requests, which can be combined into optimal hardware units by the memory subsystem. For example, for N_T = 8192, the addresses sent to the memory subsystem result in a tightly aligned pattern:

Thread	0	1	2	3	4	...	8189	8190	8192
uint4 addr	0	1	2	3	4	...	8189	8190	8192

Note that the straightforward choice—a serial access pattern from within each work-item—results in widely dispersed concurrent accesses when issued across all active threads; this is a worst-case scenario for the GPU. Here, N_I is the number of uint4 items per thread:

uint4 addr	0	1	2	3	...	N_I-4	N_I-3	N_I-2	N_I-1
Thread	0	0	0	0	...	0	0	0	0
uint4 addr	N_I	N_I+1	N_I+2	N_I+3	...	$2N_I$-4	$2N_I$-3	$2N_I$-2	$2N_I$-1
Thread	1	1	1	1	...	1	1	1	1

As an example, for N_T = 8192 and N_I = 128, the addresses sent to the memory subsystem are widely dispersed:

Thread	0	1	2	3	4	5	6	7	...
uint4 addr	0	128	256	320	512	640	768	896	...

On the CPU, this pattern is nearly ideal, particularly when running only a few CPU work-items with large numbers of N_I. Each work-item reads sequentially through its own portion of the dataset; this allows prefetching and per-core cache line reads to be most effective. As a rule of thumb, it is desirable to use per-thread column-major access on the GPU and per-thread row-major access on the CPU. Row-major and column-major access can be implemented in a single kernel through different strides—a kernel can switch at run time without cost.

Both patterns are shown in the following code example, where nItemsPerThread is the overall number of uint4 elements in the input buffer, divided by the number of threads:

```
__kernel void singleBinHistogram (__global uint4 *Image,
                                  __global uint *Histogram,
                                  uint nItemsPerThread )
{
    uint id = get_global_id(0);
```

```
    uint nWItems = get_global_size(0);
    uint i, idx; uint bin = 0;
    uint val = SOME_PIXEL_VAL;
#ifdef GPU_PEAK_READ_PERF
    // with stride, fast
    for( i=0, idx=get_global_id(0); i<nItemsPerThread; i++, idx+=nWItems) {
#else
    // serial, slow on GPU, fast on CPU
    for( i=0, idx=0; i<nItemsPerThread; i++, idx+=1 ) {
#endif
        if( Image[idx].x == val ) bin++;
        if( Image[idx].y == val ) bin++;
        if( Image[idx].z == val ) bin++;
        if( Image[idx].w == val ) bin++;
    }

    Histogram[id] = bin;
}
```

When executed with at least 8192 work-items and a work-group size of 64, this kernel reaches near hardware peak performance (on AMD GPUs), as shown in Figure 7.1.6.

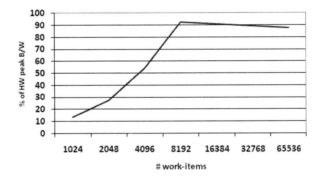

Figure 7.1.6 Bandwidth per number of work-items.

Getting around the Scatter Bottleneck

On the CPU, reads and randomly indexed writes can be performed at roughly the same speed. The GPU, on the other hand, excels when massively parallel writes can be coalesced into large blocks, just as was shown for reads in the previous section. Also, the total read-modify-write latency to __global memory can be a contributor. For a straightforward parallel histogram implementation, where each thread creates a sub-histogram in __global memory, as in the following code example, scatter turns out to be a bottleneck.

```
__kernel void multiBinHistogram ( __global uint4 *Image,
                                  __global uint *Histogram,
                                  uint nItemsPerThread ) {
    uint id = get_global_id(0);
    uint nWItems = get_global_size(0);
    uint i, idx;

    for( i=0, idx=get_global_id(0); i<nItemsPerThread; i++, idx+=nWItems )
    {
        Histogram[ id * NBINS + Image[idx].x ]++;
        Histogram[ id * NBINS + Image[idx].y ]++;
        Histogram[ id * NBINS + Image[idx].z ]++;
        Histogram[ id * NBINS + Image[idx].w ]++;
    }
    ...
}
```

Optimizing __local Memory Access

A powerful way to address the GPU scatter bottleneck is to direct scatter into __local memory. This memory is available to all work-items in a work-group, and its lifetime is that of the group.

It is fast for the following reasons:

- It typically is on-chip (cf. `clGetDeviceInfo(CL_DEVICE_LOCAL_MEM_TYPE)`) and very low latency. In essence, it is a user-manageable cache.
- It supports a large number of concurrent data paths: one for each compute unit and more for multiple banks on each compute unit, resulting in an aggregate bandwidth up to an order of magnitude higher than __global memory.
- It allows the use of hardware atomics, so that random access RMW cycles can be performed without having to worry about expensive, explicit synchronization between the global set of threads.

The __local memory size per work-group (and by extension, per compute unit) is given by:

```
clGetDeviceInfo( ..., CL_DEVICE_LOCAL_MEM_SIZE, ... );
```

This gives a total __local size per GPU device as `CL_MAX_COMPUTE_UNITS` * `CL_DEVICE_LOCAL_MEM_SIZE`.

A straightforward implementation for the histogram algorithm would be to simply have a sub-histogram instance per __local memory and to let all threads in that group contribute to that single instance, as shown in the following example code:

```
__kernel void histogramLocal( __global uint4 *Image,
                              __global uint *Histogram,
                              __local uint *subhists,
                              uint nItemsPerThread ) {
```

```
uint id = get_global_id(0);
uint nWItems = get_global_size(0);
uint i, idx; uint4 temp;
// initialize __local memory
...
// scatter loop
for( i=0, idx=tid; i<nItemsPerThread; i++, idx+=nWItems ) {
   temp = Image[idx];

   atom_inc( subhists + temp.x );
   atom_inc( subhists + temp.y );
   atom_inc( subhists + temp.z );
   atom_inc( subhists + temp.w );
}
barrier( CLK_LOCAL_MEM_FENCE );
// reduce sub-histogram and write out to __global for further reduction
...
}
```

This approach performs very well for randomized input data, since the collective scatter operations from all threads are distributed over the __local banks. Unfortunately, real application images can consist of large swaths of identical pixel values—a black background, for example. The resulting simultaneous atomic read-modify-write access by many threads into a single bin quickly leads to severe contention and loss of performance.

This is where __local banks become effective as the hardware provides multiple banks that can be accessed at the same time. On AMD GPUs, addresses of adjacent 32-bit words map to adjacent banks. This pattern repeats every N_B addresses, where N_B is the number of available banks.

For $N_B=32$, the __local bank layout looks like this:

uint addr	0	1	2	3	...	28	29	30	31
bank	0	1	2	3	...	28	29	30	31
uint addr	32	33	34	34	...	60	61	62	63
bank	0	1	2	3	...	28	29	30	31

The goal is to map the set of running threads to as many banks as possible. In the histogram case, an easy way to do this is to maintain N_B copies for each bin and use the local work-item ID to steer simultaneous writes to the same logical bin, but into separate banks.

The resulting bins are then combined after the read-scatter phase of the kernel. The optimal number of copies for each bin can be experimentally determined, but it is less than or equal to N_B. The value of N_B cannot be queried via OpenCL and is obtained from the hardware spec. For recent AMD GPUs, it is 32.

```
#define NBANKS 32
```

```
// subhists is of size: (number of histogram bins) * NBANKS
__kernel void histogramKernel( __global uint4 *Image,
                               __global uint *Histogram,
                               __local uint *subhists,
                               uint nItemsPerWI ) {
    uint id = get_global_id(0);
    uint ltid = get_local_id(0);
    uint nWItems = get_global_size(0);

    uint i, idx; uint4 temp;

    uint4 spread = (uint4) (NBANKS, NBANKS, NBANKS, NBANKS);
    uint4 offset = (uint4)(ltid, ltid, ltid, ltid);
    offset &= (uint4)(NBANKS-1, NBANKS-1, NBANKS-1, NBANKS-1);

    // initialize __local memory
    ...
    // scatter loop
    for( i=0, idx=tid; i<nItemsPerWI; i++, idx+=nWItems ) {
        temp = Image[idx] * spread + offset;
        atom_inc( subhists + temp.x );
        atom_inc( subhists + temp.y );
        atom_inc( subhists + temp.z );
        atom_inc( subhists + temp.w );
    }
    barrier( CLK_LOCAL_MEM_FENCE );
    // reduce sub-histograms, and write out to __global for further reduction
    ...
}
```

By spreading out read-modify-write accesses in this manner, contention is greatly reduced, if not removed. The resulting performance gain for a test image consisting of identical pixels is an order of magnitude.

OpenCL Command Profiling

In the previous sections, a selection of techniques for optimizing OpenCL programs have been described. But how should we time changes made for performance? In general, Windows' performance counters work well, and for more detailed profiles, tools such as AMD's CodeAnalyst Performance Analyzer or GPU PerfStudio help. In addition to these, OpenCL provides the ability to query profiling information for specific commands executed via a command queue on a device.

By default profiling is not enabled, but it can be explicitly requested at the creation of a command queue, with the following flag:

```
CL_QUEUE_PROFILING_ENABLE
```

Alternatively, profiling can be enabled for a command queue with the following API call:

```
queue.setProperty(CL_QUEUE_PROFILING_ENABLE, CL_TRUE);
```

Generally, commands are enqueued into a queue asynchronously, and the developer must use events to keep track of a command's status, as well as to enforce dependencies. Events provide a gateway to a command's history: They contain information detailing when the corresponding command was placed in the queue, when it was submitted to the device, and when it started and ended execution. Access to an event's profiling information is through the following API call:

```
event.getProfilingInfo<cl_profiling_info>();
```

Valid values of the enumeration `cl_profiling_info` are `CL_PROFILING_COMMAND_QUEUED`, `CL_PROFILING_COMMAND_SUBMIT`, `CL_PROFILING_COMMAND_START`, `CL_PROFILING_COMMAND_END`.

Conclusion

OpenCL is a technology for describing data- and task-parallel programs that can use all compute resources, including CPUs and GPUs. While it is straightforward to get applications to run using OpenCL, it is not always simple to get the expected performance. In this article, we have outlined a number of techniques that can be used to optimize OpenCL programs. These optimizations are not a guarantee for performance; instead, they should be seen as a toolkit to be considered when optimizing an application.

References

[Gaster09] Gaster, Benedict R. "Introductory Tutorial to OpenCL." August 2009. ATi Stream Technical publications. n.d. <http://developer.amd.com/gpu/ATIStreamSDK/pages/TutorialOpenCL.aspx>.

[Munshi09] Munshi, Aaftab, ed. "The OpenCL Specification." Version 1.0. Khronos OpenCL Working Group, August 2009.

7.2

PhysX GPU Rigid Bodies in Batman: Arkham Asylum

Richard Tonge, NVIDIA Corporation,
rtonge@nvidia.com

Ben Wyatt and Ben Nicholson,
Rocksteady Studios

One of the goals of the PC version of *Batman: Arkham Asylum* was to improve the realism and dynamism of the game environment by adding GPU-based physics effects, including cloth, fluids, and rigid body–based destruction. With fluids, we were able to add volumetric smoke and fog, which moves around players and other characters as they progress through it. With cloth, we were able to bring to life the piles of paper littering the admin areas of Arkham Asylum. These piles appear as static triangle meshes on other platforms. For rigid body dynamics, we wanted to provide large-scale destruction—for example, to demolish large concrete walls in the outdoor areas of the game. To believably break up a large wall requires the simulation of thousands of debris pieces colliding with the high triangle count environment of *Batman*. To achieve this in addition to running all the gameplay physics, graphics, and other game code on the CPU at high frame rates, it was clear that the effects would have to be run on the GPU.

For GPU acceleration of cloth and fluids, we were able to use NVIDIA PhysX, which already includes CUDA implementations of those features. For rigid body simulation, NVIDIA developed a GPU rigid body engine (GRB) implementing the subset of PhysX features we needed for *Batman*. Using GRB, physics calculations run up to three times faster than on the CPU, enabling the large-scale destruction required. This gem describes the design and implementation of GRB and its use in *Batman*.

Batman made use of NVIDIA's APEX destruction module to author and simulate destructible game objects. APEX is a layer above PhysX that allows specific effects to be authored and inserted into games easily. APEX destruction allows the artist to specify how an object breaks, with APEX doing the dirty work of creating, splitting, and destroying PhysX rigid bodies when the object is shot at, blown up, or swept away by a tornado.

In *Batman*'s Scarecrow levels, large wall panels needed to be destroyed, with the debris swept up into a tornado centered on the Scarecrow. Wall panels were imported into the APEX destruction tool, where they were broken into pieces and placed into the game using Unreal Editor. With the content pipeline in place, our task was to make a GPU rigid body engine to accelerate the subset of PhysX rigid body features used by APEX destruction.

Figure 7.2.1 Destructible wall section being placed in Unreal Editor.

Requirements

We identified the following requirements:

- **Performance.** The system must be able to support thousands of rigid bodies colliding and interacting with the game environment in real time.
- **Parallelism.** The system must be designed to use thousands of GPU threads to get good GPU performance and allow scaling to future GPUs.
- **API.** The API should be similar to PhysX rigid body and support all features and API calls made by APEX destruction.
- **Interaction with PhysX.** The game will use PhysX (CPU) rigid bodies for game-play objects (for example, Batman). GRB should support one-way interaction with PhysX bodies. (PhysX bodies should move GRBs but not vice versa.)
- **Shapes.** GRB should support the PhysX shapes used in *Batman*—that is, triangle meshes, convex meshes, spheres, capsules, and boxes.

- **Multi-threading.** The simulation should occur asynchronously to the game thread to allow unused GPU resources to be utilized whenever they occur in the frame and avoid having the game thread wait for GRB to complete.
- **Buffering.** The game should be free to change the scene while the simulation is running without disrupting the simulation.
- **Streaming.** *Batman* uses a single scene for the whole game and streams in adjacent levels as the player moves around. This means that additions to the scene have to be fast.
- **Authoring.** It should be easy to author and tune content. Artists should be able to specify which game objects collide with GRBs and which don't.

Shape Representation

The static environment is represented by the original geometry used in the game—triangle meshes, convex meshes, boxes, and so on. Dynamic objects have a sphere-based representation made by voxelizing the object geometry. Color Plates 13 and 14 show how shapes in *Batman* are represented by voxel-generated spheres in GRB. Although spheres are used to represent the collision geometry of dynamic objects, the dynamics are still done on rigid body coordinates.

Dynamics Algorithm

One of the most important requirements was that the algorithm be highly data parallel to allow efficient GPU implementation. Initially, the dynamics method from [Harada07] seemed like a good choice. In this method, spring and damper forces are applied at contact points to prevent penetration. The forces are integrated explicitly, which means that they can be calculated in parallel. In a sense, this method is maximally parallel, because there are as many threads as contacts.

Unfortunately, like other penalty methods, this method is hard to tune. In this method, the spring stiffness must be set high enough so that penetration is avoided for all incoming velocities. Penalizing penetration with springs injects unwanted energy into the system, so a damping parameter has to be tuned to dissipate the extra energy. Although tuning these parameters is reasonable for simple collisions—for example, between two spheres—it quickly becomes intractable for multiple simultaneous collisions each having multiple contacts. Also, because the method is an explicit method, the stiffness dictates a maximum time-step size for which the simulation is stable. [Harmon09] addresses some of these problems, but the method is far from real time.

To avoid these problems, we decided to use an implicit constraint-based method similar to that used in PhysX. In this method, instead of producing a spring and damper per contact point, the collision detection code produces a set of rules called *constraints*. These constraints are fed into a constraint solver, which iteratively finds a new set of velocities for the bodies. Its goal is to find velocities that won't move the bodies into penetration (violate the constraints) in the current time step. Compared to [Harada07], implementing this method has the additional complexity of parallelizing a constraint solver. The parallelization will be described in a later section.

Pipeline

The following is a high-level description of the pipeline.

- Transform spheres into world space using body transformation matrices.
- Find sphere-sphere overlaps, producing contacts.
- Find sphere-mesh overlaps, producing contacts.
- Evaluate force fields, such as wind, explosions, tornados, and so on.
- Update body velocities by applying force fields and gravity.
- Generate constraints from contacts.
- Solve constraints producing modified velocities and position corrections.
- Update body positions using position corrections.

Transform Spheres into World Space

The spheres are rigidly attached to the rigid body reference frame. For this reason, in each frame the spheres have to be transformed from their local frame to world space. For a particle with position $\mathbf{r}$ belonging to a rigid body with transformation matrix $\mathbf{M}$, we calculate the world space position as follows:

$$\mathbf{r}_{\text{world}} = \mathbf{M}\mathbf{r}$$

Sphere-Sphere Collision Detection

The dynamic objects are represented by grids of spheres, so we use sphere-sphere tests to determine the points of contact between them. We use the same size spheres for all the dynamic objects in the scene, so the sphere radius is a global parameter σ. A pair of spheres separated by vector $\mathbf{r}_{ij}$ are overlapping if $|\mathbf{r}_{ij}| \leq 2\sigma$. In this case, the contact normal $\mathbf{n}_c$, position $\mathbf{p}_c$, and separation ϕ_c are defined as follows.

$$\mathbf{n}_c = \mathbf{r}_{ij} / |\mathbf{r}_{ij}|$$
$$\mathbf{p}_c = \mathbf{r}_i - \frac{\mathbf{r}_{ij}}{2}$$
$$\phi_c = |\mathbf{r}_{ij}| - 2\sigma$$

In the case, where the two spheres are in almost the same position ($|\mathbf{r}_{ij}| \leq \varepsilon$, where ε is a small positive number), we use an arbitrary contact normal $\mathbf{n}_c = (1,0,0)$. Note that when the spheres are penetrating, the "separation" is negative.

Sphere-Mesh Collision Detection

The static environment is mainly composed of non-convex triangle meshes, so we also have to test for sphere-triangle contact. For each sphere and potentially colliding triangle, we first need to check whether the center of the sphere is already behind the triangle. Ignoring contact in this case helps avoid the situation where some of a body's spheres are trapped on one side of a triangle and some on the other, and it also simplifies the computation of the separation. Given sphere center $\mathbf{p}_s$, triangle vertices $(\mathbf{v}_0, \mathbf{v}_1, \mathbf{v}_2)$, and triangle normal $\mathbf{n}_t$, the sphere center is behind the triangle if:

$$\mathbf{n}_t \cdot \mathbf{p}_s < \mathbf{n}_t \cdot \mathbf{v}_0$$

If a sphere and triangle survive this test, then we next need to calculate world coordinates $\mathbf{p}_t$ of the closest point on the triangle to the center of the sphere $\mathbf{p}_s$. For details on how to do this, see [Ericson05]. We generate a contact for a sphere and triangle if $|\mathbf{p}_s - \mathbf{p}_t| \leq \sigma$. The contact normal, position, and separation are given by the following:

$$\mathbf{n}_c = (\mathbf{p}_s - \mathbf{p}_t)/|\mathbf{p}_s - \mathbf{p}_t|$$
$$\mathbf{p}_c = \mathbf{p}_t$$
$$\phi_c = |\mathbf{p}_s - \mathbf{p}_t| - \sigma$$

In the case that the sphere center is on the triangle $|\mathbf{p}_s - \mathbf{p}_t| \leq \varepsilon$, we set the contact normal $\mathbf{n}_c$ to the triangle normal instead.

We use a uniform grid data structure to avoid having to test every sphere against every triangle in the mesh. This is described later in this gem.

Evaluate Force Fields

Force fields are used in *Batman* to blow around debris and implement tornado effects. GRB supports the same interface as PhysX for specifying and evaluating force fields. See [Nvidia08] for more details.

Calculate Unconstrained Velocities

For a body with velocity $\mathbf{v}$, we step the acceleration due to force fields $\mathbf{a}_f$ and gravity $\mathbf{a}_g$ through time step h to get the unconstrained velocity $\mathbf{v}^*$. We also apply a global damping parameter η.

$$\mathbf{v}^* = (1 - \eta h)[\mathbf{v} + h(\mathbf{a}_f + \mathbf{a}_g)]$$

Each body's inertia matrix I is calculated in its local frame, so we need to transform it to the world frame as follows:

$$\mathbf{I}_{world}^{-1} = \mathbf{R}\,\mathbf{I}^{-1}\,\mathbf{R}^T$$

where $\mathbf{R}$ is the orientation matrix of the body.

Generate Constraints

For each contact, the constraint solver needs a coordinate frame $[\mathbf{b}_0 \quad \mathbf{b}_1 \quad \mathbf{b}_2]$ in which to apply the constraint forces. We'll refer to these three vectors as *constraint directions*. The X-axis is aligned with the contact normal $\mathbf{b}_0 = \mathbf{n}_c$, and the other two axes are arbitrarily chosen orthogonal axes in which the friction forces will be applied.

Consider a contact with position $\mathbf{p}_c$, normal $\mathbf{n}_c$, and separation ϕ_c. Let the position of the contact relative to the center of masses of body a and body b be $\mathbf{r}_a$ and $\mathbf{r}_b$, their final (constrained) velocities be $[\mathbf{v}_a^{cl}, \mathbf{v}_a^{ca}]$ and $[\mathbf{v}_b^{cl}, \mathbf{v}_b^{ca}]$, their inertia be $\mathbf{I}_a$ and $\mathbf{I}_b$, and their masses be m_a and m_b.

Each non-penetration constraint has the following form, known as the *velocity Signorini condition*:

$$(v_0 \geq 0 \text{ and } f_0 = 0) \text{ or } (v_0 = 0 \text{ and } f_0 \geq 0)$$
$$v_0 = \left[\mathbf{v}_a^{cl} + \mathbf{v}_a^{ca} \times \mathbf{r}_a - \left(\mathbf{v}_b^{cl} + \mathbf{v}_b^{ca} \times \mathbf{r}_b\right)\right].\mathbf{b}_0$$

Here, v_0 is the component of relative velocity of the two bodies at the contact point along the contact normal, and f_0 is the magnitude of the impulse calculated by the constraint solver to satisfy the constraint. The condition ensures that the bodies are either separating or resting. Additionally, if the bodies are separating, then the solver must not apply any impulse; and if the bodies are resting, then the solver must apply a non-adhesive impulse. The calculation of the friction impulses will be described later.

The constraint solver solves each constraint independently. To do this, it needs to calculate $f_j^* = av_j$, the magnitude of the impulse to apply along direction $\mathbf{b}_j$ needed to zero the relative velocity along that direction, given initial relative velocity v_j. The constant a is the reciprocal of the effective mass and is precomputed as follows:

$$a_j = \left[(\mathbf{r_0} \times \mathbf{b_j})^T \mathbf{I}_{0,\text{world}}^{-1}(\mathbf{r_0} \times \mathbf{b_j}) + m_0^{-1} + (\mathbf{r_1} \times \mathbf{b_j})^T \mathbf{I}_{1,\text{world}}^{-1}(\mathbf{r_1} \times \mathbf{b_j}) + m_1^{-1}\right]^{-1}$$

Solver

The task of the solver is as follows: Given a set of bodies with unconstrained velocities $\mathbf{v}^*$ and a set of constraints, find impulses to apply to the bodies such that the resulting velocities will (approximately) satisfy the constraints. As with most game physics engines, GRB uses an iterative projected Gauss-Seidel solver. Given an unlimited number of iterations, the constraints will be solved exactly. In *Batman*, we terminate after four iterations, so although the velocities may slightly violate the constraints, we can bound the amount of time the solver will take.

Let the number of constraints be m. If friction is used, then m is the number of contacts multiplied by three. In this section, we'll assume that the constraint directions and all the other constraint parameters are concatenated into arrays of length m. The solver iterates over the constraints, solving each in isolation.

Solver algorithm:

Zero f, the impulse accumulator for each constraint

For each iteration

    For i = 0 to m

        Calculate the impulse required to prevent relative motion along constraint direction i

        Clamp the accumulated impulse to satisfy the Signorini or friction constraint

        Add impulse to impulse accumulator

        Apply impulse to update the velocities of the constrained bodies

Calculate Impulse Required to Prevent Relative Motion Along Constraint Direction i

Given $[\mathbf{v}_a^l, \mathbf{v}_a^a]$ and $[\mathbf{v}_b^l, \mathbf{v}_b^a]$, the linear and angular velocities of the two bodies constrained by constraint i, and $\mathbf{r}_a$ and $\mathbf{r}_b$, the position of the contact in the frames of body a and body b, the relative velocity along the constraint direction $\mathbf{b}_i$ is given by the following:

$$v_{rel} = \left[\mathbf{v}_a^l + \mathbf{v}_a^a \times \mathbf{r}_a - \left(\mathbf{v}_b^l + \mathbf{v}_b^a \times \mathbf{r}_b\right)\right].\mathbf{b}_i$$

In other words, v_{rel} is the velocity of the contact point on body a minus the velocity of the contact point on body b projected onto the direction $\mathbf{b}_i$. We can now multiply by the inverse effective mass a_i to get f^d, the additional impulse required to satisfy the constraint in isolation:

$$f^d = a_i v_{rel}$$

Clamp the Accumulated Impulse to Satisfy the Signorini Constraint

Constraint i is either a non-penetration constraint or a friction constraint. For non-penetration constraints, we clamp to prevent adhesion as follows:

$$f_{new} = max(0, \mathbf{f}_i + f^d)$$

For friction constraints, we approximate the Coulomb friction cone with a pyramid aligned to the friction constraint directions. This allows us to calculate the friction impulses separately. For a friction constraint with friction coefficient μ, we look up $\mathbf{f}_j$, the impulse applied at the corresponding non-penetration constraint, and then clamp to the friction pyramid as follows:

$$f_{new} = max\left(-\mu\mathbf{f}_j, min\left(\mathbf{f}_i + f^d, \mu\mathbf{f}_j\right)\right)$$

Apply Impulse to Update the Velocities of the Constrained Bodies

We now apply the clamped impulse to the two bodies involved in the constraint.

$$\mathbf{v}_0^l += (f_{new} - \mathbf{f}_i)m_0^{-1}\mathbf{b}_i$$
$$\mathbf{v}_0^a += (f_{new} - \mathbf{f}_i)\mathbf{I}_{0,\text{world}}^{-1}(\mathbf{r}_0 \times \mathbf{b}_i)$$
$$\mathbf{v}_1^l -= (f_{new} - \mathbf{f}_i)m_1^{-1}\mathbf{b}_i$$
$$\mathbf{v}_1^a -= (f_{new} - \mathbf{f}_i)\mathbf{I}_{1,\text{world}}^{-1}(\mathbf{r}_1 \times \mathbf{b}_i)$$
$$\mathbf{f}_i = f_{new}$$

Update Positions

The solver calculates a new velocity for each body. To apply velocity ($\mathbf{v}_{\text{lin}}$, $\mathbf{v}_{\text{ang}}$) to a body with position $\mathbf{p}$, orientation quaternion $\mathbf{q}$, and time step h, we use the following:

$$\mathbf{p} := p + h\mathbf{v}_{\text{lin}}dt$$
$$q := \left[\cos\left(\tfrac{\theta}{2}\right), a\sin\left(\tfrac{\theta}{2}\right)\right] * q$$

where $a = \mathbf{v}_{\text{ang}}/|\mathbf{v}_{\text{ang}}|$ and $\theta = |h\mathbf{v}_{\text{ang}}|$.

GPU Implementation

Amdahl's law dictates that if you parallelize less than 100 percent of your code, your speedup will be at best the reciprocal of the proportion not parallelized. For example, if 80 percent of the code is parallelized, the speedup will be no more than 5×, even though the GPU might be significantly more than five times faster than the CPU. So our initial aim was to port all stages of the GRB pipeline to the GPU. In the end, we ported all pipeline stages except for force field calculation to the GPU. The reason that we didn't port force field calculation is that the PhysX API allows the user to write custom force evaluation kernels in C. Linking artist-generated kernels into the GRB CUDA code was not supported with the available tool chain. An advantage to running almost all of the pipeline on the GPU is that most of the data can be kept in the GPU's memory. This is an advantage because data transfer between CPU memory and GPU memory introduces latency and unnecessary synchronization with the CPU.

The pipeline stages can be divided into those that are easily parallelized and those that are not. The stages in the first category are transform particles, find sphere-sphere contacts, find sphere-mesh contacts, update velocities, generate constraints, and update body positions. For example, in transform particles, each GPU thread is assigned a single particle. The calculation of each particle is independent, and as there are typically more than 10,000 particles in *Batman*, the GPU is well utilized. Similarly, each thread is assigned one particle in the collision detection stages. In the sphere-sphere stage, each thread is responsible for finding nearby particles; and in the sphere-triangle stage, each thread looks at nearby triangles. Again, each thread can do this without synchronizing with any other. In order to concatenate the contacts produced by each thread, we allocate memory for a fixed number of contacts per thread.

We used four contacts per sphere in *Batman*. Once this fixed number of contacts has been generated, further contacts are discarded. Discarding contacts could result in unwanted penetration, but in *Batman* this is rarely visible. Another way to do this would be to use a scan (prefix sum) operation [Harris07] to allocate space for the contacts. However, this requires running the collision kernels twice—once to calculate the number of contacts and again to fill in the contact data. For the easily parallelized stages, the CUDA port was very quick. In most cases it was as simple as removing an outer `for` loop, adding the `__device__` keyword, and compiling the body of the `for` loop with the CUDA compiler. Most of the loop bodies compiled with little or no changes.

The only pipeline stage that is not easily parallelized is the constraint solver, and that will be discussed in one of the following sections.

CUDA Voxelizer

Voxelization is the conversion of an object into a volume representation, stored in a three-dimensional array of voxels. A voxel is the three-dimensional equivalent of a pixel, representing a small cubical volume. Since GRB represents objects as a collection of spheres, we use voxelization to generate an approximate sphere representation of the convex objects generated by APEX destruction. Each covered voxel generates a single sphere.

The voxelizer isn't strictly part of the pipeline because it is only run when dynamic objects are first loaded. However, *Batman* levels are streamed, so object loading has to be as fast as possible. For this reason we decided to use a GPU voxelizer.

Initially, we implemented an OpenGL voxelizer, similar to that described in [Karabassi99]. However, this required creating a separate OpenGL context, and there was significant overhead in transferring data between OpenGL and CUDA, so we decided to write a CUDA implementation instead.

Since the shapes generated by APEX destruction were all convex meshes, this was considerably simpler than writing a general-purpose triangle mesh voxelizer. The basic algorithm used was to convert each triangle in the convex mesh into plane equation form. This way, it is simple to determine the distance of a point from any plane by performing a simple dot product. The plane data is sent to the GPU using CUDA constant memory. We then launch a kernel with one thread per voxel. Each thread loops over all the planes, calculating the distance to the plane and keeping track of the minimum distance and sign. If the point is inside all the planes, then we know it is inside the object. By discarding points more than a maximum distance away from the nearest plane, we can modify the thickness of the voxelized skin of the object.

Although this algorithm was efficient for large volumes, for GRB we typically needed only a coarse voxelization (perhaps only 83 voxels), which didn't generate enough threads to fill the GPU. For this reason, we developed a batched voxelizer that voxelized a whole collection of convex shapes in a single kernel invocation.

One issue was that the original voxelizer would sometimes generate overlapping spheres for the initially tightly packed groups of convexes generated by APEX destruction, causing the objects to fly away prematurely. This was due to performing the voxelization in the local space of the convex object. By modifying the voxelization to be performed in world space, we ensured that the spheres generated by voxelization fitted together exactly with no overlaps.

Spatial Data Structures

To avoid having to test each sphere for collision against every other sphere and each sphere against every triangle in each frame, we use a spatial data structure to cull out all but nearby spheres and triangles. Because the spheres are all the same size, we use a uniform grid whose cell size is set to the sphere diameter. So for each sphere, we can find potentially overlapping spheres by querying only the 3^3 cells surrounding it. The triangles are also put into a uniform grid, but a separate grid is used to allow the cell size to be tuned separately. When the triangle mesh is loaded, a voxelization process is used to identify which cells the triangle passes through. Each intersection cell is given a pointer to the triangle. In *Batman*, triangle meshes are streamed in as the user progresses through the levels. Initially, we updated the triangle grid incrementally each time a new mesh was loaded, but we found out that regenerating the whole grid from scratch at each mesh load was more efficient. As the spheres are used to represent moving objects, the sphere grid has to be rebuilt each frame. Like [LeGrand07, Green07] we use a fast radix sort [Satish09] to do this. The grid size used for both grids is 64^3. A simple modulo 64 hash function is used so that the world can be bigger than 64^3 cells.

Solver

Unlike the other stages, the projected Gauss Seidel solver isn't easy to parallelize. The reason for this is that each constraint reads and writes the velocities of two bodies, and each body can be affected by more than one constraint. For example, consider a stack of three spheres resting on the ground. Each body is affected by two constraints, except for the top body. If the constraints were executed in parallel by separate threads, then each body (except the top body) would be overwritten by two threads. The final value of the velocity of each body would depend on the exact order in which the constraints accessed the body, and the effect of one constraint would not be taken into account in the calculation of the other.

To get around this problem, the solver has two phases, both of which run on the GPU. The first divides the constraint list into batches of constraints that can be executed in parallel. In each batch, all bodies are modified by just one constraint. The second executes the batches in sequence, using one thread for each constraint in each batch.

We make the assumption that any system can be solved in 32 or fewer batches. The goal is that each body be modified only once in each batch and that the number of batches used be minimal. Each body is given an unsigned integer called a *batch bitmap*. Bit i set means that the body is modified in batch i.

Initially, all the batch bitmaps are set to zero. In the first phase, each constraint is processed by a thread in parallel. Each thread calculates the logical or (disjunction) of the batch bitmaps of its two bodies. If a bit in the result is zero, then it means that batch doesn't modify either body, so the constraint can be processed in this batch. So, the thread finds the first zero bit in the result and attempts to atomically set it in the two bodies. If the atomic set fails (because another thread has allocated the body to the batch in the meantime), then it starts again to find a new bit that is not set for both bodies. If all the bits are set in the disjunction of the two bitmaps, then more than 32 batches are required, and the constraint is discarded.

Conclusion

To test the speedup of GRB, we ran the second Scarecrow level from *Batman* with and without GRB. When the level is run without GRB, both the gameplay and destruction rigid bodies are run on the CPU, and when the level is run with GRB, the gameplay bodies are simulated using PhysX on the CPU, but the 1,600 debris chunks are simulated on the GPU using GRB. The following timings are for the 1,600 debris chunks in both cases. In both cases, the debris rigid bodies collide with each other, the gameplay rigid bodies, and the tens of thousands of triangles that make up the static environment. Because force fields are not simulated on the GPU in either PhysX or GRB, the force field calculation is excluded in both cases.

The test was run for the first 900 frames starting at the second-to-last checkpoint of the level, where a large concrete wall is destroyed and carried away by a force field. The timings are from a representative frame captured after all the chunks have been loosened from the wall. Because the timings are of the physics pipeline only, they don't contain graphics processing time or any other game code. The timings were taken on an Intel Core 2 Quad running at 2.66 GHz with the graphics running on a GTX260 and the physics running on a second GTX260.

GRB physics frame time (1,600 bodies)	16.5ms
PhysX physics frame time (1,600 bodies)	49.5ms
Speedup	3.0x

In a real game, GRB running on a GPU can achieve a threefold performance increase over PhysX running on a CPU.

Acknowledgements

GRB was written by Richard Tonge, Simon Green, Steve Borho, Lihua Zhang, and Bryan Galdrikian. We'd like to thank Adam Moravanszky, Pierre Terdiman, Dilip Sequeira, Mark Harris, and all the other people who indirectly contributed to GRB.

The GRB Batman destruction content was designed by Dane Johnston and Johnny Costello, and the code was integrated into the game by James Dolan, David Sullins, and Steve Borho.

References

[Ericson05] Ericson, Christer. *Real-Time Collision Detection*. Morgan Kaufmann, 2005.

[Erleben04] Erleben, Kenny. "Stable, Robust, and Versatile Multibody Dynamics Animation." PhD thesis. Department of Computer Science, University of Copenhagen, 2004.

[Green07] Green, Simon. "CUDA Particles." NVIDIA Corporation. Whitepaper, 2007.

[Harada07] Harada, Takahiro. "Real Time Rigid Body Physics on GPUs." *GPU Gems 3*. Addison Wesley, 2007.

[Harmon09] Harmon, David, et al. "Asynchronous Contact Mechanics." *SIGGRAPH '09: ACM SIGGRAPH 2009 papers* (2009): 1–12.

[Harris07] Harris, Mark. "Scan Primitives for GPU Computing." *ACM SIGGRAPH/ Eurographics Conference on Graphics Hardware* (2007): n.p.

[Karabassi99] Karabassi, Evaggelia-Aggeliki, et al. "A Fast Depth-Buffer-Based Voxelization Algorithm." *Journal of Graphics Tools* 4.4 (1999): n.p.

[LeGrand07] LeGrand, Scott. "Broad-Phase Collision Detection with CUDA." *GPU Gems 3*. Addison Wesley, 2007.

[Nvidia08] "NVIDIA PhysX SDK 2.8.1 Documentation." NVIDIA Corporation, 2008.

[Satish09] Satish, Nadathur, et al. "Designing Efficient Sorting Algorithms for Manycore GPUs." *Proceedings of the 23rd IEEE International Parallel & Distributed Processing Symposium* (2009): n.p.

7.3

Fast GPU Fluid Simulation in PhysX

Simon Schirm and Mark Harris,
NVIDIA Corporation

sschirm@nvidia.com, harrism@nvidia.com

Over the past several years, physically based simulation has become an important feature of games. Effects based on physical simulation of phenomena such as liquid, smoke, particulate debris, cloth, and rigid body dynamics greatly increase the level of realism and detail in a game. These effects can be expensive to simulate using traditional sequential approaches, especially in a complex game engine where the CPU is already handling many expensive tasks. On the other hand, there is a lot of data parallelism in many physical simulations, and the GPUs in most modern PCs and consoles are powerful parallel processors that can be applied to this task. Simulating fluids and particles on the GPU enables games to incorporate complex fluids and particle effects with tens of thousands of particles that interact with the player and the game scenery.

NVIDIA PhysX is a real-time physics engine for games that uses the GPU in concert with the CPU to accelerate physically based simulation of particle systems, fluids, cloth, and rigid body dynamics [NVIDIA09a]. The GPU-accelerated portions of the engine are implemented using the C for CUDA language and the CUDA run-time API. The standard C and C++ language support in the CUDA compiler makes programming, debugging, and maintaining the complex algorithms used in PhysX much easier and ensures that they can be integrated efficiently with the CPU portions of the engine. For more information on CUDA, see [NVIDIA09b].

In this gem, we present the algorithms and implementation details for the particle and fluid systems in PhysX. We describe the features of each system and then present an overview of the algorithm and details of the implementation in CUDA. Figure 7.3.1 and Color Plate 15 are examples of the results of the techniques described in this gem.

Figure 7.3.1   Real-time GPU-accelerated Smoothed Particle Hydrodynamics (SPH) water simulation in PhysX. There are more than 60,000 particles in the simulation. The rendering is performed using a screen-space splatting technique.

Particle Systems

Particle systems are ubiquitously used in games to create a variety of effects. Particles can be used to represent media ranging from highly granular materials, such as leaves, gravel, and sparks, to more continuous media, such as smoke or steam. Particle effects in games are typically tailored to interact as lightly as possible with the scene in order to reduce computational overhead. This is done, for example, by applying pre-computed forces to the particles in a way that doesn't require any intersection tests or collision detection. The range of effects that can be achieved is therefore significantly limited. One goal of PhysX is to relax these restrictions by moving expensive but highly parallel calculations to the GPU, enabling particles to interact with geometrically rich and dynamic scenes.

Fluids

Real-time simulation of fluids can dramatically increase the realism and interactivity of smoke, steam, and liquid effects in games. The PhysX SDK supports the simulation of gaseous and liquid fluids by adding support for particle-particle interactions to its particle systems. Inter-particle forces are defined so that the volume the particles occupy is approximately conserved over time.

PhysX fluid simulation is built on top of the particle system component, sharing the same collision algorithm and spatial partitioning data structure. Like particle systems, fluid motion is not practically limited to a box domain; particles and fluids can spread throughout a game level.

Robust Particle Collisions

PhysX particles are allowed to interact with arbitrary triangle meshes in a game scene, and therefore we need an algorithm that can robustly handle particle collisions with these meshes. This is particularly challenging in the presence of inter-particle forces, which tend to literally push particles into all the edge and corner cases. Our algorithm has the following properties.

- Penetration and artificial energy loss are minimized so that particles don't leak or stick as shown in Figure 7.3.2: Left.
- A configurable collision radius is provided.
- High-velocity collisions are handled. (The collision radius is usually small compared to the distance a fast particle travels per time step.)
- Particles on thin static objects cannot be pushed through by dynamic objects penetrating the static geometry, as shown in Figure 7.3.2: Right.

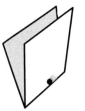
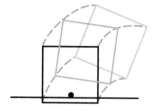

Figure 7.3.2   Left: Particles don't stick or leak in edge cases.
Right: Particles don't fall through static meshes when pushed by dynamic objects.

The PhysX particle collision algorithm is based on a mixed approach that makes use of both continuous and discrete collision detection, as illustrated in Figure 7.3.3.

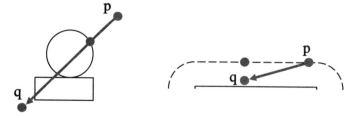

Figure 7.3.3   Left: Continuous collision detection (CCD) with multiple shapes.
Right: A discrete collision detection test between a particle and geometry.

The linear path of the particle motion is tested for intersection with any dynamic or static objects in order to find the first impact location. For dynamic objects, the intersection test must be handled with extra care. Each particle's original position **p** is transformed into the local space of the moving object according to its original pose. The target position **q** is correspondingly transformed according to the target pose of the object, as shown in Figure 7.3.4. Now the linear path defined by the transformed local positions **p'** and **q'** is tested against the object in its local space. This is just an approximation, since the motion path of the particle observed from the moving dynamic geometry would generally be curved. Nonetheless, this approximation has the nice property that the test is topologically correct when multiple compound geometries are involved. Practically, this means that a particle-filled hollow box doesn't leak particles when shaken.

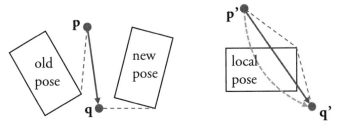

Figure 7.3.4   Left: Continuous collision detection with a dynamic shape.
Right: The same situation as on the left, but relative to a moving shape.
Instead of intersecting the curved particle path, a linear approximation is used.

In addition to the continuous collision test, the sphere defined by the target particle position and radius is tested for intersections with nearby geometry, as shown in Figure 7.3.3: Right. Both results are combined to calculate an appropriate collision response for the particle.

The collision algorithm must gracefully handle cases in which particles could get trapped between penetrating scene objects, as shown in Figure 7.3.2: Right. In practice, it makes sense to give collisions with static objects precedence over collisions with dynamic objects. This is achieved by dividing the collision algorithm into a first pass handling dynamic objects and a second pass handling static objects.

Particles are often continuously pushed against scene geometry by gravity or fluid forces. In these cases, the particle path intersects close to the particle's current position. Correct continuous collision detection will prevent a particle from sliding along object boundaries. One way to overcome this is to correct the velocity of the particle and check its new path for potential collisions again for the rest of the time step. This can be repeated until the end of the time step is reached and the final position of the particle is found. For a particle in a corner, this iteration might take forever. To solve this problem, our algorithm remembers the surfaces a particle collided with in the previous time step and uses them in the current time step to correct the particle velocity in a pre-process to collision detection. In practice, it turns out that storing two planes—called *surface constraints*—per particle is enough to provide good results in most cases.

Fluid Simulation with Smoothed Particle Hydrodynamics

To simulate a fluid, one must compute the mass (and other field values) carried by the fluid through space over time. There are two fundamental approaches to fluid simulation:

- Eulerian simulations track fluid field values at fixed locations in space—for example, on a grid.
- Lagrangian simulations track fluid field values at locations moving with the flow—for example, by using particles.

In PhysX, using particles has several advantages.

- Particles are already used in games, which eases the integration.
- Particles enable seamless collisions with static geometry and rigid bodies with no boundary resampling.
- Mass conservation is trivially achieved by associating a constant mass with each particle.

The approach we use in PhysX is called *Smoothed Particle Hydrodynamics* (SPH), which is a Lagrangian simulation technique that was originally developed to simulate the motion of galaxies [Monaghan92] and later applied to free-surface fluid flow simulation. SPH is an interpolation method that allows field values that are defined only at particle positions to be evaluated anywhere in space [Müller03]. The method is based on the Navier-Stokes equations, which describe fluid motion by relating continuous velocity, density, and pressure fields over time. The two equations enforce conservation of mass and momentum. Since mass is conserved by using discrete particles, we only use the momentum equation. In Lagrangian form, it reads as follows:

$$\frac{d\mathbf{v}_i}{dt} = \mathbf{g} - \frac{\nabla p|_{\mathbf{x}_i}}{\rho_i} + \frac{\mu \nabla^2 \mathbf{v}|_{\mathbf{x}_i}}{\rho_i} \qquad (1)$$

All terms in Equation (1) are derived from local field properties at the location x_i of particle i. The mass of each particle is constant over time. $\frac{d\mathbf{v}_i}{dt}$ represents the acceleration of the particle, and the three terms on the right-hand side describe contributions to the acceleration.

1. External acceleration $\mathbf{g}$, including gravity and collision impulses.
2. Force due to the fluid pressure gradient $\nabla p|_{\mathbf{x}_i}$.
3. Force due to the viscosity of the fluid, given by the Laplacian of the velocity field $\nabla^2 \mathbf{v}|_{\mathbf{x}_i}$ weighted by the scalar viscosity of the fluid μ.

The pressure and viscosity terms each represent a so-called "body force," which is a force per unit volume. To convert a body force into acceleration using Newton's second law, it must be normalized by the mass density ρ_i at the location of the particle, as shown in Equation (1).

The particles act as sample points for the continuous physical fields. Radially symmetric kernel functions are used to reconstruct smooth fields from the discrete particle samples, hence the name *Smoothed Particle Hydrodynamics*.

To evaluate a field value at a certain location, the contributions of the overlapping kernel functions at each nearby particle are summed up, as shown in Figure 7.3.5. Correspondingly, the pressure gradient and the velocity Laplacian can be derived using the kernel functions, as described by [Müller03]. Choosing kernels with a finite non-zero domain is crucial to accelerating the search for nearby particles.

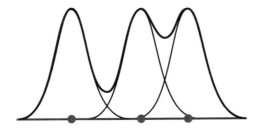

Figure 7.3.5   A one-dimensional field reconstruction formed by the summation of overlapping kernels for each particle.

To compute the acceleration on each particle in the fluid, we need to evaluate Equation (1) at the particle position by summing up the kernel contributions from all overlapping particles. In practice, this requires evaluating three physical fields: density, pressure, and viscosity. This can be done in two passes: one to evaluate the density field and another to evaluate pressure and viscosity, which both depend on density. After evaluating Equation (1) in this way, we have an acceleration that can be used to integrate the velocity and position of the particle over the time step.

For further details on SPH and our application of the method, see [Müller03].

Fluid Simulation Algorithm

Figure 7.3.6 shows an overview of the fluid simulation pipeline. First, the spatial domain that is covered by the particles is approximated with a set of bounds. These are inserted into the broad phase along with the bounds of static and dynamic objects in the scene. In parallel with the broad phase, the SPH phase computes fluid forces and uses them to update the particle velocity. The particle collision phase uses the output of the broad phase and the SPH phase to compute collisions with dynamic and static objects and applies velocity impulses to resolve any penetration. Finally, the positions of all particles are updated using their newly computed velocities.

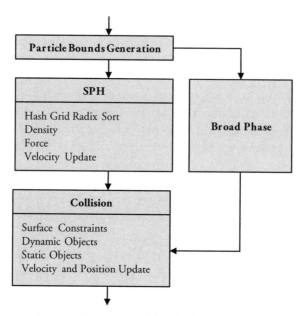

Figure 7.3.6   Particle pipeline overview.

Particle Bounds Generation and the Broad Phase

To support efficient collision detection between particles and static geometry and rigid bodies present in the scene, we need to avoid testing all possible particle-object pairs for intersections. The so-called *broad phase* collision detection algorithm compares the spatial bounds of scene objects to find all potentially colliding pairs. Checking the bounds of all individual particles would overload the broad phase. Therefore, we generate bounds for groups of spatially coherent particles. The particles are associated with a particular particle group based on a hash grid similar to the one used for finding neighbors in SPH but with much coarser grid spacing. The particle collision algorithm uses the output of the broad phase, a set of pairs of overlapping particle groups and scene objects, to find the intersections of individual particles with scene objects. The broad phase can run in parallel in a separate CPU thread while the GPU executes the SPH phase, since the result of the broad phase is only needed before the collision phase starts.

SPH Phase

The SPH phase computes the density and force at each particle position x_i. The force computation evaluates the influence of all other particles in a neighborhood around x_i. In order to find neighboring particles efficiently, we use a *hashed regular grid* to accelerate finding nearby particles. A hashed grid implementation similar to the one used in PhysX is demonstrated in the "particles" sample in the NVIDIA CUDA SDK [Green09], as described by [Teschner03].

Hashed Grid Data Structure

Building the hashed grid data structure requires two steps. The first step computes a hash index for each particle such that all particles in the same grid cell have the same hash index. The second step sorts all particle data by hash index so that the data for all particles in the same hash cell is contiguous in memory.

To compute the hash index, each particle position (x, y, z) is discretized onto a virtual (and infinite) 3D grid by dividing its coordinates by the grid cell size and rounding down to the nearest integer coordinates $(i, j, k) = ([x/h], [y/h], [z/h])$. These coordinates are then used as input to a hash function that computes a single integer hash index. Our hash function is simple; it computes the integer coordinates modulo the grid size and linearizes the resulting 3D coordinates, as shown in Listing 7.3.1. This simple hash function has the important property that given a hash index, computing the hash indices of neighboring cells is trivial, because neighboring cells in the virtual grid map to neighboring cells in the hash grid (modulo the grid size).

LISTING 7.3.1   The virtual grid hash function. Note that `GRID_SIZE` must be a power of 2.

```
int3 gridPosition(float3 pos, float cellSize)
{
    int3 gridPos;
    gridPos.x = floor(pos.x/cellSize) & (GRID_SIZE - 1);
    gridPos.y = floor(pos.y/cellSize) & (GRID_SIZE - 1);
    gridPos.z = floor(pos.z/cellSize) & (GRID_SIZE - 1);
    return gridPos;
}
int hash(int3 gridPos)
{
    return (gridPos.z * GRID_SIZE + gridPos.y) * GRID_SIZE + gridPos.x;
}
```

The hash values for each particle are computed in a CUDA C kernel that outputs an array of hash indices and an array of corresponding particle indices. These are then used as arrays of keys and corresponding indices, which we sort using the fast CUDA radix sort of [Satish09]. For each hash grid cell, we also store the sorted indices of the first and last particle in the cell, to enable constant-time queries of the particles in each hash cell. After the key-index pairs are sorted, we use the sorted indices to reorder the particle position and velocity arrays. Reordering the data arrays is important because it ensures efficient, coalesced memory accesses in subsequent CUDA computations.

Using parallel sorting to build this "list of lists" grid structure is more efficient than building it directly (in other words, by appending each particle to a list for each grid cell) in parallel, because we don't know *a priori* which cells are occupied and how many particles are in each cell. An advantage of using a radix sort is that multiple non-interacting fluids can be combined within the same virtual grid at low additional cost, because doubling the number of fluids only adds one bit to the sort key length. We simply process the particles of all fluids together in parallel and append the fluid ID above the most significant bit of the hash index. Then when we sort the particles, they will be sorted first by fluid ID and then by hash index. This enables us to do all subsequent steps in the simulation of all fluids in parallel. To reduce sorting cost, we sort using only as many bits as we need to represent our chosen grid resolution, which currently is $\log_2 N_f + 18$ bits (64×64×64 grid), where N_f is the number of fluids.

With the use of a hash, we can handle an unlimited grid. Therefore, the fluid is not confined to a box but can flow anywhere in the scene. Naturally, in a widely dispersed fluid, particles from far-apart cells may hash to the same index. If many non-interacting particles hash to the same index, we will perform unnecessary work to evaluate their Euclidean distance, but in practice this has not been a problem. For more on evaluating hash functions and hash table size, see [Teschner03].

Computing Density and Force

Once the hashed grid is built, it can be used to quickly find all particles near to each particle. Thus, we can evaluate the density and force by finding the cell each particle resides in and iterating over the 27 neighboring cells in 3D. At each neighboring cell, we perform a hash table lookup to find the list of particles in each cell. Using these particles, we can compute the sum of the influences of each neighboring particle, as shown in Listing 7.3.2.

LISTING 7.3.2 Pseudocode for evaluating a smoothing kernel at a particle's position

```
SumOfSupportFunctions(float3 pos, float cellSize)
{
   int3 gridPos = gridPosition(pos, cellSize);
   for (int i = -1; i <= 1; i++)
     for (int j = -1; j <= 1; j++)
       for (int k = -1; k <= 1; k++) {
           gridPosition += int3(i, j, k);
           particles = hashTableLookup(hash(gridPosition))
           foreach particle p in particles {
               sum += supportFunction(pos, p.position);
           }
       }
}
```

The procedure in Listing 7.3.2 can be applied to both of the steps required to compute the body forces in Equation (1). First, it is used to compute density using the density kernel function. Then, the density is used to compute pressure and viscosity using the pressure and viscosity kernel functions. For details of these kernel functions, see [Müller03].

Parallel Implementation in CUDA

The four SPH steps shown in Figure 7.3.6 are implemented using one CUDA C kernel each to compute the particle hash, the density, and the force at each particle, plus a radix sort, which is implemented using multiple CUDA C kernels as described in [Satish09], and a kernel that finds the starting and ending indices of particles in each cell and reorders the particle position and velocity arrays using the sorted indices.

The particle hash kernel simply computes the hash index for each particle given its 3D position using the function in Listing 7.3.1. We launch as many GPU threads as there are particles in the scene and compute one hash per thread. After sorting the particles by hash index using the radix sort, we launch another kernel, again with one thread per particle, to reorder the particle position and velocity arrays. This kernel also compares each particle's hash index against those before and after it in the sorted array. If it is different from the index before it, then we know this is the first particle in a cell, so we store this particle's index in the sorted array to a "cell starts" array at the cell index. If it is different from the index after it, then it is the end of a cell, so we store its index in a "cell ends" array.

The density and force kernels also process one particle per thread. Each thread runs the procedure given in Listing 7.3.2. The density kernel uses the density support function given in [Müller03] as its support function to compute a scalar density per particle. The force kernel computes two 3D force sums, one using the pressure gradient support function and one using the viscosity Laplacian support function, both given in [Müller03]. The hashTableLookup function in Listing 7.3.2 simply reads the indices at the cell's index in the cell start and cell end arrays to get a range of particle indices to read from the sorted particle position and velocity arrays.

We make several optimizations to our CUDA C kernels to ensure best performance. First, we pack together the data for all active particle systems or fluids into large batches so that the CUDA kernels can process all particles at once. This improves utilization of the GPU in the presence of multiple small particle systems. We add a small amount of padding between the end of one particle system's data and the beginning of the next to ensure that each particle system begins on an aligned boundary, and we use structures of arrays (SOA) rather than arrays of structures for the particle data. This means that instead of having an array of particle structures containing particle position, velocity, and other data, we have an array of all particle positions, an array of all velocities, and so on. These optimizations ensure that parallel thread accesses to the data arrays are coalesced by the GPU [NVIDIA09b]. Finally, the density and force kernels bind a texture reference to the data arrays so that the spatially coherent but non-sequential access pattern of these kernels can benefit from the texture cache hardware on the GPU [NVIDIA09b].

Particle Collision Phase

The collision phase uses the particle positions and updated velocities from the SPH phase (which includes external accelerations, such as gravity) to compute intersections with scene geometry and rigid bodies and to prevent penetration. The collision algorithm is composed of the following sequence of stages:

1. Surface constraint collision
2. Collision detection with dynamic rigid body shapes
3. Dynamic collision response

4. Collision detection with static rigid body shapes
5. Static collision response
6. Update velocity and position

Within each stage we can treat particles independently, and therefore we typically use one CUDA thread per particle. The particle data as well as any temporary per-particle storage is laid out as structures of arrays (SOA) for efficient coalesced memory access. As with the SPH stage, in order to improve the utilization of the GPU, each CUDA kernel processes multiple particle systems together in one batch.

Surface Constraint Collision
The first collision CUDA kernel loads up to two surface constraints from the previous time step for each particle, if available. From the current particle position and velocity, we compute a target position. The target position is projected out of the surface to get a motion path that is not in conflict with the surface the particle is in contact with. The target position is then passed on to the next stage.

Collision Detection with Static and Dynamic Shapes
Intersection tests for static and dynamic shapes can be handled with the same set of CUDA kernels, treating a static shape as a special case of a dynamic shape that doesn't move. The collision detection described in this section is therefore executed twice—first for dynamic shapes and then for static shapes.

For each spatially coherent group of particles, we need to find all relevant intersections with all shapes that are provided by the broad phase for this group. To improve execution coherence on the data-parallel GPU architecture, we run a different CUDA kernel for each shape type. Our collision algorithm handles collisions with capsules, convex meshes, and triangle mesh shape types, so we have three shape-specific collision kernels.

Each shape-specific kernel iterates over its shapes by looping over batches of shape data (capsule extents and radii, triangles, or planes depending on shape type) that are loaded by all threads cooperatively from global device memory into fast on-chip shared memory. Then, for each loaded batch, each thread tests one particle for intersection with all shapes in the batch and aggregates the contact information.

In the case of triangle meshes, an additional optimization improves GPU utilization when there are more triangles than particles in the spatial group. Instead of using one thread per particle, it is more efficient to parallelize across triangles (in other words, run one thread per triangle). However, since particles may collide with multiple triangles, we would need to store contact information per particle-triangle pair, which is not memory efficient. Our approach is to perform parallel early-out tests for which the results (one bit per test) can be stored very efficiently. This is done as follows. For each triangle, all particles are investigated to find the ones that potentially collide, ruling out the others with a relatively cheap conservative intersection test. The per-particle contact generation can then skip triangles for which the early-out test had a negative result.

Collision Response and Particle Update

After the dynamic shape collision detection, a CUDA kernel computes a collision response from the aggregated surface contact information and updates particle target positions accordingly. After the static shape collision detection, the collision response kernel is executed again, providing the final particle position.

Fluid Rendering

Displaying materials in games that are represented as particles requires very different approaches depending on the material. Granular materials, such as gravel, leaves, or sparks, can be rendered using instanced meshes or billboard techniques, such as impostors. Gaseous fluids are typically displayed using a billboard per particle and various blending methods. Adding environmental shadowing and self-shadowing improves the realism with some added performance cost. The "Smoke Particles" sample in the NVIDIA CUDA SDK demonstrates this technique [Green09]. Rendering liquids based on particle simulation is particularly challenging, since a smooth surface needs to be extracted.

Screen-Space Fluid Rendering

Extracting a surface from a set of points is typically done using the grid-based marching cubes algorithm [Lorensen87], which creates the surface by marching through voxels and generating triangles in cells through which an isosurface is found to pass. This method, however, doesn't provide real-time performance for the resolution and particle count we are targeting. A real-time alternative is the approach described by [Müller07], which simplifies the marching cubes to marching squares to generate a surface mesh in screen space. A further simplification is to avoid any polygonization of the surface and work entirely at the pixel level. This is the approach used in the demo shown in Figure 7.3.1 [NVIDIA08].

Our screen-space rendering approach is as follows.

1. Render the scene to a color texture and to the depth buffer.
2. Render all particles to a depth texture as sphere point sprites.
3. Render the particle thickness to a "thickness" texture with additive blending.
4. Smooth the depth texture to avoid a "particle appearance."
5. Compute a surface normal texture from the smoothed depth using central differencing.
6. Use the normal, depth, and thickness to render the fluid surface into the scene color texture with proper depth testing, reflection, refraction, and Fresnel term.

These steps are all implemented in a standard graphics API using pixel and vertex shaders. The smoothing step is very important; without it, the fluid will look like a collection of discrete particles. There are multiple ways to implement this smoothing.

The basic approach used in Figure 7.3.1 is to smooth the depth texture using a separable Gaussian blur filter. This is inexpensive but can lead to a somewhat "blobby" appearance. A more sophisticated approach is to apply curvature flow, as described by [van der Laan09]. Their technique achieves much more smoothing in areas of low curvature, while maintaining sharp details. A comparison of the two techniques is shown in Color Plate 16.

Performance

We measured the performance of the PhysX particle fluid demo shown in Figure 7.3.1 and Color Plate 16 on a PC with Intel Core 2 Quad CPU and an NVIDIA GeForce GTX 260 GPU. The demo was run with a screen resolution of 1024×768 and an average of about 60,000 particles. Figure 7.3.7 presents the results. The time taken for rendering and CUDA kernels in PhysX is about balanced; on the other hand, the PhysX SDK work executed on the CPU contributes relatively strongly. This can be improved by moving all of the per-particle processing onto the GPU. The executions of the CUDA kernels take 8.2 ms on average. For SPH, the summation passes over particle neighbors that compute density and force take most of the time. For collision, the largest portion is contributed from collisions with the static triangle mesh.

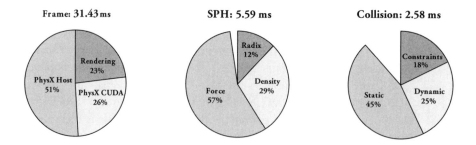

Figure 7.3.7   Left: Overall frame run time. Middle, right: Cuda kernel run time for SPH and collision phases. The gaps display contributions from remaining kernels of the respective phase. "Radix" refers to the radix sort kernels.

Acknowledgements

The CUDA fluid simulation implementation and the ideas behind it are the fruits of the efforts of a large team. We would like to thank all the members of the NVIDIA PhysX team and others at NVIDIA for their contributions, especially Steve Borho, Curtis Davis, Stefan Duthaler, Isha Geigenfeind, Monier Maher, Simon Green, Matthias Müller-Fischer, Ashu Rege, Miguel Sainz, Richard Tonge, Lihua Zhang, and Jiayuan Zhu. We would also like to thank Gareth Ramsey and Eidos Game Studios for the use of Color Plate 15.

References

[Green09] Green, S. "Particles." and "Smoke Particles." n.d. NVIDIA CUDA SDK version 2.3. n.d. <http://www.nvidia.com/object/cuda_get.html>.

[Lorensen87] Lorensen, W. E., and H. E. Cline. "Marching Cubes: A High Resolution 3D Surface Construction Algorithm." *Computer Graphics* 21.4 (July 1987): n.p.

[Monaghan92] Monaghan, J. J. "Smoothed Particle Hydrodynamics." *Annual Review of Astronomy and Astrophysics* 30 (1992): 543–574.

[Müller03] Müller, M., et al. "Particle-Based Fluid Simulation for Interactive Applications." *Symposium on Computer Animation* (2003): 154–159.

[Müller07] Müller, M., S. Schirm, and S. Duthaler. "Screen-Space Meshes." *Symposium on Computer Animation* (2007): 9–15.

[NVIDIA08] NVIDIA Corporation. "Fluids: Technology Demo." 2008. NVIDIA. n.d. <http://www.nvidia.com/content/graphicsplus/us/download.asp>.

[NVIDIA09a] NVIDIA Corporation. "NVIDIA PhysX." 2009. NVIDIA. n.d. <http://www.nvidia.com/object/physx_new.html>.

[NVIDIA09b] NVIDIA Corporation. "NVIDIA CUDA Programming Guide." 2009. NVIDIA. n.d. <http://www.nvidia.com/cuda>.

[Satish09] Satish, N., M. Harris, and M. Garland. "Designing Efficient Sorting Algorithms for Manycore GPUs." *Proceedings of IEEE International Parallel and Distributed Processing Symposium* (2009): to appear.

[Teschner03] Teschner, M. et al. "Optimized Spatial Hashing for Collision Detection of Deformable Objects." *Proceedings of VMV* (2003): 47–54.

[van der Laan09] van der Laan, W., S. Green, and M. Sainz. "Screen Space Fluid Rendering with Curvature Flow." *Proceedings of the 2009 Symposium on Interactive 3D Graphics and Games* (2009): 91–98.

INDEX

License Agreement/Notice of Limited Warranty

By opening the sealed disc container in this book, you agree to the following terms and conditions. If, upon reading the following license agreement and notice of limited warranty, you cannot agree to the terms and conditions set forth, return the unused book with unopened disc to the place where you purchased it for a refund.

License:

The enclosed software is copyrighted by the copyright holder(s) indicated on the software disc. You are licensed to copy the software onto a single computer for use by a single user and to a backup disc. You may not reproduce, make copies, or distribute copies or rent or lease the software in whole or in part, except with written permission of the copyright holder(s). You may transfer the enclosed disc only together with this license, and only if you destroy all other copies of the software and the transferee agrees to the terms of the license. You may not decompile, reverse assemble, or reverse engineer the software.

Notice of Limited Warranty:

The enclosed disc is warranted by Course Technology to be free of physical defects in materials and workmanship for a period of sixty (60) days from end user's purchase of the book/disc combination. During the sixty-day term of the limited warranty, Course Technology will provide a replacement disc upon the return of a defective disc.

Limited Liability:

THE SOLE REMEDY FOR BREACH OF THIS LIMITED WARRANTY SHALL CONSIST ENTIRELY OF REPLACEMENT OF THE DEFECTIVE DISC. IN NO EVENT SHALL COURSE TECHNOLOGY OR THE AUTHOR BE LIABLE FOR ANY OTHER DAMAGES, INCLUDING LOSS OR CORRUPTION OF DATA, CHANGES IN THE FUNCTIONAL CHARACTERISTICS OF THE HARDWARE OR OPERATING SYSTEM, DELETERIOUS INTERACTION WITH OTHER SOFTWARE, OR ANY OTHER SPECIAL, INCIDENTAL, OR CONSEQUENTIAL DAMAGES THAT MAY ARISE, EVEN IF COURSE TECHNOLOGY AND/OR THE AUTHOR HAS PREVIOUSLY BEEN NOTIFIED THAT THE POSSIBILITY OF SUCH DAMAGES EXISTS.

Disclaimer of Warranties:

COURSE TECHNOLOGY AND THE AUTHOR SPECIFICALLY DISCLAIM ANY AND ALL OTHER WARRANTIES, EITHER EXPRESS OR IMPLIED, INCLUDING WARRANTIES OF MERCHANTABILITY, SUITABILITY TO A PARTICULAR TASK OR PURPOSE, OR FREEDOM FROM ERRORS. SOME STATES DO NOT ALLOW FOR EXCLUSION OF IMPLIED WARRANTIES OR LIMITATION OF INCIDENTAL OR CONSEQUENTIAL DAMAGES, SO THESE LIMITATIONS MIGHT NOT APPLY TO YOU.

Other:

This Agreement is governed by the laws of the State of Massachusetts without regard to choice of law principles. The United Convention of Contracts for the International Sale of Goods is specifically disclaimed. This Agreement constitutes the entire agreement between you and Course Technology regarding use of the software.